D1514786

NATIONAL HOUSING FINANCE SYSTEMS

A COMPARATIVE STUDY

NATIONAL HOUSING FINANCE SYSTEMS

A COMPARATIVE STUDY

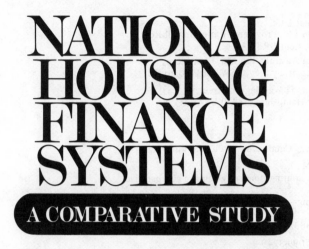

Mark Boleat

CROOM HELM
London · Sydney
Dover, New Hampshire
In Association With
The International Union of
Building Societies and Savings Associations

© Mark Boleat 1985
Croom Helm Ltd, Provident House, Burrell Row,
Beckenham, Kent BR3 1AT

Croom Helm Australia Pty Ltd, First Floor,
139 King Street, Sydney, NSW 2001, Australia

Croom Helm, 51 Washington Street,
Dover, New Hampshire, 03820 USA

British Library Cataloguing in Publication Data

Boleat, Mark
National housing finance systems: a comparative
study.
1. Housing — Finance
I. Title
338.4'33635   HD7287.55

ISBN 0-7099-3249-9

Printed and bound in Great Britain
by Billing & Sons Limited, Worcester.

CONTENTS

PREFACE

The International Union is extremely proud to present this definitive publication on housing finance. The Union is fortunate that Mark Boleat, Deputy Secretary-General of The Building Societies Association in Great Britain, had the interest and talent to undertake this project and was willing to devote the necessary time. We are also indebted to The Building Societies Association for the secretarial and logistical assistance provided to Mr Boleat in connection with this publication.

The book presents for the first time, in one convenient source, vital information and statistics on home financing systems not only in the principal developed countries of the world, but also in many of the smaller nations and those with newly emerging systems of housing finance.

For some years the International Union has published an international Fact Book presenting certain relevant statistics on building society and savings and loan type institutions. The publication of this book by Mr Boleat will make the publication of a Fact Book redundant. It is contemplated that hereafter the statistical information on housing finance systems world-wide will be provided through a type of statistical supplement to this book.

The author, Mark Boleat, has written a number of books on housing finance, including *The Building Society Industry*, published by George Allen & Unwin in 1982. He has spoken at several international conferences.

Mr Boleat was born in Jersey, Channel Islands. He was educated at Lanchester Polytechnic (first class honours degree in Economics) and the University of Reading (MA in Contemporary European Studies). He was elected Associate of The Chartered Building Societies Institute in March 1978, and Fellow in April 1983.

In 1972, Mr Boleat taught economics at Dulwich College, and in 1973 was Research Economist with the Industrial Policy Group. In 1974 he joined The Building Societies Association as Assistant Secretary (Public Relations). He was appointed to his present position of Deputy Secretary-General of the Association in 1981. He has particular responsibility for various policy matters and external relations. Even before the publication of this book, he was recognised internationally as a thorough student of housing finance systems and contemporary developments in the field of banking institutions generally.

The International Union is a world-wide organisation of building societies and savings and loan associations. In its membership are national and multi-national organisations of these institutions, individual building societies and savings and loans, and individuals interested in housing finance and thrift institutions generally. The Union dates from 1914 and has its principal offices in Chicago, Illinois in the USA.

Norman Strunk, Secretary-General
International Union of Building Societies and Savings Associations

INTRODUCTION

This book describes the process by which personal savings are transformed into loans for house-purchase, and the institutions which intermediate between investor and borrower. Most of the book comprises country studies, some more detailed than others. These studies describe the importance of institutional finance in the house-purchase process, the share of the housing finance market taken by various types of institution, and finally the various institutions themselves. The institutions are classified largely into deposit taking institutions and mortgage banks, and, as far as possible, the ownership of the institutions is described, something which is particularly important where they are subsidiaries of other financial institutions.

Housing finance systems cannot be studied in isolation, and it is necessary to describe briefly the housing market in each country, and also the banking sytem.

The book is intended as a reference book, and, for this reason, includes detailed statistics on key variables such as housing tenure, shares of the housing finance market, and assets and liabilities of housing finance institutions. The primary sources are used as far as possible, and the precise source is stated under each table for ease of future reference.

The individual country studies do not claim to be original. Rather, the intention has been to bring together, on as consistent a basis as possible, relevant published data. Where the required data is included in one publication, then the author has had no hesitation in drawing freely on this, giving due acknowledgement in the text. Where a complete chapter is devoted to one country, then it is the intention that the chapter should comprehensively describe the housing finance system of the country. Where a number of countries are included within a chapter, then briefer descriptions are generally given.

The treatment of individual countries is regrettably not consistent. There are three main reasons for this -

(a) Countries with specialist housing finance institutions tend to be more easy to study, simply because more reliable data is available.

(b) More generally, some countries produce better data than others. This is a particular problem in respect of developing countries, where lack of data has unfortunately prevented anything other than a cursory description of the housing finance systems in a number of countries.

(c) Most of the book uses information written in English, although a limited number of French publications have also been used as sources. The book is therefore biased towards countries which produce information in English. This includes not only the English speaking countries, but also the Scandinavian countries, West Germany and Japan. The book is particularly weak in respect of Spanish speaking countries.

In addition to the country studies there are four important general chapters. The first chapter describes the theory of housing finance. Chapter 2 analyses the particular problems of housing finance in developing countries, Chapter 15 includes a theoretical analysis of housing finance in the context of economic integration and Chapter 29 comprises international comparisons. With the exception of Chapter 2, these chapters include some original material, and Chapter 29, in particular, is based on the whole of the research for the book. An understanding of Chapter 1 will greatly facilitate the comprehension of the chapters dealing with industrialized countries, and an understanding of Chapter 2 is similarly helpful in respect of developing countries.

Mark Boleat
June 1984

ACKNOWLEDGEMENTS

This lengthy book has been made possible only with considerable assistance from a number of sources. At the end of each chapter is a list of institutions and individuals who have given specific help in respect of that chapter. It is necessary to acknowledge more general assistance which has been received from a number of people.

I have been encouraged to write this book by Norman Strunk, Secretary-General of the International Union of Building Societies and Savings Associations. He has provided me with invaluable assistance, including data and contacts, and has painstakingly read drafts of each of the chapters, frequently drawing my attention to areas where improvement was needed. I must also thank the Assistant Secretary-General of the International Union, Eugenia Potwora, for the administrative assistance which she has given, particularly during a visit to the USA in 1983. George Cardis, Vice-President of the Institute of Financial Education, Eric Carlson, Special Advisor to the International Union, and Roy Green, Executive Vice-President of the United States League of Savings Institutions, provided me with considerable help when I was in the USA in terms of information, contacts and facilities. George Cardis has been particularly helpful in respect of Latin American countries, and Eric Carlson has done much to point me in the right direction in respect of developing countries. He introduced me to Peter Kimm of the United States Agency for International Development, and Bertrand Renaud of the World Bank, both of whom provided me with a wealth of information. Bertrand Renaud has also offered helpful comments on a number of draft chapters.

The book has been a major logistical exercise because of the need to gather information from a number of countries and to seek comments on drafts. I am grateful to my employers, The Building Societies Association, for allowing me to draw freely on its resources, and to meet the not inconsiderable postage and photocopying costs which have been incurred.

Among the institutions which have provided information in respect of a number of countries I must thank the International Savings Banks Institute in Geneva, which includes in its membership a number of housing finance lenders. I am most grateful to the Bank of England for help in obtaining material published by a number of other central banks. I have drawn extensively on the material in two libraries in London, that of the London School of Economics and Political Science and the Statistics Library of the Department of Trade. My colleagues Adrian Coles, Head of the Association's

Economics and Statistics Department, and Tricia McLaughlin, Press Officer, have read earlier drafts of various chapters and have pointed to inconsistencies which had eluded the author and to the need to clarify certain sections. I am most grateful for their assistance.

My colleague John Murray, Assistant Secretary at the BSA, carefully checked the final manuscript and has handled the publication of the book and liaison with the co-publishers Croom Helm, to whom I must also express my thanks for publishing the book so promptly. Janet Ross helped prepare the manuscript (or more precisely the disks) for publication.

Finally, and most importantly, I must thank my secretary, Helen Burling, who worked quite above and beyond the call of duty in preparing and correcting successive drafts and for handling voluminous correspondence, and generally for her cheerful and conscientious work which enabled me to concentrate on research and drafting. Helen has played a major part in the preparation of this book, and I gratefully acknowledge my debt to her.

Many others have assisted in one way or another in helping to prepare this publication and I hope that they will forgive me if I do not mention them all by name.

Technical Notes

1. As far as is possible, data has been presented in as comparable a manner as possible. However, little attempt has been made to adjust published figures, and it needs to be recognised at the outset that there are substantial differences in the variables which are considered in respect of each country. This is particularly true in respect of loans for house-purchase. In some countries data is available in respect of mortgage loans for all purposes. In other countries specific data is available for mortgage loans on housing, and yet other countries have data on loans for housing regardless of whether they are secured in any way.
2. The problem mentioned above is particularly acute in respect of market shares. Where published data is available only for mortgage debt generally, then it is probable that some institutions, particularly those that deal predominantly with the personal sector, have a much larger share of the market in respect of loans to individuals.
3. The book publishes, wherever possible, aggregate balance sheets for housing finance institutions, and, in some cases, individual balance sheets as well. The use of the balance sheet is particularly appropriate in analysing housing finance institutions because it shows where funds come from and where they go. It also clearly enables the size of the institution to be seen.
4. Where possible, for specialist housing finance institutions income and expenditure accounts are shown. These are particularly significant in showing mortgage losses, if any, and also management expenses.

5. Where international data are used, the major source has been the Organisation for Economic Co-operation and Development (OECD). All the industrialized countries are members of OECD, the main objective of which is to contribute to economic progress. The OECD is one of the major sources of comparative national statistics, and the expression 'OECD average' is frequently used in the context of economic variables.

6. Under each table exchange rates are given for the national currency in respect of both American dollars and British pounds. The exchange rates are given as at the end of the period to which the table applies. The exchange rates have been taken from a number of sources, largely the British government publication *Financial Statistics* and the UN publication *International Financial Statistics*. Different sources give slightly different exchange rates, and the figures should be treated accordingly.

7. The expressions gross national product (GNP) and gross domestic product (GDP) are used frequently. These are measures of the output of an economy, and when presented in per capita terms are an indication of living standards. However, comparison of living standards between countries is immensely difficult, and changes in exchange rates can have a major effect on per capita figures when expressed in a single currency. There is a theoretical discussion of this point in Chapter 2.

8. Where possible abbreviations are avoided, and are used only when the full meaning of the abbreviation has been given. The abbreviation 'm' means million and 'bn' means 1,000 million, that is, an American billion.

CHAPTER 1

HOUSING FINANCE – AN OVERVIEW

Introduction

The purpose of a housing finance system is to provide the funds which home-buyers need to purchase their homes. This is a simple objective, and the number of ways in which it can be achieved is limited. Notwithstanding this basic simplicity, in a number of countries, largely as a result of government action, very complicated housing finance systems have been developed. However, the essential feature of any system, that is, the ability to channel the funds of investors to those purchasing their homes, must remain.

This introductory chapter provides a theoretical framework for housing finance systems and, in so doing, attempts to reduce the systems to the bare essentials. The framework developed in this chapter can subsequently be used to analyse the housing finance system of any country.

The Requirements of a Housing Finance System

The basic requirement of any housing finance system is that it should be able to attract funds from people who have a surplus of financial assets and channel these to those who wish to borrow. It is helpful at this stage to discuss briefly the typical pattern of saving and borrowing for a household over its life cycle.

For the first 20 or so years of their lives most people have no saving of any significance and those financial accounts which are held aim to do no more than provide a simple mechanism by which funds can be transferred or they are designed to teach young people how to manage their money. As a young person begins to receive an income, so he is likely to begin to accumulate very modest savings. Often the savings will be with a specific aim in mind, such as a motor car or a holiday. By the early 20s the thoughts of many people are turning to house-purchase and setting up a house generally, and, again, there might be specific saving for this purpose. However, the amount of such saving is likely to be comparatively modest, simply because incomes are at a relatively low level and other expenditure is at a comparatively high level.

As soon as people purchase their first house, then they become substantial net borrowers. House-buyers will, typically, make a down payment but this is unlikely to be more than 25% of the purchase price, and in some countries it is substantially less than this. It is obvious from this that the potential sav-

1

ings of house-buyers are not nearly sufficient to fund the loans which those house-buyers subsequently require. As the household becomes more mature income is likely to increase, and, after a time, expenditure will fall. Later on in life people may find that substantial capital sums come their way, perhaps from maturing insurance policies or inheritances. By the time people reach retirement age they are likely to have substantial financial assets and very little borrowing. During their retirement many people are heavily reliant on income from their investments in order to maintain their living standards.

Summarizing, the typical household will be a modest net lender until a house is purchased, will then be a substantial net borrower with the extent of indebtedness falling over time until, later on in life, the household becomes a substantial net investor. This pattern is illustrated in the diagram below.

Diagram 1   The Life Cycle of Savings

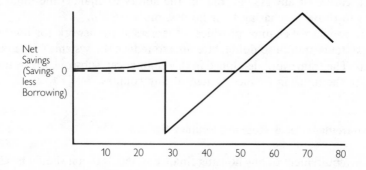

It follows from this analysis that any housing finance system, if it is to meet fully the requirements of the population, must attract funds from those who are not potential home-buyers. Basically, the system has to transfer savings from elderly people who hold most savings to younger people who are net borrowers. It is a relatively easy task to show that the bulk of personal savings are held by the elderly, and considerable statistical information in support of this is now available. Table 1.1 shows savings balances held at financial institutions in the USA in 1982.

It will be seen that under 7% of savings balances were held by those under the age of 35, who are those most likely to be purchasing homes. By contrast, nearly half of savings were held by those over 65 and nearly three quarters by those aged over 55. A similar picture exists in other countries. In Britain, the *Family Expenditure Survey 1982* shows that 51% of all investment income was received by households aged over 65 and a further 25% was received by households with a head of household aged between 50 and 65. These figures are remarkably similar to those for the USA. A more recent market research survey in Britain shows that those over the age of 55 account for 74% of savings, but just 9% of borrowing.

Table 1.1   Savings Balances Held at Financial Institutions, USA, 1982

Age Group	Median Savings $	Percentage of Total Savings Balances
18 – 24	1,840	0.9
25 – 34	3,830	5.8
35 – 44	6,720	8.1
45 – 54	12,310	12.2
55 – 64	24,960	25.4
65 & over	34,740	47.5
All	16,680	100.0

Source: *The 1982 Savers Survey*, United States League of Savings Institutions, 1983, Table 8.
Note: At end-1982 there were $1.62 to the pound.

The extent to which home-buyers will be able to put in a substantial deposit themselves, and thereby need to rely less on the savings of others, depends essentially on the housing system of a country. In those countries where there is a substantial market rented sector this is likely to house the younger sections of the population for a considerable number of years. The United States is one such country, and of married coupled households under the age of 25 over 80% are tenants, and of the 25-29 age group 60% are tenants. Not until the 30-34 age group does the proportion of owner-occupiers overtake the proportion of tenants. In Japan, cheap rented housing is available for low income families and when incomes exceed a certain level the housing must be vacated. The effect of this was that in 1978 only 17% of households with a head of household age of under 29 were owner-occupiers and even in the 30-39 age group the proportion was just 46%. These figures compare with an overall level of owner-occupation of 60.4%. In New Zealand, where rented housing is less readily available, 70% of households with a head of household age under 26 are tenants. At the other end of the range is the United Kingdom where very little rented housing is available on the market, and subsequently people purchase their first homes at an early age. In 1980, over 50% of households with a head of household age of between 25 and 29 were owner-occupiers, double the proportion of other countries, even where the overall level of owner-occupation is higher.

The interaction between housing and housing finance is clear. If there is no rented sector of housing available to young households then they will seek to become owner-occupiers much earlier than they would naturally choose to, given a free choice. In countries where this is the case, the United Kingdom representing the extreme example, the housing finance system has to be able to provide high percentage loans to young people.

More generally, of course, the higher the level of owner-occupation, the greater is the need for finance to fund house-buyers. Here, however, the rela-

3

tionships are not quite as firm as might seem to be the case at first sight. Switzerland stands out as having an exceptionally low level of owner-occupation but a very high ratio of mortgage debt to national income. A number of other factors have to be examined in looking at the overall demand for house-purchase finance, even given a certain level of owner-occupation. One such factor is government policy towards housing finance. In most countries loans for house-purchase are favoured in one form or another. In some countries, such as Sweden, there is a direct government subsidy to most home-buyers. In other countries, France being a notable example, home-buyers with incomes below a certain level qualify for subsidized loans. In most countries, mortgage interest can be offset against income tax liability. In only a few countries, including Canada and Australia, is there no significant government assistance for home-buyers. The overall demand for housing finance must, to some extent, reflect the price of that finance, and the more heavily subsidized that mortgage loans are, either directly or indirectly through tax relief on mortgage interest, the greater is likely to be the demand for those loans.

Any housing finance system has to be able to provide loans over a long period. It is a sign of a sophisticated system that long term loans are available. Even some advanced countries did not, until recently, have housing finance systems that provided for loan terms to be in excess of ten years, France being the best example. Long term loans are essential, simply because the size of a loan needed to purchase a house is very high in relation to the income of the borrower, generally between two and three times his income, and a short repayment term imposes an intolerable burden in terms of repayments. However, long term loans present prudential problems for the institutions making those loans. The recipe for banking disaster is to borrow short term and lend long term. A housing finance institution must overcome this problem, either by raising its funds on a long term basis or, alternatively, by ensuring that the rate of interest on its long term loans can be changed in line with the rate of interest on the short term savings which it has attracted.

This problem has become particularly acute over the last 20 or so years, as both rates of inflation and interest rates have risen and become more volatile. This is illustrated in Table 1.2.

It will be seen from the table that the average inflation rate doubled between 1960-67 and 1967-73, and nearly doubled again in 1973-80. Short term interest rates more than doubled from 1966-70 to 1973-80 and long term rates almost doubled. Not only have short and long term interest rates tended to rise over the period, but they also became more volatile. The first major problems arose with the substantial rise in rates between 1971 and 1974. A second problem emerged at the end of the 1970s and the early 1980s.

Inflation presents a problem, primarily because of the effect which it has on long term interest rates. As the table illustrates, long term rates bear a close relationship with the rate of inflation. As inflation increases, it follows that the repayments on long term loans must also increase and this can cause

Table 1.2   Inflation and Interest Rates, OECD Average, 1966-80

Year	Percentage Increase in Consumer Price Index, All OECD Countries	Nominal Interest Rates; Major OECD Countries	
		Short Term %	Long Term %
1966	3.5	5.3	6.2
1967	3.1	4.7	6.3
1968	4.0	5.3	6.5
1969	4.8	5.4	7.2
1970	5.6	7.2	8.0
1971	5.3	5.5	7.5
1972	4.7	4.9	7.3
1973	7.8	7.9	8.2
1974	13.4	4.8	10.1
1975	11.3	8.0	9.8
1976	8.7	8.6	10.0
1977	8.9	7.7	9.6
1978	8.0	7.5	9.3
1979	9.9	9.7	9.9
1980	12.9	11.9	11.8
1981	10.6	13.8	14.1
1982	8.0		
1960-67	2.7	4.4	5.5
1967-73	5.4	5.8	7.3
1973-80	10.4	9.0	10.1

Sources: *Historical Statistics 1960-80*, OECD, 1982, Tables 8.11, 10.6 & 10.8: *Main Economic Indicators*, OECD, February 1983.

Note: The Organisation for Economic Co-Operation and Development (OECD) comprises most of the industrialized countries and is a major source of international statistics. The 'major OECD countries' are the USA, Japan, West Germany, France, the UK, Italy and Canada. Figures for short term interest rates exclude France until 1970, and figures for long term rates exclude Japan in 1966. The inflation figures are weighted averages; the interest rate figures are simple averages.

what is known as a frontloading problem, that is, repayments are initially at a high level in relation to income, but inflation rapidly reduces the real value of repayments over time. When inflation goes above a certain level, consideration has to be given to index-linking, that is, increasing the debt year by year in line with the index of inflation and charging a lower nominal rate of interest, typically 2-3%. Index-linking has operated successfully only in countries with very high inflation rates—above 50%.

The rise in short term interest rates, and also the variation of those rates, causes considerably more problems for financial institutions which have borrowed short and lent long. Where the institution has borrowed on a short term basis and has lent long term at fixed rates of interest, then the critical problem arises of a mismatch of assets and liabilities. This problem has been acute in the USA where government regulation forced housing finance lenders to borrow short term yet lend long term at fixed rates. As short term rates rose rapidly towards the end of the 1970s and in the early 1980s, the institutions, because they were not able to issue loans at variable rates, encountered considerable financial difficulty, which has been overcome only by substantial expense of government money and a restructuring of the industry. Where lending institutions are able to vary the rate of interest on existing loans, then they have, in general, been able to avoid the worst effects of high and fluctuating interest rates. However, to this extent, they have merely passed the risk from themselves to their borrowers. In some countries, notably the United Kingdom, this has been readily accepted, and significant fluctuations in interest rates have been accommodated without too much difficulty. In other countries, rapid movements in short term interest rates have necessitated government intervention to moderate the effects on existing home-buyers. Canada is a good example in this respect.

Whatever system of housing finance is employed, the problems of inflation and high and volatile interest rates have to be faced and overcome. Some systems enable these problems to be overcome better than others, either in respect of the borrower or the institution, but seldom both simultaneously. Frequently it seems entirely fortuitous as to which housing finance system is in operation, and in particular as to whether interest rates are fixed or variable. The powerful economic forces of inflation and rising interest rates have caused major re-examinations of housing finance systems in a number of countries and there are now signs of a convergence of the types of system. In particular, it is increasingly difficult to obtain long term loans with no provision for an interest rate variation.

Sources of Funds

When reduced to basics there is only one source of funds for any one housing finance system, that is the personal sector. An economy can be divided into four sectors: the corporate sector, the government sector, the overseas sector and the personal sector. The corporate sector is generally, although not invariably, a net borrower and to the extent that individual institutions within a sector have surplus funds, then these are likely to be deposited elsewhere in the corporate sector. The government sector is invariably a net borrower, and has very little surplus funds available. However, governments do provide some funds for house-purchase, either in the form of a loan or a subsidy. The overseas sector is the counterpart of the balance of payments. If there is a balance of payments surplus, then there is an outflow of funds from the country, and if there is a balance of payments deficit it follows that there must be a corresponding inflow of funds. The personal sector is the major net supplier of funds to the other sectors, but far more importantly is the extent of what can be called intermediation within the personal sector. That is, at any one time, a large proportion of the personal sector will be net investors and a large proportion will be net borrowers. Some people, for very good reasons, may have both a substantial holding of savings and substantial borrowing. However, most households have either limited savings and substantial borrowing or substantial savings and only limited borrowing. This is partly because most people still regard a debt as being something undesirable and which they wish to avoid.

The personal sector does not necessarily provide funds directly to housing finance institutions. In most countries, life insurance companies and pension funds account for a considerable proportion of the savings of the personal sector. Often such saving is forced by government regulation or legislation and, at the very least, it is contractual. Nevertheless, the fact remains that in all countries both pension funds and insurance companies have substantial sums of money at their disposal which they can invest in a variety of ways, one of which is to provide funds for the housing market.

Types of Housing Finance System

Introduction

It has been established that to work effectively any housing finance system has to raise money from those who do not intend to borrow and be able to lend it over long periods of time. There are just four routes by which this can be achieved, two of which can be only partially successful and which do not make full use of the intermediation process-

(a) The direct route, by which those who need funds to acquire a home obtain those funds directly from individuals with surplus financial assets, either because of a personal relationship or because of a business relationship, for example, a vendor may supply funds to a purchaser.

(b) A contractual route by which part, but not all, of the funds which a home-buyer requires are raised from the savings of other potential home-buyers, or from other contractual savings schemes.

(c) The deposit financing route, by which short term savings of individuals are channelled into long term loans by intermediaries, generally retail banks, either generally or which specialize in the provision of housing finance.

(d) The mortgage bank route, by which institutions making mortgage loans fund these by bond issues, which are purchased by institutional investors and, to a much lesser extent, by individuals.

These four types of system will now be considered in detail, but it is important to note at this stage that these are the only four types of system, although there is scope for substantial variation on them. The four systems are illustrated in diagram 2.

Diagram 2   Types of Finance Systems

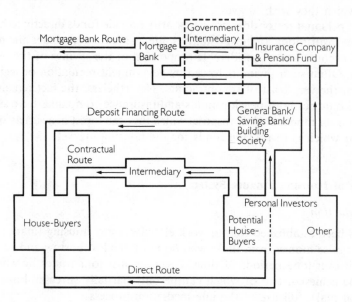

The Direct Route

In an economy where there is no well developed housing finance system, the funds which house-buyers require may be obtained directly from other individuals with funds which are surplus to their requirements. In many cases funds will be obtained from a relative. Typically, older people will lend money to their children to enable them to purchase homes. Even in advanced countries it is not unknown for parents to help their children purchase their homes, perhaps by the provision of a substantial down payment. This route, of course, is an extremely ineffective form of financial intermediation, because it is unlikely that the requirements of the borrower will match exactly those of the lender. Nevertheless, in the absence of any alternative, the direct route is one which is used in less advanced economies and also in the more advanced economies by those who are not able to use established financial mechanisms.

Somewhat paradoxically, even in advanced countries the direct route has been used increasingly in recent years by vendors providing funds to purchasers. The vendors do not, of course, lend money to purchasers, but, rather, sell a house but do not insist on taking the full purchase price immediately. Part, or even all, of the purchase price may be deferred for some years. The effect is that the vendor is making a loan to the purchaser, even if this is not what actually happens. This financing technique is known as 'creative financing' and was used extensively in the USA in the late 1970s and early 1980s when the traditional housing finance system was breaking down for a variety of reasons. It has also been used in Sweden and, to a lesser extent, in other countries. This mechanism is used in similar circumstances to relatives providing funds to home-buyers, that is, the institutional framework is not adequate to meet demand. However, it occurs not because the institutional framework has not been developed but, rather, because it is prevented from operating, generally by government regulation.

It is not possible to say much more about the direct method of financing because, almost by definition, no statistics are available and no institutions are involved. All that can be said at this stage is that direct financing is used extensively in the less developed economies but is used in more advanced economies only when normal institutions are prevented from operating effectively.

The Contractual System

The point has already been made that the savings of potential home-buyers are not adequate to provide all the finance which home-buyers need. However, this does not mean that funds gathered from potential home-buyers cannot provide part of the finance which is required. Formal contractual systems exist in a number of countries, most notably, West Germany through special institutions, the Bausparkassen, and in France throught the housing savings system, which can be operated by a large number of financial institutions. The essence of any contractual system is that regular savings are made over a period of years and receive an interest rate at below the market level, following which the investor becomes entitled to a loan, again at an interest rate below a market level. Generally, government bonuses are available to those who take part in contractual savings schemes. Arguably, it is the bonuses which make the schemes attactive.

These schemes are best suited to those countries where people do not purchase their first houses until a relatively late age. The system would be no use in a country like the United Kingdom, for example, where households seek to purchase their first homes at a young age, before they have had an opportunity to accumulate significant savings. The system works very well in countries like West Germany and France, where there is a substantial rented sector which most young people are content to use until such time as they settle their roots firmly, and that can often be in their mid-30s.

However it is used, the contractual system can still not provide more than a proportion of the funds which a home-buyer requires, perhaps 40% of the purchase price at a maximum. The system therefore has to be used in tandem with one of the other systems. In practice, loans provided on the contractual basis are frequently used to repay loans obtained on the open market in anticipation of a contractual cheap loan being made available. To the extent that this occurs, then the contractual system is being used partly as a method of tax-efficient saving rather than funding house-purchase. Because the contractual system needs to be operated in tandem with other systems, the institutions that operate it generally are either controlled by other financial institutions (as in the case of West Germany) or they are themselves general institutions, as is the case in France.

In developing countries a variant of the contractual system is the use of social security funds to provide housing loans. These funds are likely to be large in relation to other institutional sources of funds and may be the only substantial source of funds. Typically, people are allowed effectively to borrow their contributions to the funds or the funds may lend directly to those who have contributed. Brazil makes the most extensive use of this system; among the other countries using social security funds for housing loans are Mexico and The Philippines.

The Deposit Taking System

Perhaps the most common system of housing finance is for deposit taking institutions to use a proportion of those deposits to make house-purchase loans. There are a variety of types of deposit taking institution and they can, broadly speaking, be subdivided into commercial banks, which offer the complete range of banking facilities, savings banks which deal largely, although not exclusively, with the personal sector, and specialist housing finance organisations known as building societies or savings and loan associations typically, which deal almost entirely with the personal sector and which generally differ from savings banks by providing a savings service rather than a money transmission service.

All of these institutions operate by raising deposits and then lending these deposits in a variety of ways. The important point is that the deposit taking comes first and then the institution has to decide what to do with the funds. This means that house-purchase loans may be competing with loans for other purposes and if the interest rate is not at an appropriate market level, then shortages may well occur.

The deposit financing system generally means the employment of a variable rate on the house-purchase loan. This is because deposit taking institutions usually do not have long term fixed rate funds with which they can make matching long term fixed rate loans.

The Mortgage Bank System

The final type of housing finance system can be described as the mortgage bank or mortgage bond system. Through this system an institution will make loans to house-buyers, generally at fixed rates of interest, and it will seek to fund those loans by selling bonds on the capital markets at the going market rate. Almost by definition, such a system must meet the demand fully, unless there are artificial restrictions on interest rates, or indeed on the supply of bonds to the market. This system can, of course, work effectively only where there is an active bond market in which private sector institutions can participate. In some countries, for example the United Kingdom, the bond market has been dominated by the government, because of special tax rules applying to government securities. It is not therefore open for institutions to fund house-purchase loans through bond issues, because they simply cannot compete with existing instruments.

The mortgage bank system does not entail the raising of any retail deposits, and it follows that institutions which use this system do not have the branch networks that the banks have.

Typically, bonds issued by mortgage banks are purchased by financial intermediaries, such as insurance companies and pension funds, and also banks. Indeed, in some countries, for example Sweden, financial institutions are required to purchase a certain quantity of mortgage bonds. It is also possible that bonds will be purchased directly by individual investors.

There is a refinement of this system, one which is rapidly developing in the United States. A new institution, not shown on the diagram, then appears on the scene. That institution in the United States is called a mortgage bank, which is a singularly inappropriate name, as the institution is not a bank in any sense of the word. An American mortgage bank makes and services loans, but immediately sells them to an institutional investor, having previously insured them or obtained a government guarantee. This refinement can be regarded merely as one variation of the mortgage bank route, except that the bank itself becomes a mere servicing organisation, selling loans to investors rather than raising funds from investors. Alternatively, it can be regarded as a very sophisticated direct route between investors and house-buyers, the improvement on the simple direct route being that the investor has a marketable security which he is able to sell at any time.

Types of Housing Finance Institution

Introduction

There are five basic types of housing finance institution, two of which are general financial institutions which make house-purchase loans, the other three of which are specialist. In a number of countries, one or perhaps two types of institution predominate, the United Kingdom being a good example. In other countries, such as the USA and West Germany, most of the types of institution exist. It should also be noted that in many countries there are substantial government agencies in the housing finance market, New Zealand and Norway being good examples. However, a government owned institution is merely a type of institution and does not make the institution itself any different. Typically, the government institutions are mortgage banks. It is now necessary to discuss fairly briefly the five types of housing finance institution.

General Banks

General banks can be described by a number of other terms, including joint stock banks, commercial banks and deposit taking banks. These institutions are full service banks, providing the complete range of retail, wholesale and, generally, international banking business. Deposit taking is a major part of the business of some of these banks, but a more minor part of the business of others. Most general banks have a presence in the mortgage market. A typical position is one where perhaps 20% of outstanding mortgage debt is held by general banks, either directly through house-purchase loans or indirectly through ownership of bonds issued by housing finance organisations. Also, a general bank will typically have about 20% of its domestic assets in house-purchase loans.

Most of the big banks in the world have a significant mortgage portfolio. In some countries, France, Italy, Japan and Switzerland for example, the banks are the dominant lenders. There are various ways of measuring the size of banks, and under one definition the French Crédit Agricole is one of the largest banks in the world. Alternatively, it can be regarded as merely a loose grouping of 3,000 small banks. The Crédit Agricole is the largest single house-purchase lender in France.

Not only are the general banks significant lenders in their own right, but in many countries they own specialist institutions, which will be described subsequently. For example, Australian commercial banks own savings banks (in New Zealand as well as in Australia), Dutch general banks own mortgage banks, and in West Germany the large deposit taking banks have an interest in the specialist Bausparkassen and the mortgage banks. The complicated inter-relationships make it difficult at times to analyse the precise nature of the role of banks in the housing finance market.

Savings Banks

A savings bank can be defined as an institution which raises its funds almost entirely from the personal sector and which uses these funds to lend to the personal sector and also to small businesses. In developing countries the funds are frequently passed on to the government. In some countries, particularly France and West Germany, savings banks are huge organisations and provide a full banking service to individuals and to small businesses. In other countries, for example the United Kingdom, savings banks are relatively small compared with other institutions and have no significant role in the housing finance or indeed in other markets.

The savings banks have a particularly large share of the housing finance markets in Spain, Italy, New Zealand and Japan. Typically, house-purchase loans will account for between 20% and 50% of the assets of savings banks, although there are substantial variations. In some countries the savings banks, for various reasons, cannot make direct loans to home-buyers, but indirectly they can finance house-purchase loans through buying bonds issued by mortgage banks, in some cases by mortgage banks which are owned by the savings banks. This happens in Sweden, for example, and in Denmark the savings banks are major purchasers of bonds issued by specialist mortgage banks.

In some countries, regional groupings of savings banks own specialist housing finance organisations. Germany is a good example, where the savings banks are grouped together in Landesbanks which, in turn, control Bausparkassen and mortgage banks.

Specialist Savings Banks

Some savings banks devote almost all of their lending to house-purchase. Such institutions are generally not called savings banks as such, but rather are called building societies in the United Kingdom, Australia, South Africa and New Zealand, mortgage loan companies in Canada, and savings and loan associations in the United States and South America. The dividing line between what might be called a general savings bank and a specialist building society (the term being used here to embrace savings and loan associations) is a very blurred one. The main distinction between the two types of institution is that the specialist building society will probably have about 80% of assets in mortgage loans compared with a much smaller proportion for the more general savings banks.

There has, however, been a significant increase in some countries in competition between savings banks and building societies over the last few years. This has reached such a stage in the United States that savings banks and savings and loan associations are virtually indistinguishable and indeed it is comparatively easy for an institution to switch from one type of organisation to the other.

Contractual Institutions

The one advanced industrialized country where there are substantial contractual institutions is West Germany. The Bausparkassen play a major role in the financing of house-purchase, although they provide only a proportion of the funds to each home-buyer. Although the Bausparkassen are specialist institutions, it should be noted that they are not independent, and indeed the nature of the contractual savings system is such that independent institutions are unlikely to be very effective. The Bausparkassen are largely owned by the regional organisations of savings banks and also the large deposit taking banks. However, there are one or two independent institutions.

In France there are specialist deferred credit institutions, but in practice these hardly exist, except on paper, instead being part of more general financial institutions or specialist mortgage banks. The point has already been made that the French contractual system for housing finance is operated by general financial institutions rather than specific ones.

Mortgage Banks

The function of mortgage banks has largely been explained already in the section on the mortgage bank system. In some countries, mortgage banks are completely independent institutions, Denmark being a good example, while in other countries they are owned by one of the other types of institution listed above. A mortgage bank will not have a substantial branch network, because it is not a deposit taking institution. However, one cannot be a successful housing finance institution unless there is a way of attracting customers, and, for this reason, mortgage banks have to work through other institutions as their agents. These institutions will invariably be another financial institution, hence the ownership patterns which have been described previously.

The Role of Government

Perhaps the major effect which government in advanced industrialized countries has on housing finance is indirect, that is, various actions taken by government indirectly affect the way that housing finance is provided and the nature of the housing finance market. Among such factors are -

(a) Housing policy. The more that owner-occupation is encouraged the greater the demand for house-purchase finance. If young people are encouraged to be owner-occupiers there is a demand for large percentage loans.
(b) The tax treatment of housing and mortgage interest will influence the demand for house-purchase loans.
(c) The regulation of the financial system may influence the nature of the housing finance market.

In many cases, government has left private sector institutions to deal with the market as they find it, and there is no direction of these institutions to achieve certain housing finance objectives. This is true, for example, in the United States and in Britain. However, even in those countries the housing finance market is influenced indirectly by government. For example, the savings banks in Britain have been almost alone of savings banks in not being significant house-purchase lenders. This is because they were seen, until recently, as merely devices for collecting money which was then handed on to government.

All governments regulate and some have chosen to regulate the housing finance market with more vigour than others. In the United States, savings and loan associations were forced to lend at fixed rates of interest and this caused severe financial problems when the general level of interest rates increased. In Canada, interest rate controls on the banks effectively eliminated them from the market for quite a significant time. In Britain, direct credit controls on the banking system in the 1960s and 1970s inhibited the ability of the banks to compete for mortgage business.

In some countries, government provides for specific regulation of the mortgage market. This is true in France, where all institutions have to meet certain requirements, and in many countries there are limits on the loan to value ratio, types of security that might be accepted and so on.

In some countries government institutions themselves play a major role. In countries such as France the major banking institutions are, in any event, nationalised and thus housing finance is provided to a significant extent through public sector bodies. However, this in itself does not necessarily represent any significant difference from the same type of institution in private hands providing housing finance.

What is more interesting are specific housing finance bodies which can be imposed somewhere on diagram 2, typically as an intermediary between other financial intermediaries and a mortgage bank. The government intermediary may itself take on the role of the mortgage bank. This happens in Japan where the Housing Loan Corporation, the biggest single housing finance lender in the world, accepts loans from the Trust Fund Bureau, which in turn obtains them from the postal savings system. With these funds it makes direct house-purchase loans. The State Housing Bank in Norway obtains its funds through borrowing directly on the capital markets and from the government. The New Zealand Housing Loan Corporation funds its activities through a government budget appropriation, rather than through raising the funds on commercial terms. In general, the main effect of the imposition of the government intermediary is to extend the number of stages in the intermediation process except, of course, where the normal intermediaries are government owned.

In some countries, public sector bodies are given the task of stimulating a secondary mortgage market. Only one country, the USA, has a highly sophisticated secondary market and here three separate government institutions have roles in making that market. However, these institutions do not change any of the basic ways in which housing finance can be provided. They merely oil the wheels of one of the other systems.

Recent Developments

Fluctuating Interest Rates

The point has already been made briefly that interest rates have been more volatile in recent years and this is illustrated in Table 1.2. If anything this table understates the volatility because it represents an average for a major industrialized country and figures for individual countries show even more marked variations. For example, in Italy, average short term interest rates rose from 5.5% in 1972 to 16.5% in 1976. In the United States they increased from 5.3% in 1977 to over 16% in the middle of 1982, before falling back to single figures by the end of that year. In the United Kingdom short term rates increased from 7.5% in 1977 to 15.8% in 1979, before falling back into single figures in the middle of 1982.

Fluctuating interest rates present problems for any financial institution. If the institution is borrowing funds on a short term basis to lend at fixed long term rates, then the obvious problem is a mismatch of assets and liabilities. This problem has been acute in the USA, where the savings and loan associations have incurred serious financial difficulties. The solution has been the introduction of a variable rate mortgage. In many other countries, a greater degree of variability in interest rates has had to be introduced. In Canada, for example, rates used to be fixed for five years at a time, but that interval quickly came down to one year as borrowers became unwilling to commit themselves to high rates for five year periods. In Britain, which has adopted the most variable system, the frequency of interest rate changes has become greater.

In general, it can be said that the trend towards greater instability of interest rates has, not surprisingly, increased the use made of the variable rate mortgage and this trend is likely to be one which will continue.

Greater Competition Between Specialist and General Financial Institutions

In general, it has been the English speaking countries, with the exception of Canada, which have had financial systems divided into general banks and specialist housing finance intermediaries. On the continent of Europe, in particular, the same institutions tend to provide normal banking services and housing finance loans, albeit, in some cases, through a subsidiary. In the English speaking countries, and, to a lesser extent, in other countries, there has been a marked increase in competition between the various types of financial institution, and, in particular, between the specialist housing finance bodies and banks.

There are a number of reasons for this. One is simply consumer preference. As a result of increasing affluence, institutions able to offer a package of financial services have found that these have been easier to market than single services, even if they are more costly.

A second factor has been the increasing emphasis placed on monetary policy to control the economy, and the recognition by the monetary authorities that monetary policy cannot be implemented through the banking system alone. Credit controls on banks were fairly common in the 1960s and 1970s, but increasingly have been dismantled in the recognition that they could not, on their own, be effective.

A third factor in this respect has been the significant advances in technology which have made it easy for small institutions to be able to offer a wider range of financial services without going to considerable expense or buying in vast amounts of expertise. In particular, the advent of the automated teller machine and electronic funds transfer systems makes it possible for institutions other than banks to offer a retail banking service.

The greater competition has tended to diminish the activities of specialist housing finance institutions. They have had to diversify in order to compete, and, in some cases, that diversification has gone to such an extent that what were previously housing finance bodies have changed themselves and their names to banks.

Committees of Inquiry

The factors mentioned in the previous paragraph have contributed to the establishment, again, especially in the English speaking countries, of committees of inquiry into the financial systems and to major legislative reforms. The committees of inquiry have come up with very similar conclusions, notwithstanding their widely differing origins. In the USA, such is the legislative process that major changes take a considerable time and discussions on financial reform began in the early 1960s with the Commission on Money and Credit. This was followed by the Hunt Commission which reported in 1972. The weight of opinion at that time was that reform was needed in the financial system, which was very antiquated, in particular through its reliance on direct controls on interest rates and also through the limitation of financial institutions, largely speaking, to operating within individual states. However, Congress was not easily persuaded that change was needed and it took the crisis in the savings and loan industry, caused by rising interest rates, before substantial reforms could be implemented. The Depository Institutions Deregulation and Monetary Control Act 1980 gave savings and loan associations wider powers while, at the same time, providing for removal of their interest rate advantage over the banks. This was followed by the Depository Institutions Act of 1982 which, effectively, abolished the distinction between savings and loan associations and savings banks, and, more generally, gave considerbly wider powers to the associations.

In the United Kingdom, the Wilson Report, published in 1980, called for the removal of artificial impediments to competition between banks and building societies. The report was not acted on directly, but influenced the climate of opinion and was followed by an easing of controls on the banking system and consideration being given to new building society legislation.

In Australia, the Campbell Commission produced a comprehensive report on the financial system in November 1981. The Committee recommended the abandonment of a wide range of direct controls and a shift of reliance on open market methods of intervention in domestic and financial markets. It recommended the abolition of all interest rate controls and asset controls on the banks, savings banks and building societies.

In South Africa, the De Kock Commission Report followed a similar line, suggesting that a building society should become more closely integrated into the financial system generally.

CHAPTER 2

HOUSING FINANCE IN DEVELOPING COUNTRIES

Housing finance in developing countries is a very different subject from housing finance in industrialized countries. In the latter one can study the mechanism by which housing finance systems operate, that is, the institutional process by which funds are transferred from those who have a financial surplus to those who need to borrow to buy a house. There is the almost implicit assumption that people can afford to buy houses and that there are financial institutions which will help them do so.

In the case of developing countries neither of these assumptions holds good. In many countries there is still acute poverty and, at best, shelter may mean little more than a roof over one's head. In most developing countries, financial systems are not well developed and there is a mutual suspicion between those financial institutions which do exist and ordinary people. The question is not how institutions intermediate between investors and borrowers, but rather the extent to which they do so, and how a more efficient intermediation process can be encouraged.

The evidence suggests that both housing and housing finance have much to contribute to the development of poorer economies generally. Significant progress is most likely to be made by specialist institutions which seek to bring together the informal and formal sectors of the economy.

A number of agencies have helped to contribute to the spread of best practice in the developing countries. Foremost among these has been the Office of Housing of the United States Agency for International Development. The World Bank, and its related organisation the International Finance Corporation, have played a significant role. Contributions have also been made by the United Nations, the Commonwealth Development Corporation, and other international and national bodies.

Population, Living Standards and Urbanization

Developing countries have a very wide range of per capita incomes. It is difficult to compare living standards between countries, and even more so when the countries are at varying stages of development. At very low income levels much of the output of the agricultural sector is not traded and therefore does not enter into the statistics and this means that comparisons based on prevailing exchange rates are likely to overstate the differences in wealth between rich and poor countries. Nevertheless, such comparisons are all that can be attempted in this chapter. Table 2.1 show GNP per capita in selected industrialized and developing countries and also population figures.

Table 2.1 Population and GNP per Capita, Industrialized and Developing Countries

Country	Population		GNP per Capita		Exchange Rate
	1981	1970-80 Growth	1981	1970-80 Real Growth	Deviation Index (1975)
	million	% p a	US$	% p a	
West Germany	62	–	13,450	2.7	0.88
USA	230	1.0	12,820	2.1	1.00
France	54	0.5	12,190	3.0	0.91
Japan	118	1.2	10,080	3.4	1.10
United Kingdom	56	0.1	9,110	1.8	1.11
Italy	56	0.5	6,960	2.5	1.12
Spain	38	1.1	5,640	2.6	1.36
Brazil	121	2.1	2,220	5.9	1.58
South Korea	39	1.7	1,700	7.5	2.54
Colombia	26	1.9	1,380	4.0	2.83
Philippines	50	2.7	790	3.7	2.51
Thailand	48	2.6	770	4.2	2.61
Kenya	17	4.0	420	2.4	1.95
India	690	2.1	260	1.5	3.23

Source: *1983 World Bank Atlas*, World Bank, 1983.
Note: At end-1981 there were $1.91 to the pound.

The final column shows a 1975 calculation of the exchange rate deviation index; that is, a measurement of the extent to which the official exchange rate differs from an accurate measurement of relative purchasing power. Standards of living can be compared by multiplying GNP per capita at current exchange rates by the index. The indices relates to 1975 only but are unlikely to have changed significantly since then. Generally, it can be seen that the poorer the country the more the official exchange rate overstates the relative poverty of the country.

The table is sufficient to show huge differences in GNP per capita between the industrialized countries and the developing countries. The more prosperous industrialized countries have a GNP per capita figure more than ten times that of the poorest countries and over five times that of the more prosperous South American and Asian countries (Japan excepted). With such differences in economic output, and therefore in living standards, it is reasonable to expect similar huge differences in respect of the provision of housing.

Table 2.1 also usefully illustrates the second major problem of developing countries, a rapid rate of population growth. All the developing countries listed had higher rates of population growth in the 1970s than all of the industrialized countries listed. Population growth was particularly high in Kenya.

The differences between rich and poor countries can be illustrated more clearly by examining world population analysed by reference to the income group of each country. Table 2.2 shows the position.

Table 2.2   GNP and Population by Income Group, 1980

Income Group $ per year	Population Million	GNP US$ bn	Average GNP per capita US $
8,270 & over	630	6,851	10,874
3,540-8,269	141	767	5,435
830-3,539	655	1,133	1,730
360-829	396	211	533
Under 360	2,056	505	245

Source: *1983 World Bank Atlas*, World Bank, 1983.
Note: At end-1980 there were $2.35 to the pound.

The table shows that in 1980 the 630 million people living in countries with a GNP per capita in excess of $8,270 had an average GNP per capita some 50 times that of the 2,056 million people living in countries with a GNP per capita under $360.

The rapid growth in population in the developing countries together with industrialization has contributed to the phenomenon of urbanization, that is, a huge increase in the population living in urban areas. It is estimated that the urban population of developing countries is growing by some 8% a year. The consequence is a sharp rise in the number of large cities. India typifies this pattern. Between 1960 and 1980 the number of Indian cities with a population in excess of 500,000 increased from 11 to 36 and the percentage of the population living in these cities rose from 26% to 39%.

This brief description of the problems of developing countries is sufficient to show that housing and housing finance systems have to be seen in the following context -

(a) A very poor population.
(b) A rapidly growing population.
(c) Very rapid urbanization.

However, all developing countries should not be seen as being similar. Table 2.1 shows that a range of GNP per capita figures from $2,220 in Brazil to $260 in India. Some of the developing countries, especially in Central and South America, have been suffering from acute inflation, while in Africa and Asia this has not been a major problem.

Housing

The chapters of this book dealing with industrialized countries assume, with some justification, that the housing stock is in global terms adequate for the size of the population. Attention is then focussed on housing tenure and housing policy. In the case of developing countries there is a massive housing problem in respect of the number of units let alone their quality.

The more wealthy industrialized countries have, on average, over 400 dwellings per 1,000 inhabitants, and even the poorer countries in Southern and Eastern Europe have about 300 dwellings per 1,000 inhabitants. In India the figure is nearer 230 but this is hardly a fair comparison because of the small size of most dwellings in India. In 1971 in India nearly half of all households lived in one room and fewer than a quarter had three or more rooms.

In some ways the problem facing developing countries is similar to that which the industrialized countries experienced in the 19th century. A rapidly growing population together with a shift from agriculture to industry has led to urbanization. The existing housing stock, already inadequate, has not been able to cope. Overcrowding has increased, squatter settlements have been built, and land has been subdivided. Local authorities have seldom had the resources available to provide basic services such as sewerage and water supply.

It is the urbanization which creates major housing problems as much as the population increase itself. There are two reasons for this -

(a) In rural areas there is scope for much more individual initiative to create improved housing conditions than there is in urban areas.

(b) In all urban areas there is a rich section of the community and the daily contact between this and low income groups concentrated in very poor housing can make for social and political problems.

There is some dispute as to whether it is right that resources in a very poor country should be devoted to housing. It may be argued that housing is less important than food and furthermore that expenditure on housing is something of a luxury when there is a need to improve the productive potential of the country. Conversely, it may be argued that housebuilding is a legitimate industry to promote because it uses few imports, relies on low technology, is labour intensive, and may stimulate other domestic industries.

In fact, empirical evidence suggests that there is a relationship between GDP per capita and the proportion of total output invested in housing (Burns, L S, and Grebler, L, 'Resource Allocation to Housing Investment: a Comparative International Study', *Economic Development and Cultural Change*, October 1976). At very low levels of income a small proportion of output (about 1.5% of GDP) is spent on housing because the priority is for other commodities, particularly food. As incomes increase so there is likely to be urbanization and greater investment in housing reaching a peak of 7-8% of total output. When a basic minimum adequate standard of housing has been provided the proportion of output devoted to housing then declines. The richest countries tend to have the lower proportions of output allocated to housing, simply because they have already built up an adequate stock over the years.

It is commonly argued that the major problem with respect to housing in developing countries is that poor people simply cannot afford it. This argument has been disputed in a World Bank paper (Churchill, A, *Shelter*, World Bank, 1980). Churchill argued -

'Adequate shelter can be provided within the constraints of income. The question really turns upon the definition of the word adequate. Experience has shown that safe water, disposal of human and solid wastes, protection from the environment, and security can technically be provided in quantity and quality sufficient to ensure the provision of a secure and healthy environment at a cost low enough to meet the income constraint of lower income groups. For those at the lowest end of the income scale, this means public standpipes, pit latrines, and traditional forms of housing, built with traditional materials. In Upper Volta, for example, where the income per capita is US$110, water is being supplied at a cost of US$30 (at 1977 prices, inclusive of capital and production costs), a household and shelter unit itself at a maximum of US$265, for a total of US$295. If the provision of technically sound shelter is feasible in this, one of the countries in which costs are highest and incomes are lowest in the world, it should be feasible anywhere."

The paper went on to suggest that the problems do not lie in technical feasibility or costs but rather in social acceptability to decision takers.

The publication argues that most public programmes aimed at providing shelter have failed for the following reasons-

(a) Standards have been too high in relation to ability to pay with the result that large subsidies have been required.
(b) Governments have been reluctant or politically unable to enforce collection of rents and mortgage payments.
(c) Shelter units have been provided far from sources of employment and often without complementary social infrastructure.
(d) Little account has been taken of the ways of living of low income communities, and few attempts have been made to involve them actively in solving their shelter problems.

Before leaving this brief description of housing problems in developing countries the phenomenon of clandestine development should be noted, that is, people take matters into their own hands and build themselves homes, generally on the outskirts of the major urban centres and in contravention of various laws and regulations. Often such homes are fairly primitive, but this does not necessarily follow. Such settlements are known by a number of terms including shanty towns and they are likely to develop in countries other than the very poorest where there are pressures for urbanization, in particular jobs in urban areas but not in rural areas, but inadequate facilities for an influx of population into existing urban centres. This phenomenon occurs in countries as wealthy, in relative terms, as Portugal, and is not confined to the poorest countries of the third world. This informal aspect of the housing system cannot be easily measure and, as will be seen subsequently, is matched by an informal housing finance system.

Financial Systems and Housing Finance

The previous chapter indicated that there are just four types of housing finance system: the direct system, the contract system, the deposit taking system and the mortgage bank system. In the case of poorer countries it is the direct system which predominates. Informal housing finance systems are, by definition, difficult to describe, simply because little data are available about them.

As a general rule the more developed an economy the greater is the extent of financial intermediation, that is the degree to which investing and borrowing is done through the intermediation of financial institutions, rather than directly between borrower and lender. The great service that financial intermediaries perform is to bring together borrowers and lenders whose requirements can never be identical. They can take in varying amounts of money on varying terms to suit a variety of depositors and they can lend varying amounts on varying terms to suit a variety of borrowers.

Table 2.3 illustrates this point by comparing the total assets of financial institutions as a percentage of GNP together with GNP per capita.

Table 2.3   Financial Systems in Industrialized and Developing Countries

Country	Financial Aggregates as Percentage of GNP 1977-78	GNP per capita 1978 US $
USA	221	9,590
West Germany	145	9,580
France	112	8,260
Japan	204	7,280
United Kingdom	199	5,030
Spain	122	3,470
South Korea	123	1,160
Brazil	57	1,910
Nigeria	39	560
Philippines	74	560
Thailand	63	490
Bolivia	17	510
Kenya	57	330
India	58	180

Source: International Finance Corporation, reproduced from Renaud, B, *Housing and Financial Institutions in Developing Countries*, World Bank Discussion Paper, 1982.
Note: At end-1978 there were $1.92 to the pound.

It will be seen that in the industrialized countries, financial aggregates are higher than GNP (although it must be stressed that there is no direct relationship between the two) and in some cases financial aggregates are more than twice GNP. By contrast, in developing countries, financial aggregates are much lower in relation to GNP. However, it is significant that there are quite major variations between the developing countries, Bolivia standing out as having a very low figure and India and South Korea having comparatively high figures.

There are a number of reasons for the underdeveloped state of financial systems in developing countries. The first, and most obvious, is that if people have few financial assets then they do not require financial institutions to look after them. Many people in developing countries are also suspicious of financial institutions, especially where, as is commonly the case, they are government controlled.

A brief study of the formal financial systems of developing countries reveals certain basic similarities. In nearly all developing countries the commercial banks, frequently government owned, hold by far the largest share of personal deposits. However, the banks lend comparatively little to the personal sector. Most countries have a nationalised savings bank system, often run through post offices. In the poorest countries the funds collected in this way are on-lent to the government which is likely to need all the finance it can obtain. As a country becomes more developed so the national savings system may be allowed to lend and the scope increases for private sector institutions such as savings and loan associations.

Housing finance in developing countries is dominated by informal systems of financing. For example, a survey of low income housing in Cartagena, Colombia (Strassman, W P, *The Transformation of Urban Housing*, John Hopkins University Press, 1983) found that less than 10% of low income housing had any debts against it. The common pattern was one in which there was a slow accumulation of funds which determined the pace of construction. Also, many of those who improved housing did so with the aid of remittances received from members of their families who worked outside the country. In India (which is studied in detail in Chapter 22) it is estimated that only 6-7% of housing investment is financed by institutional means. Generally, under 20% of housing investment in developing countries is financed by financial institutions.

It is therefore necessary to study in some detail, in as much as this is possible, how informal housing finance systems work. The following description draws heavily on a study by James Christian (Christian, J W, *Housing Finance for Developing Countries*, International Union of Building Societies and Savings Associations, 1980). In terms of employment, the informal sector is characterised by family ownership of businesses, reliance on indigenous resources, small scale operations, labour intensive technology, skills acquired outside the formal education system, and unregulated and competitive markets. In the housing sector the simplest manifestation of the informal sector is people building their own homes, perhaps using indigenous materials. Illegal development is a more extreme manifestation.

The simplest form of housing finance in the informal sector is financing within families. People draw on current income or borrow from relatives in order to buy building materials or pay contractors to begin building a home. As more income or borrowing becomes available so more can be spent on the house. In countries where brides are entitled to receive a dowry, funds for housing construction are frequently raised by selling part of such dowries. Also, of course, much of the housing construction is conducted by the members of a family and their relatives.

Trade credit is another part of the informal housing finance system. It is not regarded as a loan as such but is merely reflected in the price of the product, effectively a hire purchase arrangement. Contractors who offer trade credit may themselves be financed, to some extent, by the formal sector of the economy.

The most formal form of informal finance is the rotating credit society by which members contribute a set amount each week or month. Each member of the society has the right to borrow the funds under some established procedure. In Africa and the Middle East lots are frequently drawn to decide who should have access to the funds and normally no interest is charged. In Asian countries interest is generally charged and access to funds is determined by bids rather than by drawing lots. These institutions are, of course, very similar in nature to the early building societies in the United Kingdom and similar institutions in other countries.

Where there are formal housing finance institutions in developing countries these are generally very small when measured against the size of the housing stock or the population although they may appear large when compared with other financial institutions. One significant difference between industrialized and developing countries is that general financial institutions, ie banks, in the developing countries tend to have little role in housing finance simply because such business is inconvenient for them and they have other more profitable outlets for their funds. Housing finance must therefore be provided by specialist organisations. The major question that has to be faced is what sort of organisation should these be, what contribution can they make to economic development and, finally, how can they be structured to work most efficiently. The next section of this chapter deals in detail with the requirements of housing finance systems in developing countries.

The Requirements of Housing Finance Systems in Developing Countries

The point has already been made that the financial systems of developing countries are less sophisticated than those of the more advanced industrialized countries. Many people will have no contact with financial institutions at all and there is comparatively little available expertise in respect of management of financial institutions. House-purchase loans to individuals pose even greater problems than other loans for four reasons -

(a) A house-purchase lending function implies a relatively large number of small loans and this imposes high transaction costs. Many of the people to whom loans are made will not be familiar with financial institutions and, again, this means higher transaction costs. Potential borrowers may not have permanent employment and this increases the possibility of arrears and losses.

(b) The problem of maturity transformation, that is, raising short term deposits and making long term loans, has not been easiliy overcome in some advanced industrialized countries, such as the USA. It is asking a great deal of a financial system of a developing country to overcome effectively this particular problem. Certainly, variable interest rates are likely to be viewed with considerable suspicion.

(c) Many developing countries have severe inflation problems, partly because governments have willingly used, or have been forced into using, deficit financing with the inevitable increase in inflation after a time lag. As Chapter 1 has illustrated, inflation makes it difficult to operate a housing finance system effectively.

(d) Because housing finance institutions deal with households, the question of public confidence in them arises. Even in industrialized countries many people are suspicious of banks and other institutions and those institutions which are most successful probably owe part of that success to the fact that they have been in existence for a very long period of time. Institutions in developing countries cannot claim such a pedigree.

Ideally, the housing finance system of a developing country should aim to meet three criteria -

(a) Housing finance loans should be made available at an affordable rate of interest.

(b) The financial institutions themselves should be viable and should not be operated in a way which might endanger that viability.

(c) The financial institutions and the housing finance system generally should contribute to the overall economic development of the country, in particular the housing sector. The clear inter-relationships between housing finance and housing itself must be recognised. An efficient housing finance system can, itself, help to reduce housing problems.

Experience suggests that both housing and housing finance systems in developing countries must recognise three distinct strata of the market. The first is the high income strata which can be catered for adequately by existing institutions. The second strata is what might be termed as the subsidized middle class, that is, people who could perhaps obtain a loan on commercial terms but who, in practice, have been the major beneficiaries of government subsidies. The third strata is the informal private sector comprising the poorest sections of the community who seldom are touched by government programmes, even when these are specifically targetted at them. Policy needs to differentiate quite clearly between those who can be helped to help themselves and those who have to be assisted financially. Experience suggests that the poor can best be helped through direct programmes aimed at them and explicitly subsidized out of the state budget. No useful purpose is served by encouraging financial institutions to lend too far down the income scale, thereby threatening their own long term viability. However, financial institutions can be encouraged to provide loans to the middle class in a way that retains their viability.

Broadly speaking, there are seven ways in which money can be raised to finance house-purchase lending activities in developing countries -

- (a) Tax revenue.
- (b) What might be called, technically, public saving, which in practice is likely to mean monopoly profits made by nationalised industries.
- (c) Inflation, which has the effect of reducing the real value of debt over time.
- (d) Savings of the corporate sector.
- (e) Inflow of foreign capital.
- (f) Mandatory savings systems.
- (g) Personal savings.

Again, experience suggests that it is unwise to rely on the public sector through budgetary allocations which may be financed by taxation or other sources. In practice, any institution dependant on the state may find that it is forced to lend to lower income groups thereby threatening its viability. Also, funds from the government are likely to dry up when the inevitable economic crisis occurs. Governments of developing countries have a large number of priorities many of which seem more pressing than providing housing assistance to people other than the very poorest.

Neither the corporate nor the foreign sector can be relied on to provide significant funds for house-purchase loans. Their priority and expertise must be in the financing of industrial and agricultural investment.

Mandatory savings schemes have been used in a number of countries, notably Mexico, Singapore and Brazil, but it is difficult to measure the success of such schemes. By definition, funds are raised and these can be used for any purpose. Whether this is an efficient mechanism in terms of providing people with what they want, and in terms of contributing to economic development generally, is another matter.

The personal sector is the obvious sector to encourage as the primary source of finance for house-purchase loans. In many developing countries this sector is not tapped to any significant extent. At first sight it might seem that there is not much scope for raising savings from people who are poor. However, poverty is a relative not an absolute term, and even in the poorest countries some the poorer people in those countries may be net savers and their savings can be used to finance loans to others. For example, in Sri Lanka and Malaysia, over 10% of those in the lowest income deciles have savings. Moreover, people may be encouraged to save specifically if they have the home ownership objective in mind. Indeed, there is evidence that the only reason why some poor people will save is so they can buy their own homes. It is significant that most of the housing finance systems in the industrialized countries arose out of mutual clubs where people did provide the savings used to finance their loans. As time went on so more sophisticated systems could be introduced. There is, therefore, much to be said for encouraging housing finance institutions which rely on taking deposits from the personal sector. This enables a new source of funds to be tapped (and therefore does not divert resources from other sectors) and may well encourage the growth of saving generally. Moreover, financial institutions will have greater knowledge of their market for loans if they have potential borrowers as their investors.

The main management question which therefore must face housing finance institutions in developing countries is how they can increase the flow of savings from the personal sector and most efficiently use these funds for house-purchase lending. James Christian suggests that what is important is that there should be a linkage between the informal sector of the economy and the formal sector. Savings institutions should try to work within the established framework and should not try to impose a system imported directly from an advanced industrialized country. Christian suggests a number of approaches by which the formal and informal sectors can be linked -

(a) An 'outreach' programme. Mobile branches of formal sector institutions can make regular scheduled visits to squatter areas to collect savings and receive loan applications. Existing employees of the financial institutions can be offered commission for generating new accounts and servicing loans in informal sector communities during their off duty hours. The formal sector institution can enter into agreements with a network of agents who are not employees of the institution to act as intermediaries between the institution and the local communities.

(b) The offering of 'mutual accounts' in the names of villages or other communities rather than individuals.

(c) Informal rotating credit societies or similar arrangements can become affiliates of a housing finance institution. This approach may make maximum use of existing informal arrangements, but it requires a substantial modification of the method of operation of the financial institution itself.

The affordability problem can be eased by encouraging owners to rent out part of their homes, something which is done to a large extent anyway. Certainly any restrictions on letting could be very damaging.

The point has already been made that specialist institutions are more likely to be successful in promoting housing finance systems in developing countries. The reasons for this need to be emphasized at this stage. The first is simply that special expertise is required and this can best be provided by specialist rather than by general institutions. Probably a more important point is that where a financial institution is able to make loans for house-purchase and for other purposes then, in practice, it is likely to neglect the housing market because more profit can be made through other forms of lending. There are examples of housing banks which have been set up in various countries, which, after a few years, have ceased to have anything to do with housing despite their names.

This analysis rather suggests that there is no role for government but this would be going too far. One problem in developing countries is that governments have been unstable and policies cannot be relied on for any period of time. This creates more problems in the housing finance sector than in almost any other because of the long time scale which is required to develop and implement policies. A number of areas have been identified where governments can make a positive contribution to the encouragement of housing finance in developing countries -

(a) Housing must specifically be identified as a priority and it must be recognised that this does not conflict with the overall objective of economic growth. However, it needs to be recognised that housing cannot be as important a priority as industry or agriculture.

(b) Obviously, any legal constraints which prevent the housing finance institutions from operating with maximum efficiency, including working with the informal sector, should be removed. In particular, any problems over land tenure must be resolved. This problem tends to be more critical the poorer the country.

(c) Deposit insurance may be necessary if there are doubts as to the viability of financial institutions. Experience shows that, even in industrial countries, this can be a very effective way of encouraging the development of a housing finance system.

(d) Equally, on the mortgage side, mortgage insurance might be a useful weapon, partly to help standardize lending procedures, but also to encourage lenders who perhaps otherwise might be unduly cautious.

(e) Perhaps the worst mistake that a government can make is to attempt to impose artificially low interest rates, and it is not only governments of developing countries that have been guilty in this respect. This is likely to lead to a misallocation of resources and may often be combined with forcing lenders to lend to people who cannot afford repayments. Allowing interest rates to operate at their market levels and providing subsidies to the poorest is far more likely to lead to the efficient allocation of resources and the growth of a viable housing finance system. In particular, it must be recognised that if interest rates are too low, savings will not be attracted.

(f) Management is particularly important in developing countries, and government can obviously make a contribution by providing for the training of staff in financial institutions. As will be seen subsequently a number of institutions in the industrialized countries have made a significant contribution in this respect.

The World Bank and International Finance Corporation

The World Bank and International Finance Corporation are the leading international organisations concerned with the promotion of housing and housing finance. The International Finance Corporation is part of the World Bank group, but operates in a different way and is best described separately.

The World Bank

The World Bank comprises two bodies, the International Bank for Reconstruction and Development (IBRD) and the International Development Association (IDA). However, they share the same staff and can be considered, for the most part, as one organisation.

Both organisations have as their objective 'to promote economic progress in developing countries by providing financial and technical assistance, mostly for specific projects in both public and private sectors'.

The IBRD was conceived at the Bretton Woods conference in 1944, at the same time as the International Monetary Fund. The Bank was duly established in 1945 in Washington DC, USA with the objective of helping to finance the reconstruction and development of its member countries. Currently it has 144 members, the most significant non members being the USSR, Czechoslovakia and Poland. It is owned by the member governments who have voting rights in accordance with their proportion of the total share capital.

IBRD lends only to credit worthy borrowers in the developing countries. It lends for a number of activities including agriculture and rural development, energy, education, transportation, urban development, water supply, sewerage, health and nutrition. It obtains its funds on the international financial markets and lends over long terms, generally 15 to 20 years. Its lending commitments in 1982 were $10,330 million and it had 150 projects in operation.

The International Development Association (IDA) is sometimes known as the 'softloan' part of the World Bank. It lends only to governments of poorer countries, its loans are over long terms, generally 50 years, and no interest is charged although there is an annual administration fee. It is financed by grants from governments, largely those of the more prosperous countries, although also of the oil producing countries.

The World Bank initiated its urban lending programme in 1972. It identified as its primary objective the assistance of member governments in developing approaches to the efficient and equitable provision of urban services and employment. Four secondary objectives were identified -

(a) To demonstrate low cost technical solutions for shelter, infrastructure and transport which the urban population could afford and which could be improved over time.
(b) To demonstrate that it was possible to provide services for most of the urban poor on a non subsidized basis.
(c) To demonstrate the feasibility of comprehensive urban planning and investment procedures.
(d) To demonstrate the reproduction of projects incorporating these objectives, that is, that they should be self-financing and self-sustaining.

In 1975 the publication *Housing Sector Policy Paper* set out four conditions for urban lending by the World Bank -

(a) The government should have a commitment to help the urban poor.
(b) The government should guarantee land tenure to project benificiaries.
(c) The government should improve pricing policies and reduce subsidies so that projects could recover their costs.
(d) The government should agree that projects should be integrated within a broad approach to urban planning and investment.

The Bank's shelter projects have fallen into two groups: slum upgrading projects, and sites and services projects. Throughout, the approach of the World Bank has been different from that of many governments, through its use of private savings and self help efforts. Early projects in Botswana, El Salvador, Jamaica, Kenya, Peru, Senegal and Tanzania were focussed on sites and services. Slum upgrading projects involve the improvement of infrastructure, in particular water supply, sanitation, roads, footpaths, drainage and electricity. Both types of project require that households receive security of land tenure thereby providing an incentive for the mobilisation of savings. Such projects were generally deemed to have been successful. Between 1972 and 1981 36 urban shelter projects were approved by the Bank. The total project costs were $1,906 million and lending by the World Bank totalled $942 million.

The Bank identified a number of major problems with such projects, some of which have already been touched on in the early part of this chapter-

(a) The organisation of projects, especially those which cut across a number of governmental units.
(b) The acquisition of land for new development and the subsequent guaranteeing of secure tenure to households.
(c) Cost recovery, especially for some sites and services projects.
(d) Efforts by some agencies to design and provide services at higher standards than agreed initially.
(e) Project management where a range of services have to be provided.

The Bank has, in the course of its urban programme, developed substantial expertise. The Bank's publications provide a wealth of analytical and descriptive material on urban housing problems in developing countries and have in themselves played a major role in promoting training and increasing understanding of the problems.

In a study of its urban lending programme over its first ten years, the Bank concludes that its projects have demonstrated low cost technical solutions and sound financial principles that should help public institutions deal with housing issues, but it emphasizes the need for the encouragement of private housing markets to work more effectively. Projects being considered are designed to use the advantages of both public and private sectors. The Bank is also seeking to strengthen local institutions so that they can relieve the pressure on the Bank itself and on other lenders and stimulate further private investment in the urban sector.

The International Finance Corporation

The International Finance Corporation (IFC) was established in 1956 with the objective 'to promote economic progress in developing countries by helping to mobilise domestic and foreign capital to stimulate the growth of the private sector'.

The IFC is primarily concerned with financial markets rather than with urban projects as such, although a significant part of its activity has been directed towards financial institutions in the housing field.

IFC has more than 120 members and authorized capital of $650 million. Following a capital injection in 1978 it has grown substantially over the past few years. By the end of 1982 it had approved investments of $4.7 billion in more than 650 ventures.

In 1971 the IFC established its Capital Markets Department which provides the necessary assistance for the development of financial markets including advisory services and financial support. It is recognised that the development of financial markets must accompany economic development generally, a point already made earlier in this chapter. The Capital Markets

Department acts both as an adviser and as an investor. It has invested in 32 institutions or mechanisms in 18 developing countries, covering a wide variety of areas including housing finance, financing of small businesses and venture capital financing.

Its technical assistance programme has included the preparation of a number of policy papers, studies of the financial sector in various countries, advice on the regulatory, fiscal and institutional framework, and assistance in drafting various laws and regulations.

The investment in housing finance institutions is seen as being an important aspect of the overall objective of contributing to the development of financial systems. IFC has five objectives in the financial sector -

(a) Increasing the supply of medium and long term funds.
(b) Broadening competition by encouraging housing finance institutions as primary lenders, and long term savings institutions as secondary investors in mortgage loan instruments.
(c) Introducing financial innovations such as new mechanisms for making housing loans.
(d) Encouraging private sector involvement in housing finance.
(e) Mobilising additional resources for housing.

The IFC sees itself as a catalyst, bringing together the various public authorities, private sector institutions and any foreign partners. It will provide technical assistance to encourage an appropriate regulatory and supervisory framework and will also invest directly in institutions. It stresses the need for prudent policies to be pursued so as to ensure that the institutions remain independent.

The IFC has been involved in six housing projects, in Colombia, the Lebanon, Bolivia, India, Senegal and Indonesia. IFC's interests in the projects in Colombia, Lebanon and Bolivia have been sold. One of the projects, a savings and loan corporation in Colombia, was deemed to have been successful. The other two, the Bank of the Near East in Lebanon and the Banco Hipotecario Nacional in Bolivia, were deemed to have moved away from their original objectives towards commercial banking operations, a danger mentioned previously.

The project in Colombia illustrates the successful way in which private finance can be encouraged. The Corporación Colombiana de Ahorro y Vivienda, generally known as Davivienda, was the IFC's first investment in a specialist housing finance institution. It arose out of Colombia's national development plan of 1971-74. Previously, the main sources of housing finance had been the government, through a subsidized central mortgage bank, and short term high rate financing from private sector institutions. IFC invested in a private stock company, the chief sponsor of which was a broadly held commercial bank. Other financial institutions also invested in the bank. The system expanded rapidly, helped by indexation, provided for by the government. IFC felt the project had gone sufficiently well to sell its shares in 1976.

The IFC's largest investment has been in the Housing Development Finance Corporation (HDFC) of India. The Indian housing finance system and this institution are described in detail in Chapter 22. The IFC's role was to participate in the financing of HDFC and it also plays an active role on the board of directors and it gives technical assistance.

The IFC's experience has led it to believe in the necessity to have specialist institutions for the reasons outlined earlier in this chapter. Its own experience has been that institutions which could engage in other banking activities did so. The IFC also suggests that experience with institutions with significant government participation is that they can be forced to focus on low income housing needs at the expense of their long term viability.

The Agency for International Development

The largest single institution which has the objective of encouraging the development on housing and housing finance systems in developing countries is the Office of Housing and Urban Programmes of the United States Agency for International Development (AID). The office is headed by Peter Kimm. AID operates primarily by providing technical assistance and by guaranteeing loans made by private sector American institutions to finance projects in developing countries. This Housing Guarantee Programme originated in the early 1960s although it has changed in emphasis several times. In the early 1970s policy required that resources should be used specifically to serve the needs of low income families and in 1978 the authorizing legislation was amended to allow financing of related community facilities and services.

AID's shelter policy has five basic objectives -

(a) To ensure that low income families have access to secure land tenure, basic services and housing they can afford.
(b) To develop systems for financing shelter and urban development with minimum subsidy requirements.
(c) To encourage and facilitate an increased role for the private sector in low income shelter production.
(d) To develop institutions capable of sustaining a level of production of shelter appropriate to the needs of the population, with special emphasis on meeting the shelter needs of the urban poor.
(e) To encourage the preparation and implementation of national housing policies that reflect these four basic objectives.

The Housing Guarantee Programme finances projects including upgrading of slums, sites and services, core housing, low cost housing units, and community facilities and services.

Since its inception AID has authorized $1.7 billion in Housing Guarantee loans for projects in 44 nations. In 1983 Housing Guarantee loans of $142 million were authorized for projects in Bolivia, El Salvador, India, Ivory Coast, Jamaica, Kenya, Panama, Peru and Sri Lanka. The project in Bolivia can illustrate the type of work which AID does. A $15 million loan was approved in 1983 to strengthen the private housing finance system. The government of Bolivia will borrow the money and on-lend to 12 associations in the savings and loan system and a co-operative. The institutions will use the resources to expand lending to low income families. AID will provide technical support.

A major part of the work of AID is the provision of technical assistance and research. Where a Housing Guarantee loan is made then one or more American technicians will be seconded to the appropriate institution for a period of about two years.

There are also a number of individual research projects not linked to the Housing Guarantee Programme. For example, a study in Sri Lanka proposed to strengthen the role of the private sector in decisions relating to the type of housing to be produced and it suggested transferring the financing of housing programmes from a public sector institution to the semi public sector State Mortgage and Investment Bank. One objective of this would be to expand the role of that institution as a primary lender. In 1983 technical projects took place in 40 countries.

AID has a major role in the provision of training and to this end it organises seminars and sponsors individual training programmes. AID also sponsors conferences which, over the years, have proved to be one of the main forums in which housing and housing finance experts get together. The proceedings of these conferences also provide valuable information. In 1982 alone AID co-sponsored or participated in 11 conferences held in Afria, Asia and the Americas.

The United Nations

The United Nations has had only a very limited involvement in the promotion of housing and housing finance systems, and many good intentions have led to little in the way of concrete results. Much effort has been devoted to considering the establishment of an International Housing Finance Corporation but nothing has emerged nor does anything seem likely to emerge.

The United Nations Economic Commission for Europe, based in Geneva, did some work on housing policy and finance in the 1950s and 1960s although this was not related to developing countries. Some studies were done and reports were written in respect of developing countries in the 1950s and 1960s but the efforts were fairly haphazard and it was the World Bank which increasingly took the lead at the international level.

In 1972 a UN conference on the human environment was held in Stockholm, Sweden, and this set the pattern for a number of similar conferences. Following this conference it was agreed that an international institution should be established. Under the direction of the United Nations Environment Programme the UN Habitat and Human Settlements Foundation was founded in 1975. This was merged into the UN Centre for Human Settlements (Habitat) in 1978. This organisation is based in Nairobi, Kenya.

Before its demise the Foundation operated in some 30 countries, generally by providing seed capital and giving technical assistance. It helped to establish housing finance systems in a number of countries, it conducted studies in several countries and it organised study tours.

The Centre for Human Settlements operates primarily through research and technical co-operation projects. At any one time some 200 projects are taking place. Recent work in the housing finance field has included case studies on the financing of human settlements, research on the role of community based finance institutions and case studies on credit unions and housing co-operatives.

Eric Carlson, who over the years has been active in most of the United Nations work, has described the progress of the UN in this area as follows -

'There appears to be little progress in the UN system at the present time regarding matters of housing finance. Certainly this progress is not commensurate with the major efforts expended at various levels to mobilise support for the two aborted projects, the International Housing Finance Corporation and the UN Habitat and Human Settlements Foundation. Whether any significant United Nations activity in support of housing finance development will take place in the 1980s and beyond is ultimately up to the nation-states who comprise UN membership. The search for a constituency to support such efforts undoubtedly will continue.'

(For a detailed history of UN involvement in housing finance see the paper by Eric Carlson in the proceedings of the IUBSSA Congress held in 1983.)

Other Institutions

The International Union of Building Societies and Savings Associations

This organisation is described in detail in Chapter 27. It is, basically, an international trade association for specialist housing finance institutions. Its main functions are to provide for an exchange of information. Until 1982 it employed no full time staff and therefore was not in a position to do the sort of work which AID and the World Bank has been doing. However, it does take a major interest in housing finance in developing countries through its

Housing Finance Development Committee which is chaired by Lalit Pandit of Kenya. The International Union has helped to serve as a catalyst in bringing together developing and industrialized countries and it has frequently provided a forum at which the particular problems of the developing nations can be discussed. Its publications have also been useful in this respect, in particular, that by James Christian, referred to earlier in this chapter. Recent activities have included the co-sponsoring, with the Agency for International Development, of a 1983 conference in the Caribbean. It is also helping to promote an African Union of Building Societies and Housing Finance Institutions. The International Union took a significant step forward in respect of its work in developing countries in 1983 when Eric Carlson, one of the leading experts in this field, was appointed a special advisor on his retirement from the United Nations.

The International Savings Banks Institute

This organisation is described in detail in Chapter 28. It has certain similarities with the International Union of building Societies and Savings Associations in that it is an international trade association. However, unlike the International Union, it has, for many years, had a very active full time staff based in Geneva, Switzerland and one of its functions is to encourage the development of savings bank systems in the developing countries. An interesting feature of its work is the encouragement of bilateral co-operation between developing countries. The Institute has helped to arrange for a linking of institutions in developing countries with those in industrialized countries. For example, savings banks in West Germany have linked with savings banks in Kenya, Thailand and Tunisia. Among the recent activities of the ISBI has been its involvement, together with the United Nations and the savings banks association in Sweden, in missions to various countries, aimed at studying savings systems and capital formation processes.

The ISBI also arranges seminars and training programmes, generally in conjunction with its member institutions.

One savings bank which has taken a particular interest in developing countries is Cariplo. This bank, based in Milan, Italy is the largest savings bank in the world; it is described in detail in Chapter 11. It has set up a training centre, FINAFRICA, in Milan, to promote banking and savings banking in Africa. In the 1980/81 year nearly 200 bank employees and managerial staff from African countries followed training courses at FINAFRICA, and various seminars were held. Specialists from FINAFRICA also made visits to savings institutions in developing countries.

Commonwealth Development Corporation

The Commonwealth Development Corporation (CDC) is a British government body, based in London, the primary objective of which is to assist the development of the economies of overseas countries. CDC operates largely, but not exclusively, in British Commonwealth countries. It works predominantly through providing finance on commercial terms. At the end of 1983 CDC had £40.9 million invested in housing finance projects, 8.1% of its total investments. CDC provides both equity and loan finance; in the case of housing finance, equity participations are most common.

Among CDC projects at the end of 1983 were -

(a) A £2 million loan to the Barbados Mortgage Finance Company.
(b) A £3 million loan to the Banco Central de Costa Rica—for on-lending to a body which provides mortgage finance for lower and middle income housing.
(c) Equity and loan finance in the Dominica Mortgage Finance Co.
(d) Equity (100%) and loan finance in the Guyana Mortgage Finance Co.
(e) Equity and loan finance in the Caribbean Housing Finance Corporation.
(f) Equity finance in the Hong Kong Building and Loan Agency.
(g) Equity and loan finance in the Housing Finance Co of Kenya.

CDC is participating in the establishment of Shelter Afrique, described in Chapter 26.

United States Trade Associations

The two trade associations for savings and loan associations in the United States, the United States League of Savings Institutions and the National Council of Savings Institutions, particularly the latter, have for many years played a significant role in encouraging housing finance in developing countries. This they have largely done through the provision of expert advice, and ad hoc technical assistance. They have also worked under contract for AID and, over the years, have built up a significant volume of expertise.

Bibliography

Capital Markets—Mobilizing Resources for Development, International Finance Corporation, 1983.
Commonwealth Development Corporation, Report and Accounts, 1983, 1984.
Christian, J W, *Housing Finance for Developing Countries*, International Union of Building Societies and Savings Associations, 1980.
Churchill, A, *Shelter*, World Bank, 1980.
Eighth Conference on Housing in Africa, Agency for International Development, 1982.
Housing Guarantee Program Annual Report—Fiscal Year 1983, Office of Housing and Urban Programmes, US Agency for International Development, 1984.
Learning by Doing—World Bank Lending for Urban Development, 1972-82, World Bank, 1983.
Les Cahiers de l'Urbanisme et du Logement, January 1983.
Proceedings, International Union of Building Societies and Savings Associations, XVI World Congress, Melbourne, Australia, October 1983.

Renaud, B, *Housing and Financial Institutions in Developing Countries*, World Bank Discussion Paper, 1982.
The Role of Specialised Housing Finance Institutions in the Financial System: The IFC Approach, International Finance Corporation, 1982.
The World Bank and International Finance Corporation, World Bank, 1981.
Urban Edge, World Bank, May 1983.

Acknowledgements

This chapter draws very heavily on the publications listed in the bibliography. The publications of James Christian and Bertrand Renaud were used extensively in the theoretical section. The sections on the various institutions are little more than summaries of reports prepared by those institutions.

The author is indebted to a number of people who provided information and who willingly gave up time to explain the work of their organisations and to discuss problems of housing finance in developing countries. In particular -

Eric Carlson, special advisor to the International Union of Building Societies and Savings Associations, for helping to arrange meetings with others as well as for his advice and comments.
Bertrand Renaud of the World Bank.
Peter Kimm and his colleagues at AID.
Harold Dunkerley of the World Bank.
James Christian of the United States League of Savings Institutions.
The author is indebted to Bertrand Renaud of the World Bank for his comprehensive and helpful comments on an earlier draft of this chapter.

CHAPTER 3

UNITED KINGDOM

The United Kingdom is different from most other countries in that there is no market rented sector of housing; rather there has been a sharp polarization between rented accommodation, provided by local authorities on the basis of need, and owner-occupied accommodation available on the open market. Both these sectors have expanded at the expense of private rented accommodation, which is now almost negligible. As affluence has increased, so the demand for the owner-occupied housing has grown in relation to the demand for local authority rented housing.

Because there is no market rented sector many households have to purchase houses at a very early age, and the housing finance system has had to accommodate this. Typically, new households purchase their first house before they are 25. Housing finance in Britain is dominated by the building societies, which account for some 75% of outstanding debt. They operate on the deposit taking principle, and, indeed, in the savings market occupy the place that in many of the other countries is taken by specialist savings banks as such. All building society operations are at a variable rate of interest, and this has helped British societies overcome fluctuations in the general level of interest rates more successfully than their counterparts in some other countries.

Introduction

The United Kingdom occupies an area of 241,000 sq kilometres. Its population in mid-1982 was 56,300,000. Although the country is quite densely populated, a higher proportion of the land area is usable than in many other countries.

The United Kingdom comprises England, Wales, Scotland and Northern Ireland. The United Kingdom without Northern Ireland is referred to as Great Britain. It is unfortunately the case that some statistics refer to the United Kingdom, while others refer to Great Britain, and little can be done to overcome this problem. For example, in this chapter, figures for housing largely relate to Great Britain, whereas those for building societies relate to the whole of the United Kingdom. However, as Northern Ireland is relatively small in terms of population compared with the UK (only 1.2% of the United Kingdom population live in Northern Ireland) this problem is not too great in practice.

The United Kingdom is a monarchy, and has two Houses of Parliament. Since the war, government has alternated between the two principal parties, the Conservative Party and the Labour Party. A Conservative Government was elected to power in May 1979, and was re-elected in June 1983. Politics and housing are closely related in Britain, because the polarization of the housing tenures has been associated with the two political parties. The Conservatives are seen as the supporter of owner-occupation, and Labour as the supporter of council accommodation.

It is well known that the United Kingdom has performed relatively badly in economic terms compared with most other advanced countries, and it has been moving steadily down the 'league table'. Over the period 1960 to 1980, real GDP per capita increased by an average of 2.0% a year, compared with an average for all OECD countries of 3.1%. Similarly, the average rate of increase of consumer prices over the same period was 8.8% a year, compared with the OECD average of 6.1%. Both short and long term interest rates have tended to be slightly more volatile than in other countries.

Housing

Housing Policy and Housing Tenure

The UK industrialized before most other countries, and the development of housing reflects this. At the beginning of the twentieth century almost 90% of British households lived in privately rented accommodation with the remainder owning their own homes. In 1915 rents were restricted for the first time, and subsequently legislation has made it very unattractive for private landlords to make accommodation available, by controlling rents and by giving almost total security of tenure. In the inter-war period, local authorities began providing accommodation for rent, and there was substantial building for sale. By 1938, 32% of homes were owner-occupied, 10% were rented from local authorities and the remaining 58% were still in the private rented sector. These trends continued in the post-war period, and by 1970 owner-occupation had increased to over 50% of the total and local authority renting to nearly one third.

By this time there was virtually no rented accommodation freely available on the market, although a limited 'black market' has always existed, especially in London. Rents for local authority housing have been kept to a low level with the result that there has been an excessive demand, and housing has had to be allocated on the basis of need. This, increasingly, has forced people to become owner-occupiers if they wish to exercise any degree of choice in their housing, and also if they cannot demonstrate that they are 'in need'. It also has to be said that owner-occupied housing has enjoyed distinct tax advantages through being exempt from Capital Gains Tax, and, more importantly, interest on mortgage loans (up to £25,000 since 1974 and £30,000 since

1983) qualifies for tax relief at a borrower's highest marginal tax rate.

The Conservative Government, elected in May 1979, implemented a policy of selling local authority housing to sitting tenants at discounts ranging from 33% to 50%. Since that time the rents on council houses have also been increasing quite sharply, thereby further encouraging the move from council housing to owner-occupied housing. However, tenants below a certain income are shielded from the full effects of rent increases by rent rebates, and the overall effect is that there is an even sharper polarization of the tenures, with all but the poorest people becoming owner-occupiers.

Some 500,000 local authority houses, about 7% of the total, were sold to their owners between 1979 and 1983, and the policy looks set to continue for a few years. As a result, the proportion of houses which are rented from local authorities is tending to decline. Table 3.1 shows trends in housing tenure for Great Britain from 1971 to 1982.

Table 3.1   Housing Tenure, Great Britain, 1971-82

Year	Number of Houses	Percentage of Total		
		Owner-Occupied	Rented from Public Sector	Private Rented & Other
1971	18,833,000	50.1	30.4	19.5
1976	20,124,000	53.3	31.7	15.0
1979	20,822,000	54.6	31.9	13.5
1980	21,025,000	55.4	31.6	13.0
1981	21,189,000	57.4	30.4	12.2
1982	21,328,000	59.0	29.3	11.7

Source: *Housing and Construction Statistics 1972-82*, HMSO, 1983, Table 9.3.

A survey carried out for The Building Societies Association in March 1983 (*Housing Tenure*, The Building Societies Association, 1983) shows the extent to which there is an unmet demand for owner-occupied housing. At the time of the survey 62% of all adults (as opposed to households) were owner-occupiers, but 77% said that owner-occupation was their ideal tenure in two years' time, and 78% expected to be owner-occupiers within 10 years. Demand for and expectation of council accommodation was virtually negligible among those under the age of 35. However, the survey also showed that while nearly half of council tenants wanted to be owner-occupiers, only 14% said it was likely that they would buy the homes in which they were living. There is, therefore, likely to be a major problem of 'difficult to let' council accommodation, especially some of the less desirable flats in inner city areas.

Housebuilding

The United Kingdom has devoted a comparatively low proportion of its GDP to investment in residential construction, this partly reflecting the fact that housing conditions in Britain were better than those in other countries in the immediate post-war period. Over the period 1960 to 1980, residential construction accounted for 3.4% of GDP, compared with an OECD average of 5.4%. In recent years there has been a very sharp decline in housebuilding for a number of reasons -

(a) The problem of lack of numbers of houses has been overcome.
(b) There has been a switch of emphasis away from demolishing older housing and replacing it with new building, to one of rehabilitating older housing as far as possible.
(c) The government has provided considerably less funds for the construction of local authority housing.
(d) The recession, as in other countries, has caused a sharp reduction in housebuilding.

Table 3.2 shows trends in new house completions from 1978 to 1983.

Table 3.2   New House Completions, Great Britain, 1979-83

Year	Public Sector	Private Sector	Total
1978	131,000	149,000	280,000
1979	104,000	140,000	244,000
1980	107,000	127,000	234,000
1981	84,000	113,000	197,000
1982	49,000	121,000	171,000
1983	50,000	138,000	188,000

Source: *Housing and Construction Statistics*, HMSO, Table 1.3.

Houses built in the public sector are almost entirely for rent, while those built in the private sector are largely for sale. A significant decline in public sector housebuilding is apparent. Private sector housebuilding picked up markedly in 1983 as the economy showed the first signs of moving out of recession.

Housing Finance

The Housing Finance Market

The pattern of housing tenure is such that most households wish to become owner-occupiers at a very early age. In 1980, 33% of households under the age of 25 were owner-occupiers, and in the 25-29 age group the proportion was 53%. Most young people obviously are not able to accumulate a high deposit, and therefore need high percentage loans. The contract system therefore cannot work in Britain. Moreover, there is only a limited private bond market, largely because of the favourable tax position of government bonds. This means that housing finance has necessarily to be provided by the savings bank system, and is reliant on short term deposits.

Table 3.3 shows trends in net loans for house-purchase from 1979 to 1983.

Table 3.3   Net Loans for House-Purchase, United Kingdom, 1979-1983

Year	Building Societies		Monetary Sector		Local Authorities		Other		Total
	£m	%	£m	%	£m	%	£m	%	£m
1979	5,271	82	597	9	293	4	301	5	6,462
1980	5,722	78	593	8	461	6	515	7	7,291
1981	6,331	67	2,265	24	268	3	434	5	9,480
1982	8,147	58	5,078	36	554	4	335	2	14,114
1983	11,041	75	3,602	24	-292	(2¹)	370	3	14,721

Source: *Financial Statistics*, April 1984, HMSO, Table S.5.
Note: At end-1983 there were £0.70 to the dollar.

It will be seen that building societies suffered a declining market share from 1978 to 1982, but enjoyed a sharp recovery in 1983. The only other significant lenders have been the banks, especially since 1981. However, the volume of their activity showed a sharp down turn in 1983. The role of banks and building societies will be explained in more detail in the following sections.

In the early 1970s, local authorities were quite significant mortgage lenders, mainly to people buying cheaper older houses. However, in 1975, local authority lending was cut back as part of a move to control public expenditure generally. Building societies have since co-operated with local authorities on a variety of housing schemes, and have taken over much of the lending previously done by the authorities. The fairly significant increase in local authority lending in 1982 and 1983 is explained by the sales of local authority houses, some of which are financed by local authority mortgages. To this extent there is a merely a transfer of debt from one part of local authority accounts to another.

Table 3.4 shows in detail loans for house-purchase outstanding as at the end of 1983.

Table 3.4   Loans for House-Purchase Outstanding, United Kingdom, End-1983

Institution	Amount Outstanding £m	Percentage of Total
Building societies	68,227	75
Monetary sector	14,238	16
Local authorities	4,184	5
Insurance companies & pension funds	2,364	3
Other public sector	1,717	2
Total	90,730	100

Source: *Financial Statistics*, April 1984, HMSO, Table S.5.
Note: At end-1983 there were £0.70 to the dollar.

It will be seen that although the monetary sector has accounted for a high proportion of net loans in recent years, its share of balances outstanding is only 16%. After the local authorities the only other significant lenders are the insurance companies and pension funds, and the figure relates almost entirely to insurance companies. The insurance companies in Britain largely withdrew from the mortgage market sometime before their counterparts in other countries. They now do only a limited amount of lending, generally in conjunction with endowment policies. In some cases they will 'top up' building society loans. Unlike in other countries, there is no secondary market which enables insurance companies and pension funds to finance indirectly house-purchase loans.

All mortgage loans in Britain are at a variable rate of interest, and there are generally no limitations on the extent to which rates can be varied. Societies and banks are also willing to make high percentage loans, sometimes up to 100%, but loans in excess of 80% generally have to be supported by an insurance company guarantee. There is no significant state guarantee system. A distinguishing feature of the housing finance market in the United Kingdom compared with other countries is that a high proportion of loans is on existing rather than new dwellings. In 1983, for example, only 13% of building society loans were on new houses, and as many as 27% were on houses built prior to 1919. Again, this reflects, to a large extent, the lack of a private rented sector, and new households often set up home in a cheap old house or flat, which they may occupy for only a few years before moving on to a larger home.

The Savings Market

Not only are building societies the principal providers of housing finance loans, but they are also the major holders of short term personal savings. Table 3.5 shows the distribution of personal sector liquid assets at the end of 1983.

Table 3.5   Personal Sector Liquid Assets, United Kingdom, End-1983

Institution	Amount £m	Percentage of Total
National Savings	18,543	11.8
National Savings Bank deposits	6,072	3.9
Tax instruments	116	
Local authority temporary debt	296	0.2
Sterling sight deposits with monetary sector	21,602	13.7
Sterling time deposits with monetary sector	31,581	20.1
Foreign currency deposits with monetary sector	1,704	1.1
Deposits with building societies	77,482	49.2
Total	157,396	100.0

Source: *Financial Statistics*, March 1984, HMSO, Table 9.4.
Note: At end-1983 there were £0.70 to the dollar.

It will be seen that building societies had 49.2% of the market, whereas the monetary sector, which includes the trustee savings banks, had a market share of 34.9%. The commercial banks have been less concerned with the personal sector than some of their counterparts in other countries, but they have also been subject to constraints on their ability to raise deposits and to make loans, in the name of monetary policy. They were largely freed from these constraints in 1980 and 1981, since when they have been more aggressive in the savings market but, as yet, they have made no inroads into building societies' market share.

Within the monetary sector are the trustee savings banks which, over the last ten or so years, have been moving gradually from the public sector into the private sector. Until fairly recently they operated only on the liabilities side of the balance sheet, handing over all the funds they received to the government. They are now becoming fully fledged banks, and hence are counted in the monetary sector as a whole. They have effectively merged into one group. However, they remain very much smaller than their counterparts in other countries, particularly on the continent of Europe.

The government is active in the savings market through National Savings. The National Savings Bank is operated through post offices, and National Savings Certificates are made available in post offices and also through banks. The certificates are generally for five year periods and are designed to be attractive to higher rate taxpayers. The government uses National Savings not so much to provide a savings service to the public, but rather to help fund the government borrowing requirement.

Building Societies

It has already been seen that building societies dominate both the housing finance market and also the short term personal savings market. They are collectively an enormous industry with over 25 million adult investors (57% of the total adult population) and nearly six million borrowers (about a quarter of all households). It is proper, therefore, to focus attention on the development and role of these organisations.

History

The first known building society was established in Birmingham in 1775. The early societies were small groups of people who clubbed together resources to build themselves homes, hence the name 'building society'. In the mid-nineteenth century building societies evolved gradually from this simple type of organisation into financial institutions. This they did first by beginning to borrow money from those who did not want a house, so as to speed up the process of housing those who did, and by introducing the concept of interest on both sides of the balance sheet. By the mid-nineteenth century, the early 'terminating societies' were being replaced by permanent societies. The first building society legislation was introduced in 1836, and in 1874 there was a comprehensive Act governing societies which, in essence, is still in effect today.

At the turn of the century building societies were still comparatively small organisations, but the twentieth century has been characterised by a rapid growth, combined with a sharp reduction in their numbers. Individual societies have merged together, and some have gone out of existence, but the structure of the industry today, and, indeed, the names of some of the leading societies, still owes much to the history of the industry.

The Legal and Administrative Framework

Building societies are distinct legal entities subject to special laws. They are governed by the Building Societies Act 1962 and various statutory instruments. The Act provides that the purpose of a building society is to raise funds for members to lend to members on the security of freehold or leasehold estate.

Building societies are mutual institutions owned by their investors and borrowers. For most practical purposes, anyone who invests in a building society becomes a member of that society, and is entitled to play a part in the affairs of the society.

Building societies are very restricted by law as to what they can do. In effect, they are able only to accept savings which are raised for the purpose of making loans. They can offer a limited range of services which are incidental to these, but cannot, for example, raise money with the specific intention to invest it in the financial markets, nor can they make any loan unless there is a security in the form of freehold or leasehold estate.

Societies are required to maintain a reserve ratio (in the terminology of other countries a net worth ratio or capital ratio) which varies according to their size, but is a maximum of 2.5% and is under 1.5% for the largest societies. Societies must also maintain a minimum liquid assets ratio of 7.5%. The manner in which societies can invest their liquid assets is closely controlled by law.

Building societies are supervised by the Registry of Friendly Societies, and not by the Bank of England which is responsible for the supervision of the banks. The Chief Registrar of Friendly Societies has duties laid on him by law, and he is also able to use informal pressure when he wishes to do so.

The Structure of the Industry

Table 3.6 shows the distribution of building societies by asset size at the end of 1983.

It will be seen that the five largest societies control over half of the total assets of the industry, and the next 11 control more than a quarter. Table 3.7 lists these societies.

Table 3.6   Classification of Building Societies by Asset Size, Great Britain, End-1983

Assets	Number of Societies	Percentage of Total	Total Assets £m	Percentage of Total
Over £3,500 million	5	2.4	47,807	55.7
Over £1,000 million Up to £3,500 million	11	5.3	24,482	28.5
Over £225 million Up to £1,000 million	20	9.7	7,696	9.0
Over £50 million Up to £225 million	41	19.9	4,323	5.0
Over £2 million Up to £50 million	84	40.8	1,544	1.8
Under £2 million	45	21.8	16	-
Total	206	100.0	85,868	100.0

Source: The Building Societies Association.
Note: At end-1983 there were £0.70 to the dollar.

Table 3.7   Largest 16 Building Societies, United Kingdom, End-1983

Society	Base	Branches	Total Assets £m	Percentage of Total	Mortgages £m
Halifax	Halifax	627	16,782	19.5	13,482
Abbey National	London	670	14,313	16.7	11,264
Nationwide	London	517	7,348	8.6	5,773
Leeds Permanent	Leeds	459	4,832	5.6	3,923
Woolwich Equitable	London	380	4,542	5.3	3,700
National & Provincial	Bradford	335	3,918	4.6	3,079
Anglia	Northampton	376	3,202	3.7	2,633
Alliance	Brighton	203	2,791	3.3	2,161
Bradford & Bingley	Bingley	230	2,687	3.1	2,118
Leicester	Leicester	243	2,477	2.9	1,928
Britannia	Leek	239	2,376	2.8	1,757
Cheltenham & Gloucester	Cheltenham	135	2,042	2.4	1,510
Bristol & West	Bristol	158	1,574	1.8	1,047
Yorkshire	Bradford	151	1,214	1.4	915
Gateway	Worthing	144	1,138	1.3	887
Northern Rock	Newcastle	124	1,064	1.2	853
All societies		6,644	85,868	100.0	67,535

Source: Balance sheets of societies.
Notes: 1.   The Halifax figure relates to January 31 1984, the Leeds Permanent and Woolwich Equitable figures relate to 30 September 1983, and the Anglia figures relate to 4 April 1983.
    2.   At end-1983 there were £0.70 to the dollar.

It will be noted that only three of the largest 16 societies are based in London, this very much reflecting the historical development of the industry. The five largest societies have branches throughout the country and are able to take advantage of economies of scale, particularly in respect of marketing. Most of the next 11 societies also branch throughout the country, although their representation is patchy in some areas.

Below the largest 16 societies are a group of regional societies, and then local societies. Most of these societies confine their branches to fairly tightly confined areas.

There are no restrictions on branching, and the pattern of the industry is that in any one large centre of population there may be branches of 16 national societies and ten regional and local societies. The number of branches of building societies has, in fact, been rising very rapidly in recent years, from 3,696 at the end of 1976, to 6,748 at the end of 1983. Most of these branches are located in main shopping areas, and there has been some criticism of the rapid growth of building society branches. Over the last two years there has been a very significant slowdown in the rate of branch expansion.

The Operation of the Industry

Partly because of their legal framework, building societies operate in a very simple way. Basically, all that they do is to raise savings from the public and on-lend the bulk of these to home-buyers, while retaining an adequate proportion in liquid assets. The aggregate balance sheet for the industry at the end of 1983 is shown in Table 3.8.

Table 3.8 Building Societies, United Kingdom, Assets and Liabilities, End-1983

Liabilities	£m	%	Assets	£m	%
Shares and deposits	78,489	89.7	Mortgages	68,227	78.0
Borrowing	1,973	2.3	Cash &	17,663	20.2
Other liabilities	3,559	4.1	investments		
Reserves	3,485	4.0	Offices	944	1.1
			Other	671	0.8
Total	87,506	100.0	Total	87,506	100.0

Source: The Building Societies Association.
Notes: 1. At end-1983 there were £0.70 to the dollar.
2. The figures are for the end of the calendar year and differ slightly from those in the previous tables.

The table shows that building societies had reserves of 4.0% of total assets, representing a significant increase on the figures for the three previous years. Borrowing is a fairly new development for building societies. From 1980 some societies began to issue negotiable bonds, and others raised syndicated bank loans. However, the amount raised by the end of 1982 was comparatively small. From May 1983, societies were able to pay interest gross on certificates of deposits and from October 1983 they could pay interest gross on large time deposits. Effectively, these changes allowed societies to use the capital markets for the first time and they made considerable use of these facilities in 1983. The proportion of liabilities in the form of borrowing will probably rise significantly over the next few years.

Shares are best considered as deposits in the generally accepted sense of the word, and certainly are so considered by the depositor. Until very recently over 80% of the shares held in building societies were in the form of ordinary or paid up shares, which are analogous to passbook deposits in most other countries. Money could be paid into and out of these accounts at any time, and an attractive rate of interest is paid.

During the mid-1970s, term accounts became popular. With these accounts, a rate of interest of a fixed differential (up to 2%) above the variable ordinary share rate was paid in exchange for a fixed term, initially two, but later up to five years. However, the nature of term accounts has subsequently changed considerably. Now most have an early withdrawal facility, which can be exercised by giving three months' notice or by incurring a three month penalty. By the end of 1983, 23.5% of building society savings balances were in the form of term shares.

Over the last few years, the most popular form of account has been the short notice account, under which a higher rate of interest is paid in exchange either for seven or 28 days' notice of withdrawal or a seven or 28 day interest penalty. During 1982 and 1983, there were substantial transfers of money from ordinary building society accounts into this new form of account. Societies also offer a regular savings account, which is particularly attractive to those saving the deposit for a first home. Table 3.9 shows the distribution of building society savings accounts at the end of 1983.

Table 3.9   Distribution of Building Society Savings Accounts, End-1983

Type of Account	£m	%
Ordinary accounts	35,400	45.1
High interest accounts	20,600	26.3
Term accounts	18,400	23.5
Regular savings accounts	2,100	2.7
Other accounts	2,000	2.5
Total	78,500	100.0

Source: The Building Societies Association.
Note: At end-1983 there were £0.70 to the dollar.

The rate of interest on all building society accounts is variable, and has to be changed in line with market conditions. The financial services offered by building societies are still fairly primitive compared with those offered by other savings institutions. Their legal constraints are such that it is not easy for societies to issue cheque books, although one or two societies are now experimenting in this area. One or two societies also have cash dispensers, and urgent consideration is being given to a shared system for the whole industry. Most societies make available third party cheques, and these are quite popular. However, for the most part, the savings service offered by building societies is simply to provide an attractive home for savings which are readily accessible in person or by post.

Table 3.8 shows that nearly 80% of building society loans are in the form of mortgages, and most of the remainder are in cash and investments. The point has already been made that the manner in which societies can invest their liquid funds is closely circumscribed. Basically, societies can invest only in named banks and in public sector securities. The remaining assets are held in the form of offices and other assets such as computers.

The balance between mortgages and cash and investments is interesting because societies seem to hold a much higher amount of liquidity than their counterparts in other countries, and, also, well above the minimum requirement. One reason for this is that societies do not have recourse to any lender of last resort, nor is there a secondary mortgage market on which they can raise funds quickly. They maintain liquidity at a high level so as to be able to meet commitments, and, when the inflow of funds is running at a high level, so liquidity is built up such that it can be run down when inflow falls off. In fact, in the first six months of 1983, societies ran down liquidity ratios by an average of three percentage points so as to maintain lending in the face of falling net receipts of new money.

Perhaps the most interesting feature of building society operations is the variable rate nature of the mortgage, and the manner in which societies set the mortgage rate merits particular attention.

The point has already been made that the funds which building societies attract are all short term, and, given the volume of funds which they need to meet mortgage demand, this is inevitable. It follows that when there is a significant change in the general level of interest rates, so there is an immediate effect on the inflow of funds into societies. Societies must react to changes in competing rates if they are to avoid having either an embarrassing inflow of funds which they are unable to lend out profitably or a deficiency of funds such that huge mortgage queues develop. Building societies do not, in fact, react to every change in interest rates because to do so would be, to say the least, disturbing to their borrowers, who could suddenly find that they might have to meet, at short notice, huge increases in repayments. Societies therefore tend to ride modest changes in the level of interest rates. One way that societies have of overcoming the effects of changes in interest rates is to use their liquidity as a stabilization mechanism. The point has already been made that liquidity was run down during the early part of 1983 to enable lending to be maintained, notwithstanding a deficiency of inflow. A similar pattern has occurred at other times.

Moreover, building societies do not act autonomously in changing interest rates. The trade association for building societies, The Building Societies Association, to which societies accounting for some 99.9% of the assets of the industry belong, gives advice to its members on rates of interest they should pay and charge. The Council of the Association normally meets monthly, and rates of interest are always on the agenda. A change in advised rates will be made only if building society rates are well out of line. The increasing volatility of interest rates in the recent past has meant that there have been more and more changes in the advised rates, and two or three a year are now quite common. Societies inform borrowers of changes either by writing directly to them advising the new repayment or by a simple press advertisement, although this is frequently followed up by a personal letter to each borrower. Borrowers readily accept that their mortgage rate can change quite drastically in a short time period, and take account of this when deciding what size loan to ask for. When interest rates increase substantially societies may be willing to allow the existing repayment to continue to be made for a short period, with a resultant lengthening of the maturity of the loan or even an increase in debt. Perhaps surprisingly, the rapid increase in mortgage rates which societies have been obliged to implement in recent years have not led to significant difficulties on the part of borrowers in meeting mortgage repayments.

The nature of the system by which interest rate changes are agreed has been changing significantly in recent years, a development related to the changing nature of their liabilities. Until the mid-1970s there was a fairly rigid cartel with all the large societies paying the same rate on the main product, the ordinary share, and charging the same rate on mortgages. The new forms of account were developed partly because societies were not free to vary rates on the basic product, which, as a result, has declined in importance. Successive agreements on interest rates were made until, in October 1983, the Association decided to reduce the status of its rates from recommendations to advice, and the requirement on societies to give notice of changes in key rates was ended. Societies are now free to decide their own interest rate structures, although the question is still discussed. In March 1984 a collective decision was taken and implemented to bring down interest rates.

The most significant increases were from 1978 to 1979, when borrowers had to face an increase in their rate from 8.5% in June 1978 to 15% by December 1979. Conversely, in little more than eight months in 1982, borrowers were able to enjoy a decrease in mortgage rates from 15% to 10%.

The variable rate nature of their operations means that it is exceptionally difficult for a building society to run into financial problems, especially those caused by borrowing short and lending long. In effect, societies do no such thing, because the rate of interest on their loans can be changed at almost no notice, and therefore they are lending on a short term, not a long term, basis. Because societies are able to move the rates on all of their assets and liabilities (with the exception of their liquid assets) together they can afford to maintain a relatively narrow margin between lending and borrowing rates and they do not need substantial reserves. Table 3.11 shows the income and expenditure account for building societies in 1983.

Table 3.10   BSA Recommended and Advised Rates of Interest, 1973-84

Year	Date of Recommend- ation	New Mortgages Effective Date	Rate %	Ordinary Shares Effective Date	Rate %	Gross Equivalent %
1973	12 January			1. 2.73	5.60	
	16 March			1.4.73	6.30	9.00
	4 April	4.4.73	9.50	1.5.73	6.75	9.64
	14 August	14.8.73	10.00			
	14 September	14.9.73	11.00	1.10.73	7.50	10.71
1975	24 April			1.6.75	7.00	10.77
1976	9 April	9.4.76	10.50	1.5.76	6.50	10.00
	8 October	8.10.76	12.25	1.11.76	7.80	12.00
1977	15 April	15.4.77	11.25	1.5.77	7.00	10.61
	10 June	10.6.77	10.50	1.7.77	6.70	10.15
	23 September	23.9.77	9.50	1.11.77	6.00	9.09
1978	13 January	13.1.78	8.50	1.2.78	5.50	8.33
	9 June	9.6.78	9.75	1.7.78	6.70	10.00
	10 November	10.11.78	11.75	1.12.78	8.00	11.94
1979	13 July	1.1.80	12.50	1.8.79	8.75	12.50
	22 November	22.11.79	15.00	1.12.79	10.50	15.00
1980	12 December	12.12.80	14.00	1.1.81	9.25	13.21
1981	13 March	13.3.81	13.00	1.4.81	8.50	12.14
	9 October	9.10.81	15.00	1.11.81	9.75	13.93
1982	12 March	12.3.82	13.50	1.4.82	8.75	12.50
	5 August	5.8.82	12.00	1.9.82	7.75	11.07
	12 November	12.11.82	10.00	1.12.82	6.25	8.93
1983	22 June	22.6.83	11.25	1.7.83	7.25	11.36
1984	16 March	16.3.84	10.25	1.4.84	6.25	8.93

Source: *Building Societies in 1982*, The Building Societies Association, 1983 and BSA.
Notes: 1. The mortgage rates shown are gross and apply to annuity advances to owner-occupiers. The gross equivalent ordinary share rate shows the value of the recommended/advised (net) rate to a basic taxpayer.
2. Since 1972 changes in recommended/advised mortgage rates have applied immediately for new loans. The rates on existing loans are normally changed on the first of the month following the month of the recommendation or as soon as practicable thereafter. In the case of an increase in rates, many mortgage deeds require between one and three months' notice before the change can be implemented. The rate recommended on 13 July 1979 was unusual in that the date for implementation was deferred until 1 January 1980. In the event this recommendation was superseded by that made on 22 November 1979 and thus the 12.50 per cent rate never became effective.

It will be seen that management expenses were a relatively low proportion of total expenditure. A significant figure is that for income tax on interest. Building societies have a special arrangement with the government whereby they discharge the basic rate tax liability on their investors' interest at a special 'composite' rate of tax. This rate is the average of borrowers' liability to tax, and in the year 1983/84 was 25%, compared with the basic rate of

Table 3.11   Building Societies, United Kingdom, Income and Expenditure, 1983

	£m	£ per £100 Mean Assets
Normal Income		
Mortgage interest	6,928	8.68
Investment & bank interest	1,429	1.79
Other	234	0.29
Total	8,591	10.77
Normal Expenditure		
Management expenses	994	1.25
Share, deposit and loan interest	5,465	6.85
Income tax on interest	1,827	2.29
Corporation tax	98	0.12
Total	8,384	10.51
Normal income less normal expenditure	207	0.26
Investment profits and other exceptional or non-recurrent items	475	0.60
Added to general reserves	682	0.85

Source: The Building Societies Association.
Notes: 1. At-end 1983 there were £0.70 to the dollar.
2. The figures are estimates, based on returns provided by the largest 16 societies.

tax of 30%. This means that 83% (25%/30%) of the interest received by building society investors is received by those liable to tax. This special arrangement is sometimes seen as giving building societies an advantage, but it is doubtful whether it does so. It does mean that societies are able to offer to taxpaying investors a rate of interest higher than the cost of their funds, but the opposite is true in the case of non-taxpaying investors. A similar arrangement is to be applied to banks and other deposit taking institutions from April 1985.

It will be noted that, in 1983, building societies obtained more profits from exceptional items than from their normal business activities. This is slightly misleading because to a large extent societies have taken income from their investments in the form of capital appreciation rather than interest. A change in the tax rules governing societies' returns on investments, announced in February 1984, will mean that in future more of the income from investments will be recorded in normal income.

The Future of Building Societies

Building societies have changed little in their method of operation in the past 50 years. What they have done is to become extremely efficient at being specialist savings banks and mortgage lenders. Societies have been able to be successful partly because the markets in which they operate have been growing rapidly, and they have had to face comparatively little competition. Neither the banks nor the savings banks have been as competitive as has been the case in other countries. However, there have been signs of a change in this situation in recent years, a development which is common in a number of countries. Building societies are not well placed to respond to aggressive competition from other institutions, because of the constraints under which they operate. To take a simple example, if the banks wish to enter the mortgage market then they can do so, and in addition to offering mortgage loans, they can offer a package of services including bridging loans, which may be unsecured, loans to finance the purchase of furniture, an insurance broking service and an estate agency service. Building societies can offer none of these additional services.

Societies also find that their legal constraints prevent them from playing as wide a role as they would wish in the housing market. One encouraging feature of housing in Britain in recent years has been that the various institutions are increasingly operating together, and societies are now working with house-builders and local authorities in a wide variety of schemes. However, societies as yet have no power to hold land nor can they make, for example, unsecured loans, which would be extremely useful in helping people maintain and improve their homes. It is anticipated that there will be new building society legislation within the next four or five years, and this legislation is expected to give building societies wider powers. In anticipation of this, The Building Societies Association published, in January 1983, a discussion document, *The Future Constitution and Powers of Building Societies*. The Association proposed that societies should continue to be mutual institutions, but that there should be certain changes in their constitution so as to make the existing system work more effectively. There is something nonsensical about a mutual organisation of millions of people, as are some of the large building societies, and the theoretical constitution under which societies operate and the way they operate in practice now bear little relation to each other. However, no solution to this problem can be seen, and the preference is to remain with the present system, while trying to make it more effective.

On powers it was proposed that building societies should be able to offer in-house a wider range of services directly related to their mainstream business including surveying, conveyancing and estate agency. More radically, it was also proposed that societies should also have power to set up subsidiaries in the field of banking, insurance and property development.

The report attracted considerable comment and stimulated a wide ranging debate on the future of the industry. In February 1984 the Association published its definitive proposals in a report *New Legislation for Building Societies*. This argued that building societies needed new legislation for three reasons -

(a) The constitution of societies was no longer appropriate for huge organisations.

(b) The law prevented societies from making as great a contribution as they would wish to dealing with housing problems.

(c) The market for financial services is changing rapidly and societies are legally inhibited from providing the range of services that their competitors can offer and which they will need to offer to respond to competition.

The report suggested modest changes to the constitution of societies and argued in favour of societies retaining their mutual status.

On powers the following recommendations were made -

(a) Societies should be able to own the equity of houses being purchased under shared ownership (part renting, part buying) schemes.

(b) Societies should be able to hold land for the purpose of housing development.

(c) Societies should be empowered to offer services related to housing development including estate agency, structural surveys, conveyancing and insurance broking.

(d) Societies should be allowed to offer accounts with modest overdraft facilities and should be able to have a limited percentage of their assets in unsecured loans.

(e) Societies should be empowered to offer insurance.

(f) Societies should be able to offer additional services directly or through subsidiaries.

(g) Societies should be permitted to operate in the other countries of the European Community.

The most significant recommendation is (d) which replaces the previous view that societies should be allowed to own subsidiaries able to offer banking services. If implemented, the recommendation would allow societies to offer a full range of retail banking services including cheque books, credit cards, cash dispensers and personal loans.

Banks

The structure of the banking industry in Britain is very different to that of the building society industry. Outside of Scotland, the market is dominated by the four large clearing banks, National Westminster, Barclays, Midland and Lloyds. Table 3.12 lists the largest British retail banks.

The banks provide a complete banking service to both businesses and individuals. However, the banks have tended to be less active in the personal market than in the corporate market, partly because of the balance sheet constraints to which they have been subject. The appearance of their offices and also their opening hours are far less attractive to the consumer than are those offered by building societies.

Table 3.12   UK Banks, End-1983

Bank	Assets Bank £m	Group £m	House-Purchase Loans £m	Domestic Deposits Savings £m	Total £m	Branches
National Westminster	32,497	60,017	2,500	5,449	23,797	3,235
Barclays	26,798	64,904	3,200	5,673	24,301	2,912
Midland	26,801	52,613	1,150	4,600	11,800	2,345
Lloyds	18,185	38,432	1,905	5,418	14,607	2,400
Royal Bank of Scotland	6,098	11,077	N/A	1,500	5,900	874
Trustee Savings Banks		9,606	910	7,393	8,223	1,612

Source: Annual reports and banks.
Notes: 1. At end-1983 there were £0.70 to the dollar.
2. Figures for Royal Bank of Scotland are as at 30 September 1983, figures for the trustee savings banks are as at 20 November 1983.
3. The figures for house-purchase loans should be regarded as being approximate only.

The table shows that savings deposits held by the banks are relatively small when compared with their total assets. The trustee savings banks are, in fact, the largest holders of savings deposits within the banking sector, even though they are only the sixth largest banking group.

However, banks are able to offer a wider range of services than building societies, and the majority of building society customers also find it necessary to have a bank account.

Until the last few years, the banks played only a small part in the housing finance market, generally confining their activities to making bridging loans to tide people over the period when they were moving house. As the balance sheet constrictions were removed in the late 1970s, and more particularly in 1980 and 1981, so the banks saw the mortgage market as being a profitable new outlet for their funds, and also one means by which they might recover their share of the personal savings market which, over the years, they had been losing to building societies. The banks entered the mortgage market with considerable publicity, and, moreover, at a time when building societies were not meeting the demand for mortgage finance. (At this stage it is important to note a peculiar feature of bank operations. The banks do not pay interest on current accounts and it is estimated that the cost of managing these accounts is about 10% of the average balance. This means that when short term interest rates are above 10% the banks can operate a current account service quite profitably, but when interest rates fall below about this level the service becomes less profitable, and can indeed be very costly. Charges cover only a small proportion of the costs of providing the current account service.

When the banks came into the mortgage market interest rates were well above 10%, and mortgage lending was therefore particularly attractive.)

The banks rapidly made inroads into the mortgage finance market, and by the final quarter of 1981 accounted for some 40% of new loans. However, the banks had misjudged the market, and they reached lending targets set in terms of the proportion of their balances they wished to hold in mortgage loans much more quickly than had been anticipated. Also, interest rates declined, and, for a time, the mortgage rate was considerably below not only the cost of managing current account funds but also other short term rates. As a result, during the second half of 1982 and the early part of 1983, the banks drastically reduced their mortgage lending, thereby incurring considerable adverse publicity. It seems likely that bank mortgage lending will settle down at perhaps 20% of the total market, above the level of the late 1970s, but well below the 40% achieved in the final quarter of 1981.

Assessment

Perhaps by accident rather than by design the British housing finance system has proved to be one of those most able to cope with the severe fluctuations in interest rates and inflation which have been encountered over the past few years. The variable rate mortgage has enabled building societies to borrow on a short term basis and lend long term, without the risks that are normally inherent in borrowing short and lending long. Societies have, therefore, not encountered the financial difficulties that have been met by savings and loan associations in the USA, which have been forced to borrow short and lend long with fixed interest rates.

The system has also preserved equity between borrowers. Unlike in countries where there are fixed rates of interest, all borrowers at any one time are paying a similar rate, and borrowers are not expected to guess the future course of interest rates. An inevitable consequence of this is that the borrower may be subject, suddenly, to a significant change in his mortgage repayments as his variable mortgage rate rises or falls. In theory, this might be thought to cause problems, but in practice this is not the case, partly because of the way that societies have handled increases in rates. Also, the variable rate mortgage is ingrained in the system, and people anticipate when they take out a loan that the mortgage rate may rise, and budget accordingly.

Arguably, the variable rate mortgage has also helped preserve stability in the housing market. When rates have risen sharply, borrowers have not been deterred from purchasing as they would be if interest rates were fixed, because they have had the knowledge that when interest rates generally come down then their rates will also fall.

The main distinguishing feature of the British system is the complete dominance in the retail savings market, as well as in the housing finance market, of one type of institution, the building society, offering a very limited range of services. Market forces are likely to force building societies to diversify, in particular, to offer integrated packages of financial and home-buying services which are inceasingly being demanded in the market place.

Bibliography

Boleat, M J, *The Building Society Industry*, George Allen & Unwin, 1982.
Boleat, M J, *Building Societies, A Descriptive Study*, The Building Societies Association, 1982.
Building Society Factbook 1984, The Building Societies Association, 1984.
Building Societies and the Savings Market, The Building Societies Association, 1983.
BSA Bulletin, The Building Societies Association, quarterly.
Housing Tenure, The Building Societies Association, 1983.
New Legislation for Building Societies, The Building Societies Association, 1984.

CHAPTER 4

UNITED STATES OF AMERICA

The housing finance system of the USA merits particular attention for a number of reasons -

(a) The USA is by far the biggest economy in the world, and developments in the American economy, for example, with respect to interest rates, affect other economies.
(b) There has been a tendency for developments in financial institutions in the USA to be followed by similar developments in other countries.
(c) The American housing finance system is the most developed, particularly in respect of the secondary market.

However, housing finance in the USA is more complicated than in almost any other country, and this makes it difficult to analyse. The problem is a circular one, that is, it is difficult to understand any part of the system until one understands the whole system. For this reason, and, also, for the other reasons set out above, this chapter is long and it is repetitive in parts.

The USA has a tradition of owner-occupation and home-ownership is frequently referred to as being the 'American dream'. That accommodation which is not owned is, for the most part, rented privately. Until recently housing finance was provided largely by the deposit taking route, by specialist savings and loan associations (S&Ls) and mutual savings banks. However, the institutions effectively had to borrow short and lend long, and this caused severe financial difficulties. There has been a massive reform of the financial system as a whole, and housing finance in particular, in the past few years. The secondary market has been growing in importance compared with the primary market, and the role of traditional deposit taking intermediaries has been diminishing. Savings and loan associations are tending to diversify into general institutions or to narrow their activities to originating and servicing loans.

Introduction

The USA occupies an area of 9,160,000 sq kilometres, that is, it is slightly smaller than Canada. In 1982 its population was 232 million. The population has been increasing at a fairly rapid rate, about 1% a year, largely because of continued immigration.

The USA is a federal republic comprising 50 states, and the District of Columbia, in which the nation's capital, Washington DC, is situated. The states have considerable autonomy, including in respect of financial institutions. Until very recently, it was the general rule that banks and savings and loan associations could have branches only in their state of origin.

Executive power is largely in the hands of a president elected for afour-yearly term. Congress, comprising the Senate and the House of Representatives, is probably the most important legislative body in the world, and has a major influence on law making. Political power has alternated between the Republicans and the Democrats and it has not always been the case that the party holding the presidency has also controlled Congress. However, party politics is less important in the USA than in most other countries.

The USA enjoys a very high standard of living; GDP per capita is higher than in any other large country, with the exception of West Germany. In the period 1960-80 real GDP per capita grew by 3.5% a year, compared with an average for all other OECD countries of 4.6% a year. Inflation and interest rates have tended to be below the levels of other countries, although both have been at high and volatile levels in the recent past. There are grounds for arguing that it was American policy, with respect to deficit financing, in the 1960s that contributed to high and volatile inflation and interest rates in the 1970s, and thereby to problems for specialist housing finance institutions. Paradoxically, the problems have been worse in the USA than in any other country.

Housing

Housing Tenure

The USA has a tradition of home-ownership. This reflects the historical development of the country, with settlers continually moving to new areas and building homes on land which previously had no defined owner. By the beginning of the century, when no more than 10% of people in Britain were living in their own homes, nearly half of Americans were owner-occupiers. As the USA became more industrialized in the early part of the twentieth century, so the amount of rented housing increased, especially in the cities, but the number of owner-occupied homes also increased as new areas were settled. By 1930, 47.8% of housing units were owner-occupied, but the proportion fell to a low point of 43.6% in 1940. Owner-occupation increased markedly in the 1940s, but in recent years the rate of growth has slowed down. In 1980, 65.6% of units were owner-occupied, although there has subsequently been a slight decline. Table 4.1 shows trends in housing tenure from 1890 to 1981.

As in most other countries, owner-occupation is higher in rural areas (82% in 1980) than in urban areas (59%). Nearly 90% of rented units are in the

Table 4.1 Housing Tenure, USA, 1890-1981

Year	Owner-Occupied Units		Rented Units		Total Occupied Units
	No	%	No	%	No
1890	6,066,000	47.8	6,624,000	52.2	12,690,000
1910	9,301,000	45.9	10,955,000	54.1	20,256,000
1930	14,280,000	47.8	15,625,000	52.2	29,905,000
1950	23,560,000	55.0	19,266,000	45.0	42,826,000
1970	39,886,000	62.9	23,559,000	37.1	63,445,000
1975	46,867,000	64.6	25,656,000	35.4	72,523,000
1980	52,516,000	65.6	27,560,000	34.4	80,076,000
1981	54,342,000	65.3	28,833,000	34.7	83,175,000

Source: Bureau of the Census.

private rented sector, and most of these are in the hands of small landlords. Some 60% of rented units are in structures with less than five units each. The private rented sector is particularly important in cities, where it houses young and transient members of the population. Real rent levels have, in fact, been declining, and, for many, rented housing is now more attractive than owner-occupied housing.

There are about 1,200,000 housing units managed by public housing authorities. This housing is largely reserved for the very poor, the median income of occupiers being less than one third of that for all families.

A recent important trend in the housing market has been the conversion of large blocks of rented apartments into 'condominiums', that is, owner-occupied units where the occupiers jointly own the freehold of the property and pay a managing agent to manage the units. The conversion of rental units to condominiums has been a controversial matter in some areas.

Housebuilding

Housebuilding in the USA has been more cyclical than in most other countries. This reflects the fact that the housing market has been relatively free from government controls, and there has been very little building by public authorities. Table 4.2 shows housing starts for the period 1978-83.

Table 4.2 Housing Starts, USA, 1978-83

Year	Private Units	Public Units	Total
1978	2,020,000	16,000	2,036,000
1979	1,745,000	15,000	1,760,000
1980	1,292,000	20,000	1,313,000
1981	1,084,000	16,000	1,100,000
1982	1,062,000	10,000	1,072,000
1983	1,703,000	10,000	1,713,000

Source: Bureau of the Census.

The table shows that public units are a very small proportion of the total. Some private units are built with public subsidy, but here again the proportion is small, 8% in 1982, although as high as 15% in 1979.

The table shows that starts of private units nearly halved between 1978 and 1982. This is a reflection of the economic cycle, and, indeed, housebuilding figures are regarded as being an early indicator of economic trends generally. It will be noted that there was a very sharp increase in starts in 1983.

Nearly 75% of starts are one family homes, and most of the remainder are blocks containing five or more family units.

Housing Policy

Housing policy can be summarized very briefly. Basically, the government has as non-interventionist a role as possible (although indirectly tax policy has influenced the market), and, in recent years, the degree of intervention and the extent to which low income people have been assisted with their housing has been declining. However, there has been considerable concern about housing policy. A number of problems have been identified -

(a) Rising interest rates and house prices have led to suggestions that the 'American dream' of home-ownership is becoming unobtainable. Between 1970 and 1982 the average price of a new house increased by 190%, and the average price of an existing house increased by 230%, while the consumer price index rose by 143%.

(b) The housing finance system has been in turmoil, and this has fed through to the housing market, and vice versa.

(c) Projects designed to help the poor to help themselves have been widely criticized, largely on grounds of ineffectiveness. Some of the public housing units have rapidly developed into low income gettos with acute social problems.

Partly in recognition of these problems, the President of the USA, in June 1981, announced the establishment of a Commission on Housing to review the housing situation and housing policy. The Commission published its report (*The Report of the President's Commission on Housing*, 1982) in April 1982. The report provides a readable and authoritative description of the housing situation and housing problems, and, moreover, it succeeds in examining housing in the context of the national economy rather than in isolation. Although the report was prepared by a Presidential Commission, that Commission worked independently of the government, and its conclusions are untainted by the "political realities" that creep into reports on housing matters. The basic philosophy of the report was freedom of choice for the individual, and minimum government intervention. It favoured the subsidizing of people in housing need rather than construction, on the grounds that this would not only help more people, but it would also be less discriminatory.

The Commission came out strongly against rent controls which have been enforced in a number of areas in the recent past. On this point, the Commission concluded-

"The Commission finds that rent control causes a reduction in the quality of the existing rental housing stock, and discourages investment in new rental property."

Among the other conclusions in the report were that there should be a reduction in the constraints imposed by the planning system, public housing projects should be restored to local control and the future of each project should be decided individually, housing finance institutions should be freed from controls under which they have operated, and tax relief on mortgage interest should be retained (mortgage interest is fully tax deductible, at a cost of $20,000 million in 1981).

The Commission's proposals have not been adopted in full, and, indeed, such is the legislative process in the United States, that it is unlikely that they can be so adopted. However, they have greatly influenced the climate of opinion, and it is estimated that over half the recommendations have been implemented or are in the process of being implemented.

Housing Finance

The point has already been made that the housing finance system in the USA is extremely complicated, and has been changing rapidly. This section briefly describes the current state of the market, and sets out short details of the institutions involved in that market. The recent developments in the market are described in the final section of this chapter, following more detailed consideration of housing finance institutions and the secondary market participants.

Until the early 1970s housing finance in the USA was quite simple. Loans were made at fixed rates of interest over 25 or 30 years. The main lenders were specialist savings and loan associations (S&Ls) (similar to British building societies), mutual savings banks and commercial banks. In the 1970s a secondary market greatly expanded, which led to the rapid growth of a mortgage banking industry, comprising institutions which made and serviced loans but did not hold them, and which also permitted institutional investors to acquire mortgage loans. Subsequently, the nature of the market has changed radically. The principal change has been a decline in the market share of savings and loan associations, matched by a sharp rise in the share of institutional investors. This is illustrated in Table 4.3.

It will be seen that the share of savings and loan associations of the one to four family mortgage market declined by no less than 14 percentage points between 1978 and 1983. This was partly caused by the conversion of mort-

Table 4.3 One-to-Four Family Mortgage Loans Outstanding, USA, 1970-83

Year	Percentage Share of Total Debt				
	Savings & Loan Associations	Savings Banks	Commercial Banks	Federally Supported Agencies & Mortgage Pools	Others
1970	41.8	14.1	14.2	8.3	21.6
1977	44.5	10.9	16.6	11.5	16.4
1978	46.2	8.1	16.8	15.5	13.4
1982	36.2	5.8	16.0	24.8	18.1
1983	32.1	7.9	15.1	31.1	13.8

Source: Federal Reserve System, *Flow of Funds Accounts.*

gages into securities. Correspondingly, there has been a rise in the market share of federally supported agencies and mortgage pools, including mortgage backed securities held by S&Ls. These will be described in detail subsequently, and, at this stage, it is sufficient merely to note that this group of mortgage holders comprises a number of government agencies, and, also, institutional investors holding mortgage loans backed either by a government guarantee or a guarantee given by one of the semi-government agencies.

However, Table 4.3 is not sufficient to show the state of the mortgage market because it fails to show the extent of secondary market activity. This can best be illustrated by looking at the mortgage market for a short time period. Table 4.4 shows activity in mortgage loans on one to four family housing in 1983.

Table 4.4 Mortgage Loans to One-to-Four Family Homes, USA, 1983

Institution	Originations		Purchases		Sales		Net Acquisitions	
	$m	%	$m	%	$m	%	$m	%
Savings & loans	81,524	41	32,919	20	50,173	34	64,270	29
Mortgage banks	59,926	30	12,843	7	67,071	45	5,698	4
Commercial banks	42,357	21	3,276	2	13,859	9	31,775	14
Savings banks	10,732	5	2,406	1	2,603	2	10,535	5
Federal agencies	3,180	2	25,347	15	9,646	7	18,881	9
Mortgage pools	0	-	85,949	51	4,044	3	81,905	37
S&L investment agencies	986	-	5,072	3	0	-	6,057	3
Others	740	-	521	-	719	-	542	-
Total	199,445	100	168,333	100	148,115	100	219,663	100

Source: *Survey of Mortgage Lending Activity*, December 1983, HUD.
Notes: 1. At end-1983 there were $1.44 to the pound.
2. Originations + purchases—sales = net acquisitions.

In most countries institutions which make mortgage loans hold them. In the United States, by contrast, many mortgage loans are originated and subsequently sold, and, as the table shows, in the period under consideration sales of mortgages were equal to 74% of loan orginations. The table shows considerable differences between institutions' shares of originations and of net aquisitions of loans. The saving and loan associations originated 41% of loans by volume, but they were substantial net sellers of loans and they accounted for only 29% of net acquisitions of mortgage debt. However, it should be noted that many of the loans sold in this period had been originated in previous periods. The mortgage bankers originated 30% of mortgage loans, but were large net sellers and accounted for just 3% of the increase in debt. Federal agencies and mortgage pools did not originate any loans, but between them accounted for over half of the increase in debt.

The complicated nature of the American housing finance system is now apparent. It is not simply a question of analysing the institutions which make mortgage loans; rather, it is necessary to analyse those institutions, the institutions which trade in mortgage loans and the various devices which make mortgage loans marketable. Even this is a somewhat complicated process, because it is market developments which have contributed to a significant extent to the growth of secondary market activity at the expense of traditional housing finance activity.

The Savings Market

The United States savings market, like the housing finance market, is extremely sophisticated and has been undergoing considerable change in recent years as will be discussed subsequently. At this stage it is helpful merely to note the distribution of time and savings accounts Table 4.5 shows the position.

Table 4.5 Over-the-Counter Savings, USA, End-1983

Institution	Amount $bn	Percentage of Total
Commercial banks	1,115	56
Savings and loan associations	632	32
Mutual savings banks	170	9
Credit unions	75	4
Total	1,992	100

Source: Federal Home Loan Bank Board, *Journal*, February 1984, Table 5.1.2; *Federal Reserve Bulletin*, February 1984, Table 1.37.
Note: At end-1983 there were $1.44 to the pound.

It will be seen that commercial banks accounted for over one half of the market with savings and loan associations having a third. The main trend in market shares in recent years has been the growth in the share of the commercial banks (from 47% in 1970) at the expense of the mutual savings banks (which had a 16% market share in 1970).

However, what has been more relevant has been the change in the nature of personal savings. Ten years ago most savings were in the form of passbook accounts with regulated rates of interest. A combination of inflation and high and volatile interest rates has made the consumer far more interest sensitive and most personal savings are now held in short term instruments yielding a money market related rate of interest.

Savings and Loan Associations

Introduction

Savings and loan associations, also known as savings associations or savings and loans (S&Ls for short), are the major specialist housing finance institutions in the USA. Until a few years ago the S&Ls were fairly similar to British, Australian and South African building societies. However, economic forces and regulatory changes have combined to change radically the nature of the S&L industry. This section briefly sets out the industry's position today while the transition from the period when the S&Ls were traditional specialist housing finance institutions is covered in the final section of this chapter. (A number of associations have recently converted to federal savings banks; they continue to be counted as S&Ls in some of the statistics used in this chapter.)

History

In 1831 immigrants into the USA from England established the Oxford Provident Building Association in a suburb of Philadelphia, Pennsylvania. This was modelled on the British terminating building society. The concept rapidly spread to other states and in 1848 the first steps towards establishing permanent associations were taken. Unlike in the United Kingdom, where building societies have retained their original name notwithstanding its irrelevance to their present functions, building and loan associations gradually changed their names to savings and loan associations as they moved away from the original function of building houses for their members.

As in Britain, the industry had a chequered history in the second half of the 19th Century and there were a number of notable failures. In 1893 the US League of Building and Loan Associations (now the US League of Savings Institutions) was founded, partly in response to concern at the activities of some housing finance organisations. The industry, like the banking industry, suffered greatly in the great depression because of the decline in savings deposits and foreclosures of existing mortgages. No less than 2,800 institutions went out of business, mostly through voluntary liquidation or mergers with others.

The modern industry owes its origin to legislation in the 1930s. In 1932 the Federal Home Loan Bank Act was enacted, which provided for a central reserve credit agency to supplement the resources of the S&Ls. In 1933 the Home Owners Loan Act became law with the aim of tightening controls over S&Ls. It provided for institutions to be chartered at federal as well as at state level, and it gave regulatory power to the newly created Federal Home Loan Bank Board. However, the Act also provided for detailed regulation, arguably contributing to the problems which the industry has experienced in the late 1970s and early 1980s. In 1934 the National Housing Act provided for the establishment of the Federal Savings and Loan Insurance Corporation (FSLIC) to insure deposits in S&Ls.

Subsequently, the industry grew rapidly and without difficulty until the last few years. Although many new laws and regulations were enacted it was not until 1980 that there were fundamental reforms in the regulation of the industry.

Constitution and Structure

The point was made in the introduction to this chapter that the 50 states have considerable powers, including in respect of financial institutions. Until the early 1930s state authorities were responsible for chartering and regulating banks, S&Ls and other financial institutions. Since the 1930s S&Ls have been able to choose whether to be federally chartered or chartered at state level. In practice there has been little difference between the two types of chartering although at times it has been advantageous for institutions in some states to switch from one form of charter to the other.

S&Ls can either be mutually owned, like British building societies, or they can have some form of permanent stock ownership. Until the 1970s only state chartered associations were allowed to operate as stock associations, but now existing federal associations may convert to stock form and it is now possible to establish new federal associations on a stock basis. Perhaps more fundamentally for the future of the industry, it is now also possible for S&Ls to convert to savings banks and a number have taken this step (partly for tax reasons) while others refer to themselves as savings associations rather than S&Ls.

It is helpful to note at this stage that California has an important role in the S&L industry. Stock associations are particularly strong in California. In the 1970s they were given more freedom by state chartering than their federally chartered counterparts. More recently, however, it has been advantageous for some Californian associations to convert to federal chartering. California used to account for well over half the stock associations but this is likely to change given the new regulations.

Table 4.6 shows the types of S&Ls as at the end of 1983.

It will be seen that most S&Ls are state chartered although the federally chartered organisations account for nearly two thirds of assets. 76% of institutions were mutual and these accounted for 58% of the assets of the industry. However, in 1982 the mutual associations had accounted for 69% of assets; the reasons for the significant change will be explained subsequently.

All federal associations are required by law to have their savings accounts insured by the Federal Savings and Loan Insurance Corporation (FSLIC); insurance of accounts is optional for many state chartered associations but the vast majority elect to take advantage of it.

There are a number of regulatory bodies to whom the institutions are

Table 4.6 Types of Savings and Loan Associations, End-1983

	Number	Percentage of Total	Assets $m	Percentage of Total
Type of Charter				
Federal	1,553	44	499,254	65
State	1,960	56	272,451	35
Total	3,513	100	771,705	100
Type of Ownership				
Stock	833	24	325,213	42
Mutual	2,680	76	446,492	58
Total	3,513	100	771,705	100

Source: *'84 Savings and Loan Sourcebook*, USLSI, 1984.
Note: At end-1983 there were $1.44 to the pound.

responsible. The most important in the Federal Home Loan Bank Board (FHLBB) which was created in 1932. An important function of the Federal Home Loan Bank System is to link S&Ls to the capital markets by providing a source of liquidity. More importantly, the Board is the chartering and regulatory authority for federally chartered associations, and it also manages the FSLIC. This latter body has a particular responsibilty for monitoring the activities of S&Ls and has been heavily involved in promoting mergers of troubled institutions in recent years. S&Ls have to obey both state and federal laws and there have, at times, been conflicts between the two. It is possible for federal law to pre-empt state laws under certain circumstances.

A major feature of the regulation of financial institutions in the USA has been a restriction of branch offices to individual states. The McFadden Act of 1927 effectively prevented financial institutions from branching across state borders. In some states there has even been a limitation on branching within the state. This has made for fragmented banking and S&L industries. At the end of 1983 there were 3,513 S&Ls, the number having fallen fairly sharply from 4,613 at the end of 1980 and 5,669 at the end of 1970. It follows that most associations are small and serve only a local market.

Table 4.7 shows the distribution of S&Ls by size at the end of 1983 and Table 4.8 lists the 15 largest associations.

Table 4.7 shows that over 63% of associations had assets of under $100 million each and that the 136 associations with assets in excess of $1,000 million accounted for 49% of the assets of the industry. This compares with the situation in Britain where the largest five societies account for 56% of the assets of the industry.

Table 4.8 shows that the seven largest associations, and ten of the largest 15, are based in California. The five largest are all in the Los Angeles area. The concentration in the industry is better measured by looking at the position within a state. The five largest associations in California account for nearly 50% of the assets of the industry in that state, which is their market, and 11% of the assets of the entire industry.

Table 4.7 Distribution of S&Ls by Size, USA, End-1983

Asset Range	Number	Percentage of Total	Assets $m	Percentage of Total
Under $10m	360	10	1,453	-
$10m and under $100m	1,866	53	81,858	
$100m and under $500m	999	28	212,546	28
$500m and under $1,000m	152	4	103,822	13
$1,000m and under $5,000m	121	3	221,214	29
$5,000m and over	15	-	150,812	20
Total	3,513	100	771,705	100

Source: *'84 Savings and Loans Sourcebook*, USLSI, 1984.
Note: At end-1983 there were $1.44 to the pound.

Table 4.8 Largest 15 Savings & Loan Associations, USA, End-1983

Association	Base	Savings $bn	Total Assets $m	Total Assets % of Total
American Savings	Stockton, Ca	18,262	21,524	2.80
Home Savings of America	Los Angeles, Ca	15,507	19,747	2.53
Great Western Savings	Beverly Hills, Ca	13,194	17,097	2.22
California Federal	Los Angeles, Ca	11,060	14,125	1.84
Glendale Federal	Glendale, Ca	7,366	9,712	1.26
First Nationwide Savings	San Francisco, Ca	5,851	8,385	1.09
World Savings	Oakland, Ca	5,767	8,192	1.06
First Federal	Detroit, Mi	4,580	7,993	1.04
Empire of America	Southfield, Mi	5,873	6,984	0.91
City Federal	Elizabeth, NJ	4,908	6,733	0.88
Home Federal	San Diego, Ca	5,091	6,669	0.87
Talman Home Federal	Chicago, Ill	5,073	6,299	0.82
Anchor Savings Bank	Northport, NY	5,187	6,036	0.78
Gibraltar Savings	Beverly Hills, Ca	3,692	5,824	0.76
Imperial Savings	San Diego, Ca	3,924	5,490	0.71

Source: United States League of Savings Institutions, *Savings Institutions*, March 1984.
Note: 1. At end-1983 there were $1.44 to the pound.
         2. Abbreviations of states are: Ca, California; Mi, Michigan; NJ, New Jersey; Ill, Illinois; NY, New York.

The structure of the industry has been changing radically in the last few years. In 1983, seven of the largest ten associations were engaged in merger activity. Until 1983, Home Savings of America had been the largest association. In 1983 two associations were created which are similar in size to Home Savings. American Savings, the fourth largest, and State Savings, the eighth largest, merged to create the largest S&L, which is part of the Financial Corporation of America. Also Great Western, the second largest, and Financial Federation, which owns the $3,000 million United S&L merged, although the merged association remained the third largest.

The rapid merging is producing a more concentrated industry. At the end of 1983 the five largest S&Ls had 10.65% of the total assets of the industry compared with 8.04% the year before.

At the end of 1983, the S&Ls had a total of 18,098 branches. The number had increased fairly rapidly, from just 4,318 at the end of 1970 to 16,733 at the end of 1980 and 18,712 at the end of 1982. The financial difficulties which the industry faced caused the downturn in 1983.

The Operation of the Industry

The operation of the S&L industry is best explained by examining the balance sheet. Table 4.9 shows the aggregate balance sheet for the end of 1983 (this includes figures for all FSLIC insured institutions (eg S&Ls which have converted to federal savings banks) and the total assets figure is therefore higher than other figures in this chapter).

Table 4.9 All FSLIC Insured Institutions, Assets & Liabilities, End-1983

Liabilities	$m	%	Assets	$m	%
Savings deposits	203,656	25	Mortgage loans	521,308	64
Savings certificates	467,401	57	Mortgage backed		
FHLB advances	57,253	7	securities	90,902	11
Other borrowed money	41,258	5	Other Loans	29,098	4
Other liabilities	16,620	2	Cash and investments	109,923	13
Net worth	32,980	4	FHLB stock	6,000	1
			Investment in service		
			corporations	8,196	1
			Buildings & equipment	11,347	1
			Other assets	42,294	5
Total	819,168	100	Total	819,168	100

Source: *'84 Savings and Loans Sourcebook*, USLSI, 1984.
Note: At end-1983 there were $1.44 to the pound.

On the liabilities side of the balance sheet the big difference between American institutions and other specialist housing finance institutions is the fairly high proportion of liabilities in the form of borrowed money. 7% of funds were borrowed from the Federal Home Loan Bank system and 5% were borrowed from other sources. Net worth was a not untypical 4% of assets but this figure conceals a rapid decline in the net worth ratio in recent years.

The composition of savings deposits requires a fairly detailed study. Table 4.10 gives a snapshot of the position at the end of 1983. A dynamic picture is presented in the final section of this chapter. However, to illustrate the difficulty of analysing a moving target, money market deposits, which totalled 6% of balances at the end of 1982 totalled 18% just six months later, in June 1983.

Table 4.10 Distribution of Savings Deposits in FSLIC Insured Institutions, End-1983

Type of Account	$m	%
Passbook	82,000	12
Transaction (NOW)	7,000	1
Money market	114,000	17
Certificate	387,000	58
$100,000 minimum certificate	81,000	12
Total	671,000	100

Source: Federal Home Loan Bank Board.
Note: At end-1983 there were $1.44 to the pound.

The passbook account is the traditional savings and loan account and was responsible for some 80% of liabilities ten years' ago. Money can be paid into and withdrawn from passbook accounts at any time and in this respect the account is similar to the British ordinary share account. Interest rates on passbook accounts have been regulated and until the recent deregulation had not risen higher than 5.5% since 1966 even when money market rates had been substantially higher.

In the 1970s savings certificate accounts became more important, by which a rate of interest higher than the pass book rate was paid on fixed term fixed rate accounts with minimum denominations of $1,000 or higher. By 1975 these accounts were responsible for more than half of total liabilities but by the end of 1983 the proportion was negligible.

A six month money market certificate was first authorized in 1978 as a means of helping S&Ls attract funds, as market interest rates rose above the regulated levels which they were allowed to pay. These certificates have a $10,000 minimum, are at a fixed rate linked to the going six month Treasury bill auction rate, and have a six month maturity. By June 1981 these certificates accounted for 40% of liabilities, but by the end of 1983 the proportion had fallen to 19%.

For investors with less than $10,000 a 30 month 'small saver' certificate became available at the beginning of 1980. This certificate is similar to the six month certificate except that it has no minimum balance and a longer term.

The certificates with a $100,000 minimum are known as 'jumbo CDs' and S&Ls have been free to offer these on whatever terms they consider appropriate.

The two types of account that merit particular attention are the transaction accounts and the money market accounts. The transaction accounts, also known as NOW (Negotiable Order of Withdrawal) accounts, are basically an interest bearing chequeing account. These were offered by some S&Ls, particularly in the New England states, in the late 1970s and have subsequently been given nationwide authority. Although the balances are fairly small this does not necessarily indicate their importance in the financial operations of the S&Ls as the interest spread on these accounts is higher than on money market related accounts.

The money market account is of significance largely because it was authorized only in December 1982, yet by the end of 1983 it had attracted $114,000 million. The money market account is very simply a call account paying a money market related rate of interest and with limited cheque writing facilities.

It is now necessary to study the assets part of the balance sheet. Mortgage loans as such accounted for 64% of total assets figure and securities backed by mortgages for a further 11%.

The following section of this chapter will explain the nature of the secondary market in mortgages in detail and at this stage it is sufficient to note that S&Ls are not only able to hold loans which they make but they also hold loans made by other lending institutions, and, as will be shown subsequently, they sell many of the loans which they make.

In addition to making loans on mortgage, S&Ls also are permitted to make loans to purchasers of mobile homes ($3,857 million at end-1983), home improvement loans ($5,490 million), loans secured on savings accounts ($3,195 million), loans for education purposes ($2,465 million), and consumer loans generally ($14,091 million). Investment in service corporations is a particularly interesting aspect of S&L operations. Until 1980, S&Ls could invest up to 1% of their assets in service corporations to undertake business in related areas such as consumer finance, mortgage banking, insurance and so on. That proportion was increased to 3% in 1980. Service corporations have become increasingly important as a source of income for S&Ls, especially as mainstream business has been under pressure. At the end of 1982, S&Ls had 3,000 service corporations. 43% were engaged in real estate development and sales, 24% in mortgage lending, 24% in insurance, 17% in acquisition of improved real estate and 13% in property management (many were involved in more than one of these activities).

Table 4.11 shows the aggregate income and expenditure account for FSLIC insured institutions for 1982 and 1983.

The major features of the assets and liabilities are well illustrated in this table, which also shows the severe financial difficulty which the S&L industry experienced in 1982. An important feature of income is the high proportion of other income, reflecting the fact that increasingly S&Ls are deriving their income other than by onlending money deposited with them. The importance of other income has increased dramatically in recent years, from 5.7% of total operating income in 1975 and 10.8% in 1981 to the 1983 proportion of 18.0%.

Operating expenses are slightly above those of British building societies, but this is not surprising, bearing in mind the much wider range of activities in which the S&Ls are engaged. It will be seen that net income, after taxes, in 1982 was -$4,271 million, the second year in succession in which a substantial operating deficit had been incurred. However, the figures for 1983 show a marked recovery.

Table 4.11 FSLIC Insured Institutions, USA, Income and Expenditure 1982-83

	1982 $m	$ per $100 Mean Assets	1983 $m	$ per $100 Mean Assets
Normal Income				
Mortgage interest	50,771	7.55	53,131	7.08
Investment interest	8,152	1.21	9,265	1.24
Loan fees & discounts	2,789	0.41	4,837	0.64
Other income (net)	9,796	1.46	14,756	1.96
Total	71,509	10.64	81,992	10.93
Normal Expenditure				
Operating expenses	10,104	1.50	12,757	1.70
Interest on savings	58,600	8.72	59,687	7.96
Interest on borrowed money	11,653	1.73	9,544	1.27
Total	80,357	11.96	81,988	10.93
Normal income less normal expenditure	(-8,848)	(1.31)	4	-
Non-operating income (net)	2,979	0.44	2,728	0.35
Net income before taxes	(-5,869)	(0.87)	2,732	0.36
Taxes	(-1,598)	(0.24)	687	0.09
Net income after taxes	(-4,271)	(0.64)	2,045	0.27

Source: *'84 Savings and Loan Sourcebook*, USLSI, 1984.
Note: At end-1983 there were $1.44 to the pound.

The United States League of Savings Institutions

The United States League of Savings Institutions (USLSI) is over 90 years old and is a particularly powerful trade association in a country where the political system makes the work of trade associations very important. S&Ls accounting for over 99% of the total assets of the industry belong to the League. The League has had to adapt in recent years and most recently has changed its name from the United States League of Savings Associations, so as to allow savings banks including those that were previously S&Ls to be members.

The League is based in Chicago but it has has a substantial Washington office. The League provides the usual trade association services to members and it produces a wide range of publications. Recently it has been heavily involved in electronic funds transfer systems, as well as the major legislative and regulatory changes to which the industry has been subject.

Mutual Savings Banks

Mutual savings banks have always been similar to S&Ls and the two are often described together under the general heading of 'thrifts'. Until recently, savings banks operated in only 17 states, largely the mid-Atlantic and New England states. They have been particularly strong in New York State and Massachussets. Correspondingly, S&Ls have been weak in these areas.

At the end of 1982 there were some 400 mutual savings banks. Their deposits are usually insured by the Federal Deposit Insurance Corporation (FDIC) which also insures deposits in commercial banks. They can elect to be members of the Federal Home Loan Bank system, in which case they have to be FSLIC insured, and at the end of 1982 131 were members.

The main differences between the balance sheets of S&Ls and savings banks have been that the savings banks have had a lower proportion of their assets in mortgages (between 50% and 75%), and also a lower proportion of their liabilities have been at market related rates. However, trends in the savings bank industry have been virtually identical with those in the S&L industry.

Savings banks have rapidly been losing market share to S&Ls. In 1950, the savings banks were 32% larger than the S&Ls but now they are less than a quarter of the size.

Until 1978 all savings banks were chartered at state level and until 1982 all were mutual. However, the Garn/St Germain Depository Institutions Act of 1982 made provision for stock savings banks and also made it fairly easy for institutions to convert from an S&L to a savings bank and vice versa. A number of S&Ls have already converted and others are expected to do so. The distinction between savings banks and S&Ls has therefore virtually disappeared and it is likely that increasingly figures will be produced for the entire 'thrift' industry. The point has already been made that some statistics for S&Ls include former S&Ls that are now savings banks. Increasingly, statistics are now being produced for FSLIC insured institutions which comprise S&Ls, federal savings banks and some mutual savings banks.

This trend has been recognised in the institutional framework. It has already been noted that the United States League of Savings Institutions changed its name in 1982 from the United States League of Savings Associations so as to be able to have savings banks as members. The National Association of Mutual Savings Banks, which is based in New York, has merged with a smaller association for S&Ls, the National Savings and Loan League, based in Washington, to form the National Council of Savings Institutions.

Commercial Banks

The American commercial banking industry has been heavily influenced by legislation which has, in particular, limited severely the extent to which banks may operate outside their state of origin. The result has been the existence of many thousand banks, most of which are very small. Even the largest banks, such as Citicorp and BankAmerica, which are the two largest banks in the world, are not yet able to operate throughout the entire country. The commercial banks offer a full range of banking services to the individual, and, to a lesser extent, to the corporate customer, although here again regulations have limited the extent to which commercial banks can engage in investment banking. For much of the 1960s and 1970s the banks were inhibited, by interest rate controls on their deposits, in the extent to which they could compete with savings and loan associations and mutual savings banks.

The banking industry has been changing in character over the last few years, largely because of regulatory reform. That reform has allowed a limited amount of cross-border activity, and a particularly significant development has been the indirect entry of the banks into housing finance through the acquisition of savings and loan associations in one or two cases, and through the purchase of mortgage banking companies. The banks also do a limited amount of direct lending and, as Table 4.5 showed, they are major deposit taking institutions.

Table 4.12 shows key data for the largest commercial banks. With the exception of BankAmerica, which is based in San Francisco, they are all based in New York.

Table 4.12 Largest Commercial Banks, USA, End-1983

Bank	Consolidated Assets $bn	Domestic Total $bn	Deposits Savings $bn	Domestic Branches	Housing Loans $bn
Citicorp	134.7	28.9	15.5	980	12.2
BankAmerica	121.2	63.5	18.4	1,231	16.5
Chase Manhatten	81.9	23.3	6.5		1.3
Manufacturers Hanover	64.3	18.1	5.5		1.3
JP Morgan	58.6	16.0	7.9		0.6
Chemical	51.2	19.7	6.4	265	1.8

Source: Annual Reports.
Notes: 1. At end-1983 there were $1.44 to the pound.
2. The figures for savings deposits and housing loans are not comparable and need to be interpreted in the context of the following paragraphs.

The Citicorp annual report records 'shelter' loans in the US of $12.2 billion. A figure of $10.8 billion is given for mortgage and real estate loans in domestic offices, managed by Citicorp's Individual Banking business, which deals almost entirely with individuals. Citicorp has a mortgage banking subsidiary, Citicorp Person to Person, which provides mortgage finance in 30 states; its 'shelter' portfolio was $4 billion at the end of 1983. Citicorp acquired a large S&L in California in 1982, and in 1983 it acquired two S&Ls, First Federal of Chicago (assets of $4 billion) and Biscayne of Miami (assets of $1.8 billion). Each of these S&Ls was in financial difficulties and the mergers occurred under the supervision of the authorities. The S&L in California, now named Citicorp Savings, is immediately owned by the mortgage banking subsidiary. The figure in the balance sheet for savings deposits is defined as including 'all savings deposits' and includes savings held in S&L subsidiaries.

The BankAmerica figure for deposits is for individual savings and time deposits. The figure for housing loans is that given for 'real estate-mortgage' loans, and includes loans not for housing. It will be seen that BankAmerica is a larger retail bank than Citicorp.

The Chase Manhatten figure for housing loans is in respect of one to four family mortgage loans; total real estate loans were $2.6 billion. The group runs a mortgage bank subsidiary, Chase Home Mortgage Corporation, which originates, packages, sells and services loans in 28 states. The figure for savings deposits is in respect of savings accounts, negotiable order of withdrawal accounts, money market deposits and savings certificates.

The Manufacturers Hanover figure for savings deposits is for retail time deposits; the figure for housing loans is for residential mortgage loans.

The JP Morgan figure for deposits is for time deposits other than from banks and official bodies. The figure for housing loans is for loans secured by real estate.

The Chemical Bank figure for housing loans is for loans secured by mortgages on real estate. The figure for savings is that given for savings deposits.

The Secondary Mortgage Market

An Introduction to Secondary Markets

A primary market is one where buyer and seller deal directly with each other; for example, where a building society or an S&L makes a loan to a house-purchaser then that transaction is part of the primary market.

Participants in any primary mortgage market are the individuals who buy homes and the lenders who originate the loans for the properties being purchased. A secondary market is a market place in which mortgage loans can be traded after having been originated by a primary lender; for example, an S&L may make a loan to a home-buyer and then sell that loan to an institutional investor such as a pension fund. Where mortgage loans are traded the borrower normally maintains his contractual relationship with the lending institution and continues to make payments to that institution. It is the beneficial ownership of the mortgage, that is, in effect, the right to receive repayments of principal and interest, which is sold.

In a primitive housing finance market, borrowers normally obtain their funds directly from private individuals, often relatives, who have savings. In more sophisticated markets private investors, and perhaps also institutions, lend money to intermediaries which use it to fund mortgage loans which they originate and service. In a highly developed market the mortgage origination and servicing becomes a function in its own right and to the extent that organisations undertaking this do not wish to hold loans then they will sell them to investors. It is possible for the financial intermediary to be completely bypassed through a secondary market. The essential difference between an intermediary, such as a building society or an S&L, and an institutional investor is that the former has to raise funds while the latter actually has funds because of the nature of its business (for example, in the case of pension funds and insurance companies) or personal circumstances (in the case of individuals).

The USA has a very developed secondary mortgage market, Canada and France have less developed markets, and few other countries have any significant secondary market. It is therefore important to examine what circumstances are likely to lead to the development of a secondary market. Basically, a secondary market will develop where some institutions are unable to secure profitable outlets for their funds through traditional means, and where housing market institutions develop a capacity to originate and service loans greater than their capacity to hold such loans. In the USA the original rationale behind the secondary market was to overcome the regional imbalances caused by restrictive legislation. In very simple terms, the bulk of savings were raised in the long-established centres in the East Coast, particularly New York, while the demand for funds was largely in the rapidly developing South and West of the country, in particular, California. In a country like the UK, with unified financial markets, the nationwide operation of banks and other financial institutions would ensure the necessary transfer of funds between areas. However, the USA has never had a nationwide banking system and the secondary market developed to enable borrowers in the West and South to borrow the surplus funds held in the East.

It would, of course, be perfectly possible for those institutions with surplus funds to invest to seek to become direct participants in the mortgage market. However, pension funds and, to a lesser extent, insurance companies do not naturally have the expertise and resources needed to service a mortgage market. Pension funds, in particular, operate generally from one office while mortgage market participants must have a wide network of branches.

Experience suggests that if the economic conditions necessitate the establishment of a secondary mortgage market then that market will develop, although some assistance from governmental or quasi-governmental organisations is generally required. If a mortgage is to be attractive to an investor then it has to be seen to be a sound investment. This is normally achieved in two ways -

    (a) By the establishment of uniform lending criteria. The secondary market in the USA has led to the adoption of standard criteria and also the adoption of standard forms for mortgage applications and valuations. Governmental bodies have played a major role in the establishment of uniform criteria and forms because they have largely determined which mortgages will be eligible for the secondary market.

    (b) By the existence of mortgage insurance, which effectively guarantees the loan. In the USA and Canada mortgage insurance has been pioneered by governmental bodies and effectively they have made the mortgage instrument as secure as any government investment.

It is helpful to explain briefly how the secondary market works. A loan will be made initially, perhaps by an institution which has its own supply of funds (for example an S&L), or perhaps by an organisation specialising in making and servicing loans, in which case it will raise its funds through short term borrowing. When it has a number of similar loans it will package them and either sell the entire package, or what is known as a 'participation' in the package, by which the purchaser secures the right to, say, 90% of interest and capital repayments. It goes without saying that the rate on loans traded in this way must be attractive compared with other investments. The mortgage originator will normally continue to collect repayments, and will handle any problems that arise with the loan. The institutional investor can, if he wishes, make a subsequent sale of his interest in the loan package.

The Nature of the Secondary Market

The point has been made that if mortgage loans are to be traded then their marketability is greatly assisted by insurance. The secondary market in the USA developed initially in respect of loans insured by the Federal Housing Administration (FHA) or guaranteed by the Veterans' Administration (VA). FHA was created in 1934 and is an agency within the Department of Housing and Urban Development. Interest rate ceilings are set for loans for which FHA insurance can be obtained. The borrower pays an annual insurance premium of 0.5% of the average principal outstanding over the year. The VA guarantees loans made by private lenders free of charge to eligible veterans of the US armed forces.

Since 1970 private mortgage insurance companies have become more important and by 1981 they accounted for some 35% of the market. Loans which are not insured or which are privately insured are referred to as conventional loans. As will be seen subsequently, the market for the various types of loan varies considerably. Private mortgage insurers also play a role in the secondary market by finding investors for packages of loans which they have insured.

The nature of the secondary market is shown quite well in Tables 4.3 and 4.4. Table 4.3 shows that the percentage of outstanding debt held by federally supported agencies and mortgage pools (broadly speaking, debt which has passed through the secondary market) rose from 8.3% in 1970 to 24.8% in 1982. Table 4.4 shows that in 1983 sales of one to four family mortgage loans were equal to 84% of originations. In round terms some 40% of all mortgages originated are now traded on the secondary market; the high figures in 1983 reflects the securitization of mortgages made in previous years.

The Mortgage Banking Industry

Table 4.4 shows that mortgage bankers originated 30% of loans by volume in the first four months of 1983, but that they accounted for only 4% of net acquisitions of loans. This summarizes the activities of mortgage bankers, ie, they are institutions which originate but which do not hold loans. Basically, mortgage bankers borrow money from a bank or raise money through other short term instruments. They then make mortgage loans which they pool together and sell to investors in the secondary market, using the proceeds to repay the loans. After the loans are sold the mortgage banker usually continues to collect monthly repayments which are then passed on to the investor purchasing the loans.

Mortgage bankers operate predominantly by using VA and FHA insured loans, although they have become more willing to offer conventional mortgages. In 1982 they accounted for 29% of total orginations of one to four family mortgage loans. They have accounted for well over three-quarters of originations of FHA/VA loans and their share of conventional originations has risen from under 2% in the early 1970s to 17% in 1982. As the secondary market has become significantly more important so mortgage bankers as major participants in that market have also grown in size. In addition to their role in the residential market, mortgage bankers also arrange finance for commercial developments.

There are about 800 mortgage companies. They have no fixed constitution. A little over a third are owned by banks, about a quarter are controlled by savings and loan associations and other institutions, and about 40% are independent organisations. A savings and loan association can either have a mortgage banking subsidiary which may well operate outside of its state of origin, or it may undertake a mortgage banking function as part of mainstream business, ie, the S&L originates and sells loans but these are recorded as being in the books of the S&L rather than a subsidiary.

Table 4.13 lists the largest mortgage banks as at 30 June 1982.

Table 4.13 Largest Mortgage Banks, USA, End-June 1982

Company	Base	Mortgages Serviced $m	Number
Lomas & Nettleton Financial	Dallas	12,075	489,000
Weyerhaueser Mortgage	Los Angeles	7,761	194,000
Banco Mortgage	Mineapolis	6,121	119,000
Manufacturers Hanover Mortgage	Farmington Hills, Mich	6,012	204,000
Suburban Coastal	Wayne, NJ	5,310	109,000
Advance Mortgage	Southfield, Mich	4,683	186,000
Colonial Mortgage Service	Philadelphia	4,474	125,000
Wells Fargo Mortgage	San Francisco	4,293	75,000
Kissell	Springfield, Ohio	4,057	153,000

Source: *American Banker*, October 12, 1982.
Note: At end-June 1982 there were $1.74 to the pound.

The largest companies are on a par with the largest S&Ls in terms of the volume and number of loans serviced. It will be noted that there are substantial differences in the ratio of the amount of loans to the number of loans serviced. Where the number of loans is large in relation to the amount, for example, for Lomas & Nettleton and Manufacturers Hanover, it is reasonable to assume that there is a concentration on residential mortgages. When the number of loans is small in relation to the amount, for example, for Suburban Coastal, there is likely to be a higher proportion of commercial loans.

Some of the names in Table 4.13 are familiar in other financial industries. Wells Fargo and Manufacturers Hanover are both large banks, the latter being listed as the fourth largest American bank in Table 4.12.

Since June 1982 the mortgage banking industry has grown much larger and the structure of the industry has been changing. One interesting development has been that Norwest Mortgage, formerly Banco Mortgage Company, has set up a subsidiary, the Residential Funding Corporation, which buys loans from mortgage banks and other institutions and finances them by issuing conventional securities. Housebuilders, real estate brokers and retailers are among the other institutions which are developing significant mortgage banking functions.

The financial structure of mortgage banks is very different from that of the traditional housing finance organisation. A typical building society or savings and loan will make mortgage loans in any one year equal to perhaps 20% of its assets. A mortgage bank will expect to make loans over 20 times its assets.

Table 4.14 shows the distribution of mortgage banks' assets and liabilities at end-1982.

Table 4.14 Distribution of Mortgage Banks' Assets & Liabilities, USA, End-1982

Liabilities	%	%	Assets	%
Commercial paper	54.9		Cash	2.1
Notes payable to banks	20.3		Other marketable securities	1.0
Other current liabilities	9.0		Receivables	4.0
Total current liabilities		84.2	First mortgages	45.7
Non-current liabilities		3.5	Construction loans	20.7
Preferred stock	0.1		Other loans	11.0
Common stock	1.0		Non-current assets	15.5
Retained earnings	6.2			
Paid in surplus	5.1			
Total stockholders' equity		12.3		
Total		100.0	Total	100.0

Source: *Financial Statements and Operating Ratios for the Mortgage Banking Industry 1982*, Mortgage Bankers Association of America, 1983, Table 4.02.

It will be seen that, unlike a building society or an S&L, liabilities are largely obtained on the wholesale markets, and mortgages are a low proportion of assets. The difference between a mortgage bank and an S&L is perhaps better illustrated by the income and expenditure figures, which are shown in Table 4.15.

Table 4.15 Income and Expenditure, Mortgage Banks, USA, 1982

	Percentage of Total
Income	
Loan administration fees	28.7
Loan origination fees	22.0
Interest income	41.6
Other income	7.8
Total	100.0
Expenditure	
Personnel	25.2
Interest	33.0
Other	24.5
Total	82.9
Net operating income	17.1
Non-recurring gain	0.4
Taxes on income	7.3
Net income	10.2

Source: *Financial Statements and Operating Ratios for the Mortgage Banking Industry 1982*,
Mortgage Bankers Association of America, 1983, Table 1.02.

The table shows that over a half of the income of the mortgage banks was accounted for by fees, while interest payments accounted for only a third of the expenditure.

The trade association for mortgage bankers is the Mortgage Bankers Association of America which is based in Washington DC, and which has been in operation since 1914. It has over 1,800 members including specialist mortgage companies, banks, S&Ls, life insurance companies, mortgage insurers, and other relevant organisations.

Government National Mortgage Association (GNMA)

The secondary mortgage market has been promoted largely through the activity of several government and semi-government organisations. A particularly important organisation in this respect is the Government National Mortgage Association (GNMA), often referred to as 'Ginnie Mae'. This is a wholly owned government body operating within the Department of Housing and Urban Development. It was established in 1968 and has as its principal function to increase the supply of credit to low and moderate income housing through the secondary mortgage market.

GNMA works through the mortgage backed securities programme by which privately issued securities, backed by pools of mortgages insured by FHA,

VA and FmHA (Farmers Housing Administration), are guaranteed. The programme works as follows. A mortgage lender (generally a mortgage bank) applies to GNMA for approval to become an issuer of GNMA securities and for a commitment to guarantee securities. The lender originates or acquires loans and packages them into pools. Relevant documents are then submitted to GNMA which will approve the issuance of securities. The issuer is fully responsible for the marketing and administration of the securities, including the monthly payment of principal and interest to investors.

GNMA earns income through a monthly guarantee fee of 0.06% on the outstanding balance of the securities issued. A GNMA guarantee effectively means that the security is government guaranteed and therefore highly marketable. Futures on GNMA securities are in fact traded in the financial futures market in Chicago.

In 1983 GNMA guaranteed mortgage backed securities to the volume of $50,000 million.

Federal National Mortgage Association (FNMA)

The Federal National Mortgage Association (FNMA or 'Fannie Mae') is a major secondary market institution in a quite different way from GNMA. The latter merely guarantees loans and does not hold them while FNMA purchases loans on the secondary market. At the end of 1983 FNMA's loan portfolio was $78,256 million making it one of the two largest holders of mortgage loans in the world and nearly four times the size of the largest S&L. In 1982, it purchased loans to the value of $17,554 million.

FNMA was created by Congress in 1938 as a wholly owned government corporation. In 1968 its functions were separated into GNMA and a new FNMA owned by private shareholders. Initially FNMA purchased FHA and VA mortgage loans only but since 1970 it has also been authorized to purchase conventional (ie privately insured and uninsured) mortgage loans, and these now account for half of its activity.

FNMA purchases loans from authorized institutions such as S&Ls and mortgage banks at rates set daily by reference to money market conditions. FNMA obtains its own funds through issues of debentures and short term discount notes. More recently it has begun to sell mortgage backed securities, backed by its own portfolio of loans. In this way the beneficial ownership of the loans it purchases is sold. In effect, FNMA is a huge S&L, except that it raises funds and purchases loans on a wholesale basis. Accordingly, it has also suffered an earnings crisis and it recorded a loss of $105 million in 1982.

Federal Home Loan Mortgage Corporation

The Federal Home Loan Mortgage Corporation (also known as FHLMC, the Mortage Corporation, and, most commonly, 'Freddie Mac') was created by Congress in 1970 with the function of developing and maintaining a nationwide secondary market for residential conventional mortgages. The

Corporation purchases loans, traditionally at fixed rates, but now also at adjustable rates, predominantly from S&Ls but also from other thrift institutions and mortgage and commercial banks. It then resells the loans largely by means of Mortgage Participation Certificates (PCs) representing undivided interests in specified mortgage pools. It also offers a Guarantor programme, by which it purchases loans from a lender and then sells PCs, based on these loans, to the same lender, effectively transforming a loan into a marketable instrument. This arrangement is often called a 'swap'. In August 1982, S&Ls held 45% of PCs, pension funds 18% and insurance companies 10%. The Corporation guarantees the timely payment of interest and ultimate collection of principal to investors purchasing its securities. It obtains its income from the difference between the interest earned on the mortgages purchased and the interest payments it makes to investors in its securities, largely PCs. By buying and selling loans at a positive spread, rather than holding them in its own portfolio, Freddie Mac has avoided interest rate risks.

The Corporation has grown massively in importance in the last few years as the secondary market has become more significant. Table 4.16 shows its activity in 1981, 1982 and 1983.

Table 4.16 Federal Home Loan Mortgage Corporation Activity, 1981-83

	1981 $m	1982 $m	1983 $m
Purchases of mortgages	3,744	23,671	22,952
Sales of mortgages	3,529	24,169	19,691
Loan portfolio at end-year	5,170	4,670	7,576
Total assets at end-year	6,321	8,029	8,964

Source: Federal Home Loan Mortgage Corporation, 1983 Annual Report.
Note: At end-1983 there were $1.44 to the pound.

It will be seen that the volume of activity rose some six fold between 1981 and 1982 and in 1983 the Corporation was the largest single purchaser of mortgages and seller of mortgage securities. However, the table shows also that the Corporation maintains only a modest loan portfolio which contrasts it sharply with FNMA.

The Corporation has played an important role in securing uniform lending standards and documentation. It has increased in significance partly because of its willingness to purchase both fixed rate loans and also adjustable rate loans, and to provide a market for securities based on these instruments. Thus while it has become increasingly difficult for S&Ls to make and hold fixed rate loans because of the risk of borrowing short and lending long, Freddie Mac can effectively enable an S&L to transfer the interest risk from itself to institutional investors generally who are willing to hold marketable fixed rate securities.

Crisis and Reform

Introduction

What has been described so far in this chapter is a complicated and confusing housing finance system. To understand how the present situation has been reached and likely future developments, it is necessary to analyse in detail, and almost as a separate subject, the massive crisis with which the S&L industry has been faced in the recent past. It is that crisis which has precipitated major changes in statute, regulation and attitudes.

The Crisis

In the 1960s and 1970s S&Ls operated fairly comfortably by raising money on passbook accounts and onlending those funds to home-buyers. Government regulations have been such that loans have had to be at fixed rates of interest. However, this did not pose any problems as the long term rate at which mortgage loans could be made was comfortably above the short term rate on savings.

A significant step was taken in 1966 when the Interest Rate Adjustment Act gave the Federal Home Loan Bank Board power to fix the maximum rate that could be paid on different types of savings account. Previously, such a power had applied to commercial banks only. By custom, the maximum rate fixed for S&Ls, and also for mutual savings banks, was allowed to exceed the rates which could be paid by the commercial banks. In 1975 Congress gave statutory authority to this differential(originally 0.5%, but later 0.25%) and prohibited the regulatory agencies from eliminating the differential on existing types of account without Congressional consent. The well-meaning intention of this differential was to enable housing finance institutions to raise substantial funds for house-purchase in competition with the commercial banks and to protect against inordinate increases in the cost of funds.

However, the regulated rates lagged behind market rates of interest and changed very little. Between 1970 and 1980 the rate of interest which could be paid on passbook accounts was increased just twice, and then only to 5.5%. As interest rates began to rise and became more volatile so passbook accounts became less attractive to the investor and increasingly funds were placed in longer term accounts, albeit with fixed rate ceilings.

By the late 1970s it had become clear that S&Ls could no longer continue to raise an adequate volume of funds to finance their lending activities with the regulated rates of interest. The growth of money market mutual funds (MMMFs) exemplified the problem. Because banks, savings banks and S&Ls were prohibited from paying a market rate of interest on call money, investors sought other means of obtain market rates that, at one stage, were three times regulated rates. The MMMFs allowed small investors to participate in money market rates through a concept similar to a unit trust. They attracted money by post, invested the proceeds in short term instruments and allowed instant withdrawals including, in many cases, through a cheque book. In January 1980, these funds held assets of $55,000 million; by July 1981 the figure had increased to $142,000 million.

The first response was in May 1978 when S&Ls were authorized to issue a new short term flexible certificate known as the Money Market Certificate (MMC). This was a short term instrument with a minimum deposit of $10,000 and a fixed maturity of six months. The rate of interest was fixed but at issuance was tied to the going rate for six month Treasury bills. S&Ls were permitted to pay 0.25% more than the banks on this account. The account proved remarkably attractive and accounted for 10% of balances by the end of 1978, 27% by the end of 1979, and 37% by the end of 1980.

The rise in market interest rates together with the popularity of the MMC led to demands for a market related certificate for the small investor. After an abortive attempt with a four year certificate, in 1980 a 30 month certificate was introduced, known as the Small Saver Certificate. The minimum balance was $1,000 and thrifts could pay 0.5% below the average yield on 30 month US Treasury securities, while the maximum rate for commercial banks was 0.75% below.

The six month and 30 month certificates were therefore at market related, albeit regulated, rates of interest. S&Ls were also able to raise funds through what were known as Jumbo CDs with a $100,000 minimum denomination. The rate on these certificates was completely unregulated.

The overall effect of the change of regulations was to transform the liability distribution from one comprising largely passbook accounts at regulated rates to one where the bulk of funds were held at market interest rates. This trend up to the end of 1981 is shown in Table 4.17.

Table 4.17 Distribution of S&L Savings Balances, USA, 1966-81

| Date | Regulated Interest Rate Accounts | | Market Interest Rate Accounts | | |
| | Passbook and Lower Yielding Accounts | Fixed Rate Ceilings | 6 Month | 30 Month | Jumbo CDs |
	%	%	%	%	%
31.10.66	88	12			
31.12.70	59	41			
31.12.75	44	56			
31.12.77	38	62			
31.12.78	32	58	10		
31.12.79	25	40	27	1	6
31.12.80	21	24	37	10	8
31.12.81	19	13	43	16	9

Source: United States League of Savings Associations.

The table shows that from the end of 1977 to the end of 1981 the proportion of savings balances at money market rates rose from 0 to 65% while the proportion at regulated rates fell from 100% to just 32%.

This liberalization of the liability side of the balance sheet of S&Ls was not, however, accompanied by any liberalization on the asset side. Although mortgage loans could be made at unregulated rates of interest the loans were at fixed rates, and the average yield could therefore rise only as new loans replaced existing loans. The problem was accentuated because holders of existing low interest loans obviously had no wish to repay them and it was often possible for such loans to be sold together with a house, the borrower being able to increase the selling price accordingly. The overall effect was a sharp rise in the yield on new loans but only a modest rise in the yield on the whole loan portfolio, and not nearly sufficient to counterbalance the rise in the cost of funds. The result was a substantial deficit in 1981 with a significant decline in the ratio of net worth to total assets. The trend is illustrated in Table 4.18.

Table 4.18 The S&L Earnings Crisis, USA, 1977-81

Year	Average Return on New Loans %	Average Return on All loans %	Average Cost of Funds %	Average Interest Spread %	Net Surplus in Year $m	Net Worth at Year-End	
						$m	% of Assets
1977	8.82	8.26	6.44	1.82	1,442	25,184	5.7
1978	10.59	8.50	6.67	1.87	1,835	29,057	5.6
1979	12.46	8.86	7.47	1.39	1,608	32,638	5.6
1980	14.39	9.34	8.94	0.40	417	33,391	5.3
1981	14.73	9.91	10.92	(1.01)	(1,546)	28,395	4.3

Source: United States League of Savings Institutions.

The table shows that while the average return on new loans rose from 8.82% in 1977 to 14.73% in 1981, the average return on all loans rose much more modestly from 8.26% to 9.91%, and a substantial negative interest spread resulted.

The Depository Institutions Deregulation and Monetary Control Act 1980

The earnings crisis made it apparent that the S&Ls were unable to compete within the prevailing legislative framework. Liabilities were at a market rate of interest and were short term while the institutions had little choice but to lend long term and had a large portfolio of long term low interest loans. The first response was the Depository Institutions Deregulation and Monetary Control Act (DIDMCA) of 1980. This sought to address the basic problems of the thrift industry. The DIDMCA had two major features. The first was the planned phase out of the interest rate ceilings imposed for certain categories of deposit; this would automatically entail the ending of the thrifts' differential over the commercial banks. This was to be achieved over a maximum period of six years. Combined with this was a significant increase in the powers of S&Ls. The Act -

(a) Authorized the issuance of interest bearing chequing accounts.
(b) Authorized investment of up to 20% of assets in consumer loans, corporate debt securities and commercial paper.
(c) Eased or removed lending restrictions.
(d) Expanded authority to invest in service corporations from 1% to 3% of assets.
(e) Granted authority to invest in mutual funds, to issue credit cards and to engage in trust operations.

The Act also increased the ceiling for accounts which could be insured from $40,000 to $100,000 and sought to pre-empt usury ceilings on mortgage loans applied in certain states.

This legislation was considered to be radical at the time but it soon became apparent that it was not adequate to deal with the acute problems with which S&Ls were faced.

Adjustable Rate Loans

Throughout the 1970s informed commentators were expressing concern at the risks which S&Ls were running by borrowing short and lending long. The S&L industry pressed for greater authority to issue variable rate loans but Congress was unimpressed, regarding the traditional 30 year fixed rate mortgage as being part of the American heritage. Significantly, the successful way in which the variable rate loan had been used in other countries, notably the United Kingdom, and the Canadian experience, much closer to home, with rollover loans, did not have a significant effect on the debate. By early 1981 all that was permitted for federally chartered institutions was a loan on which the rate of interest could rise by no more than 0.5% a year. However, in some states, notably California, the state chartered S&Ls had greater authority to issue variable rate loans.

In April 1981 the Federal Home Loan Bank Board authorized S&Ls to offer adjustable mortgage loans (AMLs) on terms far more liberal than anyone had expected. Basically, institutions were freed to decide their own loan terms, save for the important condition that changes in interest rates must be governed by the movement of an interest rate index which is not under the control of the lender.

This was a significant measure because it enabled S&Ls to resume lending again with safety, but it did nothing to overcome the basic problem of portfolios still heavily weighted with low interest fixed rate loans. The mortgage market also experienced a sudden shock and borrowers faced a bewildering array of choice of loans instead of the one traditional fixed rate loan to which they had been accustomed. Secondary market institutions had to adapt so as to provide a market in new types of instrument. However, somewhat paradoxically, the secondary market assumed even greater importance, partly because many consumers prefer the fixed rate loan and this can be offered now with safety only through the secondary market, as thrift institutions are no longer in a position to hold a large portfolio of fixed rate loans.

The Industry and the Housing Market, 1981-83

Table 4.18 showed how the industry moved into crisis from 1977 to 1981. The worst effects of the crisis were felt in 1981 and 1982 with the recovering beginning to show through in 1982. Table 4.19 shows the key figures for the industry from 1980 to 1983.

Table 4.19 The S&L Industry, USA, 1980-83

	1980	1981	1982	1983
Net receipts of new savings	$42,094m	$14,339m	$38,002m	$108,922m
Mortgage loans closed	$72,537m	$53,283m	$54,298m	$132,356m
Net income after taxes	$798m	-$4,725m	-$4,264m	$6,086m
Net worth at end of year	$33,391m	$28,395m	$26,157m	$30,758m
Total assets at end-year	$629,829m	$664,167m	$706,045m	$769,316m
Net worth ratio at end-year	5.3%	4.3%	3.7%	4.0%

Source: *'83 Savings and Loan Sourcebook*, United States League of Savings Institutions, 1983;
       Federal Home Loan Bank Board.
Note: At end-1983 there were $1.44 to the pound.

It will be seen that the net worth ratio declined by a third in 1981 and 1982 as a result of the substantial operating losses incurred in those two years. However, there was a significant recovery in 1983.

Bearing in mind the scale of the problem, the S&L industry came through the crisis in better shape than might have been expected. However, this was achieved only at considerable cost. Of the 4,002 S&Ls in existence at the end of 1980, 843 had disappeared by the end of 1982. 88 associations actually failed in 1981 and a further 254 failed in 1982. The rate of voluntary mergers doubled and there were 437 supervisory and assisted mergers between the beginning of 1980 and mid-1983. The cost to the Federal Government insuring agencies alone in 1982 was $2,000 million. This assistance was generally given by compensating the institution taking over a weak S&L to take account of the fact that the market value of the mortgages being taken over was substantially less than the book value.

More than 80% of S&Ls recorded losses in 1982 and it is estimated that if all mortgage loans at below market rates of interest had to be revalued to the market level, then S&Ls would have had negative net worth of some $40,000 million at the end of 1982, although this figure represents a marked improvement in the end-1981 figure of $57,000 million.

The improvement began to become apparent towards the end of 1982, as interest rates fell. The three month Treasury bill rate, which had averaged

14.03% in 1981, fell to under 8% by the end of 1982 and the cost of S&Ls' liabilities was moderated accordingly. The S&L industry returned to profitability in 1983.

However, some S&Ls will not be restored to health and the number of mergers will continue to run at a high level, with government assistance being required in many cases. By the end of 1984 it is anticipated that there will be fewer than 3,000 S&Ls. Moreover, if interest rates rise substantially, the crisis could re-emerge. It is also estimated that over 800 associations will qualify for capital assistance (described subsequently) totalling some $1,200 million in 1983 and perhaps another $250 million will be required in 1984.

The housing market was, of course, affected by the crisis in the housing finance industry, as well as more directly by the rise in interest rates which has a direct effect on the profitability of housebuilding. Mortgage lending by S&Ls fell from $101,000 million in 1979 to $73,000 million in 1980 and to $53,000 million in 1981 and, although there was some increase in secondary market activity, in general the availability of housing finance loans fell and the cost rose.

Borrowers were particularly reluctant to take on long term loans at what were perceived to be high rates of interest, and adjustable rate loans were either not available or were viewed with suspicion. This led to what was euphemistically called 'creative financing'. In over half of all house transactions, part of the funds were provided by the vendor, in effect by deferring part of the purchase price. The funds were made available at a comparatively low rate of interest but only for a short term, generally under five years. It was the hope that these sort of arrangements could be refinanced when interest rates returned to more normal levels.

Table 4.2 shows that starts of private housing units fell from 2,020,000 in 1978 to 1,745,000 in 1979, 1,292,000 in 1980, 1,084,000 in 1981, and to 1,062,000 in 1982. In 1982 confidence returned to the housing market with the fall in interest rates. By the beginning of 1983 this was beginning to feed through to housing starts and starts in the year of 1,713,000 marked a 60% increase on the 1982 level.

The Garn/St Germain Act

The DIDMCA had been hailed as the most significant legislation for the housing finance industry since the 1930s. However, in 1982 came the more far reaching Garn/St Germain Depository Institutions Act (the Act, in common with many other Acts of Congress, is named after its sponsors). The Act included the following provisions -

(a)   The authorization of a new savings account, directly competitive with money market funds.
(b)   The pre-emption or severe limitation of state imposed restrictions on the ability of S&Ls to enforce due-on-sale clauses in loan contracts.

(c) The completion of the phasing out of the interest differential by the beginning of 1984, and of all controls by 1986.

(d) Capital assistance for institutions with deficient net worth.

(e) An easing of the requirements for conversions from state to federal charter and vice versa and also from S&Ls into savings banks.

(f) Expanded authority to invest in consumer, commercial and agricultural loans and other investments.

(g) Removal of loan to valuation ratio limits and the restriction to lending on first mortgage.

(h) The permitting of investment in tangible personal property for lease or sale up to 10% of total assets.

The Act has had a major effect on the S&L industry and on the housing finance market and some of its effects have already been noted. In particular, the money market deposit account grew to represent 17.9% of liabilities by June 1983, futher confirming the almost total integration of S&Ls with the rest of the financial system.

Many institutions have taken advantage of the easier criteria which have to be met in order to change charter or even form of organisation. In 1983 72 S&Ls converted from mutual to stock ownership, raising $2,700 million of additional capital. There have been several subsequent conversions and indeed some of the amounts being raised by S&Ls match any previous raising of capital by private industry. In view of the precarious state of health of the S&L industry, this has been a remarkable achievement.

A major development has been the conversion of S&Ls into federal savings banks. In the first quarter of 1983, there were no fewer than 50 applications for such conversion. One reason why S&Ls wish to convert is that existing tax laws are such that an S&L must have 82% of its assets in mortgages and Treasury securities if it is to minimize its tax burden. For savings banks, the proportion is 72%. More philosophically, some institutions consider that it is better to trade under the name of a savings bank rather than an S&L. The federal savings bank is a new type of institution, different from mutual savingsbanks in terms of ownership and nearer to the S&L in terms of operations.

A New Housing Finance Market

A new type of housing finance market has emerged and it is one that is very different from the traditional market. In little more than five years, housing finance in the USA has changed from a system based on specialist housing finance intermediaries to a system wholly integrated into the financial markets.

As far as the consumer is concerned he has a range of types of loan from which to choose. Fixed rate loans are still very popular and there are a variety of adjustable rate loans on the market. Most of them provide for some limitation on the extent to which the rate can be increased and on the intervals between changes. It is said that there are over 100 types of loan and it seems fairly certain that there will be pressures for standardization in the next few years. The consumer is still prepared to pay a premium for fixed rate loans; at the beginning of 1984 adjustable rate loans were on offer, typically, at two percentage points below the rate on fixed interest loans. During the course of 1983 the proportion of loans made by S&Ls on an adjustable rate basis by S&Ls rose from 23% to 55% and this new mortgage instrument is therefore readily accepted, particularly by lenders, although the premium that has to be paid for fixed rate loans remains large. It may reflect expectations about future interest rates.

Mortgage loans are made available by a wide variety of institutions and nearly half of loans which are originated are sold. The process of originating and servicing loans has been partially divorced from that of holding loans and a number of new institutions are entering the market in addition to the traditional mortgage bankers. Retailers, housebuilders and realtors (estate agents) have all found it profitable to be able to offer to their customers mortgage loans which can immediately be financed on the secondary market.

S&Ls have seen their traditional role move away from them very rapidly but they have not been slow to react. The traditional S&L, that is, an institution which makes and holds long term fixed rate loans, financed by short term liabilities, is regarded as being dead. The complete integration of the liabilities of S&Ls into the financial markets generally means that the cost of liabilities is now far too volatile to risk holding large amounts of fixed rate loans. S&Ls therefore have to adapt in one of a number of ways.

If an S&L wishes to make fixed rate loans then, increasingly, it must do this acting as a mortgage banker, selling the loans on the secondary market and deriving its income from fees rather than interest. The S&L servicing the largest amount of loans for others is Commonwealth Savings of Houston, which, at 30 June 1983, serviced loans of $4,384 million while having assets of only $417 million. However, this is an exceptional ratio. If an S&L intends to remain as an institution raising savings to make mortgage loans then it must do this largely on a variable rate basis so that assets and liabilities are matched. Such an S&L may also find it necessary to make fixed rate loans to those who want them and then to sell those on the secondary market. S&Ls are not likely to regain the share of loan originations that they had in the 1970s, but their expertise in this area combined with the new instruments available to them means that they will probably continue to have 40-50% of the market for originations, although their share of holdings of loans is likely to be smaller, and a significant proportion of their mortgage portfolio will be in the form of securities backed by mortgages.

Larger S&Ls with substantial branch networks and which wish to continue to grow are likely to develop into full service retail financial institutions and many will convert to the savings bank charter or, at the least, will refer to themselves as savings associations rather than S&Ls. Among the services already offered by many large S&Ls are -

(a) A telephone bill paying service.
(b) A money market chequing account.
(c) Trust services.
(d) Brokerage services.
(e) Home equity loans, which are being marketed aggressively at present.
(f) Insurance services.
(g) Lease financing.

Although the S&L industry is gradually returning to a healthy position, thanks largely to a decline in the general level of interest rates, many more S&Ls will be merged. If interest rates turn upwards again then the critical problems which confronted the industry in 1981 and 1982 may re-appear, because many S&Ls still have a large volume of low interest fixed rate loans.

The secondary market is likely to continue growing in importance with the majority of loans being traded. Government involvement in the secondary market is expected to diminish, with the Federal Home Loan Mortgage Corporation moving to private ownership and the Government National Mortgage Association being gradually run down. The Mortgage Corporation will, however, continue to grow in importance as the mortgage instrument is increasingly 'securitized', and loans are transferred from the originator/servicer to the investment institution.

Assessment

The United States experience shows the inherent dangers of -

(a) Imposing controls on interest rates, for however good intentions, when controlled rates are likely to be way out of line with market rates.
(b) Borrowing short and lending long.

It is a sad commentary on the way that financial institutions in the USA are regulated that it took a major earnings crisis to force change in the situation. The housing finance market in the USA has changed more significantly in the last five years than it would normally be reasonable to expect change in a period of 30 years—because of the crisis which developed in the late 1970s and early 1980s.

Effectively, the USA is moving away from almost total reliance on the deposit taking system to a system which includes use of the mortgage banking principle, with the further refinement that the process of originating and servicing loans has been separated from that of holding loans.

These developments merit careful consideration in other countries with similar financial systems, in particular, the United Kingdom, Australia, South Africa and New Zealand, because experience suggests that trends in the USA can be used to forecast trends in those countries. However, the special circumstances that affected the USA, that is borrowing short and lending long and restrictions of interstate banking, do not apply in those countries, and therefore while the direction of change may well be the same the magnitude and timing are likely to be very different.

Bibliography

Carron, A S, *The Rescue of the Thrift Industry*, The Brookirgs Institution, 1983.
Colton, K J, 'The Nation's System of Housing Finance', in *AREUEA Journal*, Volume 11, No 2, Summer 1983.
Federal Home Loan Bank Board Journal, passim.
'84 Savings and Loan Sourcebook, United States League of Savings Institutions, 1984.
Savings Institutions, United States League of Savings Institutions, passim.
Secondary Mortgage Markets, Federal Home Loan Mortgage Corporation, Vol 1, No 1, February 1984.
'Special Secondary Mortgage Market Supplement', *Savings Institutions*, January 1984.
Struyk, R J, Mayer, N and Tuccillo, J A, *Federal Housing Policy at President Reagan's Midterm*, The Urban Institute, 1983.
The Report of the President's Commission on Housing, 1982.
The Secondary Market in Residential Mortgages, Federal Home Loan Mortgage Corporation, 1983.
Thygerson, K J and Colton, K W, *Revolution in Housing Finance*, Federal Home Loan Mortgage Corporation, 1983.
Tuccillo, J A, with Goodman, J L, *Housing Finance—A Changing System in the Reagan Era*, The Urban Institute, 1983.

Acknowledgements

The co-operation of the United States League of Savings Institutions, the Federal Home Loan Bank Board, the Federal Home Loan Mortgage Corporation and the Mortgage Bankers Association of America in providing information for this chapter is gratefully acknowledged. The chapter has drawn heavily on the *'84 Savings and Loans Sourcebook*, published by the United States League of Savings Institutions.

The author thanks the following who commented on an earlier draft of this chapter -
Henry Cassidy, Director, General Research, Federal Home Loan Bank Board; Thomas King, Director of Research, Federal Home Loan Mortgage Corporation.

CHAPTER 5

CANADA

Canada has a tradition of owner-occupation and for many years the majority of households have been owner-occupiers. The level of owner-occupation is lower in the major centres of population than in the rural areas.

Housing finance is provided largely, but not entirely, by the savings bank system, but, unlike in the other English-speaking countries, general financial institutions are responsible for most mortgage loans. No less than six different types of institution each have between 10 and 21% of the mortgage market.

Changes in market shares have resulted largely from changes in government regulations, particularly with respect to involvement of the banks. Also, there is a limited secondary market and this has been used in particular by the government to divest itself of public sector holdings of mortgages.

The distinguishing feature of mortgage finance in Canada until recently was the five-year mortgage rollover; that is loans were provided on the basis that the rate of interest would be changed in line with market rates every five years. This system worked well until interest rates began to fluctuate more frequently over the last few years, and as a consequence shorter mortgage terms have been introduced.

Introduction

Canada is the second largest country in the world with a land area of 9,976,000 sq kilometres. The population at the end of 1982 was 24,453,000 and unlike in some other advanced industrial countries the rate of population growth has been fairly rapid in recent years, about 1% per year. About 75% of Canadians live in urban areas and the main centres are Montreal, Toronto, Vancouver and Ottawa (the capital). Canada retains the status of :a dominion with the British monarch as Head of State. The country is a federation and the individual provinces have considerable powers. The federal government, based in Ottawa, has a two chamber parliament. The major political parties are the Liberals and Conservatives. The Liberals have held power for most of the post-war period.

Canada is now one of the most prosperous countries in the world, although its economic performance in recent years has tended to lag behind those of the other advanced countries. Over the period 1960-80 real GDP per capita grew by 3.1% p a, the same as the OECD average, but over the period 1973-

80 growth fell a little below the OECD average. Inflation in Canada has been slightly lower than average over the period 1960-80; consumer prices increased by an average 5.3% per year compared with the OECD average of 6.1%. Until the last few years short and long term interest rates tended to be more stable than in other countries, but in 1981 and 1982 this trend changed markedly.

The Canadian economy is closely integrated with the United States economy and consequently economic trends in the two countries are similar.

Housing

The Housing Stock and Housing Tenure

There has been a very rapid rate of housebuilding in Canada in the post-war years with the result that a high proportion of the housing stock is relatively new. As recently as 1951 Canada had an excess of houses over households and that excess has continued to grow.

Because Canada is thinly populated houses tend to be large, detached and fairly well spaced out. The relatively modest price of land means that people may have the choice of a fairly substantial house outside of a city centre or an apartment within a town. Over half of all houses in Canada are single detached dwellings and nearly a third are apartments. 89% of single detached dwellings are owned and 92% of apartments are rented.

Table 5.1 shows the housing tenure pattern revealed by the 1981 census.

Table 5.1 Housing Tenure, Canada, 1981

Tenure	Urban Areas		Rural Areas		All	
	No	%	No	%	No	%
Owned	3,650,415	56	1,491,520	84	5,141,940	62
Rented	2,855,680	44	283,905	16	3,139,590	38
All	6,506,100	100	1,775,430	100	8,281,535	100

Source: 1981 Census of Canada, *Occupied Private Dwellings*, Statistics Canada.

The percentage of owner-occupied dwellings has been growing modestly, from 60.3% in 1971 to 61.8% in 1976 and to 62.1% in 1981. There is a significant regional variation in housing tenure. The two large French-speaking cities of Montreal and Quebec have the lowest rates of owner-occupation of the metropolitan areas. In Montreal only 41.7% of houses were owner-occupied in 1981 and in Quebec the figure was 50.5%. These two cities also have a higher than average proportion of dwellings in the form of apartments.

Housebuilding

The rate of housebuilding has fallen markedly since 1978, largely as a consequence of economic conditions generally. Table 5.2 shows how completions fell from a peak of 246,533 in 1978 to 133,942 in 1982, although the figures for 1983 show a significant increase.

Table 5.2 Dwelling Completions by Type of Dwelling, Canada, 1978-83

| Year | Type of Dwelling | | | | |
	Single Detached	Semi-Detached	Row	Apartment & Other	Total
1978	106,195	19,155	26,644	94,539	246,533
1979	112,105	18,071	18,860	77,453	226,489
1980	90,720	13,675	13,398	58,375	176,168
1981	98,412	12,831	13,252	50,501	174,996
1982	54,720	8,480	16,082	54,660	133,942
1983	95,230	7,129	9,747	50,812	163,008

Sources: *Canadian Housing Statistics 1983*, CMHC, 1984, Table 7.

Housing Finance

Trends in the Housing Finance Market

The Canadian housing finance market has been characterised by significant changes in market shares, resulting partly from legislative changes. The position has now been reached where no type of institution has more than a quarter of the market, and six types of institution have at least 10% each. Table 5.3 shows trends in the distribution of mortgage loans outstanding.

Table 5.3 Distribution of Mortgage Loans Outstanding, Canada 1940-82

| Institution | Percentage of Outstanding Loans | | | | | | |
	1940	1950	1960	1970	1980	1981	1982
Trust companies	9	6	7	12	21	21	21
Chartered banks	-	-	10	5	15	13	9
Credit unions	-	-	4	4	12	12	11
Life companies	44	50	36	25	13	13	14
Government agencies	21	26	21	24	11	11	11
Estates, trusts and agency funds of trust companies	-	-	6	9	8	8	8
Loan companies	18	15	7	9	10	13	17
Pension funds	-	-	3	3	5	5	5
Other	8	3	7	8	4	5	4

Source: *Canadian Housing Statistics 1983*, CMHC, 1984, Table 78.

It is helpful at this stage to describe very briefly the institutions listed in Table 5.3. The major lenders are described in more detail subsequently.

Trust companies originally conducted estate and trust business. However, they rapidly developed deposit taking and real estate functions by accepting trust deposits and offering guaranteed investment certificates.

The chartered banks are similar to large commercial banks in other countries. They provide a full retail and wholesale banking service.

Credit unions are larger in Canada than in any other advanced country and they have been growing rapidly in recent years. They operate in a similar way to credit unions in other countries, but tend to be more sophisticated, and have taken the role that in other countries is performed by savings banks.

The life insurance companies operate on a similar basis to those in other countries. As Table 5.3 shows the life companies were the major lenders in the mortgage market until 1950, but recently they have been reducing the level of their activity in the residential housing sector, particularly lending on single detached units.

The figures for government agencies largely relate to mortgages being held by the Canada Mortgage and Housing Corporation, a government owned crown corporation whose operations are described in detail subsequently.

The estates, trusts and agency funds of trust companies purchase mortgage loans including those made by trust companies themselves.

Loan companies are similar in their method of operation to trust companies in that they accept deposits. Unlike trust companies they also raise money through debenture issues. Many loan companies are in fact associated with, and, in some cases, are owned by, trust companies and chartered banks.

Pension funds are similar to those in other countries, and like the estates, trusts and agency funds of trust companies they do not originate mortgage loans, but rather purchase them from the issuing institutions.

The early development of housing finance in Canada was similar to that in Britain. Building societies developed in the middle of the 19th century and operated in a way similar to British terminating building societies. The Building Societies Act 1859 gave legal status to the permanent type of building society. By the late 19th century, societies were fairly sophisticated financial intermediaries. However, by the end of the century they had largely disappeared and trust companies had moved in to the mortgage business. In 1897 a Loan Corporations Act removed the legal distinction between building societies and other loan companies. Significantly the loan companies raised much of their funds on the British capital market, reinvesting the proceeds in Canadian mortgage loans.

The trust companies were authorized to act as trustees for investments in 1912, and, in 1921, they were authorized to accept deposits for investment, and could guarantee rates of interest on their deposits for a fixed term. The mortgage market was an obvious outlet for their funds.

As in the United States the life companies tended to dominate the mortgage business in the first half of the 20th century. In fact, before trust companies developed into major mortgage lenders themselves they acted as 'correspondents' for the life companies—selling policies, collecting premiums and introducing investments. By the early 1940s, the life companies accounted for over 40% of all mortgage lending but, as already been noted, their market share has declined steadily subsequently.

The first significant legislation on housing finance was The Dominion Housing Act 1935 which permitted loans to be made for up to 80% of valuation, compared with the previous limit of 60%. In 1944, The National Housing Act established the Central Mortgage and Housing Corporation (CMHC), now Canada Mortgage and Housing Corporation, and in 1954 The National Housing Act (NHA) marked the beginning of the modern era of housing finance. This provided for loans for 90% of the value of the house with the top one third of the loans being insured by the government. The rate of interest under which loans under the Act could be made was stipulated by the government, and was changed from time to time to reflect market conditions. At the same time the chartered banks were permitted to make loans insured under The National Housing Act, and this marked their entry into the mortgage market. Their market share rose from 0 in 1948 to 12% in 1958. Although the banks were permitted to make NHA loans they could not charge more than 6% interest. As interest rates rose above this level in the late 1950s so the banks withdrew from the mortgage market, and their share of outstanding loans fell to 4% in 1968. The trust companies increased their lending, counteracting the decline in lending by the chartered banks and the long term decline in lending by the insurance companies.

The 1967 Bank Act removed the 6% interest limitation and permitted banks to make NHA insured loans at the current rate permissible, and also to make, for the first time, conventional loans; that is uninsured loans which cannot be for more than 75% of the value of the property. In 1970, the banks were permitted to make conventional loans for over 75% of valuation on the same basis as other institutions. In the 1960s the Mortgage Insurance Company of Canada was formed to provide mortgage insurance, and in 1969 the government abolished the maximum rate, thereby allowing NHA loans to be made at the going market rate of interest. Table 5.3 shows how the banks have greatly expanded their share of the mortgage market since 1970 and they are now the largest single type of lender.

The most significant recent change has been in the role of CMHC, which has been divesting itself of its mortgage portfolio, largely through sales to other lenders. Market developments are described in detail in the following section.

It is helpful at this stage to disaggregate the mortgage market a little because the institutions differ markedly in the type of mortgage lending which they undertake. Table 5.4 shows mortgage loan approvals by type of institution and type of loan for 1983.

It should be noted that this table applies to mortgage loans approved, and not to the net increase in mortgage loans outstanding. Some of the loans approved will have subsequently been sold to mortgage holders. The table shows that the life companies still dominate the market for non-residential mortgages, and they also have a significant share of the market for new

Table 5.4 Mortgage Loans Approved, Canada, 1983

Institution	New Residential Construction		Existing Residential Property		Non-Residential Property		Total	
	$Cm	%	$Cm	%	$Cm	%	$Cm	%
Chartered banks	1,900	36	7,459	43	533	14	9,891	38
Life insurance companies	594	11	863	5	2,260	61	3,717	14
Trust companies	1,251	24	4,962	29	495	13	6,708	26
Loan companies	818	16	3,598	21	416	11	4,832	18
Others	650	12	454	3	-	-	1,104	4
Total	5,212	100	17,336	100	3,703	100	26,252	100

Source: *Canadian Housing Statistics 1983*, CMHC, 1984, Table 35.
Note: At end-1983 there were $C1.25 to the US dollar and $C1.79 to the pound.

residential construction mortgages. The chartered banks and trust companies are the largest lenders for existing residential property. One point of
interest is that there was a marked increase in lending on existing residential
property in 1983, to $C17,336 million from $C7,582 million the year before.

The Terms of Mortgage Loans

Mortgage loans are available on demand in Canada, and, by definition, the
mortgage rate is therefore set at a market clearing level. Moreover, there is
no tax relief on mortgage interest, although the Conservative government did
announce a scheme for tax relief in the late 1970s which, in the event, was
not implemented.

For new dwellings, loans initially are made to the developer so as to enable
him to finance construction, and, at a later stage, they will be transferred
to the purchasers. This is in contrast to the position, for example, in Britain,
whereby developers normally raise funds from the banking system in order
to finance construction, and the building society enters the picture only when
the house is purchased. The purchasers of secondhand houses can invariably
'assume' the loan of the vendor, and it is not necessary for the loan to be
redeemed and a new loan taken out. Generally, further finance will be required,
and if the two loans are to be at different rates of interest then a blended
rate may be calculated.

The main distinguishing feature of the Canadian housing finance system
has been the 'rollover'. The normal method was for loans to be granted at
the prevailing rate of interest, with a 25 year amortization schedule. However, the term of the loan was not 25 years, but rather was five years, and
at the end of that period the loan became repayable. The borrower was therefore assured of a fixed rate of interest for five years. At the end of the five
year period the borrower could automatically renew his loan at the going rate.
The system worked very well when interest rates were relatively stable, and
the system could even accommodate steadily rising interest rates. However,

it could not accommodate the wild fluctuations in interest rates that have been experienced since 1980. Table 5.5 shows quoted mortgage rates on new loans by institutional lenders by quarter since 1978.

Table 5.5 Mortgage Rates Quoted by Institutional Lenders, Canada, 1978-83

Year	Quarter (%)				Average %
	1	2	3	4	
1978	10.32	10.38	10.43	11.24	10.59
1979	11.21	11.09	11.75	13.85	11.97
1980	13.81	14.62	13.68	15.16	14.32
1981	15.40	17.61	20.55	19.04	18.15
1982	18.66	19.05	18.71	15.00	17.86
1983	12.97	12.56	12.89	12.23	12.66

Source: *Canadian Housing Statistics 1983*, CMHC, 1984, Table 79.

The problems with the five year rollover are obvious. For example, a borrower taking out a loan in the third quarter of 1975 will have rolled over his loan in the third quarter of 1980 at a rate of 13.68%. A borrower taking out his loan a year later would have rolled his loan over at 20.55%, seven percentage points more. Besides creating obvious inequities between borrowers, some borrowers were placed in financial difficulty, and also borrowers generally became unwilling to commit themselves for five year periods.

The lending institutions reacted by offering loans with three year terms, two year terms, one year terms and, exceptionally, six month terms. Borrowers were thus enabled to 'gamble' on interest rates. If they believed that rates would fall then they would take out a short term loan, whereas if they believed that rates would rise they would take out a longer term loan. As interest rates fell towards the end of 1982 and in early 1983 so the longer terms became popular again. However, loans that have an interest rate which varies monthly according to market interest rates are also available.

To cope with the problem of rolling over loans at higher rates of interest the Canada Mortgage Renewal Plan (CMRP), announced in 1981, has provided assistance to home-owners facing financial difficulties on the renewal of their mortgages. Assistance of up to $C3,000 per year was available for households renewing mortgages between 1 September 1981 and 12 November 1982. In June 1982 the plan was modified from what had been a deferred interest and grant formula to a simple nontaxable grant. The plan was extended until the end of 1983.

The Canadian financial institutions have matched assets and liablilities so as to avoid the problem of borrowing short and lending long. With the fixed five year term, guaranteed investment certificates for five year periods were issued to provide the funding. Borrowers were not permitted to redeem prematurely without substantial penalty, something which is essential in a fixed rate system. As mortgage terms have reduced so shorter term certificates were offered, and the institutions have been anxious to continue matching assets and liabilities in this way.

The role of mortgage insurance merits brief mention. By law loans cannot be made for more than 75% of valuation without mortgage insurance, and mortgage insurance is also essential for the smooth operation of the secondary mortgage market. Most mortgage insurance is provided by the Canada Mortgage and Housing Corporation under the National Housing Act. One private insurance company, Mortgage Insurance Company of Canada, has however been rapidly increasing its market share. Mortgages are insured by a premium being levied on the entire loan amount rather than on the excess amount above a certain threshold.

The Secondary Mortgage Market

The secondary mortgage market in Canada has developed primarily because lending institutions developed a capacity to originate, process and service loans greater than their capacity to hold loans in their own portfolios, and also because the pattern of savings shifted with more money being held with pension and other investment funds and insurance companies. The secondary market has been made possible by NHA insurance, which is, effectively, as good as a government guarantee.

Investing institutions wishing to purchase NHA insured mortgages normally do so directly through contacting the lending institution. Normally an entire package of loans would be purchased. It is not uncommon for separate parts of particular organisations to trade loans; thus the trust and pension funds managed by the trust companies purchase loans made by the trust companies, and some of the chartered banks effectively sell loans from their lending departments to their subsidiary mortgage loan companies. However, such transactions are always at arm's length. Mortgage loans have proved to be a good investment because the rate of interest on them has been in excess of competing interest rates, for example on corporate bonds and government bonds.

Table 5.6 shows transactions in the secondary mortgage market in 1983.

The table shows that the major sellers of loans were chartered banks followed by trust companies. The major purchasers were loan and other companies and then other corporate bodies. There was a significant development in the secondary market in 1977 when CMHC decided to sell off a considerable proportion of its loan portfolio. In 1977 and 1978, CMHC loan sales totalled $C644 million.

The Canadian secondary mortgage market remains relatively unsophisticated compared with that in the USA, but this is to be expected as the circumstances which have given rise to the American market, in particular the confinement of lending institutions to operating in fairly small areas, do not apply in Canada. Mortgages are generally sold once only from issuer to holder and are not subsequently resold. Attempts have been made to stimulate a more active secondary mortgage market but have not been successful.

Table 5.6 Sales and Purchases of NHA Mortgages, Canada, 1983

Institution	Sales		Purchases	
	$Cm	%	$Cm	%
Chartered banks	1,606	75	45	2
Life insurance companies	60	3	87	4
Trust companies	312	15	189	9
Loan and other companies	149	7	780	37
CMHC	4	-	-	-
Pension funds	-	-	246	12
Other corporate bodies	2	-	684	32
Unincorporated bodies	-	-	101	5
Total	2,133	100	2,133	100

Source: *Canadian Housing Statistics 1983*, CMHC, 1984, Table 28.
Note: At end-1983 there were $C1.25 to the US dollar and $C1.79 to the pound.

The Personal Savings Market

Table 5.7 shows personal sector savings and time deposits in Canada at the end of September 1983.

Table 5.7 Savings Deposits, Canada, September 1983

Institution	Amount Held $Cbn	Percentage of Total
Chartered banks	103.3	42
Trust companies	45.9	19
Local credit unions	33.5	14
Mortgage loan companies	22.3	9
Government savings banks	6.3	3
Quebec savings banks	3.8	2
Canada savings bonds	31.4	12
Total	246.7	100

Source: Statistics Canada, *Financial Institutions*, 3rd Quarter 1983; *Bank of Canada Review*, November 1983, Tables 8 & 48.
Notes: 1. At end-September 1983 there were $C1.23 to the US dollar and $C1.85 to the pound.
2. The figures are taken from two separate sources and may not be strictly compatible.

The table shows how the chartered banks dominate the market. It is significant that chartered banks, trust companies, credit unions and mortgage loan companies all provide a complete retail financial service, including chequeing accounts as well as deposit accounts. There is therefore fierce competition in the savings market. The structure of the Canadian personal savings market is very different from that in other English speaking or indeed West European countries. There are no specialist savings banks and no specialist building societies. The question of competition between general and specialist institutions has therefore not arisen to the same extent as in the other English speaking countries in particular because, in effect, the institutions have always competed with each other across the whole range of retail business.

Housing Finance Institutions

Trust Companies

Trust companies were established and grew rapidly under provincial legislation in the late 19th and early 20th centuries. The point has already been made that originally they conducted estate and trust business, but gradually they secured a deposit taking function. Trust companies operate under the Trust Companies Act 1970 as amended or corresponding provincial legislation. At the end of 1982 there were 77 trust companies (excluding those that do not do business with the public), the number having increased fairly rapidly in recent years from 65 in 1975.

Trust companies have power to accept funds against guaranteed deposit receipts for a fixed term of five years or less, and they can invest these funds in specified assets including mortgages, company stocks and bonds and government bonds. Trust companies that accept public deposits must belong to the Canada Deposit Insurance Corporation, which was established in 1967, and which provides deposit insurance up to a maximum of $C60,000 per depositor.

Trust companies provide a complete retail financial service including agency, trust, estate planning, insurance, life assurance, deposits and chequing services. They also provide services to companies including the handling of securities. At the end of 1982, the trust companies managed estates, trusts and agencies funds of $88,808 million. In terms of the residential housing market a significant function of the trust companies is their real estate brokerage service. At the end of 1982, trust companies had 958 deposit taking branches and 391 real estate branches.

Table 5.8 shows the assets and liablilities of trust companies at the end of September 1983.

It will be seen that term deposits accounted for 67% of liabilities and savings deposits for 21%. Over half of term deposits had a maturity of between one and five years. Residential mortgage loans accounted for 49% of assets, below the 80% which is common for specialist housing finance organisations, but well above the 10% or 15% which is common for banks. As the trust companies have been losing market share in the mortgage market so they have diversified into commercial and personal lending, but the extent to which they can do this is restricted by legislation—two thirds of assets must be in certain qualifying categories including mortgage loans and government and other qualifying bonds.

Table 5.8 Trust Companies, Assets and Liabilities, September 1983

Liabilities	$Cm	%	Assets	$Cm	%
Savings deposits	11,013	21	Cash & demand deposits	512	1
Term deposits	34,535	67	Investments	15,646	30
Loans and notes	583	1	NHA mortgages	5,047	10
Other liabilities	3,350	6	Conventional residential		
Shareholders' equity	2,402	5	mortgages	20,136	39
			Non-residential		
			mortgages	4,858	9
			Personal loans	2,028	4
			Other assets	3,656	7
Total	51,883	100	Total	51,883	100

Source: Statistics Canada, *Financial Institutions*, 3rd Quarter 1983, ·Table 9.
Note: At end-September 1983 there were $C1.23 to the US dollar and $C1.85 to the pound.

The largest trust company is Royal Trust which had total assets of $C10,613 million and mortgage assets of $C5,475 million at the end of 1983. This is followed in size by the Canada Trust and the Canada Permanent Trust.

Mortgage Loan Companies

At the end of 1982 there were 44 mortgage loan companies. Some of these were owned by trust companies, some by chartered banks and others were independent. Mortgage loan companies operate under the Loan Companies Act 1970 as amended or under corresponding provincial legislation. The deposit taking and mortgage lending functions of the mortgage loan companies are similar to those of the trust companies, although they also raise some funds through debentures. Table 5.9 shows the combined balance sheet for mortgage loan companies at the end of September 1983.

Table 5.9 Mortgage Loan Companies, Assets & Liabilities, End-September 1983

Liabilities	$Cm	%	Assets	$Cm	
Demand deposits	592	2	Cash & demand deposits	222	1
Term deposits	21,662	58	Investments	5,647	15
Loans and notes	7,692	21	NHA mortgages	8,691	23
owing to affiliated			Conventional residential		
companies	3,912	11	mortgages	19,585	53
Debentures	975	3	Non-residential		
Other liabilities	345	1	mortgages	1,709	5
Shareholders' equity	1,932	5	Personal loans	102	-
			Other assets	1,154	3
Total	37,110	100	Total	37,110	100

Source: Statistics Canada, *Financial Institutions*, 3rd Quarter 1983, Table 17.
Note: At end-September 1983 there were $C1.23 to the US dollar and $C1.85 to the pound.

It will be seen that the mortgage loan companies have a more diversified source of funds than the trust companies, while on the assets side they specialise far more on mortgages. The mortgage loan companies are, in fact, more similar to specialist building societies than are the trust companies in respect of the assets side of the balance sheet.

The largest single mortgage loan company is the CIBC Mortgage Corporation which is owned by the Canadian Imperial Bank of Commerce. This had total assets of $C7,235 million at the end of October 1983. Mortgage assets accounted for $C6,606 million (91% of the total). Most of the largest companies are, in fact, owned by the banks, and companies associated with the banks account for 77% of the assets of all mortgage loan companies.

Chartered Banks

There are 12 Canadian owned chartered banks, although 58 foreign owned banks also compete in the Canadian financial markets. The chartered banks are all joint stock companies. The five largest account for some 85% of business. Table 5.10 lists these banks.

Table 5.10 Largest Chartered Banks, October 1983

Bank	Group Assets $Cm	Mortgage Assets $Cm	Individuals' Canadian Deposits $Cm	Branches
Royal Bank of Canada	84,682	8,376	33,499	1,536
Canadian Imperial Bank of Commerce	68,112	8,056	25,209	1,640
Bank of Montreal	63,194	5,163	21,365	1,218
Bank of Nova Scotia	54,809	3,886	N/A	1,200
Toronto Dominion Bank	42,448	4,748	14,405	993

Source: Annual Reports.
Notes: 1. At end-October 1983 there were $C1.24 to the US dollar and $C1.85 to the pound.
2. Of the mortgage assets, well over half were accounted for by mortgage loan company subsidiaries.

The banks are all federally chartered and operte under the Bank Act, which is revised at approximately ten yearly intervals. Over the years the Bank Acts have allowed greater freedom for banks, and it has already been noted how they have been progressively freed from the restrictions that prevented them competing on equal terms in the mortgage market. The banks operate throughout the entire country, and compete extensively with each other. At the end of 1982, they had 7,378 branches, a very high concentration of branches per head of population. Their dominance of the financial markets is indicated by the fact that they have many more deposit accounts than the entire Canadian population.

The chartered banks offer a complete banking service to both corporations and individuals. Table 5.11 shows the combined assets and liabilities of the chartered banks at the end of 1983.

Table 5.11   Chartered Banks, Canadian Assets & Liabilities, End-1983

Liabilities	$Cm	%	Assets	$Cm	%
Personal savings deposits	101,486	49	Residential		
Demand deposits	19,538	9	mortgages	31,980	15
Non personal notice & term/	44,457	21	Other loans	119,602	56
deposits			Financial assets	40,206	19
Other liabilities	29,024	14	Other assets	19,976	9
Shareholders' equity	14,085	7			
Total	208,590	100	Total	211,764	100

Source: *Bank of Canada Review*, February 1984, Tables 7 & 8.
Notes: 1.   At end-1983 there were $C1.25 to the US dollar and $C1.79 to the pound.
2.   Assets and liabilities differ slightly from each other; the difference is made up in foreign currency liabilities and assets.

It will be seen that loans accounted for well over half of the assets of the banks, and residential mortgages for 15%, the figures here including those for the mortgage loan company subsidiaries.

To some extent the banks have used mortgage lending as a "loss leader" to help bring them in other business, and also to spread overheads more widely. They were particularly responsible for many of the innovations in the mortgage market, but they have tended to bring their terms and conditions more into line with those of the trust companies. They have sought to match assets and liabilities in a similar manner to the trust companies, and some have tried to hive off activity as far as possible to subsidiary mortgage loan companies. Indeed, increasingly, mortgage loan activity has been transferred to mortgage loan companies, some of which now account for over 90% of the respective bank group's mortgage lending.

Credit Unions

The point has already been made that credit unions have a greater role in Canada than in any other developed country, and over half the population belong to a credit union. As in other countries the unions can serve only their own members, and members must share a common bond, such as employer or geographical location. The biggest credit unions are based in British Columbia, where the chartered banks are correspondingly weaker. The Vancouver City Savings Credit Union is the largest credit union in the world, and had assets at the end of 1981 in excess of $1,000 million. Table 5.12 shows the aggregated balance sheet for credit unions at the end of June 1983.

It will be seen that the credit unions raise most of their funds through demand and term deposits and are similar in this respect to the other financial institutions. Over a third of their loans are in the form of conventional residential mortgages, and, as is to be expected, a fairly high proportion of their assets are personal loans. A significant feature of the balance sheet of

Table 5.12 Local Credit Unions, Assets & Liabilities, June 1983

Liabilities	$Cm	%	Assets	$Cm	%
Demand deposits	16,576	46	Cash and demand deposits	4,307	12
Term deposits	14,588	40	Investments	4,938	14
Loans	852	2	Personal loans	6,052	17
Accounts payable	1,005	3	Other non-mortgage loans	2,958	7
Other liabilities	223	1	NHA mortgages	250	-
Members' equity	2,836	8	Conventional residential		
			mortgages	13,279	37
			Non-residential mortgages	3,135	9
			Other assets	939	3
Total	35,858	100	Total	35,858	100

Source: Statistics Canada, *Financial Institutions*, 3rd Quarter 1983, Table 23.
Note: At end-June 1983 there were $C1.23 to the US dollar and $C1.91 to the pound.

the credit unions is their relatively large allowance for bad debts on residential mortgage loans.

The Canada Mortgage and Housing Corporation and Government Policy

CMHC merits particular attention because it has no direct counterpart in the other English speaking countries. The Corporation was created as the Central Mortgage and Housing Corporation in 1946, and it changed its name to its present title in June 1979. It is a crown corporation with its head office in Ottawa, and with five regional and seven provincial offices. Its executives are appointed by the government. Its function is to implement specific economic and social housing objectives of the government. Some of its roles have been carried out over a number of years unaffected by policy changes, while others have had to adapt to changing circumstances. One of the long term functions of the Corporation is to carry out research and statistical work relating to the housing market. It publishes *Canadian Housing Statistics* annually, an excellent publication which brings together both financial and housing data.

Under the National Housing Act 1954 CMHC is able to insure mortgage loans, and the point has already been made that it is the principal mortgage insurer.

The government has experimented with various housing initiatives, including an assisted home-ownership programme and an assisted rental programme, neither of which were deemed to be successful. A graduated repayment mortgage, introduced in 1978, did prove to be more successful.

CMHC is a direct lender on a last resort basis. The section on the secondary mortgage market noted that CMHC has been divesting itself of its mortgage portfolio. This is part of a longer term programme to introduce more private sector capital into what were previously public sector activities.

One general form of assistance which is available to all home-owners are the Registered Home-Ownership Savings Plans. These provide taxpayers with a convenient method of tax free savings to purchase an owner-occupied home. Any approved institution can offer this scheme, but the funds have to be held in trust companies. Any Canadian resident taxpayer can contribute a maximum of $C1,000 a year, and can put into the scheme up to a lifetime maximum of $C10,000. The yearly contributions are tax deductible, and income on the investment is not taxed while it is retained in the plan. Both income and capital are not taxed if the capital is used for the purchase of an owner-occupied home. Table 5.13 shows figures for registered home-ownership savings plans from their inception at the beginning of 1975 until the end of 1982.

Table 5.13 Registered Home-Ownership Savings Plans: 1 January 1975 to 31 December 1982

Plans issued by:	
Trust companies	599,171
Credit unions authorized to act as trustees	50,974
Plans of corporations acting through trust companies:	
Chartered banks	871,834
Credit unions	251,634
Mutual funds	11,380
Under deposit plans with banks	235,023
Total	1,980,025

Source: *General Information Bulletin*, August 1983, Trust Companies Association of Canada.

Assessment

The Canadian financial system has been less compartmentalised than the systems in other English speaking countries, and the problems that those countries are now experiencing do not therefore exist in Canada. The housing finance market is closely integrated into the financial markets generally, and housing does not receive the preferential tax treatment that is common in other countries.

The mortgage rollover was a very successful practice while interest rates were relatively stable or drifted upwards. However, the system could not cope with violent fluctuations in interest rates, such as those that were experienced in the 1980s. The system adapted well to the new circumstances through a shortening of mortgage terms in the short term. Borrowers could not cope with huge increases in repayments which the system sometimes threw up, and short term government subvention has been necessary. The institutions themselves have been able to ride the problems caused by fluctuating interest rates without severe strain because they have matched assets and liabilities.

Bibliography

Boleat, M J, *The Canadian Housing Finance System*, 2nd Edition, The Building Societies Association, 1980.
Canadian Housing Statistics 1983, Canada Mortgage and Housing Corporation, 1984.
Canada Mortgage and Housing Corporation Annual Report, 1982, Canada Mortgage and Housing Corporation, 1983.
Bank Facts 1982, The Canadian Bankers Association, 1982.
General Information Bulletin, August 1983, Trust Companies Association of Canada.
Melton, C R, *The Canadian Mortgage Market*, International Research Paper No 2, International Union of Building Societies and Savings Associations, July 1979.
NHA Insured Mortgages as an Investment, Canada Mortgage and Housing Corporation, 1978.
The Chartered Banks of Canada, The Canadian Bankers Association, 1982.

Acknowledgements

The following institutions provided information which has been used in this chapter -
Canada Mortgage and Housing Corporation
Trust Companies Association of Canada
The Canadian Bankers' Association
The assistance of the following in commenting on an earlier draft of this chapter is gratefully acknowledged -
Canada Housing and Mortgage Corporation
A R Cooper, Director, Financial Affairs, The Canadian Bankers' Association

CHAPTER 6

AUSTRALIA

Australia is very similar to the United States and the United Kingdom in respect of housing, housing finance and trends in the financial system. The country has experienced a high level of owner-occupation for many years, and government intervention in the housing market is less than in almost any other industrialized country.

Housing finance is provided through the deposit taking system, largely by savings banks and building societies. As in the United States, there have been controls on interest rates, and some savings banks and all building societies have been able to operate only in their state of origin. Following a detailed enquiry into the Australian financial system the various controls are being dismantled, and housing finance is becoming more closely integrated into the financial system generally.

Introduction

Australia is a huge island continent occupying an area of 7,682,000 sq kilometres, some thirty times the size of the United Kingdom. However, most of the country is uninhabitable, and the population is heavily concentrated on the south and east coasts, and, to a lesser extent, the south west coast.

The population in mid-1982 was 15,200,000. A high proportion of the population is concentrated around the two major cities of Melbourne and Sydney. The other major centres of population are Brisbane, Adelaide and Perth. The capital, Canberra, is mid way between Sydney and Melbourne. The population has been growing rapidly by international standards, partly because of immigration. The annual rate of growth in the 1970s was 1.4%.

Australia recognises the British monarch as Head of State, and the central government is generally referred to as the Commonwealth. The individual states have considerable autonomy, including in respect of housing and financial institutions. Australia is similar to the United States but different from Britain in this respect.

Political power in Australia has alternated between the Liberal Party (Conservatives) and the Labour Party. A Labour government was elected to power in 1983. The attitude of the new Labour government to reforms in the financial system seems likely to be different from that of its Liberal predecessor, which had prompted a major inquiry into the financial system.

Australia is one of the most prosperous countries in the world and in addition to a high material standard of living, the very low density of population, even allowing for the uninhabited parts of the country, makes for a pleasant living and working environment. GNP per capita in 1981 was US$11,080, similar to that in many of the West European countries.

Housing

Compared with other industrialized countries the Australian government has played only a minor role in the provision of housing. Perhaps this partly reflects the high standard of living generally, and adequate space, which means that less government intervention is necessary in order to house the poorer sections of the community. Australia has had a very strong tradition of home-ownership, and those people who do not live in owner-occupied accommodation generally rent privately although some accommodation is available from state government agencies. Table 6.1 shows trends in housing tenure from 1947 to 1981.

Table 6.1 Trends in Housing Tenure, Australia, 1947-81

| 30th June Year | Number of Dwellings | Proportion of Occupied Private Dwellings | | |
		Owner-Occupied %	Rented %	Other %
1947		53.2	43.9	2.9
1961	2,602,000	72.7	25.2	2.1
1966	3,010,000	73.0	25.2	1.8
1971	3,464,000	70.0	26.9	3.1
1976	4,039,000	68.4	25.9	5.7
1981	4,534,000	70.1	25.7	4.2

Source: Australian Bureau of Statistics.

It will be noted that owner-occupation has declined modestly since 1966, although there has been a recovery since 1976. Two main reasons have been put forward to explain the decline until the mid-1970s -

(a) The population has become more mobile, and there has been a particularly strong shift of population to new mining towns where dwellings have been provided rent free or at a modest rent.

(b) There has been a growing tendency for young people to leave home earlier, and to set up households with others in rented accommodation until such time as they wish to settle down and purchase a home.

Housebuilding in Australia has not shown the same strength of cyclical fluctuation as has been the case in most other countries. The level of construction has been very high compared with, for example, Britain, this partly reflecting the continued rapid rate of population growth, in particular, the immigration of established households.

Table 6.2 shows trends in dwelling completions for the period 1978-83.

Table 6.2 Dwelling Completions, Australia, 1978-83

Year	Private Sector	Government	Total
1978	114,300	14,600	129,900
1979	105,600	11,500	117,100
1980	119,100	10,200	129,300
1981	125,500	10,400	135,900
1982	129,000	9,300	138,300
1983	104,400	10,900	115,300

Source: Australian Bureau of Statistics.

The contribution of the government can be seen to be extremely small, and declining in recent years.

Housing Finance

Policy Towards Housing Finance

Australian governments have traditionally encouraged owner-occupation, although the financial incentives evident in other countries have not been so forthcoming. In the recent past, the debate has become politicized to some extent, reflecting the position in the United Kingdom. Tax relief on mortgage interest has not been generally available, although for much of the 1970s some tax deductability was available depending on income. A general tax deductability scheme was introduced in July 1982. Relief was limited to the standard rate of 30%, with an upper limit of $A500 in the first year, falling by $A100 steps to nothing after five years. For taxpayers with dependent children the limit began at $A800. The scheme no longer applies to new borrowers.

Assistance has been provided by helping people save the deposit for their first home. Until March 1982 the Home Savings Grant existed, by which the government made a contribution to first-time buyers according to the amount they had saved. The grant was available regardless of income. In March 1982 this scheme was replaced by the Home Deposit Assistance Scheme, which provided a maximum grant of $A2,500 (up to $A1,000 more for families with dependent children) to those who had saved at least $A2,500 over two years. The main difference from the previous scheme was that there was a means test.

The new Labour government introduced the First Home Owners Scheme (FHOS) with effect from 1 October 1983. This replaced the Home Deposit Assistance Scheme, and, also, the modest housing interest income tax rebate scheme. To qualify, applicants must not have owned a home previously, and their income must be less than 155% of the national average. People can opt either for a lump sum or an on-going subsidy for five years or a combination of the two. The total benefit also depends on the number of children, and can vary from approximately $A5,000 for a family with no children to $A7,000 for a family with two or more children. These figures compare with an average loan size of about $A38,000.

At this stage one other form of assistance to owner-occupiers should be noted. For some years, the Commonwealth government has made low interest loans to the state governments to on-lend to low income home-buyers. This is achieved largely through terminating building societies, organisations which, despite their name, have virtually nothing to do with old style terminating building societies or modern permanent societies. These organisations borrow funds from other intermediaries against a state guarantee, and on-lend these funds on preferential terms to low income eligible borrowers. There are many thousand such organisations, most of which are very small. They have been of declining importance in recent years, and their total assets are small in relation to those of the permanent building societies.

The Housing Finance Market

The housing finance market in Australia is dominated by savings banks, which are very similar to savings banks in other countries, and permanent building societies which are like their counterparts in Britain and South Africa, and similar to savings and loan associations in the USA. Table 6.3 shows trends in households' housing debt for the period 1960-83.

Table 6.3 Householders' Housing Debt, Australia, 1960-83

Institution	1960 $Am	%	1970 $Am	%	1983 $Am	%
Trading banks	196	15	297	7	899	3
Savings banks	404	30	1,898	45	14,518	51
Life offices	267	20	422	10	554	2
Permanent building societies	119	9	929	22	10,638	38
Terminating building societies	347	26	682	16	1,591	6
Total	1,333	100	4,228	100	28,200	100

Source: *Australian Financial System*, Table 2.2, Australian Government Publishing Service, 1980; Reserve Bank of Australia, *Bulletin*.
Note: At end-1983 there were $A1.12 to the US dollar and $A1.61 to the pound.

The table shows a spectacular decline in the market share of the life offices, again, very much reflecting what has happened in other countries, and the rising market share of the permanent building societies and savings banks. The growth in the market share of building societies has been particularly marked—from a mere 9% of the market in 1960 to well over one-third by 1983.

The growth of the finance market in general, and of the building societies in particular, since the early 1970s is partly attributed to the existence of mortgage insurance. Mortgage insurance dates from 1965 when the government formed the Housing Loans Insurance Corporation (HLIC). A private enterprise corporation was established at the same time, and, subsequently, two other private enterprise organisations entered the market. Mortgage insurance operates through a once only premium related to the percentage of the loan/valuation ratio. Insurance is generally required if the loan is for more than 75% of valuation, and loans of up to 90% can be insured. Notwithstanding the growth of private mortgage insurers HLIC still has over 50% of the market. In 1979, as part of a package of cut-backs, the government announced that it could see no good reason why mortgage insurance could not be provided wholly by private insurers, and that it intended to sell the HLIC to the private sector. This has been opposed by the housing finance institutions and the new Labour government has announced that it does not intend to go ahead with the sale. Instead, it has called for submissions on ways in which the HLIC's powers might be widened.

Mortgage loans in Australia are made at variable rates of interest and are repaid by the annuity system over 20 or 25 years, or, exceptionally, 30 years. However, the lending institutions have not been completely free to set their rates. The savings banks in particular have been subject to controls as have the building societies. There are, from time to time, significant differences between the states in respect of building society mortgage rates, and, indeed, interest rates generally, signifying the lack of a fully developed, regionally integrated, capital market. For example, in 1982, the predominant building society mortgage rate charged in Victoria was 15.65%, whereas in South Australia and Tasmania it was 14.25%. Spreads of up to two percentage points have existed in some years. The artificial controls, formal and informal, have meant that there has frequently been a shortage of mortgage funds, both nationally and at a state level.

The housing finance market is undergoing a major change because of the changing role in the financial institutions, which will be explained more fully subsequently. However, it is helpful at this stage to set out how the market shares of the various institutions are changing. Table 6.4 shows loan approvals to individuals for owner-occupation for financial years from 1980/81 to 1982/83. (The financial year in Australia runs from July to June.)

The table shows that the savings banks have been successful in increasing their market share quite substantially at the expense of the building societies. A principal reason for this is that some of the deposit taking and asset portfolio controls on the savings banks have been eased.

The following features applied to the pattern of lending in 1982/83 -

(a) 90% of lending was for houses rather than other dwellings.
(b) 75% of lending was for the purchase of existing dwellings, 16% for the construction of new dwellings and 9% for the purchase of new dwellings.

Table 6.4 Loan Approvals to Individuals for Construction or Purchase of Dwellings, Australia, 1980/81-1982/83

Year	Savings Banks		Permanent Building Societies		Trading Banks		Finance Companies		Total
	$Am	%	$Am	%	$Am	%	$Am	%	$Am
1980/81	2,721	36	2,415	32	953	13	593	8	7,470
1981/82	2,649	41	1,809	28	884	14	392	6	6,506
1982/83	3,512	46	1,788	23	792	10	255	3	7,681

Source: *Housing Finance for Owner-Occupation, Australia, June 1983*, Australian Bureau of Statistics, August 1983.
Notes: 1. Total figures include lending by other institutions.
2. At end-June 1983 there were $A1.14 to the US dollar and $A1.77 to the pound.

(c) There were no significant differences between the institutions in respect of the division of their lending between new construction, the purchase of new dwellings and the purchase of existing dwellings.

The Savings Market

The personal savings market in Australia is shared between the trading banks, the savings banks, finance companies and permanent building societies. The role of all of these institutions, with the exception of finance companies, will be explained in more detail subsequently. Finance companies basically provide consumer credit, housing and other loans to individuals, and are involved in leasing, factoring and similar services for business customers. Some of the larger companies are subsidiaries of or are associated with trading banks.

A recent development in Australia has been the growth of cash management trusts, similar to money market mutual funds in the United States. These began to develop in 1981, and grew during the year from nothing to $A600 million. They increased further to $A2,200 million by the end of 1982. The cash management trusts were able to grow for the same reason as the money market mutual funds in the United States, that is, market rates were above the rates which savings institutions were permitted to pay to their depositors. The growth of cash management trusts has contributed to the freeing of the financial system, and the assets of these organisations have begun to decline in the recent past.

Table 6.5 shows personal sector deposits held with the major deposit taking institutions.

The Trading and Savings Banks

Although the trading banks have a comparatively small share of the housing finance and savings markets they merit attention because they control some

Table 6.5 Estimated Personal Deposits of the Private Sector, Australia, End-1982

Institution	$Abn	Percentage of Total
Trading banks	17.8	22.3
Savings banks	27.1	34.0
Finance companies	17.4	21.8
Permanent building societies	13.7	17.2
Australian savings bonds	3.7	4.6
Total	79.7	100.0

Source: Derived from Reserve Bank of Australia, *Bulletin*, March 1983.
Note: At end-1982 there were $A1.02 to the US dollar and $A1.65 to the pound.

of the savings banks. The banking industry has been undergoing fundamental structural change, partly because of the threat of foreign bank competition, and there have been a number of significant mergers. The four largest banks are -

1. *Westpac*, formed by a merger of the Bank of New South Wales and the Commercial Bank of Australia. The Westpac Group had assets at 30 September 1983 of $A34,526 million. Westpac wholly owns the Westpac Savings Bank, formerly the Bank of New South Wales Savings Bank. This incorporates the former Commercial Savings Bank of Australia and also the New Zealand subsidiaries of the group. It had total assets of $A6,305 million at 30 September 1983, making it the largest privately owned savings bank. The Savings Bank (including its New Zealand subsidiary) had housing loans outstanding of $A2.7 billion at 30 September 1983, making it the second largest housing lender in Australia.

2. *Commonwealth*, which is owned by the Commonwealth Government. The combined assets of the Commonwealth Banking Corporation Group at end-June 1983 were $A26,201 million, of which the Commonwealth Trading Bank accounted for $A13,527 million. As at 30 June 1983 the Trading Bank had deposits of $A7,117 million and it operated through 1,315 branches and agencies. The holding company owns the Commonwealth Savings Bank, the largest single mortgage lender.

3. *Australia and New Zealand Banking Group* had assets at 30 September 1983 of $A22,726 million. It has 969 branches in Australia. It wholly owns the Australia and New Zeland Savings Bank which, at September 1983, had assets of $A3,572 million

4. *National Commercial* (also known as National Australia) has recently been formed by a merger of the Commercial Banking Company of Sydney with the National Commercial Banking Corporation. The

Group had assets of $A23,283 million at end-September 1983. It has 1,318 branches. It wholly owns the National Australia Savings Bank (assets of $A4,025 million at 30 September 1983). The Savings Bank incorporates the activities of the CBC Savings Bank which was the savings bank subsidiary of the CBC Banking Corporation.

The three banks other than the Commonwealth are joint stock companies. Their importance in the housing finance market stems partly from their direct activities and partly through their ownership of savings banks. They lend directly for relatively short terms and some of their finance supplements savings bank loans.

There are 13 savings banks in total. There are three very small banks, one operated by a New Zealand bank, and the other two operate only in Tasmania. The Commonwealth Savings Bank is owned by the Federal Government and operates throughout the country, and in three of the states there are state run savings banks. The remaining savings banks are wholly owned subsidiaries of the commercial banks; it has already been noted that two of the banks own two savings banks each. It is therefore apparent that the nature of the savings banks industry is very different from that in other countries where all banks have similar constitutions; either all are mutual or all are state owned. Also, in terms of competition the savings banks and trading banks are under the same umbrella unlike the building societies.

There have been significant changes in the structure of the savings bank industry. The savings bank subsidiaries of the trading banks were established in the late 1950s and early 1960s and now have some 40% of the market. This has been at the expense of the Commonwealth Savings Banks and the State banks. Table 6.6 lists the largest savings banks, which are also the largest house-purchase lenders.

Table 6.6 Largest Savings Banks, September 1983

Bank	Assets $Am	Branches
Commonwealth Savings Bank*	10,925	1,274
State Bank of Victoria*	7,094	531
Westpac Savings Bank	6,302	1,139
National Australia Savings Bank	4,025	
Australia and New Zealand Savings Bank	3,572	1,160

Source: Annual reports.
    *June figures.
Note: At end-September 1983 there were $A1.05 to the US dollar and $A1.79 to the pound.

The Commonwealth Savings Bank, still by far the largest savings bank in Australia, merits particular attention as the largest mortgage lender. It had housing loans outstanding of $A5,050 million at end-June 1983. During 1982/83 it accounted for 37% of all savings bank and 18% of all lending for house-purchase. It was founded in 1912, and over a period of years was amalgamated with four state savings banks. It was given its present status, as a member bank of the Commonwealth Banking Corporation, in 1939. In addition to operating through 1,274 branches and sub-branches it also has 5,500 agents. Every post office is an agent for the bank.

The State Bank of Victoria (assets of $A7,094 million at 30 September 1983) is the largest deposit taking institution and mortgage lender in Victoria. It has over 500 branches and a similar number of agencies. The other state savings banks are in South Australia and New South Wales.

Table 6.7 shows the aggregate balance sheet for savings banks at the end of June 1983. The liabilities side of the balance sheet is typical of that for any savings bank or indeed building society. Deposits of various forms accounted for some 95% of liabilities. Reserves were low, under 2% of liabilities.

Table 6.7 Savings Banks, Assets and Liabilities, Australia, June 1983

Liabilities	$Am	%	Assets	$m	%
Depositors' balances	30,018	95	Housing loans	14,518	46
All other liabilities	1,495	5	Loans to building societies	248	1
			Other loans, advances and bills discounted	2,994	10
			Commonwealth government securities	4,587	15
			Local and semi-government securities	7,008	22
			Other	1,662	5
Total	31,513	100	Total	31,513	100

Source: Reserve Bank of Australia, *Bulletin*, January 1984, Tables 10 & E3.
Note: At end-June 1983 there were $A1.14 to the US dollar and $A1.77 to the pound.

The savings banks offer passbook accounts and higher rated accounts, most of which require a period of notice before a withdrawal can be made. In June 1983 31% of deposits were in passbook accounts and 52% were in investment accounts; in June 1980 the respective proportions had been 54% and 38%.

Savings banks largely deal with the personal sector, although they do borrow from some non-profit organisations. They can provide an interest bearing cheque account to non-profit societies, and in some states they are also able to offer personal cheque facilities, but as yet this service is comparatively small.

The assets side of the balance sheet is typical of a savings bank. Approximately half of all assets are in the form of housing loans, and most of the remainder are loans to government and semi-government organisations. There have been controls over the disposition of assets, and the types of savings accounts that could be offered, but these have recently been eased.

In March 1983 the savings banks were paying from 3.75% to 5% on small passbook accounts (under $A4,000), from 5% to 6.25% on larger passbook accounts (over $A4,000), and up to 13% on longer term deposits. The maximum mortgage rate that could be charged to new home-buyers at the end of 1983 was 13.5%; this is controlled by government regulation. In fact, at that time, market interest rates were some two percentage points lower. Loans are normally for not more than 75% of valuation and the maximum term is 25 years.

Permanent Building Societies

Although the permanent building society industry has its origin in the 1850s, until the mid-1960s the industry played only a small part in house-purchase finance. The first society in Australia was established around 1850, and the oldest permanent building society still in existence was founded in Tasmania in 1858. The original societies were similar to their British counterparts and they developed in the same sort of way, growing from small organisations serving a local community to larger organisations, although because of state laws they have confined their operations to individual states.

The Structure of the Industry

In March 1984 there were 75 building societies in Australia. The number has declined fairly sharply in recent years from 190 in 1974 and 88 in June 1983.

Table 6.8 shows the concentration of the building society industry as at 30 June 1983.

Table 6.8 Structure of the Building Society Industry, Australia, 30 June 1983

Size of Society	Total Assets $Am	Share of Total Assets %
Largest four	5,600	36
Numbers 5-8	2,866	19
Numbers 9-12	1,847	12
All 88	15,387	100

Source: Australian Bureau of Statistics, *Permanent Building Societies Assets, Liabilities, Income and Expenditure, Australia 1982-83*, June 1984.
Notes: 1.   At end-June 1983 there were $A1.14 to the US dollar and $A1.77 to the pound.
2.   The figures are the aggregation of balance sheets, not all of which are for 30 June; societies with assets accounting for 89% of the total do have a 30 June year-end.

Although the four largest societies accounted for 36% of the total assets of the industry this represents a much greater degree of concentration when it is realised that societies can operate only within their state of origin. In fact, in each of the states the largest four societies account for over half the total assets of the industry; in New South Wales the proportion was 82%, in South Australia, 98% Western Australia, 94% in Queensland, 78% and in Victoria, 68%.

Table 6.9 lists the largest eight building societies as at mid-1983.

Table 6.9 Largest Eight Building Societies, Australia, End-June 1983

Building Society	State	Assets $Am
St George	New South Wales	1,884
NSW	New South Wales	1,627
United Permanent	New South Wales	1,070
Statewide	Victoria	1,011
Perth	Western Australia	968
Town & Country	Western Australia	851
Metropolitan	Queensland	606
State	New South Wales	594

Source: Australian Association of Permanent Building Societies.
Note: At end-June 1983 there were $A1.14 to the US dollar and $A1.77 to the pound.

It should be noted at this stage that there has recently been the development of co-operative links, and, in some cases, mergers between building societies in the different states. In particular, the Perth Building Society, based in Western Australia, has effectively acquired control of the Hotham Building Society in Victoria. Other links are being developed, but as yet there is some uncertainty as to how far this process can go until current proposals for legislative reform which incorporate provisions for inter-state operations receive the necessary state government acceptance.

The Regulation of Building Societies

Building societies are controlled by state law and each of the states has its own Act. In some cases, the Acts go back a long way. For example, in Tasmania there has been no legislation since 1955. The main prudential controls are as follows -

(a) Building societies can lend only on a secured basis.
(b) Effectively, 90% of a society's lending in any one year must be in the form of advances to members for housing for owner-occupation.
(c) Loans which exceed 75% of valuation must be insured.
(d) Some states have legislation similar to the special advance provisions in Britain, whereby only a small proportion of loans can be above a certain size.
(e) Minimum liquidity ratios are specified. These differ slightly from state to state but, broadly speaking, are about 10% of shares and deposits.
(f) Reserves are required either equal to a fixed proportion of the surplus arising each year or of the aggregate liabilities.

A particularly important form of regulation has been on interest rates, and there are substantial differences between the states. In New South Wales, the government fixes the maximum rate which can be paid on shares, and there is also power to fix the mortgage rate, although this has not been used. In Victoria, the government has power to fix the maximum rate of interest for advances. In Queensland, the state government prescribes the maximum rate that may be paid by a society, and there is power to prescribe the maximum rate charged on loans, although this has not been used since 1977. In South Australia, there is power to fix a maximum rate on loans, although, again, this has not been used. More generally, the Financial Corporations Act 1974 enables the federal government to determine by regulation the rates of interest which building societies, and other non-bank financial intermediaries, can pay and charge. This power has not been used, but the federal government has, in the past, not hesitated to make its views known on interest rates, and the building societies have been aware of the back-up legislative power.

Financial Operation

The permanent building societies operate in a very similar way to building societies in Britain and savings and loan associations in the United States, and, consequently, their balance sheet and income and expenditure account are very similar. Table 6.10 shows the aggregate balance sheet for Australian building societies as at the middle of 1983.

Table 6.10 Assets and Liabilities of Permanent Building Societies at 30 June 1983

Liabilities	$Am	%	Assets	$Am	%
Withdrawable shares			Owing on loans	10,697	70
at call	6,827	44	Financial assets	4,203	27
Withdrawable fixed term			Land and buildings	360	2
shares	3,252	21	Other physical assets	128	1
Deposits at call	1,524	10			
Fixed term deposits	2,916	19			
Loans	278	2			
Provision for income					
tax	52	-			
Other liabilities	13	-			
Nonwithdrawable shares	36	-			
Statutory reserves	165	1			
General reserves	271	2			
Total	15,387	100	Total	15,387	100

Source: Australian Bureau of Statistics, *Permanent Building Societies Assets, Liabilities, Income and Expenditure, Australia 1982-83*, June 1984.
Notes: 1. At end-June 1983 there were $A1.14 to the dollar and $A1.77 to the pound.
2. The figures are the aggregation of balance sheets, not all of which are for 30 June; societies with assets accounting for 89% of the total do have a 30 June year-end.

On the liabilities side of the balance sheet it will be seen that funds are raised through both shares and deposits. State laws determine the relationship between the two, but as far as the individual is concerned there is practically no difference. In recent years there has been a sharp increase in the proportion of shares and deposits raised at fixed term rather than on call. Thus, in 1977, 92% of shares and deposits were withdrawable at call. By 1981, the proportion had fallen to 67%, and by June 1983 it had fallen further to 54%. It will be seen that, in general, the building societies raise an insignificant proportion of their funds from money markets or from institutional sources, although in Western Australia the exposure to such markets and sources is much higher.

On the assets side of the balance sheet, the permanent building societies are like most other specialist housing finance institutions with 70% of their assets in the form of mortgage loans. Most other assets are short term financial securities of one form or another.

The income and expenditure of the building societies very much reflects their assets and liabilities. This is illustrated in Table 6.11.

Table 6.11 Permanent Building Society Income and Expenditure, 1982/83

	$Am	$A per $A100 Mean Assets
Income	1,579	10.87
Mortgage interest	523	3.60
Investment interest	50	0.34
Other income	2,152	14.82
Total		
Expenditure		
Share, deposit and loan interest	1,637	11.27
Management expenses	331	2.28
Other expenditure	77	0.53
Total	2,045	14.08
Surplus	108	0.74
Tax	41	0.28
Net surplus	67	0.46

Source: Australian Bureau of Statistics, *Permanent Building Societies Assets, Liabilities, Income and Expenditure, Australia 1982-83*, March 1983.

Notes: 1. At end-June 1983 there were $A1.14 to the US dollar and $A1.77 to the pound.
2. The figures are the aggregation of balance sheets, not all of which are for 30 June; societies with assets accounting for 89% of the total do have a 30 June year-end.
3. Management expenses include depreciation ($A26m), losses on sale of assets ($A3m) and bad debts ($A0.2m).

The Australian Association of Permanent Building Societies (AAPBS)

The AAPBS was founded at the national level in 1964 to facilitate the nationwide development of permanent building societies. Its members comprise state associations and individual societies. Societies accounting for over 99% of building society business are members of the Association.

The AAPBS is based in Canberra and has the usual trade association functions, including representing societies to the Commonwealth government.

Because of the importance of the states there are also state associations which liaise with the respective regulatory authorities. The 28 person council of the AAPBS comprises 15 representatives of the state association and 13 representatives of individual societies.

The Association is currently heavily involved in the reform of the financial system (discussed later in this chapter), and is trying to ensure that deregulation of building societies at state level does not lag behind deregulation of the savings banks and trading banks, some of which is at national level.

The Association has also recently been involved in the planning and development of a shared ATM network for building societies and is involved in other electronic funds transfer developments.

There are also associations of building societies in each state, reflecting the fact that the prudential control of societies is still at the state level.

The Campbell Inquiry and Financial Reform

The Establishment of the Inquiry

A significant feature of the financial systems in English speaking countries in recent years has been the establishment of committees of inquiry. In 1970, the Hunt Commission reported in the United States and precipitated a decade of debate before there was significant financial reform in 1980. In Britain, the Wilson Report was published in 1979, and although it was not acted upon, it has contributed significantly to the sum of knowledge and has added to the academic debate. In South Africa the De Kock and Du Plessis Commissions both reported during the course of 1982, and in Canada there has been the usual ten yearly discussions on the revision of the Bank Acts. In Australia a committee of inquiry into the financial system was established in January 1979 under the chairmanship of Mr J K Campbell. The terms of reference were to inquire into and to report on the structure and methods of operation of the Australian financial system, to inquire into and report on the regulation and control of the system, and to make recommendations.

The Interim Report

The Campbell Committee published an interim report in May 1980 (*Australian Financial System*, Interim Report of the Committee of Inquiry, Australian Government Publishing Service, May 1980). This report set out admirably the structure of the financial system, its methods of operation and the regulation and control of the system. The interim report also aimed to identify issues emerging from the submissions and its deliberations, but it did not make any recommendations.

The principal points noted in this report were -

(a) There has been a growing tendency for personal savings to be channelled through short term deposit taking institutions, in preference to direct holdings of company securities and other long term instruments.

(b) The banks have been losing ground to non-bank intermediaries, in particular, the building societies, and, as in other countries, the various types of financial institution have increasingly encroached on each other's markets.

(c) Concern was being expressed at the impact of interest rate controls, particularly on the housing finance market.

(d) An important question was the future role of housing finance specialists and possible diversification of their assets and services.

(e) Savings banks have been growing rapidly, and an increasing proportion of their assets have been mortgages rather than government securities.

(f) Building societies have grown rapidly since the mid-1960s because of the existence of a considerable unsatisfied demand for mortgage finance, and, also, the spread of mortgage insurance.

(g) The various groups of deposit taking institutions have argued for the removal of regulatory constraints, and have sought preservation of established special links with the authorities.

The Final Report

The Campbell Committee published its final report at the end of 1981 (*Australian Financial System*, Final Report of the Committee of Inquiry, Australian Government Publishing Service, September 1981). The report, like the Interim Report, is well written and easy to follow. One might argue that it is a model of how such official reports should be presented.

The report gave considerable attention to the question of the regulation of interest rates, and instinctively favoured deregulation -

'Investors can be expected generally to be sensitive to differentials between interest rates offered by competing intermediaries, so that failure of housing finance intermediaries to lift their rates at a time of generally rising interest rates will, other things being equal, lead to a loss of deposits to competing intermediaries. It follows that rates should be allowed to move freely according to market forces if disruption to funds flows is to be avoided.'

The report pointed out that although savings banks and building societies worked in a controlled market other institutions were prepared to lend at much higher rates, and it was marginal borrowers who tended to be squeezed out of the controlled system.

The report considered the distributional effects of interest rate controls, and observed that the flow of funds from housing finance institutions was skewed against lower income earners. Conversely, the lower income groups had a considerably greater proportion of their wealth in savings bank passbook accounts than higher income earners. Overall, the Committee concluded that interest rate controls were an inefficient and ineffective means of assisting low income potential home-buyers, with regressive distributional consequences.

The Committee favoured giving building societies, and, also, savings banks greater freedom to broaden their source of funds, including access to the wholesale markets. More generally, the Committee was against the segmentation of financial markets, and it recommended considerable liberalisation in this respect.

The report had a very free market philosophy, which was reflected in its conclusion that as an important market discipline individual institutions should be allowed to fail and should not be rescued by the government. Perhaps not surprisingly, the report also favoured the proposed sale of the Housing Loans Insurance Corporation to the private sector.

The Committee considered whether a secondary mortgage market might be beneficial to the housing finance market. It was believed that this would improve the efficiency with which funds were allocated, but it noted that there were many impediments to the development of such a market, including the availability of mortgage loans and the nature of the mortgage instrument with a variable rate and early redemption being permitted. The Committee did not believe that there was a significant role for the government in helping to expand the secondary market.

Post-Campbell Developments and the Martin Report

The Campbell Report was published at a time when the financial system was undergoing stress because of money market developments, in particular, the growth of cash management trusts. Partly in response to this, in December 1980, the government abolished deposit rate controls on the trading and savings banks. However, there remained a minimum term for which savings banks and trading banks could accept deposits on which interest was to be paid.

In March 1982, the maximum rate at which savings banks could make loans was lifted and the savings banks agreed to increase the availability of housing finance loans. In July 1982 direct controls on the banking system were removed and liquidity and investment controls on savings banks were eased in August 1982. The new Labour government, elected in March 1983, announced that it had commissioned a study of the financial system, which would take account not only of the Campbell proposals but also the government's own social and economic objectives. One of the concerns of the government was the effect that deregulation might have on housing finance and on the politically sensitive mortgage rate. On the other hand, the government was thought to wish to see greater competition in the banking industry, and one means of achieving this might be to permit building societies to have wider powers, and therefore to compete more fully with the banks.

The review group was chaired by Vic Martin, former chief executive of the Commercial Banking Corporation. Its report was published in December 1983. Broadly speaking, it endorsed the free market philosophy of the Campbell Report.

On interest rate controls, the report concluded: 'The Group regards interest rate control as an ineffective instrument for the achievement of the Commonwealth's economic and social objectives in the housing area. By impairing the availability and stability of the supply of housing finance, such controls run counter to the objective of securing an adequate supply of housing finance at reasonable rates. They are also inimical to the maintenance of a steady level of activity in the housing construction industry? The report agreed with the Campbell conclusion that rationing devices associated with interest rate controls tended to favour higher income borrowers. It was noted that in 1983 mortgage interest rates fell to two percentage points below the maximum that the savings banks could charge, indicating that the institutions have to be able to adjust interest rates downwards if market conditions so require, and also that the removal of controls would not have an upward effect on rates.

On portfolio controls, the report argued that 'the government's priority for housing suggests that the provision of housing finance should remain a principal objective of permanent building societies', but it went on to say that it saw 'scope, in terms of providing services to customers and maintaining competitiveness, for some relaxation of existing restrictions on the disposition of societies' assets'. Specifically, it recommended that building societies should be allowed to offer consumer credit.

The report considered at length the implications of inflation for housing finance. It suggested that where inflation is running at a high level attention should be directed at encouraging the development and introduction of housing loan instruments more geared to inflationary conditions.

The Labour Party had favoured the establishment of a National Housing Fund, financed by the sale of bonds to non-bank financial institutions, the proceeds of which would be channelled to savings banks and building societies for onlending to house-buyers. The group did not favour the establishment of such a fund on a compulsory basis and commented that establishing a fund on a market basis offered no advantages compared with giving housing finance institutions greater freedom to compete for deposits in the market.

The group specifically considered the merits of the introduction of a secondary mortgage market. It believed that an active and broadly based secondary mortgage market would assist the government's objectives in the housing area: 'It could be particularly valuable in attracting funds for housing from non-traditional sources and is a method much preferred to the imposition of direct controls over non-bank financial institutions or the establishment of special funds'. It identified a number of impediments to the development of such a market, including interest rate controls, the diverse nature of mortgage instruments and the variability of interest rates. It was doubtful about the use of a Commonwealth agency to develop a secondary market, but said that if interest rate controls were removed it would support action by the Commonwealth, in conjunction with the states, to facilitate the development of an industry-based agency to promote the development of a secondary market.

The group recommended the easing of interest rate controls on savings banks and greater freedom for them to attract deposits and these proposals, together with those outlined above, would, it was argued, 'significantly add to the competitiveness of the major housing institutions as repositories for savings and assist the continuation of their dominant roles in the supply of housing finance'.

The report, generally, has been well received and the expectation is that the bulk of its recommendations will be implemented—indeed, some already have been. In April 1984, it was announced that all controls on deposit interest rates and maturities would be lifted from August.

Assessment

The financial markets in Australia do not appear to have reached the sophistication of those in other industrialized countries. This can be attributed to the powerful role which the states have, and also interest rate controls, which between them have served to prevent the establishment of a unified financial market.

Building societies, and savings banks to a lesser extent, have prospered-since the mid-1960s, partly because of constraints on other financial intermediaries, particularly the banks.

There are now strong pressures to remove the differences between the finanancial institutions, to deregulate interest rates and to reduce controls on assets and liabilities. This is likely to pose problems for the building societies in the same way as it has for the savings and loan associations in the United States. On the other hand, some of the more enterprising building societies can be expected to take advantage of any greater freedom which they are offered, although a larger capital base may be necessary before there is a significant broadening of powers.

Bibliography

Australian Association of Permanent Building Societies, *Annual Report 1984*, 1984.
Australian Financial System, Interim Report of the Committee of Inquiry (Campbell Report), Australian Government Publishing Service, May 1980.
Australian Financial System, Final Report of the Committee of Inquiry (Campbell Report), Australian Government Publishing Service, September 1981.
Australian Financial System, Report of the Review Group (Martin Report), Australian Government Publishing Service, 1984.

Building Society Fact Book, 2nd Edition, Australian Association of Permanent Building Societies, 1983.
Commonwealth Banking Corporation Annual Report 1983.
'Housing Finance and the Committee of Inquiry into the Australian Financial System', *Studies in Building Society Activity 1980-81*, The Building Societies Association, 1982.
'Housing Finance and the Final Report of the Committee of Inquiry into the Australian Finanical System', *Studies in Building Society Activity 1980-81*, The Building Societies Association, 1982.
Housing Finance for Owner-Occupation, Australia, June 1983, Australian Bureau of Statistics, August 1983.
National Newsletter, Australian Association of Permanent Building Societies, passim.
Quarterly Housing Survey, Commonwealth Savings Bank of Australia.

Acknowledgements

The co-operation of the Australian Association of Permanent Building Societies and the Commonwealth Savings Bank of Australia in providing material for this chapter is gratefully acknowledged. The AAPBS *Fact Book* has been drawn on extensively and is the single most useful source of information on housing finance in Australia.

The author would like to thank Bob Elstone, Assistant General Manager, Perth Building Society, for helpful comments on an earlier draft of this chapter and John Toms, Assistant Director—Planning of the AAPBS, for comments and for providing the most recent statistics.

CHAPTER 7

SOUTH AFRICA

Housing and housing finance in South Africa are influenced by that country's policies of separate development for the various races. Owner-occupation is at a very high level amongst white residents (well over 60%), but only in recent years have black Africans been permitted to purchase homes in the urban areas.

The mortgage market has been dominated by building societies, which operate in very much the same way as their counterparts in Australia and the United Kingdom. Societies have recently had to face greater competition in the savings market from the banks, and have also begun to compete more aggressively amongst themselves. South African societies have been subject to two major inquiries in recent years. The De Kock Commission examined the financial markets generally and published an interim report specifically on building societies, while the Du Plessis Commission dealt exclusively with societies. The De Kock philopsophy of a breaking down of barriers between the financial institutions is being adopted. Unlike in other English speaking countries, co-operative arrangements are being developed between banks and building societies rather than within the two industries.

Introduction

South Africa occupies an area of 1,123,000 sq kilometres. Its population in 1982 was 25,500,000. Of this total, 4,674,000 (18%) were white, 853,000 (3%) were Asian, 17,258,000 (68%) were black and 2,715,000 (11%) were coloured.

The principal cities are Johannesburg, Cape Town and Durban. The capital is Pretoria, which is quite close to Johannesburg, in the northern-most province of the country, Transvaal.

South Africa is a republic. The government and parliament are controlled by the white population. Only whites are able to have a seat in parliament, although constitutional proposals have recently been approved which will give Asians and coloureds parliamentary representation. The National Party has been in power continuously since 1948.

GNP per capita in 1981 was $2,770; only Libya and Gabon had higher figures in Africa. The rate of growth of real GNP per capita in the 1970s was 0.7% a year. In mid-1983 the rate of inflation was 12%.

Housing

Housing standards and housing tenure differ considerably between the races, as indeed does the availability of statistical information. Land is zoned for particular races, and until 1978 black Africans were not permitted to own property in urban areas. The white population enjoys a high standard of housing, and also a high level of owner-occupation. In 1970, 64% of whites in urban areas lived in owner-occupied homes. Over 40% of Asians were owner-occupiers, while for coloureds the figure was 33%. No accurate figures are available for the black African population. Table 7.1 shows some statistics for housing for 1970 and 1980.

Table 7.1 Dwellings, South Africa, 1970 and 1980

| | 1970 Urban Areas | | | | Flats | Other | Total | 1980 |
	Paid in Full	Partially Paid	Rented & Freely Occupied	Total Houses				Total
Whites								
No, 000s	122	289	231	642	200	161	1,003	1,344
%	19.0	45.0	36.0	100.0				
Coloured								
No, 000s	25	21	150	196	12	87	295	461
%	12.8	10.7	76.5	100.0				
Asians								
No, 000s	11	13	35	59	14	13	86	135
%	18.7	22.0	59.3	100.0				

Source: *Report* of the Commission of Inquiry into certain matters relating to Building Societies in South Africa, Schedule 2, Republic of South Africa, 1982.

There have been a number of significant developments, particularly in respect of housing for black Africans, in the recent past.

In 1978, a 99 year leasehold scheme for black Africans resident in urban areas was introduced. Prior to this a 30 year leasehold scheme was in operation but was not successful.

In 1979 the government announced the integration of the scheme for low interest rate loans for black Africans with similar schemes for other races. Depending on income, loans for low income people are available at interest rates of between 1% and 9.25%.

In March 1983, the government announced that, with effect from July 1983, it would sell some 500,000 state-owned dwellings to low income families of all races, although it is anticipated that most of the beneficiaries will be black Africans. Discounts of up to 40% of purchase price are available. The scheme is very similar to that employed by the British government. The government also announced that the 99 year tenure would, in future, be extended for a further 99 years every time the property changed hands.

Building societies in South Africa have played a major role in implementing the new policies towards the housing of black African people.

Housing Finance

Building societies dominate the housing finance market, and their market share has increased significantly in recent years. Table 7.2 shows the distribution of mortgage loans outstanding in 1971 and 1981, together with available figures for 1983.

Table 7.2 Mortgage Loans Held, South Africa, 1971, 1981 and 1983

	1971		1981		1983
	Rand m	%	Rand m	%	Rand m
Building societies	2,721	56	11,085	71	14,833
Participation mortgage bonds	686	14	1,298	8	1,815
Commercial banks	437	9	1,701	11	
Land Bank	392	8	1,001	6	1,584
Long term insurers	399	8	275	2	379
Pension & provident funds	228	5	256	2	224
Total	4,863	100	15,616	100	

Source: *Report* of the Commission of Inquiry into certain matters relating to Building Societies in South Africa, Schedule 6, Republic of South Africa, 1982; *South African Reserve Bank Quarterly Bulletin*, March 1984.

Notes: 1. 1983 figures for long term insurers and pension and provident funds are for September; a figure for banks is not available.
2. At end-1983 there were 1.10 rand to the dollar and 1.75 rand to the pound.

It will be seen that building societies increased their share of the market from 56% in 1971 to 71% in 1981. Building societies are described more fully subsequently, and, at this stage, it is helpful to comment briefly on private banking institutions and participation mortgage bonds.

The banks have not been significant mortgage lenders until recently. Indeed, for most purposes, the banks were not active in the mortgage market at all. However, in August 1982, Barclays Bank announced that it would enter the mortgage market and it employed a similar strategy to that used by the banks in the United Kingdom. Although Barclays charged higher rates than building societies, the continual shortage of mortgage finance led it to be confident that it would obtain an adequate demand for its loans, and this confidence was justified. However, as in Britain, after an initial surge, bank lending for house-purchase has subsequently fallen back. Nevertheless, by the end of 1983 Barclays Bank had lent R850 million to 19,000 home-buyers.

Participation mortgage bonds represent a simple secondary market. There are 33 participation mortgage schemes in operation, through which an investor acquires a share of, or all of, the rights secured under a mortgage bond registered over immoveable property in South Africa. The number of bonds registered reached a peak of 11,270 in 1973, since when it has fallen with the number totalling 7,645 in 1980. The amount owing by mortgagors under bonds reached a peak of R1.11 billion, also in 1976, before falling back to R1.09 billion in 1979, and then increasing to a new record of R1.83 billion in 1983. However, as Table 7.2 shows, participation mortgage bonds have been taking a declining share of the total market. The bonds play only a small part in the residential mortgage market. At the end of 1983 only 12%, by amount, of bonds were on residential property, the proportion having fallen from 27% at the end of 1976. Some 78% of bonds are in respect of commercial and industrial properties.

The Savings Market

Although building societies have been successful in increasing their share of the housing finance market, they have been less successful in the savings market. Table 7.3 shows trends.

Table 7.3 Funds Invested with Selected Institutions, South Africa, 1972 & 1983

Institution	End-1972		End-1983	
	Rm	%	Rm	%
Commercial banks	3,993	39	23,589	44
Building societies	3,707	37	17,499	33
HP, savings & general banks	1,663	16	9,094	17
Merchant banks	547	6	1,555	3
Post office	237	2	1,910	4
Total	10,147	100	53,647	100

Source: *South African Reserve Bank Quarterly Bulletin*, March 1984.
Note: At end-1983 there were 1.10 rand to the dollar and 1.75 rand to the pound.

It will be seen that the commercial banks accounted for 44% of selected funds at the end of 1982, their market share having increased from 39% at the end of 1972. Building societies had suffered a corresponding decline in market share. Since 1983 the banks have been paying interest on current accounts and this has further increased their competitiveness.

The banks and building societies are competing aggressively for business, and the arrangement by which societies agreed interest rates between themselves has gradually broken down to the point where the interest rate agreement which had formerly existed between societies was abandoned in March 1983.

Building Societies

History

British settlers were responsible for establishing the building society industry in South Africa. The first terminating societies were established in Port

Elizabeth in 1855 and in Durban in 1856. The first permanent society was established in Port Elizabeth in 1874. By 1900 at least ten permanent societies had been established and, subsequently, they superseded the terminating societies.

The first building society legislation was in Natal in 1909. In 1934 legislation was enacted to regulate the activities of societies throughout the country. The Act established the office of a Registrar of Building Societies to supervise the industry, and it laid down standards for operations.

In 1934 the National Association of Building Societies and the Federation of Building Societies were formed; these two bodies merged, in 1938, to form the present Association of Building Societies of South Africa.

By the end of 1936 there were 45 permanent societies with assets totalling R73 million, together with a number of terminating societies. The number of permanent societies has fallen steadily, largely as a result of mergers, from the figure of 45 at the end of 1936 to 14 at the end of 1972 and 11 at the end of 1982. There was major building society legislation in 1965 and significant amending legislation in 1973.

Constitution

Societies are governed by the Building Societies Act 1965 as amended. Section 22 sets out the powers of societies. These are significantly wider than those enjoyed, for example, by British building societies. For example -

(a) Societies can hold shares in any limited liability company which is the owner of land, where any portion of any building on such land is being used by the society or its agent.
(b) Societies can accept cash as collateral security.
(c) Societies can maintain safe deposits for their members and others.
(d) Societies can act as insurance agents.
(e) Societies can acquire or establish limited liability companies in the field of insurance.
(f) Societies can acquire or establish property development companies.

Among the financial requirements which a society must meet are -

(a) Paid-up indefinite share capital and general reserves must amount to not less than 25% of the sum of remaining paid-up share capital, deposits, loans and overdrafts.
(b) Liquid assets must be maintained, amounting to 30% of liabilities in respect of transmission accounts, 15% of other short term liabilities, 10% of medium term liabilities and 5% of long term liabilities.

The Act contains restrictive provisions relating to mortgage lending, and it also provides for the government to prescribe the pattern of mortgage interest rates (higher rates are charged for larger loans), although not the basic rate.

In theory societies are all mutual institutions, but they can, in practice, be controlled by other institutions. Two societies, the Standard and the Trust, are effectively parts of the banks of the same names, and most other societies have strong connections with other institutions, connections which have been strengthened considerably in the recent past.

A significant aspect of building society operation are service corporations, specifically provided for in Section 22 of the Act. These operate in two principal areas; insurance and township development. The authority of a government official is required before a service corporation can be established, and he will limit the areas in which it can trade. Typically, insurance subsidiaries offer only mortgage protection and property insurance. The development companies are of more significance. Societies can invest up to R4 million in development companies, and the companies can borrow up to three times as much from the society. Although the development operations run by the largest societies are big they have not realized their full potential because of the limitations on capital.

The Structure of the Industry

There are just 11 building societies in South Africa, and the largest three (United, South African Permanent and Allied) account for 75% of the industry's assets. Table 7.4 lists the building societies together with their assets in March 1983.

Table 7.4 South African Building Societies, March 1983

| Society | Total Assets, End-March 1983 | |
	Rm	Percentage of Total
United	5,296	31.6
SA Permanent	4,117	24.6
Allied	3,054	18.2
Natal	1,627	9.7
Saambou	1,288	7.7
Standard	515	3.1
Trust	341	2.0
Eastern Province	270	1.6
South West African	105	0.6
Provincial	79	0.5
Grahamstown	71	0.4
Total	16,763	100.0

Source: Annual returns to the Registrar of Building Societies, Year ended 31 March 1983.
Note: At end-March 1983 there were 1.09 rand to the dollar and 1.63 rand to the pound.

There is no limitation on the areas in which the societies can operate. The large societies operate throughout the country. The 11 societies have approximately 800 branches between them, but these branches tend to be very much bigger than those of similar institutions in other countries.

Operations

Table 7.5 shows the aggregate balance sheet for South African building societies as at the end of 1983.

Table 7.5 Aggregate Balance Sheet, South African Building Societies, End-1983

Liabilities	Rm	%	Assets	Rm	%
Savings & transmission			Mortgage advances	14,833	80
deposits	3,991	22	Loans against shares		
Fixed deposits	6,452	35	& deposits	493	3
Tax-free indefinite			Cash & investments	2,689	15
shares	1,349	7	Property	330	2
Other indefinite shares	2,980	16	Property development		
Subscription fixed period			subsidiaries	99	1
shares	1,188	6	Other assets	26	-
Paid-up fixed period					
shares	1,539	8			
Other liabilities	657	4			
Reserves	314	2			
Total	18,470	100	Total	18,470	100

Source: *South African Reserve Bank Quarterly Bulletin*, March 1984, pages S-35 and S-36.
Note: At end-1983 there were 1.10 rand to the dollar and 1.75 rand to the pound.

The balance sheet is fairly typical of that for specialist housing finance institutions. Shares and deposits accounted for 94% of liabilities, and advances (there were 568,710 outstanding loans in March 1983) for 83% of assets. Reserves, at 1.7% of assets, have shown a significant decline since 1975, when the proportion was 2.6%. Investments have to be held in public sector securities.

Deposits account for well over half of liabilities. Savings deposits are similar to the normal building society passbook account. They are withdrawable on demand and offer a low rate of interest, typically 4%. The rate is changed infrequently.

Transmission deposits offer a very low rate of interest, 2%, but in addition to being operated through a passbook, third party cheques can be drawn and unlimited withdrawals can be made. ATM facilities (including at point of sale) are now generally available for transmission deposits, and also deposit accounts.

Fixed deposits carry a guaranteed rate of interest, depending on the period of investment. At the end of 1983 the rate was 16% for one year deposits, with slightly lower rates being paid for longer term deposits.

There are four types of paid-up shares -

(a) Tax free indefinite shares currently carry an interest rate of 9.5%. Investors can hold only R20,000 per taxpayer (husbands and wives are taxed jointly) in such shares, but the rate is attractive for higher rate tax-payers, and, moreover, is cheap money for societies. After 15 months, these shares are subject to three months' notice of withdrawal, but investors can borrow on the security of them. They accounted for 8% of shares and deposits at the end of 1983.

(b) Ordinary indefinite shares are also subject to three months' notice of withdrawal, but only after they have been held for 15 months, and for some investors interest can be tax-free.

(a) For other investors, up to one-third of the interest is free of tax. In March 1982, the rate of interest payable on this class of share was 12.5%. They accounted for 17% of shares and deposits at the end of 1983.

(c) Paid-up fixed period shares have a guaranteed rate of interest payable over five years. They have become increasingly popular, and societies normally offer the highest rates of interest on this type of account. They accounted for 9% of shares and deposits at the end of 1983.

(d) Subscription fixed period shares also enjoy whole or partial tax-free status. There is a R50,000 limit per taxpayer on investments in these accounts which, in March 1982, paid a rate of interest of 8.75%. They accounted for 7% of shares and deposits at the end of 1983.

It will be noted that a high proportion of deposits and shares with building societies offer a partial or complete tax-free return. This has helped building societies in competition with other financial institutions. However, as market rates of interest have risen sharply, so the attraction of the tax-free investments has fallen, and societies have suffered accordingly. Also, the status of tax-free and partially tax-free accounts has increasingly been questioned. There is an interesting parallel with the USA where regulation Q was effectively nullified by share movements in market interest rates.

Societies raise a proportion of their funds from institutions. At the end of 1982, 15% of shares and deposits were held by institutions, private and public companies alone accounted for 7%. The proportion of institutional money has increased modestly in recent years, from 12% at the end of 1975.

A significant feature of the assets side of the balance sheet is loans secured on shares and deposits. Where investments are made for indefinite periods, investors are generally able to borrow against the security of the investment.

Almost all lending is on the security of owner-occupied houses. Mortgage loans are made at variable rates of interest, but the mortgage rate has been politically sensitive and has generally been held well below a market level. However, in 1981 the rate was increased by a total of 3.75 percentage points, and there was a further increase of two percentage points in 1982, rates being in the range of 14.25%-16.25%. As interest rates fell towards the end of 1982 and in the early part of 1983, so mortgage rates fell a little, but they rose again at the end of 1983 to stand at 16.25%-18.75% at the end of the year.

Because the mortgage rate was held below a market clearing level Barclays Bank was able to enter the market, charging substantially more than societies, in the second half of 1982. As a means of rationing, some societies accepted applications for loans from borrowers who did not have an investment account only if a relative of the potential borrower or his company made a corresponding deposit. Societies' lending fell from R4,600 million in 1980 to R1,700 million in 1981, before recovering to R2,269 million in 1982, and rising to a peak of R4,978 milion in 1983. 66% of lending was on existing dwellings.

Table 7.6 shows the aggregate income and expenditure account for the financial year 1982/83. Again, this is typical of specialist housing finance institutions, with income largely being derived from mortgage interest, most of which is used to pay interest to investors. The management expense ratio, at 2.52%, was high by international standards, New Zealand excepted. This partly reflects the much greater range of services, particularly on the savings side, which South African building societies have offered.

Table 7.6 Aggregate Income and Expenditure Account, Building Societies, South Africa, 1982-83

	Rand m	Percentage of Mean Assets
Income		
Mortgage interest	1,994	13.02
Investment interest	122	0.80
Other income	55	0.36
Total	2,171	14.18
Expenditure		
Share, deposit & loan interest	1,707	11.15
Management expenses	386	2.52
Taxation	23	0.15
Total	2,116	13.82
Net surplus	54	0.35

Source: Derived from The Association of Building Societies of South Africa Annual Report 1983.
Note: At end-March 1983 there were 1.09 rand to the dollar and 1.63 rand to the pound.

The Association of Building Societies of South Africa

All South African building societies are members of The Association of Building Societies of South Africa, which was established in 1938. The Association is based in Johannesburg and performs the usual trade association functions. Until very recently it provided a forum in which societies got together to set interest rates. A major pre-occupation has been the two commissions of inquiry, described subsequently, and the implications of greater competition between financial institutions.

Inquiry and Reform

The De Kock Commission

One of the features of financial systems in the English speaking countries in recent years has been the establishment of commissions of inquiry. In the USA, the Hunt Commission Report of the early 1970s was followed by protracted discussion on the reform of the financial system until the far reaching legislation of the early 1980s. In Britain, the Wilson Committee provided an authoritative description of the financial system, although, for various reasons, the recommendations of the Committee were not given due consideration.

In Australia, the Campbell Committee produced a radical report into the financial system, advocating the freeing of the system and the removal of artificial constraints on individual institutions, and that report has already had a major effect on government policy.

In South Africa, there has been a general inquiry into financial institutions, conducted under the Chairmanship of Dr G P C De Kock, now the Governor of the Reserve Bank. The De Kock Commission was asked to produce an interim report dealing specifically with building societies, and this was published in December 1982. The Commission views building societies in a very wide context and its underlying theme is very similar to that found in the Campbell Report in Australia, and the Wilson Report in Britain, that is, that the artificial features of the financial system should be removed and that the various institutions should compete across a broad range of activities on fair and equal terms.

The Report recognises that recent changes in the functions and operations of societies had unquestionably altered their role in the financial markets and has created problems for the monetary authorities. It considered that building societies had a number of special privileges -

(a) They do not need share capital, and are able to pay 'dividends' out of pre-tax income.

(b) The reserve funds of societies are much lower than the capital required of a bank.

(c) Their unique capital structure means that societies can maintain a lower margin between investing and borrowing rates than other institutions.

(d) Societies are not required to hold any cash reserves against their liabilities to the public.

(e) Societies are subject to substantially lower liquidity requirements than banking institutions.

(f) Societies are not subject to supplementary liquid asset requirements.

(g) Societies are able to offer, within limits, certain tax-free accounts.

139

The Report notes that societies have evolved from traditional housing finance institutions to more wide ranging institutions. For example, they obtain nearly 20% of their funds other than from the personal sector, they offer shares and deposits on terms which make them close money substitutes, and their interest rates have become more volatile.

The Commission concluded that building society shares and deposits should be included in at least some of the monetary aggregates. It saw the merit of building societies moving their rates more in line with other interest rates than in the past, but noted that this did create a problem with respect to existing borrowers.

The Commission considered that building societies' status quo could not be maintained. It rejected the option of societies returning to their traditional role of mobilising personal savings to finance housing, and it did not favour direct government regulation in exchange for continued financial protection. Its recommended approach was that societies should continue to have a special, but evolving, role. It considered that societies should be subject to the same cash and liquid asset requirements as banking institutions, and, given this, it saw no objection to societies continuing to offer transmission accounts and savings deposits. It recommended a relaxation of restrictions on the amounts of deposits held by any one depositor, and the requirements regarding spread of maturity dates. It saw merit in the lengthening of the maturities of building society liabilities and recommended that societies should raise some of their funds from the capital markets.

The Commission thought that societies' reserve funds, at under 2% of total liabilities, were too low, and recommended a gradual build up to 4%. It suggested that urgent attention be given to a relaxation and simplification of the comprehensive legal requirements regarding building society loans.

The Commission came out against special tax treatment for building societies and recommended that the existing tax concessions on building society shares should be gradually replaced, an interesting parallel with the removal of the regulation Q differential in the USA. The Commission concluded with a warning note about the harmful effects of excessive subsidization of the costs of housing finance and pointed out that this tended to result in the capitalization of any interest rate advantage in house prices. It recommended that any state assistance to enable societies and other institutions to keep the cost of housing below free market levels should be provided only in moderation and when considered essential.

The Du Plessis Report

The Du Plessis Commission was specific to building societies and was stimulated by two rises in the politically sensitive mortgage rate in the first part of 1982 just before a general election. The Report is very different in philosophy from the De Kock Report and tends to view building societies in isolation rather than as part of the housing and financial systems. The Report provides some useful information and statistics on building societies in South Africa, and it seems that this could be its only contribution to the development of the industry.

The Commission proposed that the major objective of societies should be the financing of housing from personal savings and the encouragement of home-ownership. It viewed building societies very favourably, albeit noting that they had enjoyed some government protection, but went on to comment that societies have gradually extended their functions and that the shelter extended to them by the authorities has enhanced their competitiveness against other institutions.

The Commission suggested that there were four general directions in which building societies could develop -

(a) A return to the basic principles of self-help and the promotion of thrift.
(b) Equal competition with other financial intermediaries with all sheltering of the financing of housing being abolished.
(c) Equal competition with other financial intermediaries while the financing of housing continued to be sheltered, but in such a way as to benefit all financial institutions.
(d) Continuation of the financial sheltering of building societies together with a prescription regarding their activities to ensure that they did not compete unfairly.

The Commission criticized the extension of building society activities, and proposed that societies should reorder their activities in accordance with the precepts and principles with which they functioned in the 18th and 19th centuries. The fourth option set out above was therefore preferred.

The Commission favoured a dual system of mortgage financing such that all sheltered funds would be made available to middle and lower income groups at below the market level. The Commission concluded with a recommendation that a consultative housing finance committee should be established.

Recent Developments

In general, the De Kock Report was much better received than the Du Plessis Report, and this view seems to have been adopted both by the South African building society industry and also by the government. In March 1983, the government announced that it had adopted three broad guidelines in its approach to building societies -

(a) Societies had undergone an evolutionary change away from the traditional concept of mutual thrift institutions and were increasingly operating in the field of modern deposit taking. They should therefore be subject to the same sort of disciplines as banking institutions. At the present stage of their evolution they should still be accorded special treatment under their own Act, but that Act should be brought more into line with the format of the banking legislation.

(b) To enhance the effectiveness of monetary stabilization policy societies should be permitted and encouraged to quote realistic and market determined borrowing and lending rates in competition with other financial institutions.

(c) In realisation that a more market orientated approach could entail relatively higher mortgage rates at times, the state would be prepared to provide additional assistance to moderate the cost of financing home-ownership for certain categories in the lower and middle income groups.

The present system of allowing societies to offer partially or wholly tax-free shares is to be phased out, but the government will pay a direct interest rate subsidy to borrowers who have loans with societies and other institutions, subject to certain specified limits.

Simultaneously, the government announced two measures to assist young people buying their first homes -

(a) State assisted home owners' savings scheme. The savings limit of R10,000, which qualified for a modest 2% subsidy, would be doubled to R20,000 with effect from April 1983, and the subsidy payable on the amount saved would increase to 3%. This rate is in addition to the current savings rate of 9% paid by societies, so the effective yield is 12% pa tax free. Savings under this scheme have to be used for house-purchase.

(b) Subsidy Scheme. Individuals purchasing their first home which is a new home, costing not more than R45,000, can qualify for a subsidy of 20% of the monthly interest payment calculated on the minimum building society mortgage rate applicable.

Legislation is expected shortly and it is possible that societies' mutual status will be called into question. It is clear that building societies are to become further integrated into the financial system generally, and that as in other English speaking countries they are gradually losing their specialist status. Further developments have confirmed this view.

A significant event occurred on 20 May 1983 when it was announced that building societies would no longer co-operate in determining uniform deposit and mortgage rates, and that in future each society would be free to fix its own rates. This announcement came at a time when building society mortgage rates had been reduced to a range of 14.0% to 15.0%.

Another significant development has been the establishing of co-operative links between banks and building societies rather than within the two industries. Eleven banks and building societies, including Barclays Bank, Nedbank and the South African Permanent Building Society, have agreed to set up a shared ATM system by the end of 1984. Nedbank and the Allied Building Societies are co-operating to provide a wider range of financial services generally. A second shared ATM system is being set up by the Standard Bank, the Volkas Bank and the United Building Society. The Standard Bank and the United Building Society, together with the Liberty Life Insurance Company, are co-operating more generally over a wider range of financial services.

Assessment

The South African building society industry is developing in a very similar way to the specialist housing finance industries in the other English speaking countries. The societies have increasingly been offering a wider range of retail financial services, and have been ahead of their counterparts in Britain and Australia in this respect, albeit behind American savings and loan associations. More recently, strong links have been developed between some building societies and other financial institutions.

The mortgage rate has tended to be very politically sensitive in South Africa with the result that it has invariably been held below market clearing levels. The adoption of the De Kock Report philosophy is a recognition that this policy is unsatisfactory, and it is anticipated that building society rates will be more closely related to market rates in the future. The ending of the agreement on fixing interest rates by the major societies is another manifestation of this.

Bibliography

Boleat, M J, 'Official committees report on societies in South Africa', *The Building Societies Gazette*, March 1983.
Boleat, M J, 'Societies in South Africa ponder future role as competition grows', *The Building Societies Gazette*, December 1982.
Building Societies in South Africa, BSA Bulletin, January 1983.
Official Yearbook of the Republic of South Africa, 1983.
Report of the Commission of Inquiry into certain matters relating to building societies in South Africa (Du Plessis Report), Republic of South Africa, 1982.
The Association of Building Societies of South Africa, *Annual Report 1983*.
The Building Societies, the Financial Markets and Monetary Policy, Second Interim Report of the Commission of Inquiry into the Monetary System and Monetary Policy in South Africa (De Kock Report), Republic of South Africa, 1982.

Acknowledgements

The co-operation of the South African Embassy in London and The Association of Building Societies of South Africa in providing information for this chapter is gratefully acknowledged.

The author is indebted to Tim Hart, Director, and Joe Pietersen, Secretary, of The Association of Building Societies of South Africa for their careful scrutiny of, and detailed comments on, an earlier draft of this chapter. John Bennett, Managing Director of the Natal Building Society, also gave valuable comments.

CHAPTER 8

NEW ZEALAND

Over 70% of dwellings in New Zealand are owner-occupied, giving the country one of the highest owner-occupation rates in the world. Most of the remaining dwellings are rented privately.

Housing finance operates largely on the deposit taking system with loans being provided by savings banks and specialist building societies. However, the major lender is the government owned Housing Corporation of New Zealand which has a wide range of functions including the provision of rented accommodation and the guaranteeing of private mortgages, as well as supplying housing finance directly.

Housing finance remains relatively divorced from the financial markets generally, and frequently it is necessary to wait before it is possible to obtain a loan. There are significant differences between the mortgage rates which various categories of home-buyer have to pay at any one time.

Introduction

New Zealand comprises two principal islands occupying a total of 271,000 sq kilometres. The population was 3,176,000 in March 1981 and has been increasing only slowly in recent years with the natural increase largely being counteracted by net emigration. The principal city is Auckland, and the other major cities are Wellington (the capital), Christchurch and Dunedin.

New Zealand has the status of a dominion within the British Commonwealth, recognizing the British Queen as Head of State. It has a one chamber legislature, the House of Representatives. Political power has alternated between the National Party (Conservatives) and the Labour Party. The National Party is currently in power.

Housing

Housing Tenure

Over 70% of houses in New Zealand are owner-occupied. Table 8.1 shows housing tenure in 1981.

Table 8.1 Housing Tenure, New Zealand, 1981

Tenure	Number of Dwellings	Percentage of Total
Owned without mortgage	288,522	28.8
Owned with mortgage	423,783	42.4
Rented or leased	253,623	25.3
Free with job	21,351	2.1
Free not with job	12,546	1.3
Not specified	5,664	-
Total	1,005,489	100.0

Source: *New Zealand Census of Population and Dwellings*, 1981.

The level of owner-occupation has been increasing modestly in recent years. In 1976, 69.7% of houses were owner-occupied compared with the 1981 figure of 71.2%. Most rented dwellings are rented privately. However, the Housing Corporation of New Zealand had 60,500 tenancies as at March 1983, and therefore owns about 6% of the total housing stock. Some 16,000 units of various types are under local authority control.

In June 1983, the average price of houses in New Zealand varied from $NZ34,000 in Dunedin to $NZ62,500 in Auckland. (In June 1983 there were $NZ1.54 to the US dollar and $NZ2.32 to the pound.)

Housebuilding

As in other countries the level of housebuilding has declined in recent years, largely because of the general recession. Table 8.2 gives details of new house completions.

Table 8.2 New House Completions, New Zealand, 1978-83

Year Ended 31 March	Government Built	Private Built	Total
1978	1,900	22,300	24,200
1979	1,700	17,500	19,200
1980	1,500	14,600	16,100
1981	900	13,300	14,200
1982	300	16,000	16,300
1983	400	14,400	14,800

Source: *Report of the Housing Corporation of New Zealand*, year ended 31 March 1983.

It will be seen that almost all dwellings are built privately. The average new house is single-storied and has an area of a little over 100 sq metres. Over half of the dwellings in New Zealand have been built in the last 25 years.

The National Housing Commission

The National Housing Commission was established in 1974 with the principal functions of advising the Minister of Housing on all matters relating to housing, and to research into the housing needs of the population. It is also responsible for co-ordinating the various agencies concerned with housing in New Zealand. It has published two informative five yearly reports on the position of housing in New Zealand, and has commissioned considerable research on housing matters. The government has recently announced a review of the National Housing Commission, in particular, to examine whether its objectives still continue to be relevant, and whether it is an effective and efficient means of obtaining the objectives for which it was established.

Housing Finance

The Housing Finance Market

The housing finance market is fairly complicated and difficult to analyse. One problem is that the market itself is less sophisticated than that in other advanced countries, and, until recently, there has been a lack of adequate statistical information. It is particularly difficult to work out trends in the housing finance market, including the relative market shares of the various institutions. However, information is available in respect of registered mortgage debt. Table 8.3 shows the sources of mortgages registered by amount from 1971 to 1983.

Table 8.3 Sources of Mortgages Registered, by Amount, New Zealand 1971-83

Institution	1971 %	1974 %	1977 %	1981 %	1983 %
Government (including Housing Corporation)	23.2	17.1	17.5	26.9	23.1
Trading banks	1.0	1.0	1.5	2.2	1.1
Trustee savings banks	5.8	6.4	6.2	9.9	3.7
Building societies	10.5	9.4	6.7	6.7	6.4
Insurance companies and pension funds	9.6	8.3	8.2	8.2	8.9
Private	28.9	21.6	25.9	18.9	20.3
Producer enterprises	21.0	36.2	18.8	18.6	23.6
Other			15.2	8.6	12.7
Total	100.0	100.0	100.0	100.0	100.0

Source: 'Sources of Housing Finance in New Zealand', *Reserve Bank Bulletin*, April 1978; *New Zealand Official Year Book 1982*;
Monthly Abstract of Statistics, August 1983.
Notes: 1. 'Private' covers private individuals in 1971 and 1974, and households and non-profit organisations in 1977 and 1981.
2. 'Producer enterprises' include solicitor nominee companies; this category was separately identified from 1976 only and was previously included in 'other'.
3. Figures refer to years ending 31 March.

It is important to note that the table does not differentiate between types of mortgage loan, and it includes commercial loans as well as residential loans.

A particularly important problem in this respect is that loans by savings banks and building societies are long term, whereas private loans are short term. For example, a loan by a solicitor is likely to be at a high rate of interest for, perhaps, just three years, and will require refinancing. Also, not all mortgages have to be registered and, for this reason, the activity of the banks is understated. The table does not therefore give a good indication of trends in mortgage debt outstanding. However, it is sufficient to show the importance of the government and of private sources of finance.

Table 8.4 shows the breakdown of housing loan approvals in 1982.

Table 8.4 Housing Loan Approvals, New Zealand, 1982

Institution	Number	Percentage of Total	Amount $NZm	Percentage of Total
Housing Corporation	13,949	34	230	29
Building societies	9,344	22	195	24
Trustee savings banks	9,603	23	176	22
Life insurance offices	4,522	11	122	15
Private savings banks	2,129	5	43	5
Post Office Savings Bank	2,055	5	22	3
Total	41,602	100	788	100

Source: *Reserve Bank Bulletin*, July 1983.
Note: At end-1982 there were $NZ1.21 to the US dollar and $NZ2.32 to the pound.

The table shows that building societies and the trustee savings banks each have a little under a quarter of the market, and that the Housing Corporation is the principal lender. The three main types of organisation are described in detail subsequently in this chapter, and, at this stage, it is helpful to comment briefly on the house-purchase process.

Partly because the mortgage market in New Zealand is imperfect (in the economic sense) there is generally a shortage of mortgage finance. A two year period of saving is regarded as being almost essential to secure a mortgage from a building society or a savings bank. It is partly for this reason that solicitors and other sources of finance are important. They will frequently make a loan at a very high rate of interest, perhaps 18% at end-1983, for three years, until such time as a loan can be obtained from a savings bank or building society. House-purchasers generally need a deposit of at least 20% and normally the first loan will not be sufficient to provide the remaining funds. Typically, at end-1983, the home-buyer might obtain a first loan for $NZ25,000 for 20 years at a rate of interest of 14 or 15% and a second loan for $NZ10,000 over ten years at 16%.

There are huge variations in the mortgage rates which individual home-buyers pay. The Housing Corporation makes subsidized loans at rates of interest between 3% and 9%, while the rate, which is variable, charged by private sector institutions varies from 10% to 17%, although at end-1983 the market rate for first loans was in the range 13% to 15%. There is some concern at the seemingly arbitrary nature of the market, with some buyers being able to obtain cheap loans from the Housing Corporation, while others perhaps have to pay a high rate for two or three years from a solicitor before obtaining loans at the market rate from savings banks or building societies. This feature is illustrated by Table 8.5 which shows mortgage rates charged in June 1983.

Table 8.5 Mortgage Rate Charged by Value of New Registrations, New Zealand, June 1983

Mortgage Rate	Mortgages $NZm	Percentage of Total
Less than 8%	11.8	4
8% to under 10%	48.1	16
10% to under 12%	12.9	4
12% to under 14%	9.4	3
14% to under 16%	32.9	11
16% to under 18%	33.6	11
18% to under 20%	73.7	24
20% & over	31.1	10
Unspecified	53.6	17
Total	307.4	100
Average rate		15.28
Average rate excluding government		17.28

Source: *Reserve Bank Bulletin*, December 1983.
Note: At end-June 1983 there were $NZ1.53 to the US dollar and $NZ2.33 to the pound.

In November 1981 the government introduced controls on mortgage rates as part of a wide ranging economic package and further controls were implemented in June 1982. These have had the effect of leading to a sharp reduction in the supply of mortgage funds. In November 1983 the government announced regulations limiting the rate of interest on first mortgages to 11% and on subsequent mortgages to 14%. These regulations have subsequently been renewed until the end of August 1984.

Tax relief on mortgage interest is available to a very limited extent. First-time buyers can claim personal income tax relief of up to $NZ1,000 a year for five years against mortgage interest paid.

The Savings Market

The savings market in New Zealand is dominated by the trading banks and three varieties of savings banks. The trading banks have over 40% of personal sector deposits, and the savings banks over one third. There are four principal trading banks in New Zealand. The Bank of New Zealand (by far the largest bank with total assets of $NZ5,299 million at end-1982) is government owned and the National New Zealand Bank is a wholly owned subsidiary of the British Lloyds Bank. The ANZ Banking Group (New Zealand) is 75% owned by the Australian based Australia and New Zealand Banking Group and the Westpac Banking Corporation is owned by the Australian Westpac Group. Table 8.6 shows deposits with financial institutions over the period 1974 to 1983.

Table 8.6 Deposits with Selected Financial Institutions, New Zealand, 1974-83

| Institution | 31 March | | | | | | | |
| | 1974 | | 1977 | | 1982 | | 1983 | |
	$NZm	%	$NZm	%	$NZm	%	$NZm	%
Trading banks	2,000	42	2,883	44	6,657	46	7,524	47
Private savings banks	451	9	622	9	1,057	7	887	6
Post Office Savings Bank	1,035	22	1,158	18	1,632	11	1,725	11
Trustee savings banks	712	15	959	15	2,267	16	2,589	16
Building societies	392	8	514	8	966	7	1,077	7
Finance houses	213	4	446	7	1,786	12	2,215	14
Total	4,803	100	6,582	100	14,365	100	16,017	100

Source: *Reserve Bank Bulletin.*
Note: At end-March 1983 there were $NZ1.53 to the US dollar and $NZ2.33 to the pound.

The table shows relatively constant market shares, except for the sharp decline in the share of the Post Office Savings Bank, and the correspondingly rapid increase in the share of the finance houses. The latter factor is partly explained by the finance houses being less controlled than other financial institutions, and very much parallels the experience in Australia and the United States.

Building Societies

Constitution and Structure

The first building societies in New Zealand were established by British settlers in the 1860s and very much followed the pattern of the British terminating societies. The British Building Societies Act of 1874, and, indeed, subsequent building society legislation, has greatly influenced New Zealand legislation. However, terminating societies retained their popularity, largely because they offered to the investor the prospect of a gamble through which he could obtain an interest free loan. During the 1970s concern was increasingly expressed at the strict forfeiture rules of the terminating societies and consideration was given as to how a more rational structure could be introduced. Through various amendments to existing legislation this has now been achieved.

Building societies in New Zealand act under specific legislation as do their counterparts in the United Kingdom, Australia and South Africa. The relevant Act is the Building Societies Act 1965 as amended. Section 9 of that Act is virtually identical (except for a recent amendment) to Section l(1) of the British Building Societies Act 1962 -

'The purpose for which a building society may be established under this Act is that of raising, by the subscriptions of members, a fund for making advances to members out of the funds of the society on security by way of mortgage of land, or on the security of the shares of the members (or on other or on no security) in accordance with this Act'

The section in brackets has recently been added and will be explained subsequently.

The legislation also prohibits societies from investing in land or buildings other than for the purpose of conducting their business, provides for the rules of societies, specifies procedures governing mergers and unions, limits the total amount which may be advanced on any one mortgage or commercial property, limits the investment of surplus funds to government backed securities, provides for a Registrar to control societies and gives powers for the making of regulations. The supervisor is the Registrar of Building Societies.

There is provision for building societies to have trustee status, that is, that they can be authorized to accept deposits from trustees. To qualify for trustee status a society must have a minimum of $NZ1 million in assets, a minimum of 7.5% in liquid funds and a minimum of 2.5% in free reserves. These requirements are very similar to those needed by a British building society which wishes to qualify for trustee status.

The point has been made that concern was expressed at the practices of the terminating building societies. In particular, there was criticism of the amount that members forfeited through not maintaining their contracts, the cost of operating such institutions and the resulting low returns on savings. Terminating societies have been declining in importance for some years and most were actively promoting an allied permanent society. The problem was overcome by an amendment, in 1980, to the Building Societies Act 1965. This prohibits the sale of terminating group shares, but permits societies to conduct ballots for a minor portion of their operating profit. It was felt that this provided a way in which terminating societies could decently cease to exist. During the year ended 31 March 1981, the number of terminating societies fell from 12 to seven, and subsequently there has been a further reduction to three. All societies now have a common range of products, and, in effect, the distinction between permanent and terminating societies has been abolished.

At this stage it should also be noted that while most building societies in New Zealand are mutual, five small societies, accounting for less than 5% of the total assets of the industry, have a joint stock nature.

There was further important legislation in 1982 which could radically change the nature of building societies in New Zealand. The words in brackets in

Section 9 of the Act set out above were added so as to permit societies to make unsecured loans. Amendments provided for up to 5% of advances to be unsecured and removed the restriction which prevented societies lending on second mortgage. In order to preserve building societies as housing institutions, 85% of advances must be for housing purposes. In exchange for this freeing of asset control building societies were subject for the first time to tax on their profits. This measure marked a significant departure from the system whereby New Zealand building societies have been outside the normal financial system.

At March 31 1983 there were 34 building societies in New Zealand, of which three were nominally terminating and 31 were permanent. The number of societies has fallen rapidly from over 60 in the mid-1970s. The societies between them have some 245 branches. Table 8.7 lists the five largest societies as at June 1983.

Table 8.7 Largest Building Societies, New Zealand, June 1983

Name	Base	Assets $NZm	Branches
United	Wellington	480	65
Countrywide	Auckland	335	49
Southland	Invercargill	119	3
Southern Cross	Auckland	67	7
New Zealand Permanent	Dunedin	63	7

Source: *Building Societies in New Zealand*, BSA (NZ) Inc, 1983.
Note: At end-June 1983 there were $NZ1.53 to the US dollar and $NZ2.33 to the pound.

The total assets of the industry in June 1983 were NZ1,225 million from which it can be seen that the United Building Society accounts for 39% and Countrywide for 27%. The industry is, therefore, highly concentrated.

Building Societies Association (NZ) Inc

The Building Societies Association (NZ) Inc is the trade association for New Zealand societies. It was formed at a meeting of 20 societies on 13 April 1981. It replaced the Permanent Building Societies Association and the Terminating Building Societies Association which had catered respectively for the special interests of their different classes of members. Like other trade associations the New Zealand Association has the objectives of promoting the interests of and co-operation among societies, advancing personal thrift and home-ownership, ensuring that societies conduct their business appropriately, seeking appropriate legislative and financial measures and doing other such similar functions. The Association has 22 members, which account for 99% of the assets of the industry. It is based in Wellington and has a full-time Secretary with much of its work being done through committees. The Association has been heavily involved in consultations and amendments to the

Building Societies Act in recent years and has also been investigating the possibility of forming a guarantee corporation.

The Financial Structure of Building Societies

Table 8.8 shows the aggregate balance sheet for New Zealand building societies in 1982.

Table 8.8 Assets and Liabilities of Building Societies, New Zealand, 1982

Liabilities	$NZm	%	Assets	$NZm	%
Deposits	200	18	Advances on mortgage	760	70
Paid up share capital	791	73	Advances on shares	19	2
Other liabilities	28	3	Financial assets	246	23
Reserves	66	6	Land and building	44	4
Retained profits	4	-	Other fixed assets	14	1
			Other assets	4	-
Total	1,088	100	Total	1,088	100

Source: *Report* of the Registrar of Building Societies for the year ended 31 March 1983.
Notes: 1. At end-1982 there were $NZ1.21 to the US dollar and $NZ2.32 to the pound.
2. Figures are the aggregation of balance sheet figures for financial years ending in 1982.

The structure of the balance sheet is similar to that of other specialist housing finance organisations although there are significant differences in respect of some of the variables. In particular -

(a) Reserves are a very high 6% of total liabilities.
(b) Holdings of liquidity, at 23% of total assets, are exceptionally high. It should be noted here that building societies, like most other financial intermediaries, are required to hold a proportion of their total assets in public sector securities. As at 1 April 1982 that ratio was 11%, and it is being increased annually by 1% a year to 16% in 1987. Bearing in mind that building societies also require more-liquid funds it is clear. why societies in New Zealand have higher liquidity ratios than those in other countries.
(c) Land and buildings were 4% of total assets. In other countries a proportion of 1% to 2% is more normal. The proportion is largely a legacy of the terminating societies and is probably now declining.

The structure of liabilities merits examination in more detail, and, fortunately, more up-to-date figures are available. These are shown in Table 8.9.

The one relevant regulatory requirement is that the amount held by way of deposit must not exceed two-thirds of the value of the total mortgage and investment portfolio. The proportion shown in Table 8.9 is actually 23%, well below the maximum but some permanent societies are close to the maximum.

Table 8.9 Classification of Shares & Deposits, New Zealand Building Societies, June 1983

Table 8.9 Classification of Shares & Deposits, New Zealand Building Societies, June 1983

Category	Amount $NZm	Percentage of Total
Investing shares	395	36
Terminating group shares	297	27
Bonus balloting shares	160	15
Savings bank deposits	14	1
Call deposits	43	4
Deposits with under a year to maturity	106	10
Deposits of one year and under two years to maturity	48	4
Deposits of over two years to maturity	32	3
Capital shares	5	-
Total	1,100	100

Source: *Reserve Bank Bulletin*, December 1983.
Note: At end-June 1983 there were $NZ1.53 to the US dollar and $NZ2.33 to the pound.

Set out below are details of the various types of account-

  (a) Investing shares are standard passbook accounts and are sometimes called call or no-fixed-term shares.

  (b) Terminating group shares are no longer allowed to be issued, but they will remain in portfolios for some time, because they represent a firm contract between a member and a society. It was these shares which gave certain opportunities to 'win' a mortgage loan.

  (c) Bonus balloting shares were introduced by the legislative amendment in 1980, and are a hybrid of call and term shares with the addition of a periodic cash prize. Generally these shares require a weekly or monthly subscription over a period of three to five years and receive a rate of interest (dividend technically) one or two percentage points below that offered on call shares.

  (d) Deposits are fairly straightforward, and, as will be seen from the table, are for varying terms. Holders of deposits, unlike shareholders, are not members of societies.

  (e) Capital shares refers to the five building societies with proprietary capital.

In June 1982 the government took power to limit rates of interest which could be paid by financial institutions. In mid-1983 societies were able to pay up to 15% depending on the type of account. (The mortgage rate is also controlled.)

Table 8.10 shows the aggregate income and expenditure account for building societies for 1982.

The somewhat unusual item of payments written off needs explanation. These largely comprise depreciation and payments for ballot loan rights which

Table 8.10 Building Societies, New Zealand, Income and Expenditure, 1982

	$NZm	$NZ per $NZ100 Mean Assets
Income		
Interest on advances	90	8.79
Interest on investments	38	3.71
Other income	9	0.88
Total	137	13.39
Expenditure		
Interest on borrowings	26	2.54
Management expenses	34	3.32
Payments written off	13	1.27
Other	6	0.59
Total	79	7.72
Excess income over expenditure	58	5.67

Source: *Report* of the Registrar of Building Societies for the year ended 31 March 1983.
Notes: 1. At end-1982 there were $NZ1.21 to the US dollar and $NZ2.32 to the pound.
2. Figures are the aggregation of balance sheet figures for financial years ending in 1982.

had to be written off because of the change in the law relating to the operation of terminating societies.

The main feature of the table is the exceptionally high excess of income over expenditure, and, moreover, a profit that, until recently, was untaxed. The figure is not untypical; the aggregate profit in 1981 was $NZ36 million. The second significant feature of the table is the high ratio of management expenses to total assets, nearly double the comparable figure in other countries. This partially reflects the large investment in land and buildings.

The Housing Corporation of New Zealand and Government Policy

The Housing Corporation of New Zealand is by the far the largest mortgage lender. At 31 March 1983, it had mortgage balances outstanding of $NZ1,906 million, that is, nearly twice the total assets of all building societies. The Corporation is also the largest single landlord and the main provider of publicly rented dwellings.

The Corporation was established under the Housing Corporation Act 1974, by which the functions of the State Advances Corporation in the housing field were amalgamated with those previously performed by the Ministry of Works and Development. The Housing Corporation of New Zealand (HCNZ) is responsible to the Minister for Housing. It has two principal functions -

(a) To give financial help to home-owners through guarantees and loans.
(b) To provide publicly owned rented housing.

New Zealand

Provision of Housing Loans

The Corporation is a non-market body. It obtains its funding directly from the government, and, moreover, at a rate of interest which is subsidized. Accordingly, it can afford to make mortgage loans at well below market rates, and it naturally follows that the demand for such loans exceeds the supply, and some rationing systems therefore has to be implemented. Until March 1979, loans were made almost entirely on new houses. However, as new houses became increasingly expensive in relation to existing dwellings there was a change of policy, so as to allow first-time purchasers to buy existing homes as well. More generally, it is the government's objective to switch mortgage finance to the private sector and to move away from using the Corporation to support the housebuilding industry.

Currently, the Corporation is willing to lend to modest income families acquiring a first home. There are fairly complicated income limits which depend partly on the number of persons in the household who are working and the number of children. A minimum personal contribution of 20% is required, although in the case of new houses this can be reduced to 12.5% except for sole persons without dependants.

At this stage, it is helpful to note a number of interesting ways in which a down payment can be provided. The first is the capitalisation of family benefit (that is, taking a lump sum instead of regular payments) which the Corporation will arrange, acting as an agent for the Department of Social Welfare. Basically, the Department will determine eligibility to capitalise. The maximum capitalisation is $NZ4,000 and it is estimated that one in five applicants for a first home use this method of raising the deposit. In the 1982/83 financial year 2,451 people capitalised family benefit; the total amount involved was $NZ8 million.

A second method of accumulating the deposit is the home-ownership savings scheme. Under this scheme there is a minimum savings period of two years, and savings of up to $NZ3,000 can qualify for various benefits and tax rebates. Accounts can be held in authorized savings institutions including building societies and savings banks. In addition to benefits and tax rebates depositors can obtain a supplemented mortgage loan of up to $NZ7,500, based dollar for dollar on qualified savings. In the 1982/83 financial year 3,106 supplemented mortgage loans were authorized for a total of $NZ16.5 million. Notwithstanding these schemes it must remain the case that the deposit which low income families have to provide can be onerous. The maximum loan provided by the Corporation is $NZ30,000 or 90% of valuation for new dwellings and $NZ25,000 or 80% of valuation for existing dwellings. The Corporation has two prime mortgage rates, 7.5% for modest income earners and 9% for borrowers who do not meet the modest income criteria. There is provision for a concessional rate of 5%, based on income and family size. The rate is increased automatically after the first three years until the prime rate is reached. The rate can be reviewed annually.

The normal loan term is 30 years and repayments are by the annuity method. However, two low-start arrangements are available, one through which interest only is paid for three years and then repayments are adjusted to a 30 year table, and the second by which reduced repayments are made for three years followed by a 27 year table.

Table 8.11 shows the distribution of loans authorized by the Housing Corporation for the 1982/83 financial year.

Table 8.11 Housing Corporation Loans Authorized, New Zealand, Year Ended 31 March 1983

Purpose of Loan	Number of Loans	Percentage of Total	Amount of Loans $NZm	%
New houses	2,064	15	55	23
Existing houses	7,308	54	149	63
Home improvement	3,599	27	28	12
Refinance	210	2	3	1
Other	255	2	2	1
Total	13,436	100	237	100

Source: *Report* of the Housing Corporation of New Zealand for the year ended 31 March 1983.
Note: At end-March 1983 there were $NZ1.53 to the US dollar and $NZ2.33 to the pound.

It will be noted that over half of loans were for existing houses rather than for new dwellings. However, the average loan on existing houses was much less than on new homes. In addition\to those loans authorized, 1,245 building suspensory loans were authorized for the value of $NZ6 million. These are short term interest free loans of $NZ5,000 to first-time buyers who are building their own houses.

A second function of the Corporation in the housing finance field is the operation of a mortgage guarantee scheme. This was introduced in its present form in 1978 and enables private mortgages to be guaranteed at no cost for up to 90% of value. In the 1982/83 financial year 4,070 loans were guaranteed in this way. There is a ceiling on the rate of interest which can be charged on Corporation guaranteed loans.

The Provision of Publicly Owned Housing

At 31 March 1983, the Corporation owned 60,500 housing units, that is, about 6% of the total. The number of dwellings administered has actually declined modestly in recent years, because sales have outnumbered new dwellings completed. The average rent at 31 March 1983 was a modest $NZ27.20 per week.

Since October 1976 new tenancies have been made subject to a six year review provision by which a tenant's need for continuation of a tenancy will be reconsidered. In association with this, a notional savings scheme has been introduced by which any rent paid above a stipulated minimum should be offered as a suspensory loan to tenants wishing to acquire homes of their own. The loan can be used towards the price of a loan and written off over ten years. By March 1983, half of the housing stock of the Corporation was subject to limited tenancies. During the year 1,112 tenants obtained suspensory loans, averaging a little over $NZ2,000 each, for a total of $NZ2.4 million.

Savings Banks

Table 8.4 shows that trustee savings banks, private savings banks and the Post Office Savings Bank are all mortgage lenders. The trustee savings banks have some 22% of the total market, the private savings banks 5% and the Post Office Savings Bank 3%.

The Post Office Savings Bank was established in 1867, and operates through 1,200 post offices throughout the country. It holds some 12% of personal deposits, but has been losing market share in recent years, largely because an unattractive rate of interest has been paid. Total assets at the end of March 1983 were $NZ2,205 million. In 1977, the bank was authorized to make second mortgage loans for terms of up to ten years, and first mortgage lending was authorized in 1983.

The private savings banks are subsidiaries of the commercial banks. There are currently four savings banks. The ANZ Savings Bank (New Zealand) Ltd is 75% owned by the New Zealand subsidiary of the Australian based Australia and New Zealand Banking Group. A second Australian bank, the Westpac Banking Corporation, owns the Westpac Savings Bank (NZ) Ltd, through its Australian savings bank subsidiary. The National Bank of New Zealand owns the National Bank of New Zealand Savings Bank and the Bank of New Zealand owns the Bank of New Zealand Savings Bank. The private savings banks are governed by the Private Savings Bank Act 1964 (all were set up in that year) and operate throughout the whole of the country. The private savings banks had total assets of $NZ988 million at 31 March 1983, but this represents a considerable decline compared with the peak figure of $NZ1,160 million at the end of 1981. The Bank of New Zealand Savings Bank accounts for about half the total assets of this group.

The most important group of savings banks in New Zealand are the trustee savings banks, which, in total, are bigger than the building societies and have larger shares of both the mortgage and the savings markets. There are 12 associated trustee banks as they are now known; five were founded in the late-19th century and the others were established between 1959 and 1964. They are constituted under a 1948 Act (new legislation is expected shortly) and are administered by government appointed boards of trustees. The banks are regional, and are each confined to a designated geographical area. They have 317 branches, and their total deposits, which are government guaranteed, at the end of March 1983 were $NZ2,778 million. The savings banks have some

50% of their assets in the form of mortgages, a proportion commonly found in savings banks in other parts of the world. They normally lend over 20 or 25 years. Until recently, interest rates were fixed for five year periods, but the interval has been reduced to three years, and now to annually. In 1982/83 these banks loaned $NZ29 million on new housing and $NZ152 million on existing housing. At March 1983, they had mortgage loans outstanding of $NZ1,273 million. They are required to invest 38% of their deposits in government securities and, in addition to mortgage loans, they can also make personal loans, purchase local authority stock and make deposits in trading banks or the Post Office Savings Bank. Table 8.12 shows the aggregate balance sheet for trustee savings banks as at 31 March 1983.

Table 8.12 Trustee Savings Bank, New Zealand, Assets and Liabilities, 31 March 1983

Liabilities	$NZm	%	Assets	$NZm	%
Personal cheque accounts	86	3	Mortgages	1,273	46
Ordinary deposit accounts	951	34	Government securities	947	34
Fixed deposit & investment			Cash & fixed deposits	249	9
accounts	1,425	51	Local authority		
Other deposits	126	5	securites	20	1
Other liabilities	189	7	Other assets	289	10
Total	2,778	100	Total	2,778	100

Source: *Reserve Bank Bulletin,* December 1983.
Note: At end-March 1983 there were $NZ1.53 to the US dollar and $NZ2.33 to the pound.

Assessment

In a speech to The Building Societies Association of New Zealand in 1981, the Registrar of Building Societies said -

'There is that old story that if one flies from Australia to New Zealand on certain airlines one is advised to set their watch ahead two hours and back 20 years. The 20 years may be an exaggeration but for building societies it must be a minimum of five.'

This is, perhaps, a little unkind but nevertheless has an element of truth. For an advanced country with a high standard of living New Zealand still has a fairly primitive housing finance system. Unlike in other countries, maximum use has not been made of mortgage guarantees with the result that high percentage loans, which in other countries are made perfectly safely, are not generally available. There has been a pre-occupation with the mortgage rate at the expense of the availability of mortgages with the inevitable result that many borrowers have been fortunate to pay well below a market rate, while others are forced to pay substantially above. The evidence of the Campbell report in Australia was that it was marginal borrowers who suffered most through such a policy, and it would not be surprising if research revealed a similar result in New Zealand.

It seems only a matter of time before the trends which have been apparent in the United States, Canada, Britain and Australia also manifest themselves in New Zealand. Already the building societies are being more closely integrated into the financial markets, and the arbitrariness of the system is causing some concern.

Bibliography

Building Societies in New Zealand, Building Societies Association (NZ) Inc, November 1982.
Burtt, D J, *The Provision of Housing Finance with Special Reference to Permanent Building Societies*, N Z Institute of Economic Research for Permanent Building Societies Association of New Zealand Inc, 1979.
Home Finance, HCNZ, 1983.
Housing in New Zealand, Five Yearly Report, National Housing Commission,June 1983.
International Savings Bank Directory, International Savings Bank Institute, 1984.
New Zealand Official Year Book 1982.
Report of the Housing Corporation of New Zealand for the year ended 31 March 1983.
Report of the Registrar of Building Societies for the year ended 31 March 1983.
'Sources of Housing Finance in New Zealand', *Reserve Bank Bulletin*, April 1978.

Acknowledgements

The co-operation of the New Zealand High Commission in London, the Building Societies Association (NZ) Inc, the Housing Corporation of New Zealand, the National Housing Commission and the Associated Trustee Banks in providing information for this chapter is gratefully acknowledged.

The author acknowledges assistance given by the following who commented on an earlier draft of this chapter: The Housing Corporation of New Zealand, Robin Hyams, Secretary of The Building Societies Association (NZ) Inc, and the Reserve Bank of New Zealand.

CHAPTER 9

FRANCE

Nearly half the French housing stock is owner-occupied; the level of owner-occupation is much higher in rural than in urban areas. A significant feature of the housing market is the relatively high proportion of second homes (9.5% in 1982).

The housing finance market is complicated, involving a number of types of financial institutions, various government incentives, and government regulated loan terms. The largest lenders are the Crédit Agricole and the Crédit Foncier, followed by the savings banks and the commercial banks. Housing finance is therefore largely provided by general, rather than specialist, financial institutions. The largest specialist lender is the Union de Crédit pour le Bâtiment, which operates largely on the mortgage bank principle.

Low income families are entitled to special government aid and all households can take advantage of a contractual housing-savings scheme. About half of loans are on 'free market' terms, generally at fixed rates of interest. Many home-buyers obtain a package combining several types of loan.

There is a limited secondary market, operated under the auspices of the Crédit Foncier de France, which also has a more direct involvement in housing finance, acting as an agent for the government.

Introduction

France covers an area of 552,000 sq kilometres. Its population in mid-1981 was 53,963,000, similar to that of the United Kingdom, West Germany and Italy. A high proportion of the population, and of industrial and commercial activity, is centred around the capital, Paris.

France is a republic, with executive power resting with a directly elected President. There are two parliamentary chambers, the National Assembly and the Senate. The presidency is currently held by a socialist, with communist support. The main opposition parties are the Union of Democrats for the Republic (Gaullists) and the Independent Republicans.

The French economy has been very successful in the post-war period; living standards have overtaken those in Britain and are near those of West Germany. Real GDP per capita increased by 3.8% a year between 1960 and 1980, the second highest rate (after Japan) of the major economies and one which compares with the OECD average of 3.1%. However, the French economy has suffered occasional crises and France has experienced a slightly higher inflation rate than the OECD average. More significantly for the housing finance market, long term interest rates have been relatively high by international standards.

Housing

The Housing Stock

Regular surveys of the housing stock are carried out by INSEE (Institute Nationale de la Statistique et des Etudes Economiques (National Institute of Statistics and of Economic Studies)). Data are also available from the ten yearly censuses.

The last available figures on housing tenure are for 1978. These show that 47.7% of households were owner-occupiers. The proportion has been increasing slowly, from 41.3% in 1962 and 44.8% in 1970. Table 9.1 shows trends in housing tenure between 1970 and 1978.

Table 9.1   Distribution of Households by Tenure, France, 1970-78

| | Percentage of Total | | |
	1970	1973	1978
Owning outright	30.6	28.1	26.8
Owning/purchasing	14.2	17.4	19.9
Renting	44.1	44.3	43.9
Free accommodation	11.1	10.2	9.4
Total	100.0	100.0	100.0

Source: INSEE national housing surveys.

It will be noted that the proportion buying in relation to those owning outright has been rising steadily, a trend that is evident in many countries. The proportion of rented housing has declined only modestly since 1962, when it was estimated at 45.3%.

About 40% of rented houses are privately owned. The remainder are owned by organisations under state control. The most important of these are the public Habitations A Loyer Modéré (HLM)(moderate rent housing) organisations. These date back to 1912. They operate within local government units and both build and manage rented housing, as well as doing a limited amount of building for sale. They are managed by 20 member boards comprising representatives of the local government unit, the tenants and the local savings bank. At the end of 1979 there were 282 of these organisations owning nearly 1,500,000 dwellings. The largest two each owned more than 50,000 units.

The other major providers of rented accommodation are-

(a) 14 public construction and development offices (OPACs) which operate more widely, geographically and functionally, than the HLM offices.
They own some 250,000 units.

(b) 386 (at the end of 1979) private HLM corporations with broad powers
in the construction of social housing, which own some 800,000
dwellings.

(c) 189 (at the end of 1979) real estate finance companies.

(d) Rental co-operatives.

Owner-occupation is far more pronounced in rural areas than in the cities.
In 1975, the level of owner-occupation was 67% in rural areas, 42% in urban
areas and only 34% in Paris.

A significant feature of housing in France is the large number of second
homes. Many families have flats in Paris and second homes in the country
which they use at weekends and for holidays. Table 9.2 shows trends in the
number of principal, second and vacant homes.

Table 9.2 Evolution of the Housing Stock, France, 1962-82

	1962 000	%	1968 000	%	1975 000	%	1982 000	%
Principal homes	14,604	89.0	15,842	86.7	17,786	84.4	19,674	83.0
Vacant homes	853	5.2	1,197	6.6	1,607	7.6	1,784	7.5
Second homes	952	5.8	1,233	6.7	1,686	8.0	2,258	9.5
Total	16,409	100.0	18,272	100.0	21,079	100.0	23,716	100.0

Source: INSEE, *Economie et Statistique*, May 1983.

Another interesting feature of the French housing stock is that the level
of amenities is relatively low for an advanced industrialized country. In 1978
as many as 21% of principal residences were without an inside toilet and 23%
were without a bath or shower.

Housebuilding

Housebuilding in France has been at a very high level in the post-war period
although there has recently been a decline, partly because of general economic
trends. Table 9.3 shows trends in housebuilding starts from 1978 to 1983.

Table 9.3 Housebuilding Starts, France, 1978-83

Year	Individual Houses	Apartments	Total
1978	278,000	162,000	440,000
1979	281,000	149,000	430,000
1980	265,000	133,000	398,000
1981	251,000	149,000	400,000
1982	220,000	123,000	343,000
1983			332,000

Source: Ministry of Housing.

The number of individual houses started has been fairly stable, rising from 241,000 in 1972 to 278,000 in 1978, before falling back to 220,000 in 1982. However, the number of apartments has fallen more substantially, from 314,000 in 1972 to 162,000 in 1978 and 123,000 in 1982.

Housing Policy

French governments generally have adopted an interventionist policy. An essential feature of the economy has been regular economic plans. However, the influence of these plans has been decreasing over time. Responsibility for housing policy rests with the Ministry of Housing. The Crédit Foncier de France (CFF) has a particular responsibility to implement certain aspects of housing policy. As will be seen subsequently there are a wide variety of types of financial assistance for housing.

A central feature of the housing finance system is the equal treatment of the rented and owner-occupied sectors, although there is a general encouragement of owner-occupation. Loans can be made for housing in either sector on the same terms and individual households can qualify for housing aid depending upon their circumstances rather than the tenure of their dwellings.

Housing policy in France underwent a major change in the late 1970s when there was a move away from subsidising housing as such and a move towards subsidising individuals with their housing costs. Also, support was made available for existing as well as new housing. However, there remains a wide variety of housing aids which, at times, must be confusing to those whom the aids are supposed to benefit.

Recently there has been some concern at whether housing is unduly favoured, and, perhaps partly in recognition of this, there has been a change in the system of administering tax relief on mortgage interest. Tax relief is available for loans only for ten years. Until recently FF7,000 a year of mortgage interest could be deducted from income in calculating tax payments. Now the system has been changed such that a set maximum (FF3,500) can be deducted from tax payments. The effect of this is to reduce tax relief at higher rates of tax and interest.

Housing Finance

The Housing Finance Market

The housing finance market is complicated. It involves a number of types of institution and a number of types of loan. The complexity derives from the fact that specialized institutions are relatively unimportant, and also because of the traditional interventionist and regulatory role of the government in the French banking system. This section gives relevant statistics for 1982 and describes briefly the relevant institutions and types of loan. The various types of loan are then discussed in more detail. Subsequent sections describe the role of the Crédit Foncier and the mortgage market and the various institutions in detail.

The present system largely originated with three reforms implemented in 1977 -

(a) A decision that housing finance would be handled by existing institutions rather than specialised ones.
(b) Commercial banks were allowed to lend beyond ten years for the first time.
(c) A secondary market facility was created to encourage a lengthening of mortgage terms beyond ten years.

Table 9.4 sets out the distribution of housing loans by type of loan.

Table 9.4   Housing Loans Outstanding by Type of Loan, France, 1982

Type of Loan	FFbn	%
Aided loans for house-purchase (PAPs)	125.5	13
Other aided loans (largely for rented property)	299.2	31
Loans to developers	21.6	2
Conventional housing loans (PICs)	20.5	2
Conventional loans (PCs)	95.7	10
Loans eligible for mortgage market other than PCs	128.5	13
Principal housing-savings loans	92.1	10
Personal savings bank housing loans	25.7	3
Other loans	153.5	16
Total	962.1	100

Source: Conseil National de Crédit, Annual Report 1982, Table 4.17.
Note: At end-1982 there were 6.86 francs to the dollar and 11.11 francs to the pound.

It is important to note that nearly one third of the loans were not for owner-occupation (the FF299.2 billion of 'other aided loans' and the FF21.6 billion of loans to developers). The other types of loan can be described briefly-

(a) PAP loans are state subsidized and are available to low income households.
(b) Conventional housing loans (PIC) are no longer issued, having been superseded by conventional loans.
(c) Conventional loans are not subsidized but are made on terms (including the rate of interest) stipulated by the government. These loans are eligible for refinancing on the mortgage market.
(d) Other loans eligible for refinancing on the mortgage market must meet certain conditions but there is no stipulation of an interest rate.
(e) Principal housing-saving loans are made to those who have completed a contractual savings scheme.

(f) Other loans are largely those where no special conditions apply.

The principal categories of loan are explained in more detail subsequently. Table 9.5 shows how the total amount of loans outstanding was divided between the principal types of institution.

Table 9.5 Housing Loans Outstanding by Type of Institution, France, End-1982

Type of Institution	FFbn	%
Non-bank financial institutions		
Caisse des Prêts aux HLM et Caisse des Depots et Consignations	246.1	26
Caisses d'épargne (direct loans)	100.9	10
Crédit Foncier de France et Comptoir des Entrepreneurs	159.4	17
Banks	436.4	43
Government	15.3	2
Total	962.1	100

Source: Conseil National de Crédit, Annual Report, 1982, Tables 4.19 and 4.20.
Note: At end-1982 there were 6.86 francs to the dollar and 11.11 francs to the pound.

Again, the various institutions are described only briefly at this stage -

(a) The Caisse des Depots et Consignations (CDC) (Deposit and Consignment Office) is a public sector body which obtains funds from the savings bank system, pension funds and other institutions and which uses them to fund public capital investment and social housing.
(b) The CDC manages the Caisse des Prêts aux HLM (CPHLM) (fund for making loans to organisations which provide moderate rent housing) which, as its name suggests, funds moderate rent housing.
(c) Caisses d'épargne are savings banks.
(d) Crédit Foncier de France is a private company, but government controlled, which plays a key role in implementing government policy towards the housing market.
(e) The Comptoir des Entepreneurs (CDE) is attached to the Crédit Foncier but it operates as a commercial housing finance organisation.
(f) Banks cover a variety of different types -

(i) Commercial banks, all of the largest of which are now nationalized. The three largest (Banque Nationale de Paris, Crédit Lyonnais and Société Générale) account for over 50% of the assets of all commercial banks.
(ii) The Crédit Agricole (agricultural credit bank) now offers a full banking service and is among the largest banks in the world.

(iii) Popular banks deal mainly with small firms and professional businesses.

(iv) Mutual credit banks are similar to popular banks but have mutual status.

In terms of housing finance it is the Crédit Agricole, the savings banks and the commercial banks which are important.

Table 9.6 brings together Tables 9.4 and 9.5 by showing, for 1982, the broad distribution of types of loan by types of institution.

Table 9.6 Distribution of New Loans to Households for House-Purchase, France, 1982

	Aided Loans		Conventional Loans		Other Free Sector Loans		Total	
	FFm	%	FFm	%	FFm	%	FFm	%
Monetary institutions	7,849	18	16,969	77	35,064	62	59,882	49
Financial establishments	741	2	763	3	4,761	8	6,265	5
CPHLM	4,659	10	-	-	-	-	4,659	4
Crédit Foncier & CDE	23,795	54	134	1	1,814	3	25,743	21
CDC & CE	4,901	11	4,105	19	11,243	20	20,249	16
Assurance companies	-	-	-	-	847	2	847	1
Public bodies	228	1	-	-	997	2	1,225	1
Employers' 1% contributions	2,236	5	-	-	1,661	3	3,897	3
Total	44,409	100	21,971	100	56,387	100	122,767	100

Source: Bank of France, *Bulletin Trimestielle*, September 1983.
Note: At end-1982 there were 6.86 francs to the dollar and 11.11 francs to the pound.

Table 9.7 New Loans on New and Existing Housing for House-purchase, France, 1982

Type of Loan	New Housing		Old Housing		All Housing	
	FFm	%	FFm	%	FFm	%
Aided loans (PAPs)	31,829	37	3,152	8	34,981	28
Other aided loans	8,826	10	602	2	9,428	8
Conventional loans (PCs)	19,219	34	2,752	7	21,971	18
Housing-savings loans	10,021	12	14,323	38	24,344	20
Other free sector loans	15,147	18	16,896	45	32,043	26
Total	85,042	100	37,725	100	122,767	100

Source: Bank of France, *Bulletin Trimestielle*, September 1983.
Note: At end-1982 there were 6.86 francs to the dollar and 11.11 francs to the pound.

France

Before considering the various types of loan in detail, it is helpful to give a slightly more detailed distribution of the types of loan for house-purchase, split into new and existing housing. Table 9.7 shows the position.

The only significant additional point in this table is the separate identification of 'financial establishments', which provide a range of services less than a full banking service.

It will be noted that a high proportion of loans (69%) were on new housing. Moreover, aided and conventional loans were predominantly for new housing while free sector loans (including housing-savings loans) were for existing housing.

There have been significant changes over time in the distribution of types of loan. Since 1979 alone, housing-savings loans have doubled their market share and PAPs have also increased. Free sector loans have, correspondingly, declined in importance.

Aided Loans

Table 9.7 shows that 37% of new lending on new houses in 1982 was aided under the PAP scheme and 10% was aided in other ways. The respective proportions for old housing (8% and 2%) were much lower.

Prêts aides pour l'accession la propriété (PAPs) (aided loans) were introduced in 1978. They are dependent on a budgetary allocation, and government has recently increased the funds available for this purpose. The loans are available to households whose incomes are below certain levels depending on the size of the household, whether the spouse is working and the area of France. The loans are made largely by the Crédit Foncier, but also by institutions which have entered into an agreement with that organisation. Loans are available for principal residences only. An existing house qualifies only if there are to be substantial improvements. There are certain requirements on floor space but no price ceilings. The maximum loan is usually 72% of cost, but it can be higher depending on family circumstances. The loan term is 15-20 years, at the discretion of the borrower, and no capital repayments are required in the first two years.

At the beginning of 1983 the rate of interest on PAP loans was 9.95% for the first five years, 12.55% for the next two, and 13.70% subsequently. These rates can be changed annually.

Other aided loans are largely made under agreements reached prior to 1977 when the housing finance system was changed. They also include loans which are supplementary to PAP loans of which there are three types (not all of which necessarily involve aid) -

   (a) Prêts complémentaires des caisses d'épargne et de prevoyance (savings bank complementary loans) which are available to borrowers who have previously had a PAP. They reduce the initial deposit to 5% or 10%. The rate is 15% or 15.85%, depending on circumstances, and the loan term is up to 20 years.

(b) Aide à la constitution de l'apport personnel (ACAP) (personal deposit aid) is available to workers in certain private non-agricultural sectors who have resources well below the PAP ceiling.

(c) Prêts bonifies du Crédit Agricole pour l'habitat des agricultureurs (Crédit Agricole loans for the housing of farm workers) are available to farm workers. The loan can be for up to 80% of cost, although not exceeding 400,000 francs. The rate is 11% for the first ten years and thereafter is unsubsidized.

At this stage it is helpful to include reference to aide personnalisée au logement (APL) (personal housing aid). This dates from 1977 and is superseding 'aide à la pierre', of which PAPs are a part. Eligibility for this assistance depends on housing costs and the resources of the household. APL is available only to purchasers of houses acquired with PAPs or conventional loans. APL is normally paid directly to lenders through the social security system.

Housing-Savings

A central feature of the housing finance system in France are the épargne-logement (housing-savings) schemes through which funds for house-purchase loans are obtained from the savings of potential purchasers. As was explained in Chapter 1, such schemes can provide only a proportion of the funds which home-buyers require, and they must be used in tandem with other loans.

The scheme began in 1965 with the introduction of the comptes d'épargne-logement (housing-savings accounts). A minimum investment of FF750 is required and subsequently deposits can be paid up to a maximum of FF100,000. A rate of interest of 3.25% p a is paid, which is tax free. If the loan is used for house-purchase a government bonus of 3.25% p a is also paid, up to a maximum of FF750. After a minimum period of 18 months, the depositor qualifies for a housing loan equal to 1.5 times his deposit. The term of the loan must be between two and fifteen years. The loan carries a rate of interest of 3.25%, together with a management charge of 1.5% p a.

The accounts were generally not considered to be successful in that they were not attracting new savings. Accordingly, in 1969 the plans d'épargne-logement (housing-savings plans) were introduced. The minimum initial deposit is FF1,500 and the maximum deposit is FF150,000. At least FF2,400 must be deposited each year and the minimum savings period is five years. The rate of interest paid is 5% p a and the government bonus is 4% p a. The loan amount is 2.5 times the amount saved at a rate of interest of 5.3% p a, plus a management charge of 1.7% p a. Again, the term of the loan must be no more than 15 years. The plans rapidly became more important than the accounts. Table 9.8 shows the growth of the system.

Table 9.8   Housing-Savings Accounts and Plans, France, 1966-82

| End Year | Number of Subscribers | | Cumulative Net Deposits | |
	Accounts	Plans	Accounts FFm	Plans FFm
1966	198,336		2,577	
1970	486,642	363,380	5,878	4,284
1975	928,316	2,925,197	12,184	44,920
1980	2,644,666	4,803,050	46,288	123,799
1981	3,008,035	4,863,863	53,638	130,906
1982	3,426,382	5,032,333	61,111	139,804

Source: Ministry of Finance, *Les Notes Bleues*, various issues.
Note: At end-1982 there were 6.86 francs to the dollar and 11.11 francs to the pound.

Deposits can be made only in certain designated institutions. At the end of 1982, 76% were held with banks, 17% with savings banks and 6% with the National Savings Bank. Within the banking sector, the Crédit Agricole has the largest market share; indeed it used the scheme to enter the housing finance market.

Loans made under the scheme must be for the purchase or improvement of property. Table 9.9 shows the evolution of lending.

Table 9.9   Housing-Savings Loans, France, 1975-82

| Year | New Units | | Existing Units | | Improvements | | Total | |
	No 000	FFm	No 000	FFm	No 000	FFm	No 000	FFm
1975	75	2,935	48	2,081	27	5,823	150	5,823
1980	153	9,140	157	9,674	157	5,898	468	24,712
1981	154	10,782	168	13,545	195	8,207	517	32,534
1982	72	8,269	179	15,214	255	12,746	507	36,239

Source: Ministry of Finance, *Les Notes Bleues*, various issues.
Note: At end-1982 there were 6.86 francs to the dollar and 11.11 francs to the pound.

It is clear that the system is huge and plays a major role in the funding of house-purchase. It is estimated that over 40% of all house-purchasers take advantage of the system.

However, the point has already been made that any system which relies on the previous saving of potential borrowers can provide only a proportion of the funds required. In 1982 the average loan was FF114,178 on new housing and FF84,801 on existing dwellings. On average, the scheme can provide only 40% of loan finance required.

There is, in fact, specific provision for 'prêts complémentaire épargne-logement' (complementary housing-savings loans) and these are used by about 20% of those taking out housing-savings loans (a third of whom also have one or more additional sources of finance). These can be made by any of the institutions operating the housing-savings scheme. The maximum amount is three times the principal loan, with an upper limit of FF450,000. The loan need not be of the same duration as the principal loan but must have a term of between two and 15 years. The rate of interest is fixed by the government and is currently 15.85%.

About 35% of housing-savings borrowers also have conventional loans, one third of whom again have additional sources of finance. Conventional loans are described in the next section.

About 17% of housing-savings borrowers have PAP assistance, about half of whom also have another source of finance.

Only a fifth of housing-savings borrowers raise no additional funds and some 25 separate loan packages can be identified. However, the combinations outlined above are the most significant.

Conventional Loans

Prêts conventionées (PCs) (generally translated as conventional loans. although more correctly as agreement loans) are important in the French housing finance system and account for 20% of new lending, although only 10% of outstanding loans. PCs accompany a third of all housing-savings loans. Broadly speaking, PCs are not state aided but they are made on terms laid down by the government.

The PCs replaced prêts immobiliers conventionées (PICs) (conventional housing loans) which were introduced in 1972. Part of these loans was subsidized by the Crédit Foncier and the remainder was on free-market terms and was eligible for refinancing on the mortgage market.

The PC scheme was introduced in 1978. PCs can be offered by any institution which has signed an appropriate agreement with the government. The major lenders are monetary institutions, the Caisse des Dêpots et Consignations (CDC) and the Comptoir des Entrepreneurs (CE).

Loans are available in respect of principal residences which are new, or old dwellings which are to be improved substantially. The dwellings must be within certain floor space and cost limits.

There are no income or other restrictions on eligibility for PCs. However, a major feature of the scheme is that borrowers meeting the appropriate requirements can obtain personal housing aid (APL). About 60% of PC recipients do obtain APL.

PCs cannot be for more than 90% of cost and the loan maturity is between 10 and 20 years. The rate of interest on PCs is set by the Crédit Foncier. Most loans are at a fixed rate 1.5%-1.75% above a reference rate published quarterly by the Crédit Foncier but there are provisions for variable rate loans. At the end of 1982 the maximum rate was 14.05% for monetary institutions and 15.55% for banks.

PCs are eligible for refinancing on the mortgage market.

Free Sector Loans

As their name suggests these loans are made on terms agreed between borrower and lender. Typically, the term is 10-20 years, the maximum percentage advance is 80% and the rate of interest is fixed. However, borrowers can often choose their repayment profile.

Employers' Housing Contribution

Most employers are obliged to invest an amount equal to 1% of their salary bills in construction by various means, largely indirect although some employers make direct loans (at 3%) or build houses themselves.

The Savings Market

The savings market is, at the same time, heavily regulated, yet very competitive. Four major types of organisation, commercial banks, the National Savings Bank, ordinary savings banks and the Crédit Agricole, compete through their branch networks. There are rate controls, especially on small deposits, but the savings banks and mutual credit banks are also able to offer tax-free accounts. Table 9.10 shows personal savings and time deposits at the end of 1981.

Table 9.10 Personal Savings and Time Deposits, France, End-1981

Type of Institution	Amount FF bn	Percentage of Total
Ordinary savings banks	429.9	34
Commercial banks	253.4	20
Crédit Agricole	218.0	17
National Savings Bank	206.4	16
Mutual credit banks	69.7	5
Popular banks	40.0	3
Other	52.8	4
Total	1,270.2	100

Source: Conseil Nationale du Crédit, Annual Report, 1981.
Note: At end-1981 there were 5.72 francs to the dollar and 10.89 francs to the pound.

The Crédit Foncier and the Mortgage Market

The Crédit Foncier

The Crédit Foncier de France (CFF) is an unusual mixture of public and private control, commercial and regulatory activity. It was founded in 1852 as a mortgage bank and its principal activities have always been the granting of loans secured by mortgages and the issuing of bonds to fund these activities. However, it has accumulated a variety of functions which it exercises on behalf of the government. It has the status of a 'financial institution with special legal status'. CFF is a private corporation owned by private share-holders. However, its senior executives are appointed by the government and its activites are decided in agreement with the government.

CFF has four principal activities -

(a) Long term loans, largely under government programmes. Table 9.6 shows that 54% of PAPs outstanding at the end of 1982 were made by CFF. It also makes aided loans for rented housing. In addition, CFF makes housing loans on free market terms, and it lends to local authorities and on shipping.
(b) The implementing of public policy, including the supervision of the mortgage market and conventional loans. It also acts as a paying agent for various government housing subsidies.
(c) The provision of a full range of banking services to institutions through 20 branches.
(d) Owning and managing real estate.

CFF finances its activities through bond issues and also direct loans from financial institutions including the CDC. Table 9.11 shows the balance sheet of the Crédit Foncier for the end of 1982.

Table 9.11   Crédit Foncier, Assets and Liabilities, End-1982

Liabilities	FF bn	%	Assets	FF bn	%
Bonds over one year	48.2	34	Long term loans over		
Other long term debt			one year	115.6	82
over one year	62.0	44	Fixed assets	0.6	-
Other medium and long			Other non-current		
term debt	5.6	4	assets	3.6	3
Current liabilities	21.1	15	Current assets	21.1	15
Provisions	2.7	2			
Revaluation surplus	1.3	1			
Shareholders' funds	0.9	1			
Total	141.0	100	Total	141.0	100

Source: Annual Report, 1982.
Note: At end-1982 there were 6.86 francs to the dollar and 11.11 francs to the pound.

The Crédit Foncier has increasingly been obtaining its resources from long term borrowing, both loans and bonds. The loans it makes are largely PAPs. In 1982 PAP commitments totalled FF29 billion out of total commitments of FF31.9 billion. (In terms of size, this makes the Crédit Foncier comparable with the Crédit Agricole.) Generally, the balance sheet is typical of that for a mortgage bank, although with a higher than usual proportion of current assets, reflecting the more wide ranging activities of the Crédit Foncier.

Table 9.12 shows the income and expenditure account of the Crédit Foncier for 1982.

Table 9.12   Crédit Foncier, Income and Expenditure, 1982

	FFm	FF per 100 FF Mean Assets
Income		
Income from loans and banking	15,208	11.8
Income from investments	72	0.1
Property and other income	34	-
Value of work done internally	5	-
Total	15,319	11.9
Expenses		
Loan and banking interest	13,117	10.2
Issue expenses and other financing expenses	261	0.2
Personnel expenses	777	0.6
Supplies and services	72	0.1
Transport and travel	10	-
Taxes other than taxes on income	107	0.1
Other overhead expenses	65	0.1
Depreciation	34	-
Provisions and transfers	421	0.3
Operating profit	451	0.4
Total	15,319	11.9

Source: Annual Report, 1982.
Note: At end-1982 there were 6.86 francs to the dollar and 11.11 francs to the pound.

Interest dominates both income and expenditure, again as is normal for a mortgage bank. Management expenses are lower than for a building society but higher than for a mortgage bank, again reflecting the other functions of the Crédit Foncier.

The Comptoir des Entrepreneurs (CDE) is attached to the CFF. It is now a normal commercial organisation which provides finance for property development, including social housing. It obtains its funds from savings banks, pension funds and provident organisations.

The Mortgage Market

France has a fairly limited secondary mortgage market, which is essentially a means through which mortgage loans can be refinanced on the capital markets. The market is controlled by the Crédit Foncier and was set up in 1966. A series of regulations set out the way the market operates. Operators in the market are lending institutions of which there were, in the middle of 1983, 151, and financial institutions which provide the finance. Before a loan can be refinanced on the market it must meet various conditions with respect to the object of the loan, the duration of the loan, the rate of interest and the circumstances of the borrower. The loan must be exclusively for the construction, acquisition or major upkeep of private houses. The property must act as security for the loan. The initial term of the loan must be between 10 and 20 years. Prior to 1966, loans for house-purchase with a duration of more than 10 years were uncommon and it was the deliberate intention to have a fairly high minimum term as one purpose of the secondary market is to encourage the provision of longer term loans. PCs automatically qualify for re-financing on the secondary market. For other loans there is no maximum rate of interest stipulated. Loans financed on the secondary market are normally at fixed rates although there are provisions for variable rates. A typical rate at the end of 1982 was 16.95%.

The borrower is required, as his personal deposit, to provide at least 20% of the funds needed to complete his house-purchase. For second homes a minimum of 50% is required.

The point has already been made that mortgage debts themselves do not circulate; rather the mortgage represents security for notes (known as mobilisation bills), which have a minimum amount of FF100,000 and a maximum of FF10 million. The rate of interest on the note and the term can be freely negotiated. The normal practice is to offer securities backed by mortgages on the primary market to different institutions. The instruments can be endorsed and freely circulated.

The mortgage market is considered to have brought about fairly quickly increased scope for borrowing long term for house-purchase. This has been achieved not primarily through the re-financing of loans but largely through the establishment of fairly uniform and not unreasonable lending criteria and the ability, if necessary, to refinance the loans.

The total amount of loans eligible for the mortgage market reached FF15 billion in 1970, FF63 billion in 1975, FF174 billion in 1980 and FF229 billion in 1982. Of the total in 1982, FF79 billion (35%) were PCs.

However, only a relatively small fraction of eligible loans have been refinanced and most of these have been refinanced within the banking sector rather than between different types of institution. Table 9.13 shows loans eligible for the mortgage market and how these loans have been ultimately financed.

Table 9.13   Mortgage Market Loans, France, End-1982

Institution	Eligible Loans		Loans Financed	
	FF bn	%	FF bn	%
Banks	167	73	179.5	78
Financial institutions	30.7	13	1.2	1
Other organisations	31.3	14	36.9	16
Other types of financing			11.1	5
Total	228.7	100	228.7	100

Source: Bank of France, *Le Marché Hypothécaire*, August 1983.
Note: At end-1982 there were 6.86 francs to the dollar and 11.11 francs to the pound.

It will be seen that the banks (including the Crédit Agricole and the mutual credit banks) dominate the market for eligible loans. The financial insititutions make loans which are financed by other organisations. The other organisations which make loans are the Comptoir des Entrepreneurs, the Caisse Centrale de Crédit Co-operatif (central bank for credit co-operatives), the savings banks and the Crédit Foncier. Insurance companies and pension funds are added to this category for financing. The table shows that the secondary market is used comparatively little to refinance by one group of institutions loans made by another group.

By the end of 1972, over half of eligible loans were refinanced but the proportion has fallen subsequently and stood at just 29% at the end of 1982. This trend is largely explained by banks and savings banks raising sufficient funds through their deposit taking activities such that they do not need to refinance on the mortgage market. Table 9.14 shows the distribution of mobilisation bills (securities backed by mortgages) at the end of 1982.

Table 9.14 Mortgage Market Mobilisation Bills, France, 1982

Institution	Bills Issued		Bills Bought	
	FF bn	%	FF bn	%
Banks	20.4	44	28.5	61
Financial institutions	18.7	40	0.2	-
Other organisations	7.6	16	18.3	39
Total	46.7	100	46.7	100

Source: Bank of France, *Le Marché Hypothécaire*, August 1983.
Note: At end-1982 there were 6.86 francs to the dollar and 11.11 francs to the pound.

This table shows the market is used primarily by financial institutions to refinance their loans and by some banks to refinance their loans through other banks. The mobilisation bills are generally placed with an accepting institution and, although they can subsequently be traded, they are normally held to maturity by that institution.

Housing Finance Institutions

UCB and Other Specialist Housing Finance Organisations

The point has been made that housing finance in France is provided largely by general banking institutions. However, there are a number of specialist institutions which merit detailed study because their method of operation differs in many respects from that found in other specialist housing finance organisations.

By far the largest specialist organisation is the Union de Crédit pour le Bâtiment (UCB) (building credit union). This organisation is part of the Compagnie Bancaire group. The parent company is not a deposit taking institution (and for this reason it was not nationalized along with other banks in the early 1980s), but nevertheless counts as one of the ten largest banking establishments in France and the 50 largest in Europe. The Compagnie Bancaire owns 33% of the share capital of UCB, the Crédit Foncier owns 21% and the Federation Nationale du Bâtiment (National Building Federation) owns 15%; the remaining 31% is held by other shareholders. UCB is a public company quoted on the Paris Stock Exchange. The Compagnie Bancaire effectively controls UCB and itself is a public comany listed on both the Paris and London Stock Exchanges. The Compagnie Bancaire is 46% owned by, and is controlled by, the Paribas Group, the fifth largest banking group in France, which was nationalized in 1982.

UCB is involved in all sectors of real estate financing, but with a concentration on housing, although not solely house-purchase. UCB operates largely as a mortgage bank but there are several features of its method of operation that are worthy of note.

Table 9.15 shows the balance sheet of UCB as at the end of 1982.

Table 9.15 Union de Crédit pour le Bâtiment, Assets and Liabilities, End-1982

Liabilities	FF m	%	Assets	FF m	%
Borrowing on mortgage market	22,407	48	Loans eligible for mortgage market	22,924	49
Short term borrowing from Compagnie Bancaire	11,441	25	Other property loans	18,159	39
Other short term borrowing	5,451	12	Other loans	2,314	5
Working finance	1,648	4	Investments	811	1
Bonds	1,131	2	Cash etc	306	1
Other liabilities	2,492	5	Property	234	1
Reserves	1,291	3	Other assets	1,645	4
Capital	532	1			
Total	46,393	100	Total	46,393	100

Source: UCB Annual Report 1982.
Note: At end-1982 there were 6.86 francs to the dollar and 11.11 francs to the pound.

It will be seen that UCB obtains no funds directly from depositors. A quarter of its funds are raised through short term borrowing from the parent Compagnie Bancaire. Nearly half of funds are raised through issuing mobilisation bills, backed by mortgages, on the mortgage market. On the assets side of the balance sheet, nearly 90% of assets are in the form of property loans; holdings of investments are minimal. A significant point is that only half of assets are in loans eligible for the mortgage market and many of the other property loans are not necessarily accompanied by a legal charge.

UCB has no direct branches but, rather, operates through 70 of its own agencies, 230 exclusive agents and thousands of other agents, including 2,700 housing developers, 7,100 estate agents, 8,700 contractors and 3,600 solicitors. UCB is therefore reliant on business being introduced to it and it raises whatever funds it needs to meet its loan commitments.

In terms of size, UCB is a huge mortgage lender. In 30 years it has helped 1.5 million families purchase their homes and outstanding loans currently amount to over FF50,000 million. In 1982, 75,000 new loans, averaging FF88,000, were made. This makes UCB as large as, for example, the third or fourth largest building society in Britain. UCB not only finances the purchase or construction of new and existing housing, but it also makes loans to finance home improvements and energy saving equipment. Of the total amount of FF8,814 million lent in 1982, FF5,102 million (58%) were free sector loans, FF1,984 million (23%) were PCs and the remaining FF1,728 million (20%) were loans to developers. However, of the amount of PCs, 68% was actually lent by banks, although the whole amount was arranged by UCB.

There is considerable cross-selling of products within the Compagnie Bancaire group. The group includes real estate and development companies, a data processing company, an insurance company and organisations which finance business equipment and consumer durables. UCB itself owns Locabail Immobilier which is a leasing company.

UCB also owns entirely Compagnie Francaise d'Epargne et de Crédit (CFEC), which is a deferred credit institution operating, in theory at least, on lines similar to a terminating building society. That is, a house-buyer commits himself to regular savings for a period after which he qualifies for a loan. Unlike the housing-savings schemes, or the contractual saving scheme

Table 9.16   Union de Crédit pour le Bâtiment, Income and Expenditure, 1982

	FF m	FF per 100 FF Mean Assets
Income		
Interest & commission	6,057	13.44
Investment income	24	0.05
Other income	2	-
Profit earned in previous years	219	0.49
Exceptional items	5	0.01
Total	6,306	14.00
Expenditure		
Interest on borrowing	4,975	11.04
Management expenses (including tax of FF70 bn and depreciation of FF6 bn)	606	1.34
Losses & provision for bad debt	119	0.26
Other provisions	30	0.07
Other expenditure	21	0.04
Tax (at 50% on profit for year of FF337 bn)	170	0.38
Net income (including FF219 bn in respect of previour year)	385	0.85
Total	6,306	14.00

Source: UCB Annual Report 1982.
Note: At end-1982 there were 6.86 francs to the dollar and 11.11 francs to the pound.

in Germany, no interest is paid on savings, nor is it charged on loans. However, in practice CFEC is merely part of UCB and to the extent that deferred interest loans are given then these are merely a method of paying off a normal loan, given at the time the house is purchased. Technically, CFEC finances a number of loans, but as far as the consumer is concerned, he has obtained a straight-forward housing loan from UCB.

UCB is the single largest borrower, through the issuing of mobilisation bills, on the mortgage market, and has been taking an increasing share of this market in recent years.

The income and expenditure account of UCB is typical of that for any mortgage bank; the figures are shown in Table 9.16.

The table is a little confusing because UCB is not a bank and does not follow normal accounting conventions. The profit earned in previous years is really irrelevant to the performance in 1982 but is included in the income and expenditure account as this is taken directly from the published accounts.

A significant feature of the table is the relatively high management expense ratio, at FF1.34 per FF100 of mean assets. This is comparable with figures for institutions such as building societies and savings and loan associations which have retail outlets. The figure is high partly because UCB has to pay commission for the introduction of business and also because the fragmented nature of the housing finance market in France means that the average loan is quite small and therefore requires a disproportionate amount of administration.

A second specialist housing finance organisation merits particular attention as it is an example of cross-frontier activity in Europe. BCT Midland Bank is controlled by the Midland Bank Group of Great Britain. It had a balance sheet at the end of 1982 of FF1,190 million, so it is much smaller than UCB. This organisation largely raises its funds on the money markets and its assets are predominantly loans.

A third specialist housing finance institution is the Banque La Henin. Consolidated total assets of the bank were FF23,811 million at the end of 1982 and it lent FF7,380 million during the course of the year. Unlike UCB, the Banque La Henin is a deposit taking bank. It has three main areas of activity -

(a) Deposit taking and banking services, primarily related to property.
(b) Loans to purchasers of property.
(c) Short term loans to developers.

The Bank owns a deferred credit institution, La Compagnie Générale de Financement Immobilier (Cogefimo). This offers a savings contract similar to that of the German Bausparkassen. Savings must be made for a minimum period of 18 months and attract a rate of interest of 5%. The rate of interest on loans is 9%. The Bank operates throughout the whole country through 126 offices. Although the Bank is a deposit taking institution it operates largely as a mortgage bank.

In addition to CFEC and Cogefimo, there are two other small deferred credit institutions: le Crédit Immobilier Européan (CIE) and L'Union d'Epargne et de Crédit pour le Financement Immobilier (UNIFIMO).

Commercial Banks

The French commercial banking system has been dominated by the big three nationalized banks. These banks account for over 50% of the business of all commercial banks. Table 9.17 shows key statistics for these banks.

Table 9.17   Big Three French Commercial Banks, End-1982

	Assets FF bn		Branches
	Bank	Group	
Banque Nationale de Paris	551.9	739.4	1,947
Crédit Lyonnais	590.4	650.5	1,835
Société Générale	520.3	576.6	1,752

Source: Annual Reports.
Note: At end-1982 there were 6.86 francs to the dollar and 11.11 francs to the pound.

Traditionally the banks have not been greatly involved in the retail market, partly because of the controls to which they have been subject. However, following financial reforms in 1966 and 1967 the banks have sought to expand their share of the personal market. Between the end of 1970 and the end of 1974 the big three banks increased their number of permanent branches from 3,517 to 5,420, the number has since increased modestly to 5,570 at the end of 1982.

The Crédit Lyonnais has been the most active bank in the personal savings and housing finance markets. It held personal deposits of FF104 billion at the end of 1982 and had housing loans outstanding of FF30.2 billion. These were mainly conventional loans. Other housing loans are made by a subsidiary, Crédit Lyonnais Immobilier (CLIM).

At the end of 1982 there were 275 other deposit banks which, together, had 4,341 branches. During 1982, 39 of the largest of these banks were nationalized.

Table 9.10 showed that the commercial banks had 20% of personal savings and time deposits. However, they had a larger share of sight deposits (42% —FF160 billion).

The Crédit Agricole

The Crédit Agricole, when considered as a single bank, is one of the largest banks in the world. However, unlike other large banks its operations are almost entirely domestic.

The Crédit Agricole has its origins at the end of the 19th century when French farmers created a series of mutual lending institutions. Regional banks were established in 1899, and in 1920 the Caisse Nationale de Crédit Agricole was set up as a public agency, to supervise, co-ordinate and develop the banking side of the organisation on a national scale. The bank has gradually broadened its activities. In 1920 it was enabled to accept deposits from all sources and in the post-war years a comprehensive range of financial services was introduced. This broadening was taken further in 1982 when the banks were authorized to offer the whole range of customer services and to lend to a larger number of businesses.

The Crédit Agricole has a complicated local, regional and national network. Locally, there are more than 3,000 Caisses Locales with over 3,800,000 members. They are governed by elected boards whose main function now is to act as credit committees. At regional level there are 94 Caisses Régionales. They have boards elected by representatives of the Caisses Locales, but are strictly autonomous. They accept deposits, make loans (generally to members) and provide banking services.

At national level is the Caisse Nationale de Crédit Agricole (CNCA), an autonomous public institution responsible jointly to the Ministry of the Economy and the Ministry of Agriculture. The CNCA supervises the activities of the Caisses Régionales. It is itself controlled by a board elected by various groups including the government and the Caisses Régionales. The functions of the CNCA include -

(a) Administering funds collected through the Caisses Régionales.
(b) Conducting international business.
(c) Representing the network to the authorities.
(d) Providing central services to the Caisses Régionales.

The whole system has 10,535 offices (although only half of these are open permanently) and employs over 70,000 people.

Table 9.18 shows the aggregate balance sheet for the Crédit Agricole at the end of 1982.

This balance sheet is more similar to that for savings banks than commercial banks, reflecting the retail and agricultural bias of the Crédit Agricole's operations. It is helpful to explain the composition of savings accounts and loans in more detail. Table 9.19 shows the breakdown of liabilities to customers.

Table 9.18   Crédit Agricole, Assets & Liabilities, End-1982

Liabilities	FFbn	%	Assets	FFbn	%
Customer accounts	454	69	Loans	383	58
Interbank transactions	95	14	Interbank transactions	181	27
Other liabilities	81	12	Securities & investments	11	2
Capital, reserves & profit	33	5	Other assets	79	12
			Fixed assets	8	1
Total	662	100	Total	662	100

Source: Crédit Agricole 1982, Caisse Nationale de Crédit Agricole, 1983.
Note: At end-1982 there were 6.86 francs to the dollar and 11.11 francs to the pound.

Table 9.19 Crédit Agricole, Savings and Bonds, End-1982

Type of Account	FFbn	%
Savings certificates	95	21
Housing-savings	69	15
Passbook accounts	66	15
Time deposits & CDs	247	54
Demand deposits	140	31
Bonds	66	15
Total	454	100

Source: Crédit Agricole 1982, Caisse Nationale de Crédit Agricole, 1983.
Note: At end-1982 there were 6.86 francs to the dollar and 11.11 francs to the pound.

Savings certificates are the major type of savings account; these are largely for three and five year terms. The point has already been made that the Crédit Agricole is the market leader in the housing-savings field with a 32% market share. Passbook accounts have proved very popular in recent years, and are often used in conjunction with other accounts, particularly demand deposits.

The Crédit Agricole concentrates its lending on farming, agribusiness, housing and regional development. Table 9.20 shows the distribution of loans made in 1982.

It will be noted that housing loans accounted for nearly half of total lending, and the Crédit Agricole has over 20% of the total housing finance market. Lending is heavily concentrated towards rural areas. In 1982, 12% of housing finance went to farmers, 73% to other people living in rural areas and 15% to urban areas. Half of all housing finance went to new building, 26% to purchasers of old housing and 23% to home improvement. Housing-savings loans are the main type of loan granted by the Crédit Agricole, followed by conventional loans.

Table 9.20 Crédit Agricole, Lending 1982

Type of Loan	Amount FF m	Percentage of Total
Principal housing-savings loans	11,864	18
Conventional loans (PCs)	8,455	13
Aided loans for house-purchase (PAPs)	5,000	8
Other loans	5,199	8
All housing loans	30,518	47
Farming	23,549	36
Agribusiness	3,057	5
Regional development	7,850	12
Other loans	142	—
All loans	65,116	100

Source: Crédit Agricole 1982, Caisse Nationale de Crédit Agricole, 1983.
Note: At end-1982 there were 6.86 francs to the dollar and 11.11 francs to the pound.

Savings Banks

The savings banks account for about a quarter of the housing finance market. They are also the dominant institution in the savings market with about half the market.

At the end of 1982 there were 468 savings banks with some 6,500 branches. They are all local institutions and can be divided into two categories -

(a) Caisses d'épargne ordinaires (ordinary savings banks).
(b) Caisses d'épargne et de prévoyance (savings and provident fund banks).

The savings banks held deposits of FF435.4 billion at the end of 1982. One reason for their huge size has been their ability to offer a tax free rate of interest on passbook accounts, as a result of which they dominate this particular market and, in turn, it is their principal source of funds.

The Caisse des Dépôts et Consignations (CDC) (Deposit and Consignment Bank) is the regulatory body for the savings banks, and it also acts as a central bank and outlet for their funds. The CDC was originally created in 1816 as a public trustee but now it is controlled by the government. In addition to its supervisory responsibilities it draws funds from savings banks, social security and provident institutions. It makes loans for housing, especially that provided by public and service bodies, and public works. It also administers various pension and insurance schemes and generally is a large institutional investor.

The National Savings Bank operates through 17,000 post offices. It had outstanding deposits of FF233.9 billion at the end of 1982.

Table 9.21 shows outstanding loans of the savings banks and CDC at the end of 1982.

It will be noted that the savings banks are active in all sectors of the housing finance market; housing-savings loans and personal housing loans are particularly important. Through the CDC, the savings banks finance aided loans (PAPs) and also rented housing by loans to the HLM organisations.

Table 9.21   Savings Banks and CDC Housing Loans, End-1982

Type of Loan	Amount FF bn	Percentage of Type of Loan	Percentage of Savings Bank Loans
Conventional housing loans (PICs)	3.0	15	3
Conventional loans (PCs)	19.2	20	19
Housing-saving loans	24.8	27	25
Complementary housing-saving loans	15.8	-	16
Personal housing loans	25.7	100	25
Loans on existing houses	8.3	-	8
Complementary loans to PAP loans	4.0	100	4
Total	100.9		100
HLM loans by CDC	23.6	15	-
PAPs made through savings banks	14.6	12	-
Other CDC loans	11.5	-	
Total	49.7	-	

Source: Conseil Nationale de Crédit, Annual Report, 1982.
Note: At end-1982 there were 6.86 francs to the dollar and 11.11 francs to the pound.

Assessment

The French housing finance system is among the most complicated in the world, certainly to the student of housing finance, and quite possibly also to the consumer. A considerable part of the market is isolated from the normal financial markets, and eligibility for particular types of loan depends heavily on the resources of the purchaser and the floor space of the house.

The system is dependent on state aid and changes in budgetary appropriations, for example, in respect of PAP loans, can have a significant effect on the distribution of loans by type. The cost of subsidising housing in France is massive and is arousing concern in some quarters, especially as there must be doubt as to whether the subsidies are being most efficiently used. The intention of the reform of 1977 was to put aid more towards the individual rather than the house, but this has not been fully achieved, as can be seen by the substantial amount of PAP loans.

Specialist housing finance institutions play a relatively small part in the French system. The banking sector, which can be subdivided into the Crédit Agricole, the savings banks and the deposit banks, is by far the major lender and France represents a fairly extreme case of a housing finance system relying largely on general rather than specialist banking institutions.

The mortgage market in France has a fairly limited function in terms of refinancing loans, but there is little doubt that it has greatly encouraged the availability of longer term loans. Future evolution of this market, and indeed of the housing finance market in general, is likely to be heavily dependent on government policy.

Bibliography

Arfeuillere, G, *Economie et Financement Immobiliers*, UCB, 1983.
Bank of France, *Le Marché Hypothécaire*, Information Note No 53, August 1983.
Bank of France, *Les Principaux Mécanismes de Distribution du Crédit*, 8th edition, March 1983.
Building Societies and the European Community, France Research Group, Volume 1 (Report) and Volume 2 (Appendices), BSA, October 1980.
Compagnie Bancaire, *Compagnie Bancaire*, 1982.
Conseil National de Crédit, Annual Report 1982.
Crédit Agricole 1982, Caisse Nationale de Crédit Agricole, 1983.
Crédit Agricole, *Welcome to the World of Crédit Agricole*, 1983.
Crédit Foncier, Annual Report, 1982.
Crédit Foncier, *Crédit Foncier de France*, 1981.
Frazer, P, and Vittas, D, *The Retail Banking Revolution*, Lafferty Publications, 1982.
'Housing Finance in France', *BSA Bulletin*, January 1981.
'Le logement en 1982' in Bank of France, *Supplement Enquete de Conjoncture*, 15 April 1983.
Les Caisses d'Epargne en 1982, Union Nationale des Caisses d'Epargne de France, 1983.
'Les Comptes Financiers du Logement en 1982' in Bank of France, *Bulletin Trimestielle*, September 1983.
Ministry of Finance, 'Epargne-Logement Bilan 1982', *Les Notes Bleues*, 24-30 October 1983.
Renaud, B, *Housing Finance; The French Contractual Savings Scheme*, World Bank Internal Paper, 1982.

Acknowledgements

The Bank of France, the Crédit Agricole, the Crédit Foncier, the Centre Nationale des Caisses d'Epargné et de Prevoyance, the Ministry of Housing and Urban Development, the Banque de La Henin and the Union de Crédit pour le Bâtiment provided information for this chapter.

The author thanks the staff of UCB, particularly Emmanuel Petit and Bernard Clappier, for their help in providing information and explaining the intricacies of the French housing finance system. Jackie Riley, Economist, Woolwich Equitable Building Society, and Bertrand\Renaud of the World Bank provided valuable information and comments.

This chapter draws heavily on the Bank of France publications, *Les Prin-*

France

cipaux Mécanismes de Distribution du Crédit and *Le Marché Hypothécaire*, and on the annual report of the Conseil National du Crédit.

CHAPTER 10

WEST GERMANY

West Germany has a lower level of owner-occupation (under 40%) than the other major West European countries. The housing finance system has a number of distinguishing features -

(a) The contract system is used more than in any other country.
(b) In addition to the contract system, the deposit taking system and mortgage bank system are also used extensively.
(c) Although most housing finance loans are provided by specialist organisations, many of these are subsidiaries of banks.

The largest group of lenders are the mortgage banks followed by the savings banks and the Bausparkassen.

Introduction

West Germany occupies an area of 249,000 sq kilometres. On the East it borders East Germany and Czechoslovakia; on the South, Austria and Switzerland; on the West, France, Luxembourg, Belgium and the Netherlands; and on the North, Denmark.

The population of West Germany at the end of 1981 was 61,538,000. The population grew rapidly in the 1950s, largely as a result of immigration from East Germany, and it continued to grow in the 1960s, helped by immigration from other countries. The population peaked at 62,000,000 in 1974 since when it has declined slightly. The population is expected to continue declining into the 1990s.

A notable feature of West Germany is that no one centre of population is dominant. Rather, there are a number of large cities but none has a population of more than two million. The largest cities are West Berlin, Hamburg, Munich and Cologne. The capital, Bonn, is comparatively small, with a population of no more than 300,000.

West Germany is a federal republic. The ten Lander have considerable autonomy. There are two chambers of parliament, the Bundestag which is directly elected, and the Bundesrat, which comprises delegates of the various Lander.

West Germany has a proportional representation system and only on a few occasions since the War have one of the two major parties, the Christian

Democrats and the Social Democrats, held an absolute majority of parliamentary seats. The relatively small Free Democrat party has held a balance of power and has frequently been able to determine the composition of the government. The Social Democrats were the dominant party in the 1970s but currently a Christian Democrat/Free Democrat coalition is in power.

The recovery of West Germany after the War is frequently referred to as the 'German Miracle'. Certainly, the German economy is very strong and the standard of living is higher than in any of the other major West European countries. Over the whole period 1960 to 1980, real GDP per capita grew by 3.2% a year, similar to the OECD average. However, in recent years West Germany has consistently grown faster than the average of other economies. The major success of West Germany has been in keeping inflation under control. Between 1960 and 1980 consumer prices increased by an average of 3.9% a year compared with the OECD average of 6.1%. For the 1973-80 period, the figures were respectively 4.8% and 10.4%. In the second half of 1983, inflation was under 3%.

The low level of inflation has contributed to a stable economy, in particular, interest rates. Long term bond rates have never reached double figures and interest rates in West Germany have generally been amongst the lowest in the World as well as being stable. This has probably contributed to the nature of the German housing finance system, in particular, to the strength of the mortgage banks which work best when long term interest rates are relatively low and stable.

Housing

Housing Tenure

There is not the preoccupation with housing tenure in West Germany that there is in other countries. Perhaps partly for this reason, accurate figures are available only from five yearly studies and no long run of comparable figures is available. Table 10.1 shows housing tenure in 1978, the latest year for which reliable figures are available.

Table 10.1   Housing Tenure, West Germany, 1978

Tenure	Densely Populated Regions		Regions with Small Agglomerations		Rural Areas		All Areas	
	000	%	000	%	000	%	000	%
Owned	4,107	30	2,744	46	1,671	51	8,522	37
Rented	9,698	70	3,198	54	1,588	49	14,484	63
All	13,805	100	5,942	100	3,260	100	23,006	100

Source: *Monograph on the Human Settlements Situation and Related Trends and Policies*, prepared for UN ECE, September 1982.

It will be seen that 37% of all housing units were owner-occupied, with the proportion being much higher in rural areas than in the urban areas. What information is available suggests that the proportion of owner-occupation in 1978 was much the same as in 1960 although substantially higher than the figure of 24% which is estimated for 1950.

Although most houses are rented, West Germany has a very high proportion of dwellings owned privately. In 1978, 79% of all units were owned privately, 16% were owned by housing enterprises, 4% were owned by financial institutions and non-profit organisations, and only 3% were owned by the public sector.

The housing enterprises have as their main function the provision of rented accommodation. In 1976 there were 1,960 such organisations of which 1,311 were housing co-operatives, 555 were limited liability companies, 61 were joint stock companies and 33 were other companies. Where the limited liability company format exists the main shareholders are municipalities, commercial enterprises, trades unions, churches, public insurance companies and the Post Office. The largest housing enterprise is Neue Heimat which is largely owned by the trades unions.

Housing enterprises have been taking a declining share of the housing market. In the 1950s they owned 30% of all dwellings, by 1974 the proportion had fallen to 18%, and in 1978 it was 15-16%. Increasingly, the enterprises are concentrating on special needs rather than the provision of general housing.

West Germany has a thriving private rented sector. Those people who become owner-occupiers tend to do so later in life than in other countries. Typically, a young couple will spend perhaps the first ten years of their lives together in rented accommodation and they may well purchase only one house in their lifetimes and this is likely to be built specifically for them. During their period of renting many people build up the deposit they need for house-purchase. It may be argued that such is the high price of housing in West Germany, that the private rented sector is essential because young people cannot afford to purchase. Equally, it may be argued that it is the private rented sector which is natural. Given a free choice many people would not wish to purchase until they are in their 30s. 40% of people are in the 40—60 age group before they become owner-occupiers and another 40% are between 30 and 40. This is in sharp contrast with, for example, the position in Britain where over 60% of households are now owner-occupiers by the time they are 30.

Housing Policy

Much of what is now West Germany was destroyed during the Second World War, and it was not until the 1960s that the acute housing shortage was overcome. The government provided massive state support for house building up until the mid-1960s. The assistance was available for both rented and owner-occupied properties which met certain minimum standards and which were to be occupied by people whose incomes were below certain levels. In the mid-1960s more aid was given to owner-occupied houses, the objective being to bridge the gap between the costs and the price people could afford to pay. By 1974 30% of dwellings built with public assistance were owner-occupied.

Most of the new dwellings which were built were flats rather than houses. Over half of all dwellings in West Germany are in blocks containing three or more units. The proportion rises to 63% in the densely populated areas.

More recently, public policy has switched towards aiding individuals with high housing costs in relation to their incomes rather than the construction of dwellings as such. As in other countries, there has also been increasing emphasis on modernization and repairs rather than on new building.

The West Germans perceive a major housing problem as being the lack of low cost housing in cities, allied with the problem of providing adequate housing for young people. Arguably, these problems are less in West Germany than in some other countries where private rented housing does not exist. However, there is little doubt that housing for owner-occupation is much more expensive than in most other countries. The average house price is some 5-8 times average earnings compared with a more normal ratio of 3-4. The average house price at the end of 1982 was approximately 300,000 marks (at the end of 1982 there were 2.42 marks to the dollar and 3.92 marks to the pound).

In 1981 the government took steps to stimulate the production of new housing by increasing the depreciation allowance on rented housing, easing rent restrictions and giving tax incentives to some home-buyers.

Housebuilding

The point has already been made that in the post War period there has been extensive encouragement of new housebuilding. In 1973, no fewer than 714,000 dwellings were completed. The number of completions has since fallen back reflecting no more than the fact that the accute housing shortage has been overcome. Table 10.2 shows housing completions from 1978 to 1982.

Table 10.2 New Housing Units, West Germany, 1978-82

Year	One Family Units	Two Family Units	Multi-Family Units	Total	Percentage Built by Individuals
1978	163,000	77,000	101,000	340,000	63
1979	157,000	79,000	97,000	333,000	69
1980	160,000	89,000	114,000	363,000	68
1981	130,000	90,000	118,000	338,000	65
1982	102,000	87,000	126,000	315,000	61

Source: *Der Wohnungsbau im Spiegel der Zahlen.*

It can be seen that there has been a fairly sharp decline in completions in recent years, this partially reflecting the general economic situation. A figure in excess of 370,000 was expected for 1983. Within the total, construction of multi-family units has actually increased while the sharpest downturn has been in respect of one family units. It will be noted that individuals are responsible for the construction of over 60% of all units, although this proportion has declined considerably from the 69% level recorded in 1979.

Housing Finance

Introduction

The West German housing finance system is relatively complicated because most borrowers obtain their finance from more than one source and also because of the inter-relationships between the various institutions. It is difficult to understand any one part of the system until the whole system is studied. For this reason, this section of the chapter gives a brief description of the major financial institutions in West Germany. The following sections describe in more detail the major house-purchase lenders and the section on the Bausparkassen also describes how a typical loan package is put together.

West Germany has a large number of financial institutions and various types of institution compete to offer industry and commerce and the personal customer a full banking service. Table 10.3 sets out key statistics of the various banking groups.

Table 10.3 Banking Groups, West Germany, End-1983

Bank Group	No	Branches	Assets Dm bn
Private commercial banks			
Big branch banks	6	3,113	236.2
Regional & other banks	100	2,514	287.5
Private banks	79	261	38.1
Branches of foreign banks	58	50	64.6
Banks incorporated under public law			
Savings banks	592	17,076	632.2
Central giro institutions	12	257	470.8
Co-operative banks			
Credit co-operatives	3,754	15,816	332.6
Co-operative central banks	9	45	126.9
Mortgage banks			
Private	25	22	255.6
Public	12	6	126.9
Bausparkassen			
Private	18	18	103.8
Public	13	-	51.6
Other banks			278.5
Total	4,848	39,821	3,035.0

Source: *Monthly Report of the Deutsche Bundesbank*, March 1984, Tables 12, 21 & 26.
Note: At end-1983 there were 2.75 marks to the dollar and 3.95 marks to the pound.

West Germany

The table shows that there are six big branch banks. In fact, this is a little misleading because three of the banks are the West Berlin subsidiaries of the other three big banks, the Deutsche Bank, the Dresdner Bank and the Commerzbank. They are full service banks and operate in the housing finance market largely through their ownership of private mortgage banks.

The regional and other commercial banks differ from the big banks largely because they do not operate throughout the whole of the country. The two largest banks, the Bayerische Vereinsbank and the Bayerische Hypotheken-u Wechsel-Bank, are both based in Munich and are similar in size to the third of the big banks, the Commerzbank.

The savings banks are major financial institutions, being the largest holders of personal deposits, and also they offer a complete banking service to industry and commerce. The banks operate regionally, and, together with the Lander (state governments), own central giro institutions which themselves have become major banks. The savings banks make house-purchase loans directly. The central giro institutions have interests in the public mortgage banks and the public Bausparkassen, and do some direct lending themselves.

The credit co-operatives are similar to the agricultural credit banks in other European countries, especially France and the Netherlands. Like the savings banks, they have regional central banks and a very strong national central bank, the DG Bank. This bank owns the largest private mortgage bank, and has a controlling interest in the ownership of the largest private Bausparkasse.

As has already been noted, the private mortgage banks are largely owned by the commercial banks while the public banks are closely connected with the central giro institutions for the savings banks.

Similarly, the public Bausparkassen are offshoots of the central giro institutions. The private Bausparkassen have varied ownership patterns. The Bausparkassen are the institutions which are the specialist housing finance lenders using the contractual system.

The Housing Finance Market

All of the institutions separately identified in Table 10.3 are active in the housing finance market. There are various ways in which the market can be analysed. Many loans for housing are not secured by mortgage and it is not easy to distinguish figures for loans for housing to households from those to domestic enterprises. Table 10.4 shows a detailed analysis of loans outstanding to domestic enterprises and individuals for housing, divided between those secured by mortgage loans and other housing loans.

Table 10.4   Long Term Loans to Domestic Enterprises and Individuals on Housing, West Germany, End-1983

Types of Institution	Housing Loans Secured by Mortgage		Other Housing Loans		All Housing Loans	
	DM m	%	DM m	%	DM m	%
Mortgage banks	164,188	34	7,067	6	171,255	28
Bausparkassen	104,129	22	10,960	9	115,089	19
Savings banks	104,232	21	41,843	33	146,075	24
Central giro institutions	52,658	11	10,108	8	62,766	10
Credit co-operatives	22,162	5	31,307	24	53,469	9
Regional and other commercial banks	22,909	5	7,342	6	30,251	5
Big banks	2,740	1	15,883	13	18,623	3
Banks with special functions	10,520	2	1,646	1	12,166	2
Other	288	-	908	1	1,196	-
Total	483,826	100	127,064	100	610,890	100

Source: *Statistiche Beihefte zu den Monatsberichten der Deutschen Bundesbank*, Reihe l, March 1984, Tables 6 & 12.

Note: At end-l983 there were 2.75 marks to the dollar and 3.95 marks to the pound.

It can be seen that no one type of institution has more than 30% of the total market and there are quite significant differences between market shares in respect of mortgage loans and other housing loans. The local retail banks, the savings banks and the credit co-operatives, are particularly strong in respect of other housing loans while the more specialist mortgage banks and Bausparkassen have the largest share of the market for loans secured by mortgage.

Table 10.4 records only long term loans. In addition, at the end of 1983, medium term housing loans totalled DM62,272 million with the Bausparkassen having 25% of this market. There were also short term housing loans outstanding of DM27,093 million of which the credit co-operatives had 19% and the Bausparkassen 18%.

Broadly speaking, the mortgage banks provide long term mortgage loans at fixed rates of interest (usually for five or ten years), financed by the issuing of mortgage bonds. The Bausparkassen also provide long term loans but at low rates of interest and only after a period of contractual saving, also at low rates. They may also provide anticipatory loans at higher rates of interest prior to the availability of a contract loan. The savings banks provide medium to long term loans, at either fixed (usually for five or ten years) or variable rates of interest. However, it should be noted that the relatively low and stable interest rates which have obtained in West Germany in recent years have meant that there has, in practice, been little variation for variable interest rates and not very much difference between the rates on the various types of loan.

The Savings Market

Table 10.5 shows the distribution of savings deposits of individuals as at the end of 1983.

Table 10.5   Savings Deposits of Individuals, West Germany, End-1983

Institution	Amount DM m	Percentage of Total
Savings banks	279,900	50
Credit co-operatives	131,076	24
Big banks	44,771	8
Regional & other commercial banks	27,570	5
Postal institutions	32,273	6
Private banks	2,886	1
Other banks	8,002	1
All banks	554,727	100

Source: *Statistiche Beihefte zu den Monatsberichten der Deutschen Bundesbank*, Reihe 1, March 1984, Table 7.
Note: At end-1983 there were 2.75 marks to the dollar and 3.95 marks to the pound.

The table again shows the strength of the savings banks and, to a lesser extent, the credit co-operatives as retail banking institutions. The big banks have a very small share, just 8%, of individual savings deposits. Table 10.3 showed that the credit co-operatives had 15,816 branches and the savings banks 17,076, very substantial branch networks by any standard. For example, both types of institution have more than twice as many branches as all British building societies put together and the savings banks have almost as many branches as the American savings and loan associations.

It should be noted that Table 10.5 does not include deposits under contractual savings schemes with the Bausparkassen. At the end of 1983, these amounted to DM123,045 million, almost as much as the amount held by credit co-operatives. The Bausparkassen are therefore huge depositories for savings, albeit those specifically earmarked for housing.

Savings Banks

Structure

The savings banks (Sparkassen) in West Germany are public sector bodies. Many date back to the 19th century and they have always been under municipal control. The banks operate only in local areas. At the end of 1983 there were 592 banks and the number is not declining rapidly as is the case in many other countries. At the end of 1983, the banks had 17,076 offices between them.

While they concentrate on the personal customer, the savings banks now provide a complete banking service to industry and commerce and they have even branched out into the international field through their central giro institutions.

Because the banks are confined to operating in small areas, they are, on average, fairly small institutions. The largest, by quite a long way, is the Hamburger Sparkasse.

Table 10.6 shows the aggregate balance sheets for the savings banks as at the end of 1983.

Table 10.6   Savings Banks, Assets & Liabilities, West Germany, End-1983

Liabilities	DM m	%	Assets	DM m	%
Individuals' savings			Long term mortgage loans	104,232	16
deposits	291,097	46	Other long term housing		
Other borrowing from			loans	41,843	7
non-banks	240,798	38	Other housing loans	9,548	2
Borrowing from banks	74,251	12	Other lending to		
Bearer bonds	2,330	-	non-banks	277,218	44
Other liabilities	2,503	-	Lending to banks	153,278	24
Capital	22,209	4	Cash & bank balances	20,751	3
			Other assets	26,318	4
Total	633,188	100	Total	633,188	
					100

Source: *Statistiche Beihefte zu den Monatsberichten der Deutschen Bundesbank*, Reihe l, March 1984, Tables 1, 2 & 6.

Note: At-end 1983 there were 2.75 marks to the dollar and 3.95 marks to the pound.

It can be seen that the banks obtain 46% of their liabilities from savings deposits of individuals. Of other borrowing from non-banks, DM88,251 million was in the form of bank bonds, so a high proportion of the total funding of the savings banks comes from the personal sector. Long term housing loans account for 23% of assets of the savings banks, a relatively small proportion compared with the position in many other countries. However, this understates the savings banks' role in the housing market. For the most part they give first mortgage loans for relatively low percentages, perhaps 40% of the cost. They offer a choice of fixed (for five or a maximum of ten years) or variable interest rates. Most German consumers still prefer fixed rate loans.

In effect, the savings banks have a greater role in the housing market through their central giro institutions and the subsidiaries of those institutions. Generally a savings bank will arrange a loan package comprising a direct loan from itself together with a loan from a Bausparkassen. This aspect of the German housing finance system will be examined in more detail subsequently.

Central Giro Institutions

There are 12 central giro institutions (Landesbanken), one for each of the

Lander. They serve as regional money centres for the savings banks in their respective areas, carrying their liquidity and providing certain services. However, they have been increasingly taking on banking business directly, both domestically and internationally. They also act as municipal banks and bankers for certain states.

At the end of 1983, the central giro institutions had assets of DM470,848 million. The composition of their liabilities contrasts very markedly with that of the savings banks. They obtained only 18% of their funds from non-banks while 25% came from banks and 52% from bonds. On the assets side of their balance sheet, long term housing loans of DM62,676 million accounted for 13% of the total. These are largely financed by the issue of mortgage bonds.

The largest central giro institution by a long way is the Westdeutsche Landesbank which is based in Dusseldorf/Munster. It was formed in 1969 by a merger of a Landesbank with a provincial giro centre. The Westdeutsche Landesbank is the bank of the federal state of North-Rhine Westphalia but it also operates world wide as a full service bank. At the end of 1983, it had total assets of DM139,400 million, 30% of the total assets of all central giro institutions. The second largest is the Bayerische Landesbank which had assets at the end of 1983 of DM100,463 million, and this was followed by the Hessische Landesbank. The Westdeutsche Landesbank counts as the third largest banking group in West Germany after the Deutsche Bank and the Dresdner Bank. Bayerische Landesbank is the sixth largest banking group and the Hessische Landesbank is the tenth largest.

Co-Operative Banks

At the end of 1983 there were 3,754 credit co-operatives (Volksbanken Raiffeisenbanken) with 15,816 branches. They are mutual institutions with over nine million members. They offer all types of banking services but concentrate on taking sight and savings deposits and on making short and medium term loans to their members. Their membership is now predominantly middle class.

At the end of 1983 the credit co-operatives had total assets of DM332,663 million. Savings from individuals comprised 39% of liabilities, and over 78% of liabilities were held by non-banks. Long term housing loans comprised DM53,469 million, 16% of total assets. The credit co-operatives lend on very similar terms to the savings banks.

Most of the individual co-operatives belong to one of eight regional co-operative central banks. In turn these eight regional banks hold 80% of the share capital of the national central bank for credit co-operatives, the Deutsche Genossenschaftsbank, or, as it is generally known, DG Bank. Like the central giro institutions of the savings banks, this operates as a universal bank. At the end of 1983, the DG Bank had total assets of DM44,352 million, and the DG Bank group had total assets of DM77,665 million, making it the ninth largest banking group in West Germany.

In terms of housing finance the DG Bank is most significant through its ownership of the largest private mortgage bank, Deutsche Genossenschafts-Hypothekenbank, which is the largest single mortgage lender in West Germany. The DG Bank also holds 62% of the share capital of a holding company which, in turn, owns 39% of the share capital of the Bausparkasse Schwabisch Hall, one of the largest private Bausparkassen. The other shareholders in this institution are the various regional co-operative central banks.

Commercial Banks

Big Banks

The three big banks, the Deutsche Bank, the Dresdner Bank and the Commerzbank, seem, at first sight, to play a relatively minor role in the housing finance market. Table 10.4 showed that they had just 3% of long term housing loans, and Table 10.5 showed that they held only 8% of deposits of individuals. However, these three banks have an importance in housing finance, and indeed in the West German economy generally, far in excess of that revealed by the crude balance sheet figures. The three banks are among the 40 largest in the world and all have extensive international business as well as being full service domestic banks.

The banks undertake relatively little direct mortgage lending, instead preferring to channel their lending through subsidiary mortgage banks. The Deutsche Bank has three mortgage bank subsidiaries, two of which are the third and fourth largest. The Dresdner Bank has four mortgage bank subsidiaries and the Commerzbank has just one, but this is the second largest. The Deutsche Bank, together with its mortgage bank subsidiaries, had mortgage loans outstanding of DM27.7 billion at the end of 1983. Not all of these loans were in respect of residential housing however; in the case of one of the subsidiary mortgage banks the proportion was 73%. On the other hand the banks have housing loans not secured by mortgages. The Deutsche Bank Group had total building loans outstanding of DM47 billion at the end of 1983, DM16 billion of which were accounted for by the Bank itself. As a group it is probably the largest single lender in the country. Table 10.7 shows key statistics for the three big banks, including their mortgage bank subsidiaries.

Table 10.7   Big Banks, West Germany, End-1983

		Deutsche	Dresdner	Commerzbank
Balance sheet total				
Bank	DM bn	117.8	85.3	66.9
Group	DM bn	210.2	160.8	113.3
Branches				
Bank		1,157	952	796
Group		1,407	1,150	884
Liabilities to customers (group)				
Demand	DM bn	19.2	14.0	8.8
Notice	DM bn	35.1	29.0	24.2
Savings	DM bn	24.0	15.5	11.3
Total	DM bn	78.3	58.5	45.3
Mortgage loans				
Bank	DM bn	4.7	2.3	3.2
Mortgage banks	DM bn	23.0	14.3	8.9
Mortgage bonds outstanding	DM bn	20.9	13.6	8.6
Mortgage bank assets	DM bn	54.5	41.5	25.7

Source: Annual reports of banks.
Note: At end-1983 there were 2.75 marks to the dollar and 3.95 marks to the pound.

Regional Banks

For the most part the regional banks have little direct relevance for housing finance. However, the two largest can be considered as a special category of bank. They are the Bayerische Vereinsbank and the Bayerische Hypotheken-u Wechsel-Bank, both of which are based in Munich. They are, respectively, the fourth and seventh largest banks in West Germany. They have a special status and are able to operate as mixed type banks, engaging both in general banking and in mortgage banking. Both have large branch networks (the Bayerische Vereinsbank had 419 offices at the end of 1982 and the Bayerische Hypotheken-u Wechsel Bank had 493 branches) and they have spread their operations outside their home Lande of Bavaria.

The Bayerische Vereinsbank had assets at the end of 1983 of DM65,295 million, and the group had assets of DM113,530 million. The group includes three mortgage banks, in which the parent bank has a majority holding, including the seventh and nineth largest. The total assets of these mortgage banks were DM40.5 billion at the end of 1983. In addition, the bank itself had mortgage loans outstanding of DM9,144 million. About 75% of its mortgage loans are to finance residential construction.

The Bayerische Hypotheken-u Wechsel-Bank had total assets of DM63,900 million at the end of 1983 and the group had assets of DM97,100 million. The Bank owns two small mortgage banks.

Mortgage Banks

Table 10.4 showed that the mortgage banks are the largest group of lenders for house-purchase, and the earlier sections of this chapter have already illustrated that the banks are not independent institutions, but rather are subsidiaries of more general financial institutions. The banks lend to all sectors of the economy; housing loans account for under half of their total lending. They lend at fixed rates for 20 to 25 years. The interest rate is fixed initially for between one and ten years and then renegotiated. They lend on first mortgage which, by law, cannot be for more than 60% of the value of a property. On average, they make loans for no more than 50% of the value of property. As will be illustrated subsequently, loans from mortgage banks are frequently combined with Bausparkasse and other loans. The mortgage banks finance their housing activities by issuing mortgage bonds of similar terms and maturities to the loans which they make.

Table 10.8 shows the aggregate balance sheet for the mortgage banks as at the end of 1983.

Table 10.8   Mortgage Banks, Assets & Liabilities, West Germany, End-1983

Liabilities	DM m	%	Assets	DM m	%
Bearer bonds	226,107	55	Long term housing loans	171,255	42
Long term borrowing	101,420	25	Other housing loans	4,427	1
Other borrowing from			Loans to public		
non-banks	7,234	2	authorities	120,303	29
Borrowing from banks	50,614	12	Other loans to non-banks	55,528	14
Other liabilities	16,785	4	Loans to banks	52,865	13
Capital	9,125	2	Other assets	6,807	2
Total	411,185	100	Total	411,185	100

Source: *Statistiche Beihefte zu den Monatsberichten der Deutschen Bundesbank*, Reihe l, March 1984, Tables 1, 2, 3 & 6.
Note: At end-1983 there were 2.75 marks to the dollar and 3.95 marks to the pound.

It will be seen that the banks obtain over half their funds from bearer bonds, and most of the remainder from long term borrowing. They are not deposit taking institutions. Long term housing loans comprise 42% of their assets. Loans to public authorities account for 29% of assets.

There are 37 mortgage banks. Of these, 12 are mortgage banks controlled by each of the central giro institutions. There are four federally owned public mortgage banks. The remaining 21 are privately owned. The assets of the private mortgage banks at the end of 1983 were DM255,604 million, 62% of the assets of all mortgage banks. The 12 public mortgage banks had assets of DM155,581 million. There is a significant difference in the composition of the loans of the two types of institution. The private mortgage banks had long term housing loans outstanding of DM89,963, 35% of their total assets.

The public mortgage banks had long term housing loans of DM81,292 million, 52% of their total assets. However, these averages conceal wide variations. The public mortgage banks have a fairly similar composition of assets, with loans being fairly equally divided between housing loans and loans to public authorities. The private mortgage banks are more diverse. Some have a high proportion of assets in housing loans, while others concentrate on specific fields of activity, such as shipping or agriculture.

By far the largest public mortgage bank is the Deutsche Pfandbriefanstalt Wiesbaden/Berlin. The federal government has a majority shareholding in this organisation, the object of which is to carry out government housing policy. At the end of 1983 it had total assets of some DM50 billion, which made it the thirteenth largest banking group. However, lending for house-purchase is not a major part of its activity; mortgage loans outstanding were some DM10 billion.

The point has already been made that the private mortgage banks are subsidiaries of the commercial banks; the latter channel applications for mortgage loans to these offshoots. Table 10.9 lists the largest seven private mortgage banks at the end of 1983, together with details of their ownership and total assets.

Table 10.9   Largest Private Mortgage Banks, West Germany, End-1983

Bank	Ownership	Total Assets	Percentage of Total
Deutsche Genossenschafts Hypothekenbank	DG Bank (100%)	26,400	10
Rheinisch Hypothekenbank	Commerzbank (94%)	25,651	10
Frankfurter Hypothekenbank	Deutsche Bank (91%)	25,100	10
Deutsche Centralbodenkreditbank	Deutsche Bank (85%)	23,900	9
Bayerische Handelsbank	Bayerische Vereinsbank (76%)	16,051	6
Deutsche Hypothekenbank Frankfurt/Bremen	Dresdner Bank (84%)	15,900	6
Suddeutsche Bodencreditbank	Bayerische Vereinsbank (54%) Bayerische Landesbank Girozentrale (25%)	13,074	5
All		255,604	100

Source: Annual reports of banks.
Note: At end-1983 there were 2.75 marks to the dollar and 3.95 marks to the pound.

It will be noted that all of the banks are owned by commercial or other banks. Also, the largest mortgage banks have no more than 10% of the total market. It is significant that the seventh largest, Suddeutsche Bodencreditbank, is effectively owned by one of the two special Munich based banks and the central giro institution for Bavaria.

Bausparkassen

The Contract Savings Principle

The contract savings system was described briefly in Chapter 1. Basically, the system involves people contracting to save a certain sum after which they are entitled to receive a loan, the amount of which is related to the sum saved. Both the savings and the loan attract a rate of interest below market levels. It is the savings of potential home-buyers which are used to provide loans to those purchasing homes. Chapter 1 made the point that the system cannot provide more than a proportion of the funds which home-buyers require. Moreover, the system is not well suited to countries where people have to purchase their first homes at an early age, for example, because of the lack of rented accommodation.

In practice, contract systems are generally partially, if not wholly, dependant on some form of government bonus. Because a contract savings loan is not sufficient to enable a house to be purchased, those offering this service must generally have a strong relationship with institutions able to provide the remaining mortgage finance.

The contract system is used more extensively in West Germany than in any other country. In confirmation of the theoretical points outlined above, it can be argued that the system is successful predominantly for three reasons -

(a) There is an adequate supply of private rented accommodation which most households are content to occupy until they are in their 30s. This gives the opportunity for contract saving.
(b) The government has provided generous bonuses to those saving under a contractual scheme. The value of those bonuses has been reduced in recent years and there has been a decline in the rate of growth of Bausparkassen activity.
(c) The Bausparkassen have strong links with other financial institutions. Indeed, one third of Bausparkassen activity is undertaken by public bodies which are offshoots of the central giro institutions of the savings banks. The private Bausparkassen are, for the most part, owned by other financial institutions.

History and Legal Framework

The Bausparkassen date back to the 1920s. The first was founded in 1924 as a division of a home owners' association in the village of Wustenrot. In 1926 it converted to a limited liability company and three years later it moved to Ludwigsburg, near Stuttgart. It grew rapidly, offering a service by which subscribers committed themselves to depositing monthly contributions while the Bausparkasse undertook to make a loan equal to the difference between an agreed contractual sum and the amount saved.

Other institutions soon followed and some 400 were set up between 1926 and 1931 although many never operated. In 1931 the private Bausparkassen were placed under the control of the supervisory body for insurance companies and this encouraged a rationalization of the industry such that by 1939 only 24 remained in what is now West Germany.

From 1928, on the initiative of the German Savings Banks and Giro Association, some 20 public Bausparkassen were set up, organized under public law and working in conjunction with savings banks.

Originally the Bausparkassen attempted to provide all the finance which home-buyers required. However, for reasons which have already been explained, this proved to be impossible and during the 1930s the partial financing principle was increasingly accepted. In 1938 the government officially stated that the main activity of Bausparkassen was to grant second mortgages and they were required to amend their methods of operation accordingly. By 1939 there were some 280,000 contracts. The system continued to grow during the War. Following the currency reform of 1948 the total assets of the system were DM99 million.

The system developed rapidly following the 1952 Dwelling House Construction Premium Act, the specific aim of which was to encourage saving for housing. This provided for those who saved with Bausparkassen to receive a supplementary contribution out of public funds equal to 25-35% of the amount saved (up to a set maximum), in addition to interest due. This made Bausparkassen contracts attractive to savers as well as to potential home-buyers.

The Bausparkassen Law of 1972 placed all Bausparkassen, from 1 January 1974, under the supervision of the Federal Banking Supervisory Office. The law confines Bausparkassen to the contract saving business and related activities.

The private Bausparkassen are all members of a trade association, the Verband der Privaten Bausparkassen (Association of Private Bausparkassen), based in Bonn, while the public Bausparkassen are all members of the Bundesgeschaftsstelle der Landesbank-Sparkassen (Association of Public Bausparkassen) a branch of the Deutscher Sparkassen-und Giroverband (German Savings Banks and Giro Association), also based in Bonn.

Bausparkassen Activity

The contract saving system operated by the Bausparkassen is basically fairly simple. The saver may contract for any amount and he agrees to deposit a certain amount each year, generally 5% of the contract sum. The average sum contracted is currently about DM35,000. The saver can elect to receive interest at the rate of 2.5% or 4.5% a year. The interest paid by the Bausparkasse is tax free up to a limit of DM400 (DM 800 for a married couple). A government savings bonus of 14% (plus an additional 2% for each child under 18) of the amount saved each year is paid up to a maximum of DM800 (DM1,600 for a married couple). It is this bonus which has been cut over the years, reducing the attractiveness of Bausparkassen accounts. Until 1975 the bonus was 25%; in that year it was reduced to 23%, in 1976 to 18%, and in 1982 to the present level of 14%. The bonus is tax free. However, to be eligible for the bonus a family's taxable annual income must not exceed DM48,000 plus DM1,800 for each child under the age of 18. For a single person the annual income limit is DM27,000. These income ceilings was first set in 1975 and subsequently have not been increased. Those with incomes above the income limits can still participate in the contract system by claiming tax deductions rather than a bonus.

Once the saver has deposited a minimum of 40% or 50% (depending on tariff he has chosen) of the contractual sum he is entitled to the entire contractual amount. The loan is therefore equal to the difference between the original contractual amount and the amount saved. However, there is no automatic entitlement to a loan because there is no guarantee that the Bausparkasse will have funds available to meet the requirements of all of those who are entitled to a loan. When the demand for loans exceeds the supply, loans are distributed according to a system based on the time elapsed since the savings contract commenced and the regularity of savings.

The Bausparkasse loan carries a rate of interest of 4.5% (if the 2.5% savings rate was selected) or 5.75% (if the 4.5% savings rate was selected). It is normally repaid over 10 or 12 years. The point has already been made that the loan from the Bausparkasse will be combined with a loan from another institution. The entire package is described subsequently.

Table 10.10 shows the activity of the Bausparkassen over the period 1973-1983.

Table 10.10   Bausparkassen Activity, 1973-83

Year	Net Increase in Contracts 000	Contracts Outstanding 000	Savings Paid in DM m	Building Loans Made DM m	Total Assets Dm m
1973		13,787	19,000	21,084	70,435
1974	1,189	14,976	19,052	18,028	77,686
1975	1,121	16,097	20,241	19,298	86,952
1976	1,241	17,338	22,070	21,404	94,906
1977	1,267	18,605	23,678	23,356	102,153
1978	1,285	19,890	25,707	25,903	111,223
1979	1,297	21,187	27,863	30,990	121,932
1980	1,477	22,664	27,437	31,220	132,501
1981	838	23,502	27,134	31,744	142,979
1982	310	23,812	25,677	28,570	149,655
1983	247	24,059			155,392

Source: 'Recent Developments in Building and Loan Association Business', *Monthly Report of the Deutsche Bundesbank*, April l983; 1983 figures are from Deutsche Bundesbank.
Note: At end-l983 there were 2.75 marks to the dollar and 3.95 marks to the pound.

Several points emerge from this table -

(a) At the end of 1983 there were over 24 million contracts outstanding, an average of nearly one per household. However, for reasons which will be explained later some households have more than one contract.

(b) The net increase in the number of contracts has declined sharply since 1980, probably reflecting the reduction from 18% to 14% in the savings premium, which was announced in 1981 and which came into effect in 1982.

(c) Correspondingly, savings paid in 1982 were no higher than in 1978.

(d) Building loans made have also been relatively stagnant over the past few years.

(e) Total assets of the Bausparkassen have grown relatively modestly compared with those of other institutions. For example, between the end of 1977 and the end of 1982 the assets of Bausparkassen grew by 46.5% compared with a growth rate of 69.9% for the mortgage banks and 52.4% for the savings banks. (To the extent that these figures seem relatively small compared with growth rates of financial institutions in other countries it should be remembered that West Germany has experienced an exceptionally low rate of inflation.)

Table 10.11 shows the combined balance sheet for Bausparkassen at the end of 1983.

Table 10.11   Bausparkassen, Assets and Liabilities, End-1983

Liabilities	DM m	%	Assets	DM m	%
Deposits from non-banks			Building loans	139,169	90
under savings contracts	123,045	79	Other lending to		
Other deposits from non-banks	3,123	2	non-banks	513	-
Deposits & borrowing from banks	15,045	10	Lending to banks	13,454	9
Provisions	2,771	2	Other assets	2,256	1
Capital	6,551	4			
Other liabilities	4,857	3			
Total	155,392	100	Total	155,392	100

Source: *Statistische Beihefte zu den Monatsberichten der Deutschen Bundesbank*, Reihe 1, March 1984, Table 11.
Note: At end-1983 there were 2.75 marks to the dollar and 3.95 marks to the pound.

It will be seen that deposits under savings contracts made up 79% of total liabilities. Otherwise, the Bausparkassen are not deposit taking institutions and they have no branch networks, although they do have offices to attract new business. Building loans comprised 91% of total assets. Because the Bausparkassen take deposits only under a savings contract, they have no need to hold significant liquid assets. It should be noted that of the building loans outstanding, 20% were not loans under the contractual scheme. These loans may be bridging loans or what are called anticipatory loans, the function of which is explained subsequently.

Table 10.12 shows key statistics for the two groups of Bausparkassen.

Table 10.12   Public and Private Bausparkassen, End-1983

	Private		Public		All
Number	19	(58%)	13	(42%)	32
Total assets DM m	103,805	(67%)	51,587	(33%)	155,392
Building loans DM m	93,075	(67%)	46,094	(33%)	139,169
Number of contracts	15,897,000	(66%)	8,162,000	(34%)	24,059,000
Sum contracted DM m	577,758	(70%)	250,593	(30%)	828,351

Source: *Statistische Beihefte zu den Monatsberichten der Deutschen Bundesbank*, Reihe 1, March 1984, Table 11.
Note: In end-1983 there were 2.75 marks to the dollar and 3.95 marks to the pound.

It will be seen that the public Bausparkassen are smaller in number and in size than the private institutions. Most of the public Bausparkassen are departments of the central giro institutions of the savings banks, although some are owned by the savings banks and others have a varied ownership including organisations of public banks and regional associations of savings banks. They are generally known as Landesbausparkassen. They operate within individual states only and are generally known as Landesbausparkassen. The largest, substantially, is that for Munster/Dusseldorf, which had assets of DM14,085 million at the end of 1982. This is part of the Westdeutsche Landesbank Girozentrale group, the largest central giro institution and the third largest banking group. Table 10.13 lists the largest six Landesbausparkassen.

Table 10.13   Largest Six Landesbausparkassen, End-1982

Name	Total Assets DMm	Percentage of Total
Landes-Bausparkasse Munster/Dusseldorf	14,085	28.5
Bayerische Landesbausparkasse	8,138	16.5
Landesbausparkasse Wurttemberg	6,844	13.9
Landes-Bausparkasse Hannover/Braunschweig	5,192	10.5
Landesbausparkasse Hessen	2,702	5.5
Badische Landesbausparkasse	3,650	7.4
All	49,370	100.0

Source: LBS-Bundesgeschaftsstelle, *Jahresbericht 1982*, 1983.
Note: At end-1982 there were 2.42 marks to the dollar and 4.30 marks to the pound.

The private Bausparkassen have varied ownership patterns. Table 10.14 shows the largest seven together with details of their ownership and assets.

Table 10.14 Largest Private Bausparkassen, End-1983

Name	Base	Ownership	Assets DM m	Percentage of Total
Beamtenheim-Stattenwerk (BHW)	Hameln	German Federation of Trades Unions (50%) Civil Servants Trade Union (50%)	32,500	31
Schwabisch Hall	Schwabisch Hall	DG Bank (80%) Co-operative regional central banks (20%)	30,800	30
Wustenrot	Ludwigsburg	Private	21,000	20
Leonberger	Leonberg	Allegemeine Rentenstalt (Insurance company) (54%) Dresdner Bank (25%)	5,900	6
Mainz	Mainz	Deutscher Herold (Insurance company) (15%) Rest is privately owned	2,100	2
Badenia	Karlsruhe	Aachen-Munchener Versicherungsgruppe (59%) Karlsruher Lebensuersicherung (25%) (Insurance companies)	1,900	2
Heimbau	Cologne	Hamburg-Mannheimer Versicherung (Insurance company) (100%)	1,700	2
All	103,800	100	103,800	100

Source: Balance sheets.
Note: At end-1983 there were 2.75 marks to the dollar and 3.95 marks to the pound.

Of the 18 private Bausparkassen, 16 have the status of joint stock companies and the other three are private limited companies. They all operate on a nationwide basis. The largest is the BHW which is owned by the trades unions. The second largest is the Bausparkasse Schwabisch Hall which, as has already been noted, is owned by the DG Bank, the central bank for credit co-operatives, and the regional banks for the co-operatives. The third largest is the Wustenrot Bausparkasse. This is a wholly owned subsidiary of a holding company, Wohnungswirtschaft Wustenrot Verwaltungs- und Fiananzierungs—Gesellschaft, which had relatively modest total assets of DM 116.9 million at the end of 1982. It is helpful at this stage to explain the Wustenrot group in some detail as it illustrates the close inter-relationships between the various financial institutions in West Germany. The Bausparkasse has a 90% interest in the Hausbau Wustenrot which is a major building company. It has a 60% interest in Wustenrot Lebensversicherungs, a life insurance company, and a 100% interest in the Wustenrot Stadtebau- und Entwicklungs-Gesellschaft, which is active in urban and municipal renewal projects. It also has a 25% holding (the parent company having a 50% holding) in a private bank, the Wustenrot Bank AG fur Wohnungswirtschaft. This bank had total assets at the end of 1982 of DM5,644 million, making it about the 80th largest bank in the country. The Wustenrot's connection with the life insurance company and the bank are particularly important as it obtains much of it business from those sources and its loans are frequently combined with those of the insurance company and the bank.

Aggregated figures for income and expenditure of the Bausparkassen are not readily available. However, it is helpful to set out those figures which are available as the Bausparkassen are the only large specialist institutions in the world operating on the contract principle. Table 10.15 shows a very simplified income and expenditure account for all Bausparkassen for 1981.

Table 10.15   Income and Expenditure Account, Bausparkassen, 1981

	DM m	Percentage of Balance Sheet Total
1 Net interest received	3,908	2.86
+2 Net fees & commissions	272	0.20
-3 Administrative expenses	2,544	1.86
=4 Operating result	1,636	1.20
-5 Excess of other expenses over receipts	1,112	0.83
=6 Profit	509	0.37

Source: 'Recent Developments in Building and Loan Association Business', *Monthly Report of the Deutsche Bundesbank*, April 1983.
Note: At end-1981 there were 2.27 marks to the dollar and 4.30 marks to the pound.

Table 10.16   Income and Expenditure, Wustenrot Bausparkasse, 1982

	DM m	DM per 100 DM Mean Assets
Income		
Interest	1,187	5.72
Fees to customers	249	1.20
Other revenue	96	0.46
Total	1,532	7.38
Expenditure		
Interest	615	2.96
Commission on new contracts	88	0.42
Depreciation & adjustment	85	0.41
Staff costs	234	1.13
Operating expenses	157	0.76
Taxes etc	192	0.92
Other expenses	105	0.50
Total	1,476	7.11
Net income	56	0.27

Source: *Wustenrot Annual Report 1982*, 1983.
Note: At end-1982 there were 2.42 marks to the dollar and 3.92 marks to the pound.

This table can usefully be analysed in conjunction with a more detailed income and expenditure account for one particular Bausparkasse. Table 10.16 shows the figures for the Wustenrot for 1982.

The Wustenrot seems not untypical given the average figures for 1981. At first sight the administration expenses seem high, being above those for building societies in the United Kingdom and savings and loan associations in the USA, both of which operate extensive branch networks and which offer a limited retail banking service. However, it has to be remembered that the Bausparkassen are dealing with relatively small loans which means fairly high administration costs. Customers pay substantial fees to the Bausparkassen while they in turn pay commission on new contracts. This commission may often be paid to related organisations in the same group.

The Loan Package

It is now helpful to bring together the various types of financing to explain how an individual finances the purchase of his home. This will demonstrate the importance of the inter-linking between the various financial institutions.

It may seem at first sight that the potential home-buyer has to begin a savings contract with a Bausparkasse and not until this is completed is he able to purchase a home. Many potential home-buyers do follow this course of action but in other cases the Bausparkasse loan is seen a something desirable in its own right and it is used to pay off other short term loans from institutions with which the Bausparkassen are connected. At this stage it should be noted that normally a loan from a Bausparkasse (which will always have a second charge over the property), together with any loans secured by a first charge, cannot normally exceed 80% of the valuation of the property for loan purposes, although a slightly higher percentage can be allowed if additional security is available. The purchaser therefore has to have substantial savings in order to complete the purchase.

Set out below are various examples of loan packages -

(a) A regular customer of a savings bank may well have a savings contract with the related Bausparkasse. When he requires a loan this is likely to be made up of a package of a direct loan from the savings bank secured by a first mortgage, a contract loan from a Bausparkasse if he qualifies, or, if he does not qualify, a short term housing loan from the savings bank which will be repaid when the Bausparkasse loan becomes available. Table 10.4 shows that the savings banks accounted for 32% of 'other housing loans' at the end of 1983 and these other loans were equal to 28% of their total outstanding loans.

(b) Similarly, a customer of a credit co-operative may have a package comprising three elements: a loan from the mortgage bank subsidiary of the DG Bank (the central bank for credit co-operatives), a Bauspar-kasse loan from the Schwabisch Hall Bausparkasse (a subsidiary of the DG Bank) and a short term loan from the credit co-operative itself until the Bausparkasse loan is available. Again, Table 10.4 shows that the credit co-operatives have a large share of other housing loans (ie loans not secured by mortgage).

(c) A customer of a commercial bank is likely to have a loan directly from the mortgage bank subsidiary of the commercial bank, a Bausparkasse loan from a related Bausparkasse, and a short term loan from the bank itself.

(d) The point has already been made that the Bausparkassen have 20% of their loans other than in the form of contract loans. It is possible for a Bausparkasse to allow someone to enter into a savings contract and simultaneously to grant a short term loan which will be repaid by the contract loan perhaps four to seven years later. Indeed, the Bausparkasse could make a loan for 8-14 years to be repaid by two successive Bausparkasse contracts. The Bausparkassen do some direct business in this way but the extent to which they are able to do so is limited by the availablity of funds. Either they have to borrow funds for such direct lending outside the contract system, making them nearer to general banks, or alternatively they have to form a link with other financial institutions. Most have chosen this latter course. While it is therefore theoretically possible for the Bausparkassen to provide a complete loan package they seldom do so.

(e) A private Bausparkasse which may not have any established links with other institutions may set up subsidiaries to make direct loans which it cannot finance itself. It has already been noted in this respect that the Wustenrot owns an insurance company and a private bank, both of which make long term housing loans.

At first sight these arrangements may seem very complicated. In practice, however, they are not because a package will be put together, most likely by the institution with which the potential home-buyer has an established contact. An investor with a savings bank, for example, will find that that savings bank will be prepared to arrange a loan from the mortgage bank subsidiary from the central giro institution for the savings bank, a Bauspar-kasse contract with the Bausparkasse subsidiary of the central giro institution, and will provide direct finance itself. A single payment can be made to cover all three loans and, indeed, the borrower may not be fully aware of how his loan is financed. The precise nature of the package will depend on the cir-cumstances of the house-purchaser, in particular his tax position and whether he will qualify for a bonus or tax deduction with his Bausparkasse contract. As the Bausparkasse system has become less attractive as a result of the reduc-tion in government premiums it might be expected that fewer people will use it, preferring to rely more directly on first mortgage loans from savings banks and mortgage banks.

Assessment

The West German housing finance system is one of the most interesting in the world because it combines elements of all three types of housing finance system, the contract system, the deposit taking system and the mortgage bank system. As in other countries the whole system has adapted to meet prevailing circumstances. The growth of the Bausparkassen probably owes much to government incentives introduced in the 1950s to stimulate housebuilding. As those incentives have gradually been reduced so the role of the Bausparkassen has tended to diminish slightly.

Although the housing finance system seem complicated it is not, simply because of the close inter-relationships between the various types of institution. However, there is a considerable amount of double intermediation (ie money flowing from ultimate lender to ultimate borrower via two institutions) and although most institutions provide a comprehensive service, they do it through subsidiaries rather than directly. At first sight it may seem fairly cumbersome for a savings bank to arrange a loan with a subsidiary of a central giro institution of which it itself is a member.

The West German housing finance system has not suffered any great problems over the last few years simply because the economy itself has been very stable with inflation and interest rates being kept at levels well below those of other countries. This has enabled mortgage banks to operate effectively through making long term fixed rate loans without the problems which have arisen in other countries, and also the relative attractiveness of the Bausparkasse system to those who do not want loans has been retained. It may legitimately be argued that the housing finance system in West Germany could not have operated in any other country because West Germany alone has had the combination of low and stable interest rates, a plentiful supply of rented accommodation and two large networks of retail financial institutions, savings banks and credit co-operatives. Arguably, had West Germany not had this combination of circumstances then it might have developed a very different housing finance system.

Bibliography

Building Societies and the European Community, Report of Working Group B, West Germany, The Building Societies Association, 1978.
Federal Ministry for Regional Planning, Building and Urban Environment and Federal Ministry of Economics, *Federal Republic of Germany, Monogragh on the Human Settlements Situation and Related Trends and Policy*, prepared for United Nations Economic Commission for Europe, September 1982.

Frazer, P and Vittas, D, *The Retail Banking Revolution*, Lafferty Publications, 1982.
Lehmann, W, *Short History of the German Thrift and Home Ownership Movement*, International Union of Building Societies and Savings Associations, 1982.
'Recent Developments in Building and Loan Association Business', *Monthly Report of the Deutsche Bundesbank*, April 1983.
The Banking System in Germany, Bank-Verlag Koln, 1982.
Wustenrot Annual Report 1982 (English Edition), 1983.

Acknowledgements

The co-operation of the Deutsche Bundesbank, the London branches of German banks, the West German Ministry of Regional Planning, Building and Urban Environment, the Halifax Building Society, the Verband der Privaten Bausparkassen and the Deutsche Sparkassen—und Giroverband (German Savings Bank and Giro Association) in providing information for this chapter is gratefully acknowledged. The statistics produced by the Deutsche Bundesbank have been drawn on particularly heavily.

The author thanks the following for their helpful comments on an earlier draft of this chapter -

Dr Friedrich Brych, Justitiar, Bayerischen Landesbausparkasse
Dr Schubaus, Verband Deutscher Hypothekenbank.

CHAPTER 11

ITALY

Italy has a high level of owner-occupation, and the proportion of owner-occupied houses has increased significantly over the past 20 years. As in other continental European countries owner-occupation tends to be higher in the rural than in the urban areas.

Perhaps the most distinguishing feature of the housing finance system in Italy is its small size. Compared with other West European countries, mortgage loans outstanding are very low compared with variables such as national income or the value of the housing stock. House-purchase is financed to a large extent informally, outside of the institutional framework. That institutional framework which does exist operates through the mortgage bank system although the institutions providing the loans are either departments of the commercial banks or savings banks or they are subsidiaries of those banks. The banks make loans directly but these are not easily identifiable as being for house-purchase.

Introduction

Italy covers an area of 301,000 sq kilometres. Its population in 1982 was 56,448,000. It is therefore similar in terms of size and population to West Germany, France and the United Kingdom. The population grew quite rapidly during the 1970s, by an annual rate of 0.7%. The principal cities are Rome (the capital), Milan, Naples and Turin.

Italy is a republic. It has a bicameral parliament, elected on a direct vote. The president is elected by the parliament and regional representatives, and has some constitutional rights. The government is headed by the prime minister who is appointed by the president. Italy is well known for its frequent changes of government. Since the war the Christian Democrats have been the largest single party, but they have never had an absolute majority of parliamentary seats. The current government was formed in 1983 and is a five party coalition headed by a prime minister from the Socialist Party.

In terms of economic performance, Italy has done comparatively well in respect of growth but less well in respect of inflation and interest rates. Real GDP per capita grew by an annual rate of 3.7% between 1960 and 1980, compared with the OECD average of 3.1%. The increase in consumer prices has been significantly above the average of other industrialized countries, particularly in recent years. Between 1973 and 1980 consumer prices rose by an average annual rate of 17% compared with the OECD average of 10.4%. While other countries have been successful in bringing inflation under control in recent years, Italy has been far less successful. Consumer prices rose by 21.2% in 1980, 17.8% in 1981 and 16.5% in 1982. The high level of inflation has contributed to a steady decline in the exchange rate. The lire fell by some 44% against the dollar between 1980 and 1982.

Similarly, interest rates have been at a very high level in Italy. The central bank discount rate was in the 18%-19% range in 1982, although it fell to 17% in September 1983, and to 16% in Februry 1984. Bonds yielded over 20% in 1982, falling to 17% in mid-1983 and 16% in early 1984.

Housing

The 1981 census revealed that there were 17,547,000 first homes in Italy, of which 59% were owner-occupied. The proportion of owner-occupied dwellings has been rising rapidly. Table 11.1 shows trends in housing tenure of first homes.

Table 11.1   Housing Tenure, Italy, 1961-81

Year	Owner-Occupied		Rented		Other		Total
	No	%	No	%	No	%	
1961	5,972,000	46	6,076,000	47	984,000	8	13,032,000
1971	7,767,000	51	6,769,000	44	766,000	5	15,301,000
1981	10,350,000	59	6,221,000	36	976,000	6	17,547,000

Source: Census figures.

The change in the tenure pattern since 1971 is particularly significant.

In 1961 there were 18,537,000 households in Italy, 4,323,000 more than the number of houses and 5,505,000 more than the number of first houses. By 1981 the number of households had increased to 22,414,000, still higher than the number of houses (21,853,000) and 4,867,000 more than the number of first houses. In this respect the housing situation has improved comparatively little since 1961. A significant feature of the housing situation in Italy is the high number of second homes. The proportion increased from 8.3% in 1961 to 12.3% in 1971 and to 19.7% in 1981, probably the highest proportion in the world and relevant in the context of an excess in the number of households over the number of houses. It may also be noted that only 24% of dwellings in Italy are single family homes.

Rented housing in Italy is, for the most part, owned privately. Insurance companies and pension funds are major landlords.

Housing Policy

Although the government has not been a significant direct supplier of housing in Italy it has played an interventionist role in the housing market. There is a limited amount of subsidized rented accommodation, financed directly by the state. In addition, there is assisted housing which is constructed by private developers or co-operatives, but financed by credit institutions, with the interest costs being partly covered by the state. In certain areas there is also regulated housing, which is similar to the assisted housing. However, it is the open market housing which provides most accommodation.

The Italian housing market has been depressed in recent years, partly because of the high level of interest rates. Another factor has been a 1978 law, by which the public sector was given rights to appropriate any area as a public utility and to keep it indefinitely. This has had the expected effect of deterring development.

In 1982 a package of measures was introduced to help stimulate activity in the housing market; these included a reduction of VAT on property transfers until June 1984 and an increase in tax relief on mortgage interest, which had originally been introduced in 1972.

The Banking System

The Division into Long Term and Short Term Institutions

The central feature of the Italian financial system is the fairly rigid division between institutions with power to issue medium and long term liabilities and those with power to have short term liabilities only. Short term is defined as up to 18 months, medium term is from 18 months to five years and long term is over five years. Other significant features of banking are that all institutions operate under the same legislation, the Banking Law of 1936 as amended, and all are supervised by the central bank, the Bank of Italy. The government plays a central role in the financial system, not least through its ownership of most of the major banks.

In general the banks' operations can be short term only, and normally they are unable to lend for terms beyond 18 months. However, to a limited extent they are able to make loans up to five years, and in practice they have increasingly been allowed to make loans for longer terms. Loans of over 18 months duration are made by special credit institutions which may either be distinct organisations in their own right or rigidly defined sections of the commercial and savings banks. However, the separate institutions are mostly owned by the banks. There is, therefore, what is called the double intermediation system in Italy. Deposits are made with the banks which then lend funds to special credit institutions which then make long term loans.

The Italian banking system can be divided into the following categories of institutions -

(a) Six public chartered banks which are owned by the state and various public bodies.
(b) Three banks of national interest in which the major shareholder is the state holding company, IRI (Istituto per la Ricostruzione Industriale). These banks can operate throughout the country, and in practice are very similar to the public chartered banks. Both groups of banks operate as independent institutions notwithstanding their public ownership.
(c) 159 ordinary credit banks which have a joint stock or partnership form of ownership. Most of these are privately owned. Their number has been diminishing recently.
(d) 153 co-operative banks. In terms of their functions they are similar to ordinary banks, but they are mutual institutions.
(e) 87 savings banks and 11 pledge banks.
(f) 672 small rural and artisan banks.
(g) 27 branches of foreign banks.
(h) A postal savings system.
(i) 88 special credit institutions, largely controlled by the public chartered banks, the banks of national interest and the savings banks. The institutions are responsible for medium and long term lending.

Table 11.2 shows the total assets of the various bank groups as at the end of 1982.

Table 11.2   Bank Groups, Balance Sheet Totals, Italy, End-1982

Type of Bank	Total Assets L bn	Percentage of Total
Ordinary credit banks	221,182	28
Public chartered banks	157,433	20
Savings banks	148,842	19
Banks of national interest	125,407	16
Co-operative popular banks	95,128	12
Rural and artisan banks	18,374	2
Subsidiaries of banks	20,714	3
Total	787,078	100

Source: Bank of Italy, *Bollettino*, June 1983, Table B19.
Note: At end-1982 there were 1,355 lire to the dollar and 2,369 lire to the pound.

It will be seen that the ordinary credit banks are the largest group of banks followed by the public chartered banks, and then the savings banks and the banks of national interest. The general commercial banks (the public chartered banks and banks of national interest) are therefore smaller in aggregate than the more specialized banks, an unusual situation in international terms.

However, the largest banks are the banks of national interest and the public chartered banks, although the largest savings bank is the sixth largest bank in the country, and is only marginally smaller than the fourth and fifth largest banks. Table 11.3 lists the largest banks as at the end of 1982.

Table 11.3   Largest Banks, Italy, End-1982

Bank	Category	Assets L bn	Branches Total	Fully Function- ing
Banca Nazionale del Lavoro	Public chartered	54,762	379	244
Banca Commerciale Italiana	National interest	46,911	394	305
Banco di Roma	National interest	34,806	333	265
Istituto Bancario San Paolo di Torino	Public chartered	33,632	361	253
Monte dei Paschi di Siena	Public chartered	28,769	418	379
Cariplo	Savings	26,507	441	366
Credito Italiano	National interest	22,233	452	323
Banco di Napoli	Public chartered	21,900	489	476
Banco di Sicilia	Public chartered	14,863	317	296

Source: Annual reports of banks.
Notes: 1. At end-1982 there were 1,355 lire to the dollar and 2,369 lire to the pound.
　　　　2. Figures are for total assets less those of the special credit sections.

It will be seen that the six largest banks comprise three public chartered banks, two banks of national interest and one savings bank.

One notable feature is the relatively small number of branches owned by the largest banks when compared with their assets size. The banks have branches classed as fully functioning, and other units which either offer a counter service only or which are in the premises of other organisations.

The Savings Market

The various banking institutions are also the principal holders of household savings. However, in the recent past there has been a switch away from bank

Table 11.4   Households' Financial Saving, Italy, 1963-81

Type of Saving	Percentage of Total Outstanding			
	1963	1972	1977	1981
Bank deposits	27.9	37.6	55.4	45.9
Short term securities	-	-	2.8	13.6
Shares	23.7	6.2	10.7	8.5
Postal deposits	9.1	8.5	9.3	7.6
Notes & coins	8.9	7.9	7.3	5.8
Foreign assets	7.5	9.8	4.8	2.4
Other interest-bearing deposits and bills	1.9	3.1	2.3	1.9
Other	7.5	8.1	7.2	6.3
Total	100.0	100.0	100.0	100.0

Source: Monti, M, Cesarini, F and Scognamiglio, C, *Report on the Italian Credit and Financial System, Banca Nazionale del Lavoro Quarterly Review*, June 1983.

deposits and towards holdings of short term securities, in particular Treasury securities. This disintermediation is causing considerable concern in banking circles. There has also been a switch away from fixed interest securities, a development of relevance to the financing of house-purchase. Table 11.4 shows the changing composition of households' financial assets from 1963 until 1981.

The table shows a sharp decline in holdings of shares (equity investments such as common stock or ownership stock), a development paralleled in other countries. Bank deposits increased as a share of financial savings until 1977, but subsequently have declined sharply at the expense of short term securities.

It is helpful to analyse the composition of personal deposits by type of bank. Table 11.5 shows the figures.

Table 11.5 Personal Sector Bank Deposits, Italy, End-1982

Type of Bank	Deposits L bn	Percentage of Total
Savings banks	72,314	30
Ordinary credit banks	61,412	25
Public chartered banks	43,745	18
Co-operative popular banks	41,363	17
Banks of national interest	25,980	11
Other	4	-
Total	244,817	100

Source: Bank of Italy, *Bollettino*, June 1983, Table B16.
Notes: 1. At end-1982 there were 1,355 lire to the dollar and 2,369 lire to the pound.
         2. The personal sector comprises households, unincorporated businesses and non-profit organisations.

The table shows, not surprisingly, that the savings banks are the largest holders of personal deposits (it should be noted that the figures include deposits held by unincorporated businesses and non-profit organisations). The ordinary credit banks are the second largest holders of personal sector deposits with the larger commercial banks some way behind.

Housing Finance

The Size of the Housing Finance System

Perhaps the main distinguishing feature of the housing finance system in Italy is the relatively small size of the formal sector. By definition, this makes it difficult to analyse housing finance, because of the relatively weak role of institutions.

The Bank of Italy has attempted to estimate the importance of various forms of financing. Table 11.6 shows estimates of credit flows for new construction and repairs in 1981.

Table 11.6 Financing of Investment in Housing, Italy, 1981

Source of Funds	Amount L bn	Percentage of Total
Public funds for subsidized housing	1,038	5
Loans by special credit institutions	1,978	9
Loans by banks	3,302	15
Loans by other institutions	151	1
Domestic saving	15,754	71
Total	22,223	100

Source: Bank of Italy Report 1981 (English edition), Table 39.
Note: At end-1981 there were 1,129 lire to the dollar and 2,287 lire to the pound.

This table suggests that no less than 71% of investment in housing in Italy in 1981 was financed by domestic saving, that is, the use by individuals of their own saving. Only 25% was financed by loans. It is important to note also in this respect that the table includes both financing of investment by households and by enterprises. In 1981 of the total loans of L5,431 billion, a little over half went to enterprises, although many of these loans are subsequently transferred to households. Over 80% of direct loans to households for housing were by banks, although these are not generally recorded as formal mortgage loans.

A second way of demonstrating the small size of the formal housing finance market in Italy is to compare the amount of mortgage debt outstanding with a variable representing the size of the economy, for example, GNP. Table 11.7 shows the figures for selected industrial countries.

Table 11.7 Identified House Mortgage Debt in Relation to National Income, End-1982

Country		Identified House Mortgage Debt	GNP	Debt/GNP %
Japan	Yen bn	40,355	263,939	15
Switzerland	SF bn	132	206	64
USA	$ bn	1,254	3,073	41
UK	£ bn	76	271	28
France	FF bn	962	3,460	28
Canada	$ bn	127	357	36
Italy	L bn	26,775	465,790	6
Germany	DM bn	595	1,599	37

Sources: GNP figures are taken largely from *International Financial Statistics*, December 1983.
House mortgage debt figures are taken from the various chapters in this book.

The table needs to be treated with extreme caution and it is certain that the figures for identified house mortgage debt are not comparing like with like. Nevertheless the table is sufficient to indicate the huge differences in the size of the formal mortgage market in the various countries. Of the countries listed, Italy has by far the lowest ratio of mortgage debt to national income (although it must be stressed that there is no relationship between the two variables). One of the reasons for the relative modest size of the mortgage market in Italy is the fact that housing finance is relatively underdeveloped compared with other countries. High percentage loans over long periods are not common. The high rates of interest which have been recorded in the recent past have also deterred people from taking out loans to buy houses. However, it should be noted that the figure for Italy excludes loans by banks which cannot be identified for housing purposes but which are for this purpose.

The Housing Finance System

The point has already been made that the Italian financial system provides for a sharp division between short term banking institutions and long term lenders. However, this rigid division is less apparent in practice. Theoretically the main providers of mortgage loans should be the special credit institutions. The nature of the special credit institutions is considered in detail in the following section of this chapter.

There are provisions for some state assisted loans which can be given only by special credit institutions. Until 1978 all the schemes for assisted lending were to finance new housebuilding. Under a 1980 law assisted loans can be given to finance house-purchase or contruction by individuals. Loans are at low rates of interest, between 4.5% and 9%, depending on household income. However, the rate is linked to the consumer price index and is gradually increased over time. There are three forms of non-assisted loans -

(a) Fixed rate loans.
(b) Loans with a rate of interest variable according to an interest rate index.
(c) Loans that are indexed to prices.

Attempts have been made to formulate a contractual housing finance scheme but these have not been successful.

Mortgage rates have been at 20% in the past few years, reflecting the general high level of interest rates in the economy. Loans made by the special credit institutions now normally carry a rate of interest that is linked to money market rates and is varied at six monthly intervals. Loans are for ten years or longer. These institutions are able to make low percentage loans only, generally up to 40% of value. There is normally up to a six month waiting period for a loan from a special credit institution.

Notwithstanding their limitation to lending short term the banks (including the savings banks and the ordinary credit banks) are, by various methods, able to make some longer term loans for house-purchase and as Table 11.5 has shown are larger contributors to the financing of investment in housing (although not necessarily directly to house-buyers) than the special credit institutions. Loans are generally available from banks with a shorter waiting period and this source is used predominantly by higher income people. No reliable statistics are available on direct bank lending to finance house-purchase.

Special Credit Institutions

At the end of 1981 there were 89 special credit institutions in Italy. Of these, 47 were sections of banks (most large banks having more than one section) and 42 were separate corporate bodies. The banks own most of the capital of the separate bodies, and the sections must be operated relatively independently of the main bank, although they cannot have a separate corporate identity.

Of the 89 special credit institutions, 21 are specifically related to mortgage credit. Of these 12 are sections of banks and the remaining nine are separate corporate institutions. Table 11.8 lists the largest real estate special credit institutions as at the end of 1982.

Table 11.8 Largest Real Estate Special Credit Institutions, Italy, End-1982

Institution	Mortgage Loans Outstanding	
	L bn	Percentage of Total
Sanpaolo Bank	4,242	16
Cariplo	4,413	16
Banca Nazionale del Lavoro	3,393	13
Credito Fondiario	2,669	10
Istituto Italiano di Credito Fondiario	2,606	10
Monte dei Paschi di Siena	1,485	6
Banco di Sicilia	1,470	5
Other	6,497	24
All	26,775	100

Source: Balance sheets of institutions.
Note: At end-1982 there were 1,355 lire to the dollar and 2,369 lire to the pound.

It is necessary to describe the ownership of each of these institutions -

(a) The Sanpaolo Bank is the generally accepted abbreviation for the Istituto Bancario San Paolo di Torino, a public chartered bank. Although it is shown as the second largest institution it is accepted as being the largest since 1982. This is because it treats bad debts differently from Cariplo.

(b) Cariplo is the largest savings bank.

(c) The Banca Nazionale del Lavoro is a public chartered bank and the largest bank in Italy.

(d) The Credito Fondiario (Mortgage Credit Bank) is an organisation in its own right, owned by the three banks of national interest, Banca

Commerciale Italiana, Banco di Roma and Credito Italiano. These banks do not have special credit sections. It is the largest separate real estate credit institution, with assets of L4,321 billion at the end of 1982.

(e) The Istituto Italiano di Credito Fondiario (Italian Institute for Mortgage Credit) is also a separate organisation. It is 49% owned by the Bank of Italy, the central bank.

(f) Monte dei Paschi di Siena is a public chartered bank.

(g) Banco di Sicilia is also a public chartered bank.

The Operation of the Special Credit Institutions

Table 11.9 shows lending on housing by the real estate special credit institutions and, for comparison, total lending by all of the institutions.

Table 11.9   Net Lending by Special Credit Institutions, Italy, 1981-82

	1981 L bn	1982 L bn
Lending by real estate institutions		
On subsidized housing	652	854
On unsubsidized housing	1,890	1,605
On all housing	2,542	2,459
Lending by all institutions	13,233	14,652

Source: Bank of Italy Report, 1982, Table 39.
Note: At end-1982 there were 1,355 lire to the dollar and 2,369 lire to the pound.

It will be seen that most lending is on unsubsidized housing, although between 1981 and 1982 there was a sharp increase in lending on subsidized housing and a significant decline in lending on unsubsidized housing. This partially reflects the depressed state of the housing market and the high cost of free market mortgage loans.

Most of the lending by the special credit institutions is to housebuilders rather than to individual home-buyers. Of net lending in 1982, only L1,782 billion was to households, substantially less than the total lending on housing. The loans are given initially to housebuilders but subsequently are transferred to house-purchasers.

The special credit institutions fund their activities largely through bond issues. The real estate institutions account for about 12% of total bond issues. There has recently been a marked change in the distribution of the types of their bonds, with the financially indexed variety becoming more popular at the expense of fixed rate bonds. Table 11.10 shows the distribution of net issues of bonds in 1982.

Table 11.10   Net Issues of Bonds by Real Estate Special Credit Institutions, Italy, 1982

Type of Bond	Net Issues L bn
Fixed rate	2,170
Real indexed	170
Financially indexed	1,610
Total	3,950

Source: Bank of Italy Report, 1982.

Many of the fixed rate bonds are in respect of subsidized housing and are placed at yields below a market rate. Variable rate bonds and those with capital indexation are largely taken up by banks.

Until about 1976, the bonds were specifically called mortgage bonds and were exactly matched with mortgage loans. In other words the loan was made first and then financed by selling the bonds. Since 1976 the process has been reversed. Bonds, as opposed to mortgage bonds, are issued and the proceeeds are used to make loans. However, the effect is much the same, that is that assets and liabilities are matched.

The banks are required, through agreement with the Bank of Italy, to buy certain amounts of bonds issued by the real estate credit institutions and agricultural credit institutions. For example, in 1983 the banks had to invest 5.5% of the increase in their deposits in these bonds. However, this requirement is being eased as part of an attempt to integrate the housing finance market more fully into financial markets generally. In 1982 all the special institutions' bonds were given a special tax concession to encourage private individuals to buy them.

Table 11.11 shows the combined assets and liabilities of the real estate special credit institutions at the end of 1982.

Table 11.11   Real Estate Mortgage Credit Institutions, Italy, Assets & Liabilities, End-1982

Liabilities	L bn	%	Assets	L bn	%
Bonds	28,534	75	Mortgage loans	26,775	70
Loans from banks	166	-	Other loans	442	1
Other loans	845	2	Bad debts	1,703	4
Other liabilities	6,637	20	Bonds	2,232	6
Reserves	1,167	3	Cash & bank balances	828	2
Capital	904	2	Shares of other institutions	164	-
			Excess of market value of bonds over book value	1,384	4
			Other	4,725	14
Total	38,254	100	Total	38,254	100

Source: Bank of Italy, *Bollettino*, June 1983, Table C1.

The table is fairly typical of that for a mortgage bank. The comparatively low proportion of assets and liabilities represented by bonds and loans is explained largely by the high figures for other liabilities and assets which, to a significant extent, are transactions within a group and cancel each other out.

Compiling an income and expenditure account for the institutions is far from easy and there is no certainty that the data are comparable. Published figures certainly show wide variations around the average. Table 11.12 shows calculations for the income and expenditure account for 1981.

Table 11.12 Real Estate Credit Institutions, Italy, Income and Expenditure 1981

	Lire bn	Lire per 100 Lire Mean Assets
Income		
Interest from loans	2,682	11.4
Other interest	455	1.9
Other income	23	0.1
Net income from services	38	0.1
Total	3,198	13.6
Expenditure		
Interest on bonds	2,186	9.3
Other interest	67	0.3
Personnel expenses	178	0.8
Other management expenses	126	0.5
Provisions	465	2.0
Tax	83	0.4
Net profit	93	0.4
Total	3,198	13.6

Source: Derived from Franco, D, *Contributi Alla Ricerca Economica*, Bank of Italy 1983.
Note: At end-1981 there were 1,129 lire to the dollar and 2,287 lire to the pound.

Perhaps the most distinguishing feature of the table is the high figure for provisions and the resulting large margin between the interest paid on bonds and that received on loans. Some of these provisions are for depreciation and, to that extent, can be counted as management expenses. Generally, however, they are provisions for bad debts. Over the years there has been a significant increase in provisions in relation to mean assets, and also in management expenses. It should be noted here that there are huge differences between the management expense ratios of the various institutions. The two large separate institutions have ratios in the 0.3—0.4% range, not untypical for a mortgage bank. The sections of the banks have ratios as high as 2.0%. This could reflect different accounting policies as much as real differences. The simple interest margin increased from 1.54% in 1975 to 3.75% in 1981. Net profits have fluctuated quite considerably but have tended to be on a rising trend.

Savings Banks

It has already been noted that the savings banks are major retail institutions, holding 30% of personal sector bank deposits, more than any other type of bank. They are also significant mortgage lenders directly, making loans for up to 25 years, but no figures for this activity are readily available. At the end of 1980 there were 87 savings banks, which had 3,469 branches between them. Most are grouped into regional federations and they have a central institution, Italcasse. Unlike in other countries there is no strong merger movement. Rather, the trend has been towards the provision of services centrally. Like other financial institutions, the savings banks are public bodies with a somewhat complicated ownership and control system.

The savings bank industry is dominated by one bank, Cassa di Risparmio delle Provincie Lombarde, generally known as Cariplo. At the end of 1982, this bank had assets of L26,507 billion and it operated from 441 branches. The assets of Cariplo account for 27% of the total assets of savings banks in Italy. Cariplo merits some attention in its own right as it claims to be the largest savings bank in the world, and can rightly be considered as such if the groups of agricultural credit banks, the Crédit Agricole in France and the Rabobank in The Netherlands, are excluded. The bank was established in 1823 and its mortgage credit section dates back to 1867. Its activities are concentrated, as its name suggests, in the province of Lombardy, but it now operates throughout the country, and indeed has a significant international business, with a branch in London and representative offices in five other financial centres. Table 11.13 shows the balance sheet for Cariplo, incorporating the activities the real estate special credit section.

Table 11.13 Cariplo, Assets and Liabilities, End-1982

Liabilities	L bn	%	Assets	L bn	%
Savings deposits	5,568	16	Mortgage loans	4,413	13
Balances with customers	12,004	34	Other loans to customers	9,291	26
Bonds of mortgage			Balances with credit		
credit institutions	4,212	12	institutions	4,659	13
Other bonds	2,722	8	Cash & securities	9,089	26
Other funds	2,246	6	Investments & shares	523	1
Other liabilities	8,312	24	Other	7,089	20
Total	35,064	100	Total	35,064	100

Source: Cariplo Annual Report 1982.
Note: At end-1982 there were 1,355 lire to the dollar and 2,369 lire to the pound.

This balance sheet is not typical of that for a savings bank. Rather, it is similar to that of commercial banks. Savings deposits are a relatively small proportion of total liabilities and a high proportion of balances with customers are in the form of current accounts. On the assets side of the balance sheet, mortgage loans account for 13% of the total. The real estate credit section had total assets at the end of 1982 of L5,097 billion, loans accounting for 87% of the total.

Report on the Italian Credit and Financial System

The chapters on the English speaking countries noted that most had been subject to official committees of enquiry in respect of their financial systems in recent years and that there had been a general increase in competition between specialist and general financial institutions. The nature of financial systems in continental European countries is quite different from those in the English speaking countries but, nevertheless, similar trends can be discerned. The major European countries have also been subject to enquiries into their financial systems. In the case of Italy the enquiry was a very modest one lasting just one year and conducted by three commissioners, Mario Monti, Francesco Cesarini and Carlo Scognamiglio. The report was presented to the Italian Treasury in January 1982; an English version was published in June 1983. Some of the recommendations of the report have already been acted on.

The report describes the Italian credit and financial system and approaches to credit and financial policy in the 1980s. The report commented on the distinguishing feature of the Italian financial system, what can be described as the double intermediation process, with two institutions (one of which may be a section of the other) being involved in transforming deposits into longer term loans. The report noted that there had been a process of despecialization between the various categories of banks and also between the banks and the special credit institutions. It has already been noted, for example, that banks have been able to lend for longer terms than the 18 months which used to be normal, and the special credit institutions have also been given slightly wider fund raising powers. Another phenomenon which the Commission noted was that administrative constraints on banks, such as loan ceilings and investment portfolio constraints, had led to a certain substitution of bank loans by mortgage loans made by the special credit institutions, in particular those concentrating on industrial activity. The Commission considered that the special credit institutions should be discouraged from shorter term operations.

In line with the development of views in other countries, the Commission suggested that careful consideration should be given to leaving to interest rates, rather than to administrative controls, the task of deciding the distribution of financial resources between the short and long term needs of the financial markets and between the different institutions and operators in the market. Where direct assistance was required then this should be provided by direct payment of grants to the sectors concerned.

The Commission went into some detail on the question of the ceiling on bank loans. It commented that it was a widely held view that the ceiling had led to serious problems. Among the disadvantages it listed were -

(a) The policy has been costly in terms of the credibility of monetary policy and that by different devices the banks have always managed to evade the controls.
(b) To the extent that it is effective the ceiling means reduced availability and increased cost of credit to firms.
(c) The ceiling reduced the profitability of banks.
(d) The ceiling encouraged the intermediation by special credit institutions, and new financing channels.

Ceilings on bank lending also used to apply differentially according to the size of the loan, the economic sector in which the loan was used, and whether the loans were domestic or foreign. This discrimination had largely been abolished. The Commission recommended the abolition of the requirement that the banks should invest a certain proportion of the increase in their deposits in securities issued by special credit institutions granting housing loans or agricultural loans. Subsequently, steps have been taken to remove some of the rigidities in the Italian banking system. In June 1983 bank ceilings were replaced by 'moral' limits, and these were lifted in early 1984.

Assessment

The housing finance system in Italy is comparatively underdeveloped in relation to the state of development of the country generally. The size of the mortgage market is small compared with that in other countries and the financing of house-purchase is done to a large extent outside of the normal institutional framework. This may reflect the fact that the country is, to a large extent, still rural but it must also be a reflection of the nature of the financial system.

Theoretically, long term loans are available only from the special credit institutions but these institutions work in such a way that it is necessary for people to wait some months before they can obtain loans. The mortgage bank system has been used by these institutions but the high level of interest rates which has obtained in Italy in the recent past has deterred people from taking out long term loans. It has also encouraged the use of variable rate loans. Loans are more readily available from banks, financed by shorter term deposits, but the banks are constrained in their ability to give such loans.

Although the system does not seem well developed it is significant that Italy has a higher level of owner-occupation than France and West Germany, so clearly people have not been prevented by the system from becoming owner-occupiers.

Bibliography

Bank of Italy Report 1982 (English Edition).
Dini, L, *Housing Finance in Times of Inflation*, European Community Mortgage Federation, 1982.
Monti, M, Cesarini, F and Scognamiglio, C, *Report on the Italian Credit and Financial System, Banca Nazionale del Lavoro Quarterly Review*, June 1983.
'The Disintermediation of the Banking System in the 1980s: Problems and Prospects', *Review of Economic Conditions in Italy*, Banco di Roma, June 1982.
The Italian Banking System, Credito Italiano, 1982.

Acknowledgements

The co-operation of the Nationwide Building Society, the London office of the Bank of Italy, the London branches of the Italian banks, the Banco di Roma, and the Credito Fondiario in providing information for this chapter is gratefully acknowledged. The author is indebted to Dr Maria Luisa di Battista of the University Cattolica del Sacro Cuore, Milan, for her assistance in providing information and explaining in detail those aspects of the Italian housing finance system which are not readily apparent from the literature, and for her detailed comments on a draft of this chapter. The Research Department of the Bank of Italy also made helpful comments on the draft, and Luisa Pilla, Statistics Officer of the BSA, corrected errors in my understanding of Italian terms.

CHAPTER 12

SPAIN

For many years Spain has had one of the highest levels of owner-occupation in Europe. In 1970, the latest year for which detailed figures are available, 64% of dwellings were owner-occupied, 27.5% were rented, and the remaining 8.5% were held in some other form of tenure.

The largest lenders for house-purchase are the savings banks, which, as in other continental European countries, are very strong. They have some 60% of the market, the remainder being shared by the commercial banks and the government controlled Mortgage Bank of Spain. The latter has recently been increasing its involvement in the housing finance market, largely at the expense of the commercial banks. Loans are generally made at fixed rates of interest. The high rates of inflation and of interest which have been recorded in recent years have been causing problems for the housing market. There has been a significant change in the mortgage market over the last few years; funds can now be raised through medium term bond issues.

Introduction

Spain occupies an area of 505,000 sq kilometres. Together with Portugal it forms the Iberian peninsular. In the North East, Spain borders on France but otherwise the peninsular is surrounded by sea. Spain's population in 1982 was 37,935,000. It is less densely populated than most of the other West European countries. Spain is a constitutional monarchy with a one chamber parliament, the Cortes. In 1982 a socialist government was elected to power for the first time.

In economic terms, Spain is somewhere between most of the other Mediterranean countries and the more prosperous West European countries. GNP per capita is less than half that in France and West Germany but twice the level of Portugal and substantially higher than that in Greece.

In terms of economic growth, Spain has performed comparatively well in recent years. Between 1960 and 1980 real GDP per capita increased by an average of 4.4% a year compared with the OECD average of 3.1%. However, Spain has been less successful at keeping inflation and interest rates under control. Consumer prices increased by an average of 10.6% a year between 1960 and 1980 compared with the OECD average of 6.1%. The difference was more marked in the latter part of the period. Between 1973 and 1980 the rate of inflation in Spain was 17.9% a year compared with the OECD average of 10.4%. The high rate of inflation has contributed to a high general level of long term interest rates, and this, in turn, has caused problems in the housing market. Both inflation and interest rates have been at about 15% a year over the last few years.

Housing

There were 10,760,000 dwellings in Spain in 1981. The latest figures available in respect of tenure are for 1970. These show that 64% of dwellings were owner-occupied, 27.5% were rented and 8.5% were held in some other form of tenure. The proportion of owner-occupied dwellings increased during the 1960s.

Investment in housing in Spain has, by international standards, been high, with completions averaging over 300,000 a year in the 1970s. The government has played little direct role in housebuilding and fewer than 10% of new homes in recent years have been built by public authorities. However, about half of new houses have been built with some form of state aid. The government has adopted an interventionist policy with respect to housing construction but the effects have not always been those that were intended.

An official housing programme for 1981-83 planned the construction of 571,000 homes. In 1983 the plan was to build 195,000 homes, of which 30,000 would be publicly funded and the other 165,000 privately funded. The actual number built in 1982 was 201,000 of which 63% had some form of government subsidy.

The housing market has been very depressed in recent years, partly because of the economic depression. In early 1983 the unemployment rate in the construction industry was as high as 30% compared with the general rate of 17%.

Housing Finance

Introduction

Housing finance in Spain is provided largely on the deposit taking basis. The major lenders are the confederated savings banks which have some 60% of the market. The second major group of lenders are the commercial banks, but their market share has been declining in recent years and now stands at about 20%. The third major lender is the Mortgage Bank of Spain, a government owned body. This has been increasing its activity markedly in recent years, and has also been concentrating more on housing at the expense of its other activities. It now accounts for about 20% of the market. It also acts as an agent for the government in implementing certain housing policies and, generally, it has some similarities with the Crédit Foncier in France.

The government plays a significant and interventionist role in the housing finance market, partly through regulating rates of interest. There is also provision for the financing of what is called 'officially protected' housing. In 1978 the Law on Official Protection of Housing Units laid down certain criteria which must be met by houses which qualify for preferential finance -

(a) A maximum area of 90 sq metres.
(b) A maximum selling price related to the area of the country. In the case of rented housing the maximum rent is 6% of the selling price.
(c) Houses can be developed either by individuals or by companies, with or without the profit motive. This marked a significant liberalisation as previously official support was available only in respect of housing developed by non profit making institutions.
(d) The housing must be used as a principal residence.
(e) Low income families in protected housing can qualify for personal housing aid.
(f) Houses built by the public sector are available only to very low income families.

The scheme provides for a base loan which is available from the various financial institutions which lend for house-purchase. This can be for up to 70% of the cost for both the developer and the purchaser. The purchaser pays a rate of interest of 11% over ten years. Any difference compared with market rates, up to 3%, is made up by the government.

Personal housing aid is also available to low income families buying low cost housing under the official protection scheme. Complementary loans for 15-20% of the purchase price are available at a rate of interest of 11% over 13 to 16 years. There is a low start arrangement. These loans are available only from the public sector credit bodies. There is also provision for a zero interest loan, which has the effect of deferring the interest payment in the early years of the base loan.

Loans for house-purchase are not easily identifiable from the statistics, partly because many are made in the form of personal loans, topping up loans secured by a charge on the property.

An attempt has been made to operate a contractual system, but this has not been very successful. The current system works as follows. An individual applies to a savings bank to open a housing savings account and states the amount he plans to save as well as the period over which he intends to do so. The savings earn a rate of interest mutually agreed. Once the predetermined amount has been reached the person asks the savings bank for a corresponding loan for house-purchase. The loan entitlement is two to four times the amount saved and the rate of interest is not more than 3% above the savings rate. There are also some tax benefits. The scheme has not been successful largely because people will not commit themselves to the savings.

Recently, the government has made provision for a mortgage market under the supervision of the Mortgage Bank of Spain. The market has the following features -

(a) Lending institutions may liquidate mortgage assets through the mechanism.
(b) Loans eligible for refinancing must not be more than a certain percentage of the value of the property.
(c) Government loan insurance is available.
(d) Refinancing takes the form of mortgage bonds and certificates. The minimum maturity of the instruments is three years. Accordingly, rates of interest on loans are variable at three yearly intervals (or longer intervals when longer term bonds are issued) marking the first significant attempt to introduce variable rates into the Spanish housing finance system.
(e) Special tax concessions apply to the bonds.

These new arrangements came into effect late in 1982 and seem likely to change the nature of the mortgage market dramatically. Commercial banks have set up mortgage company subsidiaries to use the new system and they are rapidly increasing their market share. Savings banks and the Mortgage Bank of Spain can also raise funds on the market. In 1982 bonds to the value of 85 billion pesetas were issued, the savings banks accounting for 93%, the mortgage companies for 5% and the Mortgage Bank of Spain for 2%. In 1983 there were 69 separate bond issues totalling 167 billion pesetas. The savings banks accounted for 80%, the mortgage companies for 14% and the Mortgage Bank of Spain for 6%. Most issues are for 50 or 100 million peseta bonds carrying a coupon of 12-13%. The minimum amount raised is usually 500 million pesetas and the maximum amount raised in one issue has been 20,000 million pesetas. The three year term remains most common although, increasingly, bonds have been issued for four, five and six years.

In 1983 the Associacion Espanol de Entidades Operadoras en el Mercado Hipotecario (Spanish Association of Financial Participants in the Mortgage Market) was established. Initial membership included the Mortgage Bank of Spain, several savings banks and several mortgage company subsidiaries of commercial banks.

The Savings Market

The two groups of deposit taking institutions which dominate the housing finance market, the commercial banks and the confederated savings banks, are also the major institutions in the savings market. The commercial banks have some 66% of the market, the savings banks have 32% and the postal savings bank has 2%. More recently, credit co-operatives have been growing but, as yet, these take only a small share of personal deposits. Table 12.1 shows deposits in the financial system as at the end of 1982.

Table 12.1 Deposits in the Financial System, Spain, End-1982

Type of Bank	Deposits Ptas bn	Percentage of Total
Commercial banks	11,029	66
Confederated savings banks	5,267	32
Postal savings bank	298	2
Total	16,594	100

Source: Spanish Confederation of Savings Banks.
Note: At end-1982 there were 126.0 pesetas to the dollar and 204.0 pesetas to the pound.

The Commercial Banks

The commercial banks account for nearly two thirds of deposits in the Spanish financial system and some 20% of house-purchase loans. However, housing loans are relatively small in relation to total assets, accounting for a little under 7%. The commercial banks have, until recently, been taking a declining share of the mortgage market.

However, they have been taking advantage of the new secondary market facility and have established mortgage banking subsidiaries. The banks see lending for housing as being substantially less risky than lending to industry and commerce. Developers have also been anxious to encourage bank lending for house-purchase as, in effect, they have often had to provide the finance themselves, often by short term bank borrowing at high rates of interest. It is seen as being advantageous for both banks and developers for banks to take on directly the financing of house-purchase loans.

There are 100 domestically owned banks in Spain of which 24 are industrial banks. The seven largest banking groups (the banks individually own other banks) account for some 65% of the total assets of the Spanish banking system. Table 12.2 lists the assets of these banks, excluding the assets of related banks.

The Spanish banking industry has been in a state of crisis in recent years, largely as a result of bad debts. A number of banks have failed and have had to be taken over by the larger banks.

For their size, the banks have a very large number of branches, a total of 14,300 at the end of 1981. This is, for example, more than the total number of bank branches in the United Kingdom. The number of bank branches grew at an annual rate of 7% between 1978 and 1981.

Table 12.2   Spanish Banking Groups, End-1982

Bank	Deposits Ptas bn	Assets Less Contra Accounts Ptas bn
Espanol de Credito	1,468	1,783
Central	1,459	1,939
Hispano	1,104	1,747
Bilbao	1,000	1,551
Vizcaya	783	1,138
Santander	738	1,002
Popular	517	692

Source: *Financial Times*, 22 March 1983.
Note: At end-1982 there were 126.0 pesetas to the dollar and 204.0 pesetas to the pound.

Confederated Savings Banks

The confederated savings banks are by far the largest house-purchase lenders, and are, generally, major retail financial institutions. There are 81 savings banks, all of which operate on a regional basis. The largest (La Caixa) is actually larger than the seventh largest of the commercial banks. Table 12.3 lists the largest five banks as at the end of 1982.

Table 12.3   Largest Spanish Savings Banks, End-1982

Bank	Deposits Ptas bn
La Caixa	713
Caja Madrid	445
Caja Barcelona	278
Caja Postal	268
Caja Zaragosa	277

Source: Spanish Confederation of Savings Banks, reproduced from *Financial Times*, 22 March 1983.
Note: At end-1982 there were 126.0 pesetas to the dollar and 204.0 pesetas to the pound.

The postal savings bank, the fourth largest, is different from others because it operates through post offices as well as 246 of its own branches.

The 81 savings banks have 9,500 branches. They operate on a local regional basis only and are grouped into 14 regional federations. The savings banks are all members of the Spanish Confederation of Savings Banks, which acts as a trade association and which provides services to its member banks, for example, in the field of money transmission.

The savings banks are private sector non profit making institutions with no equity shareholders. They can be considered to be mutual institutions.

The savings banks raise their funds largely through deposits, primarily savings deposits, although also time deposits and sight deposits. Savings banks offer a complete retail banking service, including chequing accounts, ATMs and so on. At the end of 1982 there were nearly 42 million deposit accounts with the savings banks, more than the entire population of Spain. It is estimated that almost every adult has a savings bank account of one form or another.

On the assets side of the balance sheet the savings banks are subject to some controls. A certain proportion of their assets must be held in public funds or specific bonds (25%) and special credits (10%) including loans for low income housing. These controls are gradually being eased.

The assets side of the balance sheet is distinguished by four features -

(a) A heavy proportion of loans in obligatory investments.
(b) A preponderance of long term credit.
(c) Loans to both consumers and small businesses.
(d) A regional concentration of lending.

House-purchase loans account for about half of the total lending of the savings banks. There are five different types of loan. These are illustrated in Table 12.4 which shows lending for house-purchase by the savings banks in 1978 and 1982.

Table 12.4   Savings Bank Lending for House-Purchase, Spain, 1978 and 1982

Type of Loan	1978 Ptas bn	%	1982 Ptas bn	%
Mortgage	266	36	675	50
House-purchase access	282	38	306	23
Personal	122	16	252	19
Officially protected	74	10	118	9
Savings-housing	2	-	1	-
Total	747	100	1,352	101

Source: *Las Cajas de Ahorros Confederadas y la Financiacion de la Vivienda en Espana*, Spanish
      Confederation of Savings Banks, 1983.
Note: At end-1982 there were 126.0 pesetas to the dollar and 204.0 pesetas to the pound.

It is necessary to explain the various types of loan in detail. Officially protected loans have already been described. These are made at a rate of interest of 11% with the government paying a subsidy, currently 3%, to the lender. House-purchase access loans are made on similar terms. As the total payment to the lender of 14% is less than the market rate of interest the savings banks themselves are having to subsidize the loans. Mortgage loans, which now account for 50% of total housing lending by the savings banks, are not regulated and have been at market rates of interest—around 15% to 17% over the last few years. As the name suggests these are secured by mortgages. Personal loans are used to top up mortgage loans and are likely to be at a higher rate of interest than the mortgage loans themselves. Typically a mortgage loan will be for not more than 60% or 70% of valuation and a personal loan is required for remaining finance.

All loans have been made at fixed rates of interest. Consideration has been given to introducing variable rates and index-linked loans but, as yet, few positive steps have been taken in this direction. Mortgage terms are seldom longer than 15 years and the combination of this, together with high interest rates, helps to explain the depressed housing market. However, the savings banks are taking advantage of the new power to issue medium term bonds.

The Spanish Mortgage Bank

The Banco Hipotecario de Espana (Spanish Mortgage Bank) is a public sector body, owned and controlled by the government. It makes house-purchase loans directly and also it acts as an agent in the implementation of government policies. The Mortgage Bank does not lend for housing purposes only but recently there has been a marked switch away from other types of lending towards housing. The Bank is based in Madrid but operates also from six branches.

Table 12.5 shows the assets and liabilities of the Mortgage bank as at the end of 1982.

Table 12.5 Mortgage Bank of Spain, Assets and Liabilities, End-1982

Liabilities	Ptas m	%	Assets	Ptas m	%
Official Credit Institute	417,569	71	Loans	548,163	94
Bonds	59,439	10	Other assets	36,031	6
Deposits	3,593	6			
Other liabilities	84,250	14			
Provisions	7,617	1			
Reserves	5,805	1			
Capital	5,921	1			
Total	584,194	100	Total	584,194	100

Source: Mortgage Bank Annual Report, 1982.
Note: At end-1982 there were 126.0 pesetas to the dollar and 204.0 pesetas to the pound.

It will be seen that the Bank raises most of its funds through loans from the Official Credit Institute, a government body. The other major source of funds are bonds. The bonds are quoted on the stock exchange, have a three year term, and enjoy tax concessions. The Mortgage Bank also obtains a limited amount of funds through deposits. Over 90% of its assets are loans. Like other mortgage banks, it has no need to hold a significant amount of liquid assets.

In April 1982 the activities of the Banco de Crédito a la Construcción (Building Credit Bank) were transferred to the Mortgage Bank. This had a major effect on the balance sheet total of the Mortgage Bank which increased from 175,475 million pesetas at the end of 1981 to 584,194 million at the end of 1982. The increase of 408,719 million pesetas may be compared with the Credit Bank's total assets at the date of the transfer of 316,352 million pesetas.

The effect of the incorporation of the Building Credit Bank into the Mortgage Bank can best be seen by examining the changing composition of outstanding loans. This usefully also illustrates the growth in activity of the Mortgage Bank prior to the transfer of the Building Credit Bank. Table 12.6 shows the distribution of outstanding loans from 1980 to 1982.

Table 12.6 Mortgage Bank of Spain, Distribution of Outstanding Loans, 1980-82

Type of Loan	1980 Ptas m	%	1981 Ptas m	%	1982 Ptas m	%
Special housing	19,751	16	19,190	12	18,514	3
Social housing	19,512	16	33,882	21	46,974	8
State housing	8,447	7	40,074	25	128,867	24
Rented housing	614	1	508	-	142,535	26
Subsidized housing	-	-	-	-	74,565	14
Other housing	1,707	1	1,558	1	211,680	4
Total housing	50,031	42	95,212	59	433,135	79
General mortgage	41,978	35	36,004	22	30,154	6
Tourist sector	20,479	17	21,814	14	22,673	4
Commercial loans	6,287	5	6,555	4	7,188	1
Other loans	590	1	544	-	29,192	5
Exceptional loans	1,007	1	1,007	1	1,328	-
Total	120,372	100	161,136	100	548,184	100

Source: Mortgage Bank Annual Report, 1982.
Note: At end-1982 there were 126.0 pesetas to the dollar and 204.0 pesetas to the pound.

It will be seen that at the end of 1981 housing loans accounted for 59% of total loans, more than double the proportion of two years previously. In terms of new loans housing accounted for over 90% of the total in 1981. This has largely been at the expense of general mortgage loans, but also the various other forms of lending. (General mortgage loans are not normally for housing, are for an eight year period, and carry a mortgage rate of about 14.5%.) Within the total of housing there was a switch away from special housing towards social housing and state housing (the latter two categories coming within the definition of state protected housing). It has already been noted that loans under state protection can be for up to 70% of cost, carry an 11% interest rate and are for 12 year terms.

The effect of the transfer of the Building Credit Bank in 1982 was to increase substantially loans for state housing and to add two new categories of lending, for rented housing and for subsidized housing.

The changed nature of the Mortgage Bank makes it more appropriate to examine the income and expenditure account for 1981. Table 12.7 shows the figures.

Table 12.7   Mortgage Bank of Spain, Income and Expenditure, 1981

	Ptas m	Ptas per 100 Ptas Mean Assets
Income		
Normal interest	12,794	8.4
Other interest	896	0.6
Commission	463	0.3
Other income net	13	-
Total	14,166	9.3
Expenditure		
Interest	9,668	6.3
Management expenses	3,014	2.0
Total	12,702	8.3
Net surplus	1,464	1.0

Source: Mortgage Bank Annual Report.
Note: At end-1981 there were 96.6 pesetas to the dollar and 184.6 pesetas to the pound.

The management expense ratio seems, at first sight, to be high, for an institution which does not have any branches.

Assessment

The Spanish housing finance system is fairly typical of that for an economy at Spain's stage of development. Most funds are provided by savings banks, which operate on the deposit taking principle. The Mortgage Bank plays a significant role in housing and housing finance and is the mechanism by which the government chooses to implement some of its housing policies. The government plays little direct role in either housing or housing finance but does regulate both markets.

As in other countries there seems to be a wish to bring the housing finance market more into line with other financial markets, but the high rates of inflation and of interest which have been experienced in the recent past make this difficult. The new mortgage market, introduced in 1982, seems likely to make a major impact on the market by increasing the availability of funds and introducing periodic variability of interest rates.

Bibliography

Banco Hipotecario de Espana Memoria 1982, Spanish Mortgage Bank, 1983.
Current Trends and Policies in the Field of Housing, Building and Planning in Spain,

Ministry of Public Works and Housing, 1979.
Las Cajas de Ahorros Confederadas y la Financiacion de la Vivienda en Espana, Spanish Confederation of Savings Banks, 1983.

Acknowledgements

The co-operation of the Spanish Embassy in London, the Spanish Confederation of Savings Banks and Professor Jack Revell, University College of North Wales, in providing information for this chapter is gratefully acknowledged.

The author is indebted to Juan Santiusta, General Manager of Bancaya Hipotecario, and Pablo Alvorado, London Manager of the Banco de Vizcaya, for helping to explain the intricacies of the Spanish financial system, in particular, the recent changes in the mortgage market.

CHAPTER 13

SCANDINAVIA

The four Scandinavian countries have much in common and in many respects constitute a more natural common market than some of the more formal common markets which have been established. They are also wealthy countries; GNP per capita in Sweden, Denmark and Norway is higher than in any other European country except Luxembourg and Switzerland. However, the countries are also different from each other in a number of fundamental respects -

(a) Only Denmark is a member of the European Community.
(b) Finland and Sweden are neutral; Denmark and Norway are members of NATO.
(c) While the languages of the other three countries have some similarities, that of Finland is very different.

Banking institutions recognise the Scandinavian 'common market' but as far as housing finance is concerned the four countries are as different as any four in Western Europe. In Denmark alone the government plays no role in the housing finance market, in Norway the government dominates the market, and Finland and Sweden have more mixed systems.

Table 13.1 shows key data for the four Scandinavian countries.

Table 13.1 Scandinavian Countries, Key Data

Country	Population End-1982	GNP per Capita Mid-1981 US dollars	Proportion of Owner-Occupation	Housing Finance System
Finland	4,841,000	10,680	61% (1980)	Loans provided by government (at subsidized rates) and banks.
Norway	4,123,000	14,060	67% (1980)	Loans largely provided by State Housing Bank.
Denmark	5,116,000	13,120	52% (1980)	Loans largely provided by specialized mortgage credit institutions working on mortgage bank principle.
Sweden	8,327,000	14,870	57% (1981)	Loans largely provided by State & Urban Mortgage Bank.

Finland

Introduction

Finland has an area of 338,000 sq kilometres. On the East it borders the Soviet Union, in the North West it has borders with Sweden and Norway. Its population at end-1982 was 4,841,000, 75% of whom live in urban areas. Helsinki, the capital and principal city, accommodates 10% of the population.

Although Finland has a significantly lower GNP per capita than the other Scandinavian countries, it is still high by international standards, being above that of the United Kingdom, for example.

Finland is a republic with a one chamber parliament. It has a multi-party system and each of four parties has a significant number of parliamentary seats. The Social Democrats are the largest party but have had to govern in coalition with other parties. Executive power is largely in the hands of a directly elected president.

Housing

Of the 1,838,000 dwellings in Finland at the end of 1980, 61% were owner-occupied. That proportion has been relatively constant for the past 20 years but within the owner-occupied sector a significant development has been the growth in the proportion of dwellings which are flats rather than houses. Table 13.2 shows trends in housing tenure from 1960 to 1980.

Table 13.2   Housing Tenure, Finland, 1960-80

	1960 000s	%	1970 000s	%	1980 000s	%
Owned houses	620	51	624	43	657	36
Owned flats	112	9	232	16	463	25
Provided by employer	141	12	142	10	153	8
Tenanted	329	27	405	28	384	21
Without permanent occupants	7	1	44	3	110	6
Other/unknown	2	-	16	1	70	4
Total	1,211	100	1,463	100	1,838	100

Source: *Statistics of the National Housing Board for Finland, 1949-1981*, 1983, Table 1.4.

It will be seen that the number of owned houses has been fairly constant since 1960 while the number of owned flats has quadrupled. The average price of houses on which mortgage loans were granted in 1981 was 230,000 marks (at end-1981 there were 4.3 marks to the US dollar and 8.7 marks to the pound). The average house price was 3.3 times the average annual earnings of purchasers.

Rented housing is made available by a wide variety of institutions including employers, local government and private sector institutions. Privately rented housing has been declining because of inadequate returns as a result of rent controls. Recently, local authorities have been the main providers of rented housing. One third of all rented dwellings have been built with the assistance of state subsidies (which does not necessarily mean that they are state owned). State subsidized rental units are available to low and medium income groups. Tenants who have lived in a new state subsidized rental dwelling for at least two years have the right to purchase it with the help of a state loan for 30% of the purchase price.

Table 13.3 shows trends in dwelling completions from 1978 to 1982.

Table 13.3 Dwelling Completions, Finland, 1978-82

Year	1-2 Dwelling Houses	Terraced & Row Houses	Multi-Dwelling Houses	Total
1978	18,846	11,641	24,800	55,287
1979	17,023	11,996	21,282	50,301
1980	18,128	12,365	19,155	49,648
1981	17,407	12,310	17,271	46,988
1982	31,948			47,997

Source: *Statistics of the National Housing Board for Finland 1949-1981*, 1983, Table 2.2; *Yearbook of Nordik Statistics 1983*, Table 104.

The number of completions reached a peak of 73,033 in 1974. The decline since then has been entirely in respect of multi-dwelling units (ie flats); the number of houses completed has risen.

Housing policy is the responsibility of the Ministry of the Environment, which took over this function from the Ministry of the Interior in October 1983. The National Housing Board is responsible for the planning and implementation of housing policy. It grants state loans for housing, it is responsible for the general supervision of the state subsidized housing stock, and it co-ordinates research into housing. (It publishes a number of excellent publications in foreign languages including *Housing in Finland* (1983) and a regular volume of statistics, the most recent edition of which covers 1949-81 and which was also published in 1983.) Local authorities, of which there are 461, are responsible for the implementation of housing policy at the local level, including the processing of applications for loans and grants.

Housing Finance

The state plays a major role in the housing finance market—for both owner-occupied and rented dwellings. About half of new dwellings have been built with state assistance. For owner-occupied dwellings the state makes loans for 30% to 60% of the cost of construction with the remaining loan finance being obtained from financial institutions. State loans are repayable over ten to 25 years and most enjoy an interest subsidy to keep the interest rate below the going market rate for the first ten years. Initially the rate is between 0% and 3%. Eligibility for low interest state loans depends on family circumstances.

The state provides a number of other forms of assistance to housing costs of owner-occupiers -

(a) Interest on loans for house-purchase is tax deductible.
(b) Low income owner-occupiers qualify for housing allowances.
(c) In 1981 a scheme was introduced to encourage savings for home ownership. People under the age of 35 buying their first apartment can deposit funds in a special housing budget account on which the financial institution pays a higher than normal rate of interest. In addition, the state pays a bonus of 1.75% of the amount deposited. When 20% of the cost of the dwelling has been saved, the person receives the balance as a loan from the financial institution.
(d) Subsequently, an interest subsidy scheme has been introduced for those obtaining loans through housing budget accounts. Under this scheme the state pays five percentage points of the interest for the first six years of the loan.

In addition to any entitlement to a state loan, developers obtain what are known as 'primary loans' to finance construction. Developers, in this sense, include private individuals, developers of condominiums (which may include both owner-occupied and rented units) and developers of rented property. Table 13.4 shows the sources of primary loans in 1981.

Table 13.4   Sources of Primary Housing Loans, Finland, 1981

Institution	Single Family Houses %	Condominiums %	Rental Units %
Savings banks	37	27	19
Co-operative banks	37	18	12
Commercial banks	16	20	15
Postipankki	5	19	21
Insurance companies	1	7	14
Municipalities & churches	-	1	11
Organisations & funds	-	8	9
Other	4	-	-
Total	100	100	100

Source: *Statistics of the National Housing Board for Finland, 1949-1981*, 1983, Tables 4.2, 4.3 & 4.4.

It will be seen that the institutions lend for all types of housing; the savings banks and the co-operative banks account for 75% of lending for single family homes.

It is apparent that the buyer of a new home in particular cannot obtain all the funds he needs from one source. He may have a state subsidized loan, a primary loan and a bank loan. Rates on unsubsidized loans have been in the 9% to 11% range recently. Table 13.5 shows outstanding housing loans at the end of 1980.

Table 13.5   Households' Housing Loans, Finland, End-1980

Institution	Amount m marks	Percentage of Total
Municipal governments	7,054	25
Commercial banks	7,080	25
Savings banks	6,756	24
Co-operative banks	5,451	19
Postipankki	1,143	4
Insurance institutions	526	2
Other	167	1
Total	28,187	100

Source: *The Finnish Banking System*, The Finnish Bankers' Association, 1982, Table 1.8.
Note: At end-1980 there were 3.7 marks to the US dollar and 8.7 marks to the pound.

It will be seen that the commercial banks are the major private sector lenders, although they have less of the market for primary loans than either co-operative banks or savings banks. This is because they provide 'topping up' finance, generally unsecured, where other sources of finance are not adequate to finance a transaction. Actual 'mortgage loans' (ie secured loans) are seldom for more than 20% of the house price.

The Savings Market

The commercial banks, savings banks, co-operative banks and Postipankki all have significant shares of the personal savings market. Table 13.6 sets out the position at the end of June 1983.

Table 13.6   Deposits by the Public, Finland, End-June 1983

Institution	Amount marks m	Percentage of Total
Commercial banks	35,425	34
Savings banks	29,915	29
Co-operative banks	24,475	24
Postipankki	13,064	13
Total (all institutions)	103,927	100

Source: Central Statistical Office of Finland, *Bulletin of Statistics*, 1983 IV, Table 10.
Notes: At end-June 1983 there were 5.5 marks to the dollar and 8.6 marks to the pound.

About half of savings are in savings accounts, withdrawable on demand. The other major type of investment is a 24 month deposit. All of the institutions listed in Table 13.6 offer cheque accounts, on which interest is paid. Interest rates on deposits are agreed centrally by the banks.

Housing Finance Institutions

The commercial banks are the major private sector lenders for house-purchase. There are seven commercial banks, but four of these are highly specialised and play only a small role in housing finance. Two of these are central banks for the savings banks and co-operative banks.

The three banks which have nationwide branch networks are all privately owned. Key statistics for these banks are shown in Table 13.7.

Table 13.7   Commercial Banks, Finland, End-1983

	Kansallis-Osake-Pankki (KOP)	Union Bank of Finland (UBF)	Bank of Helsinki (BH)
Total assets (m marks)	41,893	41,735	7,022
Housing loans (m marks)	5,082	4,844	908
Housing loans/assets (%)	12.1	11.6	12.9
Housing loans/loans to public (%)	20.6	22.1	22.0
Branches	443	346	113

Source: Annual reports of banks.
Note: At end-1983 there were 5.8 marks to the US dollar and 8.3 marks to the pound.

It will be noted that the three banks are very similar in terms of the importance of housing loans in the balance sheet.

The savings banks are the second largest group of private sector lenders. There were 272 savings banks at the end of 1982, the number having fallen from 327 at the end of 1970. The banks have over 1,000 branches. The banks operate under the Savings Bank Act of 1970 which allows them to offer a full range of banking services. The banks are administered by boards of trustees. One significant prudential requirement is that housing loans cannot be for more than 60% of the value of the property. The savings banks lend to small firms and agriculture as well as to households. About 30% of their assets are in housing loans, a fairly low figure by international standards.

The fragmented nature of the industry means that the Skopbank, the central bank for the savings banks, has a very important role including the handling of transactions in securities, data processing and advertising. The largest individual bank is the Suomen Tyovaen Saastopankki (The Finnish Workers' Savings Bank) which has 12% of total savings bank assets and 110 branches.

The co-operative banks are even more fragmented, there being 372 banks with 821 branches at the end of 1980. The banks operate on a regional basis and are part of the co-operative movement. Their primary function is to provide banking services for households, forestry and agriculture. They have 25% of their assets in housing loans. The largest co-operative bank is the Suur-Helsingin Osuupankki which has 5% of the assets of the industry.

The Postipankki is state owned and operates through 30 branches and 3,000 post offices. Its lending is concentrated on industry and trade; only 8% of its assets are in the form of housing loans to individuals.

Finland does have specialized mortgage credit institutions. Four of these are owned by commercial banks and lend to industry and government. The fifth is the Mortgage Society of Finland. This was founded in 1861 and in 1979 was merged with the Housing Mortgage Bank of Finland, which specialized in housing production. It operates under a specific law. The Society obtains its funds from banks, insurance companies, pension funds and bond issues, and loans money to housebuilders through branches of banks and the Postipankki. However, this institution has only a very small role in the housing finance market.

Norway

Introduction

Norway occupies an area of 386,000 sq kilometres. It borders the Atlantic Ocean on the West, Sweden on the East, and Finland and the USSR in the North East. Its population at end-1982 was 4,123,000, 71% of whom live in urban areas. The capital, and principal centre of population, is Oslo.

Norway enjoys a very high standard of living; GNP per capita is among the highest in Europe.

Norway is a monarchy with a two chamber parliament. There are a number of political parties and coalition or minority governments are common. Currently, a minority Conservative government is in power.

Housing

Norway has a very high standard of housing, partly because living standards generally are high, and partly because housing has been heavily subsidized. Detached houses comprise 42% of the total and accounted for most of the units built in the 1970s. Over two thirds of units have been built since the War, and as many as 42% since 1970.

The 1980 census showed that there were 1,523,512 dwellings in Norway. Table 13.8 shows the pattern of housing tenure in 1980 as revealed by the census.

Table 13.8   Housing Tenure, Norway, 1980

Type of Tenure	Number of Dwellings	Percentage of Total
Owned privately	756,000	50
Owned through housing societies etc	259,000	17
Rented on regular lease	178,000	12
Rented as official residence	70,000	5
Rented under other conditions	111,000	6
Not known	150,000	10
Total	1,524,000	100

Source: *Population and Housing Census 1980*, Volume 1, Housing Statistics, Central Bureau of Statistics of Norway, 1982, Table 1.

It will be noted that there is a high proportion of dwellings of unknown tenure. If these are discounted, owner-occupied dwellings comprise 74% of the total. The main trend since 1970 has been the growth of units owned through housing societies—from nothing to 17% of the total. In 1970, 53% of units were owned privately and 47% were rented.

Housing societies provide owner-occupied flats. Most rented housing is provided by non-profit making housing co-operatives. Only 5% of rented dwellings are state owned.

Housebuilding has been very stable, largely because of the interventionist role of the state. Between 1970 and 1980 the number of dwellings completed varied only between 37,000 and 44,000, although there was a decline to 34,000 in 1981. In 1981, over half of all completions were detached houses, and only 11% were flats. 70% of houses built in 1980 were for private persons who were going to live in the houses themselves, and 16% were built by housing co-operatives for renting. Public authorities account for only 3% of completions and this housing is specifically for groups such as the elderly and families in need of social care.

Government policy has been to encourage owner-occupation, and this is generally accepted by all political parties. Responsibility for housing policy rests with the Ministry of Local Government and Labour. The point has already been made that housebuilding has been relatively stable because of the role played by the state in the financing of housing. More generally, the state has intervened considerably in housing policy but, recently, there has been a switch of emphasis with more attention being given to the private sector.

There are three important state banks active in housing. By far the most important is the State Housing Bank which is effectively the central institution in the administration of housing policy. It grants loans for new dwellings and the improvement of older dwellings and it also make some loans to purchasers of existing homes. It administers housing grants schemes and several other housing programmes. The Bank is supervised by the Ministry of Local Government and Labour. The State Agricultural Bank, under the direction of the Ministry of Agriculture, grants loans for a relatively small number of houses built each year in rural areas. The State Municipal Bank, which is controlled by the Ministry of Finance, grants loans for the purchase of land and provision of infrastructure.

Housing Finance

Housing finance in Norway is dominated by the State Housing Bank, the activities of which are described in more detail subsequently. At the end of 1982 housing loans outstanding totalled Kr105.5 billion, of which state banks provided Kr51.4 billion (49%). Much of the remaining finance is in the form of personal loans and is not easily identifiable from statistics as being for housing purposes. It is estimated that at the end of 1982 the savings banks had housing loans outstanding of Kr27.5 billion (26% of the total); the commercial banks, Kr25.1 billion (24%); and the Post Office Savings Bank, Kr1.5 billion (1%).

The State Housing Bank, together with the State Agricultural Bank, has financed the purchase of some 75% of new houses (including those owned through housing societies) in the last 20 years. Recently, however, its involvement has been reduced and it now finances about 60% of purchases of new houses. The Bank provides only a proportion of the finance required, generally a maximum of 55%. The remaining finance has to be obtained from a commercial bank loan, a savings bank loan, a loan from another institution, or from personal savings. Loans from financial institutions are generally at the market rate. However, both the commercial banks and the savings banks give what are known as PSV loans for house-purchase on terms which are slightly more favourable than normal private loans.

Purchasers of secondhand houses generally obtain finance from private credit sources but in some cases loans can be obtained from the State Housing Bank. Also, existing State Housing Bank loans can, to some extent, be transferred to a subsequent purchaser of a house.

It is helpful to analyse briefly the key financial statistics for the private sector institutions, partly to show their importance in the personal saving and loan markets, but also to indicate how, indirectly, they finance the activities of the State Housing Bank. Table 13.9 shows the relevant statistics.

Table 13.9   Norwegian Financial Institutions, End-September 1983

	Commercial Banks Kr m	Savings Banks Kr m	Post Office Savings Bank Kr m	Life Insurance Companies Kr m
Deposits from public	90,041	80,229	11,913	-
Total assets	159,016	107,526	13,619	-
Loans to public	83,250	59,888	4,077	-
Loans to government	-	-	5,123	-
Bearer bonds	30,574	24,233	2,994	24,431

Source: Norges Bank *Economic Bulletin*, 1983/4, Tables 5, 9 & 10.
Note: At end-September 1983 there were 7.43 kroner to the dollar and 11.13 kroner to the pound.

It will be noted that the commercial banks are the largest financial institutions, with a little under 50% of the personal deposit market. There are 25 commercial banks, all of which are privately owned. The three largest (Den Norske Creditbank, Christiana Bank Og Kreditkasse and Bergen Bank) have

63% of the total assets of the industry, while the others operate at a regional or local level. The commercial banks have recently been taking an expanding share of the personal market. It will be noted that loans to the public form a fairly high proportion of assets and, indeed, the commercial banks do not lend directly to industry at all. However, they are obliged to purchase a specific quantity of Norwegian government bearer bonds, and they also purchase bearer bonds issued by other institutions.

There were 253 savings banks in Norway at the end of 1983; the number has been reducing rapidly as a result of mergers. In the long term it is intended to reduce the number to 50. The banks have a total of about 900 branches. Like the commercial banks, the savings banks have a high proportion of their assets in the form of loans to the public and a significant proportion is for housing purposes.

The Post Office Savings Bank is much smaller than the other savings banks and it makes only a limited amount of loans directly to the public, most of its assets being lent directly to the government and invested in bearer bonds.

It will be apparent that bearer bonds play an important role in the Norwegian financial system. The public sector accounts for half of all bonds, the government directly being responsible for some 30% of bearer bond issues.

The proceeds of the bearer bonds are used for a variety of purposes, including the financing of the state banks. It is clear that the number of stages of intermediation in the housing finance system in Norway is greater than in many other countries. The public invest in savings banks and commercial banks which purchase bearer bonds issued directly by the government or the state banks, and some of the funds which the government raise are lent direcly to the state banks. The State Housing Bank then onlends its funds to house-buyers.

The State Housing Bank

The State Housing Bank is, by a long way, the largest financial institution in Norway. In terms of operation it is more like a government department than a bank, and, in practice, it lends only for housing purposes. The Bank was established by Act of Parliament in 1946. It is wholly owned by the state and led by an appointed council and central board. It is based in Oslo but operates also from four district offices.

The Bank does not lend to housebuilders at all, but only to those purchasing houses. A loan will be made only if the dwelling is within certain cost and area limits. The maximum loan is usually Kr100,000, but this may be exceeded in certain cases.

The rate of interest, since 1982, has been 5% in the first year, rising annually to reach 10.5% in the sixth year. This corresponds to the going market rate, the intention being that interest should be subsidized for the first six years of the loan only. Loans are not repaid by the annuity method, but rather capital repayments are made separately from interest payments. The normal procedure is for redemption payments to begin after six years and to rise gradually so that the loan is repaid in full after 26 years. Loans made prior to 1982 are being adjusted to bring them into line with new loans.

The PSV scheme, mentioned earlier, provides for loans to be made by private sector institutions, but at rates agreed with the State Housing Bank. In the second quarter of 1983 the agreed rate of interest was 10.7-12.2% with the repayment period being 25 years and a redemption free period for the first five years. Dwellings qualifying for PSV loans must be of a similar standard to those qualifying for State Housing Bank loans.

The terms on PSV loans are, in fact, little different from those on commercial loans. The normal private mortgage is for 20 years with no redemption free period.

The previous table (13.9) showed how the various financial institutions contribute to government funds. Table 13.10 shows the aggregate balance sheet for all of the state banks, from which it can be seen how these funds are used.

Table 13.10   State Banks, Norway, Assets & Liabilities, End-September 1983

Liabilities	Kr m	%	Assets	Kr m	%
Bearer bond loans	26,723	22	State Housing Bank		
Loans from government	76,518	63	Loans	50,458	41
Other loans	3,266	3	Other loans	57,701	47
Other debts	8,473	2	Other assets	13,147	11
Capital & reserves	7,170	6			
Total	122,150	100	Total	122,150	100

Source: Norges Bank *Economic Bulletin*, 1983/4, Table 7.
Note: At end-September 1983 there were 7.43 kroner to the dollar and 11.13 kroner to the pound.

It will be seen that the state banks obtain nearly two thirds of their funds from the government and nearly a quarter as bearer bonds. State Housing Bank loans accounted for 41% of the total assets of all the state banks at the end of 1983.

Denmark

Introduction

Denmark has an area of 43,000 sq kilometres, over half of which (Jutland) is on the mainland of continental Europe, with a southern border with West Germany. The rest of Denmark comprises a number of islands of which Zeeland is the largest. The East coast of Zeeland is separated from Sweden by a narrow channel. Denmark's population at the end of 1982 was 5,116,000. Copenhagen is the capital and principal city; the greater-Copenhagen area accommodates nearly one quarter of the population.

Denmark is one of the wealthiest countries in Western Europe although GNP per capita is a little below that of Sweden and Norway. However, inflation and interest rates have been high compared with the other Scandinavian coutries and Western Europe in general.

Denmark is a monarchy and has a one-chamber legislature, the Folketing. The Social Democrats are currently the largest single party but a four party minority coalition, led by the Conservatives, is in power.

Housing

At the end of 1981 there were 2,180,000 houses in Denmark, of which 49% were single family houses, 42% were multi-family houses, and the remaining 9% were farm houses or other buildings. The main trend in recent years has been an increase in single family houses. Of the total stock, 75% are owned privately, 15% are owned by 650 non-profit making housing associations, 7% are condominiums and 4% are owned by central or local governments.

A little over half of principal residences are owner-occupied. Table 13.11 shows housing tenure in 1970 and 1980.

Table 13.11   Housing Tenure, Denmark, 1970 and 1980

Tenure	1970 %	%	1980 %	%
Owner-occupied				
Single family houses	35		41	
Farm houses	9		7	
Multi-family houses	5		4	
Total		49		52
Rented				
Privately owned			20	
Housing association			15	
Public sector			4	
Other			3	
Total		47		42
Unknown		4		6
Number of Dwellings		1,707,000		2,133,000

Source: *Rent Policy in Denmark*, Ministry of Housing, 1983.

The level of housebuilding has declined sharply in the recent past, from over 50,000 units in 1970, to 30,000 in 1980 and to 21,000 in 1982. Within these totals there has been a switch away from flats and towards single family homes. Table 13.12 shows trends in the contruction of new houses.

Table 13.12   Housing Completions, Denmark, 1978-82

Year	Dwellings Completed	Of Which Single Family Houses
1978	34,218	28,268
1979	31,064	26,344
1980	30,345	22,537
1981	21,925	14,737
1982	20,556	13,113

Source: *Statistisk Arbog 1983*.

Responsibility for housing policy rests with the Ministry of Housing. However, the government has a much less interventionist role than in other Scandinavian countries. It has already been noted that only a small proportion of houses are owned by public authorities, and, as will be seen subsequently, the government has no direct role in housing finance. However, owner-occupiers do enjoy tax benefits, and tenants can benefit from low interest loans for the construction of their dwellings, and rent subsidies.

Housing Finance

Housing finance in Denmark is provided largely by mortgage credit institutions which raise their funds wholly from the capital markets. The other major source of finance is that provided by those selling houses, but this is declining in importance as funds have become more readily available from the institutions. It is estimated that in 1978 the institutions accounted for 65% of housing finance with sellers accounting for most of the remainder. By 1983 the proportion was estimated at 85%, with sellers accounting for 8% and other financial institutions for 6%. The detailed operation of mortgage credit institutions is considered in the next section; this section describes the housing finance process and, of necessity, the bond market.

Construction of dwellings is generally financed by loans from commercial or savings banks. The purchaser of a house will ask a mortgage credit institution for a loan secured on the property which he intends to buy. Traditionally, the loan took the form of bonds which could be for up to 80% of the value of the property, repayable over 25 or 30 years. The bonds were sold, generally through a bank or savings bank, in the capital markets and the proceeds were used to purchase the house. Bonds carry certain fixed rates; 10% and 12% are most common. If the market rate was higher than the nominal rate then the bonds had to be sold at a discount. For example, if the market rate is twice the nominal rate then bonds can be sold only at half their face value. More commonly today, the mortgage credit institutions make cash loans which they finance by selling an appropriate amount of bonds. This change has arisen precisely because market rates have been much higher than nominal rates. and any investment loss which a borrower suffers by selling his bonds at a discount is not tax-deductible whereas mortgage interest (after allowing for notional rent received) is. Bonds are easily transferable and are quoted daily on the Copenhagen Stock Exchange.

Loans are made at fixed rates of interest and premature redemption is not permitted without substantial penalty. There have been experiments with loans on which the rate of interest is varied at intervals of five years but these have not been popular. This is a little surprising bearing in mind the high rates of interest which have prevailed in the recent past. The mortgage rate did not fall below 18% between the beginning of 1980 and the end of 1982, and for part of 1982 it was in excess of 21%. However, by the end of 1983 the rate had fallen to 14%. In 1982 the mortgage credit institutions were authorized to issue index-linked loans but, again, these have been little used in the owner-occupied sector. However, they are obligatory for non-profit housing associations.

Traditionally, the mortgage credit institutions have financed the purchase of new property, although it has been possible for loans to be transferred to subsequent purchasers. Early in 1982 the maximum percentage loan that could be granted on the transfer of dwellings was increased from 40% to 80%, and the maximum term from ten to 20 years. This led to a huge increase in loans for this purpose. Table 13.13 illustrates this trend. (All administrative limits on loans were abolished at the beginning of 1983.)

Table 13.13   Loans Made by Mortgage Credit Institutions, Denmark, 1980-83

Year	New	Owner-Occupied Housing		Other	Rental Housing	All Housing	Non Housing	Total
		Rebuilding & Extensions	Change of Ownership					
	DKrm	DKrm	DKrm	DKrm	DKrm	DKrm	DKrm	DKrm
1980	6,936	5,353	1,801	252	1,955	16,297	9,055	25,352
1981	4,542	4,708	2,625	318	2,571	14,764	6,830	21,594
1982	2,339	3,298	7,444	446	4,919	18,446	4,824	23,270
1983	4,161	5,516	15,574	639	7,446	30,051	11,709	41,760

Source: Realkreditradet, *Beretning og regnskab 1983*, 1984, Table V11.
Note: At end-1983 there were 9.95 kroner to the dollar and 14.29 kroner to the pound.

The bonds issued by the mortgage credit institutions have to be competitive (in terms of yield) with other bonds. As will be seen subsequently, the mortgage credit institutions fund activities other than housing and, effectively, the only other major bond issuer is the government. The increasing public sector deficit in recent years has meant that government bond issues have grown rapidly, contributing to the rise in interest rates and the declining demand for mortgage finance. Table 13.14 shows net purchases and sales of bonds, by type of institution, between 1981 and 1983.

Table 13.14   Danish Bond Market, 1981-83

	1981 Dkrm	%	1982 Dkrm	%	1983 Dkrm	%
Sales (net)						
Government bonds	28,996	69	44,716	75		
Mortgage bonds	11,470	27	11,333	19	27,000	31
Other bonds	1,673	4	3,186	5		
Total	42,139	100	59,235	100	86,860	100
Purchases (net)						
Post office giro & public pension funds	9,304	22	12,525	21	14,000	16
Banks and savings banks	4,914	12	11,406	19	38,900	45
Insurance companies & private pension funds	12,681	30	16,400	28	18,000	21
Business enterprises & private persons	14,897	35	(17,800	30	11,600	13
Public bodies	153	-	(			
Central bank	388	1	1,665	3	1,400	2
Foreign	- 198	-	- 571	(1)	3,000	3
Total	42,139	100	59,235	100	86,860	100

Source: Denmark Nationalbank 1982 Annual Report, Table 28; Realkreditradet, *Beretning og regnskab 1983*, 1984, Table 6.
Note: At end-1983 there were 9.95 kroner to the dollar and 14.29 kroner to the pound.

Mortgage bonds accounted for 31% of the net supply of bonds in 1983, compared with 51% in 1980, 27% in 1981 and 19% in 1982. However, they still accounted for 58% of the outstanding supply of bonds at the end of 1983, the proportion having fallen from 89% at the end of 1975. Pension funds, insurance companies, banks and private investors are the main purchasers. The savings banks have 22% of their assets in the form of bonds, and the commercial banks 17%.

The banks and savings banks participate in the housing finance market primarily through purchasing bonds, although they may also provide personal loans to 'top up' mortgage loans. The savings banks are frequently used for saving the necessary downpayment. The banks' share of net purchases of bonds has varied considerably in recent years from just 3% in 1979 to a peak of 45% in 1983. This variation is largely explained by the commercial banks whose market share varied from being negative in 1978 to 33% in 1983.

Like the other Scandinavian countries, Denmark has a strong savings bank industry. The 158 banks, which have 1,400 branches, held public deposits of DKr58.0 billion at the end of 1982, 29% of the total. The two largest savings banks, SDS and Bikuben, operate throughout the country and account for nearly 60% of assets. The Faellesbanken is the central bank for savings banks and it handles the sale and purchase of bonds, including mortgage bonds, for the banks.

The commercial banks hold a high proportion of bonds and other securities in their portfolios—they account for about 30% of total assets. The three largest commercial banks, which are relatively small by international standards, are the Den Danske Bank, Copenhagen Handelsbank and PRIVATbanken. The banks are the major deposit taking institutions, holding public deposits of DKr134.2 billion at the end of 1982, 66% of the total.

The savings banks and commercial banks compete across the whole range of banking activities. They are regulated under the same act (The Commercial Banks and Savings Banks Act 1975) and the essential difference between them is that the savings banks are independent non-profit making institutions whereas commercial banks are joint stock companies. In June 1983 the commercial banks had personal deposits outstanding of DKr150 billion, 44% of their total deposits. The savings banks' personal deposits totalled DKr66 billion, 83% of their total deposits.

Mortgage Credit Institutions

Mortgage credit institutions are a long established form of Danish organisation. The first was set up in 1797, and by 1900 they played a major role in the financing of housing and building. At this time the institutions were associations of borrowers who borrowed money on the security of mortgage against their properties, and with members being jointly liable for all debts. Each institution operated in a limited geographical area and loans were limited to 60% of the value of property.

In about 1900 second mortgage credit institutions were established which lent on the security of the 'slice' of the property between 60% and 75% of value. There was a significant change in the industry in the late 1950s when the institutions took over the government's role in the financing of housing. However, the industry remained fragmented with institutions being limited in respect of their area of operation, the types of property they could mortgage, and the types of security the could accept.

In 1970 the Mortgage Credit Act provided for the present constitution of the industry. It had three main purposes -

(a) To provide for the merging of the institutions.
(b) To enable borrowers to obtain all the finance they required from one institution.
(c) To introduce new ceilings on loans and longer repayment periods.

The institutions are non-profit making and are organised either as associations of borrowers or as proprietary institutions (ie, joint stock companies). Boards of directors comprise representatives of borrowers, bondholders, staff, the Ministry of Housing, and, where appropriate, stockholders.

There are six institutions -

Kreditforeningen Danmark (KD) (The Mortgage Credit Association, Denmark)
Jyllands Kreditforening (JK) (The Jutland Mortgage Credit Association)
Forenede Kreditforeninger (FK) (The United Mortgage Credit Institutes)
Byggeriets Realkreditfond (BRF) (The Housing Mortgage Fund)
Dansk Landbrugs Realkreditfond (DLR) (The Mortgage Credit Fund of Danish Agriculture)
Industriens Realkreditfond (IRF) (The Industrial Mortgage Credit Fund).

The first three institutions are associations of borrowers. The capital has been procured from the contributions of the borrowers (the members) to the reserve funds and the interest amounts accrued from these contributions.

The other three institutions are proprietary institutions set up during the last 25 years. The original capital basis was provided by financial institutions, trade organisations and the National Bank of Denmark. As is the case with the mortgage credit associations, the borrowers pay contributions to the credit reserve funds.

Kreditforeningen Danmark, Jyllands Kreditforening, Forenede Kreditforeninger and Byggeriets Realkreditfond lend for housing, offices, commercial buildings, hotels, and industrial and agricultural property. Kreditforeningen Danmark and Byggeriets Realkreditfond operate throughout the country. Jyllands Kreditforening operates only on the mainland of Jutland while Forenede Kreditforeninger operates only in the Danish islands. Dansk Landbrugs Realkreditfond and Industriens Realkreditfond are specialised institutions, lending for agricultural and industrial property, respectively. They have nothing to do with housing.

All six institutions are members of the Realkreditradet (The Council of Danish Mortgage Credit Institutions) which was founded in 1972. Its primary function is to ensure that the lending activities of the institutions are in accordance with the interests of the community. It also promotes co-operation between the institutes and it represents them to the authorities and to the general public.

Table 13.15 shows details of the total assets of the six institutions.

The dominant position of the Kreditforeningen Danmark is apparent. The point has already been made that the institutions lend for a variety of purposes and not just for housing. Moreover, within the housing sector, they lend to the non-profit making housing associations for the provision of rented housing as well as to owner-occupiers. During 1983, 54% of lending was on owner-occupied housing, 18% was on rented housing, and the remaining 28% was for other purposes.

The Kreditforeningen Danmark is the largest lender for housing, accounting for 43% of loans in 1983; this was followed by the Forende Kreditforeninger (21%), the Byggeriets Realkreditfond (19%) and the Jyllands Kreditforening (16%).

Table 13.15   Danish Mortgage Credit Institutions, Total Assets, 30 November 1983

Name	Total Assets Amount DKrm	%
Kreditforeningen Danmark	175,005	40
Jyllands Kreditforening	92,112	21
Forenede Kreditforeninger	84,702	19
Byggeriets Realkreditfond	63,821	14
Dansk Landbrugs Realkreditfond	18,981	4
Industriens Realkreditfond	5,573	1
All	440,197	100

Source: Realkreditradet, *Beretning og regnskab, 1983*, 1984, Table 11.
Note: At end-November 1983 there were 9.67 kroner to the dollar and 14.29 kroner to the pound.

Table 13.16 shows the aggregate balance sheet for the institutions.

Table 13.16   Mortgage Credit Institutions, Denmark, Assets & Liabilities, 30 November 1983

Liabilities	DKrm	%	Assets	DKrm	%
Bonds in circulation	405,855	92	Mortgages	326,435	74
Index-linked charge	2,193	-	Cash loans	85,167	19
Other liabilities	6,043	1	Bonds	20,893	5
Guarantee capital	1,867	-	Cash	1,770	-
Reserves	24,239	6	Commitments by guarantors	1,867	-
			Property	197	-
			Other	4,046	1
Total	440,197	100	Total	440,197	100

Source: Realkreditradet, *Beretning og regnskab, 1983*, 1984, Table 11.
Note: At end-November 1983 there were 9.67 kroner to the dollar and 14.29 kroner to the pound.

Bonds accounted for 92% of liabilities. Advances accounted for 93% of assets, most of these being mortgages (where the borrower has sold the bonds) rather than the cash loans which are now the predominant form of lending. The institutions have only modest liquid assets (5% of their assets were in bonds and only 0.4% in cash). They are not deposit taking institutions and therefore do not need liquid assets to meet withdrawals.

The aggregate income and expenditure account for the institutions is shown in Table 13.17.

Table 13.17 Mortgage Credit Institutions, Denmark, Income & Expenditure, Year to 30 November 1983

	DKrm	DKrm per 100 DKr Mean Assets
Income		
Interest on mortgages and cash loans	36,320	8.70
Index-linked appreciation	817	0.20
Interest on bond holdings	3,075	0.74
Contribution to reserves	732	0.18
Fees	95	0.02
Total	41,039	9.83
Expenditure		
Interest on bonds	36,372	8.71
Administration	976	0.23
Index-linked appreciation	817	0.02
Mortgage losses	951	0.23
Total	39,116	9.37
Profit	1,923	0.46

Source: Realkreditradet, *Beretning og regnskab, 1983*, 1984, Table 10.
Note: At end-November 1983 there were 9.67 kroner to the dollar and 14.29 kroner to the pound.

Two features of the table merit particular attention -

(a) Admininstration expenses, at 0.23% of mean assets, are much lower than those of building society type organisations, which are in the 1.25%-2.5% range. This is because the institutions are not deposit taking bodies and have no branch networks.
(b) Included in the income figure is an item 'contribution to reserves'. When a borrower takes out a loan he has to make an initial contribution to the reserves of the institution of 0.7% of the loan amount when the advance is for less than 40% of the purchase price, and 1% of the loan amount where there is a higher percentage loan. Additionally, a borrower has to make an annual contribution of 1% (1.25% for loans of more than 40% of purchase price) of current repayments of principal and interest.

Another significant feature of the table is the high level of mortgage losses. Mortgages are made on the security of the property and little regard is paid to the financial circumstances of the borrower. Unlike countries such as the United Kingdom, there is very little state assistance for borrowers who are unable to meet mortgage repayments. This factor, combined with rising unemployment and high interest rates, has led to a sharp increase in mortgage losses and possessions. The number of properties taken into possession increased from 3,298 in 1981 to 5,126 in 1983, and over the same period losses on mortgaged property increased from DKr171 million to DKr923 million.

Assessment

Housing finance in Denmark merits particular study because it illustrates the extreme case of a system being wholly integrated into the financial markets generally. Mortgage loans are always obtainable but the price of this is that they are at a market related rate. Mortgage loans are neither insured nor guaranteed, indicating that these facilities are not essential for a mortgage market to work effectively, albeit at a yield above other market rates.

The institutions have no problem in matching assets and liabilities because their loans are exactly matched by bond issues with similar terms. The only risk that the institutions run is that of losses on mortgage, to guard against which borrowers have to make a direct contribution to reserves.

One consequence of the system is that borrowers are locked into the interest rate at which they take out their loan. Mortgage rates moved gently upwards from 13% in 1975 to 21% in 1982 so existing borrowers benefitted from this arrangement. However, in 1983 rates dropped to 14% and existing borrowers committed to 30 year loans at perhaps 20% saw new borrowers able to obtain their funds at two thirds of the cost. This development may encourage shorter mortgage terms next time interest rates rise.

Sweden

Introduction

Sweden occupies 450,000 sq kilometres. It borders Norway in the West, the Gulf of Bothnia in the East and Finland in the North East. Its population at end-1982 was 8,327,000, substantially larger than any of the other Scandinavian countries. The capital and principal city is Stockholm.

Living standards are high; GNP per capita in Europe is exceeded only in Switzerland and Luxembourg.

Sweden is a monarchy. Like the other Scandinavian countries there are a number of political parties with significant parliamentary representation. The government is responsible to the unicameral Riksdag. A Social Democrat government currently holds office, albeit with support from other parties.

Housing

Previous international studies have suggested that Sweden has a low level of owner-occupation, generally put at under 40%. However, it appears that the definition of owner-occupation has been applied somewhat more rigidly in Sweden than in some other countries. Table 13.18 shows official figures for tenure in 1975.

Table 13.18   Housing Tenure, Sweden, 1975

Tenure	Number of Units	Percentage of Total
Owner-occupied	1,367,000	39
Co-operative housing society (tenant ownership)	505,000	14
Privately rented	814,000	23
Rented from public housing corporations	713,000	20
Rented from central & local government	128,000	4
Total	3,527,000	100

Source: Swedish Official Statistics, *Bostads -och byggbadsstatistisk arsbok 1980*, page 13.

Provisional figures from the 1980 census are that there were 3,667,000 units, of which 41% were owner-occupied, 14% were tenant ownership, 22% were rented publicly, 21% were rented privately and 2% were unknown.

The various types of tenure merit detailed explanation. Owner-occupied dwellings are predominantly one and two family housing; they account for 88% of dwellings in this category but only 2% of dwellings in multi-family units. The proportion of owner-occupied dwellings has remained relatively constant; it was estimated at 38% in 1945. It should be noted that owner-occupation is much higher in the rural areas than in the major urban areas (46% as against 23% in 1975).

Co-operative housing or tenant ownership has elements of both owner-occupation and tenancy. The movement originated in the 1920s when tenant associations first considered producing and managing their own dwellings. In 1923 the National Association of Tenants' Saving and Building Societies—HSB—was formed, and in 1933 a second national association, Riksbyggen, was formed by the trades unions. By 1980 there were 9,000 co-operative housing societies owning 584,000 apartments, 16% of total housing, a small proportion of which are rented. 4,000 societies are grouped into the two national associations, HSB and Riksbyggen. Members granted a right in a co-operative dwelling must pay an initial fee (in effect, the purchase price) in exchange for which they obtain the right to occupy a dwelling for an indefinite time. The member is responsible for changes and repairs to his dwelling and he pays an annual fee to cover the cost of providing common services. He is free to sell his rights at the prevailing market price and the dwelling can be used as security for loans to pay the initial fee (in effect, the purchase price). This form of housing is similar to condominiums in the USA and leasehold property in Britain and can reasonably be recorded as owner-occupied rather than rented. If so, Sweden had an owner-occupation rate of 57% in 1980, very similar to that of the other Scandinavian countries, and a significant increase on the 1945 proportion which is estimated at 43%. The increase is entirely explained by the co-operative sector.

Private rented housing has been declining in recent years; its share of the multifamily stock has fallen from 57% in 1960 to about 35% today. There are virtually no new privately rented houses. Most private landlords are old, and own and manage only one apartment block. As in other countries some privately rented blocks, especially in Stockholm, are being transformed into co-operative housing.

Public sector rented housing is largely provided by public housing corporations, also called municipal housing companies. It grew rapidly in the post-war period from 2% of the stock in 1945 to 22% in 1980. This form of housing accounted for nearly 40% of completions between 1965 and 1974 before falling to 18% in 1976 and then returning to 32% in 1982. The 450 corporations work on a non-profit basis and are controlled by local councils.

Housing policy in Sweden is the responsibility of the Ministry of Housing and Physical Planning. This is basically a policy making body; implementation of policy is largely the responsibility of the National Housing Board, at central level, and municipalities at local level.

Housing policy in the 1960s and 1970s concentrated on building as many new units as possible. One million units were built between 1965 and 1974 by the municipal housing companies, many in the form of estates of large apartment blocks. The nature of these estates has been widely criticized and there have been high vacancy rates. There has been a major switch of policy since the mid-1970s with less emphasis on building multi-family units for rent and more on repairs and maintenance to the existing stock.

Table 13.19 shows trends in dwelling completions between 1970 and 1982.

Table 13.19   New Dwelling Completions, 1970-82

Year	Multi Family Houses	One & Two Family Housing	Total
1970	75,226	34,617	109,843
1975	27,442	47,057	74,499
1976	15,671	40,141	55,812
1977	14,128	40,750	54,878
1978	13,573	40,169	53,742
1979	15,613	39,878	55,491
1980	15,902	35,536	51,438
1981	17,601	33,996	51,597
1982	18,338	26,770	45,108

Source: *Human Settlements in Sweden*, Ministry of Housing and Physical Planning, 1983, Figure IV.7.

It will be noted that production of one and two family housing rose in relation to the production of multi-family housing until 1978 but there has been a sharp reversal of this trend since then.

The government has consciously sought to follow a neutral policy with respect to housing tenure. This has been achieved by low interest rate loans being available for all housing tenures. However, over the last few years there has been a sharp rise in 'tax subsidies' to owner-occupiers. These rose 4.6 times between 1975 and 1981 compared with increases of 4.0 times in interest subsidies and only 1.7 times for housing allowances, available to low income groups in all housing tenures. Tax subsidies have risen partly because of a large number of new houses with high interest costs and also because of high marginal tax rates. Interest subsidies have risen less rapidly because of the fall in the number of multi-family houses. The rise in other subsidies has largely caused the fall in housing allowances. The government has taken action to control the rate of growth of subsidies by limiting tax relief to 50% of interest costs, whereas the highest marginal tax rate is 80%. This policy change is expected to have a major effect on the mortgage and housing markets. (Owner-occupiers can obtain tax relief on mortgage interest but pay tax on notional rental income.) More generally, there has been a lively debate on housing tenure generally, engendered by the centre-right coalition governments in the late 1970s which sought to encourage the conversion of rental units to tenant-ownership. A parliamentary commission is currently reviewing all aspects of housing policy; it is expected to report in 1984.

Housing Finance

The housing finance market in Sweden is dominated by the government and housing finance institutes, some of which are controlled by the commercial and savings banks. Funds are raised through bond issues.

The construction of houses is generally financed by loans from commercial or savings banks and is quite separate from the financing of the purchase.

Purchasers of new houses within certain standards (over 90% of houses are built to qualify) can qualify for a direct state loan through the National Housing Board. This can be for up to 25% of costs for single family owner-occupied homes, 30% for co-operative housing and 22% for private rental housing.

Purchasers of houses that qualify for state loans can obtain, from the housing finance institutes, 'basic loans' covering 70% of the cost. These loans have a 20 year term but provision is made for only partial capital repayment. Interest rates are fixed for five years at a time.

In the case of co-operative housing the initial owners have to meet at least 1% of their costs as their 'fee'. Purchasers of single family houses must provide at least 5% of the costs from their own resources, often through a savings for housing scheme run with a commercial bank or a savings bank.

The housing finance institutes obtain their funds through the sale of bonds. For loans that accompany state loans 'priority housing bonds' are issued. These are at rates of interest regulated by the state. They have generally been at interest rates a little below a market level. The government itself issues similar bonds. The banks, insurance companies and National Pension Fund agree to buy certain amounts of these bonds, and normally they are held to maturity although they can be traded. At the end of 1982 the bonds carried a rate of interest of 12.75% as against a rate of 14.25% on free market bonds. More recently, the gap between the rate on priority bonds and that on free market bonds has been closing. The funds raised in this way are onlent to home-buyers at a premium of just 0.2%.

The National Housing Board obtains its funds from the state which, in turn, raises funds through its priority bonds. It lends on the same terms as the priority loans with the one difference that the rate of interest is fixed for only one year at a time. The rate is equal to the costs of the government's own borrowing plus an administrative fee; in 1982 the rate was 13%. It is intended to move this activity outside the budget to a government mortgage bank which will issue priority housing bonds in the same way as other housing finance institutions.

Table 13.20 shows net purchases of priority housing bonds in 1983.

Table 13.20   Net Purchases of Priority Housing Bonds, 1983

Institution	Net Purchases SKrm	Percentage of Total
Private insurance companies	6,503	33
National Pension Insurance Fund	4,923	25
Commerical banks	3,903	20
Savings banks	1,836	9
Co-operative banks	445	2
Other	1,890	10
Total	19,500	100

Source: Sveriges Riksbank *Quarterly Review*, 1.1984, Tables A.1, A.3, A.4 & A.6.
Note: At end-1983 there were 8.05 kronor to the dollar and 11.56 kronor to the pound.

It will be seen that the pension funds and insurance companies are the main purchasers of bonds. Putting the priority bond market into perspective, total net bond issues in 1983 were SKr83,623 million. Priority housing bonds accounted for 23% of the total, government priority bonds for 40% and government Treasury notes for 30%. Of the insurance companies' total investment portfolio at the end of 1983, 29% was accounted for by priority housing bonds and a further 23% by priority government bonds. For the National Pension Insurance Fund the proportions were similar at 34% and 29% (including non priority bonds) respectively.

A major feature of the housing finance system is that the state gives a guaranteed rate of interest to cover both the state loan and the priority loan, the borrower receiving a subsidy to cover the difference between this rate and the actual rate. The guaranteed rate is currently3% for rented and co-operative housing, and 5.5% for owner-occupied single family housing. These rates are increased by 0.25% and 0.5% a year respectively until the nominal rate is reached. As the nominal rate has been as high as 13% the climb can take about 15 years for single family housing, and as long as 40 years for multi-family housing. In practice, however, the actual period is nearer ten years asthere are periodic rapid cuts in the subsidy on housing produced some years previously. It has already been noted that mortgage interest is tax deductible, although owner-occupiers may pay tax on imputed rental income, and that the growth in housing subsidies has been causing concern in recent years. The home-buyer is subsidized in three ways -

(a) On his priority loan and state loan he may pay a rate of interest below market levels.
(b) On both loans he receives a substantial interest subsidy, currently of eight percentage points in the first year.
(c) On that interest which he does pay he obtains tax relief.

It is necessary to comment briefly on houses which cannot be purchased with state assistance—under 10% of new houses, and secondhand houses. The housing finance institutes or banks make loans on new houses of up to 75% of cost over 20 to 30 years, with rates fixed for 2 year periods. The rate of interest can be at the priority rate but top-up finance will be at the free market rate.

Existing houses are generally financed by bank loans (often based on housing savings schemes) over 10-15 years or by loans from housing finance institutes able to make 'non priority' loans. However, the buyer can generally take over what is left of any priority or state loan. During the late 1970s a practice developed of 'seller certificates' whereby the seller agreed not to receive the full sum demanded, but rather held a certificate with a mortgage on his old house as collateral. At an agreed future date the certificate would be redeemed. This practice seems very similar to the 'creative financing' techniques employed in the USA.

Financial Institutions

Although the direct involvement of commercial banks and savings banks in the housing finance market is relatively small, these institutions merit study because the savings they collect are used to finance the purchase of priority bonds, and because of their ownership of the housing finance institutes. The Swedish banking system is very competitive and, since 1969, the savings banks have been free to compete across the whole range of banking business. At the end of 1983 the commercial banks held deposits from the non-bank sector of SKr225 billion (63% of the total); the savings banks, SKr109 billion (30%) and the co-operative banks, SKr27 billion (7%).

There are 14 commercial banks. Of these six operate provincially, two are local, and two are central institutions for the savings and co-operative banks. The two largest banks are Skandinaviska Enskilda Banken (SEB) and Svenska Handlesbanken which are described subsequently. The third largest is the Post-och Kreditbanken (PK Banken) which is owned by the state and which operates through 1,900 post offices as well as branches. The central bank for the savings banks is the fourth largest bank but it has only limited direct retail business. The other bank with a national branch network is the Gotabanken, but it is less than a quarter of the size of the two large commercial banks.

The activities of the banks in the housing finance market can be illustrated by looking at the activities of the two largest banks. Table 13.21 shows relevant data.

Table 13.21   Commercial Banks and Housing Finance, Sweden, End-1983

	Skandinaviska Enskilda Banken (SEB)	Svenska Handlesbanken
Domestic branches	365	132
Total assets	Kr132 bn	Kr119,693 m
Government bonds	Kr19,474 m	Kr24,935 m
Percentage of total assets	14.8	20.8
Housing priority bonds	Kr9,413 m	Kr9,238 m
Percentage of total assets	7.1	7.7
Housing credit institutions	SFK	Sigab
Assets	Kr10,560 m	Kr8,511
Loans on housing	Kr9,784 m	Kr8,200
Percentage of total assets	7.4	6.9
Housing bond holdings + housing credit institutions' loans	Kr19,197 m	Kr17,438
Percentage of total assets	14.5	14.6

Source: Annual reports.
Note: At end-1983 there were 8.05 kronor to the dollar and 11.56 kronor to the pound.

The Swedish commercial banks (except the central bank for savings banks) own Svensk Bostadsfinansiering (BOFAB) which is one of the housing finance institutes able to make priority loans. The state owned PK Bank has a 50% share. In 1972 SFK and certain other companies agreed to stop making priority loans, these operations to be taken over by BOFAB which would, however, also make non-priority loans. From 1983 BOFAB is not making non-priority loans, and the various banking institutions have regained their power to issue non-priority bonds.

There were 162 savings banks, with 1,425 branches, in Sweden at the end of 1982. Although they can offer the full range of banking services they concentrate their lending to municipalities and individuals. The banks have no legal owners, but are semi-public institutions. The largest bank is the Forsta Sparkbanken, formed by a merger at the beginning of 1982, and which had 132 branches and assets of Kr18,868 million at the end of 1983. As well as limited direct lending for housing, the individual banks have to purchase government and priority savings bonds in the same way as commercial banks.

The savings banks collectively own their central bank, Sparbankernas, also known as Swedbank which, in its own right, is the fourth largest commercial bank in Sweden, with assets of SKr98,748 million at the end of 1983. Sparbankernas owns Spintab (Sparbankernas Inteckningsaktiebolag), a housing finance institute able to make priority loans. This is the second largest institute and its total assets at the end of 1983 were SKr53 billion, over half the total assets of the group. Sparbankernas owns a smaller institute, Sparfi, which makes non-priority loans. This had assets of SKr7 billion at the end of 1983, but has been growing rapidly compared with Spintab and its net lending in 1983 was 30% of the total lending of the two institutions.

When account is taken of lending for housing other than through priority loans, it is estimated that in 1983 the housing finance institutions accounted for 53% of lending for housing purposes, the savings banks for 16%, the savings banks for 12%, the co-operative banks for 3% and the insurance companies for 2%.

Housing Finance Institutes

There are 11 housing finance institutes in Sweden. Only three of these, The Urban Mortgage Bank of Sweden, Spintab (owned by the savings banks) and BOFAB (owned by the commercial banks) can make priority loans. The remaining institutions (eg SFK) give loans for rebuilding, maintenance and second purchase. However, the Urban Mortgage Bank can also make non priority loans. Table 13.22 lists the largest institutions together with details of loans outstanding.

Table 13.22   Long Term Mortgage Loans Outstanding, Sweden, End-1983

Institution and Ownership	Amount SKrm	Percentage of Total
Governments	71,700	24
Urban Mortgage Bank	104,700	35
Spintab (central bank for savings banks)	48,775	16
BOFAB (commercial banks)	41,100	14
SKF (SEB commercial bank)	10,500	3
Sigab (Handlesbanken commercial bank)	8,200	3
Sparfi (central bank for savings banks)	6,337	2
Gigab (Gotabanken commercial bank)	3,100	1
PK—Kredit (PK Banken—state owned, based on post offices)	2,100	1
Other	4,300	1
Total	300,800	100

Source: Urban Mortgage Bank of Sweden.
Notes: 1. At end-1983 there were 8.05 kronor to the dollar and 11.56 kronor to the pound.
          2. The figures include some loans not for housing.

The dominance of the three institutions, and also the government, which can issue priority housing bonds is apparent.

Table 13.23 shows the aggregate balance sheet for all the institutions. Included in this table are figures for the relatively small credit companies.

Table 13.23   Housing Finance Institutions and Credit Companies, Sweden, 1982

Liabilities	Krm	%	Assets	Krm	%
Outstanding bonds	181,157	83	Advances	202,705	93
Promissory note loans	18,779	9	Cash & short-		
Short term borrowing	1,103	1	term loans	2,076	1
Other liabilities	13,931	6	Other assets	12,562	6
Capital and reserves	2,374	1			
Total	217,344	100	Total	217,344	100

Source: Annual Report of the Central Bank.
Note: At end-1982 there were 7.35 kronor to the dollar and 11.91 kronor to the pound.

The typical 'mortgage bank' nature of the balance sheet is apparent.

The Urban Mortgage Bank (Stadshypotekskassan) merits particular attention -

(a) It is by far the largest of the institutes, accounting for nearly half the assets of all institutes. It lends on about 45% of new houses. It is independent of the banks.

(b) It has a semi-mutual nature; borrowers are members, but ultimately the government would have the right to the net assets in the event of the organisation winding up.

(c) It alone is able to lend for priority and non priority purposes.

The Bank was founded in 1909; it was merged with the Swedish Housing Credit Bank in 1969. It has a two tier structure, combining a central bank and 20 urban mortgage societies, based in the major centres of population. Borrowers are members. The bank raises money in the capital markets which it lends to the societies. It is governed by a special law. At the end of 1983, the Bank had loans outstanding of Kr104,791 million, of which 39% was on single family homes, 53% was on multi-family homes, and the remaining 8% was on other property. There has been a marked change in the pattern of lending towards single family houses in recent years, and also a switch from priority to non-priority lending. The Bank obtains its mortgage business largely through introductions from the commercial banks. The banks have to purchase priority bonds and will seek a corresponding allocation of priority loans for their customers. The Bank therefore does not have to compete to attract priority mortgage business; effectively the government decides the size of the market and its allocation between the various institutions. Table 13.24 shows the balance sheet for The Urban Mortgage Bank at the end of 1983.

Table 13.24   Urban Mortgage Bank, Assets & Liabilities, End-1983

Liabilities	Krm	%	Assets	Krm	%
Priority bonds	97,828	90	Loans	104,791	97
Non priority bonds	1,174	1	Other	3,507	3
Promissory notes	4,554	4			
Other liabilities	2,162	2			
Capital & reserves	2,162	2			
Total	108,298	100	Total	108,298	100

Source: *Konungariket Sveriges Stadshypotekskassa 1983.*
Note: At end-1983 there were 8.05 kronor to the dollar and 11.56 kronor to the pound.

This balance sheet is typical of that for a mortgage bank. Bonds account for 91% of liabilities and promissory notes for 4%. It should be noted that in addition to the reserves shown in the table, the individual societies also had reserves of Kr2,635 million. No less than 97% of assets are loans, high even by mortgage bank standards.

Assessment

The Swedish housing finance system has been shaped by legislation. Loans are made by the mortgage bank system because the law prevents banks making loans. However, the state also requires banks and other institutions to purchase bonds to finance the loans, and to do so at rates of interest below market levels. Generally, the system is among the most regulated in industrialized countries. The system seems to work relatively efficiently between house-buyers but there must be doubts about the efficiency of the system with respect to equity between owner-occupiers and tenants and between the various sectors of the economy.

However, the special housing finance circuit is tending to become more integrated into the financial markets generally. The rate of interest on priority bonds has moved nearer to market rates, and lending for transfer of ownership on non-priority terms has been increasing. The housing finance institutes have led a sheltered life, having been given a monopoly of long term lending for house-purchase and being guaranteed purchasers for their bonds. The tight regulation of the system is likely to come under increasing pressure, and in the event of some of the restrictions being eased it would be open to question as to whether this would lead to the housing finance institutes, particularly the independent Urban Mortgage Bank, seeking to attract funds on the open market or whether the commercial and savings bank would seek to expand lending directly.

Bibliography

Finland

Current Trends and Policies in the Field of Housing, Building and Planning in Finland, Ministry of Interior and National Housing Board, 1980.
Housing in Finland, National Housing Board, 1983.
Statistics of the National Housing Board of Finland 1949-1981, National Housing Board of Finland, 1983.
The Finnish Banking System, The Finnish Bankers' Association, 1982.

Norway

Housing in Norway, Ministry of Local Government and Labour, 1982.
Norwegian Commercial Banks, The Norwegian Bankers' Association, 1980.

Denmark

Beretning og regnskab 1983, Realkreditradet, 1984.
Bonds Issued by Danish Mortgage Credit Associations, Kreditforeningen Danmark, 1982.
Danmarks Nationalbank, Annual Report 1982.
Financing of Housing in Denmark, Ministry of Housing, 1983.
Mortgage Financing in Denmark, Realkreditradet, 1982.
Rent Policy in Denmark, Ministry of Housing, 1983.
Results for 1983, Byggeriets Realkreditfond, 1984.
XVI World Congress of IUBSSA, *National Reports*, IUBSSA, 1983, Denmark.

Sweden

Frazer, P and Vittas, D, *The Retail Banking Revolution*, Lafferty Publications, 1982.
'Housing and Housing Policy in Sweden', *Fact Sheets on Sweden*, The Swedish Institute, 1981.
Human Settlements in Sweden, Ministry of Housing and Physical Planning, 1983.
Konungariket Sveriges Stadshypotekskassa 1983, The Urban Mortgage Bank, 1984.
Lundqvist, L J, *Housing Tenures in Sweden*, The National Swedish Institute for Building Research, 1983.
McGuire, C, *International Housing Policies*, Lexington Books, 1981.
SEB Group, Annual Report, 1984.
Sveriges Riksbank, *Quarterly Review*, 1.1984.
The Swedish Credit Market, Swedish Bankers Association.
The Urban Mortgage Bank 1983, The Urban Mortgage Bank of Sweden, 1984.

General

Savings Banks in the Nordic Countries, NCSD, 1981.

Acknowledgements

Useful information for this chapter was provided by -

The Finnish Embassy in London
The National Housing Board for Finland
The Finnish Bankers' Association
The Bank of Finland
Sparebankforeningen 1 Norge

The Royal Norwegian Embassy in London
The Royal Ministry of Local Government & Labour in Norway
The Norges Bank
The Royal Danish Embassy in London
Realkreditradet (The Council of Danish Mortgage Credit Institutions)
Byggeriets Realkreditfond (The Housing Mortgage Fund)
Christopher Sharp, General Manager, Northern Rock Building Society
The Danish Ministry of Housing
Danmarks Nationalbank
The Ministry of Housing and Physical Planning in Sweden
The Urban Mortgage Bank of Sweden
Sveriges Riksbank

The following publications have been drawn on particularly heavily -

Housing in Finland (National Housing Board)
The Finnish Banking System (Finnish Bankers Association)
Statistics of the National Housing Board for Finland
Housing in Norway (Ministry of Housing & Local Government)
The annual report of the Realkreditradet for 1983
Mortgage Financing in Denmark (Realkreditradet)
Human Settlements in Sweden (Ministry of Housing & Physical Planning)
Housing Tenures in Sweden (The National Swedish Institute for Building Research)

The author gratefully acknowledges the assistance of the following in offering invaluable comments on an earlier draft of this chapter -

Christopher Sharp, General Manager, Northern Rock Building Society
Ian MacArthur, International Department, Ministry of Housing and Physical Planning, Sweden
Torben Gjede, Director, Realkreditradet, Denmark
Henning Nielsen, Manager, BRF, Denmark
Percy Bargholtz, Economist, Urban Mortgage Bank of Sweden, commented on a draft of this chapter and together with Mats Ronnberg, Deputy Managing Director of the Bank, and Bjorn Karlberg of the Ministry of Finance, provided valuable additional information at a meeting with the author.

CHAPTER 14

OTHER EUROPEAN COUNTRIES

Switzerland

Switzerland is the richest country in Europe. It has a low level of owner-occupation (30%) but a very high level of housing finance per head of population. There are no specialist housing finance organisations; the biggest lenders are the public sector cantonal banks, followed by the big banks and other regional and savings banks.

Introduction

Switzerland is a small country, occupying an area of 41,293 sq kilometres. It is landlocked, sharing boundaries with France, West Germany, Italy and Austria. Its population in 1982 was 6,468,000; Zurich is by far the largest city, followed by Basle, Geneva and Berne, the capital.

Switzerland is the wealthiest country in Europe; in 1981 GNP per capita was $17,430, 10% higher than that in the second wealthiest country, Luxembourg. Only the oil states in the Middle East have higher national incomes per capita. Inflation has been kept under firm control, averaging 4.0% p a between 1973 and 1980 compared with the OECD average of 10.4% p a. Similarly, interest rates have been kept very low; long term interest rates have averaged under 4% since 1974.

The country is a federal republic, comprising 26 cantons which have considerable autonomy. There are a large number of political parties and for many years all the major parties have been represented in the coalition government. This factor, combined with the extensive use of referenda, has made for a stable government.

Housing

Switzerland has the lowest level of owner-occupation in Europe. In 1980, only 30% of homes were owner-occupied. Table 14.1 shows the distribution of the housing stock in 1980.

The 30% proportion marks an increase on the 1970 figure of 28%, but a decline on the 1960 level of 34%. The growth since 1970 is entirely explained by the increase in owner-occupied flats. Owner-occupation is even less pronounced in the urban areas; in none of the major cities does it exceed 10%. Co-operatives account for a significant proportion of rented housing in the cities, but most dwellings are owned privately. In 1980 65% of all dwellings

Table 14.1 Housing Tenure, Switzerland, 1980

Tenure of Units	Number of Total	Percentage
Owned houses	663,685	27.5
Owned flats	58,562	2.4
Rented or co-operative	1,618,678	67.1
Occupied with job or free	59,784	2.5
Total	2,413,185	100.0

Source: *Annuaire Statistiques de la Suisse, 1983.*

were owned by persons, 23% by co-operatives, 8% by associations and only 3% by the public sector.

A significant feature of the housing market has been the growth in the number of second homes; these increased from 5.9% of the stock in 1970 to 8.8% in 1980.

Contrary to the position in most other countries, housebuilding has been on a rising trend in recent years. Table 14.2 shows the figures for 1978-82.

Table 14.2 Housebuilding Completions, Switzerland, 1978-82

Year	Public Collectives	Construction Co-operatives	Corporate Bodies	Persons	Total
1978	1,036	2,302	7,771	12,807	23,217
1979	689	2,235	8,614	14,501	26,037
1980	638	1,921	9,841	15,887	28,287
1981	722	2,421	12,114	16,589	31,846
1982	545	2,450	12,874	16,440	32,309

Source: *Annuaire Statistiques de la Suisse, 1983.*

It will be seen that over half of dwellings have been built by individuals and most of the remainder by corporate bodies for renting. Fewer than 10% of new houses are built with any form of state aid.

Housing policy stems from the Law on Assistance to Housing and Owner-Occupiers 1975, which had as one of its objectives the encouragement of owner-occupation. Financial assistance was made available to developers of owner-occupied homes on the same basis as to developers of rented homes. Generally, policy is non-interventionist; in particular, there is a fairly free market in rented accommodation.

Housing Finance

Although Switzerland has a low level of owner-occupation, it has a very high level of housing finance. Table 11.7 shows that Switzerland has the highest ratio of housing debt to GNP in the world. There are a number of explanations for this -

(a) House prices are high and large loans are therefore required.
(b) The mortgage rate is low—it varied only from 5% to 6.2% from 1973 to 1982.
(c) Personal taxes are high, and can be reduced by having a mortgage debt on which the interest is tax deductible.
(d) Most mortgage debt is on an interest only basis and therefore is not reduced until a house is sold.
(e) The low level of inflation has meant that the real value of mortgage debt has not been reduced as much as in other countries.

Housing finance in Switzerland is provided by general rather than specialist banks and it is difficult to disentangle loans for house-purchase from other mortgage loans and other personal loans.

Table 14.3 shows key statistics for mortgage debt outstanding and the major lenders.

Table 14.3   Mortgage Debt and Banks, Switzerland, End-1982

Type of Bank	Number of Banks	Number of Branches	Total Assets SFm	Mortgages SFm	%	Of which on Family Homes SFm	%
Cantonal banks	29	1,308	119,015	51,760	39	15,901	36
Big banks	5	872	305,749	39,426	30	12,003	27
Regional & savings banks	218	1,096	51,181	27,653	21	10,914	24
Loan and raiffeisen banks	1,226	1,244	15,621	9,193	7	4,629	10
Other banks	181	241	87,503	3,748	3	1,287	3
Total	1,659	4,761	580,068	131,780	100	44,769	100

Source: Swiss National Bank, *Les Banques Suisses en 1982*, 1983.
Note: At end-1982 there were 2.05 swiss francs to the dollar and 3.32 swiss francs to the pound.

The figures for mortgages include loans on non-residential property but it is estimated that over 75% are for house-purchase. It will be noted that the market is largely shared by three different types of bank, all of which lend on similar terms. Typically, a first loan is given for up to 60% of purchase price. No repayments of principal are required and thus the debt holds constant until the property is sold. If second loans are required these usually are amortized. The banks attempt to match assets and liabilities and finance mortgage loans by savings deposits, medium term notes, mortgage bonds and debenture bonds. The mortgage rate is variable, but as interest rates generally have been very stable, so have the rates on mortgage loans.

The financing of house-purchase loans and the role of the various institutions in the personal savings market is well illustrated by Table 14.4 which shows households' assets and liabilities with the banks.

Table 14.4   Liabilities and Loans of Banks to Households, Switzerland, End-1982

Institution	Liabilities to Households		Loans to Households	
	SFm	%	SFm	%
Cantonal banks	49,350	35	45,767	33
Big banks	45,264	32	44,381	32
Regional and savings banks	28,344	20	24,161	17
Loan and raiffeisen banks	9,531	7	9,806	7
Other banks	7,405	5	9,225	7
Total	139,894	100	133,343	100

Source: Swiss National Bank, *Les Banques Suisses en 1982*, 1983.
Note: At end-1982 there were 2.05 Swiss francs to the dollar and 3.32 francs to the pound.

It will be seen that there is a marked correspondence between funds raised from the public and loans to the public for each of the types of institution.

Housing Finance Institutions

The cantonal banks, as a group, are the largest lenders for house-purchase and also the largest savings institutions. They are controlled by the regional governments in each canton, although four also have private share capital. The largest cantonal bank is that for Zurich (assets of SF22,101 million at the end of 1982) followed by those for Berne (SF8,004 million) and Lucerne (SF7,742 million). Mortgages, widely defined, account for 43% of the assets of the cantonal banks.

The five big banks are huge but their activity is largely international and commercial rather than with the personal sector. The three largest banks, all of which are privately owned, are the Union Bank of Switzerland (assets of SF106,353 million at the end of 1982), Swiss Bank Corporation (SF96,816 million) and Credit Suisse (SF73,497 million). The remaining two banks, Swiss Volksbank (a co-operative) and Bank Leu (privately owned) are much smaller. The Union Bank of Switzerland is the largest mortgage lender in the country. It had mortgage assets of SF17,016 at the end of 1982, 70% of which was in respect of residential property. All the banks are universal banks and have an importance above that which would be suggested by their balance sheets.

The regional and savings banks have a variety of legal forms. Most are co-operative or private companies but some are controlled by local authorities. Mortgages, widely defined, account for 54% of their assets. They are largely distinguished from the cantonal banks by their large number (218 as against 29) and hence small average size. Most have assets of under SF200 million. At the end of 1982 only ten had assets of over SF1,000 million and only one had assets in excess of SF2,000 million, the Aargauische Hypotheken—under Handelsbank (assets of SF3,185 million).

The loan and raiffeisen banks are co-operatives and are very similar to credit unions. Of the 1,226 institutions, 1,212 are members of the Schweizer Verband der Raiffeisenkassen and the remaining 14 belong to a local organisation in Vaud.

The Netherlands

Introduction

The Netherlands occupies an area of 41,548 sq kilometres. In the North West it borders on the North Sea, to the South on Belgium, and to the East on West Germany. The country is extremely flat and a considerable amount of it has been reclaimed from the sea; indeed, 22% of the country is below sea level.

The population of the Netherlands at the beginning of 1983 was 14,340,000 almost half of whom live in the Amsterdam/Rotterdam/The Hague area. Generally, the country is densely populated. Amsterdam is the capital but the seat of government is in The Hague. Administratively, the Netherlands consists of 11 provinces, which can be sub-divided into 842 municipalities. The country is a monarchy but political power rests with parliament and government. There are two chambers of parliament, one directly elected and the other elected by the provinces. The electoral system uses proportional representation and this, combined with a catholic/protestant split, has contributed to a multi-party system; coalition governments are invariably in power.

Housing

At the end of 1982 there were 5,072,000 dwellings in the Netherlands. Table 14.5 shows a tenure breakdown of dwellings at the end of 1981.

Table 14.5   Housing Tenure, The Netherlands, End-1981

Tenure	Percentage of Total
Owner-occupied	44
Rented from housing associations	34
Rented from local authorities	9
Rented from private institutions	5
Rented from private landlords	8
Total	100

Source: *Some Data on housebuilding in the Netherlands*, Ministry of Housing, Physical Planning and Environment, 1983.

There seems to have been a steady increase in the proportion of owner-occupied dwellings in recent years, from 35% in 1970 to 39% in 1975 and 42% in 1977, although the data are not wholly consistent. However, the proportion of owner-occupied dwellings may have fallen since 1981.

Over half of rented houses are owned by local housing associations. These are generally cheap dwellings intended for lower income groups and they are financed by public funds. Local authorities own 20% of rented dwellings. They can now develop housing for rent only if a housing association cannot take on a specific development. Most local authority rented housing is pre-war. Both local authority and housing association dwellings are heavily subsidized. Pension funds account for a significant proportion of dwellings in the privately rented sector.

Housing policy is the responsibility of the Ministry of Housing, Physical Planning and Environment, and has been very interventionist. There are complicated subsidy and rent control systems which are beyond the scope of this book. Broadly speaking, subsidies depend on the cost of the house and the income of the occupants. Until the end of 1983 they were on a diminishing annual basis; now they are fixed amounts for a number of years.

Table 14.6 shows housebuilding statistics from 1977 to 1982.

Table 14.6   Completed Dwellings, The Netherlands, 1977-82

Year	For Owner-Occupation			For Renting	Total
	Premium-Assisted	Unsubsidized	Total		
1977	33,000	27,000	60,000	51,000	111,000
1978	32,000	30,000	64,000	42,000	106,000
1979	26,000	28,000	56,000	32,000	88,000
1980	35,000	28,000	64,000	50,000	114,000
1981	30,000	17,000	47,000	71,000	118,000
1982			34,000	89,000	123,000

Source: *Some Data on housebuilding in the Netherlands*, Ministry of Housing, Physical Planning and Environment, 1983.

Note: A small number of houses for owner-occupation have been built under special provisions in the Housing Act and are included in the total for owner-occupied dwellings but not in either of the sub-divisions.

A number of points emerge from this table -

(a) Housebuilding in relation to the population has been high compared with other countries.
(b) Building of rented housing has increased in relation to building for owner-occupation, marking a sharp reversal of the contrary position which existed between 1971 and 1976.
(c) The greatest decline has been in unsubsidized dwellings for owner-occupation, the reasons for this are discussed subsequently.

Housing Finance

The most significant feature of the housing finance market in the Netherlands in recent years has been a dramatic slump in activity and reduction in house prices. Major trends are shown in Table 14.7.

Table 14.7   Housing Finance, The Netherlands, 1975-82

Year	New Mortgage Loans on Houses Gm	Owner-Occupied House Price Index 1969 = 100	Mortgage Interest Rate %
1975	21,701	202	9.9
1976	30,189	244	9.4
1977	42,124	299	8.9
1978	52,395	319	8.6
1979	44,151	300	9.7
1980	37,722	276	11.4
1981	28,806	248	12.7
1982	24,033	232	11.1

Source: Netherlands Association of Mortgage Banks.
Note: At end-1982 there were 2.67 guilders to the dollar and 4.32 guilders to the pound.

The table shows a massive slump. Between 1978 and 1982 mortgage lending declined by 54% in nominal terms and no less than 69% in real terms. House prices over the same period fell by 27% in nominal terms and 50% in real terms. However, the rise in mortgage rates was hardly dramatic, and was much less than in many other countries. Furthermore, by the end of 1982 the mortgage rate had fallen to 9%.

A number of inter-related factors have served to cause this state of affairs -

(a) House prices increased by nearly 50% between 1975 and 1977 and rented housing suddenly became more attractive than buying, leading to a sharp decline in the demand for owner-occupation. The rise in mortgage interest rates accentuated this trend.

(b) The recession in the Netherlands has fed through to the demand for owner-occupied housing. Unemployment has risen more rapidly than in any other OECD country; GNP fell by 4% between 1978 and 1982.

(c) Doubts as to the viability of some of the major mortgage lenders have added to the general lack of confidence in the market.

(d) From the beginning of 1981 full mortgage interest tax deductability was limited to loans up to G540,000. This was not, in itself, a significant measure but discussion of a possible limitation on tax relief had an unsettling effect on the market. The limiting of tax deductability of maintenance expenditure has also had an effect.

(e) The various forces have fed on each other; the initial fall in house prices led to fears of further falls and cast doubt on the viability of lending institutions.

The collapse of the property market had the greatest effect on the specialist mortgage lenders, the mortgage banks, and has contributed to sharp changes in shares of the housing finance market. Table 14.8 shows changes in the distribution of new house mortgages between 1970 and 1982.

Table 14.8   Newly Registered Mortgages on Residential Property, The Netherlands, 1970-82

	1970 %	1978 %	1982 %
Mortgage banks and bouwfonds	11	24	15
Insurance companies & pension funds	17	7	7
Savings banks	6	10	12
Co-operative & general banks	46	46	49
Other financial institutions	16	12	14
Private sources	5	1	2
Total	100	100	100

Source: Netherlands Association of Mortgage Banks.

It will be seen that the banks have nearly 50% of the total market; the greatest variation in market share has been experienced by the mortgage banks; the savings banks have achieved a steady increase in market share. However, the mortgage banks staged a strong recovery in 1983 following a restructuring of activities to concentrate more exclusively on mortgage lending. This trend is expected to continue.

Table 14.9 shows a more detailed distribution of mortgage debt outstanding (as opposed to new loans) at end-1981, in particular, splitting banks into the Rabobank and the commercial banks.

Table 14.9   Housing Debt Outstanding, The Netherlands, End-1981

Institution	Amount Gbn	Percentage of Total
Commercial banks	23.0	21
Rabobank	35.0	32
Mortgage banks	13.0	12
Insurance companies	15.0	14
Savings banks	10.9	10
Postal savings banks	7.3	7
Bouwfonds	5.3	5
Total	109.5	100

Source: Frazer, P and Vittas, D, *The Retail Banking Revolution*, Lafferty Publications, 1982.
Note: At end-1981 there were 2.47 guilders to the dollar and 4.71 guilders to the pound.

It will be seen that the Rabobank (agricultural credit bank) is the largest single lender.

The Savings Market

The Rabobank is the largest savings institution, as well as the largest housing finance lender. The other principal savings institutions are the savings banks, the Postal Savings Bank and the commercial banks. Table 14.10 shows the distribution of savings and time deposits in September 1983.

Table 14.10   Savings and Time Deposits, The Netherlands, September 1983

Institution	Amount Gm	Percentage of Total
Rabobank	55,076	41
Commercial banks	36,397	28
Savings banks	23,620	17
Post Office Savings Bank	20,733	14
Total	135,826	100

Source: Cental Bureau of Statistics, *Maandstatistick Financiewezen*, January 1984, Table 1.09.
Note: At end-September 1983 there were 2.98 guilders to the dollar and 4.47 guilders to the pound.

The Rabobank

The leading position of the Rabobank has already been indicated. As a bank, it is among the 50 largest in the world. Local rabobanks, or agricultural co-operative banks, were formed at the end of the 19th century to take deposits from, and make loans to, the agricultural community. The present structure of the system dates back to 1972 when the Co-operatieve Centrale Raiffeisen—Bank of Utrecht and the Co-operative Centrale Raiffeisen—Boerenleenbank of Eindhoven merged to form the Co-operatieve Centrale Raiffeisen-Boerenleenbank BA, known generally as the Rabobank Nederland. This functions as a central bank and service institution for its members, the 964 local rabobank co-operatives which operate as full service banks, but it is also a full line commercial bank itself. The group is completed by special finance subsidiaries including a mortgage bank. The various components of the Group are linked together, financially and legally, through a mutual guarantee system. The Rabobank system had 3,051 branches at the end of 1982 and total assets of G110,158 million.

Table 14.11 shows the aggregate balance sheet of the Rabobank Group at the end of 1982.

Of the total credits of G64,441 million (loans secured by mortgage and other debtors less debts not counted as credits, eg interest owing) 31% was to agriculture, forestry and fishing and 49% was to the private sector, most of it for house-purchase.

Included in Table 14.11 are figures for the subsidiary mortgage bank, Rabohypotheekbank. At the end of 1982 this organisation had assets of G12,488 million, of which mortgage loans accounted for G12,164 million (97%). The bank obtains nearly 60% of its funds from long term loans, 40% of them from the central Rabobank Nederland. The remaining 40% of funds are obtained from mortgage bonds, over 20% of which are held by other members of the group. About 50% of the lending of the mortgage bank is for

Table 14.11   Rabobank Group, Assets and Liabilities, End-1982

Liabilities	Gm	%	Assets	Gm	%
Savings deposits	54,759	50	Loans secured by		
Time deposits	6,293	6	mortgage	51,810	47
Negotiable paper	13,619	12	Other debtors	15,291	14
Owing to banks	13,312	12	Due from banks	17,059	15
Creditors	16,269	15	Financial assets	10,165	9
Borrowed funds	614	1	Advances to or guar-		
Capital debentures	70	-	anteed by public		
Own funds	5,221	5	authorities	12,672	12
			Equity investments	337	-
			Premises and equipment	2,825	3
Total	110,158	100	Total	110,158	100

Source: Annual Report 1982.
Note: At end-1982 there were 2.67 guilders to the dollar and 4.32 guilders to the pound.

house-purchase.

The mortgage bank lends on terms similar to other mortgage banks, that is, rates are fixed for five or ten years at a time. The local rabobanks, relying as they do on short term deposits, make greater use of the variable rate mortgage.

Commercial Banks

The commercial banks are the second largest group of housing finance lenders with a little over a fifth of the market. There are 40 general domestically owned banks but the industry is dominated by the three large banks, the Algemene Bank Nederland (ABN), the Amsterdam-Rotterdam Bank (AMRO) and the Nederlandsche Middenstandsbank (NMB). The ABN had total assets of G123,934 million at the end of 1982, making it slightly larger than the Rabobank Group although it had many fewer branches, 871. Its mortgage loans amounted to G13,636 million at the end of 1982 (11% of total assets). Over half of its mortgage loans are held through subsidiaries, the most important of which is a special mortgage finance institution, the Hypothecair Kredit. AMRO is comparable in size to the ABN and concentrates on domestic operations, while the NMB is under half the size of the two large banks.

Mortgage Banks

The mortgage banks merit particular attention both because they are specialist housing finance lenders, and because they have experienced severe financial difficulties in the recent past. Table 14.8 showed how they have lost substantial market share, from 24% in 1978 to 15% in 1982.

The first mortgage bank was founded in 1861 and in its early days the industry primarily served the agricultural community. Like the rabobanks they gradually moved into new areas. They are all limited companies; some are independent, while others are owned by more general financial institutions, including the Rabobank Group and insurance companies. Table 14.12 shows the aggregate balance sheet for the mortgage banks at the end of 1982.

Table 14.12   Mortgage Banks, Assets and Liabilities, Netherlands, End-1982

Labilities	Gm	%	Assets	Gm	%
Mortgage bonds	14,533	43	Mortgage loans	29,181	86
Other long term			Other assets	4,612	14
loans	14,303	42			
Other liabilities	4,957	15			
Total	33,793	100	Total	33,793	100

Source: Netherlands Association of Mortgage Banks.
Note: At end-1982 there were 2.67 guilders to the dollar and 4.30 guilders to the pound.

The mortgage banks, like their counterparts in other countries, are not deposit taking bodies. They raise about half of their long term funds through mortgage bonds (pandbrieven), which are publicly quoted and are traded on the Amsterdam Stock Exchange. They are on offer continuously, generally over the counter. Until a few years ago the bonds had maturities of between 20 and 40 years, but, more recently, terms of 7-10 years have been more common. The remaining funds are raised through private loans from other financial institutions. Mortgage loans have been at fixed rates of interest, in line with mortgage bonds, and have been repayable over 25 or 30 years.

The largest mortgage bank is that owned by the Rabobank; indeed during 1982 it accounted for 44% of the total amount raised by way of mortgage bonds. There have been three large independent mortgage banks, Westland Utrecht Hypotheekbank (WUH), Fiesch Groningsche (FGH) and Tilburgsche Hypotheekbank. These banks, which have not had the backing of other financial institutions, have suffered from the slump in the property market, illustrated in Table 14.7. In particular, their mortgage bonds have been seen as a risky investment.

Both WUH and Tilburgsche Hypotheekbank have been in severe financial difficulty for some time; the latter finally filed for bankruptcy in 1983. WUH lost G114.7 million in 1982 and has needed considerable assistance from other financial institutions.

Mention needs to be made at this stage of the public sector Bouwfonds, the largest of which is the Netherlands Local Authorities Building Fund. The figures for these institutions are sometimes aggregated with those of the mortgage banks. They obtain their funds directly from their constituent authorities and they are often lent at preferential rates.

Savings Banks

The savings banks in the Netherlands are comparatively small by international standards. There are about 50 non-profit making savings banks which are gradually grouping together. The largest savings bank is the Centrum Bank, formed by merger in the late 1970s. At the end of 1981 it had assets of G7,700 million and 289 branches. There is also the Post Office Savings Bank which is in the process of becoming a full service commercial bank. The total assets of the savings banks at the end of 1982 were G55,866 million, of which G21,289 million (38%) were in mortgages.

Greece

Introduction

Greece occupies an area of 131,986 sq kilometres, about 20% of which is accounted for by the various islands. The mainland is surrounded by sea on three sides and it has northern borders with Albania, Yugoslavia, Bulgaria and Turkey.

In 1982 the population of Greece was 9,792,000. Athens, the capital, had a population of 2,540,000 and the other major centre of population is Salonika with a population of just over 500,000. Greece is still predominantly an agricultural country, this sector accounting for about one third of the workforce.

Since 1975 Greece has been a republic with a unicameral parliament. Since October 1981, the socialist party (PASOK) has been in power.

Greece is poorer than most of the other countries on the mainland of Western Europe. GNP per capita is less than half that of the wealthier countries of Western Europe and significantly below that of Spain although higher than that of Portugal or Turkey. The economy has been growing more rapidly than the average for industrialized countries over the past ten years or so. However, a major problem has been inflation. Consumer prices increased by an average of 17.3% a year between 1973 and 1980 compared with the OECD average of 10.4%. The rate of increase in prices was over 19% during 1982.

Housing

Statistics on housing in Greece are not readily available. However, it is apparent that the government plays only a relatively minor role in the provision of housing and the public sector is not directly responsible for any housebuilding. The 1970 census showed that 70% of households were owner-occupiers, 25.5% were tenants and the remaining 4.5% were in other tenures. In urban areas the proportion of owner-occupiers fell to 57.6%. House building activity has been very high in relation to the size of the population. Permits were issued for the construction of 187,000 houses in 1978 and 189,000 in 1979. Since then, however, the figure has fallen quite sharply to 102,000 in 1982. Nevertheless, these figures are very high in relation to the population.

The new socialist government has a stated housing policy embracing three objectives -

(a) Increased production of housing for low and medium income groups.
(b) The establishment of new residential areas using a variety of sources of finance.
(c) Increased emphasis on maintenance and improvement.

Housing Finance and the National Mortgage Bank of Greece

The Greek financial system is dominated by commercial banks which held 71.5% of deposits at the end of 1981. The two major commercial banks are the National Bank of Greece (which handles 60% of domestic banking business) and the Commercial Bank of Greece, both of which are state controlled. The other major deposit taking institution is the Greece Post Office Savings Bank. There are no other savings banks or other retail financial institutions. The Post Office Savings Bank operates through 100 branches and 700 post offices and has over 3,000,000 accounts. It held 14.9% of deposits at the end of 1981.

The remaining 18% of deposits are held by the special status banks, the most important of which is the National Mortgage Bank of Greece. Generally, the banking system is highly concentrated, and not well developed.

In common with other predominantly agricultural communities, Greece has a comparatively underdeveloped housing finance system. Housebuilding and house-purchase is, to a large extent, financed outside of the institutional framework and this in turn contributes to the absence of reliable data about the nature of the housing finance market. Table 14.13 shows how investment in housing in Greece in 1982 was financed.

Table 14.13 Investment in Housing, Greece, 1982

Gross investment in housing	Dr 124,522 million
Bank lending for housing	Dr 44,007 million
NMBG lending for housing	Dr 31,327 million
Bank lending/gross investment	35.4%
NMBG lending/gross investment	25.2%
NMBG lending/all bank lending	71.2%

Source: National Mortgage Bank of Greece Annual Report, 1982.
Note: At end-1982 there were 70.6 drachmas to the dollar and 114.3 drachmas to the pound.

It will be seen that bank lending financed only 35.4% of gross investment in housing. This figure represented a considerable increase on the proportion of 25.8% in 1981 and just 11.8% in 1980. The table also shows that the National Mortgage Bank of Greece accounted for 71.2% of bank lending for housing. This institution dominates the institutional housing finance market in Greece.

The National Mortgage Bank of Greece (its name was changed to National Housing Bank of Greece in 1983; its old name is used in this section) is publicly owned and controlled. Technically, it is a subsidiary of the National Bank of Greece, which is nationalized. Now, it concentrates on housing but this is a fairly recent development. In 1974 only half of its lending was for housing. Its lending for other purposes, in particular the tourist sector, has been stagnant subsequently while lending for housing has increased 18 fold such that it now accounts for 95% of new lending. The Bank has set out six mechanisms by which it can help to achieve the housing objectives of the new government -

(a) The organisation of a free market of housing loans.
(b) The establishment of an effective housing saving mechanism.
(c) The financing of housing programmes for organised construction.
(d) A new priority system for the granting of ordinary housing loans.
(e) The setting up of a flexible and effective system for communicating and analysing data relating to loan and fund planning. The system will be based on electronic data processing.
(f) The organisation of a branch network throughout the country. The Bank already has 34 branches.

The Bank is an interesting mixture of mortgage bank and deposit taking institution. Table 14.14 shows the balance sheet for the Mortgage Bank as at the end of 1982.

Table 14.14 National Mortgage Bank of Greece, Assets & Liabilities, End-1982

Liabilities	Dr m	%	Assets	Dr m	%
Housing savings deposits	34,181	17	Housing mortgage loans	91,598	45
Time deposits	43,096	21	Other housing loans	11,747	6
Other deposits	7,464	4	Other mortgage loans	29,344	15
Bank of Greece	76,603	38	Other loans	10,936	5
Other loans	11,072	5	Cash & securities	16,704	8
Bank bonds	8,569	4	Other assets	41,001	20
Bond loans	201	-			
Other liabilities	13,149	7			
Retentions & provisions	2,512	1			
Profit, reserves & shares	7,444	4			
Total	201,332	100	Total	201,332	100

Source: National Mortgage Bank of Greece Annual Report, 1982.
Note: At end-1982 there were 70.6 drachmas to the dollar and 114.3 drachmas to the pound.

It will be noted that the liabilities are divided fairly equally between those from the Bank of Greece, the central bank, and deposits. A housing savings scheme is operated but this seems to be relatively modest, although there were 228,000 acounts in operation at the end of 1982. Only 4% of the amount lent is to those who have qualified by virtue of saving under the scheme.

The most notable feature of the housing savings scheme is its reliance on savings from overseas. Some three quarters of all deposits in the housing savings department are made in foreign currencies by Greek nationals working abroad, particularly in the USA, West Germany and Belgium, although also in Australia and Canada. These depositors can elect to have their savings converted into the local currency at the prevailing exchange rates or they can be held denominated in the foreign currency. The latter obviously poses an exchange risk for the Bank but this is met through the Bank of Greece which effectively absorbs the risk.

The Bank also obtains loans directly from the Bank of Greece, largely on a long term basis.

In 1982 the Bank lent Dr32,926 million to 38,000 borrowers; 95% of all loans were for housing and of the total number of loans 41% went to people eligible for workers' housing, 11% were made to people entitled to loans against the importation of foreign currency and, as has already been mentioned, 4% were made to depositors under the housing savings scheme. The rate of interest charged varied between 13% and 17% depending on the circumstances of the borrower. This rate is below market rates and the rate of inflation. Loans are generally for not more than 50% of value and are repayable within 15 years.

Table 14.15 shows the income and expenditure account for the Mortgage Bank in 1982.

Table 14.15 National Mortgage Bank of Greece, Income and Expenditure, 1982

	Dr m	Dr per 100 Dr Mean Assets
Income		
Loan interest, commission & other revenue	15,835	12.62
Income from property	51	0.04
Total	15,886	12.66
Expenditure		
Interest	13,496	10.76
Staff costs	1,008	0.80
General administrative expenses	332	0.73
Taxes & levies	115	0.26
Depreciation	99	0.08
Amortization of loans and bonds	59	0.05
Retentions and provisions	413	0.33
Tax	25	0.02
Net surplus	348	0.28
Total	15,886	12.66

Source: National Mortgage Bank of Greece Annual Report, 1982.
Note: At end-1982 there were 70.6 drachmas to the dollar and 114.3 drachmas to the pound.

A fairly high figure for retentions and provisions should be noted. These are in respect of likely depreciation of assets. It is also relevant that of the housing mortgage loans of Dr91,598 million at the end of 1982, Dr5,521 million (6%) was in respect of instalments in arrears. These comparatively high figures may possible reflect the rapid growth of the Bank as a mortgage lender. The Bank is, as has already been noted, the only significant lender for housing and it recognises its major responsibilities towards providing an efficient housing finance market and also in encouraging housing contruction.

Portugal

Introduction

Portugal occupies an area of 92,082 sq kilometres. It is part of the Iberian peninsula, bordering on to the Atlantic ocean in the West and South, and otherwise it is surrounded by Spain. In 1981 the population of Portugal was 9,496,000. Lisbon, the capital and principal city, had a population of 1,870,000. Following a revolution in 1974, Portugal became a republic. Political power is in the hands of a directly elected president and an assembly. Since the revolution Portugal has suffered from political instability, with 11 governments in the six years immediately following the revolution. Currently, the Social Democrat Party is the largest but a centre/right coalition is in power.

Economically, Portugal is one the poorest countries of Western Europe. GNP per capita is less than half that of Spain although above that of Turkey. Economic growth has also been comparatively modest over the past decade or so. Portugal's acute economic problems have been reflected in a high rate of inflation. Between 1973 and 1980 consumer prices increased by an average of 22.6% a year compared with the OECD average of 10.4%. Interest rates have been at very high levels. The central bank discount rate reached 23% in 1983 and the long term loan rate was in excess of 30%.

Housing

There is little available information on the housing stock or housing tenure in Portugal. The number of completions has been running at between 40,000 and 45,000 a year. Of houses built in 1980, 65% were funded by private individuals, 20% by private bodies and 14% by public authorities.

There has been a significant change in housing policy since the 1974 revolution. In 1975 legislation was introduced to restrict rent increases and this discouraged the building of new rented accommodation. It was intended that this should be compensated for by an increase in public sector housebuilding, but this has only partially materialized.

Fundo de Fomento da Habitacao (FFH) is the central government agency charged with the implementation of national housing policies. Its role has increased substantially since 1974 to include the construction of houses for rent. It obtains its funds directly from the central budget, but also from the credit institutions, in particular, the Caixa Geral de Depósitos.

Housing Finance and the Financial System

Table 14.16 shows details of the major financial institutions in Portugal as at the end of 1982.

Table 14.16   Financial Institutions, Portugal, End-1982

Institution	Deposits C m	Net Assets C m	Branches
Caixa Geral de Depósitos	428.0	576.7	283
Other savings & investment banks			
Banco de Fomento Nacional	51.7	171.1	20
Crédito Predial Portugués	89.0	136.0	56
Montepio Geral-Económica de Lisboa	51.9	64.2	28
Commercial banks			
Banco Portugués do Atlántico	336.9	444.2	133
Banco Posto & Sotto Mayor	256.3	325.5	119
Banco Espirito Santo e	244.1	312.9	130
Commerciale de Lisboa			
Other national banks	928.2	1,214.0	597

Source: *The Portuguese Credit Market*, Caixa Geral de Depósitos, 1983, Table 1.
Note: At end-1982 there were 0.89 contos to the dollar and 1.5 contos to the pound

It will be seen that the Caixa Geral de Depósitos is by far the largest single institution. It is also the largest mortgage lender. Its structure and functions are described in detail in the following section.

The commercial banks were all nationalized in 1975. They have only a limited involvement in housing finance although, as the table shows, they are significant deposit taking bodies.

Portugal has a relatively small savings bank industry in comparison with other countries. Of the savings and investment banks listed the Credito Predial Portugués and the Montepio Geral — Economica de Lisboa are officially classed as savings banks. The Credito Predial Portugués was founded in 1864 and was established in its present form in 1970. Traditionally, its role was an agricultural mortgage credit bank but during the 1970s it developed more general functions, particularly in the housing field. The Montepio Geral — Economica de Lisboa was founded in 1840. It is a mutual institution and incorporates a savings bank, the Caixa Economica de Lisboa. Housing and construction accounts for over three quarters of the lending of this institu-. tion. There are also 19 small private savings banks which, in effect, are local credit bodies. Their total assets do not exceed 100 million contos and they are, therefore, very small. However, they do a limited amount of lending for house-purchase.

It has been exceptionally difficult for the housing finance system to work effectively in Portugal given the high inflation and interest rates. The long term interest rate reached 22% in 1978, 26% in 1982 and 32% in 1983. The bank discount rate rose to 25% in 1983. A somewhat alarming feature of the evolution of interest rates is that the long term rate has never once fallen since 1974, and only on one occasion has the central bank discount rate fallen, and then by only 0.5%. Notwithstanding the sharp rise in market interest rates, the maximum rate payable on sight deposits has remained at 4% since 1975.

No precise figures are available on the distribution of housing finance loans between the various types of institution. However, in 1982, of the total lent for construction and housing of 138 million contos, the Caixa Geral de Depósitos accounted for 38%, the commercial banks for 28%, and other institutions for 29%. If loans to individuals only are considered there is little doubt that the Caixa's share is above 50%.

The Caixa Geral de Depósitos

Table 14.16 showed that the Caixa Geral de Depósitos is the largest single financial institution in Portugal. It was established in 1876 but now operates under a 1969 law. It has the status of a public sector credit institution and effectively it is the national savings bank as well as having wider functions. It has been growing rapidly in recent years, the number of branches increasing from 170 in 1980 to 283 in 1982. It accounts for about one fifth of the total financial system and has over 7,000,000 deposit accounts, that is, more than one for each adult.

Table 14.17 shows the balance sheet for the Caixa at the end of 1982.

Table 14.17   Caixa Geral de Depósitos, Assets & Liabilities, 1982

Liabilities	C m	%	Assets	C m	%
Term deposits	282.1	50	Real estate loans	156.0	28
Sight deposits	76.9	14	Other loans	204.3	37
Obligatory deposits	64.2	11	Cash & deposits at		
Savings deposits	3.9	1	Bank of Portugal	43.4	8
Provisions	37.7	7			
Other assets	155.2	28	Other assets	155.2	28
Other liabilities	85.2	15			
Reserves & profit	46.6	8			
Total	558.9	100	Total	558.9	100

Source: Annual Report 1982.
Note: At end-1982 there were 0.89 contos to the dollar and 1.5 contos to the pound.

It will be seen that the Caixa obtains most of its funds from deposits and, to that extent, it can rightly be considered predominantly as a savings bank. Term deposits, with a maturity of over one year, are its major source of funds. Sight deposits are surprisingly high and indeed have increased significantly in recent years, bearing in mind that the interest rate has remained at 4%.

Included in the figures are savings attracted through a postal savings system operated by the Caixa through 800 offices. However, the contribution of postal savings accounts is very small. An interesting feature of the liabilities side of the balance sheet are obligatory deposits which represent funds paid into the Caixa in respect of court orders, assignment of rents, bankruptcies and so on.

At the end of 1982, there were 6,686,000 deposit accounts with the Caixa, slightly more than half being sight deposits. It is reasonable to assume that this considerably overstates the number of investors as many will have both sight and time deposits.

Real estate loans, for both house-purchase and construction, accounted for 28% of total assets at the end of 1982. The Caixa lends for all purposes, especially to small and medium sized businesses. After housing and construction, the mining and transforming industry accounts for the highest proportion of loans outstanding, 15%, followed by central and local government with 8%.

The Caixa is by far the major lender for house-purchase, but it should be noted that as in other less industrialized countries a significant amount of housing investment is financed outside of the institutional framework, often out of savings. The high rates of interest which have obtained in Portugal in recent years have had a significant effect on the type of mortgage lending. Table 14.18 shows trends in the Caixa's real estate loans outstanding.

Table 14.18 Caixa Geral de Depósitos, Real Estate Credit Outstanding, 1980-82

	1980 C m	%	1981 C m	%	1982 C m	%
Subsidized loans for owner-occupied housing	38.5	49	67.2	57	94.2	60
Loans to builders	19.1	24	27.0	23	34.0	22
Credit without state subsidy	19.4	25	21.0	18	21.6	14
Other credit	1.2	2	3.4	3	6.1	4
Total	78.2	100	118.7	100	156.0	100

Source: Annual Report 1982.
Note: At end-1982 there were 0.89 contos to the dollar and 1.5 contos to the pound.

It will be seen that subsidized loans for owner-occupied housing accounted for 60% of outstanding loans at the end of 1982 and that the proportion has increased significantly since 1980, this reflecting the increase in long term interest rates. Correspondingly, credit without state subsidy to owner-occupiers has fallen substantially in both real and comparative terms. The Caixa made a total of 33,000 loans in respect of owner-occupied housing in 1982, including both subsidized and unsubsidized loans.

The state subsidizes loans through meeting part of the interest on loans up to 20% of the total. The Caixa also operates low start arrangements including the capitalization of interest, again, essential given the high interest rates.

It will be noted that the Caixa provides a considerable amount of finance to house builders. This is generally on a short term basis.

The Portuguese housing finance system is fairly typical of that for an economy in Portugal's state of development, that is, one in which a high proportion of the population is still employed in agriculture and the financial system is not well developed. One single institution, the Caixa, dominates the housing finance market but a considerable amount of activity is undertaken outside of the main institutional framework. Indeed, this applies to housing as well as to housing finance in that there has been much illegal building. The housing finance system cannot work effectively with interest rates in excess of 20%, and the future progress of the system must depend as much on the extent to which interest rates and inflation can be brought under control as well as on policies and performance of the Caixa.

Austria

Introduction

Austria is a landlocked and mountainous country, occupying an area of 83,850 sq kilometres, in central Europe. It has borders with West Germany, Italy, and Switzerland, and also the East European countries of Czechoslovakia, Yugoslavia and Hungary. In 1981 its population was 7,555,000, the vast majority of whom are German speaking. Vienna is the capital and the principal city, with a population in excess of 1,500,000.

Austria is a federal republic. Its 1955 constitution incorporates neutrality. There are nine individual provinces, each with considerable autonomy. Political power rests with a directly elected president and two houses of parliament. The Nationalrat is directly elected, and the Bundesrat comprises representatives of the provinces. The Socialist Party has been in power since 1970, since 1983 in coalition with the Freedom Party. The other principal party is the People's Party.

Austria is less wealthy than some of the other West European countries, but GNP per capita is, for example, above that in Britain. Its economy has performed strongly in the post war period. Between 1960 and 1980 real GDP per capita grew by 3.9% per year, compared with the OECD average of 3.1%. The annual rate of inflation was 4.9%, compared with the OECD average of 6.1%. Interest rates have been maintained at a comparatively low level. The central bank discount rate stood at 4.75% at the end of 1982. Generally, economic trends in Austria very much follow those in West Germany.

Housing

Austria has a significantly higher level of owner-occupation than its immediate neighbours of West Germany and Switzerland, although the proportion is still well below that of most of the countries in Northern Europe. Table 14.19 shows the distribution of the housing stock between the tenures as at March 1981.

Table 14.19   Housing Tenure, Austria, March 1981

Type of Tenure	Number of Inhabited Dwellings	Percentage of Total
Owner-occupied house	1,115,000	42
Owner-occupied flat	207,000	8
Tenant	1,083,000	41
Sub-tenant	34,000	1
Owned by relative	80,000	3
Other	127,000	5
Unknown	6,000	-
Total	2,652,000	100

Source: Austrian Central Statistical Office, reproduced from *Monograph on the Human Settlements Situation and Related Trends and Policies* (Austria), 1982.

It will be seen that 42% of dwellings were owner-occupied houses and a further 8% were owner-occupied flats. Since 1970, the total proportion of owner-occupied dwellings has increased from 46% to 50%. It is estimated that more than 70% of households would prefer to be owner-occupiers.

Most rented houses are owned by 'Gemeinde Wien' and by non-profit housing associations, which build for sale as well as for rent. Local and central government plays a comparatively modest role in the physical construction of housing, although, as will be seen subsequently, a more significant role in finance.

The level of housing construction has fluctuated markedly in recent years. Completions increased from 45,000 in each of 1976 and 1977 to 78,000 in 1980, before falling back. In 1980, 50% of houses completed were single family units, and most of the remainder were in blocks of flats. Also in 1980, 60% of new dwellings were built by private persons, 26% by non-profit building associations, 6% by local authorities and 8% by other institutions.

Housing Finance

House-purchase in Austria is financed to a significant extent by personal savings, with the main source of loans being Bausparkassen, which operate on the same principle as the West German Bausparkassen, which are described in detail in Chapter 10. The Bausparkassen are connected with the various groups of banks. Table 14.20 shows estimates of how dwellings completed for private individuals were financed in 1980.

Table 14.20 Financing of Dwellings Completed by Private Individuals, Austria, 1980

Total costs	AS 11,090 m
Met by -	
Own funds	63.3%
Loans	36.7%
Source of Loans	
Local authorities	29.0%
Bausparkassen	44.2%
Other loans	26.5%
Subsidies	0.3%

Source: Austrian Central Statistical Office, reproduced from *Monograph on the Human Settlements Situation and Related Trends and Policies*, (Austria), 1982.
Note: At end-1980 there were 13.9 Schillings to the dollar and 32.7 Schillings to the pound.

This table usefully shows the importance of savings, and also the major role played by local authorities and the Bausparkassen. Some 70% of new housing units are constructed with the help of public funds, which will meet between 45% and 70% of construction costs. A very low rate of interest of 0.5% is charged over a period of 47.5 years. Lower income families can obtain interest free loans. These low interest funds are made available through the individual provinces, but are provided by the central government under the Housing Promotion Act 1968.

It is necessary to describe briefly at this stage the Austrian banking system, before describing in more detail the role of the various institutions, in particular in financing house-purchase loans. Basically, the Austrian system is very similar to that in West Germany, with important roles being played by local savings institutions and their central banks. Table 14.21 shows key statistics for the major financial institutions as at the end of 1982.

Table 14.21 Austrian Financial Institutions, End-1982

Type of Institution	No	Branches	Total Assets AS bn	Share of Deposits End-1982
Joint stock banks	40	708	716	20
Provincial mortgage banks	10	79	113	2
Savings banks	133	1,105	570	31
Raiffeisen banks	960	1,470	400	21
Volksbanken	119	370	111	7
Bausparkassen	4	35	96	9

Source: Divok, F, *The Austrian Banking System*, Creditanstalt, 1983.
Notes: 1. At end-1982 there were 17.0 Schillings to the dollar and 27.6 Schillings to the pound.
2. Figures include central giro institutions for the various groups of banks.
3. 10% of deposits are held by institutions not listed in the table.

The table shows the importance of the savings banks and the Raiffeisen banks. The latter have an agricultural base, and therefore have certain similarities with the Rabobank in the Netherlands, the credit co-operatives in West

Germany and the Crédit Agricole in France. The joint stock banks are significant deposit taking institutions, but their branch networks are substantially smaller than those of the savings banks or the Raiffeisen banks.

Banks and Housing Finance

The commercial banks play little direct role in housing finance. The largest banks were all nationalized immediately after the war. The largest bank substantially is the Creditanstalt-Bankverein. This group had assets of AS338 bn at the end of 1982. The second largest is the Osterreichische-Leanderbank, the group of which had assets of AS174 bn at the end of 1982. Between them these banks account for 60% of the total assets of the joint stock banks.

The banks concentrate their lending on industry and commerce, and their loans to housing in any form are very modest. However, they are involved in the housing finance market through their connection with the Bausparkassen.

Table 14.21 shows that provincial mortgage banks have higher assets than the Bausparkassen. However, despite their name, the mortgage banks have little involvement in housing, instead concentrating their lending on the public sector. Each of the provinces has one of these banks, which now offer a full range of banking services. They have recently been switching away from loans secured by mortgage to communal loans. They raise their funds largely through mortgage bonds, although they also have some deposits.

The Raiffeisen banks, like their counterparts in most other countries, are very small. At the end of 1982, there were 960 banks, with 1,470 branches. Recently the number of individual banks has been declining substantially. There is a regional clearing bank in each one of the provinces, and a central organisation, the Genossenschaftliche Zentralbank, which, in its own right, is the sixth largest bank in Austria. This provides the usual clearing house and liquidity functions to the constituent banks, and it also engages in international business.

The Volksbanken are basically very small credit co-operatives. Like the Raiffeisen banks they have been declining in number recently, and have been expanding their range of services such that they are now virtually full banking institutions. The central banks for the Volksbanken is the Osterreichische Volksbanken-Aktiengesellschaft. Like the central bank for the Raiffeisen banks, this is connected with a Bausparkasse.

The savings banks are the major retail institutions. They date back to the early 19th century. Recently the number has been declining rapidly, from 177 to 133 in 1982. Traditionally, the savings banks have operated on a regional level only. However, banking reforms implemented in 1979 have encouraged the development of competition between savings banks, and the two largest, both of which are based in Vienna, are now opening offices in other provincial centres. These two are, by a very long way, much bigger than any of the other savings banks. The largest is the Zentralsparkasse Und Kommerzialbank, often simply known as 'Z'. This has 130 branches, and at the end of 1982 had assets of AS108 bn, making it the fifth largest bank in Austria. The second largest, Die Este Osterreichische Spar-Casse, known as 'ERSTE', has 82 branches, and at the end of 1982 had assets of AS72bn.

Mention should be made at this stage of the postal savings system, the Post-sparkasse, which in size is somewhere between the two biggest savings banks.

The savings banks collectively own their central bank, which is generally known simply as Girozentrale Vienna or 'GZ'. This is a typical central giro system, managing the liquidity of the savings banks, and generally providing services to them in fields such as underwriting and syndicated loans. It also is a major bank in its own right, being the second largest banking group in Austria. It had assets of AS195,478 million at the end of 1982.

The savings banks lend directly for housing purposes, but generally the figures for this cannot be distinguished from other bank loans to individuals. The importance of the savings banks in the housing finance system is largely through the Girozentrale's ownership of one of the largest Bausparkassen.

Bausparkassen

There are four Bausparkassen in Austria, each of which has a strong affiliation with one of the banking groups. Table 14.22 lists the Bausparkassen together with details of their base and their affiliation.

Table 14.22   Austrian Bausparkassen, End-1983

Name	Base	Affiliation	Total Assets AS m
Bausparkasse der Osterreichen Sparkassen	Vienna	Owned by savings banks	32,925
Bausparkasse Gemeinschaft der Freunde Wustenrot	Salzburg .	Partially owned by & associated with joint stock banks	26,049
Allgemeine Bausparkasse der Volksbanken	Vienna	Connected with Volksbanken	8,874
Raiffeisen Bausparkasse	Vienna	Owned by Raiffeisen banks	34,394

Source: Annual reports.
Note: At end-1983 there were 19.4 Schillings to the dollar and 27.8 Schillings to the pound.

The Bausparkassen operate the contract system in exactly the same way as their West German counterparts. They have been the most rapidly growing of the Austrian financial institutions, increasing their share of the total assets of all financial institutions from 1.4% in 1960 to 4.0% in 1970, with a further modest increase to 4.1% in 1982. This growth was helped by substantial government premiums to those saving under the contract system. They account for about 50% of the housing finance market.

The Bausparkassen offer four separate types of contract. The standard contract requires 40% of the contract sum to be saved and a loan for the remaining

60% is then available, repayable over 16 years, with capital repayments of 0.5% a month. Other repayment terms are 12 years and 21 years. The rate of interest charged on Bausparkassen loans is 6%.

Table 14.20 shows that the Bausparkassen accounted for over 44% of loans used to finance dwelling completions by private individuals in 1980. Subsequently, their market share has increased to over 50%. Generally, their loans are combined with the low interest loans available from local authorities. This is in contrast to the position in West Germany, where Bausparkassen loans are generally combined with loans from other financial institutions, with which the Bausparkassen have connections.

The point has already been made that Bausparkassen activity in recent years has been greatly influenced by the degree of government support. By 1979 a state bonus of 17% was payable. In that year it was announced that the bonus would be cut to 10% up to the maximum of AS7,000 per person. This led to a rush of new contracts towards the end of 1979 which, in turn, will lead to a huge demand for loans six years subsequently. Correspondingly, the number of new contracts fell back sharply in 1980, before recovering slightly in 1981, and more substantially in 1982. This followed a government decision to increase the bonus to 13% and to raise the maximum to AS8,000. Table 14.23 shows developments in Bausparkassen activity since 1976 and usefully illustrates the effects of the changing level of the premium.

Table 14.23   Austrian Bausparkassen Activity, 1976-82

Year	Savings New Contracts	Contracts Outstanding	Deposits AS m	Loans New Loans AS m	Outstanding Loans No	Loans AS m
1976	432,000	1,472,000	38,699	8,071	283,000	35,788
1977	417,000	1,547,000	42,645	10,604	315,000	41,606
1978	582,000	1,975,000	49,666	15,826	355,000	50,704
1979	593,000	2,393,000	62,623	18,923	400,000	61,736
1980	308,000	2,466,000	73,583	21,640	446,000	75,097
1981	424,000	2,556,000	76,606	18,352	481,000	84,924
1982	547,000	2,682,000	75,701	12,816	505,000	89,060

Sources: Various.
Note: At end-1982 there were 17.0 Schillings to the dollar and 27.6 Schillings to the pound.

The sharp increase in new contracts in 1982 is evident. However, it will also be noted that deposits actually declined, partly because a significant number of existing contracts were terminated, and also because it takes time before new contracts lead to an increase in deposits.

The Bausparkassen obtain much of their business through the banks with which they are connected.

Belgium

Introduction

Belgium is a small country, occupying 30,519 sq kilometres in Northern Europe. It has frontiers with the Netherlands, Luxembourg, West Germany and France, and its geographical location has made it a centre of trade and commerce for many years. More recently it has become the home of many leading international organisations, including the European Community and NATO.

At the end of 1982, Belgium had a population of 9.9 million. The capital and principal city is Brussels, which had a population at the end of 1982 of 995,000. The second largest city was Antwerp, with a population of 917,000. The population is divided fairly sharply between those who speak Flemish (64% of the total) and those who speak French. The language issue has been a source of political conflict over the years.

Belgium is a constitutional monarchy, comprising nine provinces. It has a two chamber parliament. The Chamber of Representatives is directly elected by proportional representation. The Senate contains representatives of the provinces. The major political parties are the Social Christian Party, the Belgian Socialist Party and the Party of Liberty and Progress. There have invariably been coalition governments in power and a frequent turnover of governments. Currently, a centre/right coalition is in power.

GDP per capita in Belgium is similar to that in the Netherlands and a little below the level in France. GDP per capita grew by 3.7% a year between 1960 and 1980, compared with the OECD average of 3.2%. Inflation and interest rates have been similar to the level for the major industrial countries.

Housing

At the end of 1981 there were 3,887,289 dwellings in Belgium. Of these 3.5% were second homes and 3.9% were unoccupied. Owner-occupied houses accounted for 61% of the total, compared with 55% in 1970 and 50% in 1961. Over 80% of rented houses are owned privately, and the government at both central and local level has little direct involvement in the provision of housing, although, as will be seen subsequently, it has a major role in the provision of housing finance.

There has been a sharp reduction in the level of housing completions in recent years. From a peak of 68,407 completions in 1979 the number fell to 28,552 in 1982. This very much parallels the situation in the Netherlands. The fall continued into 1983. The reasons for and nature of the slump in the housing market are examined in the next section.

Housing Finance

House-purchase loans in Belgium are provided largely by the state-owned savings bank, Caisse Générale d'Epargne et de Retraite (CGER), together with other savings banks. More recently the commercial banks have become significant lenders. Table 14.24 shows mortgage loans outstanding at the end of 1982.

Table 14.24 Belgian Mortgage Market, End-1982

Institution	Loans Outstanding BF bn	Percentage of Total
Para state bodies	382	42
Savings banks	254	28
Insurance companies	133	15
Commercial banks	97	11
Finance companies	41	4
Total	907	100

Source: Building societies and the European Community, Belgium, Appendix 4, BSA, 1983.
Note: At end-1982 there were 47.5 Belgian francs to the dollar and 76.9 Belgian francs to the pound.

The figures in this table need to be treated with some caution as statistics for the various institutions are not readily available. Most of the loans attributed to the para state bodies are in fact made by the CGER.

The mortgage market has been depressed for the last few years. For example, new lending by the savings banks fell from BF50 billion in 1979 to BF19 billion in 1982. The slump in the housing market has partly been caused by high rates of interest and of unemployment. The mortgage rate increased from 10% in 1979 to 15% in 1982, although it has subsequently fallen back. House prices fell in nominal terms by some 18% between 1979 and 1982, and in 1983 stood little higher than the 1977 average level.

The government has recently taken steps to stimulate the housing market. The level of VAT on new building has been cut from 17% to 6% and significant tax concessions and subsidies have been offered, which have the effect of leading to a 15-20% reduction in costs for those purchasing new houses.

A significant feature of the Belgian housing finance system is the financing of so-called social housing. Four state institutions are involved in this financing -

(a) The Société Nationale du Logement (SNL). This raises finance and channels it through 285 approved societies, which build and renovate, largely for rent, but also to a limited extent for sale.

(b) Société Nationale Terrienne (SNT) operates in a similar way to SNL, but it functions only in rural areas and small towns. It channels its funds through 54 approved societies, but it also does a limited amount of direct lending and building.

(c) The Housing Fund for the Belgian League of Large Families (LFNB) is a private co-operative which lends money to large families for various housing purposes.

(d) The Caisse Générale d'Epargne et de Retraite (CGER) is one of the largest financial institutions in Belgium and, the largest housing lender. Its functions are explained in more detail subsequently, but, at this stage, it should be noted that it makes social loans through 160 approved societies. These loans are made at a rate of 10%, which is below market rates. People can qualify for social loans only if they have held accounts with the CGER for two years. The amount of the loan is limited to 25 times the savings of various types over the previous five years.

The social housing system has been in a state of crisis for some years. Doubt has been expressed as to whether the funds are well used, and there is concern in the manner in which social loans, ie cheap loans, and subsidized rented houses are made available.

The Savings Market

Table 14.25 shows deposits in Belgium at the end of 1982.

Table 14.25   Belgian Savings Market, 1982

Institution	Deposits BF bn	Percentage of Total
Para state bodies	1,914	42
Savings banks	677	15
Commercial banks	1,915	42
Finance companies	54	1
Total	4,560	100

Source: Belgian Bankers Association.
Note: At end-1982 there were 47.5 francs to the dollar and 76.9 francs to the pound.

It will be seen that the commercial banks and the para state bodies each had 42% of the market. Of the para state bodies the CGER had 37%. The other major state body is the Crédit Communal de Belgique (CC), which is actually larger than the CGER, but it is not a significant deposit taking body. Its major function is to be a banker to local authorities, and it largely funds this activity through selling savings certificates to the public. The third major state body is the Société Nationale de Crédit l'Industrie (SNCI) which, like CC, is not a significant deposit taking body. Most of its lending is to industry.

There are three major commercial banks, the Société Générale (assets of BF1,282 billion at end-1982), the Banque Bruxelles Lambert (assets of (BF1,070 billion at end-September 1983) and the Kredietbank (assets of BF646 billion at 31 March 1983). At the end of 1982 these three banks had 3,678 branches between them.

The banks entered the mortgage market in the 1970s. Lending for house-purchase increased from BF35 billion in 1974 to BF168 billion in 1980. Loans have since stayed at about that level reflecting the generally depressed state of the market.

The private savings banks are comparatively small when compared with the CGER. They are regulated under a 1967 law which allows them to be full service banks. There are now 30 private savings banks. The largest is the Centrale des Caisses Rurales (CERA), which is a co-operative of regional savings banks within the ambit of the Belgian Farmers Co-operative. This had assets of BF199 billion at end 1982, 27% of all savings bank assets. The second largest savings bank, CDB, is a co-operative based on the trade union movement. It had assets of BF181 billion at end 1982, 25% of all savings bank assets. The third major savings bank is privately owned, An-Hyp. This had assets of BF111 billion at end 1982, 15% of all savings bank assets.

Slightly under 40% of the assets of the savings banks are invested in mortgages.

Caisse Générale d'Epargne et de Retraite

This organisation very much dominates both the retail savings market and the housing finance market in Belgium. It is state owned and controlled, and in 1980 was reorganised into a savings bank and a separate insurance company. Since 1981 the savings bank has been able to offer a full banking service. It operates through 700 branches, and also agencies in post offices.

CGER provides one third of housing finance in Belgium. It gives ordinary loans itself, and it makes social loans through approved societies. Where it lends directly it will take a first mortgage and will normally lend over 20 years. The amount lent is between 60% and 100% depending on a number of factors, including the savings record of the borrower over the previous five years. Rates are fixed, but recently consideration has been given to introducing rates which can be varied at five yearly intervals. The CGER offers a contractual savings scheme. Savings can be made for three, four or five years, and the loans are available for, respectively, three, four or five times the amount saved at a rate of interest 10% or 12.5% below the standard rate. The standard mortgage rate in 1983 was 12.75%; loans secured by insurance policies attracted a lower rate of 11.5%.

CGER lends at 10% to the institutions which onlend for social housing. It also makes direct loans to the Société Nationale du Logement.

Table 14.26 shows the assets and liabilities of CGER at end-1982.

Table 14.26 CGER, Assets & Liabilities, End-1982

Liabilities	BF m	%	Assets	BF m	%
Deposits & current accounts	497,105	64	Loans	346,031	44
Debentures & savings certificates	180,840	23	Securities	206,025	26
			Bills	132,834	17
Due to banks	51,154	7	Other assets	97,746	12
Other liabilities	34,393	4			
Reserves	782,636	100	Total	782,636	100

Source: Annual report.
Note: At end-1982 there were 47.5 Belgian francs to the dollar and 76.9 Belgian francs to the pound.

Luxembourg

The Grand Duchy of Luxembourg comprises 2,586 sq kilometres where France, Belgium and West Germany meet. Its population at the end of 1982 was 364,000. GNP per capita is higher than in any other European country except Switzerland.

Housing

At the end of March 1981 there were 128,281 households of whom 75,921 (59.2%) were owner-occupiers. Table 14.27 shows a detailed breakdown of tenure.

Table 14.27 Housing Tenure, Luxembourg, End-1981

Tenure	Number of Households	Percentage of Total
Owner-occupiers	75,921	59.2
Renting unfurnished	40,798	31.8
Renting furnished	2,720	2.1
Free renting	5,492	4.3
Sub renting	785	0.6
Other	687	0.5
Don't know	1,878	1.5
Total	128,281	100.0

Source: Ministry of Economy, *Bulletin du State*, No 2, March 1983.

The proportion of owner-occupiers has increased from 49.3% in 1947 to 54.7% in 1960 to 55.9% in 1970 and 59.2% in 1981.

The level of housebuilding has been fairly steady in recent years, at 2,000 units a year.

Housing Finance

Luxembourg is a major international banking centre. Domestically, the retail savings and housing finance market is dominated by the Caisse d'Epargne de l'Etat (State Savings Bank). This was established in 1856 and achieved its present status in 1972. It has 87 branches, more than twice as many as the next largest banking institution. It has six functions -

    (a) A savings bank.
    (b) A lender for house-purchase.
    (c) A trading bank.
    (d) The banker for the state (Luxembourg has no central bank).
    (e) An insurance fund.
    (f) A housing aid agency.

The savings bank function is particularly important. It has over 300,000 savings accounts. Deposits held by private individuals at the end of 1982 totalled 109.9 billion francs, of which 30.6 billion francs were in savings passbook accounts and 20.7 billion were in term accounts (at the end of 1982 there were 47.0 Luxembourg francs to the dollar and 76.1 Luxembourg francs to the pound).

The bank accounts for over half of house-purchase lending. At the end of 1982 it had mortgage loans outstanding of 24.8 billion Luxembourg francs. It also grants subsidized state loans and helps to finance public housing projects.

The other major housing lenders are -

    (a) The private sector pension fund which lends to its members on preferential terms.
    (b) The West German BHW Bausparkasse which lends to public servants.
    (c) The West German Wustenrot Bausparkasse.

Eire

Eire, or the Republic of Ireland, occupies an area of 69,000 sq kilometres to the west of Great Britain. Its population was 3,440,000 in mid-1981. GNP per capita is one of the lowest of the West European countries.

Housing

Eire has the highest level of owner-occupation in Europe. Table 14.28 shows house tenure in 1981.

Table 14.28 Housing Tenure, Eire, 1981

Type of Tenure	Number of Dwellings	Percentage of Total
Owner-occupied without mortgage	362,000	40.5
Owner-occupied with mortgage	231,700	25.9
Being acquired from local authority	70,200	7.8
Rented from local authority	112,800	11.5
Other rented, furnished	57,300	6.4
Other rented, unfurnished	34,100	3.8
Rent free	23,000	2.6
Unknown	4,300	2.5
Total	894,400	100.0

Source: Census of Population of Ireland 1981; 5% sample estimates housing and households, 1983, Table H.

The first three categories together give an owner-occupation proportion of 74.2%. This compares with a proportion of 55% in 1971. The increase in owner-occupation has largely been at the expense of the unfurnished rented sector.

In 1982 27,000 dwellings were completed of which 6,000 were built by local authorities.

Housing Finance

Housing Finance in Eire is largley provided by building societies and the system is very similar to that in the UK. The societies accounted for 67% of new lending in 1982, the other main lenders being the local authorities with 23% of the market. The total assets of the industry were IR£1,878 million at the end of 1982 (at this time there were IR£0.73 to the dollar and IR£1.18 to the pound sterling). Mortgage loans were IR£1,397 million, 74% of total assets, and cash and investments accounted for 24%. Funds are raised through shares and deposits from individuals.

There are 14 building societies in Ireland but the industry is dominated by the five largest which account for 93% of the total assets of the industry. These societies are the Irish Permanent (assets of IR£758 million at end-1982), Educational (IR£410 million), First National (IR£389 million), Irish Nationwide (IR£118 million) and Irish Civil Service (IR£79 million). With one exception the societies are mutual. The exception is the Irish Civil Service which has a stock ownership. In early 1984 it was the subject of a takeover bid by the second largest Irish bank. The regulatory authorities stepped in to stop the planned takeover.

The societies are subject to special legislation, the Building Societies Act 1976, and are responsible to the Registrar of Building Societies. The five large societies operate a cartel for mortgage and deposit rates.

Turkey

Introduction

Turkey is largely in Asia, but partly in Europe, and for many purposes it is regarded as a European country. It is substantially larger than any of the countries in Western Europe, occupying an area of 779,452 sq kilometres. Turkey borders on the Mediterranean and the Black Sea on three sides. That part of it which is in Europe borders with Bulgaria and Greece, with whom Turkey has been periodically in conflict. In the East Turkey borders the Soviet Union and Iran, and in the South, Iraq and Syria.

The population of Turkey in 1981 was 45.5 million. The largest cities are Istanbul, which is on the European mainland, and the capital, Ankara. Turkey has been experiencing rapid urbanisation. The proportion of the population in urban areas increased from 18% in 1950 to 41% in 1975. In the 1970-75 period the urban population grew at 5.3% a year, and the rural population at 1.3% a year. Urbanisation has brought with it the usual problem of squatter settlements.

Turkey is a republic. In recent years there has been a mixture of civilian and military government.

Living standards in Turkey are below those on the mainland of Western Europe, but above the levels in Africa and most of Asia.

Economically, Turkey experienced a rapid growth of GDP until 1975, but subsequently growth has been more moderate. Inflation has been a major problem, reaching a rate of over 100% in 1980, although falling back to 23% in 1983.

Housing

Very few statistics are available on the housing stock in Turkey. However, it is known that there is a very high level of owner-occupation. It is estimated that in 1975 77% of low income groups were owner-occupiers, mainly because they were in squatter settlements. Among the higher income groups 81% were owner-occupiers. In the middle income groups the proportion was lower, as those people who wanted and who could afford rented accommodation lived in this form of tenure. It is estimated that perhaps as many as 30% of households in urban areas live in squatter settlements, and it is generally accepted that the housing deficit has been getting worse rather than better.

The government has a relatively interventionist role in the provision of housing, but it does not provide much housing directly. Over 90% of housing investment has been by the private sector. Housing investment has been running at between 3-4% of GDP. There were 139,000 completions in 1980, but the number fell to 116,000 in 1982. Over 80% of dwellings completed are apartments.

Housing Finance

Turkey has a very underdeveloped financial system generally, bearing in mind the state of development of the economy. Financial assets are very low in relation to GNP, when compared with less industrialized countries in Asia. The financial system is dominated by the commercial banks. There are 24, and the five largest of these control 50% of assets. There are also 11 special public deposit banks owned by the government. The operating costs of the banks are comparatively high.

Within the financial system as a whole, housing finance comprises only a very small part. It is estimated that in 1970 housing credit financed less than 7% of housing investment, comparable, for example, with the figure in India.

95% of institutional housing finance is provided by the Turkiye Emlak Kredi Bankasi (Real Estate Credit Bank) (TEKB). This is one of the special public deposit banks. It builds houses and supports the building materials industry, as well as making housing loans. It is funded by bond issues and savings deposits.

Table 14.29 shows details of the major banks in Turkey, illustrating the dominant role of TEKB in the market for real estate loans.

Table 14.29   Banks, Turkey, End-1982

Bank	Status	Branches	Savings Deposits Lm	Real Estate Loans Lm	Total Assets Lm
TC Ziraat	Public deposit	1,062	338,062		890,135
Turkiye Is	Private deposit	900	349,037	11,000	783,751
Akbank	Private deposit	605	168,294	85	399,307
Yapi ve Kredi	Private deposit	595	146,919		297,710
Turkiye Halk	Public deposit	609	49,519		196,442
TEKB	Public deposit	293	51,218	31,037	188,245

Source: Turkiye Is Bankasi, *Economic Report 1982*, 1983.
Note: At end-1982 there were 186.8 lire to the dollar and 302.3 lire to the pound.

It will be seen that TEKB is much smaller than the four large banks in terms of deposits, and also that real estate loans comprise less than one sixth of total assets.

In addition to its direct lending TEKB administers two government schemes, dealing respectively with national calamities and the public housing fund. The latter body was established in 1981 and makes loans at between 5% and 11% over 13-20 years to individuals who have housing savings accounts. Banks are encouraged to accept deposits under the scheme. The two schemes between them account for 40% of the lending of the bank.

TEKB will lend only on the basis of previous savings. It will lend up to three times the amount saved, with a maximum of TL1,500,000 (at end-September 1983 there were 243 lire to the dollar and 364 lire to the pound). There is usually a waiting period of one year. The maximum loan is likely to be no more than 50% of the purchase price.

Interest rates in Turkey have been extremely high in recent years, up to 40% in some cases. Typically, TEKB will lend at 16% over 15 years, but the range of rates is from 12% to 22%. It has received a government subsidy of 14% from the interest rate rebate fund.

There is generally a huge excess demand for the funds of the TEKB, partly because interest rates have been low in real terms. The recent reduction in inflation may help to improve the situation.

Hungary

Introduction

Hungary is the only one of the East European countries which is described in this volume. The reason is simply that more data is readily available for Hungary than the other countries. It should not be assumed that Hungary is typical of the East European countries. Hungary generally is more liberal and market orientated than the other countries in the communist bloc, and this is reflected in its housing structure as well as in other features of economic and political life.

Hungary is a landlocked country occupying 93,000 sq kilometres in central Europe. It shares borders with the communist states of Czechoslovakia, Poland, the Soviet Union, Romania and Yugoslavia, and also with Austria. At the beginning of 1983 its population was 10,700,000, of whom 2,067,000 lived in the capital, Budapest. The population grew at an annual rate of 0.35% a year between 1970 and 1980.

Hungary is a republic with just one political party, the Hungarian Socialist Workers Party. GNP per capita is among the lowest in Europe for which figures are available, although it should be noted that figures are not readily available for other East European countries. Living standards are certainly below those in Greece and Portugal, the two poorest of the West European countries, although substantially above those in Turkey. However, the economy has been growing rapidly. GNP per capita grew in real terms by 4.9% a year between 1970 and 1980, higher than for any other European country except Yugoslavia.

Generally, the country has been transforming fairly rapidly from an agricultural country to an industrialized one, although it still remains predominantly agricultural. Inflation has been maintained at relatively low levels by international standards, although it did reach 9% a year in 1970 and 1980. In 1981 the figure was 4.6%.

Housing

Hungary has a higher level of owner-occupation than any West European country. However, owner-occupation does not mean quite the same thing in Hungary as in the West European countries, as will be shown in the section on housing finance. Table 14.30 shows housing tenure in Hungary in 1980.

Table 14.30   Housing Tenure, Hungary, 1980

Type of Dwelling	Number of Dwellings	Percentage of Total
Family house	2,157,000	64.4
Block of owner-occupied dwellings	210,000	6.2
Privately owned houses built by co-operatives	173,000	5.4
State dwellings	869,000	23.8
Other	8,000	0.2
Total	3,407,000	100.0

Source: *Statistical Pocket Book of Hungary*, 1983.

A total of 76% of all dwellings were owned individually, most of the remaining 24% being owned by the state. The proportion of owner-occupied dwellings increased from 66.5% in 1970 to 71.3% in 1980.

As in other European countries, the proportion of owner-occupation is higher in rural areas than in the cities. In Budapest 58% of houses are state owned, while of the 1,575,000 dwellings in villages no fewer than 1,434,000 (91%) were owner-occupied family houses.

Housebuilding has been at a very high level in Hungary. 15 year dwelling construction plans have been in operation. The current plan runs from 1975 to 1990, and envisages the production of 1,200,000 new flats, and also extensive renovations. Between 1970 and 1980 the number of families per 100 flats fell from 130 to 103, indicating a substantial reduction in overcrowding. Nevertheless, the quality of housing is still much poorer than in most other European countries. Only 24% of units have three or more rooms, and nearly a quarter of all tenants have sub-tenants.

The level of house production has remained fairly constant over recent years. 89,000 dwellings were completed in 1980 and 77,000 in 1981. A peak figure of 108,000 was achieved in 1976.

Housing and housing finance are closely linked together as both are under state control. Some of the characteristics of owner-occupied housing are described in detail in the following section. At this stage it is useful to note that rented houses are distributed according to incomes by local housing officials. A notable feature of rented accommodation is that a new tenant has to provide a contribution to the capital costs, the contribution depending on the quality of the flat and its location. The contribution is repayable when the occupier moves out. From January 1983 the amount of the contribution varied from FT7,000 to FT70,000 (in February 1983 there were 39.9 forints to the dollar and 60.8 forints to the pound). However, the contribution can be reduced by up to 80% depending on the number of dependent family members.

Housing Finance

The method by which houses are acquired in Hungary depends to a large extent on who is responsible for their construction. Table 14.31 shows dwelling construction by financial source from 1971-75 to 1981.

Table 14.31   Dwelling Construction by Financial Source, Hungary, 1971-75 to 1981

Type of Construction	1971-75		1976-80		1981	
	000	%	000	%	000	%
Flats let by councils	75	17	90	20	11	15
Flats sold by councils	56	13	55	12	6	7
Other state flats	18	4	17	4	2	2
Total state dwellings	149	34	162	36	19	25
Flats built by National Savings Bank	51	12	66	15	18	24
Dwellings built with state loans	184	42	191	42	37	49
Dwellings built without state loans	54	12	34	8	2	2
Total private dwellings	289	66	291	64	57	75
Total	438	100	453	100	76	100

Source: *Financial Conditions of Housing*, Public Finance in Hungary, No 11, Ministry of Finance, 1983 Table 3; *Statistical Pocket Book of Hungary*, 1983.

The table shows that flats let by councils have accounted for under a fifth of dwelling construction. The table also shows that only a very small proportion of flats or houses are built either without state loan or directly by the National Savings Bank.

Councils build and sell some flats directly. A 10% minimum downpayment is required. The price can be reduced by a social subsidy which varies according to the number of dependent children in the family. It can be up to 45% of costs. The loan is at a rate of interest of between 1% and 3.5%.

Where flats are built other than by the state the rate of interest is 4%. A subsidy is available as for flats built by councils. If the subsidized loan is not sufficient then a bank loan can be obtained at a market rate of interest, currently about 8%.

An interesting feature of the housing finance system is that people can get a larger discount (by having a higher subsidy) by anticipating having children. They can, therefore, get a price reduction by saying that they intend to have more children. If the children are not forthcoming within six years, then the additional subsidy has to be repaid.

The National Savings Bank is responsible for a substantial amount of housebuilding directly. These are sold on similar terms to dwellings constructed by the local councils, and are allocated by the councils.

Employers provide considerable assistance with the provision of housing-normally by an additional loan. Between 30,000 and 40,000 new flats a year benefit from employers' assistance in this way.

Owner-occupiers in Hungary do not have absolute freedom to sell to whom they choose. Most flats and houses have to be traded through local councils, housing co-operatives and other state bodies.

Where an unoccupied family home is being sold, then the buyer will be appointed by the local council. The National Savings Bank must be prepared to make a loan. The selling price will be determined by the local council, but the vendor has the right to refuse to sell if he is not satisfied by the price.

The purchaser of a family home may obtain a loan for up to 90% of the purchase price, but not exceeding FT100,000. The loan is at an interest rate of 4% over 25 years. For large families the rate of interest is reduced to 2%. An additional FT50,000 can be borrowed at an annual rate of interest of 6%.

Where privately owned flats are being sold the National Savings Bank has the right to purchase them under certain circumstances. The buyer will be appointed by which ever organisation finances the construction of the new flat for the seller. Flats are bought and resold at the prevailing market price. A transaction therefore involves a sale to the National Savings Bank and a purchase from the Bank. The terms of the loan are similar to those for state built flats.

Flats that are in private property can be sold on the free market. NSB loans are available over ten years at 8% up to FT100,000 and 10% for larger amounts. The amount of the loan may not exceed 75% of the purchase price. However, preferential terms are available where a sitting tenant buys his property.

The National Savings Bank

The Országos Takarékpénztár (National Savings Bank) was founded in 1949 and operates the full range of banking services. It handles 90% of the country's total deposits, and is the major lender to individuals, agriculture, small businesses and local governments. At the end of 1979 it had 591 branches, and it also operated through 3,200 post offices. At the end of 1979 it held savings deposits of FT140 billion in 6.2 million accounts. It is state owned, and is supervised by the Ministry of Finance.

Bibliography

Switzerland

Current Trends and Policies in the Field of Housing, Building and Planning in Switzer-land, Federal Department of Economic Affairs, 1978.
Les Banques Suisses en 1982, Swiss National Bank, 1983.

The Netherlands

Frazer, P and Vittas, D, *The Retail Banking Revolution*, Lafferty Publications, 1982.
Rabobank and Rabohypotheekbank 1982 annual reports.
Report and Appendices of the BSA Netherlands Research Group, December 1979.
Some Data on Housebuilding in the Netherlands, Ministry of Housing, Physical Planning and Environment, 1983.

Greece

National Mortgage Bank of Greece, Annual Report, 1982.
National Reports, International Union of Building Societies and Savings Associations, 1983.

Portugal

An Evaluation of Aid Shelter Programmes in Portugal, report prepared by Richard T Pratt Associates for Office of Housing, AID, USA, 1980.
Caixa Geral de Depósitos, Annual Report, 1982.
National Reports, International Union of Building Societies and Savings Associations, 1983.
The Portuguese Credit Market, Caixa Geral de Depósitos, 1983.

Austria

Banking in Austria, Girozentrale Vienna, 1983.
Divok, F, *The Austrian Banking System*, Creditanstalt, 1983.
Girozentrale Vienna, Annual Report 1982.
Monograph on the Human Settlements Situation and Related Trends and Policies, (Austria), 1982.
National Reports, International Union of Building Societies and Savings Associations, 1983.

Belgium

Building Societies and the European Community, Belgium, BSA, 1983.
CGER Annual Report 1982.

Luxembourg

International Savings Banks Directory, International Savings Banks Institute, 1984.

Turkey

National Reports, International Union of Building Societies and Savings Associations, 1983.
Turkish Monograph on Current Trends and Policies in the Field of Housing, Building and Planning (prepared for UN ECE, 1980).

Hungary

Current Trends and Policies in the Field of Housing, Building and Planning, Hungarian People's Republic Ministry of Building and Public Works, 1980.
Financial Conditions of Housing, Public Finance in Hungary No 11, Ministry of Finance, 1983.
Andrzejewski, A, and Lujanen, M, *Major Trends in Housing Policy in ECE Countries*, United Nations, Economic Commission for Europe, 1980.

Acknowledgements

Switzerland

The Union Bank of Switzerland and the Credit Suisse provided useful information for this chapter. The section draws heavily on the Swiss National Bank publication *Les Banques Suisses en 1982*.

The Netherlands

The Ministry of Housing, Physical Planning and Environment, the Netherlands Association of Mortgage Banks, the Rabobank and the Royal Netherlands Embassy in London provided useful information for this chapter. The Ministry and the Netherlands Association of Mortgage Banks made helpful comments on the section on the Netherlands.

Greece

The National Mortgage Bank of Greece and the National Bank of Greee provided useful information for this chapter. The section on Greece draws heavily on the annual report of the Mortgage Bank.

Portugal

The Caixa Geral de Depósitos provided useful information for this chapter. The section on Portugal draws heavily on its annual report and its publication *The Portuguese Credit Market*.

Austria

Information on Austria was provided by the Austrian Embassy in London, the Arbeitsgemeinschaft Osterreichischer Bausparkassen, the Federal Ministry of Construction and Technology and the London offices of the Girozentrale Vienna and the Creditanstalt. The Arbeitsgemeinschaft Osterreichischer Bausparkassen gave valuable comments on an earlier draft of the section on Austria.

Belgium

Information on Belgium was provided by the Abbey National Building Society, the Institut National du Logement, the CGER, the Belgian Embassy in London, the Société Generale and the International Savings Banks Institute.

CHAPTER 15

THE EUROPEAN COMMUNITY

The European Community is the most ambitious grouping of independent countries ever to be established. The Community developed out of the European Coal and Steel Community and now embraces all aspects of economic life and is increasingly involved in other areas, for example, foreign policy. The Community has also grown in size from its original six members in 1956 to comprise ten members now with the expectation of others joining in the near future.

While the Community has successfully secured the erosion of many barriers between countries, housing finance is still provided on a national basis and there seems little impetus for a change in this situation. This largely reflects the particular nature of housing finance which makes it less necessary for this service to be traded across state borders. The nature of housing finance, implying long term loans, also makes transnational activity particularly difficult as long as economic conditions between countries diverge markedly.

Housing Finance and Economic Integration—Theoretical Issues

The Aims of Economic Integration

The aims of economic integration are very simple. They are, broadly speaking, to take advantage of competition, economies of scale and specialisation to increase economic welfare generally.

Perhaps the strongest argument for economic integration is to enable the various economies to take greater advantage of economies of scale, this also implying greater use of specialisation. In many industries it is the case that the greater the output the lower the average cost, because overheads can be spread more widely. Equally, there are some areas which are better at producing some products than other areas. Europe can illustrate this situation very well. The availability of coal and iron ore in the Ruhr Valley in West Germany makes it sensible for steel to be produced in this area. The climate in Southern Italy makes it sensible for citrus fruits to be grown there. For West Germany to concentrate on producing steel and for Southern Italy to concentrate on producing citrus fruits and for the two commodities to be traded for each other is far more efficient than for West Germany to attempt to produce citrus fruits in an unfavourable climate and for the South of Italy to import coal and iron ore in order to make steel. The growth of world trade has encouraged such a rationalisation of activity. However, national governments, for various reasons, have sought to protect domestic producers. The intention of more ambitious economic integration arrangements is to remove such protection so as to ensure that goods are produced in the areas where they can most efficiently be produced with welfare being increased all round.

The second important aim of integration is to increase welfare simply through stimulating competition. It is generally accepted that the existence of monopoly power leads to reduced efficiency and that economic welfare is promoted if monopoly producers in each country, for example shipbuilders or steel producers, compete with each other. Indeed, when the UK was applying to join the European Community one of the great advantages to the country was seen as being the stimulus that external competition would bring.

It is as well not to lose sight of the wider aims of economic integration. Arguably, the driving force behind the European Community has been political rather than economic, that is, to ensure that the countries of Europe would be so dependent on each other that war between them could never occur again. More generally, closer contact between countries is felt by many to be desirable in its own right, regardless of whether it increases economic welfare. It is certainly the case that the political enthusiasm for European integration has developed a momentum of its own unrelated to any potential economic benefits that may accrue.

Housing Finance and Economic Integration

The question must be asked as to how housing finance fits into the general theory of economic integration. At first sight it is difficult to see how economic welfare can be stimulated by housing finance being provided across state borders, for example a British building society making a loan to a West German home-buyer. The question of economies of scale does not arise because a loan in West Germany has to be made under the terms of West German law rather than British law. The differences between the various European Community countries, for example in respect of taxation, also mean that the advantages of specialisation cannot easily be gained. Every country has to have a housing finance system whereas every country does not need to have a shipbuilding industry or motor car industry. It follows that every country must, to some extent, be specialists in housing finance and as this specialism does not arise from natural advantages such as climate or raw materials, there is no reason to expect that one country will be better at providing housing finance than another.

Much the same applies in respect of competition. The nature of housing finance is such that monopoly positions are unlikely to be developed unless they are created by the government. In this case government is hardly likely to allow such a monopoly to be broken from outside the country. Ultimately, housing finance must mean providing small loans and this makes the market particularly difficult to enter for a newcomer competing in a market in which there is already substantial competition.

This leads to the question of whether it is necessary for housing finance institutions to react to greater economic integration and whether the absence of transnational housing finance activity hinders the overall objective of creating a unified market. In the case of the latter a problem can arise only if people are hindered from moving from country to country because of the lack of transnational housing finance arrangements. It is difficult to argue that this can be the case. People who move from one country to another are generally taking a major decision to change their way of life and to move from an area in which they are established. The method by which they buy a house (as opposed to housing conditions which are more important) is not likely to be an obstacle when faced with others such as learning a new language or settling down in a new area. Also, of course, the most mobile members of the population are more likely to rent than to buy. Housing finance systems can be obstacles to economic integration only if they do prevent people from moving from one country to another and this could happen only if rented accommodation was not available and if there was a prohibition on lending to newcomers to a country. These conditions are not likely to apply between countries which wish to become more closely integrated and do not apply in the European Community.

The independent question arises as to whether it is necessary for specialist housing finance institutions to seek to operate throughout an economic community for competitive reasons. The answer to this must depend to a large extent on mobility between countries. If a large number of borrowers from one particular institution in one country are likely to move to another then if that institution is unable to provide them with consistent help in their house-purchase activities then it may lose business. People moving from one country to another quite readily accept that they have to change the banking and financial habits of a lifetime, and this must include the source of their house-purchase loan.

The position of specialist housing finance organisations is quite different from that of other institutions in this respect. A commercial bank cannot opt to operate in one country only. Its customers are likely to have an international business and will want the bank to be able to handle that. If the bank refuses it will lose the entire business. As savings banks have gradually provided a service to commerce and industry in Europe so it has been necessary for them to develop an international business as the firms which they have serviced have sought to expand exports and rely to some extent on imports. Where this international business cannot be provided directly by savings banks it may be provided by central banks representing groups of savings banks. These considerations do not apply to specialist housing finance institutions. People are not likely to require an international service from such an institution because they generally only own one house at a time and if they move from one country to another they will require a completely new loan, and financial services generally, and will not be looking for a continued service from previous financial institutions which have no great expertise in the new area.

Theoretically, therefore, it seems difficult to argue that there is a need for housing finance institutions to operate in more than one country in order for economic integration to proceed. It is significant to note, in this respect, that in many countries which have already been studied in this book, housing finance institutions are not only limited to operating within countries but often are restricted to operating in particular areas of countries. For example, until very recently savings and loan associations in the USA could not have branches outside of their state of origin and the impetus for a change in this situation had nothing to do with the mobility of the American population which has always been at a high level. The fact that people have moved from one state to another and have had to change their housing finance arrangements has not in any way hindered the establishment of a common market throughout the USA. In Australia the building societies are also limited to operating within the various individual states. In West Germany the savings banks, public mortgage banks and public Bausparkassen all operate in the individual provinces only. Indeed, West Germany illustrates very well the need or otherwise for particular institutions to operate across national borders. The savings banks are the prime holders of personal sector deposits and they provide a complete retail banking service. They are limited to operating within the individual provinces. However, the banks have also developed a comprehensive service to local industry and commerce and to help them run this service central giro institutions for each of the savings banks in each of the provinces have been established. These institutions also do international business, again assisting their member savings banks. The central giro institutions own specialist Bausparkassen and mortgage banks which, like the savings banks, can operate only within provinces. It has, therefore, been accepted in West Germany that where institutions provide a banking service to industry and commerce then it is necessary for them to be able to offer a service in other countries because business is international. Where, however, those same institutions are offering a savings service and house-purchase finance they can be restricted to operating not only domestically but to within individual provinces.

This theoretical introduction can be completed by analysing the difficulties that would be experienced by specialist housing finance institutions operating other than domestically. The difficulties arise primarily because housing finance institutions make long term loans and the problem of the exchange risk is very great and cannot easily to avoided. If, for example, a building society in the United Kingdom was able to lend to one of its borrowers moving to West Germany then it could, if it was so permitted, make a loan denominated in sterling. This would mean that the society would suffer no exchange risk. However, the borrower may be earning his income in West German currency and the rest of his budget would be denominated in Deutsche marks. Depending on exchange rate movements this might make it difficult for him to repay his loan. Any increase in the value of sterling against the Deutsche mark would automatically increase his repayments. If the building society had to sell the property in the event of mortgage default there would be no guarantee that the proceeds in Deutsche marks would be sufficient to cover the debt in sterling at the prevailing rate of exchange. If the building society chose to make a loan denominated in Deutsche marks then it would run a severe risk of exchange rate loss if the funds raised to finance the loan were denominated in sterling. If the funds were raised in Deutsche marks then the institution would, to some extent, have ceased to be a building society because it would be raising money in West Germany on West German terms. Only if there were no exchange rate movements could cross frontier loans for long terms be safely undertaken for both borrower and lender. Here, it is is important to note that fluctuations in exchange rates can be avoided only by a convergence of economic conditions rather than by international treaties or laws being passed. It will be shown subsequently that there have been quite massive exchange rate variations within the European Community.

The conclusion from this fairly basic analysis is that cross frontier lending for house-purchase is not essential for economic integration to proceed, either within or between countries, that it is not necessary for housing finance institutions to operate across national borders even where the population is mobile, and that, in any event, it is practically difficult for cross frontier loans to be made when there are sharp variations in exchange rates. It follows that progress towards cross frontier lending is likely to be slow and the analysis of what has been achieved in the European Community will confirm this.

The European Community

History

The European Community has its origins in the immediate post war years. To a significant extent these origins were political. It was felt by some that if the economies of the European countries could be integrated then the dangers of war would be sharply reduced. For West Germany the Community offered the opportunity to regain international respectability. France saw the Community as being beneficial for her large and influential agricultural sector and politically she wished to see the development of a third force in world politics, in addition to the two superpowers of the USA and the USSR.

The first formal step was taken in 1951 when the Treaty of Paris established the European Coal and Steel Community (ECSC) between Belgium,

West Germany, Italy, France, Luxembourg and the Netherlands. In 1957 the Treaty of Rome, which came into effect at the beginning of 1958, established the European Economic Community (EEC) and the European Atomic Energy Community (Euratom). These two communities had the same six member countries and the three communities together gradually came to be known as the European Community. In 1965 the Merger Treaty established, from July 1967, a single Council of Ministers and Commission for the Community.

The Community took a major step forward in January 1972 when the Treaty of Accession was signed by which the United Kingdom, Denmark, Eire and Norway agreed to become members of the Community. In the event the people of Norway rejected membership in a referendum. The other three countries joined the Community at the beginning of 1973.

In 1979 the first direct elections were held for the European Parliament, the consulative assembly in the Community. In January 1981 Greece became a member, bringing the membership up to ten. Currently applications for membership are being considered in respect of Spain and Portugal and both are likely to join the Community in due course.

Structure

The ten member nations of the Community are Belgium, Denmark, France, West Germany, Greece, Eire, Italy, Luxembourg, the Netherlands and the United Kingdom. Four institutions exist to establish and implement the policies of the Community.

By far the most important institution is the Council of Ministers which directly represents the ten member governments. Each government has a seat on the Council. There is no permanent membership although the foreign minister of each country has overall responsibility for the affairs of the Community. If, for example, a transport matter is being discussed then the Council of Ministers will comprise the transport ministers of each country. The Council is the Community's principal decision taking body and on all but minor matters unanimity is required. This means that most major issues and sometimes minor issues are subject to full international negotiations and often there is horse trading with seemingly irrelevant items being discussed together in order to ensure that each country has something to gain from each package of measures.

The Council of Ministers sits under a president, the office of which is held for six monthly terms by each member in turn.

The Commission is the permanent secretariat for the Community. It has 14 members, two from each of the large countries of France, West Germany, Italy and the United Kingdom, and one from each other member state. Commissioners are appointed for four yearly terms, in theory jointly by the national governments, but in practice individually by each government. Members of the Commission are supposed to act independently in the interests of the Community as a whole although, in practice, national considerations play a part.

Each member of the Commission is responsible for one or more of the Community's areas of activity. The Commission comprises eight specialized services and 20 directorates-general, each with responsibility for a particular area of policy. These directorates-general are divided into directorates.

The third Community institution is the European Parliament. This now has 434 members, directly elected for five year terms. Members sit in party groups rather than national delegations although, again, the national interest is never absent. The Parliament has no legislative powers but has gradually been assuming a more influential role.

The final institution of the Community is the Court of Justice which rules on questions of Community law and whether the various other institutions of the Community are acting in accordance with the treaties.

The Community is largely, although not entirely, based in Brussels, Belgium. The European Parliament meets in Strasbourg, France, the Court of Justice sits in The Hague, the Netherlands and some parts of the Commission operate from Luxembourg although the headquarters are in Brussels.

The Community's method of operation is somewhat cumbersome. Technically, both the Commission and the Council are able to issue regulations, which automatically become European Community law; directives, which are binding on member states but leave to those states the decision as to how to implement them; decisions, which are binding on those to whom they are addressed; and recommendations and opinions, which are not binding.

In practice, major decisions come into effect only after long periods of discussion. The Commission initially will prepare staff papers which are the subject of intensive debate. Eventually a draft directive will be prepared and this will be the subject of even more intensive discussion and debate. Ultimately the Council of Ministers will agree the terms of a directive which, in effect, is an instruction by themselves to themselves. Each country then has to decide how it is to implement the directive, bearing in mind that it is unlikely to agree to a directive unless it supports it, although sometimes a 'package deal' is agreed including some elements which individual countries may not want but which they are prepared to accept in exchange for other elements in the package. As will be seen in the case of housing finance, the whole process can take years even when only minor matters are being considered.

Objectives

The objectives of the European Community can be summarized as follows -

(a) To create a single market throughout the area covered by the Community.

(b) To encourage the integration of the economies of the Community countries.

(c) Generally, to promote the welfare of the populations of the Community countries.

(d) To increase understanding between the Community countries.
(e) To increase political co-operation between the governments of the Community countries.

These objectives are somewhat vague but such is the nature of the Community that no more precise definitions can be attempted. Ultimately, the progress of the Community depends a great deal on personalities and politics. Arguably, the increased contact and understanding (if not co-operation) which the Community has encouraged has proved to be one of its main benefits. Certainly the point should never be forgotten that the European Community is essentially a political body set up for political purposes and run by politicians. Progress is made on issues where there is a will to make progress and where an issue is difficult, or where it is simply not important, little progress is made.

The Progress of Economic Integration

Economic integration is not something that can be legislated. It implies a merging of economies. This can be measured, at first remove, by the growth of trade between the European Community countries and here there is no doubt that the Community has led to a substantial increase in trade. Ultimately, however, what matters is the merging of the economies themselves such that inflation rates, interest rates and growth rates are similar throughout the Community. This is a measure of the ultimate effectiveness of the Community and, moreover, it is itself a prerequisite for some forms of integration. For example, there will never be significant integration of housing finance systems as long as exchange rates move over time and interest rates vary at any one point of time. In turn, these problems can be overcome only if the economies converge and this is not dependent on decisions of the Council on Ministers.

Table 15.1 gives key statistics for the countries of the Community and this serves to indicate the major differences between the tencountries.

The table demonstrates the significant differences between the four largest members of the Community, each of which has a higher population than the other six countries put together, and those other six countries. There are considerable differences in respect of GNP per capita, the figures for Eire and Greece being less than half those of the more prosperous countries. In terms of inflation, two countries in 1982 had a rate of under 5% a year while two other countries had a rate in excess of 16% a year. In respect of long term interest rates, two countries had rates in single figures while two others were verging on 20%. During the course of 1983 the West German exchange rate appreciated by nearly 10% against that of the second major economy in the Community, France.

Table 15.1   European Community Countries

Country	Population 1983	GNP 1981 US$ bn	GNP Per Capita US$	Increase in Consumer Prices Year to End-1982 %	Long Term Interest Rates December 1982 %	Change in Weighted Exchange Rate Year to Nov 1983 %
West Germany	61,639	830	13,450	4.6	7.9	3.8
Italy	57,434	391	6,960	16.4	19.9	-1.6
United Kingdom	56,935	510	9,110	5.4	10.8	-1.6
France	54,853	658	12,190	9.7	15.8	-5.6
Netherlands	14,363	168	11,790	4.3	8.4	-0.1
Greece	9,900	43	4,420	19.1		
Belgium	9,864	118	11,920	8.1	12.7	-1.7
Denmark	5,114	67	13,120	9.0	19.6	-1.2
Ireland	3,523	18	5,230	12.3	15.5	-1.7
Luxembourg	366	6	15,910	10.4		-3.5

Source: *Monthly Report of the Deutsche Bundesbank*, December 1983, Table 11; *1983 World Bank Atlas*; OECD, *Main Economic Indicators*, February 1983.

The differences between the countries can, perhaps, be illustrated more clearly by looking at just the four large countries and the major economic variables over time. Table 15.2 shows the position.

Table 15.2   Large European Community Countries, Major Economic Indicators

	West Germany %	Italy %	France %	United Kingdom %
Change in effective exchange rate 1977-82	16.2	-23.7	-11.7	16.8
Growth of GNP per capita 1970-80 p a	2.7	2.5	3.0	1.8
Average long term interest rate, 1973-80	7.8	12.6	11.1	13.1
Average short term interest rate, 1973-80	6.2	13.8	9.8	11.0
Increase in consumer prices p a, 1973-80	4.8	17.0	11.1	16.0

Source: *Monthly Report of the Deutsche Bundesbank*, December 1983, Table 11; *1983 World Bank Atlas*; OECD, *Main Economic Indicators*, February 1983.

Again, the table shows substantial differences between the countries. Over the period 1977-1982 the West German and United Kingdom exchange rates appreciated by some 40% as against the Italian exchange rate. In terms of growth of GNP per capita the United Kingdom lagged well behind the other three countries. In respect of consumer prices the West German figure was less than half that of the other three countries. Similarly, both long and short term interest rates were lower in West Germany than in Italy, France and the United Kingdom.

Clearly the substantial increase in trade within the European Community has not been sufficient to bring about the integration of the economies and there seems little evidence to suggest that the economies are closer together now than they were when the Community was first established in 1956. Indeed, in some respects, for example variation of exchange rates, differences between Community countries have increased. This is significant in terms of housing finance if only to indicate that little progress is being made towards stability in exchange rates and interest rates, both of which are essential if housing finance is to be provided across national borders. Progress on financial integration has been even slower. A Commission report, dated 20 April 1983, commented: 'Indeed, financial markets are probably even less integrated now than in the 1960s since capital movements in the Community are less free now, and the differences between the member states are more marked'.

Housing Finance Systems in The European Community Countries

Before considering the steps which the Community has taken to promote cross frontier housing finance, it is helpful to note the different types of system in the various countries of the Community. These systems have been described in detail in Chapters 3, 9, 10, 11, 13 and 14. Table 15.3 present a brief summary of the key information for each country.

It is apparent that the differences between the countries are substantial, indeed as substantial as those between any group of ten industrialized countries. At one extreme is the British system (and also the Eire system) which relies entirely on specialist deposit taking institutions, the building societies. The system in these two countries is much nearer to the method of operation of systems in the USA, Canada, Australia, South Africa and New Zealand than it is to the systems in the continental European countries. At the other extreme, housing finance in Denmark is provided entirely on the mortgage bank principle by independent institutions. West Germany makes extensive use of the contract system but it also uses the two other housing finance systems. There is most direct government regulation of the housing finance systems of France, Italy and Greece.

The differences between the countries apply also to supervision. The British building societies and the West German Bausparkassen, for example, are regulated under special laws and are not subject to banking laws. The other West German lending institutions are controlled by a variety of bodies. In Italy all financial institutions are supervised by the Bank of Italy. In Greece

Table 15.3   Housing Finance Systems in the European Community

Country	Level of Owner-Occupation	Housing Finance System	Main Housing Finance Lenders
West Germany	37% (1978)	Contract saving/ deposit taking/ mortgage bank	Savings banks and commercial banks, and subsidiary mortgage banks and Bausparkassen
France	47% (1978)	Deposit taking/ government	Crédit Agricole (co-operative banks) and Crédit Foncier (government mortgage bank)
United Kingdom	59% (1981)	Deposit taking	Building societies
Italy	59% (1981)	mortgage bank	Mortgage bank subsidiaries of commercial and savings banks
Netherlands	44% (1981)	Deposit taking/ mortgage bank	Rabobank (agricultural co-operative banks) and general banks
Denmark	52% (1980)	Mortgage bank	Independent mortgage credit institutions
Belgium	61% (1981)	Deposit taking	Savings banks
Greece		Mortgage bank/ deposit taking	National Mortgage Bank of Greece
Luxembourg	59% (1981)	Deposit taking	State savings bank
Eire	74% (1981)	Deposit taking	Building societies

the major house-purchase lender is publicly owned.

It is clear that any attempt to promote cross frontier housing finance has to involve not only a variety of types of system, but also a variety of types of institution and regulatory bodies. The obvious danger exists that attention will be focussed on the specialist bodies, even though these are relatively unimportant in many of the Community countries.

European Housing Finance Organisations

The establishment of the European Community has encouraged the formation of several representative bodies for housing finance lenders. Indeed, the method of operation of the Community, which prefers to talk directly to European wide bodies rather than to national bodies, has stimulated the development of these organisations. This section briefly describes the constitutions and functions of the major European bodies concerned with housing finance.

European Community Mortgage Federation

Consideration was first given to establishing a body representing mortgage organisations in more than one country shortly after the end of the war, following the establishment of the Benelux economic union of Belgium, the Netherlands and Luxembourg. Contacts between the Belgian and Dutch professional organisations developed over time but it was 1967 before the European Community Mortgage Federation (ECMF) was formed in Brussels. The members of the Federation comprise organisations whose principal activities are granting housing, industrial and agricultural loans. The aims of the Federation are to study the measures which could be taken at the Community level in the field of mortgage credit, to provide the European Community with expert advice on all questions relating to mortgages, and to promote the interests of its members at the European level. The Commission of the European Community recognises the Federation as representing the mortgage sector and the Federation is a member of the Commission's advisory Committee of Credit Associations.

The Federation comprises -

(a) Six Belgian organisations including the CGER and representatives of savings banks and mortgage banks.
(b) Five West German organisations including the representative bodies for the mortgage banks and the private Bausparkassen.
(c) The Realkreditradet, the representative body for the Danish mortgage credit institutions.
(d) The Crédit Foncier together with two specialist housing finance lenders from France.
(e) The Building Societies Association and the Life Offices Association of the United Kingdom.
(f) The National Mortgage Bank of Greece.
(g) The Italian Bankers' Association.
(h) The Central Rabobank, the representative body of Dutch mortgage banks, and three other organisations from the Netherlands.

The Federation has two associate members, the Mortgage Bank of Spain and the representative organisation for mortgage banks in Norway.

The Federation is based in Brussels and has a small permanent secretariat. Most of its work is undertaken by working groups representing the various member bodies. In more detail the structure of the Mortgage Federation is -

(a) A general council, comprising all members. This is the Federation's supreme governing body.
(b) A president nominated by the general council for a period of two years.
(c) An executive committee responsible for executing decisions by the general council. This comprises a vice president, assisted by an alternate and experts, from each country.
(d) Two working parties, one concentrating on economic and financial

affairs, and the other on legal questions.
(e) The secretariat, headed by Jean Baudhuin.

The Federation's activities involve, for the most part, the studying of proposals made by the Commission, but also it initiates some studies of its own, with the objective of analysing and helping to eliminate the obstacles to the integration of housing finance systems in the Community. Among the studies which have been carried out by the Federation have been -

(a) A study on solvency ratios applicable to mortgage institutions, which was completed in 1982.
(b) A study of the incompatibilities which a credit institution would meet if it wished to operate in the countries of the Community other than its country of origin.
(c) A comparative study of the ranking of preferences and mortgages.

The European Federation of Building Societies

The European Federation of Building Societies (EFBS) was founded in Brussels in 1962 by representatives of housing finance organisations in Rotterdam, the Netherlands; Paris, France; and Bonn, West Germany. Today the Federation comprises various national associations and institutions which provide housing credit in the European countries.

The Federation has the following objects -

(a) To promote collaboration amongst its members.
(b) To study the measures necessary for the development of the European Community, and for the co-ordination of the activities of housing finance institutions, particularly with regard to the problems of supervision and taxation.
(c) To represent the interests of members in the organisations of the European Community.
(d) To study the conditions under which competition among housing finance institutions will develop in the member countries of the Community in relation to freedom of establishment and the free movement of capital.
(e) To co-operate with institutions or groups of institutions specialized in accumulating capital for the purpose of financing housing.

For the most part the members of the EFBS are in countries in the European Community but the rules of the Federation also allow institutions in countries bordering on the Mediterranean to become corresponding members.

Currently, West Germany, the United Kingdom, France, Denmark, Greece, Eire, Tunisia and Turkey have full members of the Federation, and institutions in Austria, Egypt, Finland, Israel, Norway, Sweden and Switzerland are corresponding members. It is significant that two of the full members, Tunisia and Turkey, are not members of the European Community, and that Italy, Belgium, the Netherlands and Luxembourg are not represented.

A principal function of the Federation is the organisation of biennial congresses. These give an opportunity for an exchange of views between housing finance institutions and have served to increase the understanding of the systems in the various countries represented in the Federation.

Each year the EFBS holds a general assembly which comprises all participating and corresponding members. The general assembly elects a president and a vice president, who must be from different countries. It also has power to appoint a managing director and, ultimately, is the supreme policy making body.

The affairs of the Federation are managed by a council of management comprising representatives of the various countries. Unlike the ECMF, the EFBS has no full time staff. Until 1982 the managing director was Dr Willi Dieter Osterbrauck of the Bausparkasse Heimbau in Cologne, West Germany. Since 1982 the managing director has been James Malone, Secretary of the Irish Building Societies Association. The Federation has a small office in Brussels but is run from Dublin.

Most of the work of the Federation is undertaken through three standing committees. The Legal Affairs Committee scrutinizes proposals for changes in the law which emerge from Brussels and which have some bearing on the operation of building society type organisations. It discusses various matters directly with the Commission, in particular, proposals for cross-frontier lending. Among other matters which it has recently considered have been directives covering areas such as door step selling, consumer credit, reorganisation and dissolution of credit institutions, and the harmonisation of laws relating to guarantees and indemnities.

The Economic Affairs Committee is primarily concerned with financial matters. It has studied existing operating ratios in the context of different housing finance systems, and it has also studied tax systems and currency aspects of harmonisation of housing finance. Over the past few years it has given considerable attention to a draft directive on the annual accounts of banks.

The Committee on Marketing, Advertising and Competition is concerned primarily with the exchange of information rather than dealing with detailed matters of law or finance. It has prepared studies on various aspects of housing markets, and it has also studied differences in marketing and public relations strategies between the various countries.

Savings Banks Group of the European Community

The EEC Savings Bank Group was founded in 1963. The full members of the Group are the various representative bodies for savings banks in the European Community countries; the Spanish Confederation of Savings Banks and the Caixa Geral de Depósitos (Portugal) have associate membership status.

The object of the Group is to research into, study and disseminate information and to take any necessary action to promote the aims of the EEC as regards the activities of savings banks. Its main tasks are listed as being -

(a) To inform member-organisations of developments in the European Community.
(b) To represent the interests of savings banks and savers at the European Community level.
(c) To promote co-operation at association or business level, which is particularly important for regional and local organisations.

The General Assembly of the Group comprises representatives of all full members. It meets once a year and takes all fundamental decisions. The Board of Administration sets out the general policy for the Group and meets three or four times a year. It comprises two representatives from each of the ten full members. The secretariat, which is based in Brussels, has a full time staff of 12, headed by Klaus Meyer-Horn.

Much of the Group's work is undertaken by 11 advisory bodies. The Housing, Mortgage and Municipal Credit Committee, which was set up in 1968, is concerned with the harmonisation of real estate law, mortgage security, laws governing housing finance institutions, loans to public authorities, and cross-frontier housing finance.

The publications of the Group include a detailed biennial report, a regular bulletin *EE-Epargne-Europe*, a compendium of savings banks laws and occasional research reports. The Group collects and disseminates a wide range of statistics.

Association of Co-operative Banks of the EC

The institution, which was established in 1970, is the representative body for co-operatively constituted banks in the Community. Its membership comprises relevant national bodies including major mortgage lenders such as the Crédit Agricole, the DG Bank and the Rabobank. Its objects and functions are similar to those of the Savings Bank Group. It has a 24 man Board of Directors and eight standing working parties. The secretariat, which is headed by G Ravoet, is based in Brussels.

Other European Wide Organisations

The federations described above belong to the Committee of Credit Associations of the European Community, an advisory body comprising representatives of the Commission and of the various European associations of financial institutions. In addition to the EFBS and the four institutions described previously, the following organisations are represented: the Banking Federation, the International Confederation for Small Scale Credit, the European Centre of Public Enterprises and Eurofinas.

The Commission uses this forum to discuss issues that involve more than one type of financial institution.

Community Activity on Housing Finance

Structure

The section on the European Community described the organisation of the Commission, noting that functionally it is divided into 20 directorates-general. The relevant one for housing finance is Directorate-General XV, which covers financial institutions and taxation. Currently, this is the responsibility of one of the British Commissioners, Christopher Tugendhat. The director general is O Bus Henriksen, a Dane. Within the directorate-general, directorate A is responsible for financial institutions. This is headed by Gerard Imbert who is French. It is this section of the Commission which brings forward various proposals on housing finance which are described subsequently.

First Council Directive on Credit Institutions

In 1972, before the enlargement of the Community, the Commission took its first step towards harmonising financial systems through the publication of a 'draft directive for the co-ordination of the legal and administrative provisions for the taking up and exercise of the independent operator activities of credit institutions'. This document was as ambitious as its title suggests. It sought to establish at one stroke a single legal framework for all financial institutions in the Community. The framework would include common solvency and liquidity requirements. The objective was unrealistic and the draft directive made no progress.

A less rigid draft directive was published in 1974. After lengthy discussion this became on 12 December 1977 a first Council directive (No 77/780/EEC) 'on the co-ordination of laws, regulations and the administrative provisions relating to the taking up and pursuit of the business of credit institutions'. This is a very general directive and is sometimes known as the 'umbrella directive'. It covers all financial institutions and is concerned primarily with the conditions which must be met before a credit institution can begin operating. It does not deal with the supervision or the method of operation of existing financial institutions. The objectives of the directive are listed as including the protection of savings and the creation of conditions for fair competition.

The directive applies to credit institutions although central banks and some other specialist organisations are exempted. Member states were permitted to defer application of the directive where its immediate application would cause short term technical problems. The deferment could be for a maximum of eight years, and therefore the directive must be implemented in all countries by the end of 1985. In fact, some countries, for example, West Germany, already followed the requirements of the directive and the other Community countries have not found it particularly onerous to make the necessary changes to their legislation.

The key part of the directive is article 3 which obliges member states to require new credit institutions to obtain authorisation before commencing business. It also lays down four conditions which must be complied with by a credit institution before it can be granted authorisation -

(a) It must possess its separate own funds (reserves, capital or net worth).
(b) It must possess adequate minimum own funds.
(c) There must be at least two persons who effectively direct its business.
(d) These two persons must be of good repute and have sufficient experience to perform their duties.

Article 4 of the directive provides that authorisation in a member state of an organisation whose head office is elsewhere cannot be denied because that type of organisation is unknown in that country. Article 6 requires the national regulatory authorities to establish ratios between the various assets and/or liabilities of the credit institutions with a view to monitoring their solvency and liquidity. Article 11 provides for an advisory committee of the competent authorities of the member countries to be established.

The directive is a very modest measure and has little practical significance for housing finance institutions or for other financial institutions which are embraced within it. Notwithstanding the modest nature of the directive it should be noted that it will be 13 years between consideration first being given to a directive in 1972 and all countries of the Community applying that directive in 1985. This is an indication of the leisurely pace at which progress can be expected on the harmonisation of housing finance.

In 1981 the Commission announced plans for a second directive on credit institutions, and it published a consultative document. The declared objective was to embrace a number of questions left open by the 1977 directive, or which have subsequently arisen. Three reasons were given for the need for a new directive -

(a) The first directive left the co-ordination of banking laws incomplete, pending further harmonisation measures.
(b) The regulatory authorities have drawn to the attention of the Commission problems they are facing when they are dealing with cross border credit institutions.

(c) The various credit institutions face problems when planning to set up in other countries of the Community.

The Commission indicated that the scope of the second directive would be identical with that of the first, that is that it should apply to all credit institutions. The consultative paper suggested that the second directive should define the terms used in the first directive more precisely, and deal with aspects of the capital of credit institutions, the procedure for authorisation, cross border establishment of branches and representative offices, and the supervision of cross border establishments.

The Commission has yet to finalise its thoughts on the question of the second directive, and it will be some years before the Council of Ministers agrees a final directive.

Staff Papers of Housing Credit

The two European federations dealing with housing finance have sought to encourage a special directive dealing with housing credit rather than the subject being embraced within general directives for all credit institutions. A special directive on housing credit has been promised for some time but, as yet, has not appeared. However, a number of Commission documents do make it possible to discern the way that the Commission is thinking in terms of housing finance. The policy of the Commission, although this has yet to be accepted by the Council of Ministers, seems to rest on three principles -

(a) A gradual approach.
(b) Control of housing finance institutions being exercised by the host country initially, but by the country of origin as a long term aim.
(c) The maintenance of different systems which could operate alongside each other.

The first document from the Commission on the subject was a staff paper on the co-ordination of the legal provisions relating to housing credit (XV/38/78, April 1978). This was an ambitious document concentrating on cross frontier operations by housing credit institutions. It noted the legal problem that specialist mortgage credit institutions are not generally able to lend outside of their country of origin because of domestic legislation. The paper considered whether such institutions could be defined by reference to their activities or by a listing of the relevant institutions. The problem with the latter approach is that there are few specialist institutions in Belgium, Luxembourg and Italy. The document listed the major obstacles to cross frontier operation -

(a) Foreign exchange regulations.
(b) The categories of security which can be accepted.
(c) The exchange risk.

(d) The payment of housing subsidies through domestic institutions.

(e) Restrictions on the establishment of foreign subsidiaries or branches.

It might be noted that there appears to be an undue concentration on the legal obstacles rather than the more obvious market ones. This is, perhaps, natural because little can be done at the Community level about market factors. However, it is necessary to recognise that the legal obstacles are not the only ones.

The paper proposed that there should be a special directive, to remove, as far possible, these obstacles. It was suggested, for example, that there could be a declaration that the various types of security accepted by housing finance institutions should be regarded as being equal. It also anticipated that a special directive might set out mechanisms for reducing the exchange risk and for making the necessary supervisory changes.

A second Commission staff paper 'freedom of movement in the housing credit sector', (XV/118/79, October 1979), was less ambitious, concentrating largely on freedom of establishment. It suggested that the scope for a special directive should be restricted to institutions whose activity consists of the granting of loans secured by mortgage on residential property. It did not consider that it was realistic for an organisation operating solely from its home base to conduct operations in foreign countries. It also accepted that it would be attractive for an institution to set up abroad only if it could use its own domestic system. The paper recognised that there were four problems with this approach -

(a) The compatibility of the systems for the reasons already discussed in this chapter.

(b) The question of supervision, for which it was proposed that there should be close co-operation between the member states.

(c) The structure of the capital markets, for example, regulations governing the ownership of bonds.

(d) Competitive distortions arising, for example, from the way in which monetary policy is implemented.

In 1983 the Commission published a third staff paper (XV/100/83—rev 1) on mortgage credit. This paper suggests that the promised special directive will apply to mortgage lending in general and not just to housing credit. The paper considers the following matters -

(a) Freedom of establishment where it is again proposed that any obstacle must be removed. (The Commission regards freedom of establishment as being of vital importance.)

(b) Incompatibilities in respect of legal structures, banking supervision and state intervention.

(c) Freedom of provision of services in special cases, for example, migrant workers.

(d) Refinancing through bond issues.

A draft directive is expected later in 1984 but it will be many years before a final directive is agreed and takes effect.

Cross Frontier Housing Finance Activity in The European Community

Activity by Specialist Institutions

In an article in the *CBSI Journal* (May 1982) Paolo Clarotti, who is responsible for banks within Directorate-General XV of the Commission, described four examples of cross frontier housing credit by specialist housing finance institutions.

The first, and perhaps the most important example, is activity undertaken by the West German Bausparkasse Beamtenheim-Stattenwerk (BHW). This organisation is 50% owned by the German Federation of Trades Unions and 50% owned by the Civil Servants Trade Union. It operates in the same way as other Bausparkassen but it caters predominantly for West German civil servants. It has retained this special aspect of its business with regard to cross frontier activities as West German nationals working for international bodies are regarded for housing finance purposes as being equal to those in West Germany. BHW maintains agreements with the principal international organisations in Europe such as NATO, OECD, the Council of Europe, and the various institutions of the Community. Under the terms of these agreements European civil servants are classified as having parity with West German civil servants and can therefore obtain housing loans under the same conditions as their domestic counterparts. The exchange risk, however, has to be borne by the borrower. This is often not a problem as the expatriate may be paid in a currency other than that of the country in which he is living. Technically, this activity is inconsistent with West German legislation which prohibits the Bausparkassen from lending outside West Germany, but BHW has obtained the necessary authorisation from the supervisory authorities.

BHW has established, jointly with the Wustenrot Bausparkasse, a branch in Luxembourg which operates under the same terms and conditions as branches in West Germany. However, these two Bausparkassen provide top up loans in Luxembourg for loans made by local banks rather than West German banks.

The second example of cross frontier operations is an agreement between certain central co-operative credit institutions (including the Centrale Rabobank in the Netherlands, the Caisse Nationale de Crédit Agricole in France and the DG Bank in West Germany). If a customer of any one of these institutions wishes to purchase a property in another country he applies to his own bank. Through the group, known as UNICO, the bank will contact the appropriate organisation in the other country which will grant the necessary loan in the local currency. There is, therefore, no exchange risk.

The third example is the work carried out by the San Paolo Bank of Turin, one of the largest mortgage lenders in Italy. This has branch offices in Frankfurt and Munich, West Germany, to deal specifically with Italian immigrants into West Germany who wish to build or purchase a property in Italy. The loan is taken out or repaid in West German currency but it is granted through the branch nearest the property which is being purchased or built. The exchange risk is borne by the borrower but provided he is working in West Germany then the exchange risk is reduced because both the loan and the borrower's income are denominated in the same currency.

The final example given by Mr Clarotti concerns activities on the part of West German mortgage institutions in respect of customers living in Belgium near the West German border. The operation consists simply of granting loans under West German terms to Belgian residents. The advantage to the borrowers is that they pay a lower rate of interest, albeit in exchange for a currency risk.

To these four examples can be added the National Mortgage Bank of Greece which obtains a high proportion of its funds from Greek nationals working in other countries of the Community, with the expectation that eventually a loan will be forthcoming to purchase a property in Greece. The exchange risk is borne either by the investor or the Bank of Greece (the central bank), but not by the Mortgage Bank. Other institutions in countries which export labour to other Community countries (eg the Caixa Geral de Depósitos in Portugal) also have arrangements for accepting funds from expatriates.

It will be noted that all of these examples are concerned with people who move from one country to another and most seem to rest on the assumption that the person concerned will return to his country of origin eventually. The informal linkage between groups of banks is an obvious way in which such people can be assisted without there being any risk of exchange loss or an institution taking on a few loans where the conditions are unknown to it.

Activity by General Institutions

It is only specialist housing finance institutions which are inhibited from operating across national borders. Commercial banks have for long had to develop an international business so as to be able to cater for their customers who are involved in trade. Generally, such banks do not undertake significant retail business outside of their country of origin but often it is convenient for them to do limited retail business, generally without branch facilities. Such a retail service can include the making of house-purchase loans, not least to the staff of the institution, particularly those imported from the country of origin. This principle applies generally and not just within the European Community.

London is generally recognised as the leading financial centre in Europe and most major banks have branches there. Many of these banks, for example the big West German banks, the Italian Banks and the Japanese banks, are significant mortgage lenders in their own countries and some also undertake limited lending in the United Kingdom. Often this is to their staff and it is significant in this respect that very little rented accommodation is available on the market in the United Kingdom and hence it is more necessary for people to buy homes than is the case in other countries. Some of the banks have, however, developed a more general mortgage lending function. For example, in the United Kingdom, Citibank Savings and Security Pacific, subsidiaries of American banks, have entered the residential mortgage market, and the Royal Bank of Canada has been another significant lender.

There are no obstacles facing other European banks that wish to start lending in the British market, except the obvious one of whether they can do so at a profit.

It is also open to general banks to acquire specialist housing finance institutions. The chapter on France noted that one of the big British banks, Midland, owns a specialist French housing finance lender, BCT Midland Bank. Some institutions, for example British building societies, cannot be taken over by other types of institution so this option is not open in all countries. However, it would be open to a West German bank, if it so wished, to set up a mortgage lending institution in the United Kingdom, although this could not be a building society.

To the extent that there is a demand for cross frontier housing finance operations it is most likely that in the first instance this demand will be met by general institutions which already have experience of conditions in more than one country. Specialist institutions at present have no such knowledge and are at a disadvantage to this extent when it comes to competing for cross frontier activity with general institutions. Perhaps they can best overcome this disadvantage by establishing co-operative links such as that which exists between the central banks for the credit co-operatives.

Bibliography

Boleat, M J, *The Building Society Industry*, George Allen & Unwin, 1982.
Clarotti, P, 'Cross Frontier Housing Credit' - Is it Possible?', CBSI Journal, May 1982.
European Community Mortgage Federation, Report 1981-82.
European Community Mortgage Federation, *Ten Years' Professional Action*, 1978.
'First Council Directive of 12 December 1977 on the co-ordination of laws, regulations and administrative provisions relating to the taking up and pursuit of the business of credit institutions', *Official Journal of the European Communities*, no L 322/30, 17 December 1977.
Savings Bank Group of The European Economic Community, *Report*, 1979-1980.
Vacher's European Community, September 1983.

CHAPTER 16

CENTRAL AND SOUTH AMERICA, THE INTER-AMERICAN UNION AND BIAPE

Introduction

The Central and South American states (including those in the Caribbean) can be seen as being at the boundaries of the third world and the industrialized world. Living standards are, generally, much higher than in the Asian and African countries but well below those in Western Europe and North America.

The countries have tended to experience similar economic problems and, to some extent, have been victims of their own success. As real incomes grew in the 1960s and 1970 so the countries became less eligible for loans from the International Monetary Fund on favourable terms. Extensive bank lending was undertaken without sufficient attention being given as to whether the countries could afford to repay the loans. There was the assumption on the part of many that governments simply could not go bankrupt.

The rise in oil prices and the increase in American interest rates during the 1970s had a serious adverse effect on many countries. Frequently, the preferred solution was to print whatever money was necessary, and several countries, including Argentina, Brazil, Mexico and Peru, have experienced inflation rates running into three figures.

Table 16.1 shows key data for the various countries.

It will be seen that population growth rates have been well above those for industrialized countries and these have contributed to housing problems, particularly in the cities. As in other developing countries the population growth has been concentrated in the urban areas. Between 1970 and 1983, in Latin America as a whole, urban population grew by 3.9% a year and rural population by 0.1% a year.

There is a considerable range of GNP per capita, from over $4,000 in the oil producing state of Venezuela to under $1,000 in the Central American states and also in Bolivia. Real growth rates in the 1970s have been even more variable, ranging from nearly 6% in Paraguay and Brazil to negative figures in Chile and Nicaragua.

Reliable economic data is not available for all of the countries. Nevertheless, the final two columns of the table are sufficient to show the problems which have been experienced in recent years. In mid 1983 Argentina was recording an inflation rate of 340%; Bolivia, 281%; Brazil, 126%; and Mexico, 113%.

Table 16.1   Latin America, Population and Economy

Country	Population		GNP Per Capita		Increase	Central
	1983 000	Growth 1970-83 % p a	1981 US$	Real Growth 1970-80 % p a	in Consumer Prices Year to Mid-1983 %	Bank Discount Rate Mid-1983 %
Argentina	29,346	1.6	2,560	0.7	340	
Bolivia	6,064	2.7	600	1.9	281	47
Brazil	131,822	2.5	2,200	5.9	126	95
Colombia	27,880	2.1	1,380	4.0	21	27
Costa Rica	2,397	2.6	1,430	2.6	42	30
Chile	11,687	1.7	2,560	-0.5	32	
Ecuador	8,737	3.0	1,180	5.3	11	
El Salvador	5,260	3.0	650	1.3		
Guatemala	8,000	3.3	300	1.7	16	
Guyana	810	1.0	720	1.1	16	
Honduras	4,067	3.2	600	0.5	15	
Mexico	74,981	3.0	2,250	3.1	113	63
Nicaragua	2,602	2.4	860	-2.9		
Panama	2,034	2.4	1,910	1.2	2	
Paraguay	3,405	2.4	1,630	5.9	13	
Peru	17,759	2.1	1,170	0.2	101	45
Uruguay	2,935	0.5	2,820	3.2	46	
Venezuela	15,040	2.6	4,220	2.2	5	

Source: *1983 World Bank Atlas*; *International Financial Statistics*, IMF, December 1983; Inter-American Development Bank, Annual Report, 1983.

In only two countries, Venezuela and Panama, were inflation rates in single figures. It should be noted, of course, that when inflation is runnning at levels in excess of 100% then statistics are liable to become meaningless as money loses its traditional roles as being a medium of exchange and a store of value.

Rapid inflation tends to destroy financial markets and where inflation is running at 100% there can be no normal concept of interest. No figures are readily available in respect of long term bond rates, nor does the concept mean much, particularly where there is index linking. The table shows, in respect of central bank discount rates, that where data is available the rates are at levels unheard of in industrialized countries.

Housing

The Central and South American countries are fairly similar in respect of housing tenure. Unfortunately, comparable up to date data are not readily available and it is necessary to look at figures for the early 1970s. Table 16.2 shows housing tenure for the various countries.

Table 16.2 Housing Tenure, Latin America, Around 1970

Country	Year	Dwellings Owned No 000	%	Rented No 000	%	Total No 000	Proportion Owned Rural %	Urban %
Argentina	1970	3,553	59	1,381	23	6,056		
Bolivia	1976	702	71	139	14	989		
Brazil	1970	10,632	60	3,356	19	17,629	61	60
Colombia	1973	1,858	54	1,067	31	3,472		
Costa Rica	1973	199	60	76	23	331	66	53
Chile	1970	890	53	767	45	1,690	45	55
Ecuador	1974	756	63	281	24	1,194	79	41
El Salvador	1971	314	48	142	22	655	57	35
Guatemala	1973					935		
Guyana	1970	74	57	53	41	130		
Honduras	1974	333	72	76	16	463	82	49
Mexico	1970	5,471	66	2,815	34	8,286	83	54
Nicaragua	1971	195	64	61	20	302	76	53
Panama	1970	180	63	79	28	285	87	39
Paraguay	1972	350	82	38	9	428	87	74
Peru	1972	1,868	70	445	17	2,686	83	59
Uruguay	1975	401	52	247	32	769	69	46
Venezuela	1971	1,286	70	372	20	1,827		

Source: *Statistical Yearbook for Latin America 1980*, UN Economic Commission for Latin America, 1981.
Note: Figures for the total number of housing units include units not counted as owned or rented.

It will be seen that in all the countries more than 50% of dwellings are owner-occupied and in Bolivia, Honduras, Paraguay, Peru and Venezuela the proportion exceeds 70%. Chile stands out as having the highest proportion of rented accommodation, 45%. The usual pattern of owner-occupation being higher in rural than in urban areas is apparent. The notable exception is Chile, which besides having the highest proportion of rented housing also has a higher proportion of owner-occupation in urban than in rural areas.

Housing Finance

The housing finance systems of the various Central and South American countries are fairly similar, partially refecting the influence of the USA. Until the early 1960s there were few specialist housing finance institutions. Those loans that were available to house-purchasers were generally short term high interest loans from banks. The informal system predominated with people building their own homes and where loan finance was required this was obtained from relatives or friends. The housing finance systems of Brazil and Colombia are described in some detail in the following two chapters and all that is attempted in this chapter is a brief description of the development of housing finance systems together with key data about the systems in each country.

Regrettably, lack of data in English means that the systems are not analysed in nearly the same detail as systems in other countries.

Credit for founding the housing finance movement in Latin America is generally given to an American missionary priest, Father Daniel McLellan, who worked in Peru in the mid 1950s. He recognised that Latin American culture means that there is a powerful motivation for people to own a home for themselves and their families and they are ready to make real sacrifices to do so. McLellan organised a small credit co-operative in the village of Puno, Peru, and within a few years had founded co-operative credit unions all over the country.

In 1956 a team financed by the United States Agency for International Development worked with McLellan to help him organise a specialist housing finance institution on the savings and loan association model. Consequently, in 1957, legislation was enacted in Peru to provide for a savings and loan system, and the first association began operating in 1958. However, this was of a very modest size and it was 1960 before the first effective savings and loan operation in Latin America began, in Chile. McLellan's People's Mutual Association opened in Lima, Peru in 1961 and other associations were also established in that country. In 1962 associations were established in Ecuador, Venezuela, Guatemala and the Dominican Republic, in 1964 in Bolivia and El Salvador, and in 1965 in Panama.

These early associations benefitted from technical advice from AID experts and most were begun with seed capital loans from AID. To this day the USA continues to give substantial technical assistance to the savings and loan systems in the Latin American countries. (For a comprehensive description of the early history of savings and loan associations in Latin America see: *Thrift Institution Development in Latin America*, Staff Study prepared for Subcommittee on Inter-American Economic Relationships of the Joint Economic Committee, Congress of the United States, 4 June 1970.)

It is common practice for financial data in Latin America to be given in terms of American dollars. This is partly because the high rates of inflation make the use of domestic currency inappropriate. In this chapter all figures are given in American dollars unless otherwise stated.

Table 16.3 shows key data for the savings and loan systems in the Central and South American countries, as at the end of 1983.

It must be stressed that this table does not give a comprehensive indication of housing finance systems. It records data only for formal savings and loan systems and excludes activity by banks and other similar institutions. However, the table is adequate to show the size of the formal savings and loan systems in the various countries.

The Brazilian system stands out as being by far the largest but this is not altogether unexpected given the size of the country. If the number of loans is compared with total population, a very crude indication of market penetration, then Venezuela and Brazil stand out as having the largest systems. How-

Table 16.3   Savings and Loan Systems, Latin America, End-1983

Country	Number of Associations	Number of Savers	Number of Loans	Total Assets US$ m*
Argentina	20	135,000	70,000	866
Bolivia	12	144,000	9,000	39
Brazil	94	60,000,000	1,736,000	27,018
Colombia	10	2,271,000		3,917
Costa Rica	7	84,000	23,000	100
Chile	45		68,000*	21,560
Ecuador	11	476,000	32,000	218
El Salvador	8	426,000	20,000*	42
Guatemala	1	112,000	4,000*	231
Honduras	6	82,000	9,000	97
Panama	5	97,000	3,000	59
Paraguay	6	149,000	16,000	217
Peru	23	1,313,000	30,000	185
Venezuela	27	2,504,000	130,000*	6,411

Source: Inter-American Savings and Loan Union.
Note: At end-June 1983 there were $1.55 to the pound.
         * End-June 1983 figures.

ever, figures are not readily available for Colombia but is has a higher penetration for savings accounts than the other countries except Brazil.

Those countries which have had high rates of inflation have, almost without exception, introduced index linking, because of course it is not possible to operate a housing finance system with such high rates of inflation using purely nominal interest rates. (For a detailed description of index linking in Latin America see: Cardis, G P, *Monetary Correction, Thrift Institutions and Housing Finance*, International Union of Building Societies and Savings Associations, 1983.)

In Argentina, the savings and loan system began operation in 1962. It has subsequently been subjected to a variety of regulations and these together with periodic high rates of inflation have not made for smooth operations. Initially, the savings and loan associations were responsible to the Federal Savings and Loan Bank for Housing, but since 1977 responsibility for the Associations has rested with the Central Bank.

In 1976/77 there was a general introduction of index linking, including for mortgage lending. A variety of indices have been used. The current system is based on the average costs incurred by the thrift institutions. The Argentinian industry faced considerable pressures in 1982 as a result of strains on the Argentinian economic system generally, and the government had to step in to provide temporary relief through subsidies to borrowers. In his study of the Argentinian system, Cardis concludes that indexation was used only as a palliative rather than as a powerful weapon.

In Bolivia the system comprises the Caja Central de Ahorro y Prestamo para la Vivienda (Central Savings and Loan Bank) and 12 mutual savings and loan associations, which between them have 16 branches. The whole of the system is controlled by the Central Bank. The system accounts for about 15% of savings in Bolivia, the commercial banks holding the remaining 85%.

The Caja Central was set up in 1966 and is administered largely by the individual associations although there is one government representative on the board. It acts as both a supervisory institution and a mortgage bank.

The housing finance system in Bolivia used to be indexed to the American dollar, but such was the movement in exchange rates in 1982 that this practice had to be ended. Recently, the Caja Central has raised a substantial loan from AID which in turn is being on lent to the savings and loan associations to lend to house-purchasers. The Central Bank is helping to subsidize the loan to help the profitability of the associations.

In Chile the savings and loan system was instituted in 1960. Originally there were 22 associations but these were merged in 1975 into the Associacion Nacional de Ahorro y Prestamo. Most activity in the housing finance market is now undertaken by stock housing finance institutions, the Bancos Hipotecarios y de Fomento, which operate through selling mortgage bonds. The largest single lender is the Banco Hipotecario de Fomento Nacional which has one third of outstanding housing loans. The Chilean system uses monetary correction.

In Panama the Caja de Ahorros de Panama (Savings Bank of Panama) was founded as long ago as 1934 and now operates through 27 branches. It competes with the mortgage banks and the construction loan banks to collect deposits. A major role is played by the Banco Hipotecario Nacional de Panama.

In Paraguay the savings and loan system was created by a 1971 law and began operation in 1973. Monetary correction was built into the system. There are seven mutual savings and loan associations, and also the National Bank of Savings and Loans for Housing. However, most activity is now undertaken by six private savings and loan societies for housing. In 1982 the monetary correction system was changed and rates are now fixed by the Central Bank.

Venezuela is different from the other Latin American countries by virtue of its wealth based on oil. There are 27 savings and loan institutions and the Banco Nacional de Ahorro y Prestamo. The system operates through 300 agencies.

The system in Peru dates back to 1957. There are 16 mutual associations. They obtain their funds through savings deposits and they also obtain institutional loans channelled through the Peruvian Housing Bank. It is estimated that they fund about 18% of new housing. The system uses index linking.

Uruguay does not have a savings and loan system in the same way as the other countries. The major lender is the Banco Hipothecario del Uruguay (Mortgage Bank of Uruguay) which took over the Postal Savings Bank in 1976 and which also operates through 23 subsidiaries. It collects funds through demand deposits (3% of the total), term savings (23%), indexed mortgage bonds (59%) and convertible bonds under a contractual savings scheme (15%). At the end of 1982 the bank had total assets of $960 million.

The housing finance system in Costa Rica was established in 1969. There are six mutual savings and loan associations and a regulatory central body. The associations have been under financial pressure in recent years and recorded operating losses in 1980 and 1981.

In El Salvador the system was established in 1964 and operates through profit-making corporations. The system is very large—45% of all families have accounts and the savings and loan corporations hold 47% of the country's savings.

Honduras also has savings and loan corporations, the system having been established in 1976.

Nicaragua has a mortgage bank which assimilates a previous savings and loan system.

The Inter-American Savings and Loan Union

The Inter-American Savings and Loan Union (Union Interamericana de Ahorro y Prestamo para la Vivienda) was established in 1964, following the holding of successful savings and loan conventions. The first such convention was held in Peru in 1963, and was sponsored by the Inter-American Development Bank, the Agency for International Development and the National League of Insured Saving and Loan Associations (now the National Council of Savings Institutions). The Union was established at the second Inter-American Savings and Loan Conference held in Santiago, Chile, in January 1964. The Union's objectives, broadly speaking, are to promote savings and homeownership, and to encourage co-operation between savings and loan institutions in Latin America.

The Union comprises institutions in Argentina, the Bahamas, Bolivia, Brazil, Colombia, Costa Rica, Chile, Dominican Republic, Ecuador, El Salvador, Guatemala, Honduras, Mexico, Panama, Paraguay, Peru, Puerto Rico, Trinidad, the United States and Venezuela. At the end of 1982 it had 236 members, of which 15 were central organisations, 14 were leagues of institutions, 179 were savings and loan institutions, 18 were affiliates, two were federal banks and two were international organisations.

The League is still based in Santiago, Chile and has a permanent secretariat headed by Ricardo Garcia Rodriguez.

The Union provides a wide range of statistical and other publications in Spanish, Portuguese and English. The Union provides considerable technical assistance to its members and it collaborates in training programmes.

A feature of its work is the holding of annual conferences, which enable a wide range of matters to be discussed. These conferences are partly sponsored by the Agency for International Development.

The Inter-American Savings and Loan Bank

The Banco Inter-Americano de Ahorro y Prestamo—BIAPE (Inter-American Savings and Loan Bank) is the only multi-national housing loan bank in the world. Its primary goal is to contribute to the development of savings and loan systems in Latin America by strengthening existing savings structures and establishing those where they do not exist. The impetus for its establishment came from the Inter-American Savings and Loan Union and it was founded in 1975 in Caracas, Venezuela, and operates from that country and also it runs a bank in the Cayman Islands. Its ownership is spread among 19 nations, and shareholders include 12 central housing finance organisations, 130 individual housing finance institutions, ten associations, and five bodies specialised in housing finance. The Inter-American Union, the IUBSSA, the two American savings and loan trade associations and the Spanish Confederation of Savings Banks are among the shareholders.

At the end of 1983 BIAPE had total capital and reserves of $26 million. The bank raises its funds through loans from international banking organisations and also its own security issues. Loans outstanding at the end of 1983 totalled $30 million and total assets were $42 million. The loans are to institutions in 21 different Latin American countries and are aimed at contributing to the construction of dwellings.

The Bank has obviously been affected by financial difficulties in Latin America generally, and in housing finance systems in particular. The Bank declined slightly in size in 1983, and a reduction in retained earnings and provision for loan losses of $2 million was compensated for by an increase in paid in share capital.

Bibliography

Cardis, G P and Robinson, H, *Monetary Correction, Thrift Institutions and Housing Finance*, International Union of Building Societies and Savings Associations, 1983.
Inter-American Savings and Loan Bank (BIAPE), Annual Report, 1983.
Inter-American Savings and Loan Union, 1982 and 1983 Annual Reports.
International Savings Banks Directory, International Savings Banks Institute, 1984.
National Reports, International Union of Building Societies and Savings Associations, 1983.
Proceedings of Inter-American Savings and Loan Conference, Lima, Peru, 1982, Inter-American Savings and Loan Union, 1982.
Thrift Institution Development in Latin America, Staff Study prepared for the use of the Subcommittee on Inter-American Economic Relationships of the joint Economic Committee, Congress of the United States, June 4, 1970.

Acknowledgements

The co-operation of the Agency for International Development, the Inter-American Savings and Loan Union and the Inter-American Savings and Loan Bank in providing information for this chapter is gratefully acknowledged. The author is indebted to George Cardis, Vice President, the Institute of Financial Education, and Eric Carlson, Special Advisor to the IUBSSA, for their general assistance in providing information and helping to interpret developments in Latin America. Dr Ricardo Garcia-Rodriguez, in addition to providing information, offered valuable comments on an earlier draft of the chapter.

CHAPTER 17

BRAZIL

Brazil is a very large, but still relatively underdeveloped, economy. However, GNP per capita is very much higher than, for example, in India, and it is slightly above the average for the Latin American countries generally.

The housing finance system in Brazil has three distinguishing features -

(a) It has been established from almost nothing in the early 1960s, and has grown spectacularly.
(b) The system employs full indexation of loans and savings.
(c) A large part of the system uses funds raised from a compulsory savings scheme for employees.

The formal system of housing finance, on which this chapter concentrates, largely serves the middle and upper income groups, while the poorer sections of the community use informal sources of finance.

Introduction

Brazil is a huge country, occupying 8,511,965 sq kilometres, well over a third of the total land area of Latin America, and substantially larger than, for example, India. It has borders with each of the Latin American countries, except Ecuador and Chile.

The population of Brazil in May 1983 was 125 million, 69% of whom live in urban areas. The population grew at an annual rate of 2.1% between 1970 and 1980. In terms of population, Brazil is substantially larger than all the other Latin American countries put together. The largest cities are San Paulo (8.5 million), Rio de Janeiro (5 million), Belo Horizonte (1.8 million) and Recife (1.2 million). The capital since 1960 has been the new city of Brasilia.

Brazil is a federal republic with an indirectly elected president. There are two chambers of parliament, the Federal Parliament and the Senate. The largest political party is the Social Democratic Party, but political power rests far more with the president.

GNP per capita in 1981 was $2,220, slightly below the levels of Argentina, Chile, and Uruguay, but well above the levels in Colombia, Bolivia and Peru. Real GNP per capita grew by an average of 5.9% a year between 1970 and 1980, an exceptionally high rate.

Brazil has suffered from acute inflation. In the 1950-1966 period the annual rate averaged 34%. In 1964 the rate increased to 92%, and this led to the introduction of indexation. Inflation then fell back to as low as 13% in 1973, before increasing again in the second half of the 1970s. In 1979 inflation fell back to 14%, but since then it has increased to over 100% a year since 1980, and to over 200% by the end of 1983. Obviously, this high rate of inflation has meant that there have been frequent devaluations, and it is common for economic variables in Brazil to be measured in United States dollars rather than in Brazilian cruzeiros. In this chapter figures are quoted directly from the original source; some are in dollars and others in cruzeiros. The high rate of inflation has contributed to massive international debt problems, and, for the last few years, Brazil has been faced with the possibility of defaulting on its international loans, which have now grown in size to be nearly four times the annual value of its exports.

Housing

Table 16.2 shows that there were 17,629,000 dwellings in Brazil in 1970. Of these 60% were owned and 19% were rented.

The Housing Finance System

The Financial System
The financial system of Brazil needs only a relatively brief description, because the housing finance system is a relatively independent unit. At the centre of the system are four government bodies -

    (a) The National Development Bank (BNDE).
    (b) The National Housing Bank.
    (c) The Central Bank.
    (d) The Banco do Brazil.

The National Development Bank is responsible largely for financing the needs of industry. Like the National Housing Bank and the Central Bank itself, it does not deal directly with the public but, rather, operates with institutions which themselves operate at the retail level.

Until fairly recently the Banco do Brazil, the largest commercial bank, was also the central bank, but in 1970 a separate Central Bank was established. The Banco do Brazil is 75% state owned. It has 2,755 domestic branches, and is by a long way the largest commercial bank. In particular, it is the main supplier of agricultural credit. The Central Bank and the Banco do Brazil between them form the monetary authority of Brazil.

The major private sector institutions are commercial banks and investment banks. The other principal institutions are those in the housing finance system, the housing credit companies, the savings banks and savings and loan associations. Table 17.1 shows the assets of financial intermediaries at the end of 1981.

Table 17.1   Assets of Financial Intermediaries, End-1981

Intermediary	Assets Cr Million	Percentage of Total
Commercial banks	3,555,900	29
Banco do Brazil	2,025,289	17
Investment banks	1,343,404	11
Housing credit companies	1,166,662	10
Federal Savings Bank	1,093,499	9
National Development Bank	854,534	7
Finance companies	662,589	5
State savings banks	508,810	4
State development banks	445,536	4
Savings & loans	360,715	3
National Housing Bank	79,585	1
Other	92,778	1
Total	12,189,301	100

Source: Banco Central do Brazil.
Note: At end-1981 there were 127.8 cruzeiros to the dollar and 243.5 cruzeiros to the pound.

The table shows the dominance of the banks, in particular, the huge size of the Banco do Brazil. The housing credit companies and the Federal Savings Bank are the largest of the housing finance institutions.

Formal and Informal Sectors

In common with most developing countries Brazil has informal and formal sectors of housing finance. It is estimated that the formal sector is not able to assist the poorest 25% of the population. A high proportion of this sector of the population live in very poor quality housing, often shanty towns. To the extent that they own anything other than a very basic home, then this is financed through the informal system, using loans within families or personal savings. The formal sector has fairly modest loan ceilings, and this means that the highest income groups are not able to make use of it. They obtain any funds they need to borrow either as personal loans from the banking system or from developers. The formal system of housing finance caters for the middle and upper income ranges predominantly. At this stage the formal system will be described very briefly, and the institutions which comprise that system will subsequently be described in more detail. At the centre of the formal system is the Banco Nacional de Habitacao (National Housing Bank) (BNH). This obtains its funds largely through a compulsory savings scheme.

BNH regulates the Sistema Brasilerio de Empristino e Poupanca (savings and loans system) (SBPE), which comprises a federal savings bank, five state savings banks, joint stock housing credit companies, and mutual savings and loan associations. All the funds raised and loans made are index linked.

An attempt has been made to measure the relative size of the informal and formal sectors by John Tuccillo (Tuccillo, J, *The Housing Finance System of Brazil*, 1983). Tuccillo calculated that between 1964 and 1967 the formal sector made housing loans equal to only 8% in the growth in the number of households, and that of these loans 54% were BNH popular (ie subsidized) loans. By the 1974-77 period the sector made loans equal to 46% of the growth in the number of households, and the direct contribution of the BNH popular loans had fallen to 40% of the total. Table 17.2 shows figures for the whole of the period 1964-77.

Table 17.2   Performance of Brazilian Housing Finance System 1964-77

Type of Loan	Number of Loans
BNH popular housing	522,000
BNH middle income housing	374,000
Savings and loan system	676,000
BNH construction material loans	141,000
BNH development pole housing	26,000
Total	1,739,000
Increase in urban households	6,964,000
Popular housing loans/all housing loans	30%
All housing loans/increase in urban households	25%

Source: Tuccillo, J, *The Housing Finance System of Brazil*, 1983.

The level of financial intermediation in the housing sector in Brazil is very much higher than in the poorer developing countries. In India, for example, under 10% of housing investment is financed through institutional means. However, even by 1977, intermediation was much lower than in the developed countries, where over 80% of housing investment is financed through the institutional system.

Indexation

A major feature of the Brazilian financial system is indexation. The necessity for some form of indexation has already been illustrated. Over the last few years, inflation in Brazil has been running at around the 100% level. No financial system can operate effectively without indexation when inflation is running at this sort of level. Clearly there would be a flight from money, and people would wish to hold their assets in tangible goods. Indexation effectively removes the effects of inflation, by providing for assets and liabilities to be adjusted in value to take account of rises in prices. The interest rate is then a real rate of interest rather than a nominal rate. If, for example, inflation is running at an annual rate of 20% and the nominal rate of interest is only 10%, then clearly the investor would suffer a 10% reduction in his capital, while the borrower would, in effect, be paid to borrow money. Indexation would increase the capital value of the loan and the investment by 20%, allowing a more modest real rate of interest to be paid.

Indexation was introduced in Brazil in 1964. It is not compulsory, but is operated in respect of Treasury bills, compulsory savings and also deposits in the savings and loan system. Indexation is achieved by reference to the standard capital unit (UPC). This is calculated quarterly according to the wholesale price index. Table 17.3 shows how the value of the standard capital unit has changed over the period 1964-82.

Table 17.3 Value of Standard Capital Unit, 1964-82

Year	Value of UPC 4th Quarter Cr	Depreciation in Year %	Year	Value of UPC 4th Quarter Cr	Depreciation in Year %
1964	10.00	-	1974	101.90	14
1965	15.90	59	1975	125.70	23
1966	21.61	36	1976	168.33	34
1967	27.38	27	1977	227.15	35
1968	33.88	24	1978	303.29	34
1969	39.92	18	1979	428.80	14
1970	47.61	19	1980	663.56	54
1971	58.61	23	1981	1,239.39	87
1972	68.95	18	1982	2,398.55	94
1973	77.87	13			

Source: BNH Annual Report 1981.

This table, in effect, shows the rate of inflation, although the measure used shows a slightly lower rate than the retail prices index, which has increased by about 100% a year for the last few years.

The method of indexation is somewhat crude, in that capital values of investments held at the end of each quarter are adjusted. This leads to an inflow of funds in the final month of each quarter and an outflow in the following month. However, the system does seem to have been relatively successful in allowing financial institutions to continue borrowing and lending over long terms.

The implementation of indexation was changed in 1983. Only 80% of inflation is compensated for and adjustments are now made monthly.

The National Housing Bank and The Saving and Loan System

Overview

The institutions involved in the housing finance system have already been briefly described. At this stage it is helpful to set out their relative size before considering in detail the operations of the National Housing Bank and the various institutions. Table 17.4 shows funds available to the housing finance system as at the end of 1981.

Table 17.4   Funds Available to Housing Finance System, End-1981

	Amount Cr m	Percentage of Total
Funds from public		
Savings banks	1,424,739	34
Housing credit companies	952,115	23
Savings and loans	136,058	3
Compulsory saving (FGTS) funds	1,370,521	33
Net worth	279,197	7
Total	4,158,630	100

Source: Statistical Bulletin of National Housing Bank.
Note: At end-1981 there were 127.8 cruzeiros to the dollar and 243.5 cruzeiros to the pound.

It will be seen that one third of the funds come from compulsory saving, and most of the remaining two thirds from public funds.

There is a fairly rigid segmentation not only between the various sectors of the financial market in Brazil, but also between the sectors of the housing finance market. This is illustrated in Table 17.5, which shows a very brief outline of the main sectors of the housing finance market as at February 1983.

Table 17.5   The Housing Finance System, February 1983

Type of Market	Programmes	Loans up to US $	Annual Interest Rate %	Monthly Family Income up to US $
Low income	State Companies	5,196	1-5	152
Economic	COHABS Housing Co-operatives	18,707	5.1-9.4	557
Medium	Co-operatives SBPE	28,061	9.4-9.9	886
Upper	SBPE	51,964	10	Over 1,000

Source: Tuccillo, J A, *The Housing Finance System of Brazil*, 1983.
Note: At end-March 1983 there were 417.5 cruzeiros to the dollar and 622.3 cruzeiros to the pound.

The various institutions will be described in more detail subsequently but, at this stage, it is necessary to note the COHABS, public sector housebuilding organisations, and the SBPE, which is the general abbreviation for the housing finance system.

The housing finance system operates through short term savings accounts which, as has already been noted, are index linked. The real rate of interest paid is 6% per annum. There is also provision for housing bonds, but these are now little used. Table 17.6 shows the distribution and growth of savings accounts between the housing finance institutions between 1972 and 1982.

Table 17.6 Savings Accounts, Brazil 1972-82

Institution	Number of Accounts, End-Year			Average
	1972	1977	1982	Balance End-1982 Cr
Housing credit				
companies	771,000	8,214,000	28,583,000	83,995
Savings banks	1,900,000	7,223,000	16,586,000	185,290
Savings & loan				
associations	563,000	2,911,000	3,717,000	53,097
Total	3,234,000	18,349,000	48,886,000	116,013

Source: *Banco Central do Brazil Boletim Mensal*, October 1983, Table 1.44.
Note: At end-1982 there were 252.7 cruzeiros to the dollar and 409.0 cruzeiros to the pound.

It will be seen that the housing credit companies have been growing most rapidly and account for over half of the total number of savings accounts.

The National Housing Bank

The Banco Nacional de Habitacao (National Housing Bank) (BNH) was established in 1964, and over the next few years it established a housing finance system (SFH) and a savings and loans system (SBPE). Prior to the establishment of the Bank it is estimated that government agencies had produced no more than 120,000 housing units. The BNH was intended to provide a national housing finance system, virtually from scratch. Originally, its capital was provided by the government and its resources came from a 4% levy on rents and a 1% payroll tax. However, this soon proved to be inadequate, and shortly afterwards a more comprehensive strategy was adopted embracing five principles -

(a) The indexation of savings and loans.
(b) The limiting of loans to new properties to ensure that every single loan was associated with a newly built property rather than merely the transfer of existing properties.
(c) The revitalisation of private sector housing finance institutions through indexation and also through liquidity guarantees.
(d) A compulsory savings scheme with an 8% levy on wage costs.
(e) Operation predominantly through the private sector.

BNH has a number of separate functions. The most important in quantitative terms is the mobilisation of funds through the compulsory savings scheme for the provision of low income housing. Employers are obliged to channel 8% of their payrolls through collection agents, largely the commercial banks, to the BNH. The funds are held in the names of individuals and receive an annual interest rate of 3% with full index linking. By June 1982, the FGTS (length of service guarantee fund) had accumulated balances of 19 trillion cruzeiros, and there were 41 million individual accounts. Individuals can draw on their accounts when they become unemployed, when they wish to make downpayments for a house or in order to make mortgage payments.

The funds raised in this way must be used for low income housing and infrastructure investment.

At this stage it should be noted that not only is BNH responsible for housing development, but it also has primary responsibility for sanitation and certain other aspects of infrastructure investment. FGTS funds are used for this purpose to a limited extent.

BNH does not lend directly to individuals at all, but it does make loans to the COHABS for onlending as subsidized 'popular' loans on lower income housing. The role of the COHABS is explained in more detail subsequently.

The second main function of the BNH is to control the savings and loan system (SBPE) and also to provide a liquidity guarantee for the institutions within the system. It sets and controls interest rates that the housing finance institutions can charge, and generally it is the controlling body for the COHABS, the savings banks, the housing credit companies and the savings and loan associations. All of these institutions are required to make deposits with the BNH, and these deposits are invested in Treasury securities. In this way BNH manages the liquidity of the various institutions.

BNH is wholly government owned and is organised in four separate directorates, covering housing, sanitation, land development and consumer savings. Over 80% of its direct loans are for housing purposes, and most of the remainder are for urban development of one form or another, particularly sanitation.

Table 17.7 shows BNH assets and liabilities as at the end of 1982.

The table effectively illustrates the main function of BNH, that is, in collecting FGTS deposits and using these for long term housing loans through other intermediaries. The income and expenditure account of BNH is more difficult to analyse because of the very high rate of inflation, which makes the use of mean assets more inappropriate than usual. Table 17.8 shows the figures in respect of 1981 using, as in the case of Table 17.7, American dollars rather than Brazilian cruzeiros as the currency.

Table 17.7 BNH Assets & Liabilities, End-1982

Liabilities	US$ m	%	Assets	US$ m	%
Short term housing deposits	1,083	6	Long term housing loans	13,605	82
Other short term liabilities	624	4	Other long term assets	1,216	7
FGTS deposits	12,102	73	Short term housing loans	1,457	9
Other long term liabilities	1,551	9	Other short term assets	338	2
Capital, reserves and profits	1,311	8	Fixed assets	56	-
Total	16,672	100	Total	16,672	100

Source: BNH Annual Report 1982.
Note: At end-1982 there were 252.7 cruzeiros to the dollar and 409.0 cruzeiros to the pound.

Table 17.8 BNH Income & Expenditure, 1981

	US$ m	US$ per 100 US$ Mean Assets
Income		
Income from loans	4,761	30.4
Income from investments	240	1.5
Operating revenue	355	2.3
Total	5,356	34.2
Expenditure		
Interest on FGTS deposits	3,672	23.4
Other interest	777	5.0
Administration expenses	105	0.7
Other operating expenses	374	2.4
Indexation	374	2.4
Other expenses	35	0.2
Profit	18	0.1
Total	5,356	34.2

Source: BNH Annual Report 1982.
Note: At end-1982 there were 252.7 cruzeiros to the dollar and 409.0 cruzeiros to the pound.

Housing Finance Institutions

COHABS

COHABS (Companhias da Habitacao Popular) are state or local agencies for the implementation of national housing policies through the BNH. There are 35, with there being at least one in each state. They have the role of financial institutions and also urban development agencies. Most are of the size range $3.75 million to $8.75 million, and none are larger than $40 million. The COHABS construct housing directly and they onlend money raised through the FGTS system at subsidized rates of interest. An interesting method has been developed of ensuring that recipients of subsidized loans repay them. The government subsidy is available only if repayments are made on time.

The COHABS operate with very tight margins, and effectively the rates of interest at which they work are dictated by BNH.

Savings Banks

Table 17.6 shows that the savings banks had a little over the third of the number of total accounts within the housing finance system as at the end of 1982, but that their average balance was substantially higher than that of the housing credit companies, and they hold a higher volume of deposits.

The largest single housing lender in Brazil is the Caixa Economica Federal (CEF) (Federal Savings Bank), which is owned by the federal government and operates throughout the entire country. It was originally created in 1861 and adopted its present form in 1970, when 92 savings banks were merged into the Federal Savings Bank. It was integrated into the housing finance system in 1964. It comprises a central administrative unit and 21 regional units. It has 1,359 branches and 861 service units. Table 17.9 shows the balance sheet for the Federal Savings Bank at the end of 1982.

Table 17.9   Federal Savings Bank, Assets & Liabilities, End-1982

Liabilities	Cr bn	%	Assets	Cr bn	%
Savings time deposits	2,246	67	Housing finance loans	2,055	61
Private sector demand			Mortgage loans	275	8
deposits	96	3	Other loans to private		
Other demand deposits	13	-	sector	242	7
Liabilities for advances	319	10	Other loans	254	8
Capital & reserves	430	13	Stocks & securities	218	7
Other liabilities	239	7	Cash & bank balances	90	3
			BNH deposits	206	6
			Fixed assets	145	4
			Other assets net	(143)	(4)
Total	3,343	100	Total	3,343	100

Source: *Banco Central do Brasil Boletim Mensal*, October 1983, Table 1.38.
Note: At end-1982 there were 252.7 cruzeiros to the dollar and 409.0 cruzeiros to the pound.

It will be seen that the Federal Savings Bank is very much a specialist housing finance body. It obtains 67% of its funds through savings time deposits, and does not resort to the capital markets. Housing finance loans comprise 61% of its total assets, and a further 8% are classified as mortgage loans. The bank has very few loans other than for housing purposes, and, in general, it is, by a very long way, the largest mortgage lender in the Latin American countries.

In addition to the Federal Savings Bank there are five state savings banks but, collectively, these are less than half the size of the Federal Savings Bank. At the end of 1982 they had assets of Cr1,484 billion, of which housing loans comprised Cr847 billion, 60% of the total. They operate in a very similar way to the Federal Savings Bank.

Housing Credit Companies

These institutions were established from 1964 onwards as part of the national housing finance system. They are regulated by the National Housing Bank. They obtain their funds largely from index-linked deposits, and most of their assets are in the form of housing loans. At the end of 1982 there were 61 companies, with a total of 6,878 agencies between them. They have strong connections with the commercial banks. Table 17.10 shows the aggregate balance sheet for the companies as at the end of 1982.

Table 17.10   Housing Credit Companies, Assets & Liabilities, End-1982

Liabilities	Cr bn	%	Assets	Cr bn	%
Savings deposits	2,298	70	Loans for housing		
Liabilities to BNH	696	21	acquisition	2,159	66
Reserves & capital	266	8	Loans for housing		
Other liabilities	24	1	construction	411	13
			Other housing loans	323	10
			Financial assets	457	14
			Fixed assets	60	2
			Other assets (net)	(126)	(4)
Total	3,284	100	Total	3,284	100

Source: *Banco Central do Brasil Boletim Mensal*, October 1983, Table 1.42.
Note: At end-1982 there were 252.7 cruzeiros to the dollar and 409.0 cruzeiros to the pound.

Savings and Loan Associations

In respect of their method of operation these are virtually identical to the housing credit companies; the essential difference between them is that they are mutual rather than joint stock. At the end of 1982 there were 28 savings and loan associations with 327 agencies. Their assets totalled Cr546 billion, of which housing loans comprised Cr510 billion.

The associations ran into severe financial difficulty early in 1984, and four were closed down by the Central Bank. Their joint liabilities were reported at $1.4 billion, the bulk owed to BNH. The recession is given as the cause of the problem; savings accounts have been withdrawn and many borrowers have been unable to keep up with their mortgage repayments. The number of associations has fallen to 16 and they are now less than a tenth of the size of the housing credit companies.

Assessment

Brazil can be regarded as a success story in that a savings and loan system has been established from virtually nothing, and that it has survived notwithstanding acute economic problems, in particular, severe inflation. Indexation seems to have worked fairly smoothly, and has been fair to both borrowers and lenders. However, the acute economic problems which Brazil has experienced in the last few years have finally caused strains in the housing finance system.

In his study of the Brazilian system John Tuccillo concludes that BNH has been successful in promoting low income housing, but has been less successful in mobilizing household saving. The private sector institutions have not developed as much as was intended but, nevertheless, their record is extremely good.

Bibliography

Banco Central do Brasil Boletim Mensal, October 1983.
BNH Annual Report 1981.
'Brazil's Banco Central shoots down savings banks', *Retail Banker*, 11 June 1984.
Cardis, G, *Monetary Correction, Thrift Institutions and Housing Finance*, IUBSSA, 1983.
National Reports, International Union of Building Societies and Savings Associations, 1983.
Ourivio, J C M, *The Evolution of Savings and Loan Systems in Latin America*, 1983 (unpublished).
Sandilands, R J, *Monetary Correction and Housing Finance in Colombia, Brazil and Chile*, Gower, 1980.
The Brazilian Savings and Loan System, ABECIP/CBPE, 1977.
Tuccillo, J A, *A Financial Assessment of the National Housing Bank of Brazil*, The Urban Institute, 1983.
Tuccillo, J A, *The Housing Finance System of Brazil*, 1983 (unpublished).

Acknowledgements

The co-operation of the World Bank, BNH, the Banco do Brazil and John Tuccillo, Vice-President, National Council of Savings Institutions, in providing information for this book is gratefully acknowledged. John Tuccillo offered valuable comments on an earlier draft of this chapter.

CHAPTER 18

COLOMBIA

Colombia is the poorest of the large Latin American countries, although living standards are very much higher than in many third world countries.

The housing finance system is similar to that of Brazil in that index-linking has been used extensively. Prior to 1972 the principal housing finance institution was the government owned Central Mortgage Bank. In that year a housing finance system, using saving and housing corporations, similar to American savings and loan associations, was established, and this has rapidly overtaken the Central Mortgage Bank as the main lender. There are ten corporations, the largest of which is a section of the Central Mortgage Bank. The other principal lender is the government controlled Land Credit Institute (ICT), the primary objective of which is to provide housing for low income families.

Introduction

Colombia occupies 1,139,000 sq kilometres in the North Western corner of South America. It has a long coast line, bordering the Pacific Ocean to the West, and the Caribbean to the North, and it has land borders with Panama, Venezuela, Brazil, Peru and Ecuador. The population in 1983 was 28,777,000. The population grew at an annual rate of over 3% in the early 1960s but by the late 1970s the rate had fallen to 2%. As in other Latin American countries there has been rapid urbanization. The proportion of the population living in urban areas increased from 39% in 1951 to 69% in 1983. The largest city is the capital, Bogotá, which had a population of 3,850,000 in 1978. The other pricipal cities are Medellin (1,450,000) and Cali (1,256,000).

Colombia is a republic with a directly elected president and a one chamber parliament, the Congress.

GNP per capita in 1981 was $1,380, substantially less than that in the other large Latin American countries of Brazil, Argentina, and Venezuela, but above that, for example, in Peru. GNP per capita grew at a real rate of 4% a year between 1970 and 1980. Over the same period aggregate GDP grew by more than 5% a year in real terms although there was a noticeable decline in the rate of increase during the course of the 1970s.

Colombia has suffered from high inflation, although not as high as that in other Latin American countries, and also high interest rates. Prices rose by an annual rate of between 20% and 30% in the late 1970s and early 1980s. Indexation has been in operation since 1972 and has enabled the worst effects of inflation to be minimized. The central bank discount rate has varied only between 27% and 30% since 1980.

Housing

In 1973 there were 3,472,000 occupied dwellings in Colombia. Of these, 1,858,000 (53.5%) were owner-occupied, 1,067,000 (30.7%) were rented, and 547,000 (15.8%) were held in some other form of tenure. In the urban areas, 49% of units were owner-occupied. 68% of dwellings had piped water and 58% had toilets.

Housing Finance

The Financial System

The financial system in Colombia is fairly simple. The most important institutions are the commercial banks which hold nearly two thirds of financial liabilities. There are 27 banks with 2,700 offices. By international standards the banks are comparatively small and none ranks in the largest 500 in the world. Their main function is to provide short term loans to industry and commerce. They also make some long term loans at concessionary rates, using resources provided by the central bank.

There are a number of much smaller investment banks which provide loans to industry and commerce. Traditionally, they raised their money on a long term basis but the high rates of inflation which have prevailed in the recent past have meant that, increasingly, they have had to turn to short term liabilities.

Finance companies are relatively new institutions, having been established in the 1970s. They have grown rapidly but remain very small. The other major institutions are the saving and housing corporations, the specialist housing finance bodies. Their assets and liabilities are, for the most part, index linked, and the housing finance system is sometimes known as the UPAC system, UPAC referring to the unit of account used in the index linking process.

These four types of institution alone are able to take deposits. Table 18.1 shows deposits outstanding at the end of 1982 between the four institutions.

Table 18.1 Liabilities of Colombian Financial System, End-1982

Institution	Demand Deposits Pesos bn	Certificates of Deposit Pesos bn	Savings Deposits Pesos bn	All Deposits Pesos bn	%
Commercial banks	196	132	84	412	63
Investment banks		29		29	4
Saving & housing corporations		46	123	172	26
Finance companies	45	7			
Total	196	207	207	657	100

Source: *Revista de Banco de la Republica*
Notes: 1. At end-1982 there were 70.3 pesos to the dollar and 113.8 pesos to the pound.
2. The total figure for saving and housing corporations includes 3 bn pesos of ordinary deposits.

It will be seen that the commercial banks are by far the largest institutions followed by the saving and housing corporations. However, these institutions have the largest share of the market for savings deposits.

The financial system has developed strongly in recent years and there has been a notable increase in the degree of financial intermediation. The ratio of financial saving to GDP increased from 6% in 1970 to 30% in 1982. The high rates of inflation and interest rates, together with the use of index linking in the housing finance system, have led to a sharp change in the nature of financial assets. This is illustrated in Table 18.2.

Table 18.2 Shares of Financial Assets, Colombia, 1972, 1977 & 1982

Assets	1972 %	1977 %	1982 %
Chequeing accounts	552	533	526
Savings accounts	16	18	11
Certificates of deposit	-	12	21
Housing finance system deposits	-	13	22
Mortgage bank bonds	23	5	1
Mortgage bank contractual saving	2	1	1
Finance companies	-	3	6
Investment bank bonds	1	1	2
Other assets	8	14	9
Total	100	100	100

Arango, S, et al, *El Sector Financiero Colombiana*, 1983, unpublished.

The main trends can be identified as follows -

(a) A sharp reduction in the proportion of assets held in chequeing accounts.

(b) An even more significant reduction in holdings of mortgage bonds which have become less attractive because of high inflation.

(c) Corresponding increases in holdings of certificates of deposit and deposits in the housing finance system.

The increase in inflation during the 1970s from between 10% and 15% to over 20% did not lead to any reduction in saving. This is because market interest rates have moved in line and also index linking has enabled the real value of savings to be preserved.

In 1982 a number of financial institutions, although not those which use index linking, ran into financial difficulty and had to be rescued by the central bank.

The Housing Finance System

Colombia has a relatively developed housing finance system for a country in its stage of economic development. It is estimated that the formal sector financed 45% of housing construction in 1982 compared with just 18% in 1965.

The formal sector can best be described by reference to the institutions which comprise that sector and this is done subsequently in this chapter. At this stage it is helpful to note that between 1950 and 1958 the main institutional lenders were the commercial banks. From 1958 to 1972 the lead role was taken by two government bodies, the Land Credit Institute and the Central Mortgage Bank. In 1968 the Central Mortgage Bank alone held 80% of identifiable housing debt. Since 1972 the saving and housing corporations have gained a predominant position.

Table 18.3 shows estimated housing output according to financial agency in 1981.

Table 18.3   Housing Output by Financial Agency, Colombia, 1981

Agency	Number of Units	Percentage of Total
Land Credit Institute (ICT)	20,000	16.7
Central Mortgage Bank (BCH)	10,300	8.6
Saving and housing corporations (CAVs)	21,000	17.5
National Savings Fund (FNA)	5,500	4.6
Popular & Military Housing Banks	3,000	2.5
Informal sector	60,000	50.1
Total	119,800	100.0

Source: Pachon, A, *Housing Finance in Colombia*, World Bank, 1983 (unpublished), based on research in *Urban Policy in Colombia: Selected Issues and Some Directions for Change*, World Bank, 1983 (unpublished).

Attention will be focussed initially on the informal sector which, in 1981, still acounted for half of housing output, and then on the formal institutions.

Informal Housing and Housing Finance

Chapter 2 described briefly the nature of informal housing finance systems and other chapters of this book dealing with developing countries have mentioned the importance of the informal sector. However, detailed description of the sector is made very difficult for the obvious reason that no statistics are collected and much of the activity is illegal. Colombia has been the subject of somewhat more detailed study than other countries and, accordingly, it is possible to present a brief description of the informal housing and housing finance system. The description is relevant not only in the context of the overall housing finance system of Colombia, but also as a good example of informal systems in general.

There have been a number of significant studies of the housing and housing finance markets in Colombia. Reference was made in Chapter 2 to a survey of low income housing in Cartagena (Strassman, W P, *The Transformation of Urban Housing*, John Hopkins University Press, 1983) which found that less than 10% of low income housing had any debts against it. A very detailed study, concentrating primarily on housing rather than finance, was published by the Agency for International Development in 1981 (Blaesser, B W, *Clandestine Development in Colombia*, Agency for International Development, Occasional Paper, 1981). The analysis that follows is a very brief summary of Blaesser's comprehensive study.

Blaesser's study concentrates on what is known as a 'pirate' submarket. This differs from traditional squatting in that there is an actual purchase and sale of a plot. Much of the activity is through subdivision of individual plots. Purchasers obtain proof of title to their plots although in many cases this proves defective. The subdivision is illegal primarily because it violates local regulations and zoning laws. The study concentrated on the second largest city in Colombia, Medellin.

Medellin has grown rapidly, in line with the increasing urbanization of Colombia. The population grew from 168,000 in 1938 to 773,000 in 1964 and to 1,152,000 in 1973. The first pirate subdivision was reported in 1885. Pirate activity reached a peak in the late 1960s and early 1970s. By early 1958 there were 54 pirate settlements housing 10% of the population. By 1966 the number of settlements had increased to 76, in which were living 25,700 households totalling 185,000 people, 23% of the total population of Medellin. By 1970 the number of settlements had fallen to 42 with 8.1% of the population. The reduction was influenced by a 1968 law making sub-dividing outside municipal controls a criminal offence.

Blaesser attributes the growth of the pirate sub-market to four factors -

(a) The rapid rate of growth of population.
(b) Housing standards which were too high for low income families to afford.

(c) Municipal policies generally, which have increased the cost of housing and reduced the supply for low income families.

(d) Pirate owners and sub-dividers have been able to make very high profits.

Purchasers generally acquire their lots on an instalment basis. To the extent that capital is used then the major source is personal saving followed by cesantias. This is severance pay which, by Colombian law, every employer must pay to each employee on termination of employment. The law also allows the employee to obtain advances from the employer secured by the severance pay, for specific purposes related to housing. A case study analysed the source of initial downpayments. Savings were used by 35% of purchasers, cesantias by 24%, salary by 6%, sale of previous home by 12% and loan from a relative or friend, by 24%. The actual monthly instalments are generally paid from earnings. The same case study found that 30% of purchasers began construction within one month of buying a plot, and a further 22% within a year. Only 17% of purchasers used loans to help finance the construction. Salaries, saving and cesantias, alone or in combination, were used by 60% of families.

Construction work is normally supervised by the head of the household and is a long term process. Initially, one floor is built but many then add a second floor which they rent out.

Blaesser's analysis stresses a strong sense of independence, felt by Colombians, which encourages them to seek to own their home rather than to rent. He concludes that alternative housing sub-markets cannot compete with the housing solution offered by the pirate sub-market as far as lower income people are concerned -

'It is argued that lower income purchasers in the pirate sub-market understand the commonsense proposition that ownership of a plot of land provides access to an asset which appreciates over time as well as the opportunity to construct a home in incremental stages in conformance with their needs and economic constraints. It is suggested that the lower income purchaser needs primarily spatial flexibility and financial feasibility (ie, amount and timing of payments) in his purchase of the lot; that the solutions offered by alternative housing sub-markets in Medellin have violated one or both of these criteria.'

Blaesser suggests that the pirate sub-market could satisfy public policy concerns, particularly with respect to infrastructure costs, if appropriate adjustments could be made in the legal framework governing land sub-division.

Land Credit Institute (ICT)

The Land Credit Institute (ICT) was established in 1942 with the objective of providing low income housing. It is affiliated to the Ministry of Development. Its primary purpose is to build low income housing and, as Table 18.3 showed, it is responsible for financing about 40% of dwellings built by the formal sector. It obtains its funds from its own sources, budget appropriations, borrowing from other intermediaries, foreign borrowing and compulsory investments by insurance companies, commercial banks and saving and housing corporations. This last source of funds is obtained at below market rates of interest.

By 1981 ICT had completed 383,000 units, most of which had subsequently been sold. It had 170,000 housing loans outstanding totalling 13.5 billion pesos. 54% of all outstanding loans were deliquent. ICT makes loans over 11 to 14 years at rates varying between 14% and 23% depending on the size of the loan. Loans to higher income groups are made on the same terms as those by saving and housing corporations. It provides a low start facility with payments increasing by between 10% and 15% a year.

The Central Mortgage Bank

The Banco Central Hipotecario (BCH) (Central Mortgage Bank) was established in 1932 when the commercial banks stopped making house-purchase loans directly. The original equity was provided by private banks, public credit institutions and the central bank. From its foundation until 1972 it was the only bank providing long term housing finance, and it grew rapidly. It was assisted by a requirement dating from 1949 for the banks to make compulsory investments in BCH and by a similar requirement being imposed on the social security fund in 1967. It also benefitted from preferential tax treatment of the mortgage bonds which it issued to finance its activities.

Following the establishment of the saving and housing corporations in 1972 the Bank stagnated although it has grown a little since 1978. Its bonds lost their unique tax advantage in 1974 and inflation in the second half of the 1970s reduced the attractiveness of raising funds through long term bond issues.

Mortgage bonds provided 80% of the funds of the Bank in the early 1970s but by 1981 the proportion had fallen to 23%. The largest source of funds is now the UPAC or saving and housing corporation section. This operates in the same way as other saving and housing corporations which are analysed in the next section. The Bank still obtains funds from the social insurance trust fund (classified as liabilities to the central government in Table 18.4). It offers a contractual savings scheme but this has been little used.

Table 18.4 shows the assets and liabilities of the Central Mortgage Bank as at June 1983.

Colombia

Table 18.4 Central Mortgage Bank, Assets & Liabilities, June 1983

Liabilities	Pesos m	%	Assets	Pesos m	%
UPAC section			Indexed loans	32,597	34
Savings deposits	30,928	32	Traditional loans	34,392	36
Time deposits	12,454	13	With central bank	5,883	6
Ordinary deposits	1,188	1	Other assets	23,677	25
Total	44,570	46			
Contractual saving & mortgage bonds	11,327	12			
Central government	28,616	30			
Commercial banks	8,248	9			
Other liabilities	3,788	4			
Total	96,549	100	Total	96,549	100

Source: *Revista de Banco de la Republica*, December 1983, Table 3.3.1.
Note: At end-June 1983 there were 78.5 pesos to the dollar and 121.6 pesos to the pound.

The UPAC section is similar to a building society or savings and loan association, while the remainder is similar to a traditional mortgage bank, relying on long term bond issues and funds borrowed from the government.

In 1981 BCH financed the construction of 10,300 units, equivalent in size to about 17% of the formal sector. It largely serves the highest two or three income deciles. The table shows that traditional loans accounted for a little over one third of assets. These are made at fixed rates of interest to developers and to individuals purchasing modern dwellings. The rate of interest charged in 1982 was 26%. Indexed loans are made by the UPAC section on the same terms as those made by other saving and housing corporations.

About 40% of the loans made by the Central Mortgage Bank are now made under a 'preselling' scheme. In this way loans are made to purchasers before they have actually purchased the dwelling. This is of considerable assistance to housebuilders who need to tie up less of their finance in work under construction. Preselling loans can be either traditional mortgage loans or indexed loans.

Saving and Housing Corporations

The Corporaciones de Ahorro y Vivienda (saving and housing corporations) (CAVs) were established in 1972. They were part of a national development plan drawn up by a team headed by Professor Lauchlin Currie, a Canadian born American economist, who has been a leading expert on housing finance systems. As part of the national plan and strategy, housing was to be given priority. In drawing up the plan savings and loan systems in other countries were analysed, including the American savings and loan associations and the Israeli experience with indexation.

The system was formally established in September 1972 with indexation built into the method of operation. Ten corporations were established with the banks playing a leading part in providing capital and also expertise. The indexation system has changed over time. The consumer price index is used to determine the amount of the indexation and the real value unit is referred to as the UPAC. Indexation has always been on a daily basis. Initially it was by reference to the rate of inflation in the previous three months. This was then increased to 24 months, and reduced to 12 months subsequently. Inflation linked increments to savings balances are partially tax free. There is a ceiling on the amount to which accounts can be adjusted for inflation. Since May 1983 this has been 23%, slightly below the rate of inflation. Both savings deposits and certificates of deposit, or time deposits, are index linked. Currently, savings deposits attract a rate of interest of 5% and certificates of deposit, 5.5%. Loans are made at the rate of 7.5% to individuals and 8% to developers, again index linked. The maximum loan is between 70% and 100% of the cost of the dwelling, depending on the size of the loan. The maximum loan is 7,000 UPACs.

The saving and housing corporations have grown spectacularly since their establishment and have replaced the Central Mortgage Bank as the main provider of housing finance loans. Deposits in the system accounted for over 22% of all financial assets in Colombia as at the end of 1982. By May 1983 there were 2,108,000 savings accounts, totalling 226 billion pesos (over $3,000 million).

Table 18.5 shows the assets and liabilities of the corporations as at the end of 1982.

Table 18.5   Saving and Housing Corporations, Assets & Liabilities, End-1982

Liabilities	Pesos m	%	Assets	Pesos m	%
Savings deposits	123,022	64	Loans	158,655	82
Time deposits (CDs)	46,250	24	Other assets held by		
Other liabilities	17,779	9	private sector	13,082	7
Central bank	4,664	2	Assets with central bank	11,433	6
			Other assets	8,545	4
Total	191,715	100	Total	191,715	100

Source: *Revista de Banco de la Republica*, December 1983, Table 3.5.3.
Note: At end-1982 there were 70.3 pesos to the dollar and 113.8 pesos to the pound.

This balance sheet is fairly typical of that for a savings and loan association or a building society. The figure for other liabilities of 9% of the total includes capital and reserves which were equal to 5% of total assets.

Table 18.6 lists the largest five institutions, with their assets given in American dollars.

Table 18.6   Largest Five Saving and Housing Corporations, End-1982

Institution	Assets US$ m	Percentage of Total
Banco Central Hipotecario (Central Mortgage Bank)	474	17
Corporacion Colombiana de Ahorro y Vivienda (Davivienda)	394	14
Corporacion Grancolombiana de Ahorro y Vivienda (Granahorrar)	357	13
Corporacion Cafetera de Ahorro y Vivienda (Concasa)	314	11
Corporacion Nacional de Ahorro y Vivienda (Conavi)	257	9
All institutions	2,847	100

Source: Instituto Colombiana de Ahorro y Vivienda.
Note: At end-1982 there were 70.3 pesos to the dollar and 113.8 pesos to the pound.

It will be noted that the corporation which is a section of the Central Mortgage Bank is the largest institution. The second largest, Davivienda, was mentioned in Chapter 2 as the first investment of the International Finance Corporation in a specialist housing finance institution. By 1976 IFC was sufficiently satisfied with the progress which had been made to sell its shares.

All ten institutions have a joint stock basis. At the end of 1982 they had between them 514 offices.

The central bank provides a facility, known as the housing and saving fund (FAVE), which helps the CAVs match their assets and their liabilities. The corporations make payments into the fund as necessary and can draw on it. The fund has been used, in effect, to regulate activity by requiring payments to be made into it at appropriate times.

The corporations have been successful in establishing quite a wide margin between their lending and borrowing rates. One study has suggested a gross margin as wide as 9%. Table 18.7 shows estimates of income and expenditure for the corporations (excluding the Central Mortgage Bank) in 1982.

Table 18.7   Saving and Housing Corporations, Income and Expenditure, 1982

	US$ 000
Income	
Monetary correction	194,783
Interest	83,595
Return on investments	13,378
Other income	3,824
Total	295,580
Expenditure	
Monetary correction	193,507
Interest	10,598
Savings interest	38,645
Personnel costs	16,316
Other expenditure	28,461
Net surplus	8,053
Total	295,580

Source: Instituto Colombiana de Ahorro y Vivienda.
Note: At end-1982 there were 70.3 pesos to the dollar and 113.8 pesos to the pound.

Assessment

The experience of Colombia confirms that of Brazil in showing that housing finance systems can work even when inflation is running at a high level, given an appropriate method of indexation. The system has contributed to the establishment of a fairly strong financial structure.

In common with other developing countries it may be argued that most of the benefit of the system has gone to middle income rather than to lower income groups but, in a way, this is inevitable. In a study of the housing finance system of Colombia for the World Bank, Alvaro Pachon commented on the macroeconomic issues which have been raised by the present housing finance system. These include the extent to which housing finance contributes to the development of the economy generally, the need for a rental housing market, the role of public sector institutions and ensuring that subsidies ultimately go to those for whom they are intended.

Bibliography

Blaesser, B W, *Clandestine Development in Colombia*, Agency for International Development, 1981.
Cardis, G, *Monetary Correction, Thrift Institutions and Housing Finance*, International Union of Building Societies and Savings Associations, 1983.
Pachon, A, *Housing Finance in Colombia*, World Bank (unpublished), 1983.
Sandilands, R J, *Monetary Correction and Housing Finance in Colombia, Brazil and Chile*, Gower, 1981.

Acknowledgements

The co-operation of the Agency for International Development, the World Bank and the Instituto Colombiano de Ahorro y Vivienda in providing information for this chapter is gratefully acknowledged. The chapter draws very heavily on the study prepared for the World Bank by Alvaro Pachon, which is referred to in the bibliography.

CHAPTER 19

THE CARIBBEAN

Introduction

The islands in the Caribbean are diverse in terms of history, political structure, financial systems and housing finance. The three largest islands, Cuba, Haiti/Dominican Republic (Hispaniola) and Puerto Rico, have a Spanish history, and with the exception of Puerto Rico, which is an American dependancy, they are independent states. Most of the remaining islands are independent members of the British Commonwealth. Some of the islands have a French history and Guadeloupe and Martinique are part of France. Finally, the Netherlands Antilles are Dutch.

This chapter makes no attempt to describe housing finance in all of the islands. Rather, it describes briefly the systems in three of the major states: Jamaica, Trinidad and Tobago and Barbados.

Jamaica

Introduction

Jamaica lies directly to the south of Cuba. It has an area of 11,420 sq kilometres. Its population in mid 1981 was 2,194,000 and the annual growth rate in the 1970s was 1.5%. The capital, Kingston, has a population of around 500,000.

Jamaica has a relatively weak economy compared with the other British Commonwealth islands in the Caribbean. GNP per capita in 1981 was US$1,180, less than half that in Barbados and only about one quarter that in Trinidad and Tobago. Real GNP per capita fell by an annual average rate of 2.8% during the 1970s. Inflation was a problem during the late 1970s. In 1978 consumer prices rose by 35% and by a further 29% in 1979 and 27% in 1980. However, by mid 1983 the rate had fallen to 9%.

Housing

At the end of 1980 there were 491,228 housing units in Jamaica. In 1970, 52% of units were owner-occupied and 29% were in urban areas. It was officially calculated that there was a shortage of 55,300 units and that 18,000 units a year would be needed betweeen 1980 and 2000 in order to meet demand. In the period 1972-82 only 40,250 units were completed. A peak of 7,852 units was reached in 1976 but the number fell back to 2,251 in 1981. There was then a sharp increase to 6,229 in 1982. This increase was entirely accounted for by building by Sugar Industry Housing Ltd. About 75% of new building has been by this and other public sector bodies including the Ministry of Construction, the Urban Development Corporation and the National Housing Corporation. A major problem with housing construction in Jamaica is the high costs and also high standards and expectations above those which might be expected given living standards.

The Financial System

The financial system is dominated by commercial banks which at the end of 1982 held 78% of personal savings. Remaining savings were held by building societies (14%), trust companies (6%) and merchant banks (2%). There is a strong Canadian influence in the commercial bank industry. There are no savings banks in Jamaica.

Housing Finance

For a small island, Jamaica has a fairly complicated housing finance system involving a number of private and public sector institutions.

In the public sector the Ministry of Housing has provided both construction and long term loans using finance obtained from normal government revenues. It has had a severe arrears problem with its mortgage portfolio. The National Housing Trust is funded by a levy of salaries of 3% on employees and 2% on employers. It makes housing loans at subsidized rates. Sugar Industry Housing Ltd is a public sector body which obtains its funds from the Sugar Industry Authority, sugar being one of the major industries in Jamaica.

The Jamaica Mortgage Bank occupies a particularly significant place in the housing finance system. It is government owned and obtains institutional funds from a variety of sources including the government, the Caribbean Development Bank, the National Housing Trust, the United States Agency for International Development, the Commonwealth Development Corporation and various American banks. Of its total funds of J$185 million in June 1983, 50% were in the form of foreign borrowing, 29% was borrowing from financial institutions and 10% was borrowing from the government. (In June 1983 there were J$1.78 to the US dollar and J$2.72 to the pound.) The foreign borrowing has led to substantial currency losses following the devaluation of the Jamaican dollar. These have been met by the government. In June 1983 the Bank had J$84 million outstanding in primary market loans and J$36 million outstanding in construction loans.

The role of the Jamaica Mortgage Bank has gradually been changing. The government is scaling down its primary market operations and it will no longer provide interim or long term financing to either the public or the private sector. Its primary objective now is to raise institutional funds to lend to primary institutions and it also arranges mortgage insurance.

Recently, the Bank has become a recipient of a US$25 million loan from the United States Agency for International Development. This will be used to finance various projects including starter homes, sites and services projects and squatter upgrading. The Bank will administer the loan but mortgage loans will be made through the Caribbean Housing Finance Corporation and the National Housing Trust.

The Caribbean Housing Finance Corporation is 50% owned by the Commonwealth Development Corporation and 50% owned by the Jamaica Mortgage Bank. It has obtained substantial loans from the Commonwealth Development Corporation. The main function of this organisation is to administer the existing loan portfolio of the Ministry of Construction and it is also intended that it will provide and service loans to those who purchase houses built by the Ministry of Housing. It also administers part of the loan portfolio of the Jamaica Mortgage Bank. At the end of 1983 it administered 14,000 mortgage accounts.

Building societies in Jamaica very much follow the British model, and they are the major providers of housing finance loans in the private sector. There are seven building societies which, between them, had assets of J$510 million at the end of 1982. The industry is dominated by two societies which account for 90% of total assets: the Jamaica National which had assets of J$226 million at the end of 1982, and the Victoria Mutual which had assets of J$233 million.

The societies have 28 offices and some 400,000 investors, about one account for every six people. Of their total assets at the end of June 1983 of J$ 525 million, J$417 were mortgages. They held savings at this time of J$491 million.

The other significant housing lenders in Jamaica are the trust companies which are very much modelled on their Canadian counterparts. In June 1983 they had total asset of J$314 million. Deposits totalled J$215 million and mortgage loans were J$169 million, although not all were in respect of housing.

Trinidad and Tobago

Introduction

The islands of Trinidad and Tobago lie just off the north coast of Venezuela. Trinidad has an area of 4,828 sq kilometres, and Tobago, to the north, 300 sq kilometres. The population of the islands in mid 1981 was 1,185,000 and the annual rate of growth in the 1970s was 1.3%. The capital, Port of Spain, has a population of about 250,000.

The islands are comparatively rich compared with the other islands and the Latin American mainland. GNP per capita in 1981 was US$5,670, and the real annual rate of growth in the 1970s was 3.9%.

Housing

In 1980 there were 235,000 housing units in Trinidad and Tobago. Of these, 78,000 were single detached houses. Owner-occupied dwellings accounted for 64% of the total, while 24% were rented.

The Financial System

The financial system in Trinidad and Tobago is dominated by the banks. As in Jamaica there is no significant savings bank system. At the end of 1980 the banks had personal loans outstanding for the purchase of land and real estate of $215 million and real estate mortgage loans of $179 million. The latter figure had increased to $409 million by the end of 1982. (At the end of 1982 there were TT$2.4 to the US dollar and TT$3.9 to the pound.) Individuals had bank deposits of $4,309 million at the end of 1982, 51% of which were classified as savings deposits, 39% as time deposits and 10% as demand deposits.

Housing Finance

Three separate public sector bodies are involved in the housing finance market. The National Housing Authority is responsible for the implementation of government housing policy. It builds houses for both rent and sale and provides mortgage loans at a subsidized rate of between 3% and 7%.

The National Insurance Board makes limited investments in housing as part of its portfolio. Currently, the rate of interest is 9.5%.

The specialist body is the Trinidad and Tobago Mortgage Finance Company Ltd which was established in 1965 by the Commonwealth Development Corporation and the government. The Company has grown rapidly to become one of the largest lenders in the islands. In 1982 it made 712 loans, totalling TT$105 million.

Two private sector institutions based in Trinidad are the General Building and Loan Association and the Trinidad Building and Loan Association, both of which are similar to building societies in their method of operation. The Trinidad Building and Loan Association had total assets of TT$35 million at the end of 1982.

Barbados

Introduction

Barbados is a small island to the north of Trinidad and Tobago. It occupies an area of just 430 sq kilometres. Its population in mid 1981 was 251,000, and the population had been growing at a rate of 0.5% a year in the 1970s. GNP per capita was US$3,620 in 1981, about midway between the figures for Jamaica and Trinidad and Tobago. The rate of growth of real GNP per capita in the 1970s was 3.2%.

Housing Finance

The largest group of housing lenders are the trust companies which were introduced into Barbados in the 1960s by Canadian trust companies. There are five trust companies with assets at the end of 1982 of $144 million (at the end of 1982 there were $BD2.01 to the US dollar and $BD3.25 to the pound). They obtain their funds largely through time deposits. They had mortgage loans outstanding of $96 million (almost 43% of the total). Loans on private dwellings totalled $79 million.

The banks used to be the largest housing lenders, but their market share is now about 20%. There are 45 banks, most of which are associated with American and Canadian banks. They are the largest deposit taking institutions. Their total assets at the end of 1983 were $1,211 million. Deposits held by individuals were $557 million, of which $427 million were savings deposits. Mortgage loans on private dwellings and land were $24 million.

The specialist housing finance institution is the Barbados Mortgage Finance Corporation which has about 20% of the market. This was founded in 1968. It had total assets of $48 million at the end of 1983. It obtains its funds by borrowing including from the Barbados National Bank, the Caribbean Development Bank, insurance companies, and the Commonwealth Development Corporation.

The other group of institutional lenders are the insurance companies which have about 20% of the market.

Bibliography

1982 Factbook, The Building Societies Association of Jamaica Limited, 1983.

Acknowledgements

The co-operation of the Commonwealth Development Corporation, the Inter-American Savings and Loan Union and the Building Societies Association of Jamaica in providing information for this chapter is gratefully acknowledged.

CHAPTER 20

SOUTH KOREA

South Korea has been industrializing rapidly and GNP per capita has been growing at a very fast rate by international standards.

The rapid industrialization has caused housing problems and squatter settlements are still common. The Korea National Housing Corporation has played a significant part in the production of new housing.

The mortgage market is comparatively well developed for an economy in South Korea's stage of development. The market is dominated by the Korea Housing Bank which has a hand in the financing of over half of new units. The Bank funds house-purchase loans, largely through deposit taking activities, and it also administers the National Housing Fund which provides the finance for subsidized rented accommodation.

Introduction

South Korea occupies the southern half of the Korean peninsula. In the North it borders on to North Korea and otherwise is surrounded by the Yellow Sea and the Sea of Japan. A narrow strait separates the south eastern corner of South Korea from Japan. The country occupies an area of 99,000 sq kilometres, but much of it is mountainous and generally the country has few natural resouces.

The population of South Korea in 1982 was 39,331,000. The population has been growing comparatively rapidly, from 25,000,000 in 1960 and 31,000,000 in 1970. The rate of increase was 3% a year in the early 1960s but subsequently it has fallen to 1.5% a year. The largest city is the capital, Seoul, which had a population of 8,114,000 in 1979. The second largest city is Busan with a 1979 population of 3,035,000. The rapid urbanization has led to a huge growth of population in the principal cities. Seoul had a population of just 1,000,000 in 1955, but by the year 2000 a figure of 19,000,000 is projected.

South Korea is a republic. Currently, a military government is in power.

South Korea has industrialized very rapidly, making maximum use of new technology combined with relatively low wage costs. GNP per capita was $1,800 in 1983, higher than for any of the other large Asian countries, except Japan. GNP per capita grew by the very high rate of 7.5% a year in real terms between 1970 and 1980. There was a significant fall in 1980 and 1981 but more recently an annual growth of 10% has been achieved.

South Korea

The country has experienced high rates of inflation, the figure reaching over 20% in 1981. However, the economy has successfully been brought back on course and in 1983 the rate of inflation was down to 3%.

Housing

The Housing Stock

South Korea has an inadequate housing stock in relation to the size of its population. Moreover, the difference between the number of households and the number of housing units has been increasing. This is illustrated in Table 20.1.

Table 20.1   Households and Housing Stock, South Korea, 1975 and 1982

	1975	1982
Number of households	6,340,000	7,884,000
Number of units	4,790,000	5,763,000
Excess of households over houses	32%	37%

It will be seen that between 1975 and 1982 the excess of households over houses increased from 32% to 37%. The figure for 1970 is estimated at 28% and for 1960 at 21%. However, such figures need to be interpreted very carefully. In South Korea, as in most other countries, the average size of households has been declining sharply. Indeed, a rapid growth of GNP per capita can itself contribute to an increase in the number of households for a given population. The table shows that between 1975 and 1982 the number of housing units increased by 20% and the number of households by 24%. However, the increase in the population was much smaller at 16%. Housing conditions have, on this measure, been improving.

In 1981, 87.1% of housing units were single family detached homes, 10.6% were in multi family units and 2.6% were in non residential units. In the rural areas the big majority of households are owner-occupiers. More than half of households in urban areas are renters, many occupying a room within a single family unit. In 1980 29% of all units were shared, the proportion rising to 49% in urban areas.

Housing Policy and Housebuilding

Following the civil war in the early 1950s and the resultant partitioning of Korea, South Korea received an influx of immigrants which added to its housing problem. In the 1950s and 1960s priority was given to industrial investment. Most housing investment that did take place was by the private sector.

A major feature of policy in the 1960s was the destruction of squatter settlements. This was not markedly successful and the 1970 Housing Improvement Law concentrated on conservation rather than reconstruction. In 1972 the Housing Construction Promotion Law set out a target of 2,500,000 new dwellings over a ten year period. This was subsequently reduced to 2,000,000 and the target was met. Two bodies, the Korea National Housing Corporation and the Korea Housing Bank, both of which had been formed in the 1960s, were assigned major roles. The contribution of the public sector to new housing investment increased and within the public sector the role of the Korea National Housing Corporation expanded.

The number of units constructed reached a peak of 300,000 in 1978. It fell back, partly as a consequence of the economic recession, to 150,000 in 1981 before recovering to 191,000 in 1982. The plan for 1983 was 240,000 units, of which 90,000 would be built by the public sector and 150,000 by the private sector. The Korea National Housing Corporation now contributes about half of new public sector building, local governments accounting for most of the remainder.

The ten year plan, drawn up by the Ministry of Construction, running from 1982 envisages the production of 3.2 million new units with 6% of GNP being allocated to residential construction. The number of units is planned to increase to 360,000 a year by 1986.

Korea National Housing Corporation (KNHC)

KNHC was established in 1961, the capital being provided by the government. The Corporation has received considerable assistance through the United States Agency for International Development Housing Guarantee Programme. The Corporation is supervised by the Ministry of Construction in accordance with a special law. It obtains its funds from four main sources -

    (a) Government funds from the housing lottery and housing bonds, both at low rates of interest.
    (b) Funds from the National Housing Fund administered by the Korea National Housing Bank.
    (c) Entrusted funds provided by the public and private organisations.
    (d) Its own capital and profits.

The activities of KNHC are largely confined to the construction of rental apartments for low income families. It also undertakes a limited amount of house construction for sale for the lower and middle income groups.

The Financial System

The Korean financial system is very well developed compared with those of other countries in a similar stage of economic development. The banking system has been firmly established and financial institutions are widely used by all sections of the community.

At the centre of the financial system is the central bank, the Bank of Korea, which was established in 1950. The commercial banks were strengthened in the 1950s, but following a military coup in 1961 the financial markets were reorganised and the banks were nationalized. Subsequently, the banks have been denationalized.

Currently, there are seven commercial banks with nationwide branch networks. Between them they have over 600 branches. They are deposit taking institutions, time and savings deposits accounting for over 60% of their liabilities. They are, in fact, the major holders of personal deposits. There are also a further ten local banks, with 360 branches. There are six specialist banks, all of which operate under specific laws and which between them hold some 40% of deposits. They are the Korea Exchange Bank (the largest bank in the country), the Medium Exchange Bank, the Citizens National Bank, the Korea Housing Bank, the National Agricultural Cooperatives Federation and the National Federation of Fisheries Cooperatives. Finally, there are about 200 mutual savings and finance corporations. These are small institutions which operate as mutual credit organisations. They have very little involvement in the housing finance market. Their assets at the end of September 1982 were 1,078 billion won.

Table 20.2 shows the breakdown of the increase in individuals' financial assets from 1975-79 to 1981.

Table 20.2 Increase in Individuals' Financial Assets, South Korea, 1975-79 —1981

Type of Asset	1975-79 Annual Average		1980		1981	
	Won bn	%	Won bn	%	Won bn	%
Money	262	13	264	7	10	-
Time & savings deposits	756	39	1,771	44	2,847	45
Insurance and trust funds	167	9	593	15	756	12
Deposits with investment & finance companies	77	4	10	-	59	1
Indirect assets	1,263	65	2,638	66	3,673	59
Securities	582	30	1,141	29	2,011	32
Commercial paper	73	4	211	5	639	10
Private loans	31	2	(3)	-	(43)	(1)
Direct financial assets	686	35	1,349	34	2,607	42
Total	1,948	100	3,987	100	6,280	100

Source: *Financial System of Korea*, Bank of Korea 1983, Table 38.
Note: At end-1981 there were 699 won to the dollar and 1,340 won to the pound.

It will be seen that a high proportion of the increase in financial assets has been in the form of securities, itself an indication of a relatively mature financial system.

The Korea Housing Bank and Housing Finance

Introduction

In industrialized countries over 70% of investment in housing is financed with the assistance of financial intermediaries. In the poorest countries the proportion is under 10%. In South Korea in 1982 it is estimated that 3,213 billion won was invested in housing construction of which 19% was supplied by housing finance institutions, purchasers' downpayments accounting for the remaining 81%. The Korea Housing Bank accounts for nearly 90% of long term lending for housing, so it is proper to focus attention on this institution. However, it should be noted that some short term commercial loans are used for house construction and purchase. At the end of 1982 the deposit banks had 1,401 billion won outstanding on housing, 7% of their total loans, and more than the total amount outstanding to the Housing Bank.

History and Organisation

The Korea Housing Bank was set up under the Korea Housing Bank Act in 1967. Initially, it provided housing finance loans and raised its funds through collecting deposits, sales of housing debentures, and borrowing from the government. Following the 1973 Housing Construction Promotion Law, the role of the Bank in financing public housing was increased through its use of the proceeds of National Housing Bonds.

In 1981 the Bank was, effectively, split into two separate functions. The National Housing Fund uses money raised on special subsidized terms to support public housing. The other part of the Bank continues to raise deposits and to make loans on a commercial basis. At the end of May 1983 the paid up capital of the bank was 24 billion won and total assets were 2,419 billion won. The bank employs 6,500 staff and has 126 branches.

Growth in Activity

Between 1967 and 1982 the Bank financed the construction of 790,000 housing units, 30% of the total number of units built. There has been a steady increase in its market share. In 1978 the bank financed the construction of 71,000 units, which represented 24% of the number of units completed. By 1981 the number of units financed, 127,000, represented 85% of the number of units completed. However, the proportion fell back to 61% in 1982. The planned proportion in 1983 was 65%. However, as has already been noted, the proportion of finance accounted for by the Bank is much lower.

The Bank's involvement in the financing of housing has been fairly equally divided between the public and the private sectors.

Private Housing Funds

Table 20.3 shows the sources and uses of private housing funds by the KHB in 1982.

Table 20.3   KHB, Sources and Uses of Private Housing Funds, 1982

Sources	Won m	%	Uses	Won m	%
Deposits	302,400	45	Private housing construction loans	470,000	71
Housing debentures	90,000	14			
Housing instalment savings deposits	44,200	7	Loans for builders' operation funds	40,000	6
Workmen's property formation deposits	58,800	9	Loans for housing material production	5,000	1
Loan collections	48,000	7	Commercial loans	45,000	7
Funds carried over	110,000	17	Small loans for WPFD	12,000	2
Other sources	11,800	2	Investments	53,200	8
			Fixed assets	40,000	6
Total	665,200	100	Total	665,200	100

Source: *Profile*, The Korea Housing Bank, 1983.
Note: At end 1982 there were 749 won to the dollar and 1,212 won to the pound.

It will be seen that the main source of funds, especially if funds carried over are excluded, were deposits, and therefore this part of the operation of the bank is very similar to that of a savings and loan association or a building society. The amount of deposits collected, 320 billion won (17.6 billion won was transferred to a reserve fund), represented a little over 10% of the total increase in individuals' holding of deposits during 1982. The Bank offers a full range of deposit accounts including chequeing accounts. The housing instalment savings deposits represent funds deposited under a scheme which links loan entitlement to a savings record. There are over 600,000 accounts under this scheme. Workmen's property formation deposits attract a high interest rate and a government bonus as well as entitlement to a housing loan of three times the amount saved. There are over 500,000 subscribers to this scheme.

KHB will lend to individuals, builders, partnerships and employers who provide company housing. Housing units may not exceed 330 sq metres. In 1983 the terms of private housing loans included a ten million won maximum, a 10% interest rate, repayments over three to 20 years, and a maximum 80% loan to value ratio. In practice however, the limited availability of funds means the average loan to value ratio is only 30%. Loans for collective housing are available on similar terms, except the maximum loan per unit is six million won.

Table 20.4 shows the development of private housing loans by the KHB from 1979 to 1982.

Table 20.4 KHB, Private Housing Loans, 1979-82

| Year | Individual | | Collective | | Total | |
	No	Won m	No	Won m	No	Won m
1979	8,028	21,890	18,489	43,207	26,517	65,097
1980	15,830	64,039	18,585	48,293	34,415	112,332
1981	31,743	198,776	23,019	71,085	54,762	269,861
1982	37,619	260,217	25,959	105,321	63,578	365,538

Source: *Profile*, The Korea Housing Bank, 1983.
Note: At end-1982 there were 749 won to the dollar and 1,212 won to the pound.

It will be seen that there has been a particularly strong growth in loans on individual houses. Of the loans made in 1982 nearly half were on apartment buildings.

Within the total there has been a major growth in loans for house-purchase as opposed to loans for house construction. In 1979, of the 8,028 individual loans, 5,519 were for construction. By 1982 the number of loans for construction had risen only modestly to 6,026 while the number for house-purchase had increased more than tenfold to 31,593.

The National Housing Fund

The National Housing Fund, which is managed by the KHB but which is under the direction of the Ministry of Construction, is a means by which public funds can be channelled into the construction of public sector housing. Table 20.5 shows sources and uses of the National Housing Fund in 1982.

Table 20.5 KHB, Sources and Uses of National Housing Fund, 1982

Sources	Won m	%	Uses	Won m	%
National Housing Bonds	185,800	30	KNHC	184,700	30
Government contribution	44,000	7	Local governments	108,500	18
Deposits from public institutions	43,000	7	Builders & individuals	80,900	13
Loan collections	51,700	8	Carried over	210,000	34
National housing pre-emption subscription deposits	30,000	5	Other	31,200	5
Funds carried over	198,900	32			
Reserves & other sources	74,800	12			
Total	615,300	100	Total	615,300	100

Source: *Profile*, The Korea Housing Bank, 1983.
Note: At end-1982 there were 749 won to the dollar and 1,212 won to the pound.

It will be seen that the major source of funds is national housing bonds. These were introduced in 1973. An applicant who wants to obtain a permit for gambling businesses, entertainment businesses and building construction, the registration of real estate and new private car purchase, and various other licences, must purchase a stipulated amount of national housing bonds. They are redeemable in five years and carry an interest rate of 5%, well below market rates. This is a somewhat indirect form of subsidization of rented housing. In 1983 a new form of bond was introduced. Purchase of the bonds, which are for 20 years and carry a 3% rate, leads to entitlement to purchase a condominium at a price fixed by the government.

The national housing deposit pre-emption scheme was instituted in May 1981. Under the scheme a prospective purchaser agrees to deposit a monthly instalment for a certain period of time in exchange for which he has preferential rights for the purchase of public sector houses. There are over 160,000 subscribers to these accounts. The fund also obtains some deposits from various public bodies.

The National Housing Fund can be used to finance only national housing projects. The table shows that the Korea National Housing Corporation is the major recipient of its funds. Funds are also made available to housebuilders building small dwellings, and to individuals purchasing houses, the construction of which has been financed by KHB. The maximum loan is 7.3 million won per unit, and loans have to be repaid at a rate of interest of 10% over 20 years.

Assessment

South Korea is generally regarded as being a major success story in terms of transforming an economy from an agricultural nation to an industrialized one. It has achieved spectacular rates of economic growth.

These achievements have been matched in the housing and housing finance fields. However, such has been the extent of industrialization that the problems of squatter settlements and poor housing have not been completely avoided.

The degree of financial intermediation in general, and in the housing finance sector in particular, is very high for a country in South Korea's stage of development. In terms of market share the Korea Housing Bank is one of the largest housing finance institutions in the world. It has a hand in the financing of over 60% of all new housing units and is involved in both the public and the private sectors in the provision of housing for both sale and rent. An interesting recent feature of its operations has been the splitting of its functions between unsubsidized private sector finance, funded by deposit taking activities, and a subsidized public sector.

The General Manager of the Research Department of the Housing Bank has identified six major problems with the Korean housing finance system -

(a) The demand for funds exceeds the supply, hence the necessity to restrict loans to a low percentage of cost.
(b) There is no secondary mortgage market and therefore mortgages are not liquid.
(c) Most financial institutions are not involved in housing finance at all.
(d) Housing loans are limited to small sized houses.
(e) There is no income tax deduction or tax credit for borrowers.
(f) Potential borrowers have to contribute to NHF funds before they can purchase new condominium units, and this restricts the market to those able to save.

Bibliography

Choon Bae Park, 'Housing and Housing Finance in the Republic of Korea', *Federal Home Loan Bank Board Journal*, February and March 1984.
Conference on Housing in Asia, AID, 1976.
Financial System in Korea, The Bank of Korea, 1983.
Jim Ho Kim, 'Resource Mobilization: Problems and Potentials, A Case of the Korean Housing Bank', Paper given to Asian Housing Finance Seminar, March 1984.
Korell, M, and Unger, M, *General Summary of the Housing Finance Systems of Selected Nations in the Asian and Pacific Regions*, AID, 1979.
National Reports, International Union of Building Societies and Savings Associations, 1983.
Profile, The Korea Housing Bank, 1983.
Rivkin Associates Ltd, *An Overview of Human Settlements in the ESCAP Region*, 1983.

Acknowledgements

The co-operation of the South Korean Embassy in London and the Korea Housing Bank in providing information for this chapter is gratefully acknowledged. The chapter draws heavily on the informative annual *Profile* produced by the Bank.

CHAPTER 21

THE PHILIPPINES

The Philippines are a rapidly urbanizing archipelago. In common with other developing countries the country has a high level of owner-occupation and squatter settlements are a major problem in the urban centres.

Housing finance is largely provided by the informal system. The formal institutions concentrate largely on the middle and upper income groups. Specialist housing finance institutions make a comparatively small contribution to the overall market. The government has been very active, partly through the activities of its insurance operations and, more recently, through the establishment of a secondary mortgage market and a compulsory savings scheme.

Introduction

The Philippines comprise 7,100 islands in an archipelago at the borders of the South China Sea and the Pacific Ocean. Its total land area is 297,000 sq kilometres.

The population of The Philippines was 50.74 million in mid-1982. The rate of increase was 2.64% a year between 1975 and 1980. This marked a significant diminution on the rate in previous periods. In 1980, 37% of the population lived in urban areas. The urban population has been growing at an annual rate of over 6%. The capital is Manila, the metropolitan area of which had a population of 5,925,000 in 1980, over a third of the total urban population.

Since 1972 The Philippines have been under martial law. There is a one chamber National Assembly.

In 1981 GNP per capita was $790, similar to the level in Thailand, three times that of India and half that of South Korea. GNP grew by an annual rate of 6.4% in real terms over the 1970s and real GNP per capita grew at an annual rate of 3.6%. However, the growth in real incomes has been accompanied by a marked redistribution from the poor to the rich.

In common with many other developing countries, inflation accelerated at the end of the 1970s but has since fallen back. However, The Philippines have not experienced the levels of inflation that have forced some developing countries into index-linking. The annual rate of inflation was 8% in the mid 1970s before rising to 19% in 1978 and 1979. By the end of 1983 the rate was in single figures again.

Housing

The Housing Stock

Figures on housing from the 1980 census are not yet available, and it is necessary to look at 1970 figures in most cases although some figures for 1975
are also available.

In common with most developing countries The Philippines have a high
level of owner-occupation. Table 21.1 shows details of the housing stock by
tenure in May 1970.

Table 21.1 Housing Tenure, The Philippines, May 1970

Type of Occupancy	Number of Dwellings	Percentage of Total
Owner-occupied only	5,127,589	85.3
Owner & part rented or free	145,125	3.8
Rented only	490,221	8.2
Rented & part rented or free	247,902	4.1
Total occupied	6,010,837	100.0

Source: National Census and Statistics Office, *1983 Philippines Statistical Yearbook*, Table 1.11.

It will be seen that over 85% of the stock was owner-occupied only, and
a further 4% was part owner-occupied. As for other developing countries
a high level of owner-occupation is not, in any way, an indication that there
is a satisfactory housing position. One reason for high owner-occupation is
that many people cannot afford to pay rent, and squatter settlements, however basic, are defined as owner-occupied. In most developing countries
owner-occupation is highest at the upper and lower ranges of the income
scales, and is much higher in rural than in urban areas. Figures are available
for The Philippines which demonstrate this position. Table 21.2 shows housing tenure by income and location in 1975.

Table 21.2 Housing Tenure by Income & Location, The Philippines, 1975

Income Range Pesos	Percentage of Occupied Units			
	Urban Owned	Rented	Rural Owned	Rented
Under 2,000	74	26	93	7
2,000 – 3,900	58	42	92	8
4,000 – 9,999	63	37	89	11
10,000 – 19,999	62	38	88	12
20,000 & over	66	34	93	7

Source: *The Philippines – Housing Finance*, World Bank Country Study, 1982, Table 1.4.
Note: At end-1975 there were 7.4 pesos to the dollar and 12.6 pesos to the pound.

It will be seen that owner-occupation is over 90% in the rural areas but under 70% in urban areas. In urban areas in particular there is a marked difference in the proportion of owner-occupation according to income range. Owner-occupation is actually highest in the lowest income range, simply reflecting the fact that this group cannot afford to pay for housing and therefore has to provide itself with shelter. As incomes increase so a proportion of the population is able to afford to rent if it wishes to do so. It will be noted that of the upper income groups in urban areas, 66% were owner-occupiers, a proportion that is lower than in some industrialized countries which have a lower overall level of owner-occupation.

The 1970 census showed that only 24% of dwellings had piped water, 22% had a flush toilet, and 37% had no access to a toilet at all, and 79% of houses used wood for fuel. However, there has been a significant improvement in housing conditions. In 1960 only 8% of the population had a flush toilet and 45% had no access to a toilet.

Housing Policy and Housebuilding

It is estimated that The Philippines have a deficiency of over two million dwellings and this deficiency is increasing by some 200,000 units a year. Throughout the 1970s the number of households grew more rapidly than the number of dwellings. It has been estimated that there is a need for over 500,000 new dwellings a year but there seems little likelihood of anywhere near this amount actually being built.

Most housing in constructed outside of the formal sector. In the late 1970s it is estimated that the public sector built about 10,000 houses a year and the formal private sector built between 25,000 and 30,000 dwellings a year.

There have been significant changes in responsibility for housing policy in recent years. Now, the Ministry of Human Settlements is responsible for all aspects of housing including housing finance. The National Housing Authority is the construction agency of the Ministry, and is responsible for undertaking housing development and for controlling the use of public land identified for housing purposes. The Human Settlements Development Corporation is also responsible to the Ministry and this has a particular role in developing new communities. A third agency is the National Housing Corporation which is responsible for building materials.

Housing Finance

The Financial System

The financial system of The Philippines is relatively sophisticated bearing in mind the country's stage of economic development. It has developed significantly in recent years but it remains imperfect in many respects. The system is dominated by government institutions and commercial banks. Table 21.3 shows the structure of the financial system as at the end of 1980.

Table 21.3 Structure of the Financial System: The Philippines, End-1980

Institution	Total Assets Pesos Bn	Percentage of Total
Central bank	65.4	21.1
Private commercial banks	85.1	27.4
Government commercial banks	34.6	11.1
Foreign commercial banks	18.7	6.0
Savings and mortgage banks	7.4	2.4
Private development banks	1.6	0.5
Savings and loan associations	1.6	0.5
Rural banks	5.6	1.8
Other banks	34.2	11.0
Insurance companies	27.5	8.9
Investment institutions	25.6	8.2
Other intermediaries	3.8	1.1
Total	311.1	100.0

Source: Central Bank of the Philippines.
Note: At end-1980 there were 7.6 pesos to the dollar and 17.8 pesos to the pound.

It will be seen that the central bank is itself a significant financial intermediary as well having responsibility for overseeing the financial system as a whole. However, its activities are concerned entirely with other financial intermediaries rather than with individuals or with industry and commerce.

The commercial banks are the single largest group of institutions. The sector includes both government and privately owned banks. The largest single bank is the government owned Philippine National Bank. This had assets at the end of 1982 equivalent to $6,308 million.

The category of 'other banks' is largely explained by a government body, the Development Bank of The Philippines.

It will be noted that the institutions which in advanced industrialized countries are the main providers of home loans, savings and mortgage banks and savings and loan associations, are comparatively small.

The Housing Finance Market

Most housing finance is provided by the informal system. By definition, the size of the informal system cannot be measured, nor can it be described with any degree of precision. This chapter concentrates on the formal sector while emphasizing its relatively small size. A study prepared for the World Bank (*The Philippines: Housing Finance*, World Bank, 1982) suggested that the formal financial sector could be divided into four groups -

(a) Those able to pay market mortgage rates for reasonable dwellings—

perhaps 2-3% of all households.

(b) Those able to purchase dwellings under concessionary schemes operated by the government. It is estimated that about 12% of households
come within this category.

(c) 1 or 2% of households who have assistance from their employers in
providing housing.

(d) Households whose income is just sufficient to enable them to participate in dwelling upgrading and sites and services programmes. 40%
of urban households come into this category, which is served exclusively by government programmes.

The remaining households have no choice but to use informal systems to
house themselves.

The same World Bank study identified the development of more efficient
housing finance systems as being important stimulants of housing and construction generally.

In The Philippines, in contrast to many other developing countries, the
government has made little attempt to encourage specialist housing finance
institutions. The government has played an interventionist role and has
provided finance directly.

Figures on shares of the housing finance market are not readily available.
The position can best be illustrated by using two tables, one showing the stock
of real estate loans outstanding and the other showing loans made. These
are Tables 21.4 and 21.5 respectively.

Table 21.4 Real Estate Loans Outstanding, The Philippines 1981

Institution	Date	Loans Outstanding		
		Pesos m	Percentage of Total Loans	Percentage of Real Estate Loans
Commercial banks	30 Sep	3,566	4.6	25
Thrift banks	30 Nov	2,113	30.6	15
Specialized government banks	30 Sep	3,932	16.7	28
Non bank financial institutions	30 Sep	4,557	29.1	32
Total		14,168	100.0	100

Source: *Annual Report of the Central Bank of The Philippines, 1981.*
Note: At end-1981 there were 8.2 pesos to the dollar and 15.6 pesos to the pound.

Table 21.5 Housing Finance Loans, The Philippines, 1975 & 1980

Institution	1975 Loans Granted		1980 Loans Granted	
	Pesos m	%	Pesos m	%
Commercial banks	11	3	777	40
Savings banks	2	1	108	6
Private development banks	1	—	7	—
Insurance companies	27	9	62	3
Total private sector	41	13	944	49
Government Services Insurance System	156	50	224	12
Social Security System	116	37	235	24
Development Bank	N/A		469	34
Land Bank	—	—	49	3
Total public sector	272	87	977	51
Total	313	100	1,921	100

Source: *The Philippines—Housing Finance*, World Bank Country Study, 1982, Table 3.1.
Note: At end-1980 there were 7.6 pesos to the dollar and 17.8 pesos to the pound.

The tables show that the commercial banks have rapidly increased their share of loans made and that they account for a quarter of outstanding housing loans. However, as will be explained subsequently, much of their lending is short term and to developers. The expression 'thrift banks' in Table 21.4 includes savings and mortgage banks, private development banks and savings and loan associations. The figure for specialized government banks in Table 21.4 is largely in respect of the Development Bank of The Philippines, although it also includes the Land Bank of The Philippines and the Philippine Amanah Bank. The non-bank financial institutions in Table 21.4 are the Social Security System (SSS) and the Government Services Insurance System (GSIS).

The two tables illustrate the following general picture -

(a) The Government Social Insurance and Social Security Systems have been significantly reducing their involvement in the market.
(b) To some extent this activity has been replaced by that of the Development Bank.
(c) The private sector has become more important at the expense of the public sector, this largely being explained by a huge growth in activity on the part of the commercial banks.

Private Sector Housing Finance Institutions

Commercial Banks

In 1980 there were 32 commercial banks with 1,503 offices. The number of offices has grown sharply from 996 in 1975. They raise their funds largely through time deposits. Of their total loans outstanding at the end of 1982, 4,150 million pesos (4.2% of the total) were in respect of real estate. This represents a very sharp increase compared with the 1980 figures of 2,273 million pesos and 3.1%. The banks had a further 5,076 million pesos (5.2% of total loans) of loans outstanding in respect of construction activity.

Most of the real estate loans were not to individuals for house-purchase but rather were for development. The average maturity of their housing loans is less than one year. At the end of 1981 the banks had only 121 million pesos outstanding in the form of individual housing loans. In recent years the banks have been lending at an interest rate of about 17% over not more than ten years. By the end of 1983 the rate had risen to over 21%. It is estimated that less than 3% of the population can afford loans on these terms.

Thrift Banks

The expression thrift banks includes savings and mortgage banks, savings and loan associations and private development banks. Tables 21.4 and 21.5 show that they have a relatively small share of the housing finance market. They lend on terms very similar to the commercial banks.

There are ten savings banks which between them have 249 offices, including 142 branches. Most have a joint stock form of ownership. Their assets have declined significantly since the end of 1980. Between that time and June 1982 the total assets of the banks declined from 7.4 billion pesos to 5.2 billion pesos. Housing loans account for 65% of their total loans and 84% of

Table 21.6 Savings and Loan Associations, The Philippines, Assets & Liabilities, June 1982

Liabilities	Pesos m	%	Assets	Pesos m	%
Savings deposits	965	34	Loans and		
Time deposits	774	27	advances	1,929	68
Capital accounts	764	27	Investments in		
Loans/bills payable	107	4	private sector	228	8
Other liabilities	225	8	Investments in		
			public sector	46	2
			Cash	312	11
			Other assets	321	11
Total	2,834	100	Total	2,834	100

Source: *Philippines Financial Statistics*, Central Bank of the Philippines, December 1982, Table 10f.

Note: At end-June 1982 there were 8.5 pesos to the dollar and 14.9 pesos to the pound.

their housing loans are to individuals.

The savings and loan associations have been growing very rapidly in recent years but they remain small. In 1975 there were 44 associations with a total of 69 branches and total assets of 300 million pesos. By 1980 there were 91 associations with 251 offices and total assets of 1.6 billion pesos. There are both stock and mutual associations, with the stock associations acccounting for 84% of the total assets. Most of the remaining associations are described as having a non stock status rather than a mutual status. Table 21.6 shows the assets and liabilities of the associations as at June 1982.

Government Housing Finance Institutions

Government Services Insurance System (GSIS)

The GSIS is a social security agency for employees of the government. It has power to grant loans to its members for house-purchase. These can be for up to 25 years and are at a rate of interest of between 6% and 9% depending on the size of the loan (the larger the loan the higher the rate of interest). These rates are well below market rates and are therefore heavily subsidized. GSIS also makes loans for housing development and frequently these are subsequently transformed into house-purchase loans. Between 1972 and 1980 GSIS directly financed 21,000 housing units. It has been reducing its involvement in the housing finance market in the recent past. In 1970 54% of its assets were in housing loans but by 1980 the proportion had fallen to 42%, the amount totalling 2,686 million pesos. It is intended that GSIS will eventually withdraw entirely from the house-purchase market.

Social Security System (SSS)

This is operated in a very similar way to GSIS. It has been willing to make loans to contributors to the system. However, the loans have been reserved for relatively cheap houses and have averaged no more than 70% of valuation. Loans have been made for 25 years at between 6% and 9%, again depending on the size of the loan. Between 1970 and 1980 53,000 units were financed by SSS, and generally it will lend only for houses which are being built. Like GSIS it has been reducing its house lending activity in recent years, aided by a fixed loan ceiling while house and land prices have been rising. At the end of 1980 it had housing loans outstanding of 1,593 million pesos, 20% of its total loans, compared with 40% in 1970.

Development Bank of The Philippines

This is the largest long term lender in The Philippines. The Bank is government owned and concentrates its lending on commerce and industry. It is prepared to make larger housing loans than GSIS or SSS but at a still relatively attractive rate of interest of 12-14%. It is now the single largest lender for house-purchase. It primarily serves the middle to lower middle income groups. It provides loans for construction and development as well as directly for house-purchase.

Home Development Mutual Fund (HDMF)

The HDMF is a contractual savings scheme. It is mandatory for persons employed in the formal sector of the economy, although employers can ask for exemption if they offer a better scheme themselves. The scheme became compulsory in 1981 when 1% of salaries had to be paid into the fund, with employers providing a similar contribution. The levy has subsequently risen to 3% since 1983. Interest is earned at the rate of 7.5%. A participant in the scheme can reclaim his contributions, together with interest, after 20 years. Members of the scheme are able to apply for a 25 year loan from an approved bank at a rate of interest of 9%. The maximum loan is 48 times the monthly salary.

By the end of 1983 there were over two million members of the scheme and the fund amounted to 1,730 million pesos compared with 127 million pesos at the end of 1981. The Fund is managed by the National Home Mortgage Finance Corporation.

National Home Mortgage Finance Corporation (NHMFC)

The Corporation was established in 1979 with the responsibility of establishing a secondary market. It is an agency of the Ministry for Human Settlements. It is modelled on the Federal Home Loan Mortgage Corporation (FHLMC or Freddie Mac) in the USA. It buys mortgage loans from banks and other accredited lenders, pools them and then sells what are known as Bahayan Mortgage Participation Certificates (BMPCs) which are backed by mortgages. The mortgages continue to be serviced by the originating lender. The certificates are in two categories, one offering an 8.5% tax free yield and the other offering a 14% taxable yield. Savings banks have been the main purchasers of the certificates. However, they have bought them primarily for regulatory and tax reasons rather than because of their intrinsic value. The Corporation also issues Bahayan Certificates (BCs) which are sold by auction or negotiated bids through the central bank.

It has already been noted that NHMFC administers the funds of the HDMF. It also handles any applications from members of that fund who want a mortgage loan. It will arrange the loan with an appropriate accredited institution and then refinance it.

By December 1982 55 agencies had been accredited to the secondary market. By the end of 1983 loans totalling 2,840 million pesos had been purchased of which about 40% came through HDMF. Sales of BMPCs totalled 1,000 million pesos and sales of BCs totalled 610 million pesos.

The combination of the mandatory savings scheme operated by HDMF and the secondary market activity supervised by NHMFC could prove to be the major growth area for housing finance in The Philippines. This combination is similar to the mandatory savings scheme, the FGTS, and the National Housing Bank, in Brazil.

Assessment

The study prepared for the World Bank, referred to frequently in this chapter, commented that a distinctive feature of housing finance in The Philippines is that is has not followed the conventional path of establishing specialized financial institutions at the primary level. Rather, efforts have focussed on the creation of a secondary mortgage market through the National Home Mortgage Finance Corporation. The report notes that the operations of the Corporation are closely tied to the Home Development Mutual Fund. This study also comments on the ad hoc creation of new institutions to deal with particular problems. The report concludes that the current housing finance system provides access only to the upper strata of the income distribution and even the HDMF initiative is likely to make little difference to this. It suggested the examination of alternative mortgage instruments, and the provision of a more comprehensive mortgage insurance programme than that currently available.

Bibliography

Annual Report of the Central Bank of The Philippines, 1981.
Carlson, E, *Human Settlements in The Philippines—Observations after a Decade*, 1983, unpublished.
Orendian, F B, *Shelter Finance: The Philippine Experience, Resource Mobilization Problems and Potentials*, Paper presented to Asia Housing Finance Seminar, March 1984.
Philippine Shelter System and Human Settlements, Ministry of Human Settlements, Philippines, October 1983.
The Philippines—Housing Finance, World Bank Country Study, 1982.

Acknowledgements

The co-operation of the Central Bank of the Philippines, the World Bank and Eric Carlson, Special Adviser to the International Union of Building Societies and Savings Associations, in providing information for this chapter is gratefully acknowledged. The chapter draws heavily on the excellent study prepared for the World Bank, *The Philippines—Housing Finance*.

CHAPTER 22

INDIA

India represents one of the extreme examples of the problems which developing countries face. It is still a predominantly rural and low income country, but a significant trend has been the rapid urbanization which has brought with it immense housing problems.

85% of households in India live in owner-occupied properties, but this is no indication that housing standards are at a high level. About half of all households live in one room, and three quarters of urban households lack exclusive use of drinking water and toilet facilities. Housing has not been given priority in the development of the country, and only a very low proportion of investment has been devoted to housing.

Housing finance is largely provided through the informal system with less than 10% of housing investment being financed by institutional means. The Life Insurance Corporation of India has been the biggest single lender, albeit generally through other intermediaries. More recently, a specialized housing finance intermediary, the Housing Development Finance Corporation, has been established and is making rapid progress.

Introduction

India is a large country occupying 3,300,000 sq kilometres. It borders on Pakistan, China and Burma, and surrounds Bangladesh.

The population of India in 1981 was 658.1 million. This makes India second only to China in terms of population. India is fairly densely populated with 15% of the world's population living in just 2.4% of the land area. The largest cities are Calcutta (9.16 million in 1981), Greater Bombay (8.2 million), Delhi, the capital (5.8 million) and Madras (4.3 million). There were also eight other cities with populations over one million in 1971.

The population has been growing very rapidly, having increased from 349.8 million in 1951. A major trend has been urbanization. In recent years the urban population has been growing at 3.3% a year, and the rural population at 2.2% a year. The population in each of the ten largest cities grew by more than 30% in the ten years to 1981. This is in marked contrast to the position in industrialized countries where the largest urban centres have been declining in size. However, India remains predominantly a rural country, with 76% of the population living in rural areas in 1981. The average household size is

5.7 and has tended to rise in recent years.

India is a federal republic. Each of the state governments has considerable autonomy. The federal parliament has two chambers. The Council of States comprises representatives of the various states and also people nominated by the president. The House of People is directly elected. Currently, the Congress Party is in power.

India is the poorest of the large countries in Asia. GNP per capita in 1981 was $260 compared with, for example, $10,080 in Japan, $1,700 in South Korea and $790 in The Philippines. Moreover, there is a very skewed income distribution, and substantial differences between the richest and the poorest sections of the community. GNP per capita grew at the modest rate of 1.5% a year between 1971 and 1981. The high rate of population growth means that a substantial rate of growth of GNP is needed just to maintain a constant level of GNP per capita. However, India has been successful in keeping inflation under control and prices increased by less than 10% a year throughout the 1970s.

The Indian economy has been subject to fairly rigid state supervision and regular five year plans have been drawn up. However, more recently, economic controls have been reduced and the economy is being made more open.

Housing

The Housing Stock

The most recent figures in respect of the housing stock are for 1971. Table 22.1 shows households classified by tenure status in that year.

Table 22.1 Households Classified by Tenure Status, India, 1971

Tenure	Rural		Urban		Total	
	No m	%	No m	%	No m	%
Owned	73.07	94	9.01	47	82.08	85
Rented	4.86	6	10.11	53	14.98	15
All	77.93	100	19.12	100	97.06	100

Source: Munjee, N M, *Profile on Housing*, Understanding Indian Economy, January-March 1982.

It will be seen that 85% of all households were owner-occupiers. The proportion was as high as 94% in rural areas, compared with 47% in the urban areas. In industrialized countries, owner-occupation is frequently taken as being a sign of affluence. In developing countries this is not the case and many of the owner-occupied dwellings are no more than very basic shelters.

It is generally agreed that the housing situation in India has been getting worse rather than better. The National Buildings Organisation has made the following calculations of the housing deficit.

Table 22.2   Housing and Households, India, 1961-81

Year	Households	Serviceable Housing Stock	Housing Deficit
	Millions	Millions	Millions
1961	83.5	68.3	15.2
1971	97.0	82.5	14.5
1981	120.5	99.2	21.3

Source: National Buildings Organisation, reproduced from *Monthly Commentary*, The Indian Institute of Public Opinion, 1983.

Of the total deficit of 21.3 million, 16.5 million were in rural areas and 4.8 million were in urban areas.

A good indication of housing conditions is given by Table 22.3 which shows households classified by the number of members and the number of rooms occupied.

Table 22.3   Households Classified by Number of Members and Number of Rooms Occupied, India, 1971

	Rural		Urban		Total	
	Million	%	Million	%	Million	%
Number of rooms	138		38		196	
Households with one room	37	47	10	50	47	48
Households with two rooms	22	28	5	27	27	28
Households with over two rooms	19	24	4	23	23	20
All households	78	100	19	100	97	100

Source: Munjee, N M, *Profile on Housing*, Understanding Indian Economy, January-March 1982.

It will be seen that nearly half of all households occupied only one room each. The level of overcrowding seems to have been increasing over time. A survey in 1973/74 showed that 77% of urban households lacked exclusive use of drinking water and the same proportion did not have exclusive access to a toilet. The quality of the housing stock can be illustrated by reference to the fact that over half of all houses have walls made of grass, leaves, bamboo and mud.

The housing market in India can effectively be divided into three categories-

(a)   A legal private sector which caters for the higher and middle income groups.

(b)   Public sector housing for state employees, and a limited amount of social housing for the poor.

(c)   The unregulated sector, largely comprising squatter settlements and slums generally. It is estimated that 30 million people live in dwellings officially classified as slums.

Indian companies provide some assistance to their staff with housing, either in the form of provision of rented housing, or through loans for house-purchase, generally subsidized.

Housing Policy

The provision of housing in India comes within the province of state governments. However, financial assistance comes from joint federal/state sources.

Housing has been accorded a relatively low priority in the various economic plans and has been taking a declining share of total investment. In 1950-55 housing accounted for 34% of total investment, but in the current plan, running from 1980 to 1985, the share is just 7.5%. The public sector's contribution to housing investment has fallen from 27% in 1960-65 to 12% in 1980-85. Investment in housing accounts for between 2% and 3% of GDP, a very low figure for a country in India's stage of development.

Not only has India not made significant provision for the public sector contribution to housing, but various policy measures have hindered the ability of the private sector to respond to the undoubted demand. In particular, the Urban Land (Ceiling and Regulation) Act 1976, which aimed to counter the effects of speculation, has had the not unexpected effect of reducing both land sales and development. The Rent Act is seen as being a major obstacle to the provision of rented housing. Rents have been restricted and the eviction of tenants has been made difficult as a result of which available rental space has been frozen. However, steps are being taken to exempt newly constructed housing from rent control.

Housing Finance

The Housing Finance System

Chapter 2 showed that in developing countries informal systems of housing finance predominate, that is, housing finance is provided not through institutional means but rather from sources such as personal saving and borrowing within families. India typifies this system. It is estimated that only 6% or 7% of investment in housing in India is financed by institutional means. By definition, the informal sector cannot be well documented and, to this extent, any description of housing finance in India is bound to be inadequate. The fact that this chapter concentrates on those institutional mechanisms that do exist should not allow one to lose sight of the fact that these are very small in relation to the total market.

Table 22.4 shows the development of housing loans outstanding from 1971/72 to 1980/81.

Table 22.4   Housing Finance Loans Outstanding, India

Year	Life Insurance Co of India	HUDCO	Apex Housing Societies	Primary Co-operative Societies	General Insurance Corporation	HDFC
	R m	R m	R m	R m	R m	R m
1971-72	2,631	51	1,203	815		
1974-75	4,116	337	2,025	1,259		
1977-78	5,686	1,122	2,402	1,523		
1980-81	7,919	2,672			165	298

Note: At end-June 1981 there were 8.68 rupees to the dollar and 16.84 rupees to the pound.

The various institutions will be described very briefly at this stage and in more detail subsequently. The Life Insurance Company of India (LIC) has been the major provider of funds. This is a nationalized institution, incorporating all life insurance business. Similarly, the General Insurance Corporation (GIC) conducts most general insurance in India. Apex housing societies and primary co-operative societies are co-operative organisations that, respectively, finance and build houses. The Housing and Urban Development Corporation (HUDCO) and the Housing Development Finance Corporation (HDFC) are the two specialist financial institutions, HUDCO concentrating predominantly on building for lower income groups while HDFC is a more typical financial intermediary.

The Financial System

It is necessary to say comparatively little about the financial system in India because it does not have much relevance to housing finance. The major point is that all major financial institutions are nationalized and subject to strict controls. The capital markets work under a system of credit allocation.

At the centre of the banking system is the Reserve Bank of India which itself is a financial intermediary. There are 14 commercial banks, all of which were nationalized in 1969. The banks have 39,000 branches between them, 20,000 of which are in villages. The largest bank is the State Bank of India which has 6,000 branches, making it, in terms of branches, one of the largest banks in the world. Its total assets at the end of 1982 were 243 billion rupees. As an indication of the controls under which the banks operate, 44% of all deposits have to be placed in low yielding government securities and 40% of lending must be to certain priority sectors at low rates of interest.

The banks play no direct part in housing finance. However they are under direction by the Reserve Bank of India to subscribe 1.5 billion rupees a year to housing through the various institutions. They subscribe to government guaranteed bonds issued by HUDCO and the state housing boards, and they lend to HDFC. They also provide staff loans.

In common with other developing countries India has informal money-lending institutions, operating at local level. However, these have been declining in importance as the degree of financial intermediation in the economy has been increasing.

In general, co-ordination between the various financial institutions, including the specialist housing finance bodies, has not been good and the deficiencies of the Indian financial system are widely recognised. This section can usefully be completed by showing the assets of the financial institutions. Table 22.5 shows the relevant data in respect of 1977.

Table 22.5   Assets of Financial Institutions, India, 1977

Institution	Assets Rupees m	Percentage of Total
Commercial banks	267,970	37.6
Reserve bank	141,770	19.9
Co-operative banks	98,500	13.8
Provident funds	89,000	12.5
Life Insurance Company of India	47,250	6.6
Development banks	28,680	4.0
Post Office savings system	15,230	2.1
Other institutions	23,550	3.3
All institutions	711,940	100.0

Source: Goldsmith, R W, *The Financial Development of India*, 1983.
Note: At end-1977 there were 8.21 rupees to the dollar and 15.68 rupees to the pound.

The table shows the relatively small size of financial institutions in relation to the population. The small size of the retail savings institutions is particularly apparent.

The Life Insurance Company of India

The Life Insurance Company of India (LIC) is the largest single provider of funds for house-purchase, accounting for about 50% of the institutional total. It has already been noted that LIC was formed in 1956 through the merging and nationalization of existing life insurance companies. In common with other financial institutions the LIC is strictly controlled as to the direction of its lending. 50% of the net increase in its assets must be invested in government and other approved securities, 25% must be invested in socially orientated schemes, including housing, and 10% is available for investment in the private sector. Housing accounts for about 11% of the total lending of the LIC.

Table 22.6 shows LIC outstanding housing loans as at March 1983.

Table 22.6   Life Insurance Company of India, Outstanding Housing Loans, March 1983

	Rupees m	Percentage of Total
Loans to Apex Co-operative Housing Finance Societies and other Authorities, Housing Boards and HUDCO	7,044	50
Loans to state governments	4,637	33
Loans under 'Own Your Home' Scheme	914	6
Loans on mortgage of houses	671	5
Loans to employees	387	3
LIC staff housing	249	2
Loans to co-operative societies of LIC employees	174	1
Other loans	93	1
Total	14,169	100

Source: Annual report of LIC.
Note: At end-March 1983 there were 9.97 rupees to the dollar and 14.75 rupees to the pound.

It will be noted that most of the LIC's contribution to housing is not direct. Other chapters in this book have shown how insurance companies have been taking a declining share of the mortgage market and where they are involved this is largely through indirect means, for example, secondary markets. In India the LIC makes its contribution through lending to those institutions more directly involved, in particular, the apex co-operative housing finance societies and the state housing boards. It also lends to the specialist institutions, HUDCO and HDFC.

The LIC loans have been made at rates of interest varying between 7.5% and 12%. Loans to state housing boards and to the apex societies have been at the lower rates while direct loans for house-purchase have been at market related rates, about 12%. It is understood that the delinquency rate on lending to the apex societies has been at a high level.

At this stage it may be noted that the General Insurance Company, by its very nature, has shorter term liabilities and its involvement in housing is much less than the LIC. It provides about 1,500 million rupees a year to housing, largely through loans to HUDCO and the state housing boards.

Apex Societies

There is a two tier co-operative housing finance system in India -
   (a) 18 state level apex finance societies which obtain their funds largely from the LIC. They had assets of 2,777 million rupees at the end of 1978.
   (b) Some 30,000 primary societies divided into three categories: tenant ownership housing societies, tenant co-partnership housing societies, and house mortgage societies or house construction societies.

The primary societies obtain their funds largely from the state level apex finance societies and also from central and state governments. They are very large organisations with some 16 million members in 1978 and total assets of 7,268 million rupees. The primary societies actually build houses for their members. Private builders frequently take the lead in setting up the primary societies. By June 1979 the primary societies had constructed some 236,000 houses.

The apex system is primarily a method by which housing projects are financed rather than a method by which housing finance loans are provided. Nevertheless the system usefully illustrates the type of financial intermediation in India. The LIC, a large gatherer of investment funds, makes loans to central bodies at state level which in turn lend funds to co-operative societies which are then responsible for promoting the housing project.

The apex system can be seen as a substitute for an efficient system of providing construction finance. The system is far from perfect; over a third of the primary societies have reported losses.

Housing and Urban Development Corporation (HUDCO)

HUDCO is a public sector body. It was established in 1970. It does not lend directly to individuals but rather makes loans available to others, in particular, the state housing boards which receive over 60% of its loans. Other borrowers must be approved by the state governments.

HUDCO obtains its finance through long term borrowing. Over 40% of its funds come from debentures which are government guaranteed, 20% come from borrowing from the LIC, 18% from borrowing from the GIC, and the remainder from unsecured debentures and its own equity and reserves.

HUDCO lends predominantly for projects for lower income groups. The terms on which it lends depend on the income group for which the project is aimed. Projects for the lowest income groups receive finance at a rate of 5% over 20 years, whereas projects for the higher income groups receive finance at 11.5% over ten years. HUDCO will lend up to 100% of the cost of housing for lower income groups, but only 48% of the cost for projects for the higher income groups. By March 1983 HUDCO had sanctioned 2,373 projects at a total cost of 16,600 million rupees, of which HUDCO provided 11,000 rupees, producing 1,416,000 houses.

HUDCO sets standards for the houses produced with its funds and there has been some dispute as to whether these standards have been unreasonably high for the funds available. Because many builders cannot meet HUDCO's specifications they do not take advantage of HUDCO finance to the extent that they might. In addition to providing construction finance, HUDCO also gives technical assistance.

Housing Development Finance Corporation (HDFC)

Origin and Structure

HDFC was established in 1977 as a private sector institution to make long term housing loans. The impetus for its establishment came from a development bank, the Industrial Credit and Investment Corporation (ICCI). It was supported by the Aga Khan group and the International Finance Corporation (the activities of which are described in Chapter 2). Each of these three bodies provided 5% of the initial share capital, the remainder being subscribed by banks, insurance companies, limited companies and private individuals.

Currently, HDFC has over 11,000 individual shareholders, and 119 companies have significant share holdings. The commercial banks hold 15.7% of the equity. The International Finance Corporation has a representative on the board of directors through which it maintains a continuing interest in HDFC.

HDFC has its head office in Bombay, but it now also has seven branches. It employs a total of 175 staff. In addition to its housing finance role it also has a development company subsidiary.

Growth

HDFC has grown spectacularly since its establishment in 1977. Table 22.7 shows key statistics for the period 1978/79 to 1982/83.

Table 22.7 HDFC Progress, 1978-79 to 1982-83

| Year | Loan Approvals | | Housing Loans Outstanding | Total Assets | |
	No	Amount Rupees m	Rupees m	Rupees m	Growth %
1978-79	6,665	71	13	101	
1979-80	7,255	227	101	156	55
1980-81	9,185	314	298	426	173
1981-82	11,761	440	564	691	62
1982-83	17,250	726	985	1,213	176

Source: HDFC, Sixth Annual Report, 1982-83.
Note: At-end June 1983 there were 10.07 rupees to the dollar and 15.41 rupees to the pound.

It will be seen that total assets have grown more than ten fold since 1978/79. However, spectacular growth should not disguise the relatively small size of HDFC. In 1982/83 17,000 loans were approved, a figure which needs to be compared with the population of India of 648 million.

The rapid growth of HDFC has brought in its train the inevitable management problems but, in general, these seem to have been well handled and the institution is generally regarded as being one of the great success stories in terms of the establishment of housing finance systems in developing countries. One of the objectives of HDFC, in the longer term, is to support the development of the housing finance system in a commercially viable way.

Operations

HDFC is, at this stage of its development, a mortgage bank. That is, it raises long term funds from institutional sources and lends these to home-buyers. Table 22.8 shows the assets and liabilities of HDFC as at June 1983.

Table 22.8 HDFC, Assets & Liabilities, End-June 1983

Liabilities	Rupees m	%	Assets	Rupees m	%
Loans			Housing loans		
From banks	243.7	20	Individuals	764.4	63
Life Insurance Co of India	100.0	8	Corporate bodies	175.9	15
General Insurance Co of			Co-operatives	34.4	3
India	30.0	2	Others	1.1	-
IFC	23.9	2	Investments	31.3	3
Industrial Credit &			Net current assets	183.5	15
Investment Co	2.3	-	Other assets	22.3	2
Certificates of deposit	666.0	55			
Loan linked deposits	4.7	-			
Share capital	10.0	1			
Reserves & surplus	4.3	-			
Total	1,212.9	100	Total	1,212.9	100

Source: HDFC, Sixth Annual Report, 1982-83.
Note: At end-June 1983 there were 10.07 rupees to the dollar and 15.41 rupees to the pound.

It will be seen that the main source of funds are certificates of deposit. These are issued in multiples of 1,000 rupees, subject to a minimum of 2,000 rupees. Maturity periods vary from six months to five years. The certificates of deposit have certain tax advantages in that interest on them up to 7,000 rupees qualifies for a tax deduction, and also deposits placed with HDFC are exempt from wealth tax up to a maximum of 165,000 rupees. In October 1982 interest rates varied from 9% for six month deposits to 12% for five year deposits.

HDFC's second principal source of funds are loans. The table shows that the banks have been the main source of loans, followed by the Life Insurance Company of India, the General Insurance Company and the International Finance Corporation. Since the balance sheet was drawn up, HDFC has borrowed $30 million on the US capital markets through a housing guarantee loan arranged by the United States Agency for International Development. The exchange risk is being taken by the State Bank of India. The funds raised in this way will be used to finance low income housing, generally through loans to corporate bodies which provide housing for their employees.

As yet, HDFC raises few funds at the retail level, but it is the intention that this area of its business should expand. The table shows a modest amount collected in the form of loan linked deposits. The scheme merits describing in detail because, although as yet it is only small, it is an interesting experiment to encourage personal saving for housing. The scheme is partially based on the German Bausparkasse system described in Chapter 10. It is intended to introduce a scheme very similar to the Bausparkasse arrangement; the present scheme is more flexible.

An account is opened with a minimum deposit of 200 rupees, and thereafter deposits, which need not be made at regular intervals, must be made in multiples of 50 rupees. A savings period of 18 months, three years or five years can be selected. Savings carry a 9% rate of interest. After 18 months the investor can be considered for a housing loan up to four times the accumulated savings, provided that a minimum of 3,600 rupees has been saved. The loan cannot exceed 80% of the value of the property, and the rate of interest varies from 12.5% to 14.5%, depending on the amount of the loan. Loan terms are normally between five and 15 years.

The assets side of the balance sheet shows that 81% are in the form of loans. The various types of loan available from HDFC merit description in detail. Most HDFC loans are to individuals. HDFC will lend for new residential housing of any type. Loans will not normally be for less than 7,000 rupees or more than 150,000 rupees. Loans do not normally exceed 70% of the value. The rate of interest charged is on a sliding scale depending on the size of the loan. Loans of over 20,000 rupees are charged at 12.5%, and the scale rises such that loans between 50,000 and 100,000 rupees are charged at 14%. The term of the loan is normally between five and 15 years, although 20 year terms may be offered to low income borrowers. A first mortgage is required.

By the end of 1983 HDFC had sanctioned loans of 2,250 million rupees for 68,000 units. The average loan size for individual loans has been 40,000 rupees, and a typical unit has cost 90,000 rupees. Most loans have been to individuals with incomes below the median level. Among the problems which HDFC have encountered have been ascertaining the income of potential borrowers, especially those who are self employed, the lack of familiarity with form filling, and collecting repayments from borrowers with irregular incomes. These factors, together with small loan amounts, have led to a high cost of servicing loans.

Table 22.8 shows that HDFC lends a substantial amount to corporate bodies. It is only through this way that HDFC is able to finance low income housing, because it is required to operate commercially itself. Companies, however, can subsidize the housing for their workers using HDFC loans. HDFC provides a line of credit scheme, through which it lends to a company, against acceptable security, for onlending to individual employees for housing. Alternatively, HDFC can lend directly to individual employees nominated by the company with a company guaranteeing the loans. Corporate bodies can normally obtain a loan for not more than 50% of the construction cost of a housing project. The rate of interest charged is 15% and the

repayment period is five years. Loans to individuals nominated by companies are available on much the same terms as individual housing loans
generally.

HDFC also provides a modest amount of funds for co-operative housing
societies; the terms are the same as those for individuals.

Table 22.9 shows the income and expenditure account for HDFC for 1982-83.

Table 22.9 HDFC, Income and Expenditure, 1982-83

	Rupees m	Rupees per 100 Rupees Mean Assets
Income		
Interest on housing loans	104.2	10.9
Other interest & dividends	22.9	2.4
Fees & other charges	15.6	1.6
Profit on sale of investments	1.1	0.1
Other income	0.7	0.1
Total	144.6	15.2
Expenditure		
Interest & other charges	87.1	9.2
Staff	4.6	0.5
Establishment	2.8	0.3
Other expenses	6.9	0.7
Total	101.4	10.6
Profit before tax	43.2	4.5
Less tax	14.4	1.5
Profit after tax	28.9	3.0
Profit from previous year	2.0	0.2
Profit available for appropriations	30.9	3.2
Transfer to reserves	18.8	2.0
Dividends	10.0	1.1
Balance carried forward	2.1	0.2

Source: HDFC Sixth Annual Report 1981-83.
Note: At end-June 1983 there were 10.07 rupees to the dollar and 15.41 rupees to the pound.

This is fairly typical of the figures for a mortgage bank. However, the table
should be treated with some caution, as the exceptionally high rate of growth
recorded in 1982-83 makes use of the mean asset concept less reliable than
usual. Management expenses seem to have been kept at a reasonable level,
something which is not always easy for new finanical institutions in developing countries.

Assessment

Housing and housing finance in India merit detailed study for a number of
reasons. The country represents an extreme case of a poor, predominantly
rural, nation with a major problem of rapid population growth and
urbanization.

As is typical in developing countries, housing finance is provided largely

399

through the informal system, and the institutional system is, as yet, not well developed.

HDFC represents a bold attempt to establish the nucleus of a housing finance system. Currently, HDFC is a mortgage bank, but it intends to develop its role in the retail deposit market. HDFC is still very small in comparison with the size of the overall housing finance market in India, and it will need to continue a spectacular rate of growth if it is to have a sizeable impact on the development of the financial system.

Bibliography

Housing Development Finance Corporation Limited, Sixth Annual Report, 1982-83.
Munjee, N, *Profile on Housing*, Understanding Indian Economy, January-March 1982.
National Reports, International Union of Building Societies and Savings Associations, 1983.
Parekh, D S, 'India takes first steps to evolving a housing finance system', *The Building Societies Gazette*, 1983 World Congress issue.
Private Sector Housing Finance Programme, India, Project Paper, AID, July 1981.
Shah, P P, *Operational Problems and Potential for Low Income Housing*, Paper presented to Asia Housing Finance seminar, March 1984 (unpublished).

Acknowledgements

Information on this chapter has been provided by the World Bank, the Agency for International Development and HDFC. Nasser Munjee, Economist with HDFC, provided valuable comments on an earlier draft of this chapter.

CHAPTER 23

JAPAN

Japan is the most industrially advanced of the Asian countries, and has achieved rapid economic growth in the post war period, such that standards of living are now on a par with those of the Western industrialized countries. Significant macro-economic trends have included a very high saving ratio, a high ratio of investment to domestic product, and relative success in containing inflation and interest rates.

Although it is a huge country, much of Japan is not suitable for housing or other productive uses, and pressure on the available land space has resulted in cramped housing conditions, high price of land, and, consequently, high price of housing.

The most important mortgage lender in Japan, and, indeed, the largest single lender in the world, is the Housing Loan Corporation. This public sector body obtains its funds largely from the postal savings system, and, in addition to lending to house-buyers, it also supports other forms of housing activity. The other major lenders are the city banks and the regional banks. Although house-purchase loans are funded largely by short term deposits lending is still at a fixed rate of interest, and, moreover, at one that has frequently been below other market rates.

Introduction

Japan comprises four principal islands: Honshu, Kyushu, Shikoku and Hokkaido. Its total land area is 378,000 sq kilometres. In 1982 the population was 118,390,000. The population structure of Japan is causing some concern. The birth rate has been declining, in common with trends in other advanced countries, but the death rate has been declining far more rapidly, as a result of the sharp increase in living standards. The ageing population will, in due course, cause a strain on the social services.

By any standards Japan is densely populated, but the problem is more acute because much of the land area cannot be put towards any productive use. Indeed, 67% of all the land area is classified as forest. The population is therefore tightly concentrated on the coasts. The capital city, Tokyo, has a population of 11,600,000, and there are nine other cities each with a population in excess of 1,000,000.

Japan is a monarchy with two Houses of Parliament. Since the war the

Liberal Democrats (conservatives) have been in power continuously.

Japan's economic success has been achieved notwithstanding unfavourable natural conditions. Japan has a fairly extreme climate and few natural resources, which means that it is heavily dependent on overseas trade. Between 1960 and 1980 real gross domestic product per capita increased by an average of 6.5% a year, more than twice the average for all OECD countries of 3.1%. Japan has also been relatively successful in keeping inflation under control. For example, between 1975 and the fourth quarter of 1982 consumer prices in Japan rose by 49.5%, compared with an average for the OECD countries of 93.2%. Similarly, both short term and long term interest rates have not shown the violent fluctuations that have been evident in the other industrialized countries, particularly in the last five or so years. In 1982, for example, short term interest rates averaged 7% and long term interest rates 8%, at a time when many other countries, including the United States and Britain, had interest rates well into double figures.

Housing

Many Japanese houses were destroyed during the war, and subsequently there has been a very high level of housebuilding. However, housing conditions in Japan remain relatively modest compared with those in other countries with a similar overall standard of living. A major problem in this respect is the shortage of land. This means that houses tend to be small, and fairly close to each other, and often quite some distance away from places of work. The traditional Japanese house has an open style construction with wood and straw being the major materials used. Rooms are divided by sliding doors.

The land problem means that the land component is a major part of the house price, on average about one half, compared with perhaps a quarter in, for example, the United Kingdom. House prices in Japan are very high in relation to average incomes by international standards. A three bedroomed house in the suburbs would cost perhaps five to eight times average earnings, compared with a figure of three times in the UK.

There is a history of owner-occupation in Japan, especially in the rural areas, and many homes have been handed down within a family. Owner-occupied housing as a proportion of the total stood at 71.2% in 1958, since which time it fell to 59.2% in 1973, before rising to 60.4% in 1978. The private rented sector accounts for most of the remainder, and there is a limited amount of public sector rented housing, 7.6% of the total in 1978. It is commonly believed that much Japanese housing is tied to employment, and while the proportion, 5.7% in 1978, is higher than in other countries, it is not significantly so.

There are significant regional and age variations in respect to housing tenure. In 1978, 82.5% of houses in rural areas were owner-occupied, compared with a figure of 54.3% in urban areas. People do not become owner-occupiers in Japan at as early an age as in some other countries, notably the United Kingdom. In 1978, only 17% of households with a head of household age of under 29 were owner-occupiers, and even in the 30-39 age group the proportion was just 46%. The role of the public rented sector is significant here. This is provided predominantly by local authorities and is heavily subsidized. The housing is available for low income families only, and when incomes exceed a certain level the housing must be vacated.

Table 23.1 shows trends in housing tenure from 1958 to 1978.

Table 23.1 Tenure of Dwellings, Japan, 1958-78

| Year | Number of Dwellings | Owned | Public Sector | Percentage of Total Private Sector | | Issued (Tied) |
				Exclusive Facilities	Shared Facilities	
1958		71.2	3.5	18.5		6.7
1963	21,090,000	64.3	4.6	15.3	8.8	7.0
1968	25,591,000	60.3	5.8	18.7	8.3	6.9
1973	31,059,000	59.2	6.9	22.1	5.3	6.4
1978	35,451,000	60.4	7.6	22.2	3.9	5.7

Source: Statistics Bureau, *Housing Survey of Japan*.

Japan has maintained a very high level of housebuilding in the post war period. In fact, it has devoted more resources to housebuilding than any other advanced industrial country, a point that merits noting bearing in mind that it is sometimes claimed that housing in Britain has claimed too great a proportion of national resources, notwithstanding the fact that that proportion is far below the comparable figure for Japan. Table 23.2 shows the relationship between residential construction, investment and gross domestic product for Japan, and, for comparison, the OECD countries as a whole, from 1960 to 1980.

Table 23.2 Residential Construction, Japan and all OECD countries, 1960-1980

| Period | Gross Fixed Capital Formation as a Percentage of GDP | | Residential Construction as a Percentage of Gross Fixed Capital Formation | | Residential Construction as a Percentage of GDP | |
	Japan	OECD	Japan	OECD	Japan	OECD
1960-66	31.2	20.7	16.3	25.0	5.1	5.2
1967-73	34.3	21.8	20.7	25.0	7.1	5.5
1974-80	32.0	21.8	23.5	25.8	7.5	5.6
1960-1980	32.5	21.4	20.1	25.3	6.8	5.4

Source: *Historical Statistics*, OECD, 1982, Tables 6.6 and 6.7.

It will be seen that over the whole period 1960-1980 residential construction accounted for 6.8% of GDP in Japan, compared with the average for all OECD countries of 5.4%, and, moreover, the proportion in Japan has been increasing steadily.

Table 23.3 shows trends in housing starts in Japan since 1975.

Table 23.3 Housing Starts, Japan, 1975-83

Year	Number of Starts	Public Funded	Percentage of Total Tenure Owned	Rented	Issued
1975	1,356,000	30.1	69.5	27.7	2.8
1976	1,524,000	26.0	64.6	31.1	2.3
1977	1,508,000	28.5	68.6	29.4	2.1
1978	1,549,000	38.7	69.7	28.5	1.9
1979	1,493,000	40.7	70.5	27.7	1.8
1980	1,268,000	42.9	73.0	25.2	1.9
1981	1,152,000	46.7	71.6	26.4	2.0
1982	1,146,000	50.4	70.5	27.5	2.0
1983	1,137,000	43.2	63.5	34.7	1.8

Source: Ministry of Construction, *Building Construction Survey; Monthly Statistics of Japan*, February 1984, Table E-13.

There has been a sharp rise in the proportion of housing publicly funded, such that by 1982 more than half of houses came into this category although there was a downturn in the proportion in 1983. About two thirds of new houses have been for the owner-occupier market.

An important body in the housing field in Japan is the Japan Housing Corporation, which was established in 1955. Its main function is to implement government housing policies. It raises funds from its own capital, government loans and subsidies, and the private capital markets. It builds houses for rent and for sale with its main market being middle income families. Most of its dwellings are for the rented market, but a significant proportion are built for sale, and others are bought for sale to companies to let out to their workers. In 1983 it financed the building of 386,000 units.

Housing Finance

The Housing Finance Market

Housing finance in Japan is predominantly provided by the deposit taking system; that is, house-purchase loans are funded largely through short term savings, albeit with additional stages in the intermediationprocess. There are no major private sector specialist housing finance institutions. By far the main lender is the Housing Loan Corporation, a public sector body, which obtains its funds from the postal savings system. The other main lenders are the commercial banks and also housing loan companies, which are subsidiaries of commercial banks. Table 23.4 shows housing credit outstanding at the end of 1983.

Table 23.4 Housing Credit, Selected Institutions, Japan, End-1983

Institution	Number of Loans Outstanding	Amount Outstanding Yen bn	%
Housing Loan Corporation	5,055,000	17,426	32
City banks	1,306,000	7,221	13
Regional banks	1,353,000	5,994	11
Housing loan companies	466,000	4,750	9
Shinkin banks	917,000	4,485	8
Sogo banks	654,000	3,237	6
Life insurance companies	455,000	3,196	6
Trust accounts of banks	601,000	2,523	5
Agricultural co-operatives		1,993	4
Labour credit associations	379,000	1,244	2
Other		2,000	4
Total		54,050	100

Source: *Economic Statistics Monthly*, January 1984, Bank of Japan, Table 52.
Notes: 1. The table relates to loans for individuals only, and includes loans for the purchase of residential land as well as for construction, rebuilding and purchasing houses.
2. At end-1983 there were 234.3 yen to the dollar and 336.4 yen to the pound.
3. Figures for agricultural co-operative and labour credit associations are end-November 1983 and 'other' figure is approximate.

House-purchase loans are largely provided on a fixed interest basis, although some lenders have begun to introduce variable rates. Japan has avoided the problem of borrowing short and lending long, simply because its interest rates have been more stable than those in other countries. Mortgage rates tend to be below other mortgage rates, partly because of the influence of the government Housing Loan Corporation, but also because the banks seem willing to lend at below market rates on a limited proportion of their portfolio.

In 1968 a tax exemption scheme for saving for housing was introduced, and since 1978 there has been tax deductability for interest on housing loans.

The housing finance market has grown spectacularly in recent years, particularly since 1965. One reason for the rapid growth has been the existence of mortgage insurance through the Group Credit Life Insurance System and the Housing Loan Guarantee Insurance System.

The Propensity to Save

One important feature of the Japanese economic system, and one which is relevant to the housing finance market, is the very high propensity of the Japanese to save. International comparisons of the saving ratio are fraught with difficulty, and also the saving ratio itself is not as meaningful as many commentators would suggest because it simply indicates the extent to which the funds of the personal sector are available for lending to the other sectors; that is, the government sector, the corporate sector and the overseas sector. As loans to finance house-purchase are within the personal sector the saving ratio is of relatively minor importance. Nevertheless, the ratio is important in macro-economic terms, and a high saving ratio also permits a high degree of capital investment. In the period 1960-1980, net household saving in Japan as a percentage of disposable income was 19.0%, compared with an OECD average of 10.9%. The only country with a saving ratio similar to that of Japan is Italy.

The high saving ratio has been attributed to a number of factors including -
  (a) Real incomes have been rising rapidly, and there has been a tendency for consumption to lag behind.
  (b) In Japan special salary payments, such as mid-year and year end bonuses, are relatively high in relation to basic salaries, and it seems probable that these additional payments are more likely to be allocated to saving than are normal salary payments.
  (c) The social security system in Japan is not as advanced as in other countries, and thus the people are still inclined to save for their old age.
  (d) countries, and again there has been a willingness on the part of the Japanese to save so as to be able to purchase houses and consumer durables in the longer term.

Personal saving is extensively encouraged in Japan. In April 1952 the Central Council for Savings Promotion was established, and it has taken the initiative of organising the savings movement throughout the country. The Council attempts to increase the demand for saving through discussion, it fosters money management education, and it makes available a wide variety of publications. There are also extensive tax concessions on saving, including the exemption for interest income from small savings, a special tax exemption for interest on small government bond holdings, an additional tax exemption for interest on postal savings, and also tax exemptions linked to savings for housing.

Table 23.5 shows the distribution of personal sector deposits at the end of 1983.

This table demonstrates the dominance of the postal savings system in the personal savings market. Indeed, the Japanese postal savings system is the largest savings institution in the world, with personal sector deposits over ten times larger than those of the largest British building society or American savings and loan association.

One of the main reasons for the success of the postal savings system has been the tax concessions which it enjoys, and, indeed, the entire system is now considered to be a problem, partly because it is outside the control of the monetary authorities. The postal savings system has, in fact, increased its share of personal sector deposits from 16% of the total in 1965 to nearly one third today. In addition to the general tax exemption on savings there

Table 23.5   Personal Sector Deposits, Selected Institutions, Japan, End -1983

Institution	Yen bn	Percentage of Total
Postal savings	72,101	29
City banks	42,716	17
Regional banks	41,807	17
Shinkin banks	31,943	13
Agricultural co-operatives	32,602*	13
Sogo banks	20,322	8
Credit co-operatives	10,744*	4
Total	252,239	100

Source: *Economic Statistics Monthly*, January 1984, Bank of Japan, Tables 19, 24 & 46.
Notes: 1. The figure for postal savings is made up of 65,558 billion yen of certificates and 6,543 billion yen of deposits.
2. At end-1983 there were 234.3 yen to the dollar and 336.4 yen to the pound.
* November figures.

is an additional tax exemption for postal savings, up to three million yen per depositor. Moreover, it is common for people to have accounts in more than one name so as to take maximum advantage of this exemption. There are now more than three savings accounts for every person in the country.

The postal savings system operates through post offices, although these are frequently mechanised; some 10,000 offices, over half in the country, have on-line computer facilities. The postal savings service offers a high turnover ordinary deposit account, but most of its funds are held in what is known as TD certificates (Teigaku Deposit certificates). These carried rates of interest of between 4% and 6% at end-1983.

In effect, the postal savings system operates only on the savings side of the balance sheet. Almost all of the funds which it attracts are placed on deposit in the Trust Fund Bureau, and, in turn, they are on-lent to a variety of government agencies, including the Housing Loan Corporation which is described in more detail subsequently.

The city banks, regional banks, agricultural co-operatives and credit co-operatives will be described in more detail subsequently in this chapter, and at this stage it is necessary to note only their role in the personal savings market. Time deposits are by far the most popular form of account in terms of balances outstanding, but the maturity of such deposits is frequently quite short, often only a few months.

Brief mention needs to be made at this stage of the other principal holders of personal sector savings. The Shinkin banks are credit associations similar to credit unions in other countries, and the Sogo banks (mutual loan and savings banks) are local banks that concentrate their activities on small businesses and personal customers.

Housing Finance Institutions

The Housing Loan Corporation

The Housing Loan Corporation is the biggest single mortgage lender in the world but, as has already been briefly explained, it does not obtain its funds directly from the public, but rather from the postal savings system.

The Corporation was established in 1950 with the status of a special public corporation. Its principal objective is to provide long term capital at a low rate of interest for the construction and purchase of housing. It is also the agency through which some government housing programmes are implemented, and, in this respect, it has similarities to the Canada Mortgage and Housing Corporation and the Crédit Foncier in France.

The manner in which the Corporation operates can best be explained by showing how it obtains its funds, and how these are used. Set out below is the relationship between the Corporation and the postal savings system -

	Yen bn
Postal savings had deposits outstanding at end-September 1983 of	82,487
Its deposits in the Trust Fund Bureau were -	80,466
The Trust Fund Bureau had loans to Housing Loan Corporation of	19,700

It will be seen that the postal savings system deposits almost all of its funds into the Trust Fund Bureau. This bureau is able to use the loans for the purchase of public sector securities and debentures or for loans to government related organisations. Of the total funds at its disposal at the end of September 1983 of 137,296 billion yen, 19,700 million (14.3%) were allocated to the Housing Loan Corporation. Loans to other government related organisations comprised most of the remainder of the Trust Fund Bureau's assets.

Table 23.6 shows the assets and liabilities of the Housing Loan Corporation at the end of 1983.

The table shows how reliant the Corporation is on funds obtained directly from the Trust Fund Bureau, and that it attracts almost no direct funds itself. On the other side of the balance sheet, all but a minute fraction of assets are in the form of housing loans, and over 80% are in the form of private housing loans. The Corporation is therefore very different from most other financial institutions in that it holds very little liquidity, and obtains almost all of its funds through an intermediary.

The Corporation is governed by a president, vice-president and six directors, all of whom have to be appointed by the government. The head office of the Corporation is in Tokyo, and it has 12 branch offices in the major

Table 23.6 The Housing Loan Corporation, Assets and Liabilities, End-1983

Liabilities	Yen bn	%	Assets	Yen bn	%
Owed to Trust Fund			Private housing		
Bureau	19,700	90	loans	17,003	78
Owed to Postal Life			Other housing loans	3,465	16
Insurance & Postal			Other assets	1,447	7
Annuity	469	2			
Debentures	664	3			
Reserves against					
losses	110	1			
Capital	972	4			
Total	21,915	100	Total	21,915	100

Source: *Economic Statistics Monthly*, January 1984, Bank of Japan, Table 37.
Notes: 1. The table relates to loans for individuals only, and includes loans for the purchase of residential land as well as for construction, rebuilding and purchasing houses.
    2. At end-1983 there were 234.3 yen to the dollar and 336.4 yen to the pound.

population centres. The Corporation does not lend money directly itself, but rather operates through approved financial institutions acting as agents. As at July 1983, the Corporation operated through 899 institutions (with a total of 11,241 outlets) and 142 local governments.

The main function of the Corporation is the making of loans to those who build houses for their own use. About half of the funds of the Corporation are used in this way. The Corporation will lend only on relatively modest dwellings (a maximum area of 120 sq metres). The maximum loan is seven million yen, although this can be exceeded in certain cases. Loans are normally paid by regular monthly instalments; the repayment term is typically 25 years, and until recently the annual interest rate varied from 5.5% to 7.3% depending on the income of the applicant. From October 1982 the annual rate of interest on smaller dwellings (under 110 sq metres) is 5.5% for the first ten years and 7.3% subsequently. For dwellings between 110 sq metres and 125 sq metres the rates of interest are 6.5% for the first ten years and 7.5% subsequently, and for dwellings between 135 sq metres and 150 sq metres the rate is 7.3%.

All of these rates of interest seem modest, and are at times below market rates of interest. Moreover, the funds used to finance the loans are raised on a short term basis, but the loans themselves are made over a long period. This is possible because of the non-commercial way in which the system operates. The government stipulates the rate of interest at which the Trust Fund Bureau will lend to the Housing Loan Corporation, and it stipulates the rate at which the latter will lend, therefore it can always ensure an adequate margin between the two. The important question is the rate at which the postal savings system lends to the Trust Fund Bureau, and here it should be noted that the tax incentives enjoyed by postal savings effectively enable the funds for house-purchase to be borrowed cheaply.

About one third of lending by the Housing Loan Corporation is to purchasers of existing owner-occupied housing, on terms similar to those applying for new housing. The remaining funds are allocated to a variety of housing projects including rented housing, the rehabilitation of owner-occupied housing and the acquisition and development of housing sites. Table 23.7 shows the distribution of Housing Loan Corporation loans in 1981.

Table 23.7 Housing Loan Corporation Loans, 1981

Type of Loan	Amount Lent Yen bn	Percentage of Total
Construction of owner-occupied housing	1,489	47.0
Purchase of owner-occupied housing	1,048	33.1
Rented housing	176	5.6
Development of housing sites	162	5.1
Rehabilitation of owner-occupied housing	151	4.8
Urban renewal projects	67	2.1
Multi-storied dwellings	35	1.1
Other	41	1.3
Total	3,167	100.0

Source: *General Information of the Government Housing Loan Corporation*, The Government Housing Loan Corporation, 1982.
Note: At end-1981 there were 229.4 yen to the dollar and 416.5 yen to the pound.

City Banks

The city banks are major financial institutions in Japan, but the structure of the banking industry is markedly different from that in other countries. There are 13 city banks, only six of which are based in the capital city of Tokyo. All of the banks have a nationwide operation but, for the most part, their branches are in the cities only. In August 1981, the banks had 2,634 branches between them. Table 23.7 lists the five largest city banks as at the end of March 1983.

Table 23.8 Five Largest City Banks, Japan, End-March 1983

Bank	Deposits Yen bn	Total Assets Yen bn	Domestic Branches
Dai-ichi	19,337	25,913	345
Fuji	17,663	24,106	259
Mitsubishi	16,595	23,039	210
Sumitomo	17,040	22,537	217
Sanwa	16,094	22,287	276

Source: Annual Reports.
Notes: 1. At end-March 1983 there were 237.8 yen to the dollar and 354.5 yen to the pound.
2. Figures are on a non-consolidated basis.

It will be seen that the five banks have a similar size, and, of the other banks, five had deposits of 8,000 billion yen or more. The banks raise most of their deposits from the private sector, about 90% coming from this source, and most of these are time deposits. The banks are major institutions in the financial and industrial structure of Japan, and play a significant role in industry and commerce. Their retail banking has been less developed, as is evidenced by the relatively small number of branches for the size of the banks. Only about a quarter of their deposits are held by individuals. Housing loans account for about 5% of total assets. They lend on similar terms to the Housing Loan Corporation, and rates of interest are frequently below market rates (in 1983 they averaged about 8%). This is not because the institutions are paid any subsidy, but rather because of government policy, and the fact that the banks are able to afford to charge rates which might not always cover costs because the amount of business is relatively small in relation to their total business. During 1982 and 1983 some of the banks introduced variable rate loans and allowed extended loan terms (up to 30 years) with the borrower's children being a party to the loan.

Regional Banks

The regional banks are similar in many respects to city banks, and they are frequently counted together as being 'ordinary banks'. In August 1981 there were 63 regional banks. Each of these was based in a prefecture (a local government area) but generally they extend their operations to neighbouring prefectures. The largest regional bank, the Bank of Yokohama, is marginally bigger than the smallest city bank. Although the regional banks are smaller than the city banks they have considerably more branches, a total of 5,361 in August 1981.

The banks concentrate their lending to regional companies, but they also extend loans to larger organisations based in a particular prefecture. They also provide financial services to local governments. Like the city banks less than 10% of their lending is in the form of house-purchase loans, and they lend on similar terms to the city banks.

Housing Loan Companies

The fourth biggest category of housing finance lenders are the housing loan companies, which account for about 10% of the total market. There are eight of these institutions, all of which have been established fairly recently. They are owned by groups of financial institutions including city banks, regional banks, sogo (mutual) banks, life insurance companies, security companies and the Norinchukin Bank, which is the central co-operative bank for agriculture and forestry. The first two companies were set up in 1971, one by a city bank group, and the other by a trust bank group. Other companies subsequently followed. The motive behind the establishment of these companies was that housing loans are fairly small and are labour intensive, and also require specialist knowledge. It was considered more logical to delegate this business to specialist organisations rather than to undertake it as part of mainstream banking business. The mortgage loan companies in Canada are an interesting analogy in this respect.

These companies raise their funds entirely by borrowing, generally from the parent institutions. Almost all the money they borrow is on-lent to homebuyers, with only a modest amount being kept in cash and deposits.

Other Lenders

Table 23.4 shows that the life insurance companies had 6% of the housing finance market at the end of 1983. The life companies operate in a similar way to those in other countries, and the share of their loan portfolio in the form of housing finance loans is also not untypical.

Assessment

The Japanese housing and housing finance systems comprise an unusual combination of private and public sector. The level of owner-occupation is high by international standards and the provision of public sector housing is very modest. Typically, people rent initially before becoming owner-occupiers. The main problem facing potential owner-occupiers is the high price of housing which, in turn, is caused by the shortage of land. Financial institutions do not lend on as generous terms as in other countries, but still most families seem to succeed in becoming owner-occupiers. Japan's successful macro-economic development has enabled the major problem of fluctuating interest rates to be avoided, but it must be questioned how long the system can continue by relying predominantly on short term savings, raised with tax advantages by the postal savings system, being on-lent through an intermediary to the Housing Loan Corporation. The long term ability and willingness of the banks to provide house-purchase loans at what are, effectively, subsidized rates of interest must also be questioned.

Bibliography

Banking System in Japan, 8th Edition, Federation of Bankers' Associations of Japan, 1982.
General Information of the Government Housing Loan Corporation, The Government Housing Loan Corporation, 1983.
Housing Bureau, Ministry of Construction, *Housing in Japan*, Japan Housing Association.
Ichimura, Dr Shinichi, 'Economic Growth, Savings and Housing Finance in Japan', *International Insights*, Vol 2, No 1, IUBSSA, July 1981.
'Japan: A Survey', *The Economist*, 8 July 1983.
Savings and Saving Promotion Movement in Japan, The Central Council for Savings Promotion, March 1981.
The Japanese Financial System, The Bank of Japan, Economic Research Department, 1978.

Acknowledgements

The co-operation of the Housing Loan Corporation and the London office of the Bank of Japan in providing information for this chapter is gratefully acknowledged.

CHAPTER 24

OTHER ASIAN COUNTRIES

Singapore

Introduction

Singapore is a small prosperous island, to the south of the Malaya peninsula. It occupies an area of just 618 sq kilometres. Its population in 1982 was 2,472,000, making it very densely populated. The population has been growing at an annual rate of about 1.2%.

Singapore was part of the Malaysian Federation, but it became an independent sovereign state in 1965. It is a republic, but the political system operates on non-party lines.

GNP per capita in 1981 was $5,240, higher than any other Asian state, except the oil producing countries and Japan. Real GNP per capita grew at the very high rate of 6.7% a year between 1970 and 1980. Inflation has been held at a modest level, under 3% in 1983. Singapore has made maximum use of its natural resources, and the flexibility that comes with a relatively small area and population, to become a major trading and financial centre in South East Asia. It is generally run on free enterprise lines, although, as will be seen subsequently, housing is very much under the control of the public sector.

Housing and the Housing and Development Board

Table 24.1 shows housing tenure in Singapore in 1980.

Table 24.1　Private Housing Units by Tenancy, Singapore, 1980

Tenancy	Number of Units	Percentage of Total
Owner-occupied	280,107	55
Sole tenant	167,658	33
Other tenant	34,330	7
Empty	16,285	3
Other	11,144	2
Total	509,524	100

Source: *Census of Population 1980, Singapore, Release No 6, Households and Houses*, Department of Statistics, Table 69.

Singapore has a lower level of owner-occupation than the poorer Asian countries, reflecting its ability to use its wealth to provide public sector housing. The proportion of owner-occupiers has increased markedly, the level standing at just 29% in 1970. Because it is densely populated, Singapore has very few houses as opposed to flats; less than 10% of all dwelling units are houses.

The housing sector in Singapore is dominated by a government body, the-Housing and Development Board (HDB). At the end of 1983, this managed 400,000 units, 75% of all units in the country. (The figure includes owner-occupied flats sold by the Board.) It has grown spectacularly in recent years, accounting for 35% of the total stock in 1970 and 50% in 1976.

The Board was established as a statutory body in 1960 under the Housing and Development Act. It is responsible to the Ministry for National Development. It has three divisions responsible respectively for administration and finance, building and development, and estates and land. Its operations are assisted by its exemption from planning regulations and streamlined administration in the government generally.

The Board receives its funds from the national budget, and it has been heavily subsidized. It borrows funds for property developed for sale at a rate of 6% repayable over ten years. Loans for rented property are repayable at 7.75% over 60 years. Singapore has accepted that it is right for the national budget to subsidize housing in this way, and the state is sufficiently rich to be able to afford it.

Since its establishment, HDB has continually increased the level of its production. Between 1960 and 1965 it built 55,000 houses, and for the next five years the figure was 65,000. Between 1971 and 1975 it built 110,000, and between 1976 and 1980 it built 130,000. In the current five year plan it is anticipated that HDB will build 155,000 units, and that by 1985 80% of the population will live in HDB flats.

Most HDB activity is now in respect of units for sale rather than houses for rent. It had sold 257,000 units by March 1983, meaning that over 60% of the units which it manages are now owner-occupied.

HDB launched its home-ownership scheme in 1964. This provides for loans to be available at a rate of interest, which is subsidized, of 6.25% over 20 years. HDB loans are often made in conjunction with drawings on the Central Provident Fund which is described in detail subsequently.

Table 24.2 shows the assets and liabilities of the HDB in March 1983.

It will be seen that funds are obtained almost entirely from the government, and that most assets are either land and housing or mortgage loans in respect of flats which have been sold.

Table 24.2 Housing and Development Board, Assets & Liabilities, March 1983

Liabilities	$m	%	Assets	$m	%
Government loans	6,297	74	Land and housing	10,955	
Bank loans	103	1	less capital sales	5,270	
Sundry creditors	1,440	17	net	5,685	67
Capital funds	281	3	Other fixed assets	159	2
Revenue surplus	339	4	Mortgage loans to		
			purchasers of flats	2,135	25
			Current assets	482	6
Total	8,461	100	Total	8,461	100

Source: *HDB Financial Report 82/83*, Housing and Development Board, 1983.
Note: At end-March 1983 there were 2.09 Singapore dollars to the US dollar and 3.11 Singapore dollars to the pound (all figures in this section are in Singapore dollars).

Post Office Savings Bank

This is the major retail financial institution in Singapore, accounting for some 60% of deposits. It has grown spectacularly in recent years, having accounted for just 17% of deposits in 1972. Its growth has largely been at the expense of the commercial banks. Despite its name, the Bank now has nothing to do with the Post Office but, rather, is a government owned corporation. At the end of 1983 it had 122 branches, 2,500,000 savings accounts, that is, one per person on average, and total deposits of $6,249 million.

In 1983 the Savings Bank was given power to become a full scale commercial bank. Its growth has been stimulated by the tax advantages it has enjoyed, and it remains to be seen if these will continue.

Most of the funds which the Savings Bank collects are invested in government securities, and, in this way, can be seen as an indirect method of financing the Housing and Development Board. However, it also has a 20% direct share of the market for housing finance. Its loans are made largely in conjunction with withdrawals from the Central Provident Fund.

The Central Provident Fund

This was established in 1955. It is a compulsory savings scheme, with the objective of providing retirement benefits. Currently, employees are required to contribute no less than 23% of salaries with employers contributing a further 22%. The fund had balances of $17.6 billion in June 1983, making it substantially larger than the Post Office Savings Bank. In the mid-1970s, the fund made direct loans for house-purchase. Now, however, funds can be drawn from the scheme to pay for housing, both the initial deposit and the remaining monthly instalments. It is estimated that 75% of those who purchase HDB flats use their contributions to the Central Provident Fund to help meet the costs. In 1982 withdrawals from the fund amounting to $796 million were made under the scheme. The Post Office Savings Bank works particularly closely with the Fund in this respect.

Other Financial Institutions

Banking is a huge industry in Singapore. At the end of 1982 there were 119 banks with total assets of $102 billion. The three largest banks each figure in the list of the 500 largest banks in the world; the Development Bank of Singapore (assets of $10.6 billion at end 1982), the United Overseas Bank ($9.3 billion) and the Oversea—Chinese Banking Corporation ($6.7 billion). The banks provide very little direct finance for housing, loans for this purpose amounting to $332 million at the end of 1982, but rising to $425 million by June 1983. The banks had deposits of $24,237 million at the end of 1983.

Building societies and finance companies are the other main providers of housing finance loans. In June 1983 they had housing loans outstanding of $1,035 million and deposits of $5,479 million. Finance companies account for the bulk of these figures.

Thailand

Introduction

Thailand is a large country in South East Asia. It has land borders with Burma, Laos, Kampuchea and Malaysia and it has a fairly long coastline with the South China Sea. It has an area of 513,115 sq kilometres.

The population of Thailand in 1982 was 48,847,000. The population grew at an annual rate of 2.6% a year in the 1970s. There has been less urbanization than in other Asian countries and that which has occurred has concentrated on the capital of Bangkok. The Bangkok metropolis had a population of 5,468,000 in 1982.

Thailand is a constitutional monarchy. There is a national Assembly, consisting of a Senate, appointed by the King, and a House of Representatives, elected by popular vote. Currently, a four party coalition is in power but there is a considerable military presence in the government.

GNP per capita was $770 in 1980. In the 1970s GNP grew by 8% a year in real terms and GNP per capita by 4.2% a year. Inflation reached 20% in 1980 before falling to 13% in 1981 and to 4% early in 1983.

Housing

In 1976 there were 6,863,000 housing units in Thailand. Table 24.3 shows the tenure of these dwellings.

It will be seen that 89% of dwellings were owner-occupied, a fairly typical proportion for a poor developing country. 64% of dwellings were built of wood and a further 25% of other local materials. Nearly 95% of dwellings were single detached units.

It is estimated that 25% of the population live in slums and squatter settlements, a significant proportion of them on land owned by the government.

Table 24.3 Housing Tenure, Thailand, 1976

Tenure	Number of of Units	Percentage of Total
Owner-occupied	6,080,060	89
Rented	516,950	8
Rent-free occupancy	78,810	1
Other rent-free	155,730	2
Unknown	31,710	-
Total	6,863,260	100

Source: *Statistical Yearbook Thailand 1976-1980*, National Statistical Office, Table 20.

The public sector has built very few dwellings. Responsibility for implementing housing policy rests with the National Housing Authority which was established in 1973. This obtains its funds from bank loans and the national budget. It is mainly concentrating on sites and services programmes and slum upgrading. It did build a total of 28,000 units between 1960 and 1980, most of which were for sale. The lack of an effective formal housing finance system means that the NHA has to provide the finance for these sales and the units are effectively sold on a hire purchase basis over 15-20 years at rates of interest between 6% and 12%.

The Financial System

The financial system in Thailand is dominated by the commercial banks, which have mobilized the highest proportion of personal savings and which are the largest providers of credit. The other major institutions which collect personal savings are the finance companies and the Government Savings Bank. Table 24.4 shows key data for the financial institutions in Thailand as at the end of 1980.

Table 24.4 Financial Institutions, Thailand, End-1980

Institution	Number	Branches	Household Savings Baht m	Credit Baht m	Total Assets Baht m
Commercial banks	30	1,478	163,761	218,931	300,016
Finance companies	112	32	29,309	55,348	65,147
Government Savings Bank	1	406	24,132	1,122	27,975
Government Housing Bank	1	0	1,542	8,123	10,116
Life insurance companies	12	524	5,404	2,697	6,455
Savings co-operatives	353	0	3,712	4,041	4,420
Crédit fonciers	33	0	1,152	2,420	4,103
Other	542	61	2,174	23,110	30,761
All	1,741	2,501	231,186	316,062	448,993

Source: Government Savings Bank.
Note: At end-1980 there were 20.6 baht to the dollar and 48.3 baht to the pound.

The various institutions are described in the following section.

Housing Finance

As in other developing countries there are formal and informal housing and housing finance sectors. The formal sector provides perhaps half of housing finance in terms of amount but only one third of the number of loans. It has been estimated that 70% of households in squatter settlements have built their own homes over a construction period of between four and 12 years, as finance became available. Up to one third of the cost of housing was effectively provided by direct labour. The main source of loan finance is friends and relatives.

There are rotating credit societies known as 'pia huay' in Thailand. Another interesting practice is that of share games. Typically, ten people provide a cash sum and make bids for the total amount. The successful bidder becomes a borrower and the others lend to him. The interest rate has been calculated as 3.3% per month for the lender and 3.9% per month for the borrower.

Table 24.5 shows estimates of housing finance loans outstanding from the formal institutions at the end of 1980.

Table 24.5 Housing Finance Outstanding from Formal Institutions, Thailand, End-1980

Institution	Amount Baht m	Percentage of Total
Government Housing Bank	4,790	33
Commercial banks	4,750	32
National Housing Authority	1,800	12
Finance companies	1,260	8
Credit fonciers	1,100	7
Life insurance companies	400	3
Bangkok Co-operative Housing Society	470	3
Government Savings Bank	240	2
Total	14,810	100

Source: Knight, A, *Housing Finance in Thailand*, unpublished, 1982.
Note: At end-1980 there were 20.6 baht to the dollar and 48.3 baht to the pound.

The Government Housing Bank is the largest single lender. It was established in 1953. It is wholly government owned and is responsible to the Ministry of Finance. It is largely a mortgage bank in character, obtaining most of its funds from borrowing, including from the Government Savings Bank, the Bank of Thailand and foreign banks, rather than from deposits. Table 24.6 shows the assets and liabilities of the Bank as at the end of 1982.

Table 24.6 Government Housing Bank (Thailand), Assets & Liabilities, End-1982

Liabilities	Baht m	%	Assets	Baht m	%
Time deposits	1,592	14	Loans	9,237	82
Demand deposits	52	-	Financial assets	1,516	13
Bank loans	2,728	24	Properties for sale	2	-
Borrowing	3,760	33	Physical assets	67	1
GHB bonds	2,000	18	Other assets	501	4
Other liabilities	228	2			
Equity and reserves	963	9			
Total	11,323	100	Total	11,323	100

Source: *The Government Housing Bank Annual Report 1982*, 1983.
Note: At end-1982 there were 23.0 baht to the dollar and 37.2 baht to the pound.

The Bank ran into problems in the late 1970s by overtrading. It lent money which it could not finance without borrowing at a higher rate. Subsequently it has retrenched a little and has actually declined in size. The Bank made 11,000 new loans in 1979, 12,000 in 1980, but only 7,000 in 1981 and 5,000 in 1982, of which 1,800 were to individuals. In 1982 the amount lent was 1,127 million baht compared with a peak of 2,516 million baht in 1980. Over 50% of its outstanding loans are to individuals. These are normally for a maximum of 65% of valuation but they can be for up to 80% of valuation in respect of projects where the Bank has lent to finance construction. Loans are at a rate of between 15% and 17%, depending on size, and the normal repayment term is 11-15 years. Over 20% of the Bank's loans are in overdrafts to developers in respect of projects for which personal housing loans may subsequently be made.

The commercial banks are the second largest group of lenders. Unlike in many other developing countries all but one are privately owned. The point has already been made that they dominate the financial system generally, in particular, they are the largest collectors of personal saving. They have 1,500 branches and by June 1983 their personal deposits exceeded 320 billion baht. By February 1983 their assets had increased to 448 billion baht. The largest bank, substantially, is the Bangkok Bank which has 40% of the total assets of all commercial banks.

House-purchase lending is a relatively small proportion of total bank lending. Individual loans are normally in respect of projects, the construction of which has been financed by the bank. The developer will handle the arrangements. Loans of between 70% and 80% of valuation are made at rates on interest between 18% and 19% over 10-15 years. Less generous terms are available for houses not constructed in linked projects.

The role of the National Housing Authority in housing finance has already been described. It makes loans only because this is the only way it can sell the houses which it constructs. These are made effectively on hire purchase terms.

Finance companies have been a rapidly growing type of institution, having originated only in 1969. As Table 24.4 shows, they are substantial deposit taking bodies but they also raise funds through borrowing from banks and the money markets. Housing loans are a very modest 2.4% of their total assets. Like the banks they will normally lend on projects where they have financed the construction. Loans typically are for 50-70% of valuation at a rate of interest of 18-20%. Interest rates are variable.

Credit fonciers were established in 1958 as specialist lenders on the security of land. It was the original intention that they they should be strong housing finance institutions but in common with other such institutions in developing countries which have been allowed wider powers they have taken advantage of these and only 18% of their loans are on real estate. They obtain their funds from short term borrowing and lend on very similar terms to the finance companies. The largest is the Sinkahakan Credit Foncier Credit Company which accounts for 50% of the total assets of all credit fonciers.

The Government Savings Bank is a significant institution in terms of mobilising personal saving, but almost insignificant in terms of housing finance. It had its origins in 1913 and was constituted in its present form in 1947. In 1982 it had 414 branches and a further 121 agencies. It has been very successful in mobilising personal saving and at the end of 1982 it had 11,750,000 deposit accounts. Its total deposits were 32.8 billion baht of which 59% were in 12 month time deposits and 23% in savings accounts. However, the Bank has only a very small direct lending function. Well over 90% of its assets are invested in government securities.

Sri Lanka

Introduction

Sri Lanka is an island of 65,610 sq kilometres to the south east of the southern tip of India. Its population in 1981 was 14.99 million, and had been growing at a relatively modest rate, for developing countries, of 1.7% a year in the 1970s. The capital, Colombo, is by far the largest city.

Sri Lanka is a republic. It has a Senate and a House of Representatives. Currently, the United National party is in power. In recent years there have been serious racial conflicts.

GNP per capita in 1981 was $300, meaning that Sri lanka is one of the poorer Asian countries, on a par with India. GNP per capita grew at a real rate of 2.8% a year between 1970 and 1980. The rate on inflation was 11% in 1982.

Housing

In 1971 there were 2,217,478 housing units in Sri Lanka. Of these, 19% were in urban areas, 69% were in rural areas and the remaining 11% were on estates. Well over half of the dwellings were described as semi-permanent. In 1971 there were 5.6 people per unit and 2.4 people per room. Only 9% of houses had electricity and 20% access to piped water. These figures marked only a marginal improvement on the position in 1963.

No figures are available on housing tenure but it is reasonable to assume that well over 80% of units are owner-occupied as in other poorer developing countries. There is a publicly owned rental stock of some 5,000 units.

Responsibility for housing development rests with the National Housing Development Authority, which is the developer for all government programmes. 7,000 units were built in 1982 compared with 9,000 in 1981. Most of these are sold on a hire purchase basis at a rate of interest of between 6% and 12%. The housing budget has been steadily reduced in recent years because of the general economic situation. Public sector activity now concentrates on self help projects.

In January 1984 a housing programme aimed at building one million units was initiated. It is the intention to build at least five units a month in each of the 4,000 district areas.

The Financial System

The financial system is dominated by the commercial banks. There are 11 banks, all of which are nationalised. The largest, substantially, is the Bank of Ceylon which has 500 branches. The next largest is the People's Bank.

The other major deposit taking institution is the National Savings bank. This was formed by a merger of the Post Office Savings Bank, the Ceylon Savings Bank and the Savings Certificate Fund, in 1972. It is a government owned institution and operates through 450 branches and also post offices. It attracts its funds both through savings deposits (which carried a 12% rate of interest in October 1983) and fixed deposits (which carried a 14-18% rate of interest in October 1983). The bank has over seven million individual depositors, more than half the adult population, and held deposits of nine billion rupees at the end of 1982.

The Savings Bank invests almost all of its funds in government securities, thereby funding public sector activities. Less than 10% of its funds are in loans to the private sector, including housing loans.

Table 24.7 shows deposits in the National Savings bank and the commercial banks as at June 1983.

Table 24.7 Sri Lanka, Deposits, June 1983

	Amount Rupees m	Rupees m	Percentage of Total %	%
National Savings Bank				
Savings deposits	2,563		8.4	
Fixed deposits	6,041		19.7	
		8,604		28.0
Commercial Banks				
Savings deposits	5,996		19.5	
Fixed deposits	16,096		52.5	
		22,082		72.0
Total		30,686		100.0

Source: *Central Bank of Ceylon Bulletin*, November 1983, Table 17.
Note: At end-June 1983 there were 23.0 rupees to the dollar and 35.2 rupees to the pound.

Housing Finance

The housing finance system is less developed in Sri Lanka than in most other developing countries. Housing activity is largely funded through the informal system although employers also make significant contributions. It is estimated that 80,000 housing units were produced in 1980 but only 1,800 of these were financed by the formal sector. Table 24.8 shows an estimate of housing credit extended in Sri Lanka in 1980.

Table 24.8 Sri Lanka, Housing Credit, 1980

Institution	No of Loans	Amount of Loans Rupees m	Average Size of Loans Rupees
State Mortgage and			
Investment Bank	455	27	59,000
National Savings Bank	619	9	15,000
Insurance Company of			
Sri Lanka	283	11	39,000
People's Bank	500	5	10,000
Total	1,857	53	

Note: At end-1980 there were 18.0 rupees to the dollar and 44.2 rupees to the pound.

The largest single lender is the State Mortgage and Investment Bank (SMIB). This was established in its present form in 1979 through a merger of the Ceylon State Mortgage Bank and the Agricultural and Industrial Credit Corporation. It operates through the head office in Colombo and also two branches. It also uses banks as agents for making loans outside Colombo. It raises its funds through debentures which are purchased by the financial institutions. The government makes up any difference between the cost of the bonds and the yield of mortgages. In June 1983 it had loans outstanding of 246 million rupees. It lent 74 million rupees in 1982 and 95 million in 1983. In October 1983 it made loans at between 12% and 18% for housing construction and at between 18% and 22% for the purchase of existing property.

The commercial banks stopped lending in mid-1981 as they considered that house-purchase was no longer a profitable activity for them. The People's Bank was the largest single lender within the banking sector but the largest bank in the country, the Bank of Ceylon, had also been active in this market.

The National Savings Bank is able to invest 40% of its assets in housing but in fact invests only 2% in this way. Its normal rate of interest is 15% over 20 years.

Pakistan

Introduction

Pakistan covers an area of 796,095 sq kilometres in Eastern Asia. It has land borders with Iran, Afganistan, China and India. Its population in mid-1981 was 84,501,000. The population grew by 3.1% a year between 1970 and 1980. The largest cities are Karachi (3,551,000) and Lahore (2,170,000). The capital, Islamabad, is a relatively small city with a population of just 250,000. The urban population has been growing at an annual rate of 4.5% a year.

Pakistan is a republic but it has been under martial law since 1977.

GNP per capita was $350 in 1981, similar to the level in India. Real GNP per capita grew at an annual rate of 3.7% a year in the 1970s.

Housing

Table 24.9 shows housing tenure in Pakistan as in 1980.

Table 24.9 Housing Units by Tenure, Pakistan, December 1980

	Rural		Urban		Total	
	No	%	No	%	No	%
Owned	7,461,357	83	2,405,380	68	9,866,737	78
Rented	195,507	2	777,178	22	972,685	8
Rent free	1,376,611	15	371,615	10	1,748,226	14
All	9,033,475	100	3,554,173	100	12,578,648	100

Source: *Housing Census of Pakistan 1980*, Summary Results, Population Census Organisation, 1982, Table 2.

It will be seen that 78% of all units were owner-occupied with the usual pattern for developing countries of there being a much higher level of owner-occupation in rural areas.

Housing conditions in Pakistan are among the worst in Asia. In 1980, there was an average of 6.7 persons per housing unit and 3.5 persons per room. Only 31% of houses had access to electricity, and 38% had inside access to piped water. 48% of units had outer walls comprising unbaked brick and mud.

The formal sector of the economy has been building between 40,000 and 45,000 dwelling units a year. This figure needs to be compared with a growth in the number of urban households of 150,000 units a year.

Housing Finance

The main provider of long term housing finance loans is the House Building Finance Corporation, which was established in 1952. This lends predominantly to individuals. In the recent past it has been making about 20,000 loans a year. The volume of its lending has grown from 371 million rupees in 1977-78 to 1,530 rupees in 1981/82, although the amount fell back to 1,094 million rupees in 1982-83. (In March 1983 there were 13.0 rupees to the dollar and 19.37 rupees to the pound.) HBFC stopped charging interest for its loans in 1979 as part of a government programme to end the practice of charging interest. Units are constructed on a co-ownership basis, and HBFC then receives a proportion of the imputed rent. The effect is, of course, much the same as charging interest.

The banks are the major financial institutions, and have had targets for lending to industry. At the end of 1980 they had personal loans outstanding of 713 million rupees. In 1980-81 they lent 251 million rupees on the security of real estate out of total lending of 6,286 million rupees. The banks are the major holders of personal deposits. They had over 13 million accounts at the end of 1980, with deposits in excess of 46 billion rupees.

The other major financial institution in Pakistan is the National Savings Organisation. This sells various government savings instruments through over 7,000 bank branches, 6,000 post offices and 300 national savings centres. At the end of June 1983, total net deposits in government savings schemes amounted to 30.8 billion rupees. The most popular forms of account are term deposits and prize bonds, for which there is no interest, but the opportunity to win a monthly prize. The National Savings system does not lend to the private sector at all, but, rather, all of the funds which it attracts are transferred to the government.

A major source of finance for housing investment is remittances sent from Pakistanis working abroad.

Bangladesh

Introduction

Bangladesh occupies an area of 143,998 sq kilometres. It borders on the Bay of Bengal to the south, and its land area is surrounded by India, except for a very small border with Burma.

The population of Bangladesh in mid-1981 was 87,052,000. The population grew at an annual rate of 2.5% a year between 1970 and 1980. Bangladesh has experienced very rapid urbanization. The largest city is Dacca with a population of 3.5 million. Dacca, with the second and third largest cities, Chittagong and Khulna, comprise more than half the urban population.

GNP per capita was $140 in 1981, making it one of the poorest countries in the world. GNP per capita grew in real terms by just 1.4% a year in the 1970s.

Housing

Table 24.10 shows dwelling units by tenure in 1981.

Table 24.10   Dwelling Units by Tenure, Bangladesh, 1981

Tenure	Rural		Urban		Total	
	No	%	No	%	No	%
Owned	12,037,868	94	1,217,858	60	13,257,726	90
Rented	78,557	1	663,708	33	742,267	5
Rent free	624,688	5	160,367	8	785,055	5
Total	12,743,115	100	2,041,933	100	14,785,048	100

Source: *1982 Statistical Yearbook of Bangladesh*, Bangladesh Bureau of Statistics, 1983, Table 3.73.

The table shows the usual pattern of very high owner-occupation, especially in the rural areas. However, there is a large rented sector in urban areas and squatter settlements are somewhat less common than in the other developing countries. 63% of units had walls made of straw or bamboo and a further 20% had walls of mud and unburnt brick. The government has played only a minor role in the provision of housing. 42% of units were developed by the public sector between 1973 and 1980.

Housing Finance

The specialist housing finance organisation is the Housebuilding Finance Corporation. This made loans of 437 million taka in 1982-83. (At the end of 1982 there were 24.1 taka to the dollar and 39.0 taka to the pound.) There has been a gradual decline in lending by the Corporation since 1979-80.

The banks are the major financial intermediaries. There are six banks, all of which are nationalized. The largest is the Sonali Bank. The banks have 3,800 branches between them. In June 1983 the banks had loans outstanding of 50 billion taka. Of the total, 340 million were to construction companies, and 3,981 million taka were to the personal sector. However, virtually none of the lending is for house-purchase.

The other major financial intermediaries are the Post Office Savings Bank and the National Savings Bureau. National Savings instruments are also sold through commercial banks. At the end of 1981 5,000 post offices offered limited savings bank facilities. The savings bank system is very much smaller than the commercial banks, and there is no lending function.

Malaysia

Introduction

Malaysia comprises two quite distinct areas: the Malay peninsula, which shares a northern border with Thailand, and Sabah and Sarawak which occupy the northern part of the island of Borneo, the remainder of which belongs to Indonesia. The total land area is 336,700 sq kilometres.

The population of Malaysia was 14,413,000 in 1982, 80% of whom live in the Malay peninsula. The rate of growth between 1970 and 1980 was 2.5%. Malaysia has experienced urbanization, with the proportion of the population in urban areas rising from 27% in 1970 to 33% in 1981. There has also been a very distinct rural to urban migration. The capital and largest city is Kuala Lumpur.

Malaysia is a federation, established in its present form in 1963, although Singapore seceded in 1965.

GNP per capita was $1,840 in 1981, high by Asian standards. The rate of growth in real GNP per capita was 5.1% during the 1970s, again an exceptionally high rate.

Housing

There were 2.63 million housing units in Malaysia in 1980. Between 1971 and 1980 744,000 units were built, 25% by the public sector. Notwithstanding this significant building programme, there are still significant squatter settlements. It is estimated that over one-third of housing units in urban areas are occupied by squatters, and the number of squatter units is growing at 8% a year.

Housing is integrated into general economic policy. Malaysia has had a series of economic plans. The current plan runs from 1981 to 1985. There is a target of no less than 923,000 units. It is intended that the public sector will build 43% of the units, predominantly for low income families. Private developers are required to reserve up to 50% of their housing developments for low cost housing.

Housing Finance

Table 24.11 shows the distribution of housing finance loans outstanding in 1970 and 1982.

The first point to be noted is that the housing finance system is relatively large compared with other developing countries. The table shows a huge growth in housing finance loans between the two years, and also a marked change in the distribution of outstanding loans. The reasons for these developments can be explained by examining the individual institutions.

There are 38 banks operating in Malaysia. The largest is the Bank Bumiputra (Malaysia) Behad with assets of $17,305 million at the end of 1982. The sec-

Table 24.11   Housing Finance Loans Outstanding, Malaysia, 1970 & 1982

Institution	1970		1982	
	$m	%	$m	%
Banks	88	29	3,498	37
Housing loans division	-	-	3,359	36
Building societies	194	63	1,449	15
Finance companies	26	8	1,085	12
Total	308	100	9,391	100

Source: *International Reports*, International Union of Building Societies and Savings Associations, 1983.

Note: At the end of 1982 there were 2.32 ringitts to the dollar and 3.75 ringitts to the pound.

ond largest was the Malayan Bank Berhad, with assets of $9,609 million. The commercial banks were not involved in housing finance until 1968. In that year they were required to channel 50% of savings deposits into three areas: treasury bills, approved institutions and housing loans. The guidelines have been changed several times, and most recently lending in any one year has been fixed by relation to loans outstanding at the end of the previous year. In 1983 the banks had to commit themselves to finance the purchase of at least 20,000 new units costing $100,000 each and below.

The second largest lender is the housing loans division of the treasury, which makes loans to civil servants of at least five years standing. Loans are repayable over 25 years at the rate of 4%.

Table 24.11 shows that the building societies have suffered a huge reduction in market share since 1970. However, this has occurred merely because of requirements on the banks and finance companies to lend, and the provision of heavily subsidized loans by the housing loans division. The building societies actually experienced a seven fold increase in their lending between 1970 and 1982.

There are two building societies in Malaysia. The Malaysia Building Society Berhad (MBSB) operates in the Malay peninsular, while the Borneo Housing Mortgage Finance Berhad serves Sabah and Sarawak. The MBSB was originally established in Singapore in 1950, by the Commonwealth Development Corporation, as the Federal and Colonial Building Society. After several reorganisations MBSB was established in its present form in 1972. The government is the major shareholder. MBSB is not a typical building society in that it raises most of its funds from debentures and borrowing. Table 24.12 shows its balance sheet as at the end of 1983.

It will be noted that deposits provide only 2% of funds. A major purchaser of debentures is the Employers Provident Fund to which every employee, except those covered in other schemes, has to contribute at the rate of 9% of their monthly wage. Since 1982 contributors have been allowed to withdraw part of their contributions to finance house-purchase.

Table 24.12   Malaysia Building Society Berhad, Assets & Liabilities, End-1983

Liabilities	M$ m	%	Assets	M$ m	%
Debenture loans	424	37	Mortgage loans	1,023	90
Bank Negara Malaysia loans	331	29	Net current assets	108	10
Special housing loans	167	15	Fixed assets	3	-
Deposits	19	2			
Reserves/capital	195	17			
Total	1,134	100	Total	1,134	100

Source: MBSB.
Note: At end-1983 there were 2.35 ringitts to the dollar and 3.37 ringitts to the pound.

MBSB has a variety of lending schemes. The government provides funds for the special housing loan scheme. Loans are made to low income borrowers purchasing modest houses at a rate of interest of 10%. The Society has also run a scheme for very low income families onlending funds borrowed at a rate of little more than 4% from the central bank and the Employees Provident Fund.

MBSB makes normal house-purchase loans over 15 to 20 years for between 75% and 85% of purchase price. Interest rates are 10% or 12% depending on the size of the loan.

The building society also administers a low cost housing finance programme using funds made available from the Central Bank of Malaysia and the Employees Provident Fund.

The final source of house-purchase loans are the 39 finance companies. These have been required to make loans under similar terms to their banks, and their loans are made on a similar basis.

The remaining financial intermediary in Malaysia is the National Savings Bank, which was established in its present form in 1974, based on an established network of savings banks and post offices. The Bank has one branch in each of the 14 states, but also operates through post offices. At the end of 1981 it had five million savings accounts, and the total invested was $1.2 billion. The Bank is required to invest 70% of its deposits in government securities. The remainder are invested in various stocks and government institutions. The Bank does not lend for house-purchase directly.

Bibliography

Singapore

HDB Annual Report 82/83, Housing and Development Board, 1983.
National Reports, International Union of Building Societies and Savings Associations, 1983.

Savings Banks International, 1.84, International Savings Banks Institute, 1984.
The Financial Structure of Singapore, Monetary Authority of Singapore, June 1980.

Thailand

Knight, A, *Housing Finance in Thailand*, unpublished, 1982.
The Government Housing Bank Annual Report 1982.

Sri Lanka

Central Bank of Ceylon, *Review of the Economy*, 1983.
Sri Lanka Housing Finance Study, prepared by National Savings and Loan League for AID, 1982.

Malaysia

National Reports, International Union of Building Societies and Savings Associations, 1983.

General

Korell, M L and Unger, M, *General Summary of the Housing Finance systems in the Asian and Pacific Countries*, Agency for International Development, 1979.
UN Centre for Human Settlements, Final Report, Asia and Pacific Regional Conference on Human Settlements Finance and Management, 1979.

Acknowledgements

The co-operation of the following in providing information for this chapter is gratefully acknowledged -

The International Savings Banks Institute
The Housing and Development Board (Singapore)
The Government Housing Bank (Thailand)
Alan Knight, Consultant in Housing Finance and Development
United States Agency for International Development
National Council of Savings Institutions (USA)
World Bank

CHAPTER 25

THE MIDDLE EAST

Egypt

Introduction

Egypt occupies an area of 1,000,253 sq kilometres of the north east corner of the African continent. To the north it borders on the Mediterranean, to the east on Israel and the Red Sea, to the south on Sudan and to the west on Libya.

The population of Egypt was 43,290,000 in mid-1981. It grew at an annual rate of 2.4% between 1970 and 1980. 44% of the population live in urban areas, compared with 31% in 1947. The largest city is the capital, Cairo, which had a population of 5,074,000 in 1976. The second largest city is Alexandria, with a 1976 population of 2,318,000.

GNP per capita was $650 in 1981, and the annual rate of growth in real terms in the 1970s was 5.6%. Inflation has been at a comparatively high level, and was running at 15% during 1983.

Housing

There are very few statistics available on the housing stock in Egypt. In November 1976, there were 7,300,000 housing units. It is estimated that there is a shortage of well over one million units. In 1980, 104,000 houses were built in urban areas, 72,000 of which were described as 'economic'. The current five year plan provides for 800,000 new housing units, over half of which are intended for lower income groups.

The Financial System

The financial system is dominated by nationalized and private commercial banks. There is no significant savings bank system. Table 25.1 shows the assets of financial institutions in Egypt as at June 1982.

Table 25.1   Financial Institutions, Total Assets, Egypt, June 1982

Institution	Total Assets £Em	Percentage of Total
Public commercial banks	12,645	55
Private commercial banks	5,409	24
Investment banks	3,369	15
Real estate banks	478	2
Industrial banks	310	1
Agricultural banks	761	3
Total	22,972	100

Source: Central Bank of Egypt Annual Report, 1981/82.
Note: At end-June 1982 there were 0.70 Egyptian pounds to the dollar and 1.23 Egyptian pounds to the pound sterling.

Housing Finance

The commercial banks have been successful at mobilizing saving. In particular, the Banque Misr had deposits of £E2,524 million in June 1982, and total assets of £E3,887 million. They have only a very limited role in housing finance. For example, they make loans to housing co-operatives, which build housing largely for the middle income groups.

There are three specialised real estate banks. The largest and longest established is the Crédit Foncier Egyptien, which dates back to 1880. This is a publicly owned institution and operates on fairly typical mortgage bank principles. Its balance sheet for end-June 1983 is shown in Table 25.2.

Table 25.2   Crédit Foncier Egyptien, Assets & Liabilities, June 1983

Liabilities	£Em	%	Assets	£Em	%
Central Bank			Loans	407	95
Subsidized	247	58	Cash & bank balances	11	3
Other	48	11	Investments	3	1
Deposits	59	14	Other assets	7	2
Other liabilities	24	6			
Reserves & provisions	25	6			
Capital	25	6			
Total	427	100	Total	427	100

Source: Crédit Foncier Annual Report.
Note: At end-June 1983 there were 0.70 Egyptian pounds to the dollar and 1.08 Egyptian pounds to the pound steriing.

It will be seen that the main source of funds is the Central Bank. Subsidized loans are on-lent at subsidized rates to lower income households.

The other two real estate banks are the Real Estate Arab Bank, which was established in 1948, and the Housing Development Bank, which was established in 1980 by the commercial banks as a private sector organisation.

A significant role in housing finance is played by housing co-operatives. The General Authority of Housing and Building Co-operatives borrows funds from the banking system at 9% and lends them to members of co-operatives to buy homes at 3%. These loans largely benefit the middle and upper income groups.

Jordan

Introduction

Jordan occupies a central position in the Middle East, and as such has been involved in the Middle East conflicts over the years. It has an area of 98,000 sq kilometres. It has land borders with Egypt, Saudi Arabia, Iraq, Syria, Lebanon and Israel. Jordan's territory on the west bank of the river Jordan is currently occupied by Israel. The east bank had a population of 1,152,500 in 1982, over half of whom lived in the capital, Amman.

Housing Finance

The commercial banks are the major holders of personal deposits. Their holdings totalled JD1,035 million at the end of 1983. They make only a modest contribution to housing finance. Their total loans outstanding to individuals at the end of 1983 were JD108 million.

By far the major housing finance institution in Jordan is the Housing Bank. This was established in 1973. Its objects are to promote construction and development activites generally, including promoting the construction of residential houses, encouraging saving, and encouraging the establishment of housing finance institutions. Effectively it is controlled by the government. However, it has a share capital which is widely held. The largest individual shareholder is the Kuwait Ministry of Finance, which owns 25% of the equity. Various banks in Jordan own between them 39% of the equity. The Bank is based in Amman and has 65 branches, making it the largest financial institution in Jordan in terms of branches. It is the second largest in terms of deposits.

Table 25.3 shows the assets and liabilities of the Housing Bank at the end of 1983.

It will be seen that, contrary to its name, the Housing Bank is, in fact, a retail institution, relying on savings and current accounts for 74% of its funds. It has nearly 300,000 individual accounts, and it is estimated that 12% of the population have accounts with the Bank.

At the end of 1983 savings deposits at the Housing Bank were JD82 million, compared with the banking system figure of JD134 million; at the end of 1979 the figures were, respectively, JD29 million and JD80 million. The Bank's figure for total deposits at the end of 1983 compares with the bank-

Table 25.3 Housing Bank (Jordan), Assets and Liabilities, End-1983

Liabilities	JDm	%	Assets	JDm	%
Savings, notice &			Loans	197	67
deposit accounts	179	61	Investments & cash	55	19
Current accounts	33	11	Other assets	5	2
Credit Bank advances	48	16	Equity investments	13	4
Other liabilities	10	3	Commercial centre		
Shareholders' equity	23	8	investment	17	6
			Fixed assets	4	1
Total	293	100	Total	293	100

Source: The Housing Bank, 10th Annual Report, 1983.
Note: At end-June 1983 there were 0.37 Jordanian dinars to the dollar and 0.53 Jordanian dinars to the pound.

ing system's figure of JD212 million.

The income and expenditure account for the Bank is fairly typical of that for a building society or savings and loan association, although, as is common with fairly small institutions in developing countries, management expenses are comparatively high. Table 25.4 shows the income and expenditure account for 1983.

Table 25.4 Housing Bank (Jordan), Income and Expenditure, 1983

	JD 000	JD per 100 JD Mean Assets
Income		
Interest from loans and credit facilities	15,451	5.9
Interest from bank deposits and investments	4,164	1.6
Other income	826	0.3
Total	20,441	7.8
Expenditure		
Interest paid	12,605	4.8
Personnel costs	3,585	1.4
Expenses relating to borrowers	6	—
Depreciation	443	0.2
Administrative expenses	1,588	0.6
Total	18,227	7.0
Net Income	2,214	0.8
Allocated to reserves	603	0.2
Bad debts	395	0.2
Dividends	1,100	0.4
Other	116	—

Source: The Housing Bank, 10th Annual Report, 1983.
Note: At end-1983 there were 0.37 Jordanian dinars to the dollar and 0.53 Jordanian dinars to the pound.

The Housing Bank has increased in size markedly since its establishment. Loans outstanding increased from JD61 million in 1978 to JD103 million in 1980, to JD156 million in 1982 and to JD197 million in 1983.

Although the Bank lends primarily for housing, it is not restricted to this activity. It is also not restricted to lending to individuals for housing. Table 25.5 shows the development of its loan approvals from 1980 to 1983.

Table 25.5   Housing Bank (Jordan), Loans Approved, 1980-83

Year	Housing Loans			Development Loans	Credit Facilities	All Loans	Number of Units Financed
	Individuals	Other	All				
	JDm	JDm	JDm	JDm	JDm	JDm	
1980	12	16	28	2	13	43	5,205
1981	11	23	34	4	9	48	4,466
1982	10	30	40	5	19	64	8,455
1983	10	33	43	3	45	91	7,602

Source: The Housing Bank, 10th Annual Report, 1983, Table 5.
Note: At end-1983 there were 0.37 Jordanian dinars to the dollar and 0.53 Jordanian dinars to the pound.

It will be seen that there has been a gradual reduction in the amount of loans approved to individuals. For housing loans there has been a sharp increase in other finance, which basically means finance to developers. The Bank also lends to the Housing Corporation, which is responsible for the construction of new dwellings. Of the total amount which it approved for housing in 1983, 21% was to individuals, 35% to the Housing Corporation and 37% to developers.

It is clear that the Housing Bank is something more than a housing finance institution, and it remains to be seen how it will develop. Table 25.3 shows a large investment in a commercial centre which has been absorbing a considerable amount of the Bank's resources. The centre was completed in 1983.

Israel

Introduction

Israel is situated at the western end of the Mediterranean Sea. It has land boundaries with Egypt, Jordan, Syria and Lebanon. The effective borders of the Israeli state have changed at frequent intervals as a result of the various Middle East conflicts. The state of Israel, excluding occupied areas, comprises 20,700 sq kilometres. The population at the end of 1982 was 4,023,000 and the annual rate of growth between 1970 and 1980 was 2.6%. GNP per capita was $5,160, substantially higher than its immediate neighbours. The rate of growth in real GNP per capita during the 1970s was 1.3% a year. GNP does not give a wholly accurate measurement of living standards generally, and this is particularly true in the case of Israel, where a substantial proportion of national output has been devoted to the armed forces.

The major feature of the Israeli economy has been endemic inflation. Since 1981 the inflation rate has been over 100%. It reached 132% in 1981 and as high as 191% in 1983.

Housing

Over 70% of households in Israel are owner-occupiers. Table 25.6 shows tenure as at 1978.

Table 25.6   Tenure of Households, Israel, 1978

Tenure	Number of Dwellings	Percentage of Total
Owned	658,500	71
Rented	247,400	27
Other	26,200	3
Total	932,400	100

Source: *Statistical Abstract of Israel, 1983*, Table X1/28.

Notwithstanding the conflicts with its neighbours Israel has continued to build a high number of dwellings. 33,000 dwellings were completed in 1982, 60% of which were built by the private sector.

The Financial System

The Israeli financial system is distinguished by the dominance of commercial banks and the absence of savings bank type institutions. There are 29 banking institutions in all, with 1,100 branches between them. 20 of the institutions are affiliated to five groups. The largest three groups control 90% of the banking market, and also most of the mortgage banks as well. Generally, they can be considered to be financial conglomerates. Table 25.7 lists the largest five banks as at the end of 1982.

Table 25.7   Largest Banks, Israel, End-1982

Bank	Deposits Bank ISbn	Group ISbn	Total Assets Bank ISbn	Group ISbn
Bank Leumi	440	566	671	788
Bank Hapaolim	369	382	748	749
Israel Discount Bank	173	285	275	391
United Mizrahi Bank	54	74	87	147
First International Bank	42	43	65	68

Source: Bank of Israel Examiner of Banks, *Israel's Banking System*, Annual Survey 1982, 1983, Tables I-A2 & I-A3.
Note: At end-1982 there were 33.7 shekels to the dollar and 54.5 shekels to the pound.

The banks offer index-linked savings plans, the linking being by reference to the cost of living index or the American dollar.

Housing Finance

Housing finance in Israel is provided by 15 mortgage banks. They provide nearly all mortgage loans, and also a significant proportion of development finance. 12 of the banks are subsidiaries of commercial banks and account for over 90% of activity. The banks have 50 branches and four of them have, between them, 122 mortgage counters in the branches of their parent commercial banks.

The largest mortgage bank is the Tefahot Israel Mortgage Bank Ltd which is a subsidiary of the United Mizrahi Bank, the fourth largest banking group. The parent bank has 82% of the capital, all but 2% of the remainder being held by the registry companies, as nominees, of the United Mizrahi Bank and the Bank Hapaolim. The mortgage bank has a number of subsidiaries including another mortgage bank, investment and property companies and a securities company, and it also manages provident funds and issues guarantees. Tefahot has 25 branches, not all of which offer a full service, and 15 counters in the branches of the United Mizrahi Bank. Tefahot had assets of IS39,679 million at end-March 1983, about one third of the assets of all mortgage banks.

The second largest bank is the Leumi Mortgage Bank, one of three mortgage banks owned by the Bank Leumi, the largest banking group. This had assets of IS23,341 million at the end of 1982.

Table 25.8 shows the assets and liabilities of the mortgage banks at the end of 1982.

Table 25.8   Mortgage Banks, Israel, Assets & Liabilities, End-1982

Liabilities	IS m	%	Assets	IS m	%
Bonds & other notes	40,552	35	Loans to public		
Deposits earmarked			Housing	60,785	52
for loans	27,908	24	Contractors	3,944	3
Government deposits	29,331	25	Other	5,280	4
Approved savings			Deposits for		
schemes	3,400	3	granting loans	28,690	25
Other liabilities	6,131	5	Deposits with Treasury	9,011	8
Capital notes	229	-	Securities	3,619	3
Surplus, reserves &		2	Other assets	5,259	5
capital	12,311				
Total	116,588	100	Total	116,588	100

Source: *Statistical Abstract of Israel, 1983*, Table X1X/5.
Note: At end-1982 there were 33.7 shekels to the dollar and 54.5 shekels to the pound.

The mortgage banks obtain a large part of their finance from their parent banks. A significant feature of their operations are deposits earmarked for loans. Most of these deposits are made by the parent banks, but some are also made by contractors and employers. In exchange for a corresponding deposit the mortgage bank will make a loan to a nominated person. Government deposits are made on the same basis. In such cases the depositor stipulates the term of the loan. A margin of 1-2% is usually allowed. Here, the banks are effectively operating as servicing agents for other institutions. The government is planning to reduce its own involvement in the system, instead requiring provident and social security funds to purchase mortgage backed securities issued by the mortgage banks.

Generally, the mortgage banks are not deposit taking institutions. Only the Tefahot offers a savings plan which is linked to house-purchase. A real rate of 2% is paid and a guaranteed loan is available. However, as can be seen from the table, approved savings schemes account for only 3% of the liabilities of the banks.

The assets and the liabilities of the mortgage banks are index-linked. Various indices have been used over the years, but now the cost of living index is the operative one. Accounts can also be denominated in foreign currencies. Adjustments are made to accounts monthly. The maximum real rate which can be charged on loans is 7.5%.

Mortgage bank activity has been growing rapidly over the last few years. The number of housing loans granted increased from 2,000 in 1980 to 6,000 in 1981 and 19,000 in 1982.

Bibliography

Egypt

National Reports, International Union of Building Societies and Savings Associations, 1983.
Richard T Pratt Associates, *Housing Finance in Egypt—Prospects for Development*, report prepared for Agency for International Development, 1979.
Crédit Foncier Annual Report 1982/83.

Jordan

The Housing Bank 10th Annual Report 1983.
National Reports (Supplement), International Union of Building Societies and Savings Associations, 1983.

Israel

Bank of Israel Examiner of Banks, *Israel's Banking System*, Annual Survey 1982, 1983.
Bank Tefahot Annual Report 1982/83, 1983.
National Reports, International Union of Building Societies and Savings Associations, 1983.

Acknowledgements

The co-operation of the Agency for International Development, the Crédit Foncier, the Housing Bank of Jordan and the Tefahot Israel Mortgage Bank in providing information for this chapter is gratefully acknowledged.

CHAPTER 26

AFRICA

Unfortunately it is difficult to say much about housing and housing finance in most of the African countries. Formal systems generally are not well developed and in some countries are non-existent. Very little data is available in respect of housing conditions or housing finance and only a cursory study of most countries is possible.

This chapter attempts to do no more than set out various institutional aspects of housing finance in respect of a few countries which do have formal systems, and it also describes international efforts to improve housing and housing finance systems in Africa.

Introduction

The African continent had an estimated population in mid 1980 of 459 million. In terms of population the largest countries in the continent are Nigeria (85 million in 1980), Egypt (42 million), Ethiopia (31 million), Zaire (29 million), South Africa (29 million) and Morocco (20 million). 42 of the 53 African nations had populations of under ten million each in 1980. A major problem has been rapid population growth. The annual rate of growth between 1970 and 1980 was 2.5% in Nigeria, 3.0% in Zaire, 2.0% in Ethiopia, and as high as 5.1% in the Ivory Coast.

In contrast to Latin American the population in Africa is still largely rural. In East Africa only 12% of the population live in urban areas, in Central Africa the proportion is estimated at 24% and in West Africa at 19%. However, urban populations are growing rapidly—by an estimated 6% a year.

Average GNP per capita in 1980 was $760 compared with, for example, $2,070 in South America and $11,460 in North America. Libya, with substantial oil wealth, had the highest GNP per capita, $9,630 in 1980. It was followed by the comparatively small country of Gabon ($3,810), South Africa ($2,770), Algeria ($2,140) and Namibia ($1,960). The largest country, Nigeria, had a GNP per capita of $870, again influenced by substantial oil revenues. At the other extreme Ethiopia had the lowest GNP per capita with a figure of just $130 in 1980. Growth rates varied substantially during the 1970s. The southern African states of Botswana and Lesotho, and also Tunisia and Egypt in the north, recorded an annual growth in real GNP per capita in excess of 5%, but many other countries had negative figures including Uganda, Zaire, Zambia and Zimbabwe.

Housing

The point has already been made that little data is available in respect of housing conditions in Africa. There is, however, no doubt that in most countries housing conditions remain very bad. Any reasonable estimate of housing need shows a huge deficit of housing and moreover one that cannot possibly be met by available resources. It is estimated that about half the population in urban areas live in slums, while in rural areas housing conditions are generally primitive.

Some governments have had ambitious housing plans but these have frequently run into the problem of alternative claims on resources. Increasingly, emphasis is being given to self help projects, making use of local labour and indigenous materials. International agencies have also concentrated their help in this direction.

One major problem in trying to stimulate more formal housing and housing finance arrangements has been the question of land tenure, which is considered briefly in Chapter 2. This has proved particularly difficult in Africa where the system of land ownership has tended to be based on tribes rather than on individual ownership.

The Financial System and Housing Finance

In most African countries informal systems of finance generally, and housing finance in particular, predominate. Informal systems were described in Chapter 2 and there is little that can be added at this stage.

Formal institutions, whether government run or privately owned, have tended to deal largely with the middle and upper income groups, and where government subsidies have been provided these have tended to benefit the middle rather than the lower income groups.

In many countries there have been attempts to establish savings and loan systems and there has been a general recognition of the importance of encouraging the private sector and establishing a linkage between the formal and the informal sectors of the economy.

The Role of International Organisations

A variety of international organisations have, over the years, helped to encourage the development of housing and the establishment of housing finance systems in the African countries.

Of the United Nations agencies the UN Habitat and Human Settlements Foundation is based in Nairobi. It has arranged a number of regional meetings at which housing problems have been discussed and it has financed a

number of housing finance and shelter projects. The UN Economic Com-
misssion for Africa and the UN Development Programme have also been
involved in shelter schemes and housing finance projects. The World Bank
has played a significant role as has, to a lesser extent, the International Finance
Corporation, in the area of establishing financial institutions.

The African Development Bank has 48 member countries, and it concentrates its lending on projects of benefit to several states. This tends to exclude
housing and the Bank has, in any event, concentrated its activity
predominantly on agriculture.

The United States Agency for International Development has provided
finance for shelter projects and also considerable technical assistance. Another
important function of AID has been to cosponsor regular housing conferences in Africa, which have done much to promote understanding of the major
issues.

A French body, the Caisse Centrale de Cooperation Economique (CCCE),
which was established in 1946, played a significant role in setting up housing
finance institutions in the Francophone countries before they gained their
independence. However, it is no longer significantly involved in the housing
area.

Similarly, the British Commonwealth Development Corporation (CDC) has
helped to establish mortgage finance companies, largely in what were formerly British territories. Like the CCCE it has been reducing its direct
involvement in housing but it is still involved in a number of projects and
it has played a major part in the establishment of Shelter-Afrique which is
described subsequently.

Kenya

Introduction

Kenya is on the east coast of Africa, and is bordered by Somalia, Ethiopia,
Sudan, Uganda and Tanzania, as well as having a coastline with the Indian
Ocean. It occupies an area of 583,000 sq kilometres. Its population in mid
1981 was 17,363,000 and the rate of growth in the 1970s was a very high 4.0%
a year. The capital, Nairobi, had a population of 950,000 in 1980.

Housing

Responsibility for housing policy rests with the Ministry of Housing, and the
National Housing Corporation acts as a developer on behalf of the government. It constructs rented units and also units for sale. It completed 4,100
units in 1979, 3,500 in 1980 and 2,700 in 1981.

Housing Finance

Kenya has a history of building society type institutions. At the time of independence in the early 1960s there were four building societies. However, these faced various financial difficulties and they had to be rescued by a combination of the government, other financial institutions and the Commonwealth Development Corporation (CDC). Ultimately, the CDC took over three of the societies, and in turn these were transferred to the Housing Finance Company of Kenya (HFCK), a body which is 50% owned by the CDC and 50% owned by the government. At the end of 1982 HFCK had mortgage assets of KSH1,011 million (at the end of 1982 there were 12.7 shillings to the dollar and 20.6 shillings to the pound). It lent KSH275 million in 1982, financing just over 1,000 new units. It held deposits of KSH886 million. Currently it has £7 million in loans from the Commonwealth Development Corporation. HFCK has a wholly owned subsidiary, the Kenya Building Society, which is a developer. HFCK works with the National Housing Corporation and private developers. It has been involved in the major Buru Buru project of 5,000 units outside Nairobi. The Commonwealth Development Corporation has provided finance for this project.

A second housing finance institution is Savings and Loan Kenya Ltd. This was founded in 1949 but was acquired by the country's largest bank, the Kenya Commercial bank, in 1972. Like HFCK it operates under the Banking Act. It had assets of KSH459 million at the end of 1982.

The other major specialist lender is the East African Building Society which was founded in 1959. This operates under specific building society legislation.

The major deposit taking institutions are the commercial banks, which had deposits outstanding of over KSH13,000 million at the end of 1982. They had real estate loans outstanding of KSH598 million, but not all of these will have been for house-purchase.

The other major financial institution is the Kenya Post Office Savings Bank which dates back to 1910 but which was established in its present form in 1978. It operates through 240 post offices. Like many other savings banks in developing countries it acts only on the liabilities side of the balance sheet, using all of the funds which it raises to purchase government bonds and securities. At the end of 1982 it had deposits of KSH600 million and 1,200,000 depositors.

Tunisia

Introduction

Tunisia occupies an area of 163,610 sq kilometres in the centre of the North African coastal region. To the north and east it borders on the Mediterranean Sea, to the south east on Libya, and to the west on Algeria.

Its population in mid 1981 was 6,528,000 and the annual rate of growth in the 1970s was 2.2%. 52% of the population lived in urban areas, very high by African standards, and the rate of growth of the urban population in the 1970s was 4% a year. The principal city is the capital, Tunis, which had a population of 1,233,000 in 1980.

GNP per capita in 1981 was $1,420, one of the highest figures in Africa, but still substantially below that of countries to the north of the Mediterranean. Real GNP per capita grew at the very high rate of 5.4% a year during the 1970s.

Housing

At the end of 1980 there were 1,120,000 dwelling units in Tunisia. 54% of these were in urban areas. 79% of families were owner-occupiers with the proportion falling to 59% in urban areas.

Responsibility for housing policy rests with the Ministry of Housing. The Société Nationale Immobilire de Tunisie (SNIT) (National Real Estate Company) is the development arm of the government and it administers the housing programme. In recent years it has been producing about 17,000 housing units a year.

Housing Finance

314,000 new dwelling units were completed between 1975 and 1980. Estimates have been made of the way in which these units have been financed. The figures are shown in Table 26.1.

Table 26.1 Financing of Housing Investment, Tunisia, 1975-80

Sector	Housing Investment		Number of Units		Institutional Financing	
						Percentage of
	TDm	%	No	%	TDm	Investment
'Legal' private	272	34	64,000	21	21	8
Public controlled	328	41	80,000	26	113	34
'Informal'	196	25	169,000	54	-	-
Total	796	100	314,000	100	134	47

Source: Renaud, B, *Housing and Financial Institutions in Developing Countries*, World Bank Discussion Paper, 1982.
Note: At end-1980 there were 0.42 dinars to the dollar and 0.99 dinars to the pound.

The 'legal' private sector caters for the top 20% of the income groups only. This sector is calculated to have accounted for 34% of housing investment although only 21% of units. The table shows that very little institutional finance was used by this sector, the amount equalling just 8% of the investment. The publicly controlled sector, including dwellings financed by public institutions, accounted for 41% of investment but only 26% of dwellings.

This made greater use of institutional sources of finance, the amount equalling 34% of total investment. This sector caters for the middle and upper income groups. The informal sector was calculated to have provided over half of all dwellings with 25% of investment and without using any institutional finance. This sector caters for the lower half of the income distribution. Most of the informal development has been technically illegal but some of it has been of a very high quality and it should not necessarily be associated with shanty towns as is the case in some other countries.

Caisse Nationale d'Epargne Logement (CNEL)

The Caisse Nationale d'Epargne Logement (CNEL) (National Saving and Housing Bank) was established in 1975. It is 100% state owned and operates from 16 branches. Its main purpose is to implement the financial aspects of government housing policy.

CNEL operates a contract savings scheme modelled on the West German Bausparkasse and French épargne-logement schemes. Savings contracts run for four or five years. They attract a rate of interest of 6% which includes a 2% government bonus. When the savings period is finished a loan can be obtained for twice the amount saved. Loans carry a rate of interest of 5.5% less a 1% government subsidy and have to be repaid over 10-15 years. Bridging loans will be granted until the contract loans become available. These carry an interest rate of 7% and have to be repaid within two years.

CNEL also obtains funds from borrowing. It has a right to borrow from the commercial banks at a subsidized rate of interest and it has also raised money through the United States Agency for International Development and from the government of the United Arab Emirates.

In addition to operating the contract savings scheme it also makes loans to housing developers and one of its major roles is to work in conjunction with SNIT, the latter providing construction while CNEL provides both construction finance and also some finance for ultimate purchasers.

By the end of 1982 CNEL had 127,000 savings accounts with balances totalling TD129 million. Partly because of the time lag between savings accounts being opened and loans becoming available only 20,000 loans had been made. Table 26.2 shows the assets and liabilities of CNEL as at end 1981.

CNEL manages FOPROLOS (Fonds pour le Promotion du Logement des Salariés) which aim to finance housing for low income families. They are financed by a 2% levy on wages. Loans are made at 3% over 15 years to qualifying families. At the end of 1981 there were outstanding loans of TD28.5 million.

CNEL is considered to be a successful and well managed institution. It has grown to be one of the two largest savings institutions in the country. The other is the Caisse d'Epargne Nationale Tunisienne (CENT) which oper-

Table 26.2   CNEL, Assets and Liabilities, End-1981

Liabilities	TD m	%	Assets	TD m	%
Housing savings	80	53	Housing loans	35	23
Borrowing	22	15	Bridging loans	14	9
FOPROLOS scheme	26	17	Other loans	9	6
Net worth	3	2	Construction finance	35	23
Other liabilities	19	13	FOPROLOS loans	29	19
			Cash	10	7
			Other assets	18	12
Total	150	100	Total	150	100

Source: Annual report.
Note: At end-1981 there were 0.52 dinars to the dollar and 0.97 dinars to the pound.

ates through 500 post offices. At the end of 1982 it had 500,000 depositors with total savings balances of TD100 million. CENT does not lend to the private sector; all of the funds which it collects are entrusted to the national government.

Zimbabwe

Introduction

Zimbabwe occupies an area of 391,109 sq kilometres in the central part of southern Africa. It is landlocked, sharing borders with Mozambique, Zambia, Botswana and South Africa. Its population in mid 1981 was 7,190,000, and the population grew at an annual rate of 3.2% during the 1970s. The capital, Harare (formerly Salisbury), had a population of 686,000. GNP per capita was $870 in 1981. During the 1970s real GNP per capita fell at an average rate of 1.5% a year.

Housing Finance

Zimbabwe has a strong building society industry. The societies are very similar to their British counterparts in respect of structure and method of operation. There were eight societies in the 1950s but the number has gradually been reduced to three. The largest is the Central African Building Society (assets of Z$351 million in June 1982) and the other two are the Beverley Building Society (Z$137 million) and the Founders Building Society (Z$121 million). Table 26.3 shows the combined balance sheet of the building societies as at the end of 1982.

Table 26.3   Building Societies, Zimbabwe, Assets & Liabilities, End-1982

Liabilities	Z$ m	%	Assets	Z$ m	%
Deposits	588	91	Mortgage loans	376	58
Reserves	31	5	Other loans	68	11
Other	25	4	Liquid assets	166	26
			Other assets	34	5
Total	643	100	Total	643	100

Source: Reserve Bank of Zimbabwe, *Quarterly Economic and Statistical Review*, March 1983, Tables 2.3 & 2.4.
Note: At end-1982 there were Z$1.09 to the US dollar and Z$1.76 to the pound.

The balance sheet is almost identical to that of British building societies on the liabilities side. On the assets side the figure for other loans largely represents loans made to central and local government for low income housing.

The building societies are comparatively large financial institutions, accounting for some 25% of savings in the financial system.

Shelter-Afrique

An earlier section of this chapter noted that the British Commonwealth Development Corporation and the French Caisse Centrale de Co-operation Economique have reduced their commitment to housing partly because of priorities in other areas, notably agriculture. There have been lengthy discussions as to whether a new organisation could be established to replace the work that these organisations have done. The lead in this was taken by the African Development Bank (ADB). A 1977 study favoured the creation of an autonomous regional housing finance institution in Africa. The Commonwealth Development Corporation was asked to prepare a feasibility study and on the basis of this Shelter-Afrique was established in 1983. It has four principal objectives -

(a) To mobilize capital which can be made available to national housing development institutions for approved schemes in member countries.

(b) To facilitate the investment of capital in housing and the establishment and development of viable institutions in African countries.

(c) The building up of a technical capacity which will ensure the soundness of Shelter-Afrique's own operations.

(d) To provide technical services to member governments, in particular to assist in the establishment of appropriate housing institutions.

Shelter-Afrique has 23 subscribing governments and it will also work with the United Nations Commission on Human Settlements, the Economic Commission for Africa and other agencies.

Shelter-Afrique has the status of a charter company incorporated under Kenyan law and it is based in Nairobi. Its shareholders are the 23 African governments, together with the African Development Bank, Africa-Re (African Reinsurance Corporation) and the Commonwealth Development Corporation. It is intended that investments will be made only in institutions which can afford to service the loans. Initially, investments will be directed at national institutions.

African Union of Building Societies and Housing Finance Institutions

Steps are currently being taken to establish an African Union of Building Societies and Housing Finance Institutions. The initiative to establish this organisation has been taken by Lalit Pandit of Kenya, Chairman of the International Union of Building Societies and Savings Associations Housing Finance Development Committee, and Eric Carlson, Special Advisor to the International Union. Representatives of eight countries agreed to a draft constitution for the Union in June 1983. The African Union will be open to government and private organisations concerned with housing finance in all the African countries. Consideration is also being given to establishing a Southern African Federation of Building Societies which, it is hoped, can be integrated into the African Union in due course.

Bibliography

International Savings Banks Directory, International Savings Banks Institute, 1984.
Leech, J, 'Shelter-Afrique: New Lifeline for Africa's Housing', *The Courier*, No 81, September-October 1983.
National Reports (including supplement), International Union of Building Societies and Savings Associations, 1983.
Proceedings of the Eighth Conference on Housing in Africa, 1982, AID, 1982.
Proceedings of the Sixth Conference on Housing in Africa, 1979, AID, 1979.
Proceedings, International Union of Building Societies and Savings Associations, XVI World Congress, 1983.
Renaud, B, *Housing and Financial Institutions in Developing Countries*, World Bank Discussion Paper, 1982.

Acknowledgements

The co-operation of the following in providing information for this chapter is gratefully acknowledged -

Commonwealth Development Corporation
Agency for International Development
World Bank
Lalit Pandit, Chairman, East African Building Society
International Savings Banks Institute
Eric Carlson, Special Advisor, IUBSSA
Michel Chretien, Consultant

THE INTERNATIONAL UNION OF BUILDING SOCIETIES AND SAVINGS ASSOCIATIONS

The International Union of Building Societies and Savings Associations (IUBSSA) is an international grouping of specialist housing finance organisations. Consideration was first given to establishing an international body in the late 19th Century, a modest international congress was held in 1914, a permanent body was established in 1938, and in the last few years the Union has, for the first time, had full-time staff and its own office.

The Union is not a commercial organisation, and makes no attempt to co-ordinate the activities of its members, or to act as a regulatory body. Rather, it serves as a means by which information about housing finance techniques can be disseminated, and, through its publications and conferences, it provides for an exchange of views between housing finance specialists. It also seeks to encourage the objectives of thrift and home-ownership, and it has made a significant contribution towards the development of housing finance systems in third world countries.

History

The history of the International Union has little direct relevance to the operation of housing finance institutions today. However, it merits study as a subject in its own right as it illustrates the forces that help to bring together similar organisations in a number of countries which have no obvious reason to look beyond national frontiers. It is a relatively simple matter to describe the history of the International Union because a detailed study has been published (Josephine Hedges Ewalt, *Nation to Nation — Nurturing Home Ownership*, International Union of Building Societies and Savings Associations, 1982). This part of the chapter attempts to do no more than summarize this study.

The first proposal to hold an international congress was made in 1892 and, in 1893, an ambitiously named 'World Congress of Building and Loan Associations' was held in Chicago. Although a paper was given by the British Chief Registrar of Friendly Societies the conference was otherwise attended by Americans only. Serious consideration of a more representative congress began in 1910 on the initiative of the Ohio Building Association League in the USA. In 1911 the United States League formally adopted a resolution to hold an international congress. Eventually it was decided to hold a congress in London, England, in 1914 under the auspices of The Building Societies Association (of the United Kingdom) and the United States League. Representatives were expected from the United States, Britain, Germany, Canada, Norway, France, Switzerland, South Africa, New Zealand, Ireland, Turkey, Australia and British Guyana. Unfortunately the congress coincided with the outbreak of the First World War and, in the event, was attended by just 39 representatives from the United States, Britain and South Africa. The congress set out as its objectives -

(a) To disseminate knowledge concerning the best methods of conducting financial organisations and home building companies.

(b) To secure these by legislation or otherwise.

(c) To safeguard them by such legal restrictions as may be necessary.

(d) To encourage thrift and to stimulate the building and owning of homes throughout the world.

It was agreed to hold a second international congress in San Francisco in 1915. The congress was duly held but it could hardly be called international as no people were present other than from the United States. Nevertheless, papers were presented on housing finance in a number of countries. It was agreed at this congress that subsequent congresses should be held at five yearly intervals.

In the event the international spirit seems to have died, partly because some of those who had worked so hard for the early congresses were no longer active, and partly because of the sense of isolationism which gripped the United States in the post-war period. It was not until 1931 that the third international congress was held, in Philadelphia in the USA. By this time, two men had emerged who would dominate the international scene for many years. One was Morton Bodfish, the full time chief executive of the United States League, and the other was Sir Enoch Hill, Chairman of The Building Societies Association (of the United Kingdom) and also head of the Halifax Building Society. The 1931 congress was attended by representatives of the USA, Britain, Germany and South Africa.

During the 1930s the International Union became firmly established, with three conferences being held, in London, England, in 1933, in Salzburg, Austria, in 1935, and in Zurich, Switzerland, in 1938. Representatives of 16 countries attended the London congress of 1933, but American representation was low as a result of the economic recession in that country. The London congress marked the introduction of national reports which have been a feature of each subsequent congress. The countries represented included three which no longer feature in the International Union: Czechoslovakia, Poland and Switzerland.

The fifth congress, in Salzburg, attracted a record number of participants. 18 countries were represented, including, for the first time, Bulgaria, Italy, Romania and Brazil. This marked the first occasion on which there had been true representation from Latin America although as yet there was no Asian representation. The Salzburg congress is best remembered for the issuing of a 'World manifesto of the building societies' movement which emphasized the importance of home-ownership, thrift and building societies.

The sixth congress in Zurich in 1938 represented a watershed in the history of the International Union. On the one hand the Union had progressed well and was in a position to be transformed from an ad hoc organisation into a permanent establishment, but on the other the deepening international crisis cast a cloud over the entire proceedings. Only 11 countries were represented although national reports were given for several others.

The Zurich congress adopted a new constitution for the International Union which gave it permanent status and provided for annual dues by the constituent national organisations. Morton Bodfish, still only 36 years old, was elected president of the Union.

Obviously, international contacts lapsed during the Second World War and it took a surprisingly long time after the war for the international congresses to be re-established. This was largely attributed to internal differences within the United States industry. A second national organisation of savings and loan associations, the National Savings and Loan League, had been founded in 1943 and it sought affiliation to the International Union. Effectively, the Union was under the control of the large trade association in the USA and the National League's application was not considered. The British supported the National League's application and the whole issue effectively stultified the development of the Union. It was May 1956 before the issue was resolved. A new constitution was agreed between the British and the Americans as a result of which the National League was admitted into membership. Charles Garratt-Holden, the Secretary of the British Building Societies Association, was appointed Secretary-General of the International Union and at the same time plans were made for the seventh international congress which was held in Stuttgart, West Germany in 1957. The Stuttgart congress was attended by some 450 representatives from 28 countries. Shortly after the congress the first issue of the *Union Newsletter* was issued and this has helped to spread information about saving and loan activities throughout the world. A second initiative at this time was the establishment of the Development Committee with the declared objective of arranging for the extension of knowledge of the work of the union and of its members and the giving of advice and assistance.

The eighth congress was held in Johannesburg, South Africa in 1959. At this congress the Union formally changed its name to the International Union of Building Societies and Savings Associations (omitting the words 'and loan'). It was also resolved that future congresses should be held on a three yearly basis.

Washington DC in the USA was the venue for the ninth congress held in 1962. A total of 20 countries were represented, a record, and 292 delegates attended.

Subsequent congresses have followed a fairly standard pattern and the triennial congresses have become firmly established as probably the major activity of the International Union. Congresses were held in London, England in 1965; in Sydney, Australia in 1968; in West Berlin, West Germany in 1971; in Rio de Janeiro, Brazil in 1974; in San Francisco, USA in 1977; in London, England in 1980; and in Melbourne, Australia in 1983.

In the three years prior to the 1965 London congress the president of the International Union had been Sir Hubert Newton of Britain, for many years one of the hardest workers in the development of the Union. He was succeeded by another firm believer in international co-operation, Raymond Harold of the USA. At this time the Secretary-Generalship of the International Union moved from London to Chicago, Josephine Hedges Ewalt taking over from Charles Garratt-Holden. Also at this time consideration was given to establishing a permanent office and full time staff for the Union, and also to the establishment of an international housing finance agency. The second proposal has frequently been discussed but nothing has come of it, and on the first proposal it was 1980 before the Union obtained its own office and full time staff. A significant development during the presidency of Raymond Harold was the acceptance of the International Union as a non-governmental organisation in consultative status in conjunction with the United National Economic and Social Council. The Union was greatly assisted in this application by a UN official, Eric Carlson, who subsequently was to become a special adviser to the Union.

In 1971 Norman Griggs, Secretay-General of the British Building Societies Association, took over as Secretary-General from Josephine Hedges Ewalt and for the period in which he held office he was assisted by Barbara Daniel, one of his staff in London.

The 1974 congress at Rio was significant because it was the first time in which the Union had met in a third world country. A considerable part of the congress was devoted to a discussion of housing problems and housing finance in developing countries.

Under the presidency of John Stadtler of the USA, between 1974 and 1977, the Union greatly expanded its work in third world countries. Much of this work was carried on under the auspices of the United Nations and Development Committee (as the Development Committee had become), chaired by Leonard Williams of the United Kingdom. After the San Francisco congress in 1977 Andrew Breach of Great Britain became President and Norman Griggs was succeeded as Secretary-General by Don Geyer, a staff member of the United States League of Savings Associations in Chicago. The US League is a much larger organisation than the British BSA and it decided to put its vast resources behind the International Union. The result was a significant increase in the number and quality of publications. A particulary significant innovation was the publication of a first *Factbook* in 1978; this has now become a regular publication.

In 1979 Don Geyer was succeeded as Secretary-General by Norman Strunk who was stepping down as Executive Vice President of the US League, a post he had held for 29 years. At the beginning of 1980 the International Union opened its own office in Chicago. This is staffed by Norman Strunk and an assistant secretary-general, Eugenia Portwora.

From 1980 to 1983 the Union had its first President from a third world country, Jose Carlos Ourivio from Brazil. He was succeeded by Dr Willi-Dieter Osterbrauck of West Germany who has long been a leading figure in the European housing finance scene. In the normal course of events he will be succeeded by Harry Sorensen of Australia.

Constitution

The constitution of the International Union dates from 1971, although there have been amendments in 1980 and 1983. Article 3 defines the objects of the International Union as -

(a) To foster the ideals of thrift and home ownership and to promote a higher housing standard of living throughout the world.

(b) To foster the spirit of co-operation among members by providing facilities for periodic congresses and other functions.

(c) To arouse and stimulate, on the part of governments and people throughout the world, interest in thrift, home-ownership and adequate housing.

(d) To encourage the comparative study of methods and practices and generally to encourage the universal adoption of tried and efficient standards conducive to ordered development of thrift and housing.

(e) To encourage the initiation and promotion of such legislative and other measures as may safeguard the expansion of the thrift and home financing movement or any of its components and to maintain the prestige of all the institutions in all parts of the world.

(f) To formulate and adopt such other proposals as may contribute to the attainment of these objectives, including the formation of a world housing bank or similar financial organisation.

There are two classes of membership. Full membership is available to institutions which are actively engaged in the financing of housing and the encouragement of home ownership, and national organisations which have to be recognized by the government of that country as a negotiating body for legislative and other purposes. Associate membership is available to other institutions, government and quasi-government organisations and individuals.

The officers of the Union comprise a President, a Deputy President, Past-Presidents, Regional Vice-Presidents representing national groupings of institutions officially recognized by the Union, not more than 20 other Vice-Presidents, a Secretary-General, Assistant Secretaries-General and a Congress Secretary. The presidency is held for a three year term and the President presides over meetings of the Union and acts as its principal spokesman. The Secretary-General is the chief executive officer of the Union. Most of the Assistant Secretaries-General are the chief executives of the various national organisations.

The constitution provides that a congress shall be assembled at least once every three years.

The general policy and affairs of the Union are controlled by a board of directors called a Council. It comprises the officers of the Union and representatives of each member-country. The President appoints an executive committee composed of members of the Council to administer the affairs of the Union.

Membership

At September 1983, 65 countries were represented in the International Union. Full membership comprised 430 individual institutions, 24 national organisations and three multi-national organisations. The United States had the largest number of members at 166, followed by Australia with 49, Great Britain with 43, Brazil with 35, West Germany with 18 and South Africa with 12.

The member institutions are largely specialist housing finance bodies and this means that the Union is not well represented in countries where specialist housing finance institutions are relatively weak. There is, for example, only very limited membership from France and none at all from major industrial countries such as Spain, Italy and Japan. The tendency for the boundaries between the areas of activity of different types of financial institutions to blur is likely, in the long term, to have significant implications for the membership of the International Union. The Union will probably become more concerned with housing finance as such rather than with specialist housing finance institutions.

Activities

The principal activity of the International Union has traditionally been triennial congresses. Only a relatively small number of people have been involved as officers of the Union, whereas the congresses have given opportunities for those engaged in housing finance throughout the world to exchange views with their counterparts in other countries. The congresses have become firmly established and the proceedings are most useful documents to students of housing finance. Speakers at the most recent congress, held in Melbourne, Australia in October 1983, included the Governor-General of Australia, the Australian Housing Minister, the Deputy Governor of the Bank of England, the Chairman of the Federal Home Loan Bank Board of the USA, Professor

Jack Revell, one of the leading academic experts on housing finance, Dr Maurice Mann, Vice Chairman of a major banking institution in the USA, and the Vice-Chancellor of the University of Western Australia as well as representatives from building societies themselves. The national reports provide probably the most useful single account of developments in housing finance in the three year periods before each congress. However, like other such documents, they are somewhat patchy in quality and concentrate on the role of specialist housing finance institutions, rather than on housing finance generally.

A second principal function of the International Union is the conducting of research and the preparation of publications, both of which take place under the auspices of the Research and Publications Committee. The long established *International Newsletter* comprises relevant articles, together with the usual news of personalities, conferences and so on. A more recent innovation has been *International Insights*, which contains more detailed articles on various aspects of housing finance. The regular *Factbook* has become a useful work of reference. The Union has also published a number of occasional papers on aspects of housing finance relevant to all countries. Among the most significant of such publications have been -

Christian, J W, *Housing Finance for Developing Countries*, 1982.

Ewalt, J H, *Nation to Nation*, 1982.

Cardis, G, and Robinson, H, *Monetary Correction, Thrift Institutions and Housing Finance*, 1983.

Reich, K, *Funds Transfer Systems*, 1981.

The International Union has done much to stimulate the provision of adequate housing finance systems in third world countries under the direction of the Housing Finance Development Committee, previously the United Nations and Development Committee. This it has achieved through a variety of ways, including the preparation of publications, the holding of seminars and the provision of special sessions at world congresses on the problems of third world countries. The contact which naturally occurs at congresses has led to other forms of co-operation directly between institutions with advanced housing finance systems and those countries where systems are just beginning to evolve.

Over the years there has been talk of a world housing finance bank, but nothing has ever become of this and indeed it is difficult to see how such an institution could operate more effectively than some of the existing bodies, which are described more fully in Chapter 2.

Conclusion

The International Union has made a great contribution to increasing the understanding of various types of housing finance system. Its publications are particularly useful in this respect and reach audiences that academic publications seldom manage. It is perhaps equally unfortunate that those academic publications which do exist seldom reach those actually working in the field of housing finance.

The Union has successfully brought together a number of countries, but its representation is still somewhat patchy, being dominated by the English speaking countries and West Germany. The rapid diversification of savings and loan associations in the USA has already caused one change in the constitution of the International Union, and, as this trend continues outside the USA as well as in it, it is most likely that the Union will have to reconsider its own objectives and activities. It may well find a significant wider role to play in the encouragement of international understanding of housing finance, but to achieve this it will be necessary to draw into membership general financial institutions which are significant housing finance lenders in their particular countries, such as the savings banks in France and Spain, the Crédit Agricole in France, trust companies in Canada and commercial banks in Italy.

Bibliography

Ewalt, J H, *Nation to Nation — Nurturing Home Ownership*, International Union of Building Societies and Savings Associations, 1982.
The Building Societies Gazette, World Congress 1983 issue.
Proceedings, XVl World Congress, International Union of Building Societies and Savings Associations, 1983.

CHAPTER 28

OTHER INTERNATIONAL BODIES

Introduction

Housing finance is provided on a national rather than an international basis. Indeed, in some countries, for example West Germany, the USA and Australia, many of the housing finance institutions are restricted to operating at the sub-national level. By its very nature, housing finance does not need to be provided on an international basis. Chapter 15 includes a theoretical discussion on this point. Because housing finance is predominantly national, there have not developed the range of international bodies that exist for goods and services which are traded across national frontiers, for example, coal, steel and banking. International organisations of specialist housing finance institutions tend to be small scale, either with a very small permanent staff or none at all. Some international bodies concerned with wider aspects of financial services do, however, have an interest in housing finance.

The previous chapter described in detail the work of the principal international body, the International Union of Building Societies and Savings Associations. Other chapters have described, where appropriate, the work of organisations representing institutions in more than one country at less than a global level. Chapter 15 explained the work of the two principal organisations at the European Community level, the European Community Mortgage Federation and the European Federation of Building Societies. Chapter 16 described briefly the Inter-American Savings and Loan Union, and Chapter 26 set out details of attempts to form international groupings in the continent of Africa. Chapter 2 described the work that various international bodies do to encourage the establishment of housing finance institutions in developing countries.

This chapter describes briefly various international groupings of housing finance institutions which have not yet been covered in this book, and then explains in some detail the work of the international body for savings banks, the International Savings Banks Institute.

International Bodies Concerned With Housing Finance

Asian Pacific Federation

The Asian Pacific Federation of Building Societies and Savings Associations had its origins in a meeting in Singapore held in May 1979. A second meeting was held in London during the World Congress in 1980, at which the first officers were elected. A full scale conference was held in Auckland, New Zealand in March 1982.

The objects of the Federation are listed as being -
  (a) To promote the principles of savings and home-ownership and to assist through advice, consultation and recommendations in improving housing standards amongst the peoples of the countries of the Asian Pacific area.
  (b) In collaboration with the International Union, to promote the establishment of building societies and savings associations, and to assist in the establishment of national associations of building societies and savings associations in those countries where no national association exists.
  (c) To co-operate with governments in the Asian Pacific areas and with international organisations in meeting housing needs.
  (d) To make recommendations to members in respect of uniformity of operation and standards of practice.

Membership is open both to national associations of building societies and savings associations and also to individual institutions. The rules of the Association provide for a general meeting to be held at least once every three years. The rules provide for a President, a Council of Management, an Executive Committee and a Secretary-General. Currently, the Secretary-General is Jim Larkey, the Executive Director of the Australian Association of Permanent Building Societies.

Steps are now being taken to establish a Caribbean Federation of Building Societies. The first meeting of institutions in the Caribbean area was held in June 1983, when the Building Societies Association of Jamaica hosted a conference on housing and housing finance, jointly sponsored by the International Union and the United States Agency for International Development. It is hoped that the Caribbean Federation will formally be established later in 1984.

Chapter 26 briefly describes steps being taken to set up regional associations in the African continent, and it is useful to repeat that information in this chapter. The first steps have been taken to establish an African Union of Building Societies and Savings Associations. The effort is being led by Lalit Pandit, Chairman of the Housing Finance Development Committee of the International Union and Eric Carlson, Special Advisor to the Union. Consideration is also being given to establishing a Southern African Federation of Building Societies.

International Savings Banks Institute

Previous chapters of this book have indicated the importance of savings banks in the housing finance market. In a number of countries, for example, New Zealand, Australia, West Germany, Italy and Spain, the savings banks are either the largest lenders for housing finance or, through connected organisations, they are among the largest groups. However, savings banks generally have wider functions than building societies and savings and loan associations, offering a more complete range of retail financial services, and, in some cases, also serving the needs of industry and commerce.

The International savings Banks Institute (ISBI) was founded in 1924. At the end of 1983 it had 117 direct members, embracing 3,000 savings banks, in 73 countries. The principal function of the Institute is to promote the exchange of experience and to facilitate practical co-operation among savings banks. Information on subjects of interest to savings banks is regularly collected and made available to members. The Institute holds international meetings, conferences and seminars on a wide variety of subjects, and it organises a major world congress of savings banks. It has produced a number of publications, including the *International Savings Banks Directory*, one of the major sources of information on savings banks and therefore on housing finance institutions. It also publishes a quarterly magazine *Savings Banks International*.

The ISBI has a General Assembly of 365 members, a Board of Administration of 19 members, an Executive Committee of eight members, a President and a General Manager. These institutions are assisted by 120 experts who comprise the Institute's various Committees: the Consultative Committee; National Associations Committee; Development Cooperation Committee; Savings Banks' Central Banks Committee; Marketing and Publicity Committee; Education Committee, and Business Organisation and Automation Committee.

The members of the ISBI comprise a wide range of institutions with a particularly strong representation, in terms of assets, from West Germany, and, in terms of numbers, from Africa. Among the significant mortgage lenders which are members of the Institute are the Caixa Economica Federal, the largest lender in Brazil; the Banco Hypotecario del Uruguay, a specialist housing finance institution in that country; Cariplo, one of the two largest house-purchase lenders in Italy; the Caixa Geral de Depósitos, the largest lender in Portugal; and the Commonwealth Savings Bank, the largest lender in Australia. The Inter-American Savings and Loan Bank is also a member.

The Institute is based in Geneva, Switzerland, with a staff of 21 coming from less than eight different countries in three continents. The Institute also maintains a regional office in Bangkok, Thailand, to maintain contact with its members in Asia and the Pacific. Internally the ISBI is divided into four departments.

The International Relations Department has the task of developing international relations in various fields for the benefit of ISBI members. This includes relations with other international organisations. A particularly important function of this Department is the encouragement of development co-operation. The ISBI has been a co-sponsor of an international symposium on the mobilisation of personal savings in developing countries, and it has arranged workshops for savings bank managers.

The Information Department services ISBI members with information aimed to help them in their studies and research. It is responsible for various publications including *Savings Banks International* and conference reports. It also maintains responsibility for relations with the press.

The Business Management Department co-ordinates activities and organises conferences, meetings and seminars in the areas of organisation, data processing, automation and auditing, marketing, advertising and training.

Finally, the Administration Department looks after the conference service and the technical and accounting activities of the Institute.

Bibliography

Newsletter, International Union of Building Societies and Savings Associations, December 1983.
Report 1982/83, *International Savings Banks Institute 1984*.

CHAPTER 29

INTERNATIONAL COMPARISONS

Introduction

This chapter attempts, modestly, to make some comparisons in respect of housing, the savings market and housing finance systems. For the most part the data in this chapter are taken not from previous chapters but rather from what comparative international statistics are available. To attempt to compile compatible statistics from the range of information which has been used for the country studies in this book would be a monumental task and there is no guaranteeing that the results would be very meaningful. Indeed, it is quite possible that the published international statistics are themselves far from perfect.

The chapter begins by studying housing, and then moves on the savings market and housing finance systems.

Housing

Housing Tenure

Housing tenure is obviously relevant in the context of a study of systems by which people purchase their homes. Other things being equal a higher level of owner-occupation can be expected to require a greater volume of house-purchase finance. (In fact, it is clear that other things are not equal, and some countries with a low level of owner-occupation, such as Switzerland, seem to have much higher levels of mortgage debt outstanding than countries with a very high level of owner-occupation. This point is discussed later in this chapter.)

Table 29.1 shows the proportion of owner-occupied dwellings in each of the countries studied in this book for which data are available. For comparison, GNP per capita figures at current exchange rates for 1981 and 1975 figures adjusted on a parity purchasing power basis are shown. The 1975 figures should be a reasonable indication of comparative living standards in that year and they are sufficient to show that the 'league table' of GNP per capita is broadly accurate (with the exception of the USA) although the differences between rich and poor countries are overstated.

Table 29.1 Per Capita Income Levels & Housing Tenure

Country	Owner-Occupation Percentage	Year	GNP Per Capita 1981 US$	GNP Per Capita 1975 International $
Switzerland	30	1980	17,430	
Luxembourg	59	1981	15,910	5,883
Sweden	57	1981	14,870	
Norway	67	1980	14,060	
West Germany	37	1978	13,450	5,953
Denmark	52	1980	13,120	5,911
USA	65	1981	12,820	7,176
France	47	1978	12,190	5,977
Belgium	61	1981	11,920	5,574
Netherlands	44	1981	11,790	5,397
Canada	62	1978	11,400	
Australia	70	1981	11,080	
Austria	50	1981	10,210	4,995
Japan	60	1978	10,080	4,907
United Kingdom	59	1981	9,110	4,588
New Zealand	71	1981	7,700	
Italy	59	1981	6,960	3,861
Spain	64	1970	5,640	4,010
Singapore	55	1980	5,240	
Eire	74	1981	5,230	3,049
Israel	71	1978	5,160	2,844
Uruguay	52	1975	2,820	1,811
Brazil	60	1970	2,220	3,559
Hungary	76	1980	2,100	
Paraguay	82	1972	1,630	
Colombia	54	1973	1,380	1,609
Philippines	89	1970	790	946
Thailand	89	1976	700	936
Pakistan	78	1980	350	590
India	85	1971	260	470
Bangladesh	90	1981	140	

Sources: Owner-occupation figures are taken from the various chapters of this book; GNP per capita for 1981 are taken from the *1983 World Bank Atlas*; GNP per capita 1975 figures are taken from *World Tables*, 3rd edition, John Hopkins University Press, 1983, Page 568.

The table presents a fascinating picture. The first obvious point is that the very poor countries tend to have extremely high levels of owner-occupation, typically above 80%. However, what is an owner-occupied house in a very poor country is not, of course, comparable with an owner-occupied house in a rich country, and the figures are no indication of comparative housing standards. According to the published statistics it is the country with the lowest GNP per capita, Bangladesh, which has the highest proportion of owner-occupation.

For the middle income and higher income countries it is difficult to correlate the proportion of owner-occupation with GNP per capita. It will be noted that the country with the highest GNP per capita, Switzerland, has the lowest proportion of owner-occupation of any of the countries listed, and another rich country, West Germany, has the second lowest proportion.

The second point to emerge from this table is that, generally, the English speaking countries have higher proportions of owner-occupation than the other countries with comparable GNPs per capita. Indeed, of the industrialized countries, Eire and New Zealand have the highest proportions of owner-occupation.

Some of the individual country studies have differentiated between urban and rural areas in respect of housing tenure. It is clear that owner-occupation is higher in rural than in urban areas. This helps to explain the higher proportions of owner-occupation in the less developed countries. It also helps to explain why Eire and New Zealand have higher owner-occupation proportions than other industrialized countries.

Table 16.2 shows relative owner-occupation proportions in rural and urban areas for the various Latin American countries, and with only one exception in each of the countries owner-occupation was higher in the rural than in the urban areas. There is a similar pattern in the industrialized countries. For example, in West Germany, in 1978, 46% of houses in rural areas were owner-occupied compared with 30% in urban areas. In Japan in the same year the relative proportions were 82% and 54%. In Canada in 1981 they were 84% and 56%. In the USA in 1980 they were very similar at 82% and 59%. Large cities tend to have even lower proportions of owner-occupation than urban areas generally. For example, in Paris only 34% of dwellings are owner-occupied.

One table, already given in this book, can usefully show the relationship between the proportion of owner-occupation, income levels and urban and rural areas. This was Table 21.2 in respect of The Philippines which is reproduced below as Table 29.2.

Table 29.2   Housing Tenure by Income & Location, The Philippines, 1975

Income Range Pesos a Year	Percentage of Occupied Units			
	Urban		Rural	
	Owned	Rented	Owned	Rented
Under 2,000	74	26	93	7
2,000-3,900	58	42	92	8
4,000-9,999	63	37	89	11
10,000-19,999	62	38	88	12
20,000 & over	66	34	93	7

Source: *The Philippines—Housing Finance*, World Bank Country Study, 1982, Table 1.4.
Note: At end-1975 there were 7.4 pesos to the dollar and 12.6 pesos to the pound.

The table shows that owner-occupation in the urban areas is highest in the lowest income groups. This is simply because they cannot afford any rent and therefore have to provide themselves with primitive housing. As income levels increase so some of those who can afford to do so rent. As income levels further increase, people renting are able to purchase better homes. A similar pattern exists in rural areas but it is less pronounced. Again, the table shows the very much higher proportions of owner-occupation in rural than in urban areas.

So far a picture has emerged which can be summarized as follows -

(a) The poorest countries have the highest levels of owner-occupation.
(b) There is no correlation between per capita income levels and levels of owner-occupation in the industrialized countries.
(c) Owner-occupation is higher in rural than in urban areas.
(d) Within countries the poorest people may be owner-occupiers where direct action to provide housing may be a more viable option than renting.

There is one other area which merits examination. Chapter 2 showed a life cycle of saving, demonstrating that households tend to have modest savings until they purchase a house, they then become substantial net borrowers, and over the years savings then increase until at a late age they are substantial net savers. It is useful to consider whether there is a similar life cycle in respect of housing tenure and here it is necessary to confine the analysis to the industrialized countries.

In the normal course of events one would expect young people, after they have left their parents' home, to rent. This may be while they are a student or when they are in their first job and have not yet had time to settle down. The renting is likely to continue until there is a firm wish for roots to be planted, something which is not likely to occur until after marriage. The precise age at which people become owner-occupiers is, however, influenced by the relative availability of owner-occupied and rented property. Almost by definition, if rented accommodation is not available then people will move into owner-occupation at an early age. The dwellings which in most countries would be rented, especially flats in city centres, will need to be available for owner-occupation.

In a number of countries rented accommodation is not readily available on the market, hence a high proportion of younger households are owner-occupiers. This is particularly true in the United Kingdom which has perhaps the most severe laws against private landlords. In 1980, no fewer than 53% of households with a head of household age of 25-29 were owner-occupiers and even among households with a head of household age of under 25 the proportion was 33%. This contrasts very markedy with the position in countries where rented accommodation is freely available. For example, in the USA of married couple households under the age of 25 over 80% are tenants and in the 25-29 age group the proportion is still as high as 60%. In Japan only 17% of households with a head of household age of under 29 were owner-occupiers in 1978, and even in the 30-39 age group the proportion was just 46%, compared with an overall owner-occupation proportion of 62%. In New Zealand 70% of households with a head of household aged under 26 are tenants.

The Housing Stock

It is exceptionally difficult to measure the quality of the housing stock between countries. One statistic that can be examined is the number of dwellings per 1,000 inhabitants. Figures for the West European countries and also for the USA are shown in Table 29.3.

Table 29.3   Dwellings Per 1,000 Inhabitants, Selected Countries, 1981/82

Country	1981	1982
Austria	420	
Belgium	400	
Canada	350	351
Denmark	424	427
France		437
West Germany	410	
Hungary		348
Eire	268	271
Luxembourg	382	
Netherlands	348	354
Sweden		441
Switzerland	427	437
United Kingdom	388	
United States	398	

Source: *Annual Bulletin of Housing and Building Statistics for Europe 1982*, United Nations, 1983, Table 4.

There is a strong correlation between dwellings per 1,000 inhabitants and GNP per capita. The countries with the highest figures for dwellings per 1,000 inhabitants are Sweden, Switzerland, France and Denmark. Eire has the lowest figure. The figure for Canada looks very low given living standards in that country. However, it should be remembered that the table takes no account of different sizes of houses. In Canada it may well be the case that houses are larger than in other countries and there may also be a lower proportion of second homes.

Housebuilding

Comparative housebuilding levels can be measured either by looking at housing construction as a proportion of GDP or the number of dwellings completed. Table 29.4 shows the available statistics, again largely in respect of the European countries.

Table 29.4 Investment in Residential Construction, Selected Countries, 1982

Country	Gross Fixed Residential Construction as Percentage of GDP 1982	Dwellings Completed by Type of Investor, 1982		
		Public	Private Persons	Other Private
Austria		17,000	24,000	3,000
Belgium	3.3	7,000*	20,000*	6,000*
Canada	3.6			
Denmark	3.4	1,000	10,000	10,000
Finland	5.9	5,000	16,000	26,000
France	5.7	78,000*	205,000*	107,000*
West Germany	6.1	41,000*	226,000*	98,000*
Greece	6.0*		108,000*	
Eire		6,000	21,000	
Italy	5.6*			
Netherlands	5.1			
Norway	4.5	1,000*	23,000*	10,000*
Sweden	4.2	13,000	23,000	9,000
Switzerland		1,000	16,000	16,000
United Kingdom	2.1	57,000		130,000
United States	3.1		1,006,000	
Hungary	5.7	19,000	34,000	18,000

Source: *Annual Bulletin of Housing and Building Statistics for Europe 1982*, United Nations, 1983, Tables 2 & 5.
Note: *1981 figures.

It will be seen that there are quite significant differences in respect of the percentage of GDP devoted to residential construction. In 1982 the United Kingdom had the lowest proportion, at 2.1%, while West Germany had the highest at 6.1%. The figure for any country will, to some extent, reflect the adequacy of the housing stock. In those countries where the housing stock is, in global terms, adequate in relation to the number of households there is a need for less new building than in those countries where the housing stock is still relatively modest. The comparatively high figures for Greece, Italy and Hungary need to be seen in this context. It should be noted that Japan, which is not covered in the table, has, of all the industrialized countries, the highest proportion of GDP devoted to residential construction.

The table also shows the available figures in respect of dwellings completed by type of investor. Caution is necessary in interpreting the figures because of the very different institutional structures in the various countries. The major point to come from the table is the complete absence of public sector activity in the USA, and also in Greece. The countries with the greatest public sector activity are Austria, Sweden and the United Kingdom.

Housing Policy

Developments in housing policy require a major study in themselves and it is possible here to attempt no more than a very brief summary. There has, in fact, been one such study (*Major Trends in Housing Policy in ECE Coun-*

tries, Economic Commission for Europe, 1980). This drew three conclusions from the experience of the 1970s in developed countries in Western Europe -

(a) As long as there is an acute housing shortage it is possible to rent or sell practically all dwellings but as soon as the shortage has been eliminated attention will rapidly be focussed on qualitative factors.

(b) The existence of empty dwellings should not lead one to conclude that the housing needs of the whole population have been satisfied. A correct conclusion is that policy should shift from supporting housing production to more selective support.

(c) While the level of housing production is likely to be lower the conclusion should not be drawn that the share of housing investment should correspondingly decline. There will be a need to devote more resources to improvement and modernization.

The study concluded that the most important change in housing policy has been the extension of policy to cover the entire housing stock and housing conditions rather than simply encouraging new housing construction. There has been a major shift of emphasis away from new building, especially where this involved the destruction of reasonable housing, and towards the rehabilitation of existing housing. There have also been attempts to make more efficient use of the housing stock, something which inevitably requires the cost of dwellings to reflect their value.

Although the study is now a little dated the conclusions still hold good. In the industrialized countries the problem of an acute shortage of housing has been overcome and the fact that the number of houses completed has been falling should not necessarily be a cause for concern. Attention is focussing increasingly on the quality of the housing stock and the need to improve and modernize older houses.

More attention is also being given to the question of resource allocation, both in respect of housing and housing finance. There has been a general trend towards the reduction of subsidies, certainly in respect of rented housing, and, to a lesser extent, in respect of owner-occupied housing. The major difference between the two sectors is that subsidies to rented housing have been explicit while those for owner-occupied housing have generally been implicit, that is, through tax concessions. The general trend has certainly been for a reduction in the favoured status of housing in much the same way as there has been a reduction in the favoured status of housing finance institutions.

Financial Systems and The Savings Market

Financial Systems

Again, this subject is too wide to be studied in this chapter. In respect of industrialized countries financial systems can, broadly speaking, be divided into those of the English speaking countries and those of other countries. In the English speaking countries there are commercial banks and savings bank (including building societies) which lend for house-purchase. In the United Kingdom, South Africa and the United States the institutions which have lent for house-purchase have not, for the most part, had any legal connection with the commercial banking institutions. However, this has not been the case in Australia and Canada, where subsidiaries of the commercial banks are major housing lenders. A similar position applies in New Zealand.

In the West European countries the normal pattern is for universal banks, that is banks which offer the complete range of financial services, including house-purchase loans. This may be done directly or it may be done through a range of subsidiaries concentrating on particular types of activity.

The Savings Market

There is already an excellent comparative study of the savings market in the industrialized countries (Frazer, P and Vittas, D, *The Retail Banking Revolution*, Lafferty Publications, 1982). One source of comparative data is the International Savings Banks Institute. Table 29.5 shows statistics prepared by the Institute on savings deposits in selected countries at the end of 1982. As with all international comparisons the table needs to be treated with caution, particularly in respect of the total figures for savings deposits. However, the table is sufficient to show the strength of the savings bank systems in a number of West European countries, particularly West Germany, Spain, France and Norway. Savings banks have least market penetration in the United Kingdom, Eire and the USA.

Table 29.5   Savings Deposits, Selected Countries, End-1982

Country	Savings Deposits per Capita at all Banking & Savings Institutions US$	Percentage Held With	
		Local Savings Banks	Postal & National Savings Banks
EUROPE			
Austria	6,265	32	7
Belgium	7,251	20	18
Switzerland	14,620	18	34
West Germany	7,435	43	3
Denmark	3,937	32	-
Spain	2,897	33	2
France	4,394	30	15
Great Britain	3,130	5	5

Greece	2,028	-	17
Hungary	416	12	88
Italy	2,533	24	17
Eire	2,563	6	9
Norway	4,855	47	7
Netherlands	3,995	15	13
Portugal	1,896	4	20
Sweden	4,328	36	-
Finland	3,290	31	10
AMERICA			
Bolivia	15	15	-
Peru	134	3	-
Argentina	173	-	4
USA	5,996	11	-
ASIA			
Sri Lanka	86	-	29
Japan	9,072	-	31
Malaysia	1,068	-	4
South Korea	473	45	-
Singapore	5,191	-	19
Thailand	294	-	10
OCEANIA			
Australia	3,651	17	15
New Zealand	1,839	12	7

Source: *International Savings Banks Directory*, International Savings Banks Institute, 1984.

Notes: 1. For Belgium the figure for local savings banks is that for private savings banks; that for national savings banks is for the CGER.
2. For Switzerland the figure for local savings banks is that for regional savings banks; the figure for national savings banks is for cantonal banks.
3. The figure for national savings banks for Australia is for the Commonwealth Savings Bank.

Housing Finance in Developing Countries

The Informal Sector

In developing countries housing finance is provided predominantly by the informal sector, that is outside of the institutional framework. In the poorest countries under 10% of housing investment is financed by institutional means and even in middle income countries the proportion is frequently 30% or less. Chapter 2 stressed the importance of the informal system and suggested that policy should attempt to link the informal system with more formal deposit taking housing finance institutions. The theory behind this seems quite reasonable but in practice it is not certain that much of significance has been achieved in this respect. Certainly, the informal system merits more study and it may prove to be the case that it is not desirable to formalize the informal system. The fact that over 90% of housing investment can be financed without institutional means is itself of significance and proves that housing finance institutions are not essential for houses to be built or to be purchased. In many countries it may be the case that the housing finance system is best left on an informal basis in the knowledge that as the country generally develops then so a formal system will inevitably emerge, as has happened in the industrialized countries.

Housing Finance Institutions

Each country, even the very poorest, has a commercial banking system and generally these banks account for the bulk of deposits. However, very few commercial banks in the poorest countries do any significant house-purchase lending. For the reasons set out in Chapter 2 they find such lending inconvenient and unprofitable. They may, however, finance some construction and through the provision of short term loans to the wealthier section of the community they may also finance house-purchase, although often such lending cannot be identified as such.

Most poor countries have a government-run savings bank system, frequently operated through post offices. Almost without exception the funds raised by these institutions are handed over to the central government and the institutions are not allowed to lend. As savings banks are major sources of housing finance this practice effectively rules out an obvious housing lender. As countries and financial systems develop so the savings banks are more likely to be allowed to engage in lending, and housing is an obvious area for them to begin.

Chapter 2 stressed the merits of deposit taking housing finance institutions in developing countries, pointing out that some people will save only if they have house-purchase in mind. Notwithstanding the theoretical attractions of using the deposit taking system, in practice most housing finance institutions in developing countries are based on the mortgage bank principle and have been set up either by governments or with the assistance of equity finance from commercial banks or international agencies, especially the United States Agency for International Development and the Commonwealth Development Corporation. Equity finance is essential to get such institutions off the ground and if they are to reach any reasonable size in the short term then they will need to have loan finance initially to enable them to begin lending. As the institutions develop, and as financial sophistication increases, so such institutions should increasingly be able to adopt a deposit taking role. In some of the poorer European countries, for example Greece and Portugal, the major house-purchase lenders are government institutions using a mixture of the deposit taking and mortgage bank systems. Within the developing countries the Korea Housing Bank is a good example of a mixed institution, which has become a very significant lender. Brazil has successfully used the deposit taking system notwithstanding massive inflation, and the Federal Savings Bank of that country is the largest housing finance institution in the developing countries. The progress of the Housing Development Finance Corporation in India will be watched with great interest. It has been established with equity funds from a number of sources, has obtained its funds from borrowing and is anxious to develop a deposit taking role.

The establishment of housing finance institutions has undoubtedly been assisted by international bodies, in particular, the World Bank and its affiliate the International Finance Corporation, the United States Agency for International Development and the Commonwealth Development Corporation. The developing countries have much to learn from each other and bilateral links between them have been established. Conferences sponsored by the Agency for International Development have been particularly useful in bringing together housing finance specialists from different countries.

The Use of Social Security Funds

Even the poorest countries tend to have social security funds of one form or another. Often these are substantial financial institutions, particularly because those institutions which exist in industrialized countries are not fully developed and in some cases are not even established. Funds collected by these institutions are used for a variety of purposes, and in some cases they have been significant sources of funds for house-purchase. Brazil makes particular use of such funds as does The Philippines. This may well be an effective way to increase the availability of housing finance as long as it can be done in a viable way. However, there are likely to be other calls on these funds and the continual flow of money to housing finance cannot be guaranteed. Where such funds are used it is also necessary to ensure that in the long term a more viable system can be developed.

Housing Finance Institutions in Industrialized Countries

Contract Institutions

The point was made in Chapter 1 that the contract system can provide only a small fraction of the funds which the house-buyer requires. The contract system is used extensively in only three countries: West Germany, France and Austria. In West Germany and Austria the institutions offering the contract system are specialist Bausparkassen. Significantly, none of the Bausparkassen is wholly independent. In Austria the four Bausparkassen are linked with the various banking groups. In West Germany, the public Bausparkassen are part of the central giro networks for the savings banks, and the private Bausparkassen have varied ownership including co-operative banks, insurance companies and commercial banks. The largest Bausparkasse, Beamtenkeim-Stattenwerk (BHW), is owned by the German Federation of Trades Unions and the Civil Servants Trade Union, and the second largest,

Schwabisch Hall, is owned by the co-operative banks' central banks. These links are important because they are the means by which the Bausparkassen attract business.

It is also clear from an examination of Bausparkassen activity in West Germany and Austria that the system seems heavily dependent on government bonuses or tax benefits. Indeed, arguably a savings contract which is inflexible is used in preference to more flexible methods only if there is some form of incentive. The system is therefore vulnerable to any change in government policy. The Bausparkasse system also has the disadvantage that it is continually dependent on attracting new entrants to meet the obligations to existing contract holders. Unless new entrants can be attracted the amount that can be lent to each individual at a preferential rate of interest must fall or waiting periods must lengthen. If this happens the Bausparkassen are likely to become more like savings banks, raising funds on more commercial terms so as to be able to meet the demand for loans more promptly.

In Austria Bausparkassen loans are generally accompanied by low interest loans from the municipalities. In West Germany the Bausparkassen loans are combined with loans from the banks with which the Bausparkassen are connected. Indeed, often the Bausparkasse loans are arranged by the linked banks rather than directly.

In France the contract savings system is operated by commercial banks rather than specialist institutions. The Crédit Agricole makes the most extensive use of the system. As in West Germany the contract loans have to be provided with loans from other sources, and in France they generally come from the same institution which makes the contract loan.

It may well be the case that the contract system will gradually lose market share where it is operating and it is unlikely that any industrialized country will wish to introduce a system which must embrace some form of government incentive. However, there may be scope for the Bausparkasse system to spread to developing countries where it is necessary to encourage thrift, and the promise of a housing loan may be one way of achieving this objective.

Specialist Deposit Taking Institutions

There are only a few industrialized countries where the housing finance market is dominated by specialist institutions using the deposit taking system. The United Kingdom stands out in this respect, where the building societies account for 75% of outstanding mortgage loans. Two other English speaking countries, South Africa and Eire, also come into this category. The system in the United Kingdom merits particular attention because of its sheer size. British building societies hold nearly 50% of the liquid assets of the personal sector, account for 75% of outstanding mortgage debt, and have loans outstanding to over a quarter of all households. Notwithstanding their huge size they are very specialist institutions offering basically a savings service and house-purchase loans. There are signs that the societies are now beginning to adopt a wider role in the financial markets.

General Deposit Taking Institutions

In a number of countries house-purchase loans are provided by a combination of specialist and general institutions, both working on the deposit taking principle. In Australia, for example, housing finance loans are provided by savings banks and specialist building societies. The same applies in New Zealand although here the biggest lender is a government agency.

Table 29.6   Savings Banks' Mortgage Lending—End-1982

Country	Local Savings Banks		State & Postal Savings Banks	
	% of Total Assets	Market Share %	% of Total Assets	Market Share %
EUROPE				
Austria	9.4	18.4	-	-
Belgium	31.8	N/A		
Switzerland	53.0	21.0	43.5	39.3
West Germany	21.1	40.2		
Denmark	9.8	65.2		
Spain	18.5	80.7	29.5	6.5
France	17.9	N/A		
Great Britain	7.1	0.8		
Greece	6.3	N/A		
Hungary	49.3	N/A		
Italy	3.5	65.8		
Eire	4.3	N/A		
Norway	-	-		
Netherlands	41.5	8.7		
Portugal	-	-	-	-
Sweden	42.5	25.8		
Finland	-	-		
AMERICA				
Brazil	74.0	N/A	69.3	N/A
Peru	-	-		
Argentina			1.3	1.5
USA	54.0	12.0		
ASIA				
Sri Lanka	1.2	N/A		
Japan	-	-		
Singapore	5.9	N/A		
Thailand	0.4	N/A		
OCEANIA				
Australia	29.0	20.4	28.5	33.1
New Zealand	45.6	45.8	9.5	7.5

Source: International Savings Banks Institute, *Report* 1982-83, Table B.
Notes: 1. The figure for Belgium is for the GCER, COB and CODEP.
2. For Switzerland the figures for local savings banks are for the savings banks and regional banks. Figures for national savings banks are for cantonal banks.
3. The figure for local savings banks for Brazil is for local savings banks; the figure for national savings banks is for the Caixa Economica Federal.
4. Figures for local savings banks for Australia are for two local and three state savings banks; figures for national savings banks are for Commonwealth Savings Banks.

General deposit taking institutions are probably the major group of house-purchase lenders. Canada is particularly interesting in this respect. No one type of institution has more than 20% of the market. Commercial banks, credit unions, trust companies and mortgage loan companies, most of which are subsidiaries of the banks, all provide house-purchase loans which they fund almost entirely by taking deposits.

In Western Europe, France, the Netherlands, Belgium and Spain all rely largely on the deposit taking system. In France, the Crédit Agricole, the network of agricultural credit banks, and the savings banks are the major lenders. Similarly, in the Netherlands the Rabobank, again an agricultural co-operative bank, is the largest lender although some of its lending is done through a subsidiary mortgage bank. In Belgium, Luxembourg and Portugal, state owned savings banks are the major lenders.

Outside of the industrialized countries the Latin American nations use a combination of savings and loan associations on the American model, and more general savings banks. In Brazil, for example, a savings and loan system has successfully been established but the largest lender is the Federal Savings Bank.

The importance of savings banks in the mortgage market can be assessed by using the statistics published by the International Savings Banks Institute. Table 29.6 shows the data in respect of 1982. The figures for percentage of total assets are reliable, but those for market shares should be treated with extreme caution because of differences of definition of 'the market'. For example, the proportion for Denmark seems to take account of bonds bought by savings banks from mortgage credit institutes; those for Spain seem implausibly high, and the figures for Italy look implausible generally. However, the table does usefully indicate the countries where savings banks, directly or indirectly, are particularly important in the mortgage market.

Mortgage Banks

The mortgage bank system is used most commonly in Western Europe. It is used exclusively in Denmark and, indeed, this country is probably the only one where the individual is able to obtain all of the loan finance which he requires from a mortgage bank and where these institutions are independent and dominate the market. Of the other European countries, Sweden comes nearest to this position but here most house-purchasers are able to take advantage of substantial low interest loans from the government. In Norway, the State Housing Bank, operating on the mortgage bank principle, is the main lender but again it restricts its loans to no more than about 55% of the cost of a house. Theoretically, Italy uses the mortgage bank system only but the mortgage credit institutions which make the loans are owned by the commercial and savings banks. The banks themselves are restricted to making short term loans but in practice it seems that these are used more extensively for house-purchase than the longer term loans of the mortgage credit institutions.

Government Agencies

The fact that an institution is government owned is not necessarily of any significance for the housing finance market. In some countries all of the major financial institutions are state owned, yet these may operate in exactly the same way as commercially owned institutions in other countries. For example, all of the Italian commercial banks are government owned yet they compete extensively with each other. In Spain and Greece government owned mortgage banks operate in a fairly similar way to commercial mortgage banks. This is even more true in West Germany where a high proportion of housing loans are made by public sector bodies but these act in a similar way to their private sector counterparts, and in the case of Bausparkassen are actually regulated under the same law. However, in other countries government owned bodies adopt a unique role which means that they do not operate on a commercial basis. The Housing Corporation of New Zealand, which is funded from the national budget, is one example. The Mortgage Bank of Spain and the Crédit Foncier in France to some extent operate as commercial mortgage banks but they also have more wide ranging functions imposed on them by the government.

Mixed Systems

The sytems of four countries can be regarded as unique and do not wholly fit into any of the categories described above.

Japan seemingly uses the mortgage bank system with loans being made by a government agency, the Housing Loan Corporation. However, the whole of the house-purchase process is conducted on a non-market basis. The largest savings institution in the world is the Japan Postal Savings System which is successful in attracting funds primarily because of the tax advantages which it offers. This institution is, therefore, able to pay interest rates that are otherwise below market levels. The funds that the system attracts are handed over to the Trust Fund Bureau which in turn lends to the Housing Loan Corporation for it to make its loans, generally at fixed rate of interest and through other intermediaries. The government determines the rate of interest on the funds provided to the Housing Loan Corporation. It is therefore not a typical mortgage bank in that it raise no funds through bond issues or long term borrowing. It is, rather, a government agency which uses funds raised on a non market basis.

Ten years ago the USA would have been included in the countries where housing finance loans are provided predominantly by specialist deposit taking institutions. However, housing finance in the USA has changed significantly in recent years, partly because of the crisis which was caused by the savings and loan associations (S&Ls) being forced to borrow short and lend long. The deposit taking system is still used extensively but the unique feature of housing finance in the USA is that the process of originating and servicing loans has become separated from that of holding them. Therefore, the role of the traditional financial intermediary has declined. It is now possible for those institutions close to the house-purchase process, such as housebuilders and real estate agents, to offer loans which are financed directly on the capital markets. To some extent the USA is shifting from the deposit taking system to the mortgage banking system with the one difference that the mortgage bank itself need not exist. The complicated American housing finance system may be regarded as being unique, depending on a combination of circumstances including the antiquated laws governing financial institutions in the USA, the earnings crisis which the specialist housing lenders faced and the sophistication of the financial markets generally.

West Germany, in many respects, has the most interesting housing finance system in that it uses the contract system, the deposit taking system and the mortgage bank system. It is also significant because the government adopts a minor role even though the public sector owns many of the major lenders. Certainly, the Bausparkassen system has government bonuses but otherwise it operates without significant government involvement. West Germany has been particularly successful in keeping inflation and interest rates under control and this has enabled loans for house-purchase to be provided at comparatively low interest rates and moreover at rates which are fixed in such a way as to preserve the viability of the institutions making them.

Finally, the French system merits attention. Until ten or so years ago housing finance in France was very underdeveloped for the stage of development of the country generally. That has changed and France, like West Germany, uses a combination of all three systems. The Crédit Foncier, a government agency, has a major place in the market but otherwise the major lenders are the Crédit Agricole and the savings banks.

Housing Finance Systems

It has been noted that the contract system can be the source of only part of the funds which the house-buyer requires, and that in practice any such system is dependent on a government bonus and continually requires new entrants. The merits of the deposit taking system and the mortgage bank system require more detailed analysis.

The deposit taking system has proved to be well able to cope with the significant fluctuations in inflation and interest rates which have been recorded in the 1970s in particular. This assumes, of course, that institutions match their assets and their liabilities by using the variable rate mortgage. The one country where this was not done was the USA where savings were raised on a short term basis but had to be lent long term at fixed rates. The result was predictable. As interest rates rose rapidly so the S&Ls were placed in financial difficulty and the crisis has led to a major reform of the whole industry. One consequence is that S&Ls do not now make significant amounts of fixed rate loans which they hold. Increasingly they hold variable rate loans and to the extent that they make fixed rate loans these are largely sold on the capital markets.

One strength of the deposit taking system is its basic simplicity. People invest their savings with building societies or savings banks or S&Ls or commercial banks and those same institutions lend back to people. The process is easily understood and when there are changes in interest rates to investors the necessity to change borrowers' rates is also understood. Most countries have not found difficulty in increasing rates to existing borrowers, even by substantial amounts and at short notice. The British experience is particularly instructive in this respect. At one stage mortgage rates increased in less than three years from 8.5% to 15% but this was accepted.

The mortgage bank system has the advantage of being able to tap more easily financial institutions such as insurance companies and pension funds. Generally, loans made by mortgage banks have been at fixed rates of interest. This is because the loans have been financed by bonds, also carrying a fixed rate of interest. Any housing finance system which depends on fixed rates cannot work efficiently in an environment where interest rates fluctuate markedly. The first, and most important, problem is that changes in interest rates will be reflected in changes in housing market conditions. For example, if interest rates rise from, say, 10% to, say, 15%, then the number of people who can afford loans is clearly reduced. Some potential buyers may feel that interest rates will fall and therefore do not take out loans at 15%, leading to a further reduction of demand in relation to supply. The factors that cause the increase in interest rates may also contribute to a rise in mortgage default and lending institutions may find themselves taking possession of properties which they are unable to sell. The process can easily feed on itself, encouraging a lack of confidence in the market. The process worked in a number of West European countries in the late 1970s, in particular, the Netherlands.

Such a system may also be seen to be inequitable between borrowers. Purely by chance a person may buy a house with a 10% loan over 20 years, and two years later another person buys the house next door also with a loan over 20 years but this time at 20%. Individuals cannot be expected to guess at future interest rate movements. Where loans are issued at fixed rates of interest there are bound to be considerable inequities between borrowers.

What has, in fact, occurred is that in those countries where the mortgage bank system is used rates have been fixed for shorter periods or have been made variable at set intervals. In this way the mortgage bank system and the deposit taking system have been brought closer together.

Government Regulation

The degree to which the government regulates housing finance systems is not necessarily related to government control of the institutions. The point has already been made that a number of housing finance institutions are government owned, but in effect operate as commercial institutions. In other countries there is very little government ownership of the institutions but, effectively, the whole system is regulated by the government.

In many countries housing finance is a politically sensitive area and governments have taken steps to hold down the rate of interest below market levels. The effect has been to create a shortage, and, in all probability, to deny marginal purchasers access to the market. The Campbell Committee in Australia certainly came to this conclusion.

Over the years there has been a lessening of government intervention. In the case of Australia and the USA this has taken the form of an easing of regulations. In the case of the United Kingdom, the political pressure which government used to exert on building societies to hold mortgage rates down now seems to have disappeared.

However, there are a number of countries where government regulation still plays a major part. Among the advanced industrialized countries, Sweden has the most regulated system. The financial institutions are forced to purchase bonds at slightly below market rates of interest from specialist housing finance bodies. The government itself makes low interest rate loans and also subsidizes the loans made by the housing finance institutions. The system seems to have worked without creating undue shortages but there must be doubts as to whether it is efficient.

In New Zealand there are huge differences between the mortgage rates which people pay and those fortunate enough to obtain low interest rate loans are not necessarily any more deserving than those who are not able to obtain such loans. The government controlled Housing Corporation of New Zealand makes loans at below a market rate and steps have been taken to limit interest rates generally.

In Italy, the regulation of the financial system, preventing commercial and savings banks from operating on a long term basis, has caused the creation of the special credit institutions which alone are able to make long term loans. However, they have seldom been able to meet demand and banks have been making short term loans to house-purchasers, such loans frequently being renewed.

There are many countries where there is no government regulation of the housing finance market at all. Denmark, Canada, the United Kingdom and Switzerland are among the countries in this category. However, even in those countries government policies in respect of such matters as tax relief on mortgage interest can have a major effect on the market.

It is also necessary to consider the economic performance of a country when looking at government regulation of the housing finance system. West Germany and Switzerland have been among the most successful of all countries in holding interest rates and inflation rates at modest levels. Both countries have had stable and efficient housing finance systems but arguably this is more a consequence of economic variables rather than the systems as such. In countries where there has been endemic inflation, for example Israel and Brazil, index linking has been inevitable. Generally, the higher are rates of inflation and interest, the more that governments are likely to intervene in the market.

There is a clear trend towards less intervention by governments in housing finance markets, just as there is a trend for housing finance institutions to become involved in a wider range of activities. These trends have occurred partly because of market pressures and also because of an increasing realisation on the part of government that regulation has often not been effective and, indeed, in some cases, has achieved results the opposite of those which were intended.

The Largest Housing Finance Systems and Institutions

Differences in statistical coverage and definitions make it very difficult to measure the size of housing finance systems. However, there can be no doubt that the USA has, by a very long way, the largest amount of housing finance loans, this largely reflecting the size of the country.

It is generally agreed that Switzerland has the highest proportion of mortgage debt to GNP in the world. Table 11.7 shows that proportion to be 64% compared with 41% in the USA, 37% in West Germany, 28% in the UK and 15% in Japan. At first sight this is a paradoxical situation because Switzerland has by far the lowest proportion of owner-occupation in the world and no specialist housing finance institutions. The reasons for this have been set out in the section on Switzerland in Chapter 14. The key factor is neatly summarized in a recent article on the Swiss mortgage industry.

'For Americans, it may be difficult to believe that most Swiss borrowers take out a mortgage for almost the full value of their property. This is because taxes must be paid on the 'opportunity' rental value of owner-occupied homes. Government officials estimate the rental value of a home, and the homeowner must claim this rental value as personal income. The homeowner may, however, deduct his interest payments from his declarable income. Thus, it is standard practice to take out a large mortgage, even if not essential for personal cash flow reasons, solely in order to offset additional income tax which a homeowner must pay. This is particularly true for homeowners in the higher tax brackets.'

Source: Schuster, L and Beckstrom, R A, 'The Swiss Mortgage Industry' in Federal Home Loan Bank Board *Journal*, March 1984.

It is clear that the size of the mortgage market depends on a series of factors and not just the obvious one of the level of owner-occupation. These factors are -

(a) The level of owner-occupation—the higher the level the greater the need for housing finance.

(b) The greater the rate of inflation the lower mortgage debt is likely to be in relation to GNP, on the assumption that inflation reduces the real value of the debt.

(c) The more rapid the turnover in the housing market the higher is mortgage debt in relation to GNP because new loans have to reflect current prices.

(d) If the institutional system cannot respond to the demand for loans then mortgage debt in relation to GNP will be low. This is relevant for developing countries and also in Italy.

(e) If it is attractive to have a mortgage debt, for example because of tax relief on the interest, then mortgage debt in relation to GNP will be high.

In the case of Switzerland the owner-occupation factor is swamped by the other factors. Detailed study could well show that (d) and (e) are the most important factors.

Table 29.7   Largest Housing Finance Institutions in Industrialized Countries

Country	Institution
United Kingdom	Halifax Building Society
USA	American Savings and Loan Association (largest lender)
	Federal National Mortgage Association (government agency, largest holder of loans)
Canada	Royal Bank of Canada
Australia	Commonwealth Savings Bank
South Africa	United Building Society
New Zealand	Housing Corporation of New Zealand (government agency)
Japan	Housing Loan Corporation (government mortgage bank)
France	Crédit Agricole (agricultural co-operative bank)
	Crédit Foncier (government mortgage bank)
Italy	Sanpaolo Bank (section of commercial bank)
	Cariplo (section of savings bank)
West Germany	Beamtenkeim-Stattenwerk Bausparkasse (largest single house-purchase lender)
	Deutsche Bank) (largest lending groups)
	DG Bank)
The Netherlands	Rabobank (agricultural co-operative bank)
Switzerland	Union Bank of Switzerland (commercial bank)
Greece	National Housing Bank (government mortgage bank)
Portugal	Caixa Geral de Depositos (state savings bank)
Austria	Raiffeisen Bausparkasse
Belgium	Caisse d'Epargne et de Retraite (state savings bank)

Luxembourg	Caisse d'Epargne de l'Etat (state savings bank)
Eire	Irish Permanent Building Society
Finland	Kansallis-Osake-Pankki (commercial bank)
Norway	State Housing Bank (government mortgage bank)
Denmark	Kreditforeningen Danmark (mortgage bank)
Sweden	Urban Mortgage Bank (mutual mortgage bank)
Spain	Spanish Mortgage Bank
Israel	Tefahot Israel Mortgage Bank

It is interesting, although perhaps no more than that, to list the largest housing finance institutions in various countries. Table 29.7 shows this information for the industrialized countries. For the most part, only one institution in each country is listed. However, in some countries it is far from clear which is the largest institution. This is particularly true where housing finance institutions are subsidiaries of more general financial institutions. In the case of four countries more than one institution is listed -

(a) In the USA, American Savings and Loan Association is the largest lender. The largest holder of mortgage loans is the government agency, the Federal National Mortgage Association.

(b) In France, the Crédit Agricole, the agricultural co-operative banks, and the Crédit Foncier, the government owned mortgage bank, each have about 20% of the market and it is difficult to say precisely which is the larger institution.

(c) In Italy, the largest mortgage credit institutions are those owned by the San Paolo Bank, a commercial bank, and Cariplo, the largest savings bank. They are of a very similar size.

(d) In West Germany the largest single house-purchase lender is the largest private Bausparkasse, the Beamtenkeim-Stattenwerk (BHW). However, if the figures for all the institutions are consolidated into those of the various banking groups, either the Deutche Bank or the DG bank, the central bank for the credit co-operatives, would probably count as being the largest.

The institutions can be divided into a number of broad categories -

(a) Six specialist institutions which take deposits and make loans for house-purchase, comprising two Bausparkassen, one savings and loan association, and three building societies.

(b) Five commercial banks.

(c) Four state savings banks, three of which have much wider functions than those of a traditional savings bank, and one other savings bank.

(d) Seven government owned mortgage banks and one government agency.

(e) Three privately owned mortgage banks.

(f) Three central banks for co-operative banks.

It will be noted that there is a huge diversity in the types of organisation which are the largest housing finance lenders in each country.

It may be of interest to take the analysis slightly further and point to the largest housing finance institutions in the World. Here, the problem is one of definition. The largest building society, the expression here taken to mean any institution which collects retail deposits and lends them predominantly for house-purchase, is the Halifax Building Society in the United Kingdom. The second largest, depending on how one does the calculation, is either the American Savings and Loan Association or the Abbey National Building Society in the United Kingdom.

The largest house-purchase lender is, by a very long way, the Housing Loan Corporation in Japan. This is a government owned mortgage bank but operates essentially on a non-market basis. It obtains its funds from the government and it lends through other institutions. In terms of mortgage portfolio outstanding, the Housing Loan Corporation is probably also the largest although the Federal National Mortgage Association in the United States has a very similar sized loan portfolio. The loan portfolios of these two institutions are three times as large as those of the largest building society.

A similar exercise can be done in respect of developing countries. The results are shown in Table 29.8.

Table 29.8   Largest Housing Finance Institutions in Developing Countries

Country	Institution
Brazil	Federal Savings Bank
Colombia	Central Mortgage Bank
Chile	National Mortgage Bank
Uruguay	Mortgage Bank of Uruguay
Jamaica	Jamaican National Building Society
	Victoria Mutual Building Society
Kenya	Housing Finance Company of Kenya
Tunisia	National Savings and Housing Bank
Zimbabwe	Central African Building Society
Jordan	Government Housing Bank
Egypt	Crédit Foncier
South Korea	Korea Housing Bank
Thailand	Government Housing Bank
India	Housing Development Finance Corporation
Sri Lanka	State Mortgage and Investment Bank
Pakistan	Housebuilding Finance Corporation
Malaysia	House loans division of Treasury
The Philippines	Development Bank of The Philippines

This table is far more speculative than the previous one because lack of data means that it is not always possible to identify the largest lender. In any event, in most countries the informal sector is very substantially larger than the formal sector. The main feature of Table 29.8 is the preponderance of government owned mortgage banks of one form or another. This very much confirms the point made earlier in this chapter that a mortgage bank is the correct way to establish housing finance systems in developing countries with the hope that a deposit taking function can be added later.

Assessment

It would be invidious to pick out particular countries which have efficient or inefficient housing finance systems. Efficiency can be analysed only in the context of objectives. Some countries, for example, Sweden, have taken a positive decision that housing will be heavily subsidized and it would be wrong to criticise the system on the grounds that it does rely on subsidies. Other countries take the view that housing finance loans should be provided on as free market terms as possible.

However, it is possible to assess which types of system have overcome most successfully the economic fluctuations of the past few years. The point has already been made that the West German and Swiss systems have been successful in so doing, simply because they have not had the range of fluctuations that other countries have experienced. The system used in the United Kingdom, South Africa and Australia, making maximum use of the variable rate mortgage, has also proved to be fairly successful. Not surprisingly, the system in the United States of America, combining short term deposits with long term loans, has proved to be one of the most disastrous, but now the system in operation is very different from that which existed a few years ago. Endemic inflation has had to be coped with by index linking and this seems to have been operated fairly successfully in the Latin American countries, particularly Brazil, and also Israel.

Perhaps the one general observation that one is entitled to make is that if interest rates fluctuate markedly any system which uses long term loans at fixed rates is unlikely to be successful. It may well be a matter of luck that some countries have had systems relying predominantly on variable rates while others have used fixed rates. There is certainly now a convergence of the systems and long term fixed rate loans are increasingly uncommon.

CHAPTER 30

THE STUDY OF HOUSING FINANCE

The State of Knowledge

The process by which people obtain finance to purchase their homes is vitally important. In the industrialized countries between one fifth and one third of all households are, on average, purchasing their homes with the assistance of loans from financial institutions. In developing countries it is recognised that housing finance can, modestly, help to promote economic development and the strengthening of financial institutions generally. However, it is the case that there is a marked lack of knowledge about housing finance systems, a state of affairs which this book attempts to remedy to a limited extent. There have been few other attempts to provide comparative international data, and the subject seems to have failed to interest either academics or international bodies. One notable exception has been Professor Jack Revell, Director of the Institute of European Finance at the University College of North Wales. He wrote two papers (*Flexibility in Housing Finance* and *Housing Finance —Present Problems*) both of which were published by the OECD in 1974. However, there have been a number of comparative studies of banking systems, most notably that of Patrick Frazer and Dimitri Vittas (*The Retail Banking Revolution*, Lafferty Publications, 1982).

Perhaps one reason why there has been so little written about housing finance has been because the international bodies concerned with housing finance are very modest compared with those for other industries. This reflects the point made in Chapter 28, that is, that because housing finance is not provided across national borders so there has been little need for international bodies. Even in the European Community, where there are intentions to allow housing finance institutions to operate outside of their home country, no comparative studies of the various systems have emerged.

One problem facing any student of housing finance is the different institutional structures; in some countries housing finance is effectively provided by the banking system and studies are likely to be related to housing finance in the context of the financial system generally. In other countries housing finance is provided largely by specialist institutions, separate from the banking system. In some countries the government, through ministries of housing, plays a significant role in the market, while in yet other countries it is finance ministries which are important.

The paucity of knowledge has led to a gulf between academics, practitioners, governments and international bodies. There are some valuable studies of housing finance systems, but all too often these have not been published, or they have been published in such as a way as to make them not readily accessible. Studies done for the United Nations and the World Bank, for example, are frequently well out of date by the time they are published if indeed they are published at all. When national and international bodies representing housing finance institutions publish documents these frequently fail to reach the academic market. Equally, detailed academic studies are often read by other academics only.

Responsibility For Housing Finance Systems and Sources of Information

It is reasonable to assume that information on housing finance systems in various countries can best be obtained from the appropriate regulatory department of the government. This is true in some cases but not in others. This may be because specialist housing finance institutions have a relatively modest market share, and as the banks are not considered as part of the housing finance system, their activity may not be adequately recorded.

As a general observation ministries of housing seem to be concerned predominantly with the physical aspects of housing and not with the financial aspects. One can find detailed publications on housing, produced by ministries, which contain very little reference to the housing finance market, and certainly no detailed statistics.

Central banks have proved to be perhaps the most useful source of information, and they seem to be able to take a more detached view of financial systems than government departments. Regular central bank bulletins frequently include detailed statistics for housing finance and analyses of market trends. Sometimes such statistics are more up to date that those which can be obtained from the institutions themselves.

Both the World Bank and the United Nations have been active in the study of housing finance and have produced some studies which are duly recorded in the bibliographies at the end of Chapter 2 and the end of the book. Given the number of people who work for both agencies it is reasonable to expect that much more work has actually been done and indeed this is the case. However, much of it has not been published for one reason or another. This is unfortunate because some of the unpublished studies to which the author has had access have been most useful in preparing this book. It is to be hoped that, over the years, more information can be published by these organisations, and other international bodies such as the European Commission.

Some trade associations produce reports, many of which have been used extensively in preparing the various country studies. However, the quality of such reports is variable and generally there is understandably considerable emphasis given to the institutions which the association is representing rather than to the entire housing finance market. This can often make it difficult to obtain comparable data for the groups of financial institutions, even where excellent data exist for each group.

As the study progressed greater use was made of central bank reports and also annual reports of individual institutions. The information produced in these reports is more likely to be accurate than other information, simply because of the statutory requirements. Many banks, building societies and savings and loan association now produce reports which not only describe the activities of the institution and give the necessary statistical data but also include more general information about housing and financial market developments. Again, the quality of such reports is variable. For the size of the institutions, those produced by the British building societies count as being the least informative. However, there is a good reason for this. The societies are required by law to send these reports to most of their investors and this is an expensive exercise and precludes producing informative reports such as those prepared, for example, by South African and Australian building societies and by the American savings and loan associations.

Agenda For Future Research

The introduction to this book comments that it is little more than an attempt to bring together already published information on housing, financial systems and housing finance. It is to be hoped that it will provide a base on which more detailed research can be undertaken. The research for this book has thrown up several areas where more work is required.

For industrialized countries a comparative study of housing tenure, particularly by reference to age, would usefully show the major factors that determine tenure patterns. The previous chapter suggested that in the United Kingdom there is a very high proportion of owner-occupation among younger households simply because of the lack of availability of rented accommodation. This conclusion is undoubtedly valid but it would be helpful to quantify it much more than has been possible. In the United Kingdom there have been several major research surveys into attitudes to housing tenure (the results of the most recent one are published in *Housing Tenure*, The Building Societies Association, 1983) and again it would be useful to compare these with any similar studies in other countries.

One of the more interesting conclusions of the previous chapter is that Switzerland, which has the lowest level of owner-occupation in the world, also seems to have the highest ratio of mortgage debt to GNP. Several reasons were given for this, including the tax treatment of mortgage interest. A detailed study of the size of the mortgage markets in various countries, and their relationship to economic variables such as the level of owner-occupation and GNP, could usefully illustrate the extent to which the demand for housing finance is dependent on the demand for owner-occupation, rather than the various institutional factors.

More generally, this book has shown that housing finance systems are tending to move in a similar way, with long term loans at fixed rates becoming less common, and with there being a diversification in the activities of specialist housing finance lenders. The USA has gone further down this road than any other country, helped by the crisis which the housing finance industry faced in the early 1980s. The position has now been reached whereby there are specialist institutions which do no more than make and service loans, and the traditional financial intermediary can be completely by passed. It would be interesting to attempt to study whether this is the way that other housing finance markets might develop or whether this development is peculiar to the USA.

The whole area of housing finance in developing countries merits much more detailed study. It has been possible to cover it only briefly in this book. By their very nature informal housing finance systems are more difficult to study than formal systems and the relatively weak institutional framework in most developing countries makes it difficult to obtain data. Neverthless, some research has been done, particularly by international bodies, and there is scope for this research to be brought together in a comprehensive study. A more precise idea of the way that the informal system works could help in attempts to link it to more formal deposit taking housing finance institutions which are beginning to be developed.

The Value of International Study

The simple reason why there have been no previous major comparative studies of national housing finance sytems has been that no one has seen any point in doing such studies. For any individual institution this conclusion probably still holds good because housing finance is, and is likely to remain, something provided largely on a national basis. However, for institutions as a whole a knowldge of what is going on in other countries can be of value. Over the past few years there has been a growing interest in developments in housing finance in foreign countries, exemplified by articles in specialist journals. For example, the *BSA Bulletin*, published by The Building Societies Association in the UK, has regularly included such articles and the BSA has itself commissioned four studies of housing finance markets in West European countries. More recently, the Federal Home Loan Bank Board *Journal* has published a series of articles on housing finance in various countries. Housing finance conferences for Asia and Latin America, and more recently for the Caribbean also, have been increasingly useful as sources of comparative data.

Housing finance experts are frequently quite unable to understand how systems in other countries operate. For example, the British variable rate mortgage was viewed with incredulity by American practitioners in the 1970s, who thought it would be impossible for rates of interest to be raised on existing loans without massive problems being caused. British practitioners viewed with equal incredulity the manner in which funds in the USA were raised on a short term basis and lent long term at fixed rates. The Americans learned the hard way, and it was not until the crisis of the early 1980s that variable rates were introduced.

The futility of interest rates controls is another area where lessons can usefully be learned across national frontiers. The work of the Campbell Inquiry in Australia showed fairly conclusively that the effect of artificially holding down interest rates is to squeeze out marginal buyers who are least able to react to the reduced availability of funds by providing additional resources themselves. In the USA the effect of interest rate controls was merely to store up trouble for the future and such controls have now been almost entirely eliminated. In developing countries it is universally agreed that interest rates must be allowed to find their own level notwithstanding the apparent attractions of cheap loans. Despite all this evidence, governments in both rich and developing countries persist in trying to hold down interest rates.

It is, perhaps, the developing countries which have most to learn from an examination of the housing finance systems in other countries. Here, however, research will reveal the futility of attempting to implant a system which works effectively in an industrialized country into a developing country where attitudes and institutions are so very different. It may be very tempting to believe that all of a developing country's housing finance problems can be solved merely by the establishment of a few mutual savings and loan associations or building societies, but the fact is that there have been few examples where this has happened successfully. Housing finance experts in industrialized countries have something to teach their counterparts in developing countries but they can do this only if they are fully aware of all of the circumstances in the developing countries. It may well prove to be the case that it is experts in developing countries who have most to offer to those trying to establish housing finance systems in other developing countries.

Conclusion

Housing finance is important, but this importance has not been recognised in the literature on the subject. There is a need for those involved in housing finance in one country to understand what is happening in other countries, because no system is perfect and it is always preferable if possible new techniques and policies can be studied where they have actually worked rather

487

than solely in theory.

Further research is likely to be restrained by the fact that there is no consistent set of institutions which provide housing loans. If all housing finance was provided by savings banks and all savings banks provided housing loans then no doubt the International Savings Banks Institute would already have published much research on housing finance. Perhaps there is scope for the International Union of Building Societies and Savings Associations to widen its membership to embrace all types of institution which are involved in the housing finance market, and to attempt to become a central body for the study of housing finance and for the promotion of discussion and co-operation between countries.

GENERAL BIBLIOGRAPHY

Housing

Annual Bulletin of Housing and Building Statistics for Europe 1982, United Nations, 1983.
Fuerst, J S, *Public Housing in Europe and America*, Croom Helm, 1974.
Headey, B, *Housing Policy in the Developed Economy*, Croom Helm, 1978.
Howenstine, E J, *Attacking Housing Costs*, Centre for Urban Policy Research, 1983.
'Human Settlements—Key Factor in Economic and Social Development', *Economic Bulletin for Europe* (Journal of the United Nations Economic Commission for Europe), Vol 35, No 1, March 1983.
Major Trends in Housing Policy in ECE Countries, United Nations, 1980.
McGuire, C C, *International Housing Policies*, Lexington Books, 1981.

Housing Finance

Bellinger, D and Glauner, K-H, *Das Recht der Hypothekenbanken in Europa*, C H Bech, 1981.
Boleat, M J, *Housing Finance—An International Study*, The Building Societies Association, 1982.
Cardis, G P and Robinson, H, *Monetary Correction, Thrift Institutions and Housing Finance*, International Union of Building Societies and Savings Associations, 1983.
Frazer, P and Vittas, D, *The Retail Banking Revolution* Lafferty Publications, 1982.
Howes, E, *European Building Societies*, Franey & Co, 1965.
International Savings Banks Directory, International Savings Banks Institute, 1984.
1982 Fact Book, International Union of Building Societies and Savings Associations, 1982.
Jorgensen, N O, *Housing Finance for Low Income Groups*, Bouwcentrum-Rotterdam, 1975.
Melton, C R, *Savings and Lending for Home Ownership*, International Union of Building Societies and Savings Associations, 1980.
Revell, J, *Flexibility in Housing Finance*, OECD, 1974.
Revell, J, *Housing Finance—Present Problems*, OECD, 1974.
Sandilands, R J, *Monetary Correction and Housing Finance in Colombia, Brazil and Chile*, Gower, 1980.
Studies in Building Society Activity 1974-79, The Building Societies Association, 1980.
Studies in Building Society Activity 1980-81, The Building Societies Association, 1982.
United Nations Centre for Human Settlements, Final Report, Asia and Pacific Regional Conference on Human Settlements Finance and Management, Manila, Philippines, 1979.
XVI World Congress, *National Reports*, International Union of Building Societies and Savings Associations, 1983.
XVI World Congress, *Proceedings*, International Union of Building Societies and Savings Associations, 1984.

Journals

Avance, Inter-American Savings and Loan Union.
The Banker, Financial Times Business Publishing Ltd.
BSA Bulletin, The Building Societies Association.
European Savings and Loan News, European Federation of Building Societies.
Housing Europe, Abbey National Building Society.
Newsletter, International Union of Building Societies and Savings Associations.
International Insights, International Union of Building Societies and Savings Associations.
Retail Banker International, Lafferty Publications Ltd.
Savings Banks International, International Savings Banks Institute.